20,000 QUIPS AND QUOTES

20,000
Quips and Quotes

EVAN ESAR

Garden City, New York
DOUBLEDAY & COMPANY, INC.
1968

Library of Congress Catalog Card Number 68–18096
Copyright © 1968 by Evan Esar
All Rights Reserved
Printed in the United States of America
First Edition

To that rare journalist of genius
BRUCE HORTON
whose enterprise inspired this book
and who created a daily audience
of millions of newspaper readers
for thousands of my quips

Foreword

THIS BOOK follows a tradition honored since ancient days. The creators and collectors of wise and witty sayings go back to the biblical times of Solomon about three thousand years ago. Centuries later Aristotle collected witticisms for his studies of Greek comedy. Cicero and Plutarch quote clever sayings by the Roman consul Cato the Elder, who was not only amusing in his own right but compiled the clever sayings of others. Cicero himself, a wit creator and collector, wrote extensively on the subject, and from him we learn that Caesar was one of the wittiest Romans of them all.

The Renaissance too followed this tradition. Outstanding is the Dutch humanist Erasmus, whose *Adages* were the bestsellers of sixteenth-century Europe. Rabelais was only one of many who made fruitful use of this classic, especially its witty sayings. Another leading contributor was Thomas More, the friend of Erasmus, though the great Englishman's political activities and serious writings have obscured his services to the literature of wit. Other literary giants were to join this select group a century later. One was Shakespeare, whose references to his habit of recording these "paper bullets of the brain" have curiously been ignored by his host of commentators. Another was Bacon, also a treasurer of salty sayings, who discusses the subject in the preface to his own anthology of wit as well as in his *Advancement of Learning*. Meanwhile, in distant Spain, Cervantes was gilding his masterpiece with Iberian wit and wisdom.

I have tried to make this collection not too unworthy of such a past, to lace this volume of many sentences with many sentences that speak volumes. But I have kept in mind an even more important factor—its use as a source of quotable sayings. Like the proverb, the epigram is nothing if not quotable. Thus, the *sine qua non* for inclusion in this book was quotability. Nothing here is over one sentence long. And even single-sentence wit, when overlong or complicated, has been excluded. Since witticisms are not the truth but bits and tidbits of truth, qualifying phrases tend to splinter these fragments and dim their sparkle. As a rule that satirist is most qualified whose sayings are not. An exception is Bernard Shaw who would have been even more richly represented if he had been less wordy.

Like Falstaff, a book of this kind must be a fat fellow, a source of plentiful amusement, for it must not only be witty in itself, but the cause that wit is in others. Brevity may be the soul of wit, but not of wit collections. In fact, this book is made up of three large groups of sayings. One is the inclusion of about 5000 quotations originally intended for an enlarged edition of my *Dictionary of Humorous Quotations*. Another larger group consists of witticisms which I have been coining for many years, mostly syndicated in newspapers. To these I have added a mass of quips that have been floating anonymously in our small-town press in recent years.

My desire to make this work as serviceable as possible will explain the comprehensive range of quoted sources, from minor journalists to Nobel laureates of literature. Our contemporary world is full of celebrities whose wisecracks are constantly quoted in the press and over the air. These are all too often the ephemeral gags of press agents, having little wit and less weight, and few of them appear in these pages. But where there is insight in citation, or wisdom winged with wit, especially from the world of letters, I have quoted liberally. For a good epigram not only makes a point, but a point to ponder. This book provides many such quotations that I have unearthed from the tomes of many writers.

Since it would be the height of egotism to quote myself more than others, especially when the others include our chief satirists, I have withheld my name from my own store of wit. Many years ago when first I acquired the habit of writing epigrams, I was concerned mostly with the methods of sharpening a broad statement to a point. This practice taught me that one's sense of humor is inherited, but one's wit is acquired. (The interested reader will discover scores of techniques of epigrammar in my *Humorous English*.) Later I realized that techniques merely help one to create clever effects but do little to give an individual outlook to insight. I found in every epigrammatist worth his salt a slant revealing his unique personality. With time thousands of my non-topical witticisms appeared in print. Many of these are omitted from this collection for I have given them as alms to oblivion. Others, however, too frank or controversial for syndicated journalism, appear here for the first time.

Balancing the credited quotations and my own uncredited sayings are the anonymous quips culled from our weekly newspapers. By and large they belong to a class relished by James Thurber. *Trivia Mundi,* he wrote, was always as dear and necessary to him as her bigger and more glamorous sister, *Gloria.* Although these quips are trifles, mostly pin-pricking rather than penetrating, they add diversity to diversion.

Their purpose is to lighten the spirits, not to enlighten the mind. To make this reference book appeal on different levels, I have mixed these forgettable flashes of wit with genuine gems. However, the judicious reader will have no trouble, if I may change the metaphor, separating the few nuggets from the many nougats. All in all, this book should serve as a quip-pro-quote treasury where one man's quip becomes another man's quote.

There have always been historians and there has always been wit, but never historians of wit. Since scholars have studied the proverb and the aphorism but have neglected the comic saying, a quick survey here should prove of interest.

The evolution of the single-sentence witticism involves two separate but related processes: the rise of wit and the rise of the detached saying. A striking illustration of the emergence of wit out of wisdom lies in the word *wit* itself. Of old English origin, originally it stood for the mind and the mental faculties, and then its meaning gradually veered from the wise to the amusing. Another proof that after wisdom comes wit lies in the history of the proverb. Man had been creating proverbs for centuries (for example, *honesty is the best policy*) before he began to twist them (for example, *honesty is the best policy, but not the best politics*). Man's sense runs in serious proverbs, his sense of humor in twisted ones. By the same evolutionary process, other ancient forms of wisdom, like the fable and the riddle, have been turned into forms of wit.

Ages before Shakespeare revealed that brevity is the soul of wit and Einstein discovered his equation of energy, ideas in the mind of man have gravitated toward the compression of expression. The first dominant type of wise saying was the dark saying, a double-edged sentence that could cut either way, and that enabled man to cope with a world full of dark mysteries. During the next stage the proverb prevailed, when words had lost their magic power and the familiar experiences of daily life taught him simple truths. This was followed by the aphorism when man learned through his intellect to mock the motives underlying human behavior. Finally, as society grew more complex and man more sophisticated, the epigram came into prime popularity. Here wit and wisdom were interwoven to reveal the tragicomic nature of truth so that nothing in life was too sacred for laughter. Thus, what the dark saying was to ancient man, the proverb to medieval man, the aphorism to modern man, the epigram is to contemporary man.

This growth pattern does not mark fixed ages but rather broad stages when particular types of sayings were dominant. Just as man coexists with less highly developed species, so the epigram coexists with other pointed sentences. But as each type of saying unfolded, the comic element became more pronounced. More wit pervades the proverb than the dark saying, and more wit the aphorism than the proverb.

The nomenclature of such sentences has always been a matter of indiscriminate usage. The Bible occasionally uses dark saying and proverb interchangeably. Some 2500 years ago Hippocrates called his collection of medical sentences aphorisms. The ancient Greeks and Romans used adage and apothegm to cover a variety of pithy wisdom and wit, and later writers soaked in classical tradition, like Erasmus and Bacon, followed their example. Duty demands that lexicographers find distinctions in meaning and usage among such terms, but these distinctions are ignored today as in the past by everyone else.

Currently the most popular words of English origin for witty detached sentences are *quip* and *witticism.* In 1677, when the word *quip* seemed to be going out of literary favor after more than a century of use, Dryden coined the substitute *witticism,* from witty and criticism. He apologized for the new word, unaware that it was to win standard acceptance. The term *epigram,* equally current with the others, is of ancient Greek birth, and originally represented a serious inscription. In Dryden's time it used to mean a short clever verse, but later came to mean a witty general notion.

In the seventeenth century, while the proverb still retained its European primacy, La Rochefoucauld, Pascal and La Bruyère thrust the French aphorism into prominence. The English were still pursuing their poetic tradition, forging satire into short verses rather than prose sayings. By the next century, with the rise of the essay and novel, the English aphorism took off with Swift, Lord Chesterfield (and before him his grandfather Lord Halifax) and Samuel Johnson. Everywhere, as life was growing less countrified and more citified, the proverb began to lose ground.

But in colonial America, a century behind Europe culturally, the proverb was almighty and Ben Franklin was its prophet. The following nineteenth century saw America try to catch up with aphoristic Europe by writers like Emerson and Thoreau. The influence from abroad on the literary aphorism also pervaded the popular witticism. This was largely due to the rise of our humorous periodicals like *Puck, Judge* and *Life,* following the fashion of comic journalism in Europe. No less seminal were other native influences: the newspaper paragraphers from George Prentice to Ed Howe; the crackerbarrel philosophers from Josh Billings to Kin Hubbard; and the comic lecturers from Artemus Ward to Mark Twain.

Since then America has become a democracy distempered by wisecracks, to paraphrase Carlyle, chiefly because our most plentiful sources of wit, daily journalism and broadcasting, equate satire with gaglines. However, as magazines narrow the gulf between journalism and literature, they contribute a good deal to epigrammar. Meanwhile, barely a sprinkle of academic wit has fallen during the reign of scholarship that has saturated this country in recent decades. As always, literature steeped in satire remains a fertile source of quotations. In Robert Frost, America for the first time produced a great poet who was equally at home in literature and wit, to whom words were amusing toys as well as divine tools.

Centuries ago, before education played so universal a part in life, few people wrote too much. Today, overwriting is the common curse of civilized mankind. Under the guise of information and knowledge, we are offered the vague and verbose, the big word and the bigger sentence where the less you mean, the more you say. This reverses the *multum in parvo* of the witticism, which spares the unnecessary adjective and the excessive phrase. For wit cannot be strengthened by being lengthened. In van der Rohe's dictum, less is more. A good epigram always says more than a page; if it doesn't, it isn't a good epigram. A dozen words dressed in wit will often outlast a hundred thousand padded out in a volume, like Voltaire's "The Holy Roman Empire was neither holy, nor Roman, nor an empire."

The brevity of wit not only runs counter to our age of overwriting, but its style seems to violate some of our canons of good prose. Exaggeration is as natural to it as imagery is to poetry, for to make a clever point you must stretch a point. Wit delights not in freshness of phrase nor in lively figures of speech but in everyday expressions. The least colorful usage characterizes the comic saying, general words like *do* and *have* and *make* and *get* because they are the common coin of the common people. Indeed, there's nothing so rare as meeting a rare word in an epigram. In this the epigram follows the proverb, and even the aphorism which is sometimes wrought in imaginative magic, like the sayings of Blake.

Akin to brevity and style is the sequence of words in a witticism. The rule is: common words in capsule form in comic sequence. Many of these sayings are condensed jokes: the opening is the rug you step on, the closing is the unexpected pull of the rug from under you. Some climb to a climax: a single word after the last one blunts the effect. Others are framed in analogy, reversal or contrast. Whatever the structure, wit is always expressed in the most economical order while humor need carry no particular verbal economy or order.

Form and content are inseparable in the better epigrams, the full flavor depending as much on one as on the other. What is said is the food for thought, and how it is said is the salt. In the best specimens, above the what of matter and beyond the how of manner is the overtone, a provoking idea that trails after the words and vibrates in the mind.

Caricature and satire are the two chief weapons in the war of wit. There is far more caricature in word than in line, though the term still carries the pictorial suggestion of the past. We have come a long way since the seven deadly sins of early Christianity: pride, greed, lust, anger, gluttony, envy and laziness. In modern caricature these sins of the Christian fathers have become faults of character, and have grown into seventy times seven. Nowadays they are usually personified, embracing species as varied as the cynic, the know-it-all, the reformer and the egotist. Nowadays, too, we have a deeper understanding of sin as a social vice. We ridicule not just one extremist, like the miser, but also the opposite extremist, like the spendthrift. Both the saint and the sinner are caricatured, the optimist and the pessimist, the radical and the reactionary. The epigrammatist makes extremes meet, and out of their friction with society, comes the brilliance of his gems.

As society evolves, so do its caricatures. In ancient humor the silent person was even more popular a theme than his talkative counterpart, for life was mainly agricultural, and labor often meant long hours spent in solitary occupation. As society grew more gregarious, and education and leisure more universal, man developed into a talking machine. Thus, in contemporary humor the silent individual is seldom lampooned while his opposite number has been specialized in the chatterbox, the windbag, the hypochondriac, the braggart, the gossip, the bore, the backseat driver, and others—talkers all.

Complementing the caricature of the individual is the satire that ridicules his institutions and customs. Caricature is apt to be the wit of the literate, satire the wit of the literati. Everything from politics to religion, from education to art, is the butt of critical comment and, for the satirist, to comment on life is not to commend it. No established practices of society are immune from his wit and twit. Both democracy and Communism are mocked, youth and age, labor and management. Only when something ceases to be a subject of interest does it cease to be an object of satire. Target number one, of course, is marriage—before, during and after—from dating through divorce.

These caricatures and satires have much to teach the behavioral scientist if he will but recognize their value. Here are mirrored the contemporary prejudices of the public. Here is what the community at large really thinks about traditional values, exaggerated naturally to sharpen the cutting edge of truth. And how it really feels about widespread changes that are constantly replacing older ways of living, for the tapestry of wit follows the decorative design of life itself.

Why does man delight in such ridicule? If self-preservation is a law of nature, may it not be that wit is a built-in preservative to keep man and his society from self-destruction? We need no psychiatrist to tell us that where the human mind breaks down there is no laughter, save the wild laughter of hysteria. In a world where gravity acts on bodies, levity acts on minds. Still fresh in our memory is the fatal madness of a nation where self-caricature and satire were verboten. Reformers come and go, but wit reforms forever. Once upon a time we reformed ourselves into Prohibition until ridicule reformed us out of it. It is the uncensored sense of humor of a people which is the ultimate therapy for man in society.

This sense of humor, which is inseparable from the mind of man, is linked in some way to his well-being. It seems to be a self-correcting mechanism regulating his destiny. After all, life is a game played on us while we are playing other games. And the laws of nature make up some cryptic form of cosmic comedy. Or, to put it in theological terms, God is the supreme humorist, and it is his divine sense of humor that we men call fate.

EVAN ESAR

Subject Index

(With Cross References to Related Entries)

20,000 QUIPS AND QUOTES

ABANDON

An artist never really finishes his work; he merely abandons it.
— *Paul Valéry*

There's nothing smart about winning a girl; shaking one is the real test. — *Kin Hubbard*

The reason more wives than husbands leave home is that few men know how to pack their own suitcases.

Many a man whose wife deserts him, throws himself on the mercy of the quart.

It is the exceptional woman who goes out of a man's life without slamming the door.

Some men desert their families, but most missing fathers are merely looking for a parking place.

Many a man begins his marriage by running away with a girl; many another ends it by running away from her.

There are two reasons why men leave home: wives who can cook and won't, and wives who can't cook and do.

None but the brave desert the fair.

A woman is a creature that's expensive when picked up, but explosive when dropped.

ABILITY

A woman has to be twice as good as a man to go half as far.
— *Fannie Hurst*

The capacity for getting into trouble and the ability for getting out of it are seldom combined in the same person.

The ability to speak several languages is an asset, but the ability to keep your mouth shut in one language is priceless.

You can't judge the ability of a doctor by the amount of praise the undertakers give him.

The chief ability of an executive should be his ability to recognize ability.

There is a lot of difference between the man who is not able and his brother who is notable.

Many a young man resembles both his parents: his mother's ability for spending money, and his father's ability for not making it.

Ability is a good thing but stability is even better.

ABSENCE

Failing to be there when a man wants her is a woman's greatest sin, except to be there when he doesn't want her. — *Helen Rowland*

A day away from some people is like a month in the country.
– *Howard Dietz*

This is neither here nor there— nor elsewhere. – *Damon Runyon*

When a man doesn't go straight home, his wife's remarks do.

Parents usually know where a teen-age son is: he's in the family car; but they don't know where the car is.

Habits are hard to change; many a man whose wife is away hates to go home just the same.

To some people freedom of religion merely means a choice of churches to stay away from.

Half the world doesn't know how the other half lives: the women can't keep track of the men.

Nowadays the girl who marries for a home hardly ever stays in it.

The one absent from the bridge party gets the most slams.

Another husband who is hard to live with is the one whose wife can never find him.

Home is where the college student home for the holidays isn't.

The only way some women can keep their husbands at home nights is by going out themselves.

Absence makes the heart grow fonder—of the other fellow.

You can never tell about husbands: they are here today, gone tomorrow, but where are they tonight?

You appreciate some people most when they deprive you of the pleasure of their company.

There are some people who are always in the conversation when they are not there.

Many a person livens up a party simply by staying away.

Some women spend the first part of their lives looking for a husband, and the last part wondering where he is.

Absence makes the heart grow fonder, but presents brings better results.

ABSENT-MINDED

No man knows what absent-mindedness really is until he finds himself dialing his own telephone number.

It's absent-mindedness when you forget, but it's gross negligence when your wife forgets.

Many an absent-minded businessman takes his wife to dinner instead of his secretary.

When a man has a vacant look, it's usually because a girl is occupying his mind.

The trouble with absent-minded professors is that they are never absent-minded enough to forget to flunk anyone.

When an absent-minded man kisses a woman by mistake, it's usually his own wife.

ABSTINENCE

Once during Prohibition, I was forced to live for days on nothing but food and water. — *W. C. Fields*

Abstinence is the best rule of conduct to follow, but only if taken in moderation.

There are men who can take a drink or stay alone.

Most men on the water wagon feel better off.

The man who doesn't smoke, drink, or eat grass is not a fit companion for man or beast.

Teetotalers are always conspicuous by their abstinence.

Quaff and the world quaffs with you, abstain and you drink alone.

To an ascetic the pleasure of dying without trouble is well worth the trouble of living without pleasure.

Just when you take your seat on the water wagon, some friend you haven't seen for years calls you up.

Abstinence makes the heart grow fonder.

ABSURD

There is nothing so absurd that some philosopher has not already said it. — *Cicero*

There's only a step from the sublime to the ridiculous, but there's no road leading back from the ridiculous to the sublime.
— *Lion Feuchtwanger*

The intelligent man finds almost everything ridiculous, the sensible man almost nothing. — *Goethe*

There is nothing so absurd as knowledge spun too fine. — *Franklin*

In politics, an absurdity is not a handicap. — *Napoleon*

Look for the absurd in everything, and you will find it.
— *Jules Renard*

Almost all absurdity of conduct arises from the imitation of those whom we cannot resemble.
— *Samuel Johnson*

Man is the only animal that speaks, except when he talks like an ass.

Men are ridiculous when they think they cannot do without women; women are ridiculous when they think they can do without men.

The shortest distance between two points is going from the sublime to the ridiculous.

When people suddenly become prosperous, they also become preposterous.

ABUSE

I do not waste my time in answering abuse; I thrive under it like a field that benefits from manure. — *Henry Labouchère*

There's a big difference between criticism and abuse, but many people don't know it.

When argument fails, try abuse.

You must not think that because a woman abuses her husband, she will allow you to do so.

ACCENT

Your accent should betray neither your mother's birthplace nor your father's income.

The accent is on youth today, but the stress is on parents.

If Paul Revere had been a poor rider, Americans would all be talking with a British accent.

Man is the only animal to whom an accent is important.

ACCIDENT

The cause of most traffic accidents is high h.p. and low I.Q.
— *Olin Miller*

All great calamities on land and sea have been traced to inspectors who didn't inspect. — *Kin Hubbard*

Another reason for highway accidents is that the new car models are faster, while the pedestrians are still made in the same old models.

There are only two kinds of liars in car accidents: both drivers.

There would be less accidents in the home if people would spend enough time there to learn their way around.

Many an accident is the result of looking only one way before crossing a one-way street.

Millions of people in the United States escaped being in car accidents last year, several of them having also escaped the year before.

There's no place like home— for accidents.

Car accidents usually result from one person being in too great a hurry and the other not being in a hurry at all.

Accidents are usually caused by three kinds of dangerous drivers: urban, suburban and bourbon.

The best thing to do when the brakes on your car fail is to run into something cheap.

Many accidents in the home occur in the kitchen, many in the bathroom, but most occur in the bedroom.

Some people drive as if they were anxious to have their accident quickly and get it over with.

There would be far fewer accidents if we could only teach telegraph poles to be more careful.

Most accidents are caused by motorists when their cars are in high and their minds are in neutral.

Many a pedestrian is struck down by a hit-and-rum driver.

Since most accidents happen in the home and in traffic, the surest way to be safe is to leave home and sell your car.

Some women learn to drive by taking lessons, but most learn accidentally.

Traffic accidents could be reduced to a minimum if only the cars that are fully paid for were allowed on the roads.

A jaywalker often reaches the other side of the street, but rarely reaches the other side of seventy.

Most accidents are caused by people, and most people are caused by accidents.

Two heads are better than one —except in a head-on collision.

Many an accident occurs when a man is driving under the influence of his wife.

Although trees and telegraph poles are often involved in car accidents, they are the only ones that have never lost a case in court.

When you're run down, the best thing to take is the license number.

Another reason for the high accident rate is that many a motorist of today is driving the car of tomorrow on the highway of yesterday.

The reckless driver never puts off till tomorrow the accident he can have today.

ACCOUNTING

In filling out an income tax return, let an accountant instead of your conscience, be your guide.
                              — Will Rogers

An accountant is a man hired to explain that you didn't make the money you did.

Bookkeeping taught in one lesson: Never lend them.

An accountant is a man who is always dealing in numbers, but who doesn't count much when his wife is around.

ACCURACY

Accuracy is to a newspaper what virtue is to a lady, but a newspaper can always print a retraction.   — Adlai Stevenson

To give an accurate description of what has never occurred is the proper occupation of the historian.
                              — Oscar Wilde

The female of the species is more accurate than the computer: a woman will often put two and two together and get a man's number.

ACHIEVEMENT

Nothing is ever accomplished by a reasonable man. — Bernard Shaw

It is better to be a nobody who accomplishes something than a somebody who accomplishes nothing.

When the worm turns, that is all it accomplishes.

Don't put things off—put them over.

To accomplish something important, two things are necessary:

a definite idea, and not quite enough time.

A man achieves according to what he believes.

It's surprising what an amount of nothing some people can accomplish.

There are two types of doers: those smart enough to know it can be done, and those too foolish to know it cannot.

Most of us are inclined to measure our achievement by what others have not done.

A man can do more than he thinks he can, but he usually does less than he thinks he does.

It is the man who has done nothing who is sure nothing can be done.

The more accomplishments you have, the less you are apt to accomplish.

Somebody is always doing what somebody else said couldn't be done.

The more a man talks about what he is going to do, the less he talks about what he has done.

The quickest way to do many things is to do only one thing at a time.

If you have talent and work hard and long, anything in the world can be yours—if you have enough money.

A man with enterprise accomplishes more than others because he goes ahead and does it before he is ready.

ACQUAINTANCE

An acquaintance that begins with a compliment is sure to develop into a real friendship.
— *Oscar Wilde*

The mere process of growing old together will make our slightest acquaintances seem like bosom friends. — *Logan P. Smith*

By the time you reach middle age, you've already met so many people that every new acquaintance reminds you of someone else.

ACTION

What you do speaks so loud that I cannot hear what you say.
— *Emerson*

Think like a man of action, and act like a man of thought.
— *Henri Bergson*

The world is divided into people who do things and people who get the credit; try to belong to the first class—there's far less competition. — *Dwight Morrow*

We are much beholden to Machiavelli and others that write what men do, and not what they ought to do. — *Francis Bacon*

The expression *divine service* should cease to be applied to church attendance and be applied instead to good deeds.
— *G. C. Lichtenberg*

The man who never does anything he doesn't like, rarely likes anything he does.

Actions speak louder than words, but not so often.

An ounce of performance is worth more than a pound of preachment.

All things come to him who waits, but they come sooner if he goes out to see what's wrong.

What you do doesn't count: it's what the other fellow does when you do what you do.

If you want a thing to be well done, let your wife do it herself.

Every man should do as he likes, and if he doesn't, he should be made to.

If you want to have what you have not, you must do what you do not.

Actions speak louder than words, and they tell fewer lies.

The go-getter likes to do everything at once; the procrastinator likes to do nothing at once.

Do it now! There may be a law against it tomorrow.

Sitting down on a tack is often more useful than having an idea; at least it makes you get up and do something about it.

The man who believes he can do it, is probably right, and so is the man who believes he can't.

ACTIVITY

It is not enough to be industrious; so are the ants—what are you industrious about? *— Thoreau*

All things come to him who hustles while he waits.

Some men are always up and doing—up to no good and doing someone.

A live wire usually acquires wealth and success—and ulcers.

Activity itself proves nothing: the ant is praised, the mosquito swatted.

Nothing stagnates like activity.

Many a man who thinks he's a human dynamo is probably more like an electric fan.

The young tell you what they are doing, the old what they have done, and everyone else what they are going to do.

Many a go-getter never stops long enough to let opportunity catch up with him.

ACTOR

Father Time is the make-up man responsible for the physical changes that determine the parts the average actor is to play.
— Fred Allen

The moment an actor is off with one wife, he is on with another.
— Mencken

You have to work years in hit shows to make people sick and tired of you, but you can accomplish this is a few weeks on television. *— Walter Slezak*

A ham is simply any actor who has not been successful in repressing his natural instincts.
— George Jean Nathan

The fool cannot be a good actor, but a good actor can act the fool.
— *Sophocles*

I deny that I ever said actors are cattle; what I said was that actors should be treated like cattle.
— *Alfred Hitchcock*

An actor is a sculptor who carves in snow.   — *Edwin Booth*

Show me a great actor and I'll show you a lousy husband; show me a great actress, and you've seen the devil.   — *W. C. Fields*

An actor's success has the life expectancy of a small boy about to look into a gas tank with a lighted match.   — *Fred Allen*

There are three kinds of actors: able, unable, and lamentable.

An actor is a man with an infinite capacity for taking praise.

Many an actor who plays a millionaire when the curtain goes up, borrows ten dollars when the curtain goes down.

To be an actor and get paid for it is one way of turning conceit into profit.

Never turn your back on an actor; remember, it was an actor who shot Lincoln.

Many an actor does the stage more ham than good.

An actor must have a lot of experience to act as if he had none.

To an actor, a small role is always better than a long loaf.

The actor holds the mirror up to nature, and sees in it only the reflection of himself.

All the world's a stage, with a lot of bad actors hugging the spotlight.

An actor is a man who clasps the woman he loves in his arms, looks tenderly into her eyes, and tells her how wonderful he is.

Many an actor who thinks he is acting is merely misbehaving.

Acting is pretending, and the most difficult part for an actor is pretending he is eating regularly.

Actors live expensively to impress other actors who live expensively to impress them.

By the time many an actor gets the kind of a role he can sink his teeth into, he hasn't any teeth.

When an actor isn't thinking about himself, he is probably thinking of what others are thinking about him.

When you spend an evening with an actor, the night has a thousand I's.

An actor always likes to save you the trouble of finding out for yourself how wonderful he is.

All the world's a stage, with all the players giving stage directions.

If an actor isn't the subject of the conversation, he isn't listening.

ACTRESS

An actress is not a lady; at least, when she is, she is not an actress.
— *Bernard Shaw*

We used to have actresses trying to become stars; now we have stars trying to become actresses.
— *Laurence Olivier*

What a strange notion for an actress to want to be a chaste woman! — *Jules Renard*

Every woman under thirty thinks she is an actress, and every actress thinks she is under thirty.

An actress doesn't change her name when she marries; she makes up for it by changing her husbands.

The girl who has half a mind to become an actress doesn't realize that that's all it requires.

The private life of an actress is often like her public life—one scene after another.

Many an actress thinks she is the constant subject of admiration by people who don't even know she exists.

ADAM

Adam wanted the apple only because it was forbidden; the mistake was in not forbidding the serpent— then he would have eaten the serpent. — *Mark Twain*

Adam created two beings; Jehovah and Satan—yea, in his own image created he them.
— *Clarence Day*

It was a non-smoker who committed the first sin and brought death into the world and all our woe. — *Robert Lynd*

Let us be grateful to Adam: he cut us out of the blessing of idleness and won for us the curse of labor. — *Mark Twain*

Adam should have been adamant.

Adam was created first to give him a chance to say something.

If all flesh is grass, then Adam was the fodder of mankind.

Adam had one consolation when he fell: a crowd didn't laugh at his mishap.

If there's no such thing as a new joke, Adam must have been the greatest of all comedians.

The winter of Adam's discontent came directly after his fall.

There was only one indispensable man in all history, and that was Adam.

The history of the world is full of self-made men, but only Adam was a self-maid man.

ADAM AND EVE

None of us can boast much about the morality of our ancestors: the records do not show that Adam and Eve were married.
— *Ed Howe*

The first parents of the human race ruined themselves for an ap-

ple—what might they not have done for a truffled turkey?
— *Brillat-Savarin*

"My dear, we live in a time of transition," said Adam as he led Eve out of Paradise. — *W. R. Inge*

Conversation between Adam and Eve must have been difficult at times because they had nobody to talk about. — *Agnes Repplier*

A learned Jesuit of Antwerp once proved that Adam and Eve spoke Dutch in Paradise.
— *Edmund Gosse*

Adam blamed Eve, Eve blamed the serpent, and the serpent hadn't a leg to stand on.

Adam was the only man who never had to listen to his wife tell about all the other men she could have married.

It wasn't an apple from the tree that started the trouble in the Garden of Eden; it was the pair on the ground.

God made Eve out of Adam's rib so that He might be able to shift half the blame on him.

The price of fruit today is cheap compared to what an apple cost in the Garden of Eden.

God must have been disappointed in Adam—He made Eve so different.

Adam and Eve were the first of all unions to defy management.

Adam and Eve lived thousands of years B.C.—Before Clothing.

Don't feel sorry for Adam and Eve; no one wants to live in a garden after the fall.

No marriage is perfect: even Adam and Eve raised Cain.

What Adam and Eve started, atom and evil may end.

ADAPTATION

Both the cockroach and the bird could get along very well without us, although the cockroach would miss us most.
— *Joseph Wood Krutch*

He who trims himself to suit everybody will soon whittle himself away.

If at first you don't suceed, try doing it the way your wife told you.

If the equality of the sexes is ever achieved, it will take time for the men to adjust to their new rights.

If you can play bridge or golf as if they were merely games, you're too well-adjusted to be normal.

ADJECTIVE

Pick adjectives as you would a diamond or a mistress.
— *Stanley Walker*

As to the adjective, when in doubt, strike it out. — *Mark Twain*

Advertising has put an end to the power of the most powerful adjectives. — *Paul Valéry*

ADMIRATION

Nature gives a man virtues when she wants him to be admirable, but gives him success when she wants him to be admired.
— *Joubert*

Americans adore me and will go on adoring me until I say something nice about them.
— *Bernard Shaw*

I've always taken off my hat to people who could do things I couldn't; that's why I've gone through life bareheaded most of the time.   — *Lord Vansittart*

I have received excessive admiration and respect from my fellow-men through no fault of my own.
— *Einstein*

A man admires a woman not for what she says, but for what she listens to.
— *George Jean Nathan*

Hero worship is usually harmless, except when the hero himself shares in it.

A girl admires men for their looks, strength or intelligence, but when she marries, it's usually for love.

The best way to make admirers is to make a fortune.

A man is never surprised when a woman admires him, but is always surprised when she admires another man.

A man's silent adoration is not enough for a woman; she wants to hear the service.

A man admires a woman for what he thinks she is; a woman admires a man for what she thinks he has.

A fool always finds a bigger fool to admire him.

The man who puts a woman on a pedestal is in danger of getting kicked in the face.

ADMISSION

To err is human, but to admit it isn't.

No man is really successful until his mother-in-law admits it.

If you are willing to admit faults, you have one less fault to admit.

A gossip is usually first with the news, but last with an admission of error.

A woman's idea of meeting her husband halfway is to admit she's wrong if he admits she's right.

A man is as old as he feels, and a woman is as old as she feels—like admitting.

It's as hard to admit that your enemy has many virtues as to admit that you have many faults.

If a man is willing to admit he's a fool, the chances are he isn't.

Unlike most people who won't admit their faults, I'd gladly admit mine—if I had any.

ADOLESCENCE

The sooner you treat your son as a man, the sooner he will be one.
— *John Locke*

The trouble with the juvenile is not that he is not as yet a man but that he is no longer a child.
— *Eric Hoffer*

Nowadays youngsters act as if adolescence were a last fling at life instead of the introduction to it.

Adolescence is the time in life when a girl loses her faith in fairy tales and begins to believe in love.

Adolescence is the best substitute ever invented for experience.

Adolescence begins when children stop asking questions—because they know all the answers.

Adolescence is the period when the younger generation begins to ruin cars, and cars begin to ruin the younger generation.

Adolescence is the age when a child feels his parents should be told the facts of life.

Parents worry about their adolescent children because they still remember what they used to do during adolescence.

Adolescence is the period when you can't tell the girls from the boys by the clothes they wear.

Adolescence is the period when girls stop making faces at boys and start making eyes.

Adolescence is the age when a youngster starts to eat again even before the dishes have been washed.

The adolescent girl who thinks only of boys will soon outgrow such foolish thoughts—and think only of men.

Adolescence is the period when youngsters ask questions that parents *can* answer.

Adolescence is that period in a youngster's life when his parents become more difficult.

Adolescence is the period when a teenager discovers that hard work takes all the fun out of earning money.

Puberty is the in-between age when a youngster is too old to say something cute, and too young to say something sensible.

Adolescence is the period when you are always starting things you can't finish, like phone calls.

Adolescence is the period when people are too young to give advice and too old to take it.

Adolescence is a period of rapid change: between the ages of 13 and 18 a parent ages 20 years.

A youngster's adolescence sometimes begins before his father's adolescence ends.

Adolescence is the period when a boy stops quoting his dad and starts criticizing him.

Adolescence is the time in life when a youngster is well informed about anything he doesn't have to study.

Adolescence is the period when your parents whom you highly regarded have somehow become greatly retarded.

When an adolescent gets some money, the first thing he wants is a car; and when he gets a car, the next thing he wants is some money.

Adolescence is the period when a youngster objects to his parents' having their own way.

ADULT

A boy becomes an adult several years after he thinks he does, and several years before his parents think he does.

A grownup is one who has stopped belonging to the younger generation and has started complaining about it.

What television needs are less adult Westerns and more adult sponsors.

You have to be grown up to realize that you are only young once—upon a time.

ADULTERY

A Southern colonel is a gentleman who would rather commit adultery than mention the word before a lady. — *Ellen Glasgow*

You can't tell your friend you've been cuckolded; even if he doesn't laugh at you, he may put the information to his personal use.
— *Montaigne*

A hundred years ago Hester Prynne of *The Scarlet Letter* was given an A for adultery; today she would rate no better than a C-plus.
— *Peter De Vries*

It would amuse me to learn that my father was cuckolded, and that I am not really his son.
— *Jules Renard*

When a Roman was returning from a trip, he used to send someone ahead to let his wife know, so as not to surprise her in the act.
— *Montaigne*

If marriage is honorable, wherefore should cuckoldom be a discredit, being derived from so honorable a root? — *William Congreve*

Cuckoldry is getting to be so frequent that it will soon become the customary thing. — *Montaigne*

You cannot pluck roses without fear of thorns, nor enjoy a fair wife without danger of horns. — *Franklin*

An adulterer always has three problems: the woman he loves, the woman who loves him, and his wife.

A wife may be a necessity, but another man's wife is certainly a luxury.

The lover who has a key to a married woman's apartment doesn't always know what he's letting himself in for.

Usually the man who runs off with another man's wife simply wants to borrow her.

Marriage is a game full of intimate fun; it's also the game where most cheating is done.

Men often marry to keep other men from getting the woman they desire; they are not always successful.

When the husband comes in at the door, the lover flies out of the window.

Many a corespondent wishes that half the things he is accused of were true.

To avoid trouble, always consult your wife before starting a love affair.

When you see a loving couple who have been married for many years, they are probably not married to each other.

Many a wife is true to her husband—kind of.

Sometimes it's easier for a husband to keep the wolf from the door than to keep his wife from the wolf.

Conscience makes cowards of us all, and time, cuckolds.

Variety is the spice of life, including married life.

Nothing makes a woman more furious than the discovery that her husband has been deceiving her while she has been doing the same to him.

It takes two adults to commit adultery.

To stop adultery is impossible; in fact, you cannot even make it unpopular.

In wedlock nowadays, there are too many keys given to outsiders.

The husband who always catches his wife in the act is probably the man on the flying trapeze.

ADVANCE

I will go anywhere, provided it be forward. — *David Livingstone*

The process of advancement is interesting: it isn't that you get bigger to fit the world; the world gets smaller to fit you. — *T. S. Eliot*

It doesn't matter how bold you are when the dangerous age is past.
— *Noel Coward*

You often hear of a man in advance of his age, but never of a woman in that condition.

Women want men to make little advances to them before marriage, and big advances afterwards.

One way to give a man a chance to rise in the world is to knock him down.

The man who is forward with women is usually backward about getting married.

When a girl finds that she's not the only pebble on the beach, she becomes a little bolder.

The man who is ahead of his time is probably waiting somewhere for his wife.

The best way of getting ahead of most people is by getting along with some and getting around others.

It is hard to get to the top if the boss has no daughter, and even harder if he has a son.

The most positive way to progress to the top is to start at the bottom and never stop.

A man will often take a girl to some retreat in order to make advances.

If you want to get ahead, don't rest on your laurels; no one learns to spell by sitting on a dictionary.

Some girls are so far ahead of the times that being modern seems very old-fashioned to them.

ADVANTAGE

Next to knowing when to seize an opportunity, the most important thing in life is to know when to forgo an advantage.   — *Disraeli*

It's them as take advantage that get advantage in this world.
                        — *George Eliot*

A clever man can turn bad luck to his advantage, but a fool can turn even good luck to his disadvantage.   — *La Rochefoucauld*

It is the greatest of advantages to enjoy no advantage at all.
                        — *Thoreau*

In America, the young are always ready to give to those who are older the benefits of their inexperience.   — *Oscar Wilde*

Men don't take advantage of opportunities; men are the opportunities to be taken advantage of.

Many men are successful because they didn't have the advantages other men had.

If you don't get the better of yourself, someone else will.

Sometimes a millionaire's son overcomes the obstacle of having no obstacles, and succeeds in spite of his advantages.

There's one advantage in being a fool: you needn't be lonely.

ADVENTURE

When you're safe at home, you wish you were having an adventure; when you're having an adventure, you wish you were safe at home.   — *Thornton Wilder*

Marriage is an adventure, like going to war.   — *Chesterton*

ADVERSITY

Sweet are the uses of adversity —your enemy's adversity.

No matter what kind of trouble a man has, he is sure to prefer some other kind.

The best thing for children is to have the television set go out of order now and then to teach them how to stand up under adversity.

The only man who sticks closer to you in adversity than a friend is a creditor.

ADVERTISING

If advertising encourages people to live beyond their means, so does matrimony.　　— *Bruce Barton*

Doing business without advertising is like winking at a girl in the dark: you know what you are doing but nobody else does.
　　— *Ed Howe*

The most improbable products— toilet paper, for example—cannot be advertised without the cooperation of some voluptuous female.
　　— *Joseph Wood Krutch*

You can tell the ideals of a nation by its advertisements.
　　— *Norman Douglas*

The vice-president of an advertising agency is a bit of executive fungus that forms on a desk that has been exposed to conference.
　　— *Fred Allen*

Advertising may be described as the science of arresting the human intelligence long enough to get money from it. — *Stephen Leacock*

Advertising has made America great, but then advertising makes everything look great.

Advertising is like marriage: there may be a better way, but what is it?

Advertising is usually a trick to get you to spend money by telling you how much you can save.

There are two things that never live up to their advertising: sin and circuses.

Sweet are the uses of advertisement.

When funnier-sounding ailments are invented, advertised products will cure them.

In buying a car be sure you get the best; any one of the car advertisements will tell you which that is.

The businessman who is not afraid to ad venture, is the one most likely to succeed.

Advertising is the only kind of news found in the daily papers that's always on the bright side.

Stopping your advertising to save money is like stopping your watch to save time.

The best things in life are free— no wonder they are never advertised.

If you want to find people eager to work, look in the classified ads.

If your business is not worth advertising, then advertise it for sale.

He who calls a spade a spade won't last long as an advertising copywriter.

The advertiser has to sell the consumer on the product before the shopkeeper can sell the product to the consumer.

The chief drawback of advertising is that it shows us thousands of ways to spend money but few ways to earn it.

ADVICE

In those days he was wiser than he is now—he used frequently to take my advice.
　　— *Winston Churchill*

Advice is seldom welcome, and those who need it the most, like it the least. — *Chesterfield*

There is some advice that is too good—the advice to love your enemies, for example. — *Ed Howe*

Don't give a woman advice: one should never give a woman anything she can't wear in the evening. — *Oscar Wilde*

Consult: to seek another's advice on a course already decided upon. — *Bierce*

People who are sensible enough to give good advice are usually sensible enough to give none. — *Eden Phillpotts*

In matters of marriage and religion I never give advice, for I will have no man's torments in this world or the next laid to my charge. — *Chesterfield*

If you want to save money, don't eat anything: this advice is impractical, but so is most good advice. — *Ed Howe*

There's nothing more futile than advice, especially advice on how to handle women.

The best time to give advice to your children is while they're still young enough to believe you know what you're talking about.

Friendly advice has cost many a man his friend.

To give advice to those who know is superfluous; to give it to those who do not know is useless.

The woman who is clever enough to ask a man's advice is seldom foolish enough to follow it.

I am always giving myself excellent advice, but I am incapable of taking it.

We hate to have some people give us advice because we know how badly they need it themselves.

The man who follows other people's advice always ends up making other people's mistakes.

There's nothing more common than giving poor advice, and nothing more rare than taking good advice.

The worst men often give the best advice.

Advice to persons about to give advice: Don't!

Advice never hurt anyone, neither the person who gives it, nor the person who doesn't take it.

Advice when most needed is least heeded.

There's no fool like the fool who is always taking advice, except the fool who is always giving it.

You sometimes wonder how some people have any advice left to give when they keep passing it out all the time.

Don't hesitate to give advice; it passes the time, and nobody will follow it anyway.

Everyone is unselfish when it comes to giving advice.

The older generation that's always giving advice to the younger should be reminded that gray hair is a sign of age, not wisdom.

There's nothing so rare as the ability to take good advice, except the wisdom to give it.

The fool asks the wise for advice, but the wise ask the experienced.

When some people give you a piece of advice, you wonder what's wrong with it.

Advice is bad when it's good, because good advice saves you from the most valuable mistakes.

Men often pay good money for bad advice.

There are two kinds of men who never amount to much: those who never take advice from anybody, and those who always take advice from everybody.

It is harder to give advice to yourself than to others, but just as useless.

If at first you don't succeed, you'll find everyone giving you advice.

You don't have to take a person's advice to make him feel good —you merely have to ask him for advice.

We always admire the intelligence of those who ask us for advice.

The trouble with advice is that you never know whether it is good or bad until you no longer need it.

Never take any advice, including this.

It's funny about advice: the better it is, the harder it is to take.

Advice is an opinion given by someone who can't use it to someone who won't.

When a person asks you for advice, try to give him the kind he wants.

We give people advice for their own good because it makes us feel better.

If you can tell the difference between good advice and bad advice, you don't need advice.

You can give a man good advice, but not the sense to take it.

AFFECTION

In nine cases out of ten, a woman had better show more affection than she feels.
                              —Jane Austen

A slight touch of friendly malice and amusement towards those we love keeps our affections for them from turning flat. *— Logan P. Smith*

If his tie is still in place, a man can't be too affectionate.

AGE

I refuse to admit I'm more than fifty-two even if that does make my sons illegitimate. *— Lady Astor*

A man is sane morally at 30, rich mentally at 40, wise spiritually at 50—or never.
                         — William Osler

Women deserve to have more than 12 years between the ages of 28 and 40.   — *James Thurber*

The women of Greece counted their age from their marriage, not from their birth.   — *Homer*

The best years are the forties; after fifty a man begins to deteriorate, but in the forties he is at the maximum of his villainy.

— *Mencken*

She may very well pass for forty-three—in the dusk, with a light behind her.   — *W. S. Gilbert*

A woman is the only creature that remains in her twenties between teen-age and middle-age.

A woman's age doesn't really matter; what matters is how long she has been at that age.

A woman is never quite so old as her dearest friend says she is.

Sometimes the happiest period in a woman's life are the years when she is twenty-nine.

He had known her for many years—in fact, ever since they were the same age.

Man knows his age, woman calculates hers.

Girls who don't marry by twenty-eight, usually stay at that age until they do.

The seven ages of woman are her own and six guesses.

The best way to tell a woman's age is not to.

A woman never seems to know her own age but always knows the ages of her friends.

Age gives people away: it tells on them.

Another thing that's usually marked down is a woman's age.

A woman stops telling her age when her age starts telling on her.

He who is not healthy at 20, wealthy at 40, or wise at 60, will never be healthy, wealthy, or wise.

It's always a good idea to act your age even if you hesitate to tell it.

Twenty-nine is a wonderful age for a man to be, and for a woman to stay.

Age doesn't really matter—unless you're a cheese.

There are more women of 30 going on 29 than there are women of 29 going on 30.

A woman's age is like the speedometer of a used car for sale: it has been set back, but you don't know how far.

A clever wife doesn't lie about her age: she just says she's as old as her husband, and then lies about his age.

Why do women think they get wiser with the years, but not older?

Thirty is a nice age for a woman, especially if she happens to be forty.

A woman cannot stop time in its flight, but she can fix her own age.

Women age quicker than men, but less often.

The thing women hate most to leave them is the age of twenty-nine.

It's always difficult to tell a woman's age—at least, it is for her.

The sweetest age in the world is sixteen, or whatever age your daughter is.

No woman is just the age she would like to be.

The little girl who once was five going on six has grown up now and is 29 going on 28.

A man's age commands respect, a woman's demands tact.

Age creeps up on a woman, but never quite catches up with her.

Most women try to conceal their age because most men don't act theirs.

At the age of 40 an Eskimo woman is very old; in the United States a woman at that age would be about 28.

The three ages of men are underage, overage and average.

The best way to tell a woman's age is—when she's not around.

When a woman begins to show her age, she begins to hide it.

A woman's age is her own business, and she certainly knows how to mind her own business.

A woman is as young as she feels—you'll believe.

AGING

The only thing some people do is to grow older.　　　— Ed Howe

I must be getting old because the women I meet now always look younger to me than they really are.
　　　　　　　　　　— Sacha Guitry

When a fellow begins to complain of the immodesty of women, he's getting pretty well along in years.　　　— Kin Hubbard

As we grow older, our bodies get shorter and our anecdotes longer.　　　— Robert Quillen

To grow old is to pass from passion to compassion.　— Camus

A man is getting old when the gleam in his eye is merely the sun reflected in his glasses.

Aging is the process of growing old, hastened chiefly by the eternal struggle to remain young.

The surest sign of growing old is when you begin to regret the sins you did not commit.

Growing old has one advantage: you'll never have to do it over again.

You are getting old when you find yourself using one bendover to pick up two things.

It is woman's fate to keep on growing older long after she is old enough.

Another trouble with growing old is that you stop feeling your oats and start feeling your corns.

Growing old isn't so bad, especially if you consider the alternative.

Widowers grow old alone; and so do husbands whose wives have given up having birthdays.

Geriatrics is the science that helps you to live longer without growing older.

You're getting old when, of two evils, you choose the one that gets you home earlier.

The older we grow, the more we realize that no one who is as young as we are, is old.

Before some women age a lot, they age a lot of men.

Don't worry about your age: remember, every time you grow a year older, so do all your friends.

Don't complain that you aren't as young as you used to be: you never were.

Another sign of age is when you begin to spend more time talking with your druggist than with your bartender.

Growing old has its compensations: all the things you couldn't have when you were young you no longer want.

As we grow older, work seems a lot less fun, and fun seems a lot more work.

You're getting old when you feel on Saturday night the way you used to feel on Monday morning.

When you grow older, you don't grow wiser; you merely learn to hide your ignorance better.

Geriatrics is the branch of medicine that seeks to add years to your life as well as life to your years.

As a man grows older, he either talks more and says less or talks less and says more.

Another drawback about growing old is that the younger generation keeps getting younger.

AGNOSTICISM

Don't be an agnostic—be something.   — Robert Frost

Agnosticism is nothing new; what is new is agnostic culture.
                            — Malraux

I don't know if God exists, but it would be better for His reputation if He didn't. — Jules Renard

An agnostic is an irreligious person who stays away from church religiously.

Although there are dozens of religious denominations in this country, many persons cannot find one to suit them.

AGREEMENT

Agreement is brought about by changing people's minds—other people's.   — S. I. Hayakawa

There is no conversation more boring than the one where everybody agrees. — *Montaigne*

We like a man to come right out and say what he thinks—if we agree with him. — *Mark Twain*

I have never in my life learned anything from any man who agreed with me.
— *Dudley Field Malone*

When men and women agree, it is only in their conclusions; their reasons are always different.
— *Santayana*

The fellow that agrees with everything you say is either a fool or he is getting ready to skin you.
— *Kin Hubbard*

The man who agrees with everybody is not worth having anybody agree with him. — *Lord Palmerston*

You may easily play a joke on a man who likes to argue—agree with him. — *Ed Howe*

To have a person agree with everything you say is worse than living alone.

When a man agrees with his wife, it is sometimes due to experience, but more often to expedience.

Nobody agrees with the opinion of others; one merely agrees with one's own opinion expressed by others.

When diplomats say they agree in principle, it means they agree in nothing else.

When a married couple always agree, one of them is the boss.

Most of us are too fond of people that agree with us—and of food that doesn't.

The only thing that two politicians agree on is what the third politician should give to charity.

Always agree with a woman before you start telling her she's wrong.

The only way you can sometimes achieve a meeting of minds is by knocking a few heads together.

The most difficult problem in mathematics is to make the date of a woman's birth agree with her present age.

Isn't it strange that in political matters it is only the intelligent people who agree with us?

A good way to get people to agree with you is to keep your mouth shut.

AIM

Many a man has an excellent aim in life, but no ammunition.
— *C. C. Colton*

You aim for the palace and get drowned in the sewer.
— *Mark Twain*

Whenever you have an aim you must sacrifice something of freedom to attain it.
— *Somerset Maugham*

You're not driving your car after you pass eighty miles an hour —you're aiming it.

The girl who seems to be throwing herself at a man is really taking careful aim.

The bull's-eye is the last part of the target to wear out.

If a man's aim in this world is good, the chances are that he will miss fire in the next.

Don't hurl defiance unless your aim is good.

When a wife misses her husband, she should aim more carefully next time.

Many a man has the right aim in life, but hasn't enough courage to pull the trigger.

Don't aim too high if your stock of ammunition is low.

It isn't enough in business to aim to please; one must constantly improve one's marksmanship.

AIR

Fresh air is good if you don't take too much of it; most of the achievements and pleasures of life are in bad air.
        – Justice O. W. Holmes

The air is free, but not when you advertise over it.

In this automobile age our national air comes near being carbon monoxide.

When a man sets out to air his knowledge, he is always able to supply the wind.

A civilized country is one whose inhabitants must go to a backward area in order to breathe pure, clear air.

The air is just as free as it ever was, but it now costs more to be able to breathe it.

Another good way to reduce air pollution is to get political candidates to make fewer and shorter speeches.

There's nothing wrong with an air of importance, provided it is sung instead of worn.

AIR CONDITIONING

Many an executive goes from his air-conditioned office in an air-conditioned car to his air-conditioned club to take a steam bath.

Hell carries no terrors for us any longer because nowadays everyplace is air-conditioned.

Air conditioning is most useful during months that have no R in them.

The chief virtue of an air conditioner is that the neighbors can't borrow it.

AIRPLANE

Nowadays the airlines have so many types of planes that a person can ride on everything but schedule.

Speed isn't everything: modern planes fly so fast, you hardly have time to get acquainted with the hostesses.

With modern jets you can have breakfast in Los Angeles, lunch in New York, dinner in London, and baggage in Rome.

The only way to pass motorists at a safe distance is to travel by air.

Many a timid person won't take a trip by plane until the law of gravity has been repealed.

Times change: today the successful executive has to be a man with an infinite capacity for taking planes.

Two other places the airplane has brought closer together are this world and the next.

Aviation is making the earth smaller and smaller, but you still can't fall and miss it.

It isn't the cost of your private plane—it's the upkeep.

Jet planes have superseded the propeller planes, thus proving that pull will get you far, but push will get you farther.

Another good way to insure yourself against auto accidents is to take the plane.

Airplane travel is so swift that it enables you to have dinner in New York and heartburn in Los Angeles.

An airplane is the only place where you cannot walk out on a dull movie.

Progress is wonderful: in bad weather modern jets whisk you faster than ever to someplace hundreds of miles from where you want to go.

ALARM CLOCK

The man who invented the alarm clock believed people slept too long or worked too little.

The only thing worse than hearing the alarm clock in the morning is not hearing it.

Some men have alarm clocks; others have their wives' elbows.

Of all daylight-saving plans, the best by far is an alarm clock.

When an alarm clock wakes a man up, it makes him feel not like the early bird, but like the worm.

An alarm clock is a device that wakes you up just in time to go back to sleep.

What this country needs is an alarm clock that can be set on Saturday night to ring Monday morning.

The man who invented the alarm clock probably did more than anyone else to arouse the working classes.

An alarm clock is built with a mechanism to scare the daylights into you.

ALCOHOL

I have taken more out of alcohol than alcohol has taken out of me.
      — Winston Churchill

Man is the only machine that needs to be lubricated with alcohol.

Alcohol is a good preservative for almost everything but secrets.

Man has been exhorted to love his enemies, but so far alcohol is the only enemy he has learned to love.

Alcohol is like success: both are all right until they go to your head.

ALCOHOLIC

The trouble with many an alcoholic is that he has no desire to become anonymous.

What every drunk needs is to get more blood into his alcohol stream.

An alcoholic is anyone who will drink with anyone to anyone.

An alcoholic is the only sponge that never fills up on water.

You cannot keep both yourself and your business in a liquid condition.

Many an alcoholic doesn't really like to drink: it's just something to do while getting drunk.

An alcoholic finds it hard to battle his way to the top, but easy to bottle his way to the bottom.

The higher a drunk feels in the evening, the lower he feels in the morning.

The man who drinks to drown his sorrows is trying to put out a fire with oil.

The reason an alcoholic finds it hard making both ends meet is that he is busy making one end drink.

An alcoholic's favorite drink is always the next one.

Many an alcoholic would go on the wagon if he could only find one with a bar.

An alcoholic is a person who drinks like a fish, but not the same thing.

An alcoholic has his mind always on drink, and has drink always on his mind.

Rich men are alcoholics, poor men are drunks.

Drink should never be given to the man who is given to drink.

An alcoholic is a man who never puts off till tomorrow the drinking he can do today.

An alcoholic never feels fit as a fiddle because he always gets tight as a drum.

An alcoholic is constantly irritating his family because he is constantly irrigating himself.

An alcoholic always drinks to forget, but never forgets to drink.

ALIBI

A woman with a few children always has an alibi.
                              — Kin Hubbard

An alibi is first cousin to an excuse, and they're both mighty poor relations.

Some men spend half their lives telling what they are going to do, and the other half explaining why they didn't do it.

College students specialize in all fields of study, but most of them major in alibiology.

The man who fails to live up to his own expectations never fails to give himself a satisfactory alibi.

The husband with an iron-clad alibi is never as well off as the husband with a diamond-studded one.

The wife who listens to every word her husband says is probably looking for a hole in his alibi.

An alibi is the proof that you did do what you didn't do so that others will think you didn't do what you did.

The man who loves to fish usually has a wife who would rather listen to his alibis than clean fish.

There's nothing like flowers if you want a strong plea to accompany a weak alibi.

ALIMONY

Alimony often enables a woman who lived unhappily married to live happily unmarried.

Some women aren't particular what men they marry; one man's alimony is as good as another's.

To some women marriage is always a gamble because they never know in advance how much their alimony will be.

If marriage is a lottery, alimony must be a sort of gambling debt.

When a man is being sued for alimony, he suddenly discovers how rich he is.

The man who has only one opinion about marriage is probably paying alimony on it.

Alimony is a great improvement in a woman's lot because it comes in regularly, never quarrels, and never complains about the food.

Marry in haste, and pay alimony at leisure.

Divorce often turns a short matrimony into a long alimony.

Many a woman's idea of economy is never to live beyond her alimony.

Two can live as cheaply as one can pay alimony.

Many a man falls behind in his alimony payments because his second wife doesn't earn as much as he had expected.

Alimony often keeps matrimony from being a failure.

Alimony is the fine levied on a man who won't stay single and can't stay married.

'Tis better to have loved and receive alimony than never to have loved at all.

Alimony is like paying installments on your car after it is wrecked.

Love has its compensations, and they are usually called alimony.

Alimony takes pay out of the man's paycheck, and work out of the woman's housework.

There are few things as rare as a day in June, and one of them is the man who is always ahead in his alimony payments.

The girl who marries a man for his money sometimes has to divorce him to get it.

Some women make money, and some make alimony.

Alimony is the fee a woman charges for name dropping.

Many a man makes the first payment on the alimony before he makes the last payment on the engagement ring.

ALLOWANCE

Another thing a small boy is constantly outgrowing is his allowance.

Many a youngster gets an allowance while his father doesn't.

Don't criticize your wife's clothes too freely—make allowances for them.

Parents can afford to give their child an allowance, but what breaks them are the fringe benefits.

Don't give your son all the allowance you can afford; keep back some to bail him out.

One of the first things a child learns at school is that some other child is getting a bigger allowance.

Husbands give allowances, and wives make them.

The allowances you give your children never do as much harm as the allowances you make for them.

Allowance is the name given to the bribe that the older generation gives the younger generation to live with it.

Don't ruin your little son by giving him an allowance—how will he feel later when he marries and doesn't get one?

Almost any youngster can manage on his allowance—until he needs more money.

ALPHABET

Alphabetically speaking, it's the eyes of a woman that disturb the ease of a man.

Our wise old ancestors knew we would always be making mistakes, so they put the letter x in the alphabet for xxxxxing out.

Children start kindergarten these days with a big advantage: they already know two letters of the alphabet—TV.

The alphabet of love consists of avowals and consents.

A lawyer can usually do more with two or three letters than a writer can with the whole alphabet.

ALTRUISM

An altruist is one who would be sincerely sorry to see his neighbor's children devoured by wolves.
— *Mencken*

The most popular form of altruism is giving to others the advice you cannot use yourself.

Unselfish women make the best wives—and the worst husbands.

An altruist is a human being who has a greater love for the species than for specie.

AMATEUR

An amateur is a young man who, when flattering women, is afraid of overdoing it.

The two most difficult careers are entrusted to amateurs—citizenship and parenthood.

An amateur is an athlete who insists on cash and won't take a check.

AMATEUR AND PROFESSIONAL

Any amateur can start a love affair, but only a professional knows how to break it off.

Another field where professionals face too much amateur competition is the business of marriage counselling.

They always talk about professional women because there is no such thing as an amateur woman.

Sex is the only field where the amateur is favored and the professional disapproved.

One picture is worth a thousand words, but only if the picture is by a professional photographer and the words by an amateur writer.

It takes a little experience to kiss like a professional, but a lot of experience to kiss like an amateur.

AMBIGUITY

Those who write clearly have readers, those who write obscurely have commentators.   — *Camus*

The man who uses big words is afraid that if people knew what he was talking about, they'd know he didn't know what he was talking about.

The man who wants to appear deep usually uses high-sounding words.

Doubletalk is absolutely necessary for art critics, otherwise they'd be found out.

AMBITION

If ambition doesn't hurt you, you haven't got it.
— *Kathleen Norris*

The wise man is cured of ambition by ambition. — *La Bruyère*

Ambition often puts men upon doing the meanest offices: so climbing is performed in the same posture with creeping. — *Swift*

Many a man's ambition is to marry a rich girl who is too proud to have her husband work.

The height of the average girl's ambition is just about six feet.

Ambition doesn't always pay: the man whose wife drives him to go out and look for a new job often ends up by looking for a new wife.

The ambitious girl starts out to make a name for herself, but she usually ends up by accepting some man's.

Ambition is the only disease that laziness can cure.

If you can't bear to have your face stepped on, don't try to climb the ladder of success.

All men want to suceed; some want to succeed so badly, they're even willing to work for it.

Remember this on your way up: the biggest dog was once a pup.

Ambition is a person's strong desire to work so that he can live later without work.

No persons stoop so low as those most eager to rise high in the world.

Beware of ambition—it can drive you into a lot of work.

AMERICAN

As an American, I naturally spend most of my time laughing.
                    — Mencken

I've seen many American women who look like queens, but I have never seen an American man who looks like a king.
                    — Hermann A. Keyserling

Americans are like a rich father who wishes he knew how to give his sons the hardships that made him rich.   — Robert Frost

A citizen of America will cross the ocean to fight for democracy, but won't cross the street to vote in a national election.
                    — Bill Vaughan

The ordinary American is a pure abstraction, like the sociological monster known as the average man who has two and a half children.
                    — Herbert J. Muller

Being a Virginian is a profession, and being a South Carolinian is a trade to be worked at, but Kentuckianism is an incurable disease.   — Irvin S. Cobb

Census figures show the average American is getting younger, thus proving the average American is a myth.

An American is a man who is proud of his right to say what he pleases, and often wishes he had the courage to do so.

About the only time an American citizen hears from his government is when he gets a tax bill.

It is the right of every American male to bear arms, and of every American female to bare the rest of her anatomy.

Most Americans drive last year's cars, wear this year's clothes, and live on next year's earnings.

AMERICAN AND ENGLISHMAN

The Americans are the illegitimate children of the English.
— *Mencken*

An Englishman does things because they have been done before; an American does things because they haven't been done before.
— *Mark Twain*

In England I would rather be a man, a horse, a dog or a woman, in that order; in America, I would reverse the order. — *Bruce Gould*

An Englishman is much like an American, with the volume turned down.

An American lifts his hat to ladies in an elevator; an Englishman elevates his hat to ladies in a lift.

AMUSEMENT

Life would be tolerable but for its amusements. — *Bernard Shaw*

Happy is the father whose child finds his attempts to amuse it amusing.   — *Robert Lynd*

Life is worth living, but only if we avoid the amusements of grown-up people. — *Robert Lynd*

When at home, try to amuse yourself; when visiting, try to amuse others.

The only things more amusing than some of our statues are some of our statutes.

ANCESTOR

I would like to be like my father and all the rest of my ancestors who never married. — *Molière*

Everyone has something ancestral, even if it is nothing more than a disease.   — *Ed Howe*

The man who hasn't anything to boast of but his illustrious ancestors is like a potato—the only good belonging to him is underground.   — *Thomas Overbury*

You can't choose your ancestors, but that's fair enough; they probably wouldn't have chosen you.

People who brag about their ancestors talk as if they had selected them themselves.

A person's pride in his ancestors increases in proportion to the distance.

Some mighty disagreeable contemporaries have turned out to be glorious ancestors.

Our ancestors were overworked and undereducated so that we might be underworked and overeducated.

The man who boasts about his ancestors of a century ago is not likely to become an ancestor they will boast about a century hence.

The further back you can trace your descent, the longer you have been descending.

Some people can trace their ancestry back hundreds of years, but cannot tell you where their children were last night.

ANECDOTE

A good story is always worth repeating, but not to the same person.

The man who doesn't laugh at a funny story is probably not employed by the man who told it.

The difference between an old man and an old woman is that one is in his dotage and the other in her anecdotage.

Many a man wouldn't listen to your story if he didn't think it was his turn next.

ANESTHETIC

To be in love is merely to be in a perpetual state of anesthesia.
       — *Mencken*

The only way to reform some people is to chloroform them.
       — *Thomas C. Haliburton*

The liquor tax is the only tax ever imposed that provides its own anesthetic.

The woman who is given an anesthetic before the operation, should be given another afterwards to keep her from talking about it.

Modern art is a form of esthetics that looks as if it were painted under anesthetics.

ANGEL

Angels can fly because they take themselves lightly.   — *Chesterton*

You never see angels with beards because men who get to heaven make it only by a close shave.

Many a man treats his wife like an angel—nothing to eat and less to wear.

If man is little lower than the angels, the angels should reform.

Beware of the girl who looks like an angel: sooner or later she will play the devil with a man.

Nowadays what the pedestrian needs more than legs are wings, and he often gets them.

Marriage seldom seems to teach a woman that only an angel should keep harping.

ANGER

A man who has never made a woman angry is a failure in life.
       — *Christopher Morley*

Anger is seldom without an argument, but seldom with a good one.
       — *Halifax*

Speak when you're angry—and you'll make the best speech you'll ever regret.

Nothing makes a woman angrier than when her husband pretends to believe her when he knows she is lying to him.

Hitting the ceiling is the worst way to get up in the world.

Hell hath no fury like the lawyer of a woman scorned.

Marriage gives a woman a new roof over her head, and the right to raise it occasionally.

Anger improves nothing, except the arch of a cat's back.

When an irresistible force meets an immovable object, both women get mad.

Never quarrel with a person who is angry, but give him a soft answer instead: it will make him madder than anything else you could say.

It usually takes two people to make one of them angry.

Anger is an uncontrolled feeling that betrays what you are when you are not yourself.

Hell knows no fury like that of the woman you are trying to stop from making a fool of herself over a man.

Righteous indignation is the ability to be mad without swearing.

No animal in the world has as little sense as a man when he gets mad.

Control yourself: remember that anger is only one letter short of danger.

Ask a woman how old she is if you want to see her rage.

There are two things you should never be angry at: what you can help, and what you can't.

If you want to know where a man really stands, see him when he's beside himself.

Hell hath no fury like a woman who has waited an hour for her husband on the wrong corner.

When angry, shake your finger, not your fist.

Marriage often makes a woman money-mad—at her husband.

Don't fly into a rage unless you are prepared for a rough landing.

When angry, take a lesson from modern science: always count down before blasting off.

ANIMALS

The hippopotamus looks monogamous—he looks as if he would have to be.   *— Will Cuppy*

Man is the only animal that knows that animals grow old.
— G. C. Lichtenberg

What really happened to the buffaloes is just what you might expect if you've ever seen one in a zoo—the moths got into them.
— Will Cuppy

Pity the poor animals; but for their shape they might be human.

The only creature that can keep his feet on the ground while his head is in the clouds is the giraffe.

We no longer believe that people can change themselves into animals, yet the world is full of men who make hogs and asses of themselves.

Animals are not as stupid as people think; for example, they have no lawyers.

Man is the only animal that feels insulted when called an animal.

ANNIVERSARY

An anniversary is the day on which a husband behaves as he always should.

The most welcome surprise you can give your wife on your anniversary is to remember it.

With history piling up so fast, almost every day now is the anniversary of something awful.

A married couple may reach their golden wedding anniversary without ever having thought of divorce, but not without ever having thought of murder.

An anniversary is the yesterday you forgot to buy your wife a gift.

Why is it that married couples celebrate their wedding anniversaries while divorced couples don't celebrate their divorce anniversaries?

A silver wedding is the day on which a married man celebrates twenty-five years of work under the same boss.

Golden wedding anniversaries are joyous occasions because the happy couple is usually out of debt by then.

Some husbands have no talent for remembering anniversaries, while with others it's a gift.

Another man who doesn't bear a grudge is the husband who forgets his wedding anniversary.

A golden wedding anniversary is lots of fun and laughter, created in part by the original wedding pictures.

Some husbands forget anniversaries; others save a lot of money pretending that they do.

A movie star celebrates her fifth wedding anniversary after she has been married five years—or five times.

The man who never forgets his wedding anniversary is probably a bachelor.

ANNOY

Nothing upsets a woman like somebody getting married she didn't even know had a beau.
— *Kin Hubbard*

An irritable man is like a hedgehog rolled up the wrong way, tormenting himself with his own prickles. — *Thomas Hood*

When a woman after many years of married life loves her husband as much as ever, she probably annoys him in other ways too.

Women are more irritable than men, probably because men are more irritating.

There's only one thing that irritates a woman more than a man who doesn't understand her, and that's a man who does.

Before marriage, a woman is a man's aspiration; after marriage, she's his exasperation.

There's no one so annoying as the person who always says something against everyone, except the person who never says anything against anyone.

Life for a movie star is full of aggravations: if it isn't one husband, it's another.

The only thing more disturbing than a neighbor with a noisy old car is a neighbor with a quiet new one.

Some schoolchildren are always trying; others are always very trying.

ANSWER

You sometimes have to answer a woman according to her womanishness, just as you have to answer a fool according to his folly.
— *Bernard Shaw*

The more you put off answering letters, the less need there is for answering them.

It's not what a man says that counts, it's what his wife answers.

No answer is also an answer.

A loud answer too turneth away wrath, but only if you're much bigger.

The shortest answer sometimes is to do it.

Some men love nothing better than to answer an unanswerable argument.

A word to the wise often gets a very long answer.

Girls who know all the answers may have learned them in questionable places.

ANT

The ant is knowing and wise, but he doesn't know enough to take a vacation.　— *Clarence Day*

The ant is the hardest-working creature in the world—when someone is looking.　— *Mark Twain*

If ants are so busy, how is it that they attend all the picnics?

All the essentials for a picnic are brought from home, except the ants.

ANTICIPATE

If pleasures are greatest in anticipation, remember that this is also true of trouble.
— *Elbert Hubbard*

The only thing more entertaining than anticipation of the unexpected is expectation of the impossible.

You can never tell what a woman is going to do, and if you could, she would probably do something else.

ANTIQUE

An antique isn't always as old as it's cracked up to be.

The woman who collects antiques is probably living in a modern apartment.

One man's junk is another man's antique.

The only modern things in an antique shop are the prices.

No one would ever want a particular antique if there were plenty of specimens around.

If it's hard to dust, it's probably an antique.

An antique is a fugitive from the junk shop with a price on its head.

Family antiques handed down from generation to generation prove that the children of your ancestors were better behaved than your own.

An antique shop is a place where there are thousands of treasures you can do without.

The price of an antique increases as its value decreases.

An antique is anything that's too old for the poor, but not too old for the rich.

Anyone can become rich if he can guess just when a piece of junk becomes a rare antique.

Only the chairs that are uncomfortable become antiques: the comfortable ones are worn out in a single generation.

An antique by any other name would not cost as much.

The old things we own are heirlooms; yours are antiques; the other fellow's are junk.

Antiques are things one generation buys, the next generation gets rid of, and the following generation buys again.

ANXIETY

It requires a great deal of inexperience to be beyond the reach of anxiety.

Anxiety isn't all bad: at least it gives you something to think about while watching television.

Don't brood: you're a human being, not a hen.

Anxiety is like sand in an oyster: a little produces a pearl, too much kills the creature.

There are only two types of girls who brood about a boyfriend: those who have one, and those who haven't.

APARTMENT

The ideal apartment is large enough to keep your wife from going home to mother, yet small enough to keep her mother from coming to you.

The trouble with modern apartments is that the walls are too thin when you try to sleep, and too thick when you try to listen.

Modern apartments are built on the principle that half as much room should cost twice as much money.

Modern apartment houses are being built with every known convenience, except low rent.

The surest way to meet your neighbors in an apartment house is to play your television set too loud too late.

An apartment house is a building full of people who are always wondering when that noisy party will end.

There's always room for a good man, unless he is looking for an inexpensive apartment.

APE

It is even harder for the average ape to believe that he has descended from man.   — *Mencken*

None of the anthropoid apes emits musical sounds, but on the other hand none of them tries to.

APHORISM

Aphorisms are salted and not sugared almonds at reason's feast.
   — *Logan P. Smith*

The more men coin wise aphorisms, the more foolish the world acts.

Another man of few words is the aphorist.

Aphorisms prick with the sharp point of truth, but with the sting removed.

APOLOGY

If I've done anything I'm sorry for, I'm willing to be forgiven.
   — *Edward N. Westcott*

An apology sometimes consists of words of regret that you really feel, but more often words of regret.

Never refuse to accept an apology; you won't be offered more than one in a lifetime, and you can keep it as a rarity.

An apology is saying the right thing after doing the wrong thing.

Man is the only member of the animal kingdom that apologizes— or needs to.

The less a man says, the more he doesn't have to apologize.

An apology is an expression of regret where the voice seldom matches the words.

An apology is a lump in the throat caused by having to eat your own words.

When a husband manages to get the last word, it's usually an apology.

Humble pie is the only pastry that's never tasty.

APPEARANCE

Being a well-dressed man is a career, and he who goes in for it has no time for anything else.
   — *Heywood Broun*

A woman can look both moral and exciting—if she also looks as if it was quite a struggle.
— *Edna Ferber*

The more clothes I put on, the better I look. — *Finley Peter Dunne*

If a girl knew she looked all right, wouldn't it save her a lot of trouble? — *Kin Hubbard*

He had so much money that he could afford to look poor.
— *Edgar Wallace*

A woman, the more serious she is about her face, is commonly the more careless about her home.
— *Ben Jonson*

The Lord prefers common-looking people: that is the reason he makes so many of them. — *Lincoln*

Getting talked about is one of the penalties for being pretty, while being above suspicion is about the only compensation for being homely. — *Kin Hubbard*

Most women try to improve their looks instead of their minds because they know most men are dumb but not blind.

Keeping up appearances is what keeps many a man down.

Many a man spends a lot of time and money beautifying his patio, and then ruins it all by appearing on it dressed in shorts.

Appearances are deceiving, but disappearances are often more so.

Appearance is an important factor in earning money, and vice versa.

Girls who look good in the best places usually get taken there.

Many a girl who looks like a million is probably looking for it too.

Women get a good deal of their looks from their parents, and even more from their cosmetics.

Many a woman looks just as young as she used to look years ago, but it takes her much longer.

Nothing improves a woman's appearance faster than a man's.

When a woman looks her age, she tries to overlook it.

Beauty fades, but a plain girl stays plain forever.

When the other fellow looks that way, it's because he's dissipated; when you look that way, it's because you're run down.

No matter what some men wear, they always look like an unmade bed.

People who have nothing else to keep usually try to keep up appearances.

Looks are deceiving, but it's better to have them deceive for us than against us.

A man's appearance shows how much he is earning; a woman's appearance shows how much she is spending.

When someone says you look like a million dollars, don't swell with pride; maybe you do look overtaxed.

The reason mature men look younger than mature women is that a woman of 40 is usually 50.

Many a woman grows old before her time trying to look young after her time.

Smart men are smarter than they look; smart women look smarter than they are.

APPEASEMENT

An appeaser is one who feeds a crocodile hoping it will eat him last.　　　— *Winston Churchill*

Appeasers believe that if you keep on throwing steaks to a tiger, the tiger will become a vegetarian.
— *Heywood Broun*

APPENDIX

The only time a man ever took anything from me was when my appendix was being removed—and then he had to use chloroform.
— *Peggy Hopkins Joyce*

An appendix is what you have taken out before the doctor decides it is your gall bladder.

If you still have your appendix at middle age, you're probably a surgeon.

It's not true that the appendix is useless; it has put thousands of surgeons' wives in fine furs.

APPETITE

Too many appetizers spoil the appetite.

Appetite is a troublesome thing: if you're too rich, you suffer from lack of it; if you're too poor, you suffer from excess of it.

The best way to improve your appetite is to go on a diet.

Gluttons don't really have good appetites, except at breakfast, lunch, dinner, and between meals.

The objection to saving for your old age is that you cannot save your appetite for your old age.

APPLAUSE

The movies enable an actor not only to act, but also to sit down in the theater and clap for himself.
— *Will Rogers*

He who seeks only for applause from without has all his happiness in another's keeping.
— *Oliver Goldsmith*

If a man accepts applause when people like what he does, he should accept hissing from people who don't like what he does.
— *Leopold Stokowski*

Politicians are applauded not for what they have done but for what they may do for the applauders.
— *Alben Barkley*

Every actor hates to be interrupted, except by applause.

APPLE

But for the apple, man would simply be a sun-tanned idler.

An apple a day keeps the doctor away, but not if it's a green one.

Adam's experience proves that the apple should be drunk as cider rather than be eaten as fruit.

An apple a day will keep the doctor away, unless he's a doctor of philosophy.

Good often comes from evil: the apple that Eve ate has given work to thousands of designers and dressmakers.

All apples look alike when pared.

An apple a day will keep the ear, eye, nose, and throat specialist, the dermatologist, and the gastroenterologist away.

APPOINTMENT

It's never too late for a woman to keep an appointment.

Appointments are a waste of time because being early wastes yours and being late wastes the other person's.

APPRECIATION

Appreciation is a wonderful thing: it makes what is excellent in others belong to us as well.
— *Voltaire*

A young man in love thinks nothing is good enough for her, except himself.

It is better to be able to appreciate things you cannot have than to have things you cannot appreciate.

In a woman's eyes, a man to be worthwhile must think her more than worthwhile.

Some girls appreciate the man who loves them and leaves them, provided he leaves them enough.

Appreciation is something that comes to a man after death, and to a woman after divorce.

APPROVAL

When a man says he approves of something in principle, it means he hasn't the slightest intention of putting it into practice. — *Bismarck*

To a teenager, it cannot be true love if her family approves of him.

A wife likes to see her husband enjoy himself, but only in the ways that she approves.

There's only one kind of tax that would win universal approval —a tax on the other fellow.

ARBITRATION

An arbitrator is the only man who is completely satisfied with the final settlement.

When an arbitrator fails to settle a dispute, both sides regard him as more traitor than arbitrator.

A mediator is the middleman who is always in the middle of a muddle.

An arbitrator should never be arbitrary.

An arbitrator is a man who listens to both sides, studies the evidence, and then mispronounces judgment.

Necessity is the mother of intervention.

Arbitration is the art of getting management and labor together not to lock horns but to lock arms instead.

ARCHEOLOGY

An archeologist is the best husband any woman can have because the older she gets, the more he is interested in her. — *Agatha Christie*

Archeology is the science of digging in the earth to try and find a civilization worse than ours.

An archeologist is a scientist who seeks to discover past civilizations while the present one is still around.

Marriage is an ancient institution and most of our knowledge of antiquity is gleaned from shattered pottery.

ARCHITECTURE

The only thing wrong with architecture are the architects.
— *Frank Lloyd Wright*

We shape our buildings; thereafter they shape us.
— *Winston Churchill*

A doctor can bury his mistakes, but an architect can only advise his client to plant vines.
— *Frank Lloyd Wright*

The architect makes an old house look better just by talking about the cost of a new one.

The architect who always talks shop is probably suffering from an edifice complex.

ARGUMENT

A long dispute means that both parties are wrong. — *Voltaire*

Behind every argument is someone's ignorance.
— *Louis D. Brandeis*

Every argument between two people is likely to sink or rise to the level of a dogfight.
— *A. A. Milne*

No matter what side of an argument you're on, you always find some people on your side that you wish were on the other side.
— *Jascha Heifetz*

He always had a chip on his shoulder that he was ready to use to kindle an argument.
— *Fred Allen*

The principal objection to a quarrel is that it interrupts an argument. — *Chesterton*

Argumentative people have one thing in common: they are always ready to dispute an indisputable fact.

The most common argument against marriage is the one between husband and wife.

A wrangler will argue with everyone, even with the man who won't talk.

Never argue with anyone: remember, he too has a right to his own stupid opinion.

There's only one thing worse than the man who will argue over anything, and that's the man who will argue over nothing.

Avoid arguments if possible, and especially avoid them if impossible.

When we wrangle, it's because we are sensitive; when others do, it's because they are quarrelsome.

When you win an argument with your wife, the argument is not over.

An argument always leaves each party convinced that the other has a closed mind.

Some women never take part in an argument—they take all of it.

The less sound a man's argument, the louder he talks.

A man can't win an argument with his wife, but he can break even by keeping his mouth shut.

Heated arguments cool friendship.

That a man may know how to argue is no proof he knows what he is arguing about.

If you are losing an argument with your wife, try a kiss.

An argument is an angry dispute in which two persons keep talking without throwing anything.

The quickest way for a peacemaker to end an argument between a man and his wife is to take sides.

When one woman argues with another, who gets the last word?

All cantankerous men are alike: they keep gnawing away on the bone of contention.

The reason women usually win arguments with men is that only dumb men are foolish enough to argue with women.

An argument seldom proves anything, except that two people differ.

The only thing worse than being on the wrong side of an argument is to be on the right side with no one listening.

There are two sides to every argument, and they're usually married to each other.

The surest sign that you haven't any sense is to argue with one who hasn't.

Some men learn quickly, while others still argue with a woman.

It takes two to make an argument, unless you have a wife.

It's surprising how many people don't find it necessary to understand things in order to argue about them.

A wife always has the last word in an argument; anything a husband says after that is the start of another argument.

Avoid disputes: you never get as much out of an argument as you put into it.

In every family there are two sides to every argument, but no end.

There is nothing so exasperating as arguing with someone who knows what he's talking about.

The only thing that starts more arguments in the home than weak coffee is strong drink.

To get the best out of an argument, stay out of it.

There are two sides to every argument, until you take one.

ARISE

I am the oldest living white man, especially at seven in the morning.
— *Robert Benchley*

Well enough for old folks to rise early—they have done so many mean things all their lives, they can't sleep anyhow.
— *Mark Twain*

My mother used to get up every morning at five A.M., no matter what time it was. — *Sam Levenson*

Many a man does the hardest work of his whole day before breakfast—getting up.

Early risers are conceited in the morning and sleepy in the afternoon.

The older generation thinks nothing of getting up at six in the morning—and the younger generation doesn't think much of it either.

Sometimes all the early bird gets is up.

It's never too late to get up in the morning—unless it's past noon.

It is human nature to grumble at having to get up early in the morning—until one morning when you can't get up.

It's hard to raise a family nowadays, especially in the morning.

Some men get up with the lark, while others want a swallow the first thing in the morning.

The rising generation may be rising, but it's mighty hard to get it out of bed.

ARMS

The moment you have a woman in your arms, you have her on your hands.

The quickest way to check a domestic quarrel is by the timely use of arms.

The length of time it takes to put your arm around a girl is not always in proportion to her size.

It is much easier to slip between a woman's arms than to slip out again.

One arm makes dangerous driving and very poor hugging.

What the average man likes about the average girl is his arms.

ARMY

In order to have good soldiers a nation must always be at war.
— *Napoleon*

Army saying: If it moves, salute it; if it doesn't move, pick it up; if you can't pick it up, paint it.

To clothe one soldier it takes the wool from two sheep and the hides from three taxpayers.

The army is another organization that gives commissions in addition to salaries.

ARRANGEMENT

Nothing is new except arrangement.　　　　— *Will Durant*

It is absurd to divide people into good and bad: people are either charming or tedious.
　　　　　　　— *Oscar Wilde*

Knowledge is getting to be more and more costly, with most of the cost required in classifying it.

People may be divided into two classes: those who divide people into two classes, and those who do not.

ARRIVAL

Another thing that seems to arrive almost before you get started is the bridge you were going to cross when you got to it.

All things come to him who waits, but not all things wait for him to come.

In fashionable society, nobody arrives until everybody else has.

It is not enough for a man to have arrived; it is necessary to know in what condition.

Nothing stops a family quarrel more quickly than the arrival of an unexpected guest.

The latest thing in clothes is the woman who is the latest to arrive at a party.

ARRIVAL AND DEPARTURE

I arrive very late at work in the morning, but I make up for it by leaving very early in the afternoon.　　— *Charles Lamb*

She was so glad to see me go, that I have almost a mind to come again, that she may again have the same pleasure. — *Samuel Johnson*

An average is struck in all things: cold welcome, warm farewell.

At a cocktail party, the guests have more friends when they arrive than when they leave.

Life is a party at which you arrive after it has begun, and depart from before it has ended.

There's no blessed event like the arrival of your baby, except the departure of your mother-in-law.

The departure of the Christmas season is always followed by the arrival of the bills.

Visitors always give pleasure— some when they come, others when they go.

If your arrival doesn't improve a party, your departure probably does.

ART

Art is a lie that enables us to realize the truth.　　— *Picasso*

Art is long, and the talk about it is even longer.
— *William J. Locke*

It is art itself which should teach us to free ourselves from the rules of art.   — *Molière*

Let art alone—she's got enough guys sleeping with her.
— *Sherwood Anderson*

All works of art should begin at the end.   — *Edgar Allan Poe*

Art is I, science is we.
— *Claude Bernard*

Art for art's sake means no more than gin for gin's sake.
— *Somerset Maugham*

There is only one valuable thing in art: the thing you cannot explain.   — *Georges Braque*

Art isn't something you marry, it's something you rape.   — *Degas*

Drawing is not what you see, but what you must make others see.   — *Degas*

All art is a kind of subconscious madness expressed in terms of sanity.   — *George Jean Nathan*

Art is to get some fun out of sex without having to work for it.
— *Robert Frost*

The highest condition of art is artlessness.   — *Thoreau*

He knows all about art, but he doesn't know what he likes.
— *James Thurber*

The rule in the art world is: you cater to the masses or you kowtow to the elite; you can't have both.   — *Ben Hecht*

There is something ghostly in all great art.   — *Lafcadio Hearn*

When my eyes become dim with age and I shall not be able to see the world around me, I can paint non-objective abstractions and abstract non-objections.
— *Boris Artzybasheff*

It's clever, but is it art?
— *Kipling*

You're not supposed to enjoy modern art: it's made to be written and talked about, not looked at.

Opinion on abstract art is divided: some people think it's a waste of time, while others think it's a waste of paint.

. Art is long but seldom long enough to make both ends meet.

The paintings of today are pretty much alike except that they aren't pretty, they aren't much, and they aren't alike.

Abstract art is a form of modern art where the artist shows great skill in his inability to paint.

Modern is a word used to describe a form of art that has no other merit.

Art is the cure for many a disease which has not yet been discovered.

A dilettante is one whose interest in art consists of a little dabble and a lot of babble.

Abstract art enables the critic to admire what he can't appreciate, and to appreciate what he doesn't like.

Art is a paradox: if you want to master it, you must become its slave.

Modern art shows that the possibilities of art are nothing compared to its impossibilities.

Whether it is art or Art depends upon whether you capitalize it or not.

Art is long, which is why we have intermissions.

Modern art is a popular style of painting which is usually abstract, abstruse, and absurd.

It's not hard to understand modern art: if it hangs on a wall, it's a painting; if you can walk around it, it's a sculpture.

ARTIST

Bad artists always admire each other's work.   — *Oscar Wilde*

There are two kinds of woman painters: one kind wants to marry, and the other has no talent either.
          — *Max Liebermann*

The artist spends the first part of his life with the dead, the second with the living, and the third with himself.   — *Picasso*

Many excellent cooks are spoiled by going into the arts.
          — *Paul Gauguin*

The true artist will let his wife starve, his children go barefoot, his

mother drudge for his living, sooner than work at anything but his art.   — *Bernard Shaw*

Every artist was once an amateur.   — *Emerson*

Of seven peasants I can make seven Lords, but I cannot make even one Hans Holbein out of seven Lords.   — *Henry VIII*

The illustrator of books is an active fiend who clips with long, sharp shears the tender wings of illusion.   — *Max Beerbohm*

An artist who theorizes about his work is no longer artist but critic.
          — *H. G. Wells*

A good artist mixes his paints with his brush; a great one mixes them with his brains.

An artist is often ahead of his time with his paintings, but more often behind time with his payments.

An artist is known by the critics he praises.

Art is long, but artists are usually short—in funds.

The difference between an artist and an artisan is about twenty-five dollars a day.

The one thing genuine artists put aside for their old age is the thought of retirement.

No good artist can live without the critic within.

The reason so many artists are poor is that there are so many poor artists.

An artist sometimes gets paid per hour, sometimes per picture, but most often perhaps.

His salary is what a commercial artist draws best.

Art is long, and artists are usually long-suffering.

It is not necessary for an artist to be crazy, but it helps.

The abstract artist who sees things he cannot paint, decides to paint things he cannot see.

ASHTRAY

What this country needs is an ashtray that looks like one.

A wife's hardest task is to convince her husband that everything is not an ashtray.

Woman's place in the home nowadays is generally near an ashtray.

Any piece of bric-a-brac looks like an ashtray to the man who smokes.

ASPIRIN

We have had two chickens in every pot, two cars in every garage, and now we have two headaches for every aspirin.
— Fiorello La Guardia

When you can't take it any longer, take an aspirin.

Aspirin is a miracle drug: a year's supply usually disappears in a month.

Some people are such bores that, if allowed to go on, they would even give an aspirin a headache.

ASSOCIATION

The people are to be taken in very small doses. — Emerson

Getting married is not a bargain made by a man and woman to keep constantly tied to each other by the tail. — Montaigne

Why shouldn't things be largely absurd, futile and transitory—they are so, and we are so, and they and we go very well together.
— Santayana

When men have to do with one another, they are like verbs—almost all verbs are slightly irregular.
— Kierkegaard

By the time a man finally learns to get along with women, he discovers he can get along without them.

It is surprising how often good sense and good luck go hand in hand.

The less you have to do with some people, the less you'll be worse off.

All weddings are happy; it's the living together afterwards that causes all the trouble.

If you can't lick them, and they won't let you join them, what then?

To keep young, associate with young people; to get old, try keeping up with them.

ASTRONAUT

The advertising world had space men in it before spacemen existed.
— *Fred Allen*

An astronaut is the only man who can see the shape of the world as it really is.

Astronauts are always eager to get off the earth, and even more eager to get back.

An astronaut is a spaceman who finds a place in the sun by reaching for the moon.

The only person who can make a trip around the world without coming home loaded with souvenirs is an astronaut.

An astronaut is a man who qualifies for outer space travel without the aid of a clergyman.

An astronaut is the only man who is hailed as a hero when he's down and out.

Sending a man to the moon is not unusual—you'll find men everywhere who have been living in the clouds for years.

An astronaut spends years in space training, then has as much trouble as the rest of us finding parking space.

An astronaut is the only man who runs around in circles—and gets somewhere.

To an astronaut, a capsule is not something you take, but something that takes you.

An astronaut is the man most likely to go far.

Only one kind of pedestrian can be sure he won't be struck by a passing car—the astronaut who walks in space.

An astronaut is a man chosen to travel in outer space because he can be trusted to keep his feet on the ground.

An astronaut is a spaceman who looks out at a maximum of space from a spaceship that has a minimum of space.

Another man who does a lot of traveling without his wife is the astronaut.

An astronaut is a man who spends most of his time on the earth preparing for the moon.

ATHEISM

Nobody talks so constantly about God as those who insist that there is no God.
— *Heywood Broun*

There is no God, but Mary is His mother.   — *William James*

I was a freethinker before I knew how to think.
— *Bernard Shaw*

God comprehends even the atheism of the atheist.   — *Gandhi*

God first created man and then woman, but the atheist created himself.

An atheist is a person whose faith is his lack of faith.

An atheist is a man who does not believe in God and wants others to share his belief.

To an atheist, cleanliness is not next to godliness because godliness is next to nothing.

An atheist cannot find God for the same reason a thief cannot find a policeman.

Many a freethinker proudly boasts: "Thank God I'm an atheist!"

An atheist is a man who can take any text in the Bible and prove that it doesn't mean what it says.

ATOM

Atomic energy is the most powerful force known to man—except woman.

An atom is the smallest thing in the world which, when split, becomes the biggest.

There is always the danger that the smashing of the atom by man will sooner or later be followed by the smashing of man by the atom.

The atom is another proof that it's the little things that count.

ATTENTION

One of the best hearing aids a man can have is an attentive wife.
— Groucho Marx

A woman will do anything to attract attention, even dress sensibly.

The man who passes a pretty girl without turning around is either blind or walking with his wife.

It's hard to get a child to pay attention to you, especially when you are telling him something for his own good.

In the old days a woman used to drop her handkerchief to attract attention; nowadays she drops her neckline.

A cat watching a mouse seems the ultimate in alert attention until you see a small town watching a widower.

The man who shrinks from attracting attention should marry.

When a woman marries, she gives up the attentions of several men for the inattention of one.

To get maximum attention, you can't beat a big blunder.

ATTIC

The surest way to dig up the past is to look for something in the attic.

An attic is a place where you keep something for ten years and then throw it away just two weeks before you need it.

An antique is a piece of furniture that has been to the attic and back.

ATTRACTION

If a woman attracts a man, she has sex appeal; if she attracts women, style; if she attracts everyone, charm.

A girl is most attractive when she is old enough to know better, but not quite old enough to be better.

Many a woman takes to a man only if she can take from him.

Women are always buying more and more clothes although they are more attractive to men with less and less.

Nothing makes a man forget a passing fancy like something fancier.

Hooking a husband is like fishing: you must wait until the fish comes to the hook, but it helps if you wiggle the bait a little.

Most girls are attracted to the simple things in life, like men.

Many a man doesn't find out what his wife really saw in him until it's all spent.

A man is often attracted to a woman by the way she talks to him, but more often by the way she listens.

It is easy to choose the lesser of two evils when the greater has fewer attractions.

Clothes make the man—if the right woman is in them.

The man who is as sound as a dollar, often falls for the girl who looks like a million.

The more a bore is attracted to you, the less attractive he becomes.

Before money was invented, what did women find attractive about men?

The flirt who attracts a man before marriage, usually distracts him afterwards.

Even the girl who doesn't want to yield to temptation, wants to feel that she is attractive enough to attract it.

Any woman can lure a man with a bikini; the trick is to be able to attract a man with your clothes on.

There are two kinds of people who are fascinating: intelligent men who know everything, and beautiful women who know nothing.

Evil was invented by good people to explain the attraction of others.

Most girls nowadays are attracted to the man who is tall, dark and has some.

If some women were twice as attractive as they try to be, they still wouldn't be half as attractive as they think they are.

A woman with a past attracts men who hope history will repeat itself.

A girl without perfume can attract a man, but a man without a cent to his name finds it hard to attract a girl.

AUDIENCE

The play was a success, but the audience was a failure.

— *William Collier*

To have great poets, there must be great audiences too.
— *Walt Whitman*

If all the world's a stage, and men and women merely players, where is the audience to come from?

The best audience a lecturer can have is one that's polite enough to cover their mouths when they yawn.

The man who is head and shoulders above the rest is sure to be sitting in front of you in the theater.

The man who likes to hear himself talk always has an appreciative audience of one.

The important thing is not that money talks, but that it has the largest listening audience.

The man higher up doesn't mean much in a theater.

Another monopolist is the man who keeps an elbow on each arm of his theater seat.

Marriage is a legal custom by which a man becomes a captive audience for his wife.

Never confuse the seating capacity of an auditorium with the sitting capacity of your audience.

All the world loves a lover, unless he's sitting in front of you in the theater.

AUTHOR

Many contemporary authors drink more than they write.
— *Gorki*

If there is a special hell for writers, it would be in the forced contemplation of their own works.
— *John Dos Passos*

Writers become idiotic under flattery sooner than any other set of people in the world.
— *Frank Moore Colby*

I have the disease of writing books and feeling ashamed of them afterwards.   — *Montesquieu*

A writer has nothing more to say after the age of forty; if he is clever he knows how to hide it.   — *Georges Simenon*

A person who publishes a book willfully appears before the populace with his pants down.
— *Edna St. Vincent Millay*

There are three difficulties in authorship: to write anything worth publishing, to find honest men to publish it, and to get sensible men to read it.
— *C. C. Colton*

Great writers are always evil influences; second-rate writers are not wicked enough to become great.   — *Bernard Shaw*

The author should keep his mouth shut when his work begins to speak.   — *Nietzsche*

There is probably no hell for authors in the next world because they suffer so much from critics in this.   — *Bovee*

The woman who writes commits two sins: she increases the number of books, and decreases the number of women.
— *Alphonse Karr*

He who wields a pen is in a
state of war.   — *Voltaire*

Practically everybody in New
York has half a mind to write a
book—and does. — *Groucho Marx*

If writers were good businessmen, they'd have too much sense
to be writers.   — *Irvin S. Cobb*

The public never has any sympathy for authors who have deprived themselves of sleep in order
to give it to their readers.
                     — *C. C. Colton*

If a writer has to rob his
mother, he will not hesitate—the
Ode on a Grecian Urn is worth
any number of old ladies.
                     — *Faulkner*

The whole duty of a writer is
to please and satisfy himself, and
the true writer always plays to an
audience of one.   — *E. B. White*

A writer is always admired
most, not by those who have read
him, but by those who have
merely heard about him.
                     — *Mencken*

Writing books is just another
business, but it's quite another
thing being an author.
                     — *La Bruyère*

A man makes his reputation not
by what he writes, but by what
others write about him.

An author achieves success
when he no longer shows his published writings to his friends.

To an author, writing is a
pleasure, especially when he
doesn't have to do it.

The author who suddenly at-
tains fame, has probably been
lucky enough to have his book
banned.

Before publishers' blurbs were
invented, authors had to make
their reputations by writing.

Many a novelist begins with a
wealth of thought and ends with
a thought of wealth.

Some impressive-looking books
are not as thick as their authors.

Writers are often paid by the
word, never by the thought.

After breaking into print, many
an author continues to be broke.

AUTHORITY

At critical times the authorities
always claim they have no authority.

Many a man who thinks he
was born to command, marries a
woman who was born to countermand.

When a man brags that he
wears the pants at home, you can
be sure his wife tells him which
pair to put on.

The only time a married man
speaks with authority is when he
talks with his wife.

Give some politicians a taste
of authority, and they really eat
it up.

You can't trust a woman: no
sooner does she promise to obey
than she starts to take command.

The family of today doesn't need more authority: what it needs is to transfer the authority from the children to the parents.

Another species of optimist is the man who marries his secretary and thinks he will continue dictating to her.

The practice of putting women on pedestals began to die out when men discovered that women could give orders better from that position.

When a wife insists on wearing the pants, some other woman is probably wearing the fur coat.

All men believe in law and order as long as they can lay down the law and give the orders.

AUTOBIOGRAPHY

Autobiography is an unrivalled vehicle for telling the truth about other people.　　— *Philip Guedalla*

Disrobing in public is not to my taste; there are intellectual and spiritual pudenda as well as physical.　　— *Finley Peter Dunne*

An autobiography is the story of how a man thinks he lived.
— *Herbert Samuel*

No man is bad enough to tell the truth about himself.
— *Bernard Shaw*

There ain't nothing that breaks up homes and nations like somebody publishing their memoirs.
— *Will Rogers*

Only when one has lost all curiosity about the future has one reached the age to write an autobiography.　　— *Evelyn Waugh*

Autobiography is a popular form of fiction in which the writer is always the hero.

Autobiography is a form of literature so devised that the past can be changed in the present.

The hero-worshipers of yesterday are all writing autobiographies today.

Autobiography is the fine art of reconciling fact with fiction.

An autobiography is the story of a person whose life is an open book.

When men write about themselves, their books fall into two classes: one is autobiography, and the other, ought-not-to-be-ography.

Autobiography is a popular form of literature based on the art of self-defense.

Dead men tell no tales, but sometimes their memoirs live after them.

Autobiographies have one thing in common: the author can always be depended upon to give a good account of himself.

An autobiography is a book that describes a person's experiences, some of which are true.

AUTOGRAPH

Don't waste time collecting other people's autographs; rather

devote it to making your own autograph worth collecting.
— *Bernard Shaw*

The celebrity's autograph that is sought by fans is not always honored by banks.

There's only one thing that disturbs an author more than to ask for his autograph, and that is not to ask for it.

Another kind of practical joker is the celebrity who, when he is asked for his autograph, prints it.

AUTOMATION

If automation keeps up, man will atrophy all his limbs but the push-button finger.
— *Frank Lloyd Wright*

This may be the age of automation, but love is still being made by hand.

Man first makes the machine necessary, and then the machine makes man unnecessary.

Automation may be a good thing, but don't forget that it began with Frankenstein.

Automation is an electronic process in which more machinery provides more people with more time to be bored.

America is an auto nation which is dominated by automation.

The toughest decision a purchasing agent faces is when he is about to buy the machine designed to replace him.

Another advantage of automation is that you don't have to contribute to an office collection when it's retired.

When automation really takes over, we'll probably be working a no-hour week.

Pessimists have already begun to worry about what is going to replace automation.

Automation has opened up for thousands of skilled employees a whole new world of unemployment.

Automation is a system where electronic devices act just like human beings by doing things without using any intelligence.

When automation in the home does away with dishpan hands, it will probably be followed by push-button fingers.

If automation is so efficient, why doesn't it replace the ladder of success with an escalator?

In the approaching push-button age, the factory that works like a machine will replace the man who works like a horse.

Automation was invented by man to make work so easy that woman can eventually do it all.

Automation is controlling the world: if you get to your job without being hit by a machine, you find that another machine has replaced you.

Automation is an electronic process of producing cheaply and quickly more of the things we already have too much of.

Automation will never be in complete control until the ship of state can be steered by automatic pilot.

Automation seems to be replacing men and women of all kinds, but it will never replace the taxpayer.

AUTUMN

Autumn is a second spring when every leaf is a flower.   — *Camus*

In the autumn husbands get their fall clothes out of moth balls, and wives get theirs out of dress shops.

AVERAGE

Things average out: if you think too much of yourself, others won't.

The trouble with the average man is that he seldom increases his average.

If you are average, it means you are as close to the top as you are to the bottom.

If at first you don't succeed, you're about average.

AVERAGE MAN

I consider myself an average man, except in the fact that I consider myself an average man.
— *Montaigne*

The common man does not exist: he is an abstraction invented by bores for bores.

The average man is probably the only man who has never been photographed.

Statistics still show that the average man gets a car before a car gets him.

Many a woman thinks her husband is not an average man, but thinks he could be with a little improvement.

What the average woman wants is about twice as much as the average man has.

A statistician always talks about the average man, yet never expects to meet him.

The average man is a wonder to himself, a Romeo to some woman, and a fool to his wife.

In the morning the average woman looks like the average man feels.

AVOID

A man marries one woman to escape from many others, and then chases many others to forget he's married to one.   — *Helen Rowland*

History is the sum total of the things that could have been avoided.   — *Konrad Adenauer*

In love, there are two kinds of men to avoid: the young and spent, and the old and bent.

A man is known by the company he keeps—out of.

The trouble with trying to get away from it all these days is that most of it is portable.

A friend in need is a friend to keep away from.

Life is one dodge after another—cars, taxes, and responsibilities.

A do-it-yourselfer starts to make progress only after he learns what not to do.

As you grow older you don't have to avoid temptation—temptation avoids you.

AWAKE

Some people wake up and find themselves famous; others wake up and find themselves late.

When some preachers finish a sermon, there's always a great awakening.

Because a girl closes her eyes when she is being kissed is no sign that she is not wide awake.

Now is the time for all good men to come to.

You don't have to lie awake nights to succeed—just stay awake days.

AWKWARD

Atlas had a great reputation, but I'd like to have seen him try to carry a mattress upstairs.
— *Kin Hubbard*

There's nobody so awkward as the middle-aged man who tries to get into a car that's more compact than he is.

Some men are such clumsy dancers, they make you feel more danced against than with.

When an awkward man lends a hand, he is apt to put his foot in it.

AX

About the only people who have no axes to grind are the people who have no axes.

If you'll spend more time sharpening the ax, you'll spend less time chopping wood.

Life is full of people who have an ax to grind but cannot find an ax grinder.

BABY

Babies are such a nice way to start people.   — *Don Herold*

One cannot love lumps of flesh, and little infants are nothing more.
— *Samuel Johnson*

A baby is God's opinion that the world should go on.
— *Carl Sandburg*

We are intellectually still babies; this is perhaps why a baby's facial expression so strangely suggests the professional philosopher.
— *Bernard Shaw*

Babies do not want to hear about babies; they like to be told of giants and castles.
— *Samuel Johnson*

There's nothing like having a baby to make you realize that it's a changing world.

A baby keeps his mother from having an eight-hour day, and his father from having an eight-hour night.

A baby is a small creature who soon ceases to be an armful and grows into quite a handful.

Don't baby your husband; if you want a baby, have a new one.

Every time a bachelor picks up a baby it bends in a new place.

The only period in a person's life when he is not giving advice is infancy.

When two women feel sorry for each other, the chances are one has a baby and the other hasn't.

Out of the mouths of babes comes—cereal.

When a baby has the colic, its first instinct is to advertise.

An infant is the only creature that's more helpless than it new-born father.

There's nothing new under the sun, except a new baby.

No one can plan a family's activities like a new-born babe.

A baby is a crawling infant whose mother never knows what his mouth is going to eat next.

The nicest thing about being a baby is that everything you do is wonderful.

A baby is the only person in the house who can leave a ringing telephone alone.

All babies look alike—that is, all other people's babies.

Many a baby is born with one parent's features and the other parent's fixtures.

A baby is the only case where an addition automatically becomes a deduction.

Babies are angels whose wings grow shorter as their legs grow longer.

A man is always master in his own house—at least the first year of his life.

Sooner or later every person opens his mouth and puts his foot in, but only a baby is admired for doing it.

BABY SITTER

The young mother who gets on well with her mother-in-law, probably can't afford a baby sitter.

A baby sitter is a young girl hired to fall asleep while keeping your child awake.

When you're young, your mother tells you what time you have to be home; when you're grown up and married, your baby sitter tells you.

Children keep a family together, especially when you cannot get a baby sitter.

A baby sitter is a girl hired to solve the problem of what to do with the leftovers.

Time brings all things, including the period when you no longer have to pay girls to spend an evening with your son.

A baby-sitting teenager is expected to act like an adult while the adults are out acting like teenagers.

Some parents hire a baby sitter when what they really need is a lion tamer.

A baby sitter is someone you pay to watch television while your child cries itself to sleep.

BABYTALK

Why talk babytalk to an infant when plain English is hard enough for the poor youngster to understand?   — *John Kendrick Bangs*

The honeymoon is over when all the babytalk at home is done by the baby.

BACHELOR

Bachelors should be heavily taxed: it is not fair that some men should be happier than others.   — *Oscar Wilde*

The only good husbands stay bachelors: they're too considerate to get married.
— *Finley Peter Dunne*

Being a bachelor is the first requisite of the man who wishes to form an ideal home.
— *Beverley Nichols*

A bachelor's life is a fine breakfast, a flat lunch, and a miserable dinner.   — *La Bruyère*

A bachelor believes in love as long as it is not followed by honor and obey.

Every man has it in his power to make one woman happy—by remaining a bachelor.

A bachelor is a man who gave up waiting for the right girl and is making the best of the wrong ones.

The man who dies a bachelor has never completed his education.

Many a bachelor is still waiting for a beautiful girl who is a good cook, a good nurse and a good audience.

It's not joining himself to one woman that a bachelor dreads; it's separating himself from all the others.

A bachelor is a man who has taken out many a girl, but who has never been taken in.

No one has yet been able to figure out at just what age a bachelor becomes confirmed.

The man who understands women best is the bachelor—that's what makes him a bachelor.

A bachelor is a man who believes that the proper time for divorce is before the wedding.

A bachelor is a man who carries off all his romances without a hitch.

A bachelor is a man who looks before he leaps—and then doesn't leap.

To avoid getting tied up with one woman, a bachelor often gets tangled up with several.

A bachelor may be often mis-led, but he is never miss-led to the altar.

A bachelor never quite gets over the idea that he is a thing of beauty and a boy forever.

A bachelor is a man who is careful not to stumble into a woman's arms while running from another woman.

A bachelor doesn't marry till he has saved some money, and then to keep it saved, doesn't marry.

A bachelor is a man whose marriage vow is not to take one.

For a man to remain a bachelor calls for a cool head—or cold feet.

There are two kinds of confirmed bachelors: those smart enough not to enter into matrimony, and those foolish enough to stay out of it.

A bachelor is a man who has taken advantage of the fact that marriage is not compulsory.

Eternal vigilance is the price of bachelorhood.

A bachelor is a man who isn't fit to be tied.

A bachelor usually has his hands full trying to loosen a woman's grip.

A confirmed bachelor thinks the proper age to get married is when you are old enough to know better.

A bachelor is a man who profits by the mistake he doesn't make.

A bachelor is an investor who never puts his money into the bonds of matrimony.

A bachelor has nobody to share his troubles with—but why should a bachelor have any troubles?

A bachelor is a man who firmly refuses to allow a woman to replace him in his affections.

A bachelor doesn't really object to marriage—as long as it's not his own.

A bachelor's aim in life is not to lose his liberty in the pursuit of happiness.

A bachelor is a man who hasn't yet found a woman smart enough to understand him and foolish enough to admire him.

God created bachelors for the consolation of wives and the hope of spinsters.

A bachelor is a man whose mind is set, surrounded by women trying to upset it.

Bachelors often court trouble, but seldom end up marrying it.

A bachelor is a man who is free to choose, and chooses to be free.

A bachelor misses many wonderful pleasures, including the relief of being divorced.

A confirmed bachelor is a man who never allows a lass to lasso him.

All bachelors are unattached, but some are put together ridiculously.

A bachelor is a selfish man who is cheating some deserving woman out of her rightful alimony.

A bachelor always considers himself eligible for courtship while others always consider him eligible for marriage.

The only man who never turns to his wife when he's in trouble is probably a bachelor.

A bachelor is a man who prefers to cook his own goose.

A bachelor sometimes gets the wrong party on the phone, but never at the altar.

A bachelor is a man who never got around to marrying in his youth, but has got around it ever since.

A bachelor always leans toward the fair sex, but seldom far enough to make him fall.

A bachelor is the only man who never learns what a woman really thinks of him.

A bachelor is always willing to meet a woman halfway as long as she doesn't want to be the better half.

A bachelor is the only man who is allergic to wedding cake.

BACHELOR AND MARRIED MAN

A bachelor's virtue depends upon his alertness; a married man's depends upon his wife's.
                                    — Mencken

Bachelors have consciences, married men have wives.
                                    — Mencken

Some married men are husbands, and some are merely ex-bachelors.

The bachelor is a cagey man; the married man is caged.

Fools rush in where bachelors fear to wed.

The last thing a married man wants to do is to die; the last thing a bachelor wants to do is get married.

Next to bachelorhood, marriage is best.

If single life is bad, then double life must be twice as bad.

Another reason married men are happier than bachelors is that they already know the worst.

No matter how wise a husband is, he is sure to have made one mistake more than a bachelor.

When a bachelor wants to flatter a married man, he tells him he doesn't look it.

A bachelor blames fate for his mistakes, a married man blames his wife.

There are two kinds of marriageable men: the slick and the wed.

A bachelor can't find where he puts his things, while a married man can't find where his wife puts them.

A bachelor may be no less a fool than a married man, but he is less often reminded of it.

You can't always tell a married man just by looking at him: he may be a bachelor with a headache.

Married men have better halves, but bachelors have better quarters.

Although married men live longer than bachelors, women still prefer to marry bachelors.

A bachelor is linked with many girls, while a married man is handcuffed to only one.

The difference between a bachelor and a married man is that when a bachelor walks the floor with a baby, he is dancing.

When a bachelor falls in love, it leads to marriage; when a married man falls in love, it leads to divorce.

A bachelor is a man who has been crossed in love, and a married man has been double-crossed.

If there were only one bachelor left in the world, every married woman would still think she had married the wrong man.

BACKSEAT DRIVER

A backseat driver doesn't drive a car, but drives the man who drives one.

No man is a hero to his backseat driver.

A backseat driver is generally a woman whose husband drives by ear.

Every man has saved a lot of lives by not driving the way his wife told him to.

The only motorist who never seems to run out of gas is the backseat driver.

Many a wife drives a man to drink—from the back seat.

There are only two ways to avoid backseat drivers: drive alone, or drive a hearse.

Many accidents would be prevented if licenses were also required for backseat drivers.

Hell hath no fury like a backseat scorned.

Another traffic snarl is the criticism you get from a backseat driver.

A backseat driver is the only person who can ride through the most spectacular scenery without seeing anything but the speedometer.

Behind every successful man is a woman—usually a backseat driver.

If you're troubled by the noise in your car, why not let her drive?

Many a woman does all the driving in the family while her husband merely holds onto the steering wheel.

BACKSIDE

Even when a man occupies the most exalted throne, he still has to sit on his own behind.
— *Montaigne*

The man who bows before the ruler, shows his behind to the courtiers. — *Stanislaw J. Lec*

Every man has also his moral backside which he keeps covered by the trousers of decorum.
— *G. C. Lichtenberg*

If the word *arse* is read in a sentence, no matter how beautiful the sentence, the reader will react only to that word.
— *Jules Renard*

The man who gets too big for his breeches will be exposed in the end.

You don't have to be a carpenter to know how to put a bottom on a chair.

Nature is farsighted: she always gives bigger cushions to people who like to sit.

When a woman pours herself into an evening gown, too much shouldn't settle at the bottom.

Another thing that has to be learned from the bottom up is baby care.

BALANCE

Things even up: the more excess weight you carry around, the less time you'll probably have to carry it.

Family life is a balance sheet: parents make allowances for children, and children make deductions for parents.

There's no balancing act like tightrope walking, except being a successful mother-in-law.

Things balance out: your neighbors' troubles are not as bad as yours, but their children are worse.

All things strike a balance: a dull party, for example, gets you to bed at a decent hour.

BALD

Baldness may indicate masculinity but it diminishes one's opportunity of finding out.
— *Cedric Hardwicke*

A man is usually bald four or five years before he knows it.
— *Ed Howe*

Nothing makes a woman feel as old as watching the bald spot daily increase on the top of her husband's head. — *Helen Rowland*

A man is the first to notice that his friends are growing bald, and the last to notice that he is.

A bald spot is no asset, but it's better than no head at all.

Don't worry if your hair falls out; suppose it ached and had to be pulled out one at a time, like teeth.

Many a bald man proves that it is possible to come out on top and still be a loser.

A determined man can accomplish almost anything, except keeping his hair from falling out.

Many a man inherits only one thing from his father—a bald head.

If your hair starts to give you a great deal of trouble, don't worry; it'll come out all right.

Don't tear your hair out over a woman; it'll be harder to attract the next one if you're bald.

Within this vale of toil and sin, your head grows bald but not your chin.

Women will never be the equals of men until they have bald spots on top of their heads and still think they're handsome.

It is the bald barber who invariably has a cure for baldness.

BANK

If it's as easy to borrow money from a bank as its advertising claims, why should anyone want to rob it?

Savings banks operate on the principle that everyone should save because spending costs money.

The drive-in bank was established so that the real owner of a car could get to see it once in a while.

A bank is the place you borrow money from when you can't get it from a friend.

If money doesn't grow on trees, why do the banks continue to sprout branches?

A bank takes an interest in each employee's appearance, and an even greater interest in his disappearance.

When a poor man has too much money, he lends it to the bank; when a rich man hasn't enough, the bank lends it to him.

A bank is a place where you deposit money so that it will be there when other people want it.

BANK ACCOUNT

Some people's only interest in life comes from their bank account.

A savings account would be even more popular if it could help us save money without our having to economize.

An unexpected note falling due has knocked many a person off his balance.

If men weren't so quick on the draw, there would be more money in bank accounts.

BANKRUPTCY

When an implacable creditor meets an unpayable debtor, a bankruptcy is declared.

Bankruptcy is putting your money in your pants pocket, and letting your creditors take your coat.

If men behaved after marriage as they do during courtship, there would be far less divorces but far more bankruptcies.

Every man must work to become successful; you can't get rich on just one bankruptcy.

The man who does nothing but wait for his ship to come in will find it a receivership.

Bankruptcy is the proof that a business with a slow turnover will overturn fast.

BANQUET

When a banquet is given in a man's honor, it is sometimes hard to tell whether he is a guest or a victim.

Green peas haven't missed a banquet in fifty years.

BAR

There are some men whose wives can talk them out of anything, except a bar.

Some men are driven to drink, but most walk to a bar.

A bar is a place where one drink calls for another to keep it company.

Many a man does time behind bars because he spent too much time in front of them.

At a bar, conversations are sometimes nipped in the bud, but more often budded in the nip.

Usually when a man has trouble, he drops into a bar to drink it over.

BARBER

Two heads are better than one, especially in a barber shop.

Any man who argues with his barber should have his head examined.

A barber will give you a quick shave if you haven't time to listen to a haircut.

What makes a barber think he can mind two businesses at once?

Pity the poor barber who cuts hair all day, and then goes home and has to mow the lawn.

A barber is the only husband who talks as much as his wife.

When one barber cuts another barber's hair, which one does the talking?

During middle age, a man gets less for his money every time he goes to the barber.

Barber's maxim: you can only scalp a customer once, but you can give him a haircut every two weeks.

A barber is the only man whose conversation you can follow even though he talks over your head.

In the better barber shops everything is sterilized but the conversation.

BARGAIN

One of the difficult tasks in this world is to convince a woman that even a bargain costs money.
— *Ed Howe*

Those who marry in haste often see better bargains at leisure.

A bargain is anything you can buy today at yesterday's prices.

The woman who always gets the biggest bargains is the shoplifter.

Women may be the weaker sex, but not at a bargain counter.

It takes two to make a bargain, but only one gets it.

By reading the ads regularly, women can get bargains in everything, except husbands.

Hell hath no fury like a woman at a bargain counter.

A man never knows how hard it is to drive a bargain until he buys a used car.

BARGAIN HUNTER

It is surprising how many different things a bargain hunter would rather have than money.

A bargain hunter is a woman who is always getting at low prices things she doesn't need.

When the bargain hunter's last dollar is spent, so is she.

A bargain hunter is always hunting for goods in retail shops at less than wholesale prices.

Some women are bargain hunters, while others buy the things they need.

It takes two to make a bargain, but only one to make a bargain hunter.

A bargain hunter is always saving more money than her husband can afford.

The man who marries a bargain hunter gets no bargain.

The bargain hunter has little trouble finding a bargain, but a lot of trouble finding a use for it afterward.

BARTENDER

By the time a bartender knows what drink a man will have before he orders, there is little else about him worth knowing.
— *Don Marquis*

Every time a bartender makes a mistake a new drink is born.

The bartender who isn't a fool is a philosopher, and the bartender who isn't a philosopher is a fool.

A bartender is the only psychiatrist who never tells anyone to give up drinking.

BASEBALL

I've never heard a crowd boo a homer, but I've heard plenty of boos after a strike-out.
— *Babe Ruth*

Baseball is too much of a sport to be called a business, and too much of a business to be called a sport.   *—Philip K. Wrigley*

Knowing all about baseball is just about as profitable as being a good whittler.   *— Kin Hubbard*

Although he is a very poor fielder, he is also a very poor hitter.   *— Ring Lardner*

Baseball combines the best features of primitive cricket, lawn tennis, puss-in-the-corner and Handel's *Messiah*. *— Bernard Shaw*

Baseball is the only place in life where a sacrifice is really appreciated.

The man who wants to see a baseball game in the worst way should take his wife along.

The cream of a baseball team is either in the pitcher or in the batter.

Love and baseball go by contraries: the girl who can get to first base is always out, while the girl who never makes a hit is always safe at home.

If at first you don't succeed, try playing second base.

As a batter he has only one weakness—a pitched ball.

The trouble with baseball is that the player who knows how to bat and field best is sitting in the bleachers.

You're really getting old when you think a double-header is too much baseball for one day.

BASKETBALL

Any American boy can be a basketball star if he grows up, up, up.   *— Bill Vaughan*

Of all sports, basketball attracts the highest type of youth.

BATH

Nobody has ever thought out anything in a shower bath because it's too fast and too efficient.
    — Don Herold

Cold baths are more enjoyable if made with hot water.

There is good in everything: if the ancients hadn't neglected bathing, nobody would have invented perfume.

There's nothing certain in this world except death and taxes—and the ringing of the telephone when you're taking a bath.

The best thing about a cold shower in the morning is getting out of it.

Many a man who is a quiet dresser is a very loud bather.

There's only one thing better than a cold shower before breakfast, and that's no cold shower before breakfast.

Between the invention of the bathtub and the telephone, a person could relax in the tub for hours without being disturbed.

Anyone who tells you that he enjoys a cold shower every morning will lie about other things too.

A shower isn't the only place where if you make one wrong turn you find yourself in hot water.

People who live in glass houses shouldn't take baths.

BATHING SUIT

Some women think bikinis are immodest, while others have beautiful figures.   — *Olin Miller*

The trouble with a bathing suit is that it shows you off or shows you up.

Many a clergyman still preaches against the bikini though there's hardly anything to talk about.

The bathing suit is rapidly removing the difference between a bathing beach and a nudist camp.

Another way marriage changes a man is that he likes to see bikinis worn by all women but his wife.

The difference between one bathing suit and another is the difference between ever so little and nothing at all.

A bikini attracts no attention until someone puts it on.

The woman who is eager to show the world the stuff she's made of is probably wearing a bikini.

In bathing suits too it's the little things that count, and the littler they are, the more they count.

A bikini is a bathing suit with a lot of nothing usually worn by a girl with a lot of something.

A swimsuit is a garment that designers shortened first from the bottom, then from the top, and finally from the middle.

At the per ounce rate a bikini sells for, a man's overcoat would cost about $1000.

The bathing suit that leaves little to a man's imagination leaves a lot to his self-control.

Bikinis are worn by two kinds of women: those who should, and those who shouldn't.

Nothing seems to have done so much to improve the feminine figure as the bathing suit.

A girl puts a little into a bikini, but gets a lot out of it.

Brains may be mightier than brawn, but they don't show up so well in a bathing suit.

Some women don't have the figure to wear a bikini, but they do have the nerve.

A girl's summer wardrobe should include several bathing suits and at least one for bathing.

A bikini shows what a woman can do with almost nothing.

Many a bathing suit has led a girl into deep water.

A bikini is like a barbed wire fence: it protects the property without obstructing the view.

It's easy to make a bikini: just take three handkerchiefs and throw one away.

Women who say they have nothing to wear are often found wearing it on the beach.

Another thing that gets right down to the bare essentials is a bikini.

A bathing suit is the only garment designed for a girl to go into and come out of at the same time.

The bikini is a little bathing suit that saves a man a lot of guesswork.

The bikini that's less than a woman can wear is probably more than she can bare.

If the designers of women's bathing suits don't watch out, they will soon be out of business.

A bikini is a beach garment that has turned swimming into a spectator sport.

BATHROOM

George Moore leads his readers to the latrine and locks them in.
— *Oscar Wilde*

The father of the bride shouldn't think of it as losing a daughter, but as gaining a bathroom.

In some government bureaus, the only place where the employees know what they're doing is the washroom.

How long a few minutes are depends on whether you are in the bathroom or out.

Generally our respect for a man is in direct proportion to the number of bathrooms in his house.

The most inefficient room in a home is the bathroom—it can only seat one.

BEACH

Nowadays a woman wears less on the beach than she wears in bed.

On the beach you look only half as long to see twice as much.

There's nothing new under the sun, but on the beach there's a lot more of it showing.

If only it were warm enough to go swimming in winter when the beaches are not crowded.

Another place where girls all try to outstrip one another is the beach.

The beach is a place where a man looks his best—at girls.

There is more than the shore to see at the seashore.

If it's scenery you want, go to the mountains, or better still to the beaches.

On the beach women's bathing suits don't look like they used to, but the men look just the same.

Figures don't lie—except on the beach.

The beach is another place where lots of girls invite pursuit by showing lots of girl per suit.

BEAR

Once upon a time there were three bears: Papa Bear, Mama Bear, and Camembert.
— *George S. Kaufman*

Never pat a bear until it's a rug.

If your home is unbearable, maybe you're the bear.

The reason a polar bear wears a fur coat is because he'd look funny in a woolen one.

BEARD

He that hath a beard is more than a youth, and he that hath no beard is less than a man.
— *Shakespeare*

He looks like he swallowed a St. Bernard and left the tail hanging out.   — *Fred Allen*

Many a youngster's ambition is to grow a beard as soon as he's old enough not to shave.

Everything comes to the man who waits, including a beard.

BEAST

He who makes a beast of himself gets rid of the pain of being a man.   — *Samuel Johnson*

Of all wild beasts, preserve me from a tyrant; and of all tame, a flatterer.   — *Ben Jonson*

The animal in man that most women want to bring out is the beast of burden.

The woman who thinks all men are beasts would just love to be an animal trainer.

The brute is an imperfect animal compared to man who is a perfect beast.

BEAUTY

A man must marry only a very pretty woman in case he should ever want some other man to take her off his hands.
— *Sacha Guitry*

She was not pretty, but she might have been handsome if somebody had kept telling her that she was pretty.
— *J. B. Priestley*

She was a great beauty in her youth—a fact which she alone remembers.   — *Benjamin Constant*

The beauty of the male has not yet been portrayed by the only one who can do so—the female.
— *G. C. Lichtenberg*

Beauty is only skin deep, but it's a valuable asset if you're poor or haven't any sense.
— *Kin Hubbard*

It is not easy to be a pretty woman without creating trouble.
— *Anatole France*

I always say that beauty is only sin deep.   — *Saki*

I derive no pleasure from talking with a young woman simply because she has regular features.
— *Thoreau*

What's the use of being young without good looks, or having good looks without being young?
— *La Rochefoucauld*

Let us leave pretty women to men without imagination. — *Proust*

It is beauty's privilege to kill time, and time's privilege to kill beauty.

It's not easy for a beautiful girl to believe that love is blind.

A bathing beauty spends more time diving in front of cameras than into swimming pools.

A woman's beauty affords her less pleasure than the other woman's lack of it.

A thing of beauty is a joy— until your wife wants one like it.

When a man analyzes the quality of beauty in a girl, it's a sign he's much younger than he looks.

If a woman knows she's pretty, it's not because some other woman told her so.

The best beauty aid a woman can have is a nearsighted husband.

A beauty contest is where you can see the most beautiful, less-dressed women of the land.

Girls whose beauty gets them hired often find that's why they're fired.

A woman is never as beautiful as she used to be.

Beauty in a child is the work of nature; beauty in an adult is the work of art.

Beauty may be in the eye of the beholder, but most of us look for it elsewhere.

The beautiful is not always expensive, and the expensive is not always beautiful.

A bathing beauty is a girl you always see more of in the summer than in the winter.

When a woman's face is her fortune, it probably runs into a nice figure.

Feminine beauty is many-sided: some women should be seen from the front, some from the side and some from behind.

A good-looking girl seldom has far to look.

Beauty is only skin deep, but the impression it makes is not.

Even when a girl is as pretty as a picture, a man still likes to look at the frame.

The easier some girls are on the eye, the harder they are on the wallet.

BEAUTY SHOP

Most women leaving beauty parlors look as if they hadn't been waited on.   — *Will Rogers*

In the old days a woman's face was her fortune; nowadays the fortune goes to the beauty parlor.

A beauty salon is a place where a thing of beauty is a job forever.

In a beauty shop, women are usually busy letting their hair down while the hairdresser is busy putting it up.

The modern beauty parlor has destroyed in a few years the respect that gray hairs commanded for centuries.

BECOMING

If you are looking for trouble, tell a woman her new dress is unbecoming.   — *Ed Howe*

A woman's always ready to take what's becoming to her.

BED

Politics doesn't make strange bedfellows—marriage does.
          — *Groucho Marx*

The actor rushes from the bed to the altar almost as fast as other men rush from the altar to the bed.   — *Mencken*

I do all my writing in bed; everybody knows I do my best work there.   — *Mae West*

Lying in bed would be an altogether perfect experience if only one had a colored pencil long enough to draw on the ceiling.
          — *Chesterton*

Many women never take their figures to bed with them.

Nothing makes a bed more comfortable than the ringing of an alarm clock.

Uneasy lies the head that eats crackers while in bed.

An upper berth is where you rise to retire and get down to get up.

Breathes there the man with soul so dead, who never to a girl hath said, "Let's go to bed!"

You can get any child to run an errand for you, but only if you ask him at bedtime.

A small child will often call for a drink as soon as he goes to bed, but more often will wait until his parents have also gone.

Another good thing about marriage is that it gets young people to bed at an early hour.

Twins beds became popular when men began to realize they should not take their troubles to bed with them.

Getting children up is the lull before the storm; putting them to bed is the storm before the lull.

The only man who can take a nap on top of a bedspread is a bachelor.

Many a man gets up on the wrong side of the bed because he doesn't get into it early enough.

The best time to put the children to bed is when you can.

BEE

The bees got their governmental system settled millions of years ago, but the human race is still groping.   — *Don Marquis*

All the honey a bee gathers during its lifetime doesn't sweeten its sting.

Science has finally discovered why bees hum—they don't know the words.

Man has no sense of justice: he steals honey from the bees, and then gets sore when the bee stings him.

If bees were like human beings, would they strike for shorter flowers and more honey?

The stinger of a bee is one-tenth of an inch long, the other nine-tenths is pure imagination.

The busy bee teaches two lessons: one is not to be idle, and the other is not to get stung.

If flies are flies because they fly, and fleas are fleas because they flee, then bees are bees because they be.

BEER

Mencken, who is constantly informing his readers of his libations, drinks beer, a habit no more bacchanalian than taking enemas.
       — *Maxwell Bodenheim*

People who drink beer, think beer.

Beer not only makes you talkative, it also makes you walkative.

Beer makes you feel as you ought to feel without beer.

BEG

Beggars should be abolished: it is irritating to give to them and it is irritating not to.   — *Nietzsche*

Common people do not pray; they only beg.   — *Bernard Shaw*

Nowadays there is more begging done through the mails than with tin cups.

BEGINNING

I start where the last man left off.   — *Thomas A. Edison*

The secret of getting ahead is getting started.

The man who is waiting for something to turn up might start with his shirt sleeves.

The trouble with many people is that they take so long to start to begin to get ready to commence.

Everyone talks about middle age, but no one knows when to begin it.

It takes all kinds of people to make a world, and it's about time they got started.

The best way to win an argument is to begin by being right.

BEGINNING AND END

A poem begins in delight and ends in wisdom; the figure is the same as for love. —*Robert Frost*

Middle age is not the beginning of the end, but the end of the beginning.

News is the end of a story; the beginning is seldom printed.

A movie star's marriage always begins with a romance and ends the same way.

It's hard to know just when one generation ends and the next one begins, but it's sometime around nine P.M.

There's nothing worse than a quitter, except the man who's afraid to begin.

Matrimony begins with two people pulling together, and ends with one of them pulling out.

BEHAVIOR

With a gentleman I am always a gentleman and a half, and with a fraud I try to be a fraud and a half. —*Bismarck*

He treats a flower girl as if she was a duchess, and a duchess as if she was a flower girl.
—*Bernard Shaw*

I like men to behave like men —strong and childish.
—*Françoise Sagan*

Live so that you can at least get the benefit of the doubt.
—*Kin Hubbard*

Be intellectual with pretty women, frivolous with intellectual women, serious with young girls, and flippant with old ladies.
—*Gelett Burgess*

I never observe rules of conduct, and therefore have given up making them. —*Bernard Shaw*

How is a girl nowadays to behave: if she's too free, she's promiscuous; if she isn't, she's a prude.

We behave better to our dogs than to our fellowmen, and dogs behave better to us than to their fellowdogs.

The world would be a peaceful place to live in if we could only get human beings to stop acting like human beings.

When adults behave like children, we call them juveniles; when children behave like adults, we call them delinquent.

A lot of people get credit for being well-behaved simply because they haven't the money to be otherwise.

A husband should always treat his wife as if she were a voter and he a candidate.

The trouble with child training is that parents teach their children not how to behave, but how not to behave.

People don't change much from one generation to another; nowadays they simply don't bother to pull the blinds down.

Act your age: no woman likes a young man trying to act old, or an old man trying to act young.

BELIEVE

The public will believe anything, so long as it is not founded on truth.   — *Edith Sitwell*

Man can believe the impossible, but can never believe the improbable. · — *Oscar Wilde*

Most of our so-called reasoning consists in finding arguments for going on believing as we already do.
— *James Harvey Robinson*

Men are most apt to believe what they least understand.
— *Montaigne*

For God's sake, believe in something, even if it is only in the existence of the devil.
— *Ramsay MacDonald*

I believe it just because it is unbelievable.   — *Tertullian*

If you believe the doctors, nothing is wholesome; if you believe the theologians, nothing is innocent; if you believe the military, nothing is safe.
— *Lord Salisbury*

Some people like to understand what they believe in, while others like to believe in what they understand.
— *Stanislaw J. Lec*

Believe only half of what you hear, especially if it's a half-truth.

A woman can believe anything in the world if there's no good reason for it.

The eyes believe themselves; the ears believe other people.

The man who understands women the least believes them the most.

Half the people in the same church don't know what the other half believes.

Blessed are they who believe in something, even if it is nothing.

Some people will believe anything about you as long as it's the worst.

The woman who believes all she hears will probably tell all she knows.

A woman likes to believe she is the only one in a man's life, especially when she knows there are several others.

Believe only half of what you hear if half of what you hear is gossip.

BELITTLE

The fellow who belittles his wife in company is only trying to pull her down to his size.
— *Kin Hubbard*

Don't belittle—be big.

People who indulge in small talk usually belittle other people.

Don't belittle yourself; your friends will do it for you.

Many a husband who calls his wife the little woman should call her the belittle woman.

BENEFIT

Another great boon to the legal profession is that you cannot take it with you.

Next to television, the greatest boon to mankind is the knob that turns it off.

BESTSELLER

Don't be misled by bestseller lists: they represent the books that are bought, not the books that are read.

A bestseller is usually forgotten within a year, especially by those who borrow it.

Give a book a bad name— and it becomes a bestseller.

If you wait a year before buying a bestseller, you won't have to.

Speak no evil, see no evil, hear no evil—and you'll never write a bestseller.

A bestseller is a book that many thousands of people have read, and even more thousands pretend they have.

BETRAY

To have a good enemy, choose a friend—he knows best where to stick the knife.

A double-crosser is a person who borrows your pot to cook your goose in.

A confidence man will first do you a favor, and then do you.

Beware of the man who is always patting you on the back: he may be trying to find out where to stick the knife.

BETTING

The fellow that doesn't know what he's talking about always wants to bet you. *—Kin Hubbard*

Betting is pretty much like liquor: you can make it illegal, but you cannot make it unpopular. *—Arthur Baer*

The race is not always to the swift, nor the battle to the strong— but that's the way to bet.
—Damon Runyon

The man who is a bettor is never a better man.

At the race track you have the right to bet if you choose, but be careful how you choose if you bet.

We all love a poor loser— if we don't have any bets on him.

Many a man who would swear to the truth of a thing hesitates to bet on it.

BIBLE

Most people are bothered by those passages of Scripture they do not understand, but the passages that bother me are those I do understand. —*Mark Twain*

When I think of all the harm the Bible has done, I despair of ever writing anything to equal it. —*Oscar Wilde*

The total absence of humor from the Bible is one of the most singular things in all literature. —*A. N. Whitehead*

It is odd that God learned Greek when he wanted to turn author, and that he did not learn it better. —*Nietzsche*

No public man believes that the Bible means what it says: he is always convinced that it says what he means. —*Bernard Shaw*

During the past ten years I have stolen 75 Bibles, perhaps the national record. —*Mencken*

The Bible may be the truth, but it is not the whole truth and nothing but the truth. —*Samuel Butler*

The Bible is a good book that's even better when it's the worse for wear.

If the Bible is mistaken in telling us where we came from, how can we trust it to tell us where we are going?

Only a mother would think her daughter has been a good girl when she returns from a date with a Gideon Bible in her handbag.

The Bible is great enough to survive everything, even the hypocrites who are always quoting it.

The Bible says to multiply, but many couples prefer to divide.

Prosperity is the blessing of the Old Testament; adversity is the blessing of the New.

The Bible tells us to love our neighbor, even though he's worthless, but not to covet his wife, even though she's beautiful.

The hardest thing to believe about the Bible is that there were only two jackasses in the Ark.

BIGAMY

Every man should have two wives: one to cook for him, and another to amuse him after he has eaten. —*Ed Howe*

If all women are alike, why should any man commit bigamy?

A bigamist is a man whose better half doesn't know how the other half lives.

The best argument against bigamy is that it would leave a man no place to hang his clothes.

A bigamist is a man who has foreseen the modern trend toward doubling—two cars, two television sets, two phones.

To the bigamist, two beds are better than one.

Some men commit bigamy because they believe divorce is wrong.

A bigamist is a man who makes a second mistake before correcting the first.

Bigamy is the proof that there can be too much of a good thing.

The bigamist deserves his two mothers-in-law because he didn't take the trouble to get a divorce.

A bigamist is a man for whom life is a bed of ruses.

The bigamist is another man who has taken one too many.

Bigamy is a form of matrimony involving three people in which the ignorance of two is the opportunity of one.

A bigamist is a man who loves not wisely but two.

A man is considered singular is he has more than one wife.

A bigamist is a man who gets into trouble by turning a good custom into a bad habit.

A bigamist is a man who wants to keep two himself.

Sooner or later every bigamist discovers the futility of fighting on two fronts.

A bigamist is the only man who is counted twice in a census.

If a wife is a man's better half, what happens if he marries twice?

A bigamist is a man who makes his bed and tries to lie out of it.

A bigamist is a husband who is twice the man his wife thinks he is.

Why a man would want a wife is a mystery to bachelors; why a man would want two wives is a bigamystery.

A bigamist is a man who goes his better half one better.

BIGOT

Wisdom has never made a bigot, but learning has.
— *Josh Billings*

Bigot: one who is obstinately and zealously attached to an opinion that you do not entertain.
— *Bierce*

The mind of the bigot is like the pupil of the eye: the more light you pour upon it, the more it will contract.
— *Dr. O. W. Holmes*

A bigot is a narrow-minded man who thinks the straight and narrow path isn't narrow enough.

A bigot is always so positive that he becomes a positive nuisance.

When a bigot answers your questions, he resents when you question his answers.

Every time he opens his mouth, a bigot exposes his closed mind.

The bigot is another man who abuses the privilege of being stupid.

The man with a closed mind can get by nicely if he will keep his mouth the same way.

BILL

Anybody who has any doubt about the ingenuity and resourcefulness of a plumber never got a bill from one.   —*George Meany*

On the first of every month when bills fall due, there is no female more deadly than the mail.

The worst thing about history is that it repeats itself, especially about the first of each month.

Cheer up: birds have bills too, but they keep on singing.

Every business loses money on bad bills, except the counterfeiter's.

The man who allows his wife to run up big bills probably prefers to have trouble with his creditors than with her.

The customer is always right —until his bill is overdue.

If a wife didn't run up bigger bills, what incentive would her husband have to achieve bigger things?

Some doctors believe in shock treatments—they send them out the first of each month.

There's one bill that few of us escape—the mosquito's.

There are bigger things in life than money—bills, for example.

Another good way to reduce your bills is to put them on microfilm.

If half the world knew how the other half lives, they wouldn't pay their bills either.

Life would be a lot more pleasant if they'd place a POST NO BILLS sign on every mailbox.

Pay your medical bills promptly: at least that would be an incentive for your doctor to keep you alive.

The money you lay away for the phone bill often pays for the electric bill before the gas bill is due.

BILLBOARD

Billboard companies must have a sense of beauty, or they couldn't pick out the best views to obstruct.

Beyond the Alps lies Italy, and beyond the billboards lies America.

The autumnal colors, as you motor along the highways, are beautiful: many of the billboards are newly painted.

The billboards must go—we need the room for roadside stands, garbage dumps and auto junkyards.

BILL COLLECTOR

It's hard to convince a bill collector that there are other things than money to think of in this world.

The nicest thing about being a bill collector is that the people you call on don't return your visits.

The life of a bill collector isn't all bad: almost everyone asks him to call again.

Misery loves company, but not the company the bill collector works for.

That knocking on your door may be opportunity, but it's more likely to be a bill collector.

It's easy to tell if it's a friend or a bill collector at the door: just wait a while and if it's a bill collector he won't go away.

Not everyone trying to keep up with the Joneses is a status seeker: some are bill collectors.

A bill collector doesn't believe in putting off until tomorrow what can be dunned today.

Bill collectors always seem to call at the most inopportune times —when you are at home.

BIOGRAPHY

Every great man nowadays has his disciples, and it is always Judas who writes the biography.
— *Oscar Wilde*

It is as difficult to write a good life as to live one.
— *Lytton Strachey*

How delicate, how decent is English biography, bless its mealy mouth.   — *Carlyle*

Dead men tell no tales, but many have biographers who do.

Lives of great men all remind us how important it is to choose a good biographer.

Know thyself, but don't tell thy biographer.

A biography is the story of a famous individual describing personal experiences in his life that never happened.

Lives of great men oft remind us that we haven't returned those we borrowed.

There is only one type of biography worse than that written by a son, and that is the one written by a daughter.

Some men have been immortalized in biography, while others have been immoralized.

Lives of great men oft remind us that they were written by persons who detested the subjects of their biographies.

BIRD

If I were reincarnated, I'd want to come back a buzzard: he is never bothered or in danger, and he can eat anything. — *Faulkner*

The white blackbird is so white that it cannot be seen, and the black blackbird is merely its shadow.   — *Jules Renard*

The partridge loves pears, but not those that go with her into the pot.   — *Thoreau*

The sparrow chirps *peep*, and thinks there is nothing more to say.   — *Jules Renard*

Our national bird is the eagle, with the stork a close second.

Protect the birds: the dove brings peace, and the stork brings tax exemptions.

A bird watcher is a person who listens to birds with a pair of binoculars.

How can birds flock any other way than together?

There's no such thing as the dove of peace—it's really a mockingbird.

The duck is a bird that walks as if it had ridden a horse all day.

A bird in your hand is worth two in a tree above your new hat.

The owl is supposed to be wise, but it is not wise enough to get off the night shift.

BIRTH

If nature had arranged that husbands and wives should have children alternatively, there would never be more than three in a family.   — *Laurence Housman*

The moment you're born, you're done for.   — *Arnold Bennett*

I went to a convent in New York and was fired finally for my insistence that the Immaculate Conception was spontaneous combustion.   — *Dorothy Parker*

To my embarrassment I was born in bed with a lady.   — *Wilson Mizner*

Every child born in America is endowed with life, liberty and a share of the government debt.

A baby born during a hurricane finds out much too early what life is like.

If a new-born babe cannot think, why does it yell the moment it sees the kind of world it's in?

There is no insurance against the accident of birth.

An obstetrician can never understand why most babies have to be born at three o'clock in the morning.

The stork is charged with a lot of things which should be blamed on a lark.

The man who is born with a silver spoon, rarely makes much stir with it.

Isn't it strange that the world should be made up entirely of people who never asked to be born?

To heir is to err, especially before the wedding.

Everyone who has had to pay the costs of childbirth knows that man may be born equal, but certainly not free.

Nothing ages a woman faster than her birth certificate.

Many a man makes you wish his mother had thrown him away at birth and raised the placenta.

With more children being born every year, what is needed is not a better mousetrap, but a better rattle.

BIRTH AND DEATH

All men are born truthful, and die liars. — *Vauvenargues*

Life starts with a bottle and ends with a bier.

For many people, life begins almost the same way it ends: creation and cremation.

To be born healthy is an accident; to die healthy also takes an accident.

BIRTH CONTROL

Whenever I hear people discussing birth control, I always remember that I was the fifth. — *Clarence Darrow*

A girl's firm *no* is still the best oral contraceptive.

It's a pity that birth control cannot be made retroactive.

The man who practices birth control will never be disappointed in his children.

Children should be seen and not had.

Surgeons should not practice birth control: those who help to depopulate the world should do their share to repopulate it.

Many a wife keeps taking contraceptive pills even when her husband is out of town.

The hand that used to rock the cradle is now busy writing about planned parenthood.

People who favor birth control have nothing to lose—they have already been born.

BIRTHDAY

Marriage is the alliance of two people, one of whom never remembers birthdays and the other who never forgets them. — *Ogden Nash*

A birthday is an anniversary that tells you how old a child is, or how old his mother isn't.

Women are unpredictable: the wife who doesn't want to be reminded of her birthdays is disappointed when her husband forgets them.

A birthday is what a child deserves, a man observes and a woman preserves.

Among women, every birthday after the twentieth is the plentieth.

The only sure way to remember your wife's birthday is to forget it once.

Every woman eventually reaches the age when she doesn't want any more birthdays, but still wants the presents.

The woman who puts the right number of candles on her birthday cake is playing with fire.

Sooner or later every woman wants the same thing for her birthday: not to be reminded of it.

BITTER

Marriage is a partnership where the better half often turns into the bitter half.

Reformers are always trying to make the world a bitter place to live in.

The bitterest words are those we are forced to eat.

BLACK AND WHITE

White lies by frequent use become black ones.
— *Douglas Jerrold*

Optimist: a proponent of the doctrine that black is white.
— *Bierce*

A candidate is never as black as he is painted nor as white as he is whitewashed.

In the hands of the painter or lawyer, white becomes black.

The man who sees everything either in black or white is not using his gray matter.

White lies are the kind we tell, and black lies are the kind we hear.

BLACKMAIL

A blackmailer finds out in the present something in the past for use in the future.

A blackmailer profits not by what he knows or whom he knows, but by what he knows about whom.

Money talks, especially hush money.

The blackmailer is a person cunning enough never to write a compromising letter—or to destroy one.

Silence is golden, especially for the blackmailer.

Truth crushed to earth will rise again, unless you pay blackmail.

Money talks, and it also stops talk.

A blackmailer is the man who has a skeleton key to the family closet.

BLAME

A man always blames the woman who fools him; in the same way he blames the door he walks into in the dark.
— *Mencken*

To err is human; to blame it on someone else is even more human.

If you wish to be praised, die; if you wish to be blamed, get married.

A poor workman blames the tools, and a poor candidate blames the fools.

Every man needs a wife because he can't blame everything on the government.

If you want to avoid criticism, say nothing, do nothing, be nothing.

No man can ever rise so high in the world that he is above reproach.

Marriage is a partnership where a husband thinks it's his right to criticize, while a wife thinks it's her duty.

The man who can smile when things go wrong has probably just thought of someone he can blame it on.

Faultfinders are all the same: you never get credit for what you do, but always get criticism for what you don't.

If you never take advice, you'll never have anyone to blame things on.

There are two types of men who never profit by their mistakes: those who blame their luck, and those who blame their wives.

You are only young once; after that you have to blame your mistakes on something else.

Why is it that the man who is always accusing others is always excusing himself?

Another thing where the supply always exceeds the demand is blame.

When a man has only himself to blame, he is probably a bachelor.

BLANKET

Many a person's idea of roughing it is to sleep without an electric blanket.

One good turn gets most of the blanket.

There was once an old Indian who cut off one end of his blanket and sewed it on the other end to make it longer.

BLESSING

An optimist counts his blessings; a pessimist thinks his blessings don't count.

After you've paid your income tax, you should still count your blessings—that's about all there's left to count.

If it is more blessed to give than to receive, why are we content to let others get all the blessings?

To a movie star a blessed event is the arrival of the divorce papers.

It is only the rich who can speak in glowing terms about the blessings of poverty.

BLONDE

What happens when an irresistible blonde meets an immovable bachelor?

Gentlemen prefer blondes because blondes know what gentlemen prefer.

Love is more often blonde than blind.

Of two evils, most men choose the blonde.

Many a man's idea of a vacation is to rest quietly in the shade of a blonde.

If the truth were told about some blondes, it would be off-color.

Gentlemen prefer blondes because where there's light there's heat.

BLONDE AND BRUNETTE

Opposites attract: many a man has a brunette wife and a blonde sweetheart.

Some women are blondes, some are brunettes, and others have convertible tops.

Faint heart ne'er won fair lady, nor dark one either.

If there's a difference in temperament between blondes and brunettes, what about the women who have been both?

Never judge by appearances: the girl who looks like a dumb blonde may really be a smart brunette.

Matrimony is the only state under which every man is free to choose his own form of government—blonde, brunette or redhead.

A blonde is usually a cross between a brunette and a cosmetic counter.

By the time a man has decided which blonde he prefers, she's a brunette.

Nowadays a man can switch from a blonde to a brunette and then to a redhead, and still be going with the same girl.

Gentlemen prefer blondes, especially those who are married to brunettes.

BLOOD

Blood will tell, but often it tells too much.   — Don Marquis

When I got through with him, he was all covered with blood —my blood.   — Jimmy Durante

Some men give their blood to their country; others their spleen.   — Gelett Burgess

Blood is thicker than water, and it boils quicker too.

The best blood will at some time get into a fool or a mosquito.

In the old days doctors used to bleed patients for almost every disease—and many of them still do.

Another way to get high blood pressure is to go mountain climbing over molehills.

There's only one man who is never criticized when he lies down on the job—a blood donor.

BLUSH

As blushing will sometimes make a whore pass for a virtuous woman, so modesty may make a fool seem a man of sense.
        — Swift

Some girls blush when they shouldn't, but most girls don't blush when they should.

The old-fashioned girl blushed when she was embarrassed; the modern one is embarrassed when she blushes.

BOASTING

When I cannot brag about knowing something, I brag about not knowing it. *— Emerson*

There is one thing about hens that looks like wisdom—they don't cackle until they have laid their eggs. *— Josh Billings*

The talk of small boys among themselves consists almost entirely of boasting. *— Mencken*

Some men are born great, some achieve greatness, and others just keep still. *— Kin Hubbard*

One of the hardest things for most of us to put up with is a braggart who makes good.

The only way to cure an egotist from bragging is by surgery —amputation at the neck.

The man who boasts of his ancestry will never be able to boast of his posterity.

A blowhard never keeps his trap shut until he puts his foot in it.

With a braggart, it's no sooner done than said.

The bragger is another man who never succeeds in selling himself to others because he always gives himself away.

Beware of the man who boasts about his family; he'd boast about himself if he had anything to boast about.

No one is all bad; even the braggart has a rare virtue: he never talks about other people.

There's something about a bragger that always attracts women—to other men.

Only one man has the right to boast, and that's the man who never does.

The biggest braggers belong to three groups: those who have quit smoking, those who have quit drinking, and those who have lost weight.

A braggart always sings his own praises in a key pitched much too high.

Sooner or later every bragger gets hooked with his own lyin'.

A braggart is a fellow who keeps recalling things that never happened.

You will never hear a good word said about a bragger, unless you hear him talk about himself.

BOAT

We didn't all come over on the same ship, but we're all in the same boat. *— Bernard Baruch*

There's safety in numbers, except when you're in a canoe.

The most enjoyable way to travel by air is not by plane but by boat—sailboat.

BODY

Nature wisely prevents us from changing our bodies as we'd like to; otherwise, one man would be all eyes, another all ears, and another all penis.
— *G. C. Lichtenberg*

I have made a drawing of him so that on judgment day he'll be able more easily to identify his body. — *G. C. Lichtenberg*

To get into a bathing beauty contest, it is more important for a girl to know somebody than to have some body.

The human body is extremely sensitive: pat a person on the back and his head swells.

In the geography of the human body also, the torrid zone is the area in the middle.

The human body is the baggage everyone carries through the voyage of life, and the more excess baggage one carries, the shorter the trip.

In the movies they do things in reverse: they put beautiful frames in pictures.

BOIL

We boil at different degrees.
— *Emerson*

It takes longer to hard-boil a man or a woman than an egg.
— *Frederick Lewis Allen*

The pot must have been boiling when it called the kettle black.

A fusspot thinks the water won't boil unless she herself puts the kettle on.

A boil in the pot is worth two on the neck.

All that some women know about cooking is how to bring a man to a boil.

Nothing cooks your goose quicker than a boiling rage.

BOMB

Since the invention of the atom bomb, science spends less time studying the origin of man and more time on what his finish is to be.

H-bombs are being made smaller and smaller, but they will probably never reach the vanishing point.

The atom bomb is a weapon that has made man the only animal man now fears.

Statesmen grow tired of talking about hydrogen bombs during the cold war, yet hope the subject will never be dropped.

The H-bomb is here to stay —but are we?

Just when man started to build houses without cellars, he invented a bomb to drive us into cellars.

The atom bomb comes in three sizes: huge, stupendous, and where is everybody?

BONE

What this country needs are men with less bone in the head, and more bone in the back.

The main bone of contention in international affairs is the one above the eyebrows of its statesmen.

If a dog's prayers were answered, it would rain bones.

The difference between success and failure often depends on which you develop: backbone or wishbone.

Bumping your funny bone is no laughing matter.

The most important thing to remember in skiing is that the human body is made up of over two hundred bones, and every one of them is breakable.

Man is a creature having a spinal column, with most of the bone lumped at the top.

BOOK

Already by 1900 I could boast I had written as many books as Moses.　　　— *Winston Churchill*

Some day I hope to write a book where the royalties will pay for the copies I give away.
　　　　　　　— *Clarence Darrow*

It is easier to buy books than to read them, and easier to read them than to absorb them.
　　　　　　　　— *William Osler*

I know some people who are constantly drunk on books, as other men are drunk on whiskey.
　　　　　　　　　　— *Mencken*

My books are water; those of the great geniuses are wine— everybody drinks water.
　　　　　　　　— *Mark Twain*

This book contains much that is good and new; it's a pity that the good is not new, and the new is not good.　　— *Lessing*

A bad book is as much a labor to write as a good one; it comes as sincerely from the author's soul.　— *Aldous Huxley*

There are more books about books than about any other subject.　　　　　　— *Montaigne*

No book that will not improve by repeated readings, deserves to be read at all.　　　— *Carlyle*

When I get hold of a book I admire, I am so enthusiastic that I loan it to someone who never brings it back. — *Ed Howe*

If it weren't for the law, I would steal books; if it weren't for my purse, I would buy them.
　　　　　　　— *Harold J. Laski*

Writing a book is an adventure: it begins as an amusement, then it becomes a mistress, then a master, and finally a tyrant.
　　　　　　　— *Winston Churchill*

If well used, books are the best of all things; if abused, among the worst.　　— *Emerson*

If a law were passed giving six months to every writer of a

first book, only the good ones would do it. — *Bertrand Russell*

A real book is not one that we read, but one that reads us.
— *W. H. Auden*

Read the best books first, or you may not have a chance to read them at all. — *Thoreau*

Sartor Resartus is simply unreadable, and for me that always sort of spoils a book. — *Will Cuppy*

No man should ever publish a book until he has first read it to a woman.
— *Van Wyck Brooks*

It would be a good idea if children would write books for older people, now that everyone is writing for children.
— *G. C. Lichtenberg*

Make it a rule never to give a child a book you would not read yourself. — *Bernard Shaw*

This is the best book ever written by any man on the wrong side of a question of which he is profoundly ignorant. — *Macaulay*

The multitude of books is making us ignorant. — *Voltaire*

Good books usually make the fools more foolish, the wise more wise, and leave the majority just as they were. — *G. C. Lichtenberg*

The chief objection to new books is that they prevent us from reading the old ones.
— *Joubert*

It is with books as with men: a very small number play a very large part. — *Voltaire*

A house without books is like a room without windows.
— *Horace Mann*

One always tends to overpraise a long book because one has got through it. — *E. M. Forster*

The lowbrow often believes that a bad book is good, while the highbrow often believes that a good book is bad. — *Robert Lynd*

The real purpose of books is to trap the mind into doing its own thinking. — *Christopher Morley*

A book is a mirror: when an ass looks into it, don't expect an apostle to look out.
— *G. C. Lichtenberg*

Every abridgement of a good book is a foolish abridgement.
— *Montaigne*

A book collector is interested in the first edition, but an author is more interested in the tenth.

The really cultured person reads the newest books in science and the oldest in literature.

The three most important books in the American home are the bankbook, the cookbook and the trading stamp book.

The man who knows his wife like a book, probably means a scrapbook.

All things come to him who waits, except a loaned book.

What an author doesn't know usually fills a book.

Books should be made as appealing in childhood to a child as adultery is to an adult.

A book in the hand is worth two in the library.

Of all the guidebooks, the best one to go by on a vacation is your checkbook.

A big book may be full of faults, full of errors, full of contradictions, but it is seldom full of omissions.

The best surprise ending in literature is the borrowed book that's returned.

An anthologist is one who earns his living by taking a leaf from another person's book.

The person you can read like a book cannot be shut up as easily.

BORE

Bores bore each other too, but it never seems to teach them anything. —*Don Marquis*

Against boredom even the gods struggle in vain. —*Nietzsche*

The capacity of human beings to bore one another seems to be vastly greater than that of any other animals. —*Mencken*

The man who lets himself be bored is even more contemptible than the bore. —*Samuel Butler*

A bore is a person who talks when you want him to listen.
—*Bierce*

In the good old days before radio and television, what did people have to bore them?

There's nothing more tiresome than entertaining a person who never says anything, except a bore who talks all the time.

A bore is the man who is having a good time when he is giving others a bad time.

Money talks, and most of us wish we were in a position to be bored by it.

Bore is too mild a word for some men; they are more like pneumatic drills.

A woman's definition of a bore is any man in love with another woman.

A bore is always giving you twice as many details as you want to hear.

Those who talk without thinking always bore those who think without talking.

Nature makes the fool, but the bore belongs to civilization.

Why is it that a bore always seems to have lots of time to spare?

The secret of being a bore is not to leave anything out.

A bore never puts off till tomorrow the tedium he can spread today.

A bore always runs out of listeners faster than he runs out of conversation.

Ennui is the feeling when you're tired of doing nothing and you're too lazy to do something.

A bore is a person whose conversation it is hard to listen to but easy to yawn at.

People shrink from a bore because his capacity of utterance exceeds their capacity of sufferance.

A bore finds it easy to start talking, and even easier to get others to stop listening.

You can always rely upon a bore to make a short story long.

A bore is a man whose mother bore him and who now bores everyone else.

The bore is a person who is the easiest to approach and the hardest to get away from.

Some people are such bores, the moment you meet them, you feel as if you'd been tired of them always.

A bore's idea of conversation is a monologue.

Some men are such bores you can't stand listening to them even when they're talking about you.

A bore is a person who never likes to be alone, but makes you wish you were.

When some people sit alone with their thoughts, the process might be described as boring from within.

Recipe for being a bore: drown your tales in details.

A man bores you with what he has done; a woman with what she has said.

A bore is a person with plenty of time to spare—your time.

When a man talks as much as a woman we call him a bore.

The worst thing about a bore is not that he won't stop talking, but that he won't let you stop listening.

A bore is a person who uses his mouth to talk while you use yours to yawn.

BORROW

You need no collateral to borrow trouble.
                        —William Lyon Phelps

No debt ever comes due at a good time, yet borrowing is the only thing that's handy all the time.   *— Will Rogers*

Before you borrow money from a friend, decide which you need more.

Never call a man a fool; borrow from him instead.

Don't borrow trouble: borrow money, and trouble will come of its own accord.

If at first you don't succeed, try borrowing from another friend.

Never be at home to borrowers because if you're in, you'll be out, but if you're out, you'll be in.

No man who can borrow money easily ever wants it badly.

Happiness has one great advantage over money: friends don't try to borrow it.

Always borrow from a pessimist—he never expects it back.

If you want to borrow fifty dollars from a friend, ask for a hundred.

If you want to teach children the value of money, borrow from them.

Many a man spends half his life borrowing money, and the other half not paying it back.

The man who tries to borrow money, soon finds out how many close friends he has.

No matter how bad a man's credit may be, he can always borrow trouble.

Many a man with a big collection of books needs more shelves, but doesn't know how to borrow shelves.

BORROW AND LEND

Don't borrow or lend, but if you must do one, lend. *– Josh Billings*

It's easy to forget when you borrow money, but easy to remember when you lend it.

The borrower who goes out beyond his financial depth usually attracts the loan shark.

The man who never lends his books probably remembers how he acquired them.

BOSS

When a woman wears the pants in the family, she has a good right to them. *– Josh Billings*

The man who does not need a boss is usually the man selected to be one.

Most men don't find it necessary to bring the boss home to dinner—she's already there.

'Tis better to have loved and lost than to marry and be bossed.

Many a man never has to show his wife who's boss in his house —she has a mirror.

Many a girl would like a husband made to order—in more ways than one.

Before marriage a man declares he will be master in his own house or know the reason why; after marriage he knows the reason why.

Don't envy your boss: remember he has to get up early to see who comes in late.

Sometimes a girl marries her boss, but more often a girl bosses her marriage.

The real boss of the family is the one who can get along without the other's love.

Marriage is the only business where there are more bosses who are women than men.

The boss is the man whose son is the man most likely to succeed.

The man who claims he's boss in his own home will lie about other things too.

A man always shows himself in his work, especially when the boss is around.

There are dozens of ways for a man to get to be a boss, but marriage isn't one of them.

An adolescent waits impatiently to grow up and become his own boss—then he gets married.

Marriage is a business where the husband is the boss and has his wife's permission to say so.

There are some husbands who boss the house, but most husbands merely house the boss.

The four ages of man: bossed by mother, bossed by sister, bossed by wife, bossed by daughter.

Nothing improves a man's jokes like being a boss.

Many a husband thinks his wife thinks he's the boss.

BOTTLE

A sweetheart is a bottle of wine, a wife is a wine bottle.
—Baudelaire

'Tis better to be brought up on a bottle than to be brought down by one.

There's many a slip 'twixt the cup and the lip; the safest way is to drink out of the bottle.

Some men know only one way to open a conversation—with a corkscrew.

A good beginning is half the bottle.

Some people have no respect for age unless it's bottled.

The corkscrew opens the bottle, and the bottle opens the man.

The only one who can go into ecstasies over a bottle when it's empty is an interior decorator.

There are many ways to pull yourself out of trouble, but the worst way is with a corkscrew.

Nothing can hold liquor as well as a bottle—so leave it in the bottle.

To some men the only symbol of hospitality is a corkscrew.

BOTTOM

The only way to learn anything thoroughly is by starting at the bottom, except when learning how to swim.

Many a man who starts at the bottom likes it so well he stays there.

Many a boss's son learns his father's business by starting at the bottom—for a few days.

BOXING

The hardest thing about prize fighting is picking up your teeth with a boxing glove on.
— *Kin Hubbard*

The greatest prize in prize fighting is found by the boxer at the box office.

To be a success a prize fighter must always consider the rights of others.

The prize ring is no place for a slowpoke.

The difference between champions and other heavyweights is that the latter retire while they're still in the ring.

BOY

All my life I have loved a womanly woman and admired a manly man but I never could stand a boily boy.
— *Archibald Primrose*

Boys will be boys—and so will a lot of middle-aged men.
— *Kin Hubbard*

Nobody can misunderstand a boy like his own mother.
— *Norman Douglas*

Boys are beyond the range of anybody's sure understanding, at least when they are between the ages of 18 months and 90 years.
— *James Thurber*

A boy is a hurry on its way to doing nothing. — *John Ciardi*

When you can't do anything else to a boy, you can make him wash his face. — *Ed Howe*

A man can never quite understand a boy, even when he has been a boy. — *Chesterton*

The reason a woman knows her son will turn out to be a fine man is that he shows no signs of it.

Many a youngster is much worse than the other boys his mother warns him not to play with.

A boy is a human machine that operates on the principle of perpetual commotion.

The typical American boy would love to go to the moon, but hates to go to the supermarket for his mother.

It is a mistake to believe that because a boy is quiet, he is up to mischief; he may be asleep.

Any boy would rather have a dollar in the hand for being good than a promise of heaven when he dies.

Every small boy brings into a home a lot of happiness—also a lot of dirt, noise and junk.

The hardest crop to raise on a farm are the boys of the family.

A boy may not realize when he's falling in love, but everyone else does.

BOY AND GIRL

It wouldn't matter if boys will be boys, if we could only prevent girls from being girls.
— *Anthony Hope*

Every man is a little boy at heart, and every girl a woman.

Little girls like dolls and little boys like soldiers, but after they grow up, the girls go for soldiers and the boys go for dolls.

Boys will be boys, otherwise the girls would be disappointed.

Some babies are born to rule, while others are boys.

A tomboy is a girl who misbehaves like a boy.

Boys will be boys, but girls these days are running them a clothes second.

BOYHOOD

My brother and I devoted all our boyhood to one long argument, unfortunately interrupted by meals, schools, and work.
— *Chesterton*

He's no longer your little boy when he stops asking Pop and starts consulting the encyclopedia.

BRAINS

I not only use all the brains I have but all I can borrow.
— *Woodrow Wilson*

Brains: that which distinguishes the man who is content to *be* something from the man who wishes to *do* something. — *Bierce*

If you haven't much education, you've got to use your brains.

The brain is a thinking machine whose chief use is to find reasons to keep us thinking as we already do.

There's no tax on brains—the revenue would be too small.

A brain is no stronger than its weakest think.

Brains are not a handicap to a girl because a smart girl knows enough to hide them behind a low neckline.

The man who has more money than brains doesn't have it for long.

Brains are what make a man think he's cleverer than he is.

To pay for success you must tax your brains.

The average man's brain weighs more than a woman's because it takes more to understand a woman than a man.

BRASSIERE

Appearances are deceiving: many a girl who puts up a swell front in public is flat-chested at home.

A century ago the bustle was regarded as a stern necessity, but today it's the brassière that's up in front.

BREAD

In the Lord's Prayer, the first petition is for daily bread; no one can worship God or love his neighbor on an empty stomach.
— *Woodrow Wilson*

Man does not live by bread alone, even pre-sliced bread.
— *Denis W. Brogan*

What difference does it make to know which side your bread is buttered on—you eat both sides anyway.

We pray for our daily bread daily, instead of by the month or week, because we want it fresh.

Some people cast their bread upon the waters and expect it to return toasted and buttered.

The woman who used to bake a dozen loaves of bread a week, now has a granddaughter who complains if she has to toast half a dozen slices.

Don't loaf away your time and depend on the Lord for your daily bread; He isn't running a bakery.

Give us this day our daily bread—with caviar.

BREAK

Friendship is like earthenware: once broken, it can be mended; love is like a mirror: once broken, that ends it.   — *Josh Billings*

When an optimist breaks his leg, he is glad that it wasn't his neck.

Some actors are so bad, the only way they can get into a cast is to break a leg.

After you go through with it a few times you learn how to fall in love without sustaining any serious fracture.

BREAKFAST

The husband who has to get his breakfast downtown is liable to be late for dinner.
— *Kin Hubbard*

My wife and I tried to breakfast together, but we had to stop or our marriage would have been wrecked.   — *Winston Churchill*

Believe it or not, once upon a time all members of the family had breakfast together.

Sometimes the biggest surprise a wife can get her husband for his birthday is to get him his breakfast.

The smile that over cocktails looked ethereal is not so charming over breakfast cereal.

Breakfast is the meal during which a husband reads while his wife is talking, or a wife talks while her husband is reading.

Breakfast is the only meal to which no one is ever invited.

It's a good idea for a bride to eat breakfast with her husband, even if he prepares it himself.

Breakfast is the tollbooth through which you must pass in order to get to work.

A woman always knows what's behind the headlines: it's her husband, at the breakfast table.

Early to bed and early to rise makes a man get his own breakfast.

When an alcoholic drinks orange juice for breakfast, it is only as a chaser.

The husband who gets his breakfast in bed is probably in a hospital.

I've got my wife trained—she makes her own breakfast.

What this country needs is not more breakfast foods to make kids stronger, but a cereal to sap their energy.

Another advantage of being a bachelor is that you have to prepare only one breakfast before going to work.

Wives don't resent their husbands reading the newspaper at breakfast—at least, the wives who never get up for breakfast.

No woman is as old as she looks—before breakfast.

There's no one so exasperating as the husband who notices the burnt toast when he should be reading his paper like other husbands.

BREATHING

When some comedians are on the air, I find it hard to breathe.
— *W. C. Fields*

A tight dress sometimes affects a girl's breathing, but more often a man's.

What this country needs are fewer statesmen who are long-winded, and fewer athletes who are short-winded.

Many a woman has a slight impediment in her speech: every now and then she has to stop to breathe.

The only good thing about smog is that it enables you to see what you are breathing.

Breathing is the secret of longevity—but only if you keep it up long enough.

To avoid trouble, breathe through the nose; it keeps the mouth shut.

BREVITY

It is my ambition to say in ten sentences what others say in a whole book.   — *Nietzsche*

When it comes to briefing her husband, the average wife is seldom brief.   — *Carey Williams*

Make your business talks as short as your prayers, and you will always be a winner.
— *Ed Howe*

I don't care how much a man talks, if he only says it in a few words.   — *Josh Billings*

There's a great power in words, if you don't hitch too many of them together.   — *Josh Billings*

Some authors are so addicted to wordiness that they are capable of writing a huge volume in favor of brevity.

A good cook uses shortening before dinner, and a good speaker uses it after dinner.

Brevity is the soul of wit—that's why men laugh at fat women wearing shorts.

BRIBERY

Corrupt officials are usually close-mouthed and open-handed.

The wheels of politics never turn unless they are well-greased.

Money doesn't grow on trees, but a lot of people get it by grafting.

With corrupt officials, money is the loot of all evil.

Politics is full of sins of omission and commission, with the omission being ignored if the commission is high enough.

BRIDE

Brides aren't happy—they are just triumphant. *—John Barrymore*

When men meet a bride, they look at her face, but women look at her clothes.   *— Ed Howe*

Bride: a woman with a fine prospect of happiness behind her.
— Bierce

It looks as if Hollywood brides keep the bouquets and throw away the grooms.
— Groucho Marx

Many a bride who is given away turns out to be mighty expensive.

The latest thing in weddings is generally the bride.

Where there's smoke, there's probably a bride cooking.

Every man has his price, but brides are given away.

Remember, the most adorable bride of today will be someone's mother-in-law in the future.

Many a bride who has never held a broom in her hands sweeps up the aisle beautifully.

In some marriages the bride is given away by the press.

A movie star is destined never to be a bridesmaid but always a bride.

The modern bride dresses to kill, and she usually cooks the same way.

The father of the bride seldom objects to giving her away, but often objects to her being so expensively gift-wrapped.

BRIDEGROOM

A bridegroom is a man who spends a lot of money on a new suit that nobody notices.

A man never realizes how unimportant he is until he attends his own wedding.

There's nothing written about less than a June bridegroom.

Man worships woman, and then sacrifices himself at the altar.

A bridegroom is a man who agrees to marriage before marriage disagrees with him.

A new groom sweeps clean, and also washes dishes.

Another optimist is the bridegroom who thinks none of his habits needs reforming.

A bridegroom is a man who is never important at a wedding unless he fails to show up.

One of the first things a bridegroom learns is that a man can't fool his wife as easily as his mother.

The bridegroom who thinks matrimony is a 50-50 proposition is about to find out that he doesn't understand fractions.

A bridegroom co-stars at the wedding ceremony, but plays only a supporting role thereafter.

A bridegroom is a man who has just lost his self-control.

BRIDGE

In bridge, men like to win, but women hate to lose.
— *Charles Goren*

To have learned to play a good game of bridge is the safest insurance against the tedium of old age. — *Somerset Maugham*

Bridge is a friendly game invented by two married couples who disliked each other.

Women bridge players seldom play the game skillfully, but they always play it fluently.

There is a place for everything in this world, except four pairs of feet under a bridge table.

The most difficult of all card tricks is how to get out of making a fourth at bridge.

Some people enjoy playing bridge; others like to sit on the sidelines as noncombatants.

Anyone who thinks conversation is a lost art doesn't play bridge.

Some women always do their husbands' bidding, but only at a bridge table.

Another change the game of bridge needs is a crossbar under the table.

The old quarrel between the North and South has spread out to include the East and West, and is now called bridge.

A good talker is appreciated in any company, but not when the other three are trying to play bridge.

Bridge is a card game in which a player often loses his head and his hand at the same time.

In bridge, a good deal depends on a good deal.

Bridge is the only game that bruises more shins than hockey.

One reason why women play bridge is that they may have something to think about while they talk.

The man who doesn't know what to do with his hands shouldn't try to play bridge.

Some people play bridge with eyes and hands, while others play it with mouth and ears.

So live that you don't have to hesitate to be the first woman to leave the bridge party.

Women who play bridge are generally familiar and conversant with the game, especially conversant.

Wives who kick their husbands under the bridge table, should not wear open-toed shoes.

Many a man criticizes his wife as a bridge partner because she has a one-trick mind.

Bridge teaches a woman the art of concentration as well as the art of getting her husband's dinner ready in ten minutes.

BRIDGE CLUB

A bridge club consists of a group of women who meet to hold cards, hold teacups and hold forth.

A bridge club is a group made up of some women who talk too much, and others who are silent too little.

A bridge club consists of a handful of women who gather for a mouthful of food and an earful of gossip.

BRIDGE PRIZE

If not for bridge where would we store all the rummage we give away now as bridge prizes?

The only practical use for bridge prizes is to give them away for bridge prizes.

One of the hardest things to affect is a cry of delighted surprise upon unwrapping a bridge prize.

Junk is anything worthless, like trash, rubbish or bridge prizes.

BRIGHT

There's a bright side to everything, except the bright sayings of other people's children.

Students would reflect more if they were brighter, or would be brighter if they would reflect more.

Brightness is the mark of the full moon, but not of the lovers attracted to it.

A baby often makes your days brighter, but more often your nights.

For every person who boasts about being bright, there are a dozen persons ready to polish him off.

Another person who looks at the bright side of things is the sun worshipper.

The bright sayings of children are generally a relative matter.

The only thing needed to make children bright is for them to be your own.

BROADCASTING

In America you can go on the air and kid the politicians, and the politicians can go on the air and kid the people.
— *Groucho Marx*

My father hated radio and could not wait for television to be invented so he could hate that too.
— *Peter De Vries*

The ancient Greeks could not broadcast the Aeschylian trilogy but they could write it.

There's only one thing wrong with radio and television: it's the stuff that's broadcast.

BROTHEL

The best job ever offered to me was to become a landlord in a brothel; it's the perfect milieu for an artist to work in.
— *Faulkner*

The only place where no one ever suffers the pangs of love is a brothel.

When an unmarried man goes to a brothel, he's needy; when a married man does, he's greedy.

BROTHER

Officially, nations love each other like brothers; unofficially, they love each other like brothers-in-law.

Age and her little brother will always tell on a girl.

Girls who give advice to others go to proms with their own brothers.

Love is blind, but kid brothers are not.

BROTHERHOOD

I want to be the white man's brother, but not his brother-in-law.   — *Martin Luther King*

We live in a world that has narrowed into a neighborhood before it has broadened into a brotherhood. — *Lyndon B. Johnson*

A fraternity is the antithesis of fraternity.   — *E. B. White*

Marilyn Monroe married a Protestant, a Catholic, and a Jew, and divorced them all: that's what I call brotherhood.
— *Harry Golden*

It is easier to love humanity than to love one's neighbor.
— *Eric Hoffer*

As a young man, unable to accept the Fatherhood of God, I began to believe in the Brotherhood of Man.   — *Louis Untermeyer.*

Every once in a while you meet a person who makes you dread the coming brotherhood of man.

You can't blame a taxpayer for feeling that he is his brother's keeper.

You can't spell *brothers* and not spell *others.*

The lion and the lamb may lie down together, but the lion will be the only one to get up.

The brotherhood of man is a wonderful idea, especially when you are in need of help.

The trouble with being your brother's keeper is that he thinks you are trying to be his boss.

BRUSH

You can quiet a child by brushing his hair or using the other side of the brush on the other end of the child.

There are several million unemployed in the United States, but everyone can't sell Fuller brushes.

BUDGET

The success of a family budget depends upon the husband's power to veto his wife's bills.

A budget is a plan that enables you to pay as you go—if you don't go anywhere.

A housewife finds it easy to run a house on a budget—until the money runs out.

A family budget is usually made up of a little money and a lot of estimates.

A family budget stops you from wondering about last month's money, and starts you worrying about next month's.

The government always has trouble trying to budget, but never has any trouble to juggle it.

A budget sometimes shows how much we have to save, but more often how much we have to borrow.

A family budget tells you not how you are going to spend your money, but how you have already spent it.

A family budget is a plan that leaves you with nothing to spend —except time.

To Congress, a billion dollars is just a drop in the budget.

A budget is a financial schedule adopted to prevent part of the month being left at the end of your money.

Running a house on a budget is easily managed—until the first of the month.

A budget is a family plan whose main drawback is that it won't work unless you economize.

A budget is a plan adopted to prevent people from making the down payment on something new each month.

A budget is a detailed record of how you managed to spend more than you earned.

All that a budget does for some people is to keep them from buying a necessity today so that they can buy a luxury tomorrow.

A budget is a family plan whose success depends not on what a husband earns, but on what his wife doesn't spend.

Another way to stay within your budget is to sit back and let the rest of the world go buy.

A budget is a way of spending money without getting any fun out of it.

Living on a budget is the same as living beyond your means, except that you have a record of it.

There's only one thing wrong with a budget: it's open at the wrong end.

Every nation finds it difficult to balance a budget at the end of a sword.

Why is it that the second half of the month is harder to budget than the first half?

A budget enables you to pay as you go, but only if you go without.

A budget is a family plan where the money always runs out before the month does.

A budget is a plan adopted when you cannot support yourself in the style to which you have become accustomed.

The aim of a family budget is to get you to spend as little

the first few days after payday as the last few days.

A family budget is a plan adopted to reduce the amount of money a wife spends above what her husband earns.

BULLFIGHT

The American tourist can always be recognized at a bullfight: he's the one who cheers the bull.

A bullfight is the only sport where it is hard to lose a bet.

BUNGLE

Some homeowners are always doing things around the house that they can't.

Instead of first learning how and then doing it, a do-it-yourselfer first does it and then learns how.

The man who never has enough time to do it properly always has enough time to do it over again.

A do-it-yourselfer is another man who never has to be shown how to do a thing the wrong way.

If you want a thing to be well done, don't do it yourself.

The child who is unable to put the pieces of a jigsaw puzzle together will probably grow up to be a do-it-yourselfer.

A do-it-yourselfer never knows what he can do till he tries, and his wife is often sorry he found out.

BUREAUCRACY

There is only one giant machine operated by pygmies, and that is bureaucracy. — *Balzac*

The nearest approach to immortality on earth is a government bureau. — *James F. Byrnes*

A bureaucrat is a government official who sees his duty and gets someone else to do it.

There is very little to admire in bureaucracy, but you've got to hand it to the Internal Revenue Service.

Bureaucracy is the government of some of the people, by some of the people, for some of the people.

It takes an awful lot of people to run this country, and a lot of awful people.

A bureaucrat is a politician who has swapped his bunk for a berth.

We all work for the government, but the bureaucrat is smarter than the rest of us—he gets paid for it.

In a dictatorship there is only one dictator; in a democracy the government is full of them.

Bureaucracy is governmental officialism where the civil servant is the uncivil master.

Government officials act as if the public business of the country is the private business of the bureaucrat.

A bureaucrat's idea of cleaning up his cluttered files is to make a copy of every paper before he destroys it.

Bureaucrats are neither smart enough to run the government, nor smart enough to keep out of it.

There are a dozen taxpayers born every hour, and one government worker to live off them.

Bureaucracy is more people doing less things, and taking more time to do them worse.

With Washington taking the shirts off everyone's back, it's fortunate we have so many bureaus to keep them in.

Bureaucracy is a system of government where a citizen elects big bureaucrats who dictate to little bureaucrats who dictate to him.

When a bureaucrat makes a mistake, he often labels it *Top Secret* and files it away.

Bureaucrats are all alike: they think it's their business to delay other people's business.

Bureaucracy is a form of government where you seldom get civil service.

A bureaucrat is an official who is clothed with power and whom it doesn't fit.

BURN

To avoid burning your hands in hot water feel the water before putting your hands in.

The man who has too many irons in the fire usually gets his fingers burned.

Nowadays the midnight oil is burned in the transmission instead of the lamp.

Always spread newspapers in front of the fireplace so that if any sparks fly out they won't get on the rug.

Most of the knowledge in the world has been acquired at the expense of someone's burned fingers.

When a man is burning with love, he usually makes a fuel of himself.

A patio is the place where a man burns leaves in the autumn and steaks in the summer.

BUS

The best way to tell if a girl is really beautiful is whether she is standing or sitting in a crowded bus.

The only one who is always sure of getting a seat on the bus is the bus driver.

Americans will go anywhere, except to the rear of a bus.

Many a man can't keep his eyes off women, except when he's sitting in a crowded bus.

Country people make their own jam, but city people get theirs in the buses.

There's always room for a good man—except in a crowded bus.

Bus company officials complain of bad business when all their passengers get seats.

A seat in a crowded bus is worth two in an empty one.

Time, tide and bus drivers wait for no man.

Every bus is equipped with shock absorbers, most of which are the passengers.

Another way to get an education is to drive a school bus.

All things come to him who waits, except a seat in the bus.

A bus is a vehicle that runs twice as fast when you are after it as when you are in it.

Man is a courageous creature who ventures high in the skies and deep in the seas, yet fears to move to the rear of the bus.

BUSINESS

Half the time when men think they are talking business, they are wasting time.   — Ed Howe

The successful businessman sometimes makes his money by ability and experience, but he generally makes it by mistake.
                    — Chesterton

A friendship founded on business is better than a business founded on friendship.
— *John D. Rockefeller*

The craft of the merchant is this: bringing a thing from where it abounds to where it is costly.
— *Emerson*

One way to avoid having industrial troubles is to avoid having industries. — *Don Marquis*

My people belonged to the old-fashioned English middle class in which a businessman was still permitted to mind his own business.
— *Chesterton*

Nothing is quite honest that is not commercial, but not everything commercial is honest.
— *Robert Frost*

If you want to know how to run a big business, ask the man who hasn't any.

A businessman can't win nowadays: if he does something wrong, he's fined; if he does something right, he's taxed.

The man who uses yesterday's methods in today's work won't be in business tomorrow.

Mind your own business; if you don't, another will.

Businessmen are alike the world over: they get together and complain about bad business over the most expensive dinners.

A man is known by the company that keeps him.

The man who never has time to attend to other people's business usually has more business than he can attend to.

The businessman who keeps his nose to the grindstone will find it hard to keep his ear to the ground.

When an irresistible force meets an immovable body, a merger usually follows.

The man who works for another should not spend too much time minding his own business.

A man is judged by the company he keeps—solvent.

Women in business are a problem: if you treat them like men, they start complaining; if you treat them like women, your wife may find out.

It's bad business to talk about bad business.

There are two classes of people: those who worry about their business, and those who worry about other people's business.

Fools rush in where wise men fear to trade.

The business outlook for the businessman is often brighter than the business outlook of the businessman.

BUST

The woman who admits she's thirty-six is probably referring to her bust size.

Many a heaving bosom is nothing more than a hope chest.

Honesty may be the best policy, but falsies prove it is not always the bust policy.

The starlet who goes to dramatic school soon learns how to project—her bosom.

A large-busted woman always seems closer to you than you are to her.

BUSY

The busiest man you meet is generally the one who is trying to make a living without working for it.

If time is money, why is it that wealthy executives never seem to have a moment to spare?

If there's a job to be done, select a busy man; the other kind has no time.

Busy souls have no time to be busybodies.

If you are too busy to laugh, you are too busy.

The best recourse for a man who doesn't want to be idle is to fall in love.

A man is never too busy to talk about how busy he is.

An executive is too busy if he cannot entertain a new idea without an appointment.

The hand that rocks the cradle is usually too busy to rule the world.

All things come to him who is too busy to wait for them.

If you want to find out how busy a man is, ask him to do something for you.

The happiest people are those who are too busy to notice whether they are happy or not.

The best way to get a job done is to give it to a busy man —he'll have his secretary do it.

BUTLER

Some women won't marry a man unless he can earn enough for bread and butler.

A butler sometimes lives to serve his third degeneration.

BUTTON

Men build bridges and throw railroads across deserts, yet the job of sewing on a button is beyond them.   —*Heywood Broun*

Life is full of disappointments: nothing ever comes off except buttons.

Why is it that the wife who can see right through you doesn't notice the button missing from your shirt?

If you can't find the right button, sew up the bottonhole.

The age of automation is still young: wait until the buttons start pushing back at you.

When a man has buttons missing from his clothes, he should get married—or divorced.

The mark of a successful executive is to have more buttons on his telephone than on his suit.

Before zippers, life was chiefly buttons; now we're back again to buttons—pushing them.

About the only thing in the modern house that doesn't seem to have a button is a husband's shirt.

An oldtimer is one who remembers when buttons were sewn, not pushed.

BUY

It's good to have money to buy the things that money can buy, but it's better not to lose the things money cannot buy.
— *George Horace Lorimer*

I am the world's worst salesman; therefore I must make it easy for people to buy.
— *F. W. Woolworth*

People never buy what they need—they always buy what they want. — *Charles F. Kettering*

He who buys what he does not want will soon want what he cannot buy. — *C. C. Colton*

Credit buying has divided America into two classes: those who have all the latest appliances, and those who pay cash.

Many a husband never buys a suit on his own because he needs his wife to tell him whether he likes it or not.

The only thing some people do on time is buy.

Money cannot buy happiness, but then happiness cannot buy groceries.

The way to a man's heart is through his stomach, but the way to a woman's heart is a buy-path.

A woman buys things she cannot afford to show off to others who cannot appreciate them.

Formerly people worried about how much it took to buy something; nowadays they worry about how long.

America is a land with such a high standard of living that almost everyone can afford to buy expensive unpaid-for things.

Never put off till tomorrow what you can buy today—there will probably be a higher tax on it.

There are two ways a man can make sure of getting his wife to listen: to talk about buying something for himself, or about buying something for her.

Some people are so poor, they don't know where the next down payment is coming from.

BUY AND SELL

The best time to buy a house is when you are selling.

You never know how dear things are until you buy them, nor how cheap they are until you sell them.

According to television commercials, there are only three kinds of shopkeepers: favorite dealers, neighborhood dealers and friendly dealers.

Prices are never right: the seller thinks they are too low; the buyer, too high.

In business, you sometimes sell things below cost, but you never buy them that way.

Success is a matter of buying your experience cheap and selling it at a profit.

CAESAR

Caesar might have married Cleopatra, but he had a wife at home—there's always something.
— *Will Cuppy*

Caesars are usually killed by their own friends because they are enemies. — *Stanislaw J. Lec*

If Caesar had been a conformist, he would have said, "I came, I saw, I concurred."

CAKE

The wedding cake is the only cake which, once eaten, can give you indigestion for the rest of your life.

Beware of the girl who likes to eat her cake and have yours too.

Don't judge a woman's cooking by the cake she sends to the church bazaar.

There is nothing that broadens one like travel, except pastry.

A thoughtful bride will save a piece of her wedding cake for the divorce lawyer.

A woman grows more economical with age—at least, if you judge by the number of candles on her birthday cake.

CALENDAR

After slaving the whole year, all that some men have to show for it is a calendar.

You can get along with last year's car and clothes, but you must have this year's calendar.

The only thing you can give the man who has everything is a calendar to remind him when the payments are due.

CALM

A mind that is not only calm itself, but the cause of calm in others—that is the true college presidential ideal.
— *Frank Moore Colby*

Anyone who is calm in these hectic days probably doesn't feel well.

Taking things philosophically is easy, especially if they don't concern you.

CALORIES

The best way for a woman to watch her calories is from a distance.

What this country needs is a five-course 500-calorie dinner.

Middle age is the time in life when you are determined to cut down on your calories—one of these days.

Some women are no good at counting calories, and they have the figures to prove it.

A person on a diet should eat the calories allowed without counting the calories aloud.

CAMERA

The camera is one of the greatest liars of our time.
— *John Gunther*

The camera never lies, but it would be justified in lots of instances. — *Kin Hubbard*

A tourist abroad always forgets some things at home, but unfortunately the camera is never one of them.

There is no one so popular as a returning vacationist who lost his camera at the beginning of his trip.

Modern high-speed cameras are so fast that a man can even catch his wife with her mouth shut.

A girl can't fool a camera—which proves that a camera has more sense than a man.

CAMP

A parent will spend hundreds of dollars to send his boy to a summer camp where he can learn to make something worth a few cents.

A camp is a summer place in the country where a mother sends her children for her vacation.

Parents have their blessings: once a year they can pack up their troubles and send them to camp.

CAMPING

He who believes that where there's smoke there's fire has never tried cooking on a camping trip.

Camping is an outdoor vacation during which you have a great time in great discomfort.

Some men fish with flies on their camping trips, while others fish, sleep and live with them.

Careless campers are the forest's prime evil.

CANADA

Canadians use English for literature, Scotch for sermons, and American for conversation.
— *Stephen Leacock*

Canada's climate is nine months winter and three months late in the fall.

Canadian saying: Man wants but little here below—zero.

CANDIDATE

The lavish and shameful use of money to gain political office wouldn't be so bad if the office ever got anything out of it.
— *Kin Hubbard*

The worst thing about being the top candidate is that you have to speak last, after everyone has already said everything.
— *Adlai Stevenson*

Office seeking is a disease: it is even catching.
— *Grover Cleveland*

There is no one less candid than a candidate.

In politics, the self-made man seldom wins against the machine-made candidate.

There are some political candidates who, if their constituents were cannibals, would promise them missionaries for dinner.

In politics, familiarity breeds votes.

A candidate is a man who manages to get around before election, especially around the issues.

To the candidate running for re-election, all issues lead to the stream where horses must not be swapped in the middle of.

Every candidate is entitled to his own opinion, if you can only find out what it is.

The righteous indignation of a candidate knows no bounds when he discovers that his opponent is also playing politics.

Never judge Presidential timber by its bark.

Every now and then you meet a candidate who runs for office so hard that only a roadblock can stop him.

The good die young, but the bad live on and run for office.

A candidate's gift for gab before election usually turns into a gift for grab afterward.

Some men are born great, some achieve greatness, and some Presidential candidates are willing to have it thrust upon them.

Running for office is like courting: you say a lot of things you later wish you hadn't.

The reason women don't run for President is that by the time a woman can decide which hat to throw into the ring, the election is over.

No candidate ever gets his ear so close to the ground that he can't speak into a microphone.

A candidate is a politician who is anxious to help us out of all the trouble the other politicians have got us into.

Many a candidate pretends he would rather be righteous than President.

A candidate often promises to clean up politics before election, but too often prefers to clean up for himself afterward.

Many a candidate feels that, since his rival has been fooling the public for years, he should now be given a chance.

What this country needs are candidates who care more for the nation than they do for the nomination.

A clever politician knows that it isn't necessary to fool all the people all the time—just during the campaign.

Many a candidate who throws his hat into the ring forgets to take his head out.

Agility is a requisite for political office: every incumbent must be able to run while holding on to his seat.

When there are more than two candidates for public office, how are you to choose the lesser of two evils?

A candidate is one who shakes your hand before election and your acquaintance afterward.

A candidate is the only man who knows all the answers, especially if he is out of office.

A man never realizes how foolish and unfit he is until he runs for office and listens to his opponent's speeches.

The candidate who takes a firm stand when he runs seldom walks away with the election.

A candidate has to see both sides of an issue—otherwise, how is he going to get around it?

CANDLE

The game is not usually worth the candle that is burned at both ends.

Middle age is the time in life when you haven't enough wind to blow out the candles on your birthday cake in one breath.

CANNIBAL

Is it progress if a cannibal learns to use a knife and fork?
— *Stanislaw J. Lec*

Can the cannibal speak in the name of those he has eaten?
— *Stanislaw J. Lec*

Cannibals are not vegetarians, they are humanitarians.

Some cannibals take missionaries seriously, others take them with a grain of salt.

A cannibal has no manners: he talks when he has people in his mouth.

One man's meat is another man's poison, unless he's a cannibal.

A cannibal often eats something that disagrees with him—or someone.

When a cannibal is converted, does he eat only fishermen on Friday?

There was once a cannibal who complained he was getting fed up with people.

CAPITAL

Beauty is the capital of a girl, and capital is the beauty of a man.

Wise men profit by their mistakes, and use the profit as capital in a different business.

About the only thing you can do on a shoestring nowadays is to trip.

The world would have been better off if Karl Marx had made some capital instead of writing about it.

Many a man is in favor of capital punishment; he thinks capital deserves it.

Never let capital lie idle; remember that money talks, but it doesn't talk in its sleep.

Capital breeds interest: when a man has the one, a woman shows the other.

Rome isn't the world's most beloved capital—money is.

CAPITALISM AND COMMUNISM

The inherent vice of capitalism is the unequal sharing of blessings; the inherent virtue of socialism is the equal sharing of miseries.   — *Winston Churchill*

Under capitalism, the people have most of the automobiles; under Communism, the people have most of the parking space.

Communist countries wouldn't be so far behind capitalist countries if they didn't spend so much time fighting capitalism.

There's nothing wrong with capitalism that any Communist can't cure.

Under capitalism, the stockholders own the factories and the workers own the cars; under Communism, the workers own the factories and the bureaucrats own the cars.

CAPITAL PUNISHMENT

When we execute a murderer, we probably make the same mistake as the child who strikes a chair it has bumped into.
          — *G. C. Lichtenberg*

If you advocate the abolition of capital punishment, remember that you have all the murderers on your side.

The man who doesn't believe in capital punishment has probably never tried it.

There's no capital punishment in primitive society; otherwise for his last meal a cannibal might want to eat the warden.

Mankind may be divided in many ways; the guillotine divides it into two: heads and bodies.

The aim of capital punishment should be to reform the criminal.

Capital punishment is the law in some states and the Internal Revenue Service.

There's nothing wrong with any man that capital punishment can't cure.

CAR

What this country needs is a car that can go no faster than its driver can think.

In the United States every man is entitled to life, liberty and a car in which to pursue happiness.

Some men take good care of a car; others treat it like one of the family.

An automobile helps you see the world, but you must decide which world.

The one attachment that fits all makes of car is that of the finance company.

Not all who auto ought to.

The easiest way for a man to lose control of his car is to allow his son to get a driver's license.

Every now and then you see a car so old that it's already been paid for.

Nothing injures a car like a trade-in.

Cars are constantly being improved with more horsepower under the hood instead of more horse sense behind the wheel.

The car formerly did away with horses, and is now doing away with people.

There are many automobile accessories, but a wallet is the main one.

Every family needs at least two cars—ask the man who owns one.

A small foreign car reduces your problem of finding parking space while it increases your problem of finding the car.

Cars are constantly being made more beautiful, more powerful and more dangerous.

Cars come in three dimensions: height, width and debt.

If you give some men an inch, they'll park a foreign sports car in it.

More and more people are getting cars, and more and more cars are getting people.

The car was invented as a convenient place to sit out traffic jams.

The most exasperating car trouble is when the engine won't start and the payments won't stop.

What many a man wants in his new car is air conditioning, and what he wants out of it is his teen-age son.

Some cars are so old that the motor vehicle bureau should issue them upper and lower plates.

You can't win: the better your brakes, the greater the danger to your rear fenders.

The foreign sports models are cars for which you pay twice as much to get half as much comfort.

The youngster who borrows the family car for the night subtracts years from the car and adds them to the years of his parents.

Another device that's doing a great deal to reduce the evils of the population explosion is the automobile.

What this country needs are car pools for the parents of teen-agers who have driving licenses.

Technology has improved the modern car so much that it can now run almost as fast as the payments seem to come due.

The most common ways of losing control of your car is by keeping up your drinking, and by not keeping up your payments.

Another way to make your car run better is to have a salesman quote you the price on a new model.

The car has divided mankind into two classes: those who drive them and those who dodge them.

Nothing ages your car as much as the sight of your neighbor's new one.

You don't get into those small foreign cars—you put them on like a girdle.

Another advantage of a small car is that you can squeeze twice as many into a traffic jam.

The man who buys a used car doesn't want a cheaper car, but an expensive one that costs less.

CARDS

I always admire a Christian whose calm confidence is backed up by four aces. — *Mark Twain*

I don't object to Gladstone having the ace of trumps up his sleeve, but merely to his belief that the Almighty put it there.
— *Henry Labouchère*

Card playing is an expensive pastime, like any other game in which we hold hands.

It's extraordinary what fine poker hands you get when you're playing bridge.

When a man says he is putting all his cards on the table, count them.

A lady never cheats at cards—unless it's absolutely necessary.

An ace in the hand is worth two in the deck.

Never do business with a man who cheats himself while playing solitaire.

Almost as essential as a fourth at bridge is a fifth at a poker game.

Some women go through life never remembering what trump is.

In cards, a good deal depends upon luck, and luck depends upon a good deal.

Beware of the man who says he's going to put all his cards on the table—look up his sleeve.

Two can live as cheaply as one can play gin rummy.

Life is another game played with cards: post, greeting, punch and credit.

The only thing that enables a long-married couple to get any fun out of holding hands is a card game.

A girl should never lay all her cards on the table, or she will soon find herself playing solitaire.

Solitaire is the only game in which you can put all your cards on the table and still cheat.

CARE

Look after your wife; never mind yourself—she'll look after you.   — *Sacha Guitry*

A man is usually more careful of his money than he is of his principles.   — *Ed Howe*

He is really a mild and inoffensive character, the kind of person one should guard against.
            — *Bernard Shaw*

God takes care of fools, drunks, and the United States of America.
            — *Stephen Leacock*

I don't care to know about many things; what I care to know are the things I care about.
            — *Jules Renard*

Take care of the minutes, and the hours will take care of themselves.   — *Chesterton*

Take care of the sense, and the sounds will take care of themselves.   — *Lewis Carroll*

A man cannot be too careful in the choice of his enemies.
            — *Oscar Wilde*

Care may kill a man, but *don't care* kills more.

One of the hardest jobs a man has nowadays is trying to keep the government from taking care of him.

Another careful driver is the one who saw the driver ahead get caught.

If you walk right and drive right, you won't be left in a hospital.

Take care of the pennies and the dollars will take care of themselves; take care of neither and the government will take care of you.

Many a man cares for his mother-in-law even when he doesn't care for her.

By the time a man gets enough experience to watch his step, he isn't going anywhere.

Take care of the children, and society will take care of itself.

Every man needs a woman to take care of him so she can make him strong enough for her to lean on.

CAREER

Many girls who seek a career find one, but he isn't always tall, dark and handsome.

Sensible women earn their own living, but more sensible women let the men earn it for them.

In order to achieve success, the career woman must look like a woman, act like a lady, think like a man, and work like a dog.

A career is all right but you can't run your hands through its hair.

A girl can have both a career and a home—if she knows how to put both of them first.

You never hear of a man being asked how he manages to combine marriage with a career.

Some men carve careers, others chisel them.

The question that confronts every girl is whether she wants a career or just one husband.

A career woman is one who goes out and earns a man's salary instead of staying home and taking it from him.

CARELESS

When I began going about by car I got just as angry at the carelessness of pedestrians as I used to be at the recklessness of drivers. — *Freud*

The reckless driver always expires before his license does.

A careless motorist is a man whose wife is on her way to become a widow.

Another reckless driver is one who passes you on the highway in spite of all you can do.

If you are careless enough, your present car should last you a lifetime.

CARESS

The hardest problem of a girl's life is to find out why a man seems bored if she doesn't respond to him, and frightened if she does. — *Helen Rowland*

Many a fellow is so brazen, a girl has to slap him several times before she lets him caress her.

To please them, don't tease them; first seize them, then squeeze them.

A man's knowledge of love depends on the way he grasps the subject.

Even if you can't read some girls like a book, it's nice to thumb the pages.

Some girls think it's fun to fight against being caressed, while others take it lying down.

Many a man is all feet when he dances, and all hands when he stops.

CASE

The more lawyers, the longer the case; the more doctors, the shorter the case.

Circumstances alter cases, but in law, cases alter circumstances.

A doctor's first case may be considered a success if the widow pays the bill.

CASH

The excuse some people give for not contributing to charity is that all their money is tied up in cash.

Pay as you go, unless you are going for good.

Cold cash has a way of making the approach a little warmer.

There are still a few things you can get for a quarter—pennies, nickels and dimes.

The man who cannot pay as he goes is probably going too fast.

Cash is a purchasing plan where you pay one hundred per cent down, and nothing every month thereafter.

CASH AND CREDIT

Behind every successful man is a wife who takes much of the credit, and a government that takes most of the cash.

Formerly if you paid cash, people presumed you were thrifty, but nowadays they presume your credit is no good.

Where credit is due, give credit; when credit is due, give cash.

CAT

When I play with my cat, who knows but that she regards me as a plaything even more than I do her? —*Montaigne*

No matter how much cats fight, there always seem to be plenty of kittens. —*Lincoln*

If man could be crossed with the cat, it would improve man, but it would deteriorate the cat.
—*Mark Twain*

I call my kittens *Shall* and *Will* because no one can tell them apart. —*Christopher Morley*

Cats know how to obtain food without labor, shelter without confinement, and love without penalties. —*W. L. George*

The way to keep a cat is to try to chase it away. —*Ed Howe*

A kitten does not discover that her tail belongs to her until you tread upon it. —*Thoreau*

A cat also has nine wives.

There's more than one way to skin a cat—but not the same cat.

There would be less objection to the neighbors' cats if they could only keep in tune.

A catty remark often has more lives than a cat.

Letting the cat out of the bag is much easier than putting it back.

Never maul or tease a Maltese cat.

CATCH

Running after women never hurt a man; it's catching them that does the damage.

True happiness is found in pursuing something, not in catching it, except when it's the last train home.

No wonder a girl can't catch a ball like a man: a man is so much bigger and easier to catch.

Many a wife thinks her husband is the world's greatest lover, but she can never catch him at it.

The easiest way for a girl to catch a man is by pretending to run away from him.

Behind every successful man there's a woman—trying to catch him.

CAUSE

The little trouble in the world that is not due to love is due to friendship. — *Ed Howe*

When a woman is good to a man, it's because she loves him, or because she wants something, or just because.

There are hundreds of causes of war, the chief of which is the belief that you can lick the other fellow.

Many men owe their success to their wives; others owe their wives to their success.

Half the trouble in the world is caused by loose thinkers, and the other half by tight drivers.

The chief cause of marriage is that women dislike becoming spinsters.

CAUSE AND EFFECT

With man, every effect has its causes; with woman, its because.

A legal action that results in no damages is an example of a cause without effect.

Cause and effect can be puzzling: for example, cold feet are often the result of burnt fingers.

Many a have and have-not of today are the did and did-not of yesterday.

Behind every successful man is a woman who makes it necessary for him to make money.

CAUTION

The chief danger in life is that you may take too many precautions. — *Alfred Adler*

I have lived long enough to look carefully the second time into things I am most certain of the first time. — *Josh Billings*

Don't cry out for help at night —you might awaken the neighbors. — *Stanislaw J. Lec*

Look out for the fellow who lets you do all the talking. — *Kin Hubbard*

The young man turned to him with a disarming candor which instantly put him on his guard. — *Saki*

Look before you leap out of the frying pan into the fire.

There's no one so cautious as the man who always looks both ways before crossing a one-way street.

You have reached middle age when all you exercise is caution.

Always watch your step—even when you're not going anywhere.

Nowadays when a girl goes out on a blind date, she should eat, drink and be wary.

Always be on your guard because you are one of all the people who can be fooled some of the time.

Look before you leap, but look ahead, not behind.

Be careful you don't start something when you try to stop something.

CELEBRATION

The man who takes to drink when his wife leaves him should be careful not to overdo the celebration.

Sometimes when a man takes a day off to celebrate, he needs another day off to get over it.

Some people's idea of a celebration is to enjoy a Christmas they'll never forget and a New Year's they can't remember.

When an alcoholic wants to celebrate an occasion, does he go out and get sober?

CELEBRITY

A celebrity is one who is known to many persons he is glad he doesn't know.   —*Mencken*

When everyone is somebody then no one's anybody.
—*W. S. Gilbert*

Early to bed and early to rise, and you'll never meet any celebrities.

Figures don't lie, unless they happen to be public figures.

Today's celebrities of show business will go thundering down in history like extra drops of water over Niagara Falls.

The trouble with being in the limelight is that you cannot see what is going on around you.

A celebrity is a nonentity who has been on television twice.

You can't occupy a place in the sun without being exposed to blisters.

Many a person listed in *Who's Who* doesn't know what's what.

A celebrity is one you don't know well enough to speak to, but know well enough to talk about.

Being a celebrity means that you have to spend more than you make, on things you don't need, to impress people you don't like.

A celebrity is a somebody who is often a nobody that is well-known to everybody.

CEMETERY

The only place nowadays where a man can find a wife who doesn't smoke, drink or flirt is the cemetery.

A cemetery is the only place where people never complain about the weather.

The fence around a cemetery is foolish, for those inside can't get out, and those outside don't want to get in.

A cemetery is the only place where people don't try to keep up with the Joneses.

Every cemetery is filled with people who thought the world couldn't get along without them.

All work and no play makes Jack the wealthiest man in the cemetery.

The only place where you can find people who spend all their time minding their own business is the cemetery.

A cemetery is the only place where people don't crave for the things they can't afford.

CENSOR

As long as I don't write about the government, religion, politics, and other institutions, I am free to print anything. — *Beaumarchais*

Any country that has sexual censorship will eventually have political censorship.
— *Kenneth Tynan*

In spite of censorship, babies are still being born without clothes.

Some people wouldn't read a book even if it were banned.

A censor should think a little more above the neck, and a little less below the belt.

What makes no sense makes censors.

Censorship is an iron curtain; freedom of the press, a picture window.

The censor is another man who no's a good thing when he sees it.

The song that censors sing is made up wholly of refrains.

The high thinking of censors is usually out of all proportion to its breadth.

Censors make up for their lack of awareness of what is suitable by their extra censory perception.

Our censors will never be satisfied until we have sex repeal.

A censor is a man who never suppresses his desire to suppress the desires of other.

Every censor thinks everyone needs to be censored except himself.

A censor believes in life, liberty and the pursuit of other people's happiness.

CENTENARIAN

I've never known a person to live to be 100 and be remarkable for anything else. — *Josh Billings*

The only person who has to wait a lifetime to reach his goal is the centenarian.

If you want to live long, become a centenarian.

By the time everything he owns has finally been paid off, a man is probably a centenarian.

A centenarian is a man who has lived a hundred years, not counting time and a half for overtime.

If you drink a pint of milk every day for 1200 months, you'll live to be 100 years old.

The advantage of being a centenarian is that you are never bothered by insurance agents.

No one tries the patience of his relatives like a rich centenarian.

Centenarians are always telling tall stories because there's no one alive to disprove them.

A centenarian is a person who has lived long enough to make more mistakes than anyone else.

Half the centenarians smoke and drink too much, probably to make up for the total abstinence of the other half.

Another way to live to be 100 is to reach 99, and then live very carefully.

A centenarian never knows what his long life is due to till he signs a testimonial.

The only advantage in being a centenarian is that you have no enemies—you've outlived them all.

Centenarians seldom marry, probably because they are old enough to know better.

CERTAINTY

Convictions are more dangerous foes of truth than lies.
— *Nietzsche*

Doubt is not a pleasant mental state, but certainty is a ridiculous one.
— *Voltaire*

Nothing is certain but death and taxes, but unfortunately they don't come in that order.

Nothing is certain but death and higher taxes.

A dogmatic person is sure that he's right before making certain that he's sure.

Nothing is certain but debt and taxes.

CHANCE

Some men don't believe in taking chances, especially when they have a chance to learn something.

Drivers don't have to give the pedestrian a chance because he takes one every time he crosses the street.

If you want to be successful, you must either have a chance or take one.

A chance remark is anything a man gets the chance to say when two women are talking.

Many a man has lots of chances to get married, but refuses to take any.

CHANGE

Everyone thinks of changing the world, but no one thinks of changing himself.
— *Tolstoy*

Things do not change, we do.
— *Thoreau*

When it is not necessary to change, it is necessary not to change. — *Lord Falkland*

A woman changes a lot after marriage—her husband's habits, friends and hours.

Do not fear change, for it is an unchangeable law of progress.

In prosperity, prepare for change; in adversity, hope for one.

Marriage changes the soft-spoken bride of today into the oft-spoken wife of tomorrow.

Be careful with women who are going through a change of life, and with men who are going through a change of wife.

Many a man who has found a way to the marriage altar would like to find a way to alter the marriage.

The two critical periods in a man's life are when his voice changes and when his choice changes.

Change is not reform, any more than noise is music.

Matrimony is an institution where a woman changes her ways, and a man his woes.

It takes a woman longer to change her clothes than her mind, but she doesn't change them so often.

At every wedding there are two changeable people who vow that they will never change.

It's easy for a woman to change a male, but only while he's a baby.

God grant me the courage to change things, and the peace of mind to accept things I cannot change—and the wisdom to know the difference.

Matrimony is the process of changing a girl who was hard to get into a woman who is hard to take.

Another thing that isn't what it used to be is the older generation.

It's less dangerous to change horses in the middle of a stream than to change your mind in the middle of a street.

CHAPERON

The modern rule is that every woman must be her own chaperon. — *Amy Vanderbilt*

Nowadays you never know how a girl will turn out until her parents turn in.

A woman's place is with her children, but not when you're going out with one of her daughters.

CHARACTER

What you are thunders so that I cannot hear what you say to the contrary. — *Emerson*

A person reveals his character by nothing so clearly as the joke he resents. — *G. C. Lichtenberg*

We know but a few men, a great many coats and breeches.
— *Thoreau*

Every man has three characters: the one he shows, the one he has, and the one he thinks he has.
— *Alphonse Karr*

A man never discloses his own character so clearly as when he describes another's.
— *Jean Paul Richter*

You are only what you are when no one is looking.

A man's real character lies somewhere between the partiality of his mother and the prejudice of his mother-in-law.

Character is something you either have or are.

What a woman is depends upon what she does when she might be doing something else.

You can never tell a girl's character by her clothes because girls have more character than that.

Character is another thing that's formed in youth and reformed in marriage.

CHARACTER AND REPUTATION

Many a man's reputation would not know his character if they met on the street.   — *Elbert Hubbard*

Character is what you are; reputation is what you try to make people think you are.

Many a man pays so much attention to his reputation that he loses his character.

A public servant is always more concerned about his reputation than he is about his character.

Your character is built by what you stand for, your reputation by what you fall for.

Character is what you get; reputation is what you get caught at.

CHARITY

If you give money, spend yourself with it.   — *Thoreau*

The word *alms* has no singular, as if to teach us that a single act of charity is no charity.

Some people are so nearsighted that they can't see the need for charity until they're up against it.

Charity begins at home, and generally dies from lack of outdoor exercise.

When some people give their old clothes to charity, they should stay in them.

Many a man's idea of charity is to give unto others the things he cannot use himself.

Charity was once a virtue; now it's an industry.

Some kinds of charity are like that of the man who cast his bread upon the waters while he was seasick.

Charity begins at home, but that's no reason to treat your wife like a pauper.

The difference between charity and philanthropy is that charity can't afford a press agent.

It doesn't take very long to give till it hurts.

When it comes to giving charity, some people stop at nothing.

The Lord loves a cheerful giver, and so does everyone else.

If you are not poor enough to take charity, you are rich enough to give it.

The charity that begins at home is usually a stranger elsewhere.

A fund raiser is a man who spends his time urging you to spend your money.

Be more charitable: don't follow the path of least assistance.

The big problem is not the haves and the have-nots—it's the give-nots.

Some men leave all their money to charity; others leave theirs to charitable institutions.

If you give away your money to charity while you are alive, your relatives won't have to fight over it when you are dead.

The only charity some men support are their sons in college.

Charity begins at home and ends on the income tax return.

Some give according to their means, while others give according to their meanness.

CHARM

There are charms made only for distance admiration.
— *Samuel Johnson*

A really plain woman is one who, however beautiful, neglects to charm.   — *Edgar Saltus*

Charm is a glow within a woman which casts a most becoming light on others.
— *John Mason Brown*

A woman is always ready to describe another woman as charming, but only if the other woman is not charming.

Charm is to a woman what perfume is to a flower.

There are some women who do nothing so gracefully that it becomes something.

A woman wears a veil for the same reason that distance lends enchantment.

Charm is the power to make someone else feel that both of you are wonderful.

Charm is what everyone notices when someone has it, but no one notices when someone hasn't.

CHASE

A real man wants two things —danger and play; that's why he

pursues woman who is the most dangerous plaything. —*Nietzsche*

A man running after a hat is not half so ridiculous as a man running after a woman.
—*Chesterton*

All men are entitled to life, liberty and the pursuit of women.

All things come to him who goes after them.

A modest girl never pursues a man any more than a mousetrap pursues a mouse.

Though there are ever so many ways to pursue happiness, the idea of most men is to chase after a woman.

Some husbands never chase other women; they're too decent, too refined, too old.

The world is full of people who go through life running from something that isn't pursuing them.

Every bachelor thinks he is entitled to life, liberty and the happiness of pursuit.

A woman never chases a man —unless he's getting away.

The faster a motorist is in the pursuit of happiness, the less likely he is to overtake it.

A woman's art is to make pursuit just so difficult as not to be too difficult.

The Constitution guarantees our pursuit of happiness; it doesn't guarantee that happiness will pursue us.

CHASTITY

Of all sexual abberations, chastity is the strangest.
—*Anatole France*

The woman who has never aroused a man's desire shouldn't boast of her chastity. —*Montaigne*

You can put a chastity belt around the body, but you cannot put it around the mind.

The girl who is chaste is probably a virgin; the girl who is chased is probably not.

Many a girl will fight for her honor until the man is just about ready to give up.

CHATTERBOX

A chatterbox is a woman who, to say the least, never does say the least.

A woman is always ma'am or mom but never mum.

When two chatterboxes get together, which one listens?

A chatterbox is a friendly woman who is always ready, able and willing to give your tongue a rest.

Don't listen to a chatterbox for a minute, or you'll have to listen to her for an hour.

Breathes there a man with soul so dead who never to his wife hath said: Shut up!

The chatterbox always runs out of ideas long before she runs out of words.

A man is lucky if his wife has the last word; some wives never get to it.

A chatterbox always has plenty of poise in conversation, but never enough pause.

A woman's mouth usually works faster than her mind.

A chatterbox goes through life always missing wonderful opportunities for keeping quiet.

A chatterbox is a woman who won't stop talking until you start walking.

A chatterbox usually talks so fast that she says things before she even thinks of them.

There are two kinds of women who like to talk a lot: the married women and the single ones.

A chatterbox is known by the silence she doesn't keep.

The only man who doesn't think a woman talks too much is the man who's in love with her.

Girls who chatter don't much matter.

A chatterbox may command a large vocabulary, but she never orders it to halt.

A woman may be down but she's never out—talked.

Her constant chatter keeps a chatterbox from hearing a lot of gossip that would make her chatter more interesting.

It's hard for a woman to learn that a stiff lower jaw can be as useful as a stiff upper lip.

A chatterbox spends half her time telling you what she has told others, and the other half telling others what she has told you.

You can never get away from some women except in the middle of a sentence.

A chatterbox is a woman who goes in for small talk which comes out in large doses.

Many a man who can read his wife like a book can't shut her up like one.

The chattering of some women will never cease until they decease.

When you meet a tiresome chatterbox, you are always glad to learn she is the wife of some man you don't like.

You can depend upon a chatterbox always to speak twice before she thinks.

CHEAP

It is considerably cheaper to sit in a meadow and see motors go by than to sit in a motor and see meadows go by. – *Chesterton*

Two can live as cheaply as one, but only half as long.

Men really understand women; they merely pretend they don't because it's cheaper that way.

Whenever you buy anything for a song, watch out for the accompaniment.

Two people can live as cheaply as one what?

The world is full of cheap vacation spots; the trouble is that it costs a lot of money to get there.

The man who calls them cheap politicians has probably forgotten what his taxes are.

Many things in life are dirt cheap, but to a gardener dirt isn't one of them.

Two can live as cheaply as one, but it costs them twice as much.

CHEAT

Whoever catches the fool first is entitled to shear him.
— *Ed Howe*

A confidence man always keeps himself busy looking for someone to do.

It's about all a man can do today to keep from being done.

Cheat me once, you ought to be ashamed; cheat me twice, I ought to be ashamed.

Always do your best, but not your best friend.

A confidence man pretends to take you for what you are in order to take you for what you have.

You never know whom you can do till you try.

You can cut every man's hair many times, but you can scalp most men only once.

Some men are always up and doing—up to mischief and doing everyone.

Some men will do anything for money—except work for it.

The man who is well-to-do is usually hard to do.

A confidence man is a man with confidence in his own ability, and in the other man's gullibility.

Never put off till tomorrow those whom you can do today.

CHECK

A blank check is the only blank that can be more dangerous than a bullet.

It may be expensive to reach for the check, but it gets you home earlier.

A woman's affection is always increased by receiving a check.

Another nice thing to have in the house is an unexpurgated checkbook.

Many a woman, when she writes a check, draws on her imagination.

A system of checks and balances is all right if you have the balances for the checks.

A deadbeat never knows where his next check is coming from,

or when his last one is coming back.

Many a woman likes to curl up in a chair with a good checkbook.

Feminine logic is what leads a woman to make out a check to cover the difference when she's overdrawn.

A check for liquor is not a check for liquor.

There are many reasons for a man having his arm in a sling, but grabbing the check isn't one of them.

A joint checking account is never overdrawn by the wife; it's just underdeposited by her husband.

All that inflation means to some men is that their checks bounce higher.

Many a woman goes through life wondering why her checkbook refuses to balance.

A joint bank account is one in which a wife usually beats her husband to the draw.

CHEEK

If a pretty woman smacks me on one cheek, I will turn her the other also.   — *Josh Billings*

People who turn the other cheek are apt to end up with a red face.

When a girl permits you to kiss her on either cheek, hesitate a long time between them.

When a movie star turns the other cheek, it's because that side photographs better.

Whoever kisseth thee on thy right cheek, turn to him the other also.

There's no one so sickening as the parasite who is ready to kiss the person he flatters on all four cheeks.

CHEER

The best way to cheer yourself up is to try to cheer somebody else up.   — *Mark Twain*

The chief obstacle to cheerfulness is the person who always preaches it.

Cheer up—only a dentist has to look down in the mouth.

People will often give three cheers for something they won't give anything else for.

Some people are so cheerful that they can have a good time thinking what a good time they'd have if they were having it.

The one college cheer that fits all colleges is the check from home.

CHEMISTRY

Organic chemistry is the study of organs; inorganic chemistry is the study of the insides of organs.
— *Max Shulman*

A beautiful blonde is chemically three-fourths water, but what lovely surface tension!

One of the first things a boy learns with a chemistry set is that he'll never get another.

Sex appeal is a matter of chemistry, but you don't have to be a chemist to find the formula.

CHESS

It's hard to understand why people who have enough time to play chess want to spend it playing chess.

Age brings wisdom to some men, and to others chess.

A successful marriage is one where the husband is almost as patient with his wife as he is with his chess.

The only costume ever designed for chess players is the two-pants suit.

CHEWING GUM

Americans spend more money on chewing gum than on books; if you want to know the reason why, read some of the books.

The advantage of bubble gum is that children can't ask questions while chewing it.

CHILDHOOD

Childhood is a happy period when nightmares occur only during sleep.

Another difference between first and second childhood is that usually you have more money to spend during your second.

Childhood is the period when you're more likely to have measles than scruples.

You can't win in childhood: if you're too noisy, they punish you; if you're too quiet, they take your temperature.

Childhood is that wonderful time of life when all you have to do to lose weight is to take a bath.

A hypochondriac looks back to her happy childhood when she had everything from mumps to measles.

Childhood is the time in life when you spend strenuous days without the aid of a cocktail to ease the strain.

A juvenile delinquent is a youngster whose childhood has made him a child hoodlum.

Childhood begins with a youngster's asking where he came from, and ends with his refusing to tell where he is going.

The most awkward age is when your child is too young to be left at home alone, and too old to be left with a baby sitter.

CHILD PSYCHOLOGY

Child psychologists never punish their children; being a child of theirs is punishment enough.

Not every child psychologist is a bachelor, but every bachelor is a child psychologist.

Child psychology is the art of convincing your child that he'll have more fun playing at the neighbor's.

No wonder Cain turned out badly; his parents never read a book on child psychology.

Child psychology probably worked better in the old days when it was applied with a hand.

Brats are usually the children of parents who don't know the difference between child psychology and childish psychology.

Child psychology has discovered many excellent rules for bringing up other people's children.

The trouble with child psychologists is that they know too much about training children, and too little about taming wild animals.

Many a parent would like to use the rod on the psychiatrist who advised him to spare the child.

Every child psychologist would like to bring up his children in the way he advises other parents.

Child psychology is a science where the child is confused by psychology, and psychology is even more confused by the child.

When a mother hasn't enough will power to discipline her children, she calls her weakness child psychology.

A child psychologist starts out with learning what's wrong with his patients, and ends up with learning what's wrong with their parents.

The child who knows how to get around his parents doesn't need a child psychologist—he is one.

A child psychologist doesn't believe that parents should be on spanking terms with their children.

A child psychologist usually knows too little about the child and too much about psychology.

CHILDREN

My mother loved children—she would have given anything if I had been one.   – *Groucho Marx*

We've had bad luck with our kids—they've all grown up.
  – *Christopher Morley*

Children are given to us to discourage our better emotions.
  – *Saki*

Children enjoy the present because they have neither a past nor a future.   – *La Bruyère*

There are millions of Americans who are clever and fearless, but the trouble is they are only four years old.

Children are a great comfort in your old age, and they help you reach it faster too.

Children are at their best after they're too old to spank but before they're too clever to reason with.

Nowadays one never knows how a son is going to turn out, or when a daughter is going to turn in.

Children are excellent judges of character until they have received the benefits of education.

All children need love, especially those who do not deserve it.

To adults the most annoying thing about children is that they're so childish.

A brat is a child who has learned to get what he wants from his parents by trial and terror.

The neighbor's children are always ill-bred.

An only child usually runs everything around the house, except errands.

Pre-teen children are at an ideal age: they are too old to wake you up at night, and too young to borrow the car.

Children never put off till tomorrow what will keep them from going to bed tonight.

The only things that children wear out faster than shoes are parents.

The advantage of having many children is that one of them may not turn out like the rest.

A brat is a spoiled child who never lifts a finger, except to thumb his nose.

CHILD TRAINING

The only rational way of educating a child is to be an example —of what to avoid, if one can't be the other sort.   – *Einstein*

How the twig is bent may be less important than the way it bends itself.
– *Joseph Wood Krutch*

The reason parents no longer lead their children in the right direction is that parents aren't going that way themselves.
– *Kin Hubbard*

You can't raise your child probably unless you sometimes raise your voice.

If you are no trouble to your children now, they will be a trouble to you when they grow up.

Train a boy in the way he should go, and he will depart from it in the days of his manhood.

Child training is chiefly a matter of knowing which end of your child to pat, and when.

Every parent knows how to bring up children—that is, his neighbors'.

The hardest thing in the world to raise is a child, especially in the morning.

The proper way to bring up children is to see that they get everything that's coming to them, both good and bad.

The child who is being raised strictly by the book is probably a first edition.

Parents who bring up their children best are those who exercise most—tact, self-control and authority.

Children are harder to raise than in the past, and every generation of parents thinks so.

Train up a child in the way he should go, and when he grows up he'll show you how wrong you were.

The best way to elevate the masses is to raise children properly.

Everyone seems to know how to bring up children—everyone, that is, except parents.

Bringing up children by the book is well enough, but remember, you need a different book for each child.

The most effective factor in child training is an affirmative *NO!*

It's really unbelievable how many mistakes the neighbors can make in raising their children.

Every generation finds out from the next generation that the way it brought up its children was altogether wrong.

Time may be money, but the best thing parents can spend on their children is not money, but time.

Bring up your children in the way you think other people's children should go.

Now that we have perfected guided missiles, the only things left that need guidance are our children.

No wonder it's so difficult to raise children properly—they are always imitating their parents.

Fathers should teach their sons how to earn money because mothers teach their daughters how to spend it.

There's nothing so baffling as child training: no sooner have you taught a child to talk than you have to teach him to keep quiet.

In bringing up children, a good rule to follow is: Spend on them half as much money and twice as much time.

Some parents are so busy raising kids, they have no time to bring them up.

Train up a child in the way he should go, and before you know it, he's gone.

Child training is a matter of teaching your child to eat his food instead of wearing it.

When you feel like criticizing the younger generation, just remember who raised them.

CHIN

When in trouble, always hold your chin up—if it does nothing else, it will keep your mouth shut.

It's harder to keep your chin up after you get more than one.

Nothing is so gratifying to a wife as to see a double chin on her husband's old flame.

The woman who is overweight should make a virtue of necessity and always put her best chin forward.

If exercise eliminates fat, how does a woman get a double chin?

During middle age a firm chin usually adds a partner to the firm.

Most women would rather be two-faced than double-chinned.

CHIVALRY

The age of chivalry is past; bores have succeeded to dragons.
— *Disraeli*

In the good old days of chivalry, men stood up for women, but there were no buses then.

Chivalry is the way a husband acts toward a wife—some other man's wife.

Chivalry means removing your hat for a woman in the elevator, but not yourself from a seat in the bus.

Chivalry was the practice of going around releasing beautiful maidens from other men's castles and bringing them to your own.

Nowadays chivalry on a bus is a standing joke.

CHOICE

When you have to make a choice and don't make it, that in itself is a choice.
— *William James*

In literature as in love, we are astonished at the choice made by other people.   — *André Maurois*

A man is given the choice between loving women and understanding them.
— *Ninon de Lenclos*

A perambulator hasn't much choice of tactics against a furniture van.   — *Bernard Shaw*

Choose as a wife only the woman whom you would choose as a friend if she were a man.
— *Joubert*

Life is a constant oscillation between the sharp horns of dilemmas.   — *Mencken*

It is usually harder for a man to choose a birthday gift for his wife than it was to choose her.

Of two evils, choose neither.

A man picks a wife about the same way an apple picks a farmer.

The wife who selects everything in the home usually picks the quarrels too.

The man who is forever criticizing his wife's judgment never seems to question her choice of a husband.

Pick a winner; anyone can pick the loser.

All a young man can do about marriage is to hope the right woman will pick him out.

The woman who chooses her husband's clothes probably started out by choosing his wife.

CHRISTIANITY

Christian: one who believes that the New Testament is a divinely inspired book admirably suited to the spiritual needs of his neighbors. — *Bierce*

There has never been a kingdom inclined to so many civil wars as the kingdom of Christ.
— *Montesquieu*

People in general are equally horrified at hearing the Christian religion doubted, and at seeing it practiced. — *Samuel Butler*

We are little Christian children and had early been taught the value of forbidden fruit.
— *Mark Twain*

In reality we Christians are nothing more than a sect of Jews.
— *G. C. Lichtenberg*

A Christian is a man who feels repentance on a Sunday for what he did on Saturday and is going to do on Monday.
— *Thomas R. Ybarra*

Christian: one who is willing to serve three Gods, but draws the line at one wife. — *Mencken*

I never knew any man in my life who could not bear another's misfortune perfectly like a Christian. — *Pope*

I often think the Christian church suffers from a too ardent monotheism. — *E. B. White*

Christian: one who follows the teachings of Christ insofar as they are not inconsistent with a life of sin. — *Bierce*

A Christian nation is one that is full of churches, and full of people staying away from them on Sunday.

Man's Christianity to man makes countless thousands mourn.

Christianity has made the rape of the human body a crime, but not the rape of the human mind.

The man who criticizes Christianity, doesn't practice it; the man who practices it, doesn't criticize it.

Christmas comes but once a year, and Christianity comes but once a week.

Too many people have been inoculated with small doses of Christianity that keep them from catching the real thing.

A pious Christian will probably do anything the Lord requires of him as long as it's honorable.

CHRISTMAS

The shortest night of the year is Christmas Eve—from sundown to son up. — *Burton Hillis*

Why does the Christmas season always come when the stores are at their busiest?

There would be more Christmas spirit during Christmas if so many women wouldn't take up extra seats in the bus with their Christmas packages.

Among the joys of going home for Christmas is seeing how your old sweethearts have turned out.

If postmen had their way, they'd abolish Christmas.

Christmas is the season when you buy this year's gifts with next year's money.

Christmas is when your neighbor's television keeps you awake until the early hours of the morning playing *Silent Night*.

Christmas greetings speak of peace on earth—but they don't say where.

Christmas is the season of the year when there's nothing so shopworn as the shopper.

The first Christmas was a myrrhy Christmas.

If you want to celebrate Christmas in some way you never did before, you might try going to church.

Christmas is the season when you never know which is going to give out first—your money or your feet.

November runs into December, December runs into Christmas, and Christmas runs into money.

Christmas comes but once a year, and once a year is enough.

Christmas is the season when people take the milk of human kindness out of the deep freeze.

Christmas is a guest that always comes a month before arriving.

What most youngsters would like for Christmas is something to separate the men from the toys.

Christmas is the season when everyone goes shopping and mangles with the crowd.

Every man should spend a pleasant Christmas; usually that's about all he has left to spend.

Christmas is the season when by their fruitcakes shall ye know them.

Christmas is the season of good will when a wife gives her husband all the credit she can get.

All some men get for Christmas are their wives' relatives.

Christmas is the season when people run out of money before they run out of friends.

When Christmas is over, father usually has more tics than bonds.

CHRISTMAS CARDS

Another Christmas miracle is how everyone receives more Christmas cards than he sends.

Christmas cards prove that if there is much sentiment in business, there is even more business in sentiment.

The greatest Christmas crisis occurs when a family mixes up the lists of those who sent cards last year and those who didn't.

CHRISTMAS GIFTS

The ideal Christmas gift is money, but the trouble is you can't charge it. —*Bill Vaughan*

What I like about Christmas is that you can make people forget the past with the present.
— *Don Marquis*

There is always somebody that you are afraid not to give a Christmas gift to.

There are generally two kinds of Christmas gifts: the ones you don't like and the ones you don't get.

A woman never knows what to give her husband for Christmas until she learns how much he wants to spend for it.

The exchange of Christmas gifts ought to be reciprocal rather than retaliatory.

Anyone who ever got the right-sized gloves as a Christmas gift would have a fit.

Some Christmas gifts are just what a woman needs to exchange for what she wants.

Christmas is the season when all good men and true have presence of mind and presents in mind.

A lot of Christmas gifts are mismailed every year, and a lot more should be.

If you really want your friends to remember you next Christmas, give them a very expensive gift— or a very cheap one.

At Christmas one half the world doesn't know how the other half can afford to give such gifts.

A few more payments and the Christmas gift you gave your wife is yours.

It is better to give than to receive a Christmas gift because you don't have the bother of exchanging it.

Christmas is the season of good will to all, except to those who failed to reciprocate last year's Christmas gift.

Christmas is the season when gifts are gladly given, happily received and cheerfully refunded.

CHRISTMAS SHOPPING

Christmas is the day when you resolve to do your Christmas shopping early next year.

An oldtimer is one who remembers when you did not start to shop for Christmas until after Thanksgiving.

Do your Christmas shopping late so as to avoid the early rush.

During the Christmas shopping season the crowds are so heavy that even the men have to stand in the buses.

O for the good old days when people would stop Christmas shopping when they ran out of money!

It is never too early to do your Christmas shopping early.

CHURCH

We sing in a church—why should we not dance there?
— *Bernard Shaw*

The church is the only place where someone speaks to me and I do not have to answer back.
— De Gaulle

There is no doubt about there being something real behind the churches; unfortunately, it is a long way behind. — Don Marquis

The church is only a secular institution in which the half-educated speak to the half-converted.
— W. R. Inge

If the man who doesn't attend church because hypocrites do were consistent, he wouldn't attend anything.   — Olin Miller

We never doubt a woman's religion after we have seen her at church with old clothes on.
— Ed Howe

The Pope is an idol whose hands are tied and whose feet are kissed.   — Voltaire

The first Sunday I sang in the church choir, two hundred people changed their religion.
— Fred Allen

There are ten church members by inheritance for every one by conviction.

Most churches go on the theory that it's more desirable to have a dozing attendant than a wide-awake absentee.

You can never tell what church a man goes to by the way he acts on weekdays.

If churches had free pews, it would give everyone a chance to stay away at a minimum expense.

Churchgoers are very good Christians until you show someone else into their pew.

Men never notice the clothes women wear in church—a lot of good the services do them!

Many people go to church because they think the church needs them and not because they think they need the church.

A church bazaar is a shuttle for miscellaneous articles from one person's attic to another's.

Some women take themselves to church, but most take their clothes instead.

Absence makes the heart grow fonder, but that's not the principle to follow in loving your church.

One of the best tests of your faith is to find yourself in church with nothing less than a ten-dollar bill in your pocket.

Some families must think the Sunday church service is like a convention—they just send one delegate.

Many a man is a pillar of the church—an outside pillar.

It's harder to get men to church than women, probably because men aren't interested in what other men are wearing.

The trouble with religion is that, while most people want to go to heaven, few people want to go to church.

When ministers exchange pulpits, it is always the congregation that gets the worst of it.

Among the things a man prays for when he goes to church is a place to park.

Going to church doesn't make you a Christian any more than going to the garage makes you a car.

Many an American who wouldn't hesitate to travel to the moon is afraid to sit up in front at church.

There's many a woman who goes to church just to see who didn't.

If all the people who sleep in church were placed end to end, they would be more comfortable.

CIGAR

I make it a point never to smoke more than one cigar at a time.   — *Mark Twain*

You should treat a cigar like a mistress: put it away before you are sick of it.   — *Disraeli*

Our country has plenty of good five-cent cigars, but the trouble is they charge fifteen cents for them.   — *Will Rogers*

A good cigar is as great a comfort to a man as a good cry to a woman.   — *Lord Lytton*

No cigar is so bad that sooner or later it won't meet its match.

What this country needs is a good five-cent-cigar extinguisher.

The man who turns over a new leaf has probably changed his brand of cigars.

The difference between a strong cigar and a weak one is that the strong cigar doesn't break so easily in your pocket.

What this country needs is a good no-scent cigar.

CIGARETTE

Gold-tipped cigarettes are awfully expensive; I can only afford them when I am in debt.
            — *Oscar Wilde*

A cigarette is the perfect type of perfect pleasure: it leaves one unsatisfied.   — *Oscar Wilde*

You need a cigarette to steady your nerves after reading the statistics on the hazards of smoking cigarettes.

What this country needs is a cigarette with a built-in cough medicine.

Another reason they are called the good old days is that you could light any cigarette at either end.

According to the tobacco ads, gentlemen prefer blends.

CIGARETTE LIGHTER
What this country needs is a cigarette that will cure the smoking habit.

It is considered unlucky to light three cigarette lighters from one match.

Don't give your children matches to play with; give them cigarette lighters—they're less dangerous.

History shows that no one has ever set the world on fire with a cigarette lighter.

Life is seldom long enough for a man to find one wife, one friend, and one cigarette lighter he can depend upon.

CINEMA

I've always had a nightmare: I dream that one of my pictures has ended up in an art theater, and I wake up shaking.
— *Walt Disney*

The only way to make a good film is to know nothing about film making.   — *Jean Cocteau*

The kind of jackass who likes the movies as they are is the man who keeps them what they are.
— *Mencken*

I can't imagine anything more boring than watching yourself on the screen.   — *Ethel Barrymore*

Nothing will kill the movies, except education.   — *Will Rogers*

In ancient times a Pharaoh could maintain a good-sized empire on what it costs to make the movie about it today.
— *Bill Vaughan*

Why pay to go see a bad movie when you can watch television and see a bad one for nothing?

Times change: the movie hero of old never kissed the girl as if he were eating an overripe peach.

Westerns are popular because every girl has a 38 sweater and every man a .45 gun.

In a movie colony, instead of a father having half a dozen children, one child has half a dozen fathers.

It's a wise novelist that knows his own screen child.

Parties in a movie colony always begin with discussing a star's latest picture, and end with discussing her latest divorce.

Some of today's films are so long that it takes less time to read the book.

Some movies are so bad that they have to be seen to be depreciated.

What is so rare as a movie actor who takes a girl to a picture he's not playing in?

A critic seldom realizes how good the book is until after he sees the movie.

All's well that ends well, except in the movies.

Nowadays some movies are so long that they last longer than the marriages of their stars.

The early silent films had one great advantage: you could see a woman open her mouth without any sound coming out.

The only bright thing about some movies is the electric sign in front of the theater.

The one problem the movies have solved is that of perpetual emotion.

Why is it that the movie you are seeing is never as good as the one that is coming to the theater next week?

The censors and the movie producers ought to get together: they both can't clean up on a picture.

In the past, boring movies put you to sleep in the theater; nowadays they put you to sleep at home.

It's amazing what progress the movies have made: first they moved, then they talked, and now they smell.

Sometimes a movie is so bad, you are sorry you asked the woman in front of you to take her hat off.

Another happy ending at the movies is the last crunch of popcorn by the person sitting in back of you.

In the movies some actresses play parts while others merely display them.

Instead of releasing some pictures, they should withhold the pictures and release the actors.

Some people love to go to the movies, while others go to the movies to love.

The cinema has ruined a lot more evenings than morals.

CIRCLE

The worst way to try to make ends meet is by running around in circles.

Every woman wants to enlarge her sphere but not her circumference.

The wheel of fortune never turns for the man who is always going around in circles.

CIRCUMSTANCES

Circumstances alter cases, especially reduced circumstances.

Things don't turn up in this world until someone turns them up.

Whether circumstances make one bitter or better depends entirely upon the I.

A fortune hunter's choice of a wife depends upon circumstances—her circumstances.

CITY

A neighborhood is a residential area that is changing for the worse.   —John Ciardi

Another mistake our pioneer forefathers made was to locate the cities so far from the airports.

A large city will never be as bad as reformers think it is, nor as good as they think it ought to be.

The city is a place where you go out for a walk and get a breath of fresh air pollution.

Every city needs more park space for its children and more parking space for its grownups.

A metropolis is a large city whose inhabitants have neighborhoods but no neighbors.

The history of a city is divided into three parts: first it gets rid of animals, then plants, and finally children.

CITY AND COUNTRY

A twofold national problem is how to preseve the wilderness in the country and get rid of the jungle in the cities. *– Bill Vaughan*

I like a lot of things about the city, but I prefer the country because I don't have to wear a tie there. *– Alexander Calder*

It is in the midst of the city that one writes the most inspiring pages about the country.
– Jules Renard

Everything that's worth having goes to the city—the country takes what's left.
– Finley Peter Dunne

In the country you go to bed feeling all in and wake up feeling wonderful; in the city you go to bed feeling wonderful and wake up feeling all in.

When a politician does a great thing for the country, the chances are he has moved to the city.

There's nothing like a trip to the country; it makes you appreciate the city.

In the city there are many people, and many are lonely; in the country there are few people, and few are lonely.

The station wagon in the country usually becomes the stationary wagon in the city.

A home in the country is what a city man hopes to buy and a farmer hopes to sell.

CIVILIZATION

The end of the human race will be that it will eventually die of civilization.   *– Emerson*

You can't say civilization isn't advancing: in every war they kill you in a new way.   *– Will Rogers*

Civilization is a limitless multiplication of unnecessary necessities.   *– Mark Twain*

The fate of civilization is like needlework: you can take it up and worry about it at odd moments.   *– Frank Sullivan*

Civilization is the process of reducing the infinite to the finite.
– Justice O. W. Holmes

Civilization is a state of affairs where it takes less and less time to fly across countries and more and more time to drive across towns.

Civilization is the history of human society with a split Adam at the beginning and a split atom at the end.

Civilization is a good idea— somebody ought to start it.

Where ignorance is bliss, it's a sign of a low stage of civilization.

The highest form of civilization is the people who can endure it.

Civilization is a state of affairs where it is sometimes difficult to distinguish between war and peace.

Civilization will really begin when the power of love replaces the love of power.

Civilization is the history of human society with a Fall at the beginning and a fallout at the end.

The improvements in guided missiles, nuclear submarines and hydrogen bombs just about keeps pace with the progress of civilization.

Civilization is a high state of development where a country bans fireworks while producing hydrogen bombs.

A civilized country is one that has reached so high a stage of development that it can provide employment for millions of soldiers.

Civilization began with the self-made man, followed by the man-made machine, and will end with the machine-made him.

The three principal things that hold civilization together are the safety pin, the paper clip, and the zipper.

Civilization is a state of society where a thousand people study the line of a putt for one man who studies the line of a poet.

Civilization has finally reached the point where miracle drugs and get-well cards have a hard time keeping up with each other.

Nowadays civilization is not at the crossroads, it's at the cloverleaves.

Civilization owes a debt to women for what they inspire their husbands to do, and also for what they talk their husbands out of.

Civilization is the history of mankind beginning with a cave and ending with a fallout shelter.

CIVIL SERVICE

The man who never worries or hurries is probably in civil service.

The best way to get civil service is by waiting on yourself.

Eventually we all have to go to our everlasting rest, but some do it sooner by going into civil service.

Civil service is usually performed by uncivil servants.

Some people are employed by the government, but most of us have to work for a living.

CLASSICS

The classical authors wrote at a time when the art of writing badly had not yet been invented.
– G. C. Lichtenberg

The classics are not esteemed for getting one on in the modern

world, but for getting one pleasantly out of it.
— *Frank Moore Colby*

Books are always the better for not being read—look at our classics. — *Bernard Shaw*

Gladstone read Homer for fun, which I thought served him right. — *Winston Churchill*

A classic is a book that you like to pretend you like.

The test of a classic is its ability to outlive all the translations that are made of it.

A classic is a book everyone wants to have read, but no one wants to read.

A classic is a dry book that satisfies the thirst for knowledge.

A book becomes a classic when people who haven't read it begin to say they have.

CLAUSTROPHOBIA

The head of our advertising agency suffered from claustrophobia, so he had to stay out of Rhode Island. — *Fred Allen*

The men who invented the upper berth and the telephone booth were probably married to women who had claustrophobia.

CLEAN

A pure heart is a good thing, and so is a clean shirt.
— *G. C. Lichtenberg*

Cleanliness is next to godliness, but in childhood it's next to impossible.

Stop accumulating: everything you collect means just another thing for you to keep clean.

Some people's thoughts need washing even more than their bodies.

Many a woman slaves to clean the house so she won't be embarrassed when the cleaning woman comes.

A woman's mind is supposed to be cleaner than a man's, probably because she changes it more often.

The only thing that's harder to clean up than a small boy is politics.

The nearest some husbands get to being tidy is when they drink their whiskey neat.

CLERGY

To a philosophic eye, the vices of the clergy are far less dangerous than their virtues.
— *Edward Gibbon*

Caution for clergymen: Be ascetic, but if you can't be ascetic, then at least be aseptic.
— *Mencken*

The first clergyman was the first rascal who met the first fool. — *Voltaire*

A man who is good enough to go to heaven is good enough to be a clergyman.
— *Samuel Johnson*

To be a successful clergyman, a man must be buttered on both sides. — *Mencken*

I won't take my religion from any man who never works except with his mouth. — *Carl Sandburg*

Blessed is the clergyman who is more interested in a surplice than a surplus.

The most popular minister always plays the saint with the men, and the devil with the women.

Two's company and three's a crowd—except when the third party is the clergyman.

A clergyman is a man whose mother practices what he preaches.

Virtue is its own reward, and a clergyman's income proves it.

Some clergymen are so heavenly minded that they are of no earthly use.

The only way a minister can meet his flock is to join a golf club.

A wise doctor of divinity always administers the right kind of medicine.

The clergy have made considerable progress; it's almost as hard to get into hell these days as it was to get into heaven a century ago.

The best of ministers seldom preach, but the best of preachers often minister.

Many a minister has been criticized because on six days of the week he is invisible, and on the seventh he is incomprehensible.

A clergyman with no politics is never made a bishop.

The clergy can do nothing about rainy Sundays; they are in sales, not in management.

CLEVER

It is better to be stupid like everyone than to be clever like no one. — *Anatole France*

Mother is far too clever to understand anything she does not like. — *Arnold Bennett*

Find enough clever things to say, and you're a Prime Minister; write them down, and you're a Shakespeare. — *Bernard Shaw*

A man likes his wife to be just clever enough to appreciate his cleverness, and just stupid enough to admire it.
— *Israel Zangwill*

Most men would rather say a clever thing than do a good one.

Think twice before you speak, and the other fellow will make the clever remarks first.

A clever woman's way of getting around her husband is to hug him.

A clever husband always wins an argument with his wife, but a cleverer one doesn't.

Every executive wishes he were as clever as he thinks his secretary thinks he is.

A clever girl flatters a man by asking the kind of questions he is able to answer.

Of all the clever wives, the cleverest is the one who never lets her husband suspect how clever she is.

Sometimes nothing is the cleverest thing you can say when you want to say something clever.

Even a foolish girl is clever enough to make a foolish man think he's clever.

By the time a person is old enough to know better, he thinks he's clever enough to get away with it.

It takes a clever girl to keep a man at arm's length without losing her grip on him.

Many a woman is so clever that she manages to let no one suspect her of being half as foolish as she really is.

Some women are so clever that you can't talk with them for ten minutes without beginning to realize how brilliant you are.

When a wife laughs at her husband's jokes, it's not because they are clever, but because she is.

A clever girl always seems to know less than the man she happens to be talking to.

CLIMATE

Don't cuss the climate; it probably doesn't like you any better than you like it. — *Don Marquis*

The climate of some places is so bad that its inhabitants have to live elsewhere.

CLIMATE AND WEATHER

Climate lasts all the time; weather lasts only a few days.

Climate is what you expect, but weather is what you get.

CLIMB

The rung of a ladder was never meant to rest upon, but to enable a man to put his other foot higher.   — *Thomas H. Huxley*

Mountain climbers always rope themselves together, probably to prevent the sensible ones from going home.

Careful grooming may take years off a woman's age, but you can't fool a long flight of stairs.

India's climb to leadership in world affairs is being hampered by her sunny clime.

CLOCK

Take a lesson from the clock: it passes the time by keeping its hands busy.

An office clock is rarely stolen, probably because everyone watches it.

No matter how fast a clock may run, it always winds up at the same place.

In some homes the clock, like father, is always wrong.

A clock is a modest piece of furniture that covers its face with its hands, and runs down its own works.

CLOSET

Every man should have a bedroom closet of his own for the garments his wife can't get into hers.

Another good way to acquire more closet space is to marry off a daughter.

A woman is always complaining she has nothing to wear while also complaining she hasn't enough closet space.

The average wife is willing to share everything with her husband, except her clothes closet.

There's one thing you can always give the man who has everything, and that's extra closet space in which to keep it.

Behind every successful man is a woman—who hasn't enough closet space.

Men are trying to conquer space; clothes closets show that women are too.

CLOTHES

If a woman rebels against high-heeled shoes, she should take care to do it in a very smart hat.
— *Bernard Shaw*

Our minds want clothes as well as our bodies.
— *Samuel Butler*

Men take clothes as a matter of course; women take it as a matter of discourse.

Clothes make the man; lack of them, the woman.

The hardest thing on a woman's clothes is another woman.

The man who thinks nothing of clothes is usually married to the woman who thinks of nothing but clothes.

Clothes make the woman, but seldom the woman who makes her own clothes.

The first costume on record was a hand-me-down—from the fig tree.

If women really dressed to please their husbands, they would be wearing last year's clothes.

One woman's neckline is sometimes lower than another woman's waistline.

Tight clothes can stop a man's circulation, but with a girl, the tighter the clothes, the more she circulates.

Women may not be deep thinkers, but they are usually clothes observers.

Clothes make the man, especially when the right girl is wearing them.

Women wear clothes not to please men but to displease other women.

Clothes don't make the woman, but they often show how she is made.

A man never discovers that a woman has nothing to wear until he marries her.

The wife who is foolish enough to ask her husband's advice about clothes is seldom foolish enough to take it.

A woman's most difficult problem is to buy clothes that both reveal and conceal at the same time.

An old-timer remembers when women wore more when they went swimming than they wear today when they go shopping in the supermarket.

Clothes may not make the man, but they certainly help a woman to make him.

The little girl of today starts school with a larger wardrobe than her grandmother had when she got married.

Clothes conceal the body, but more often reveal the soul.

A man is sometimes judged by the clothes he wears, but more often by the clothes his wife wears.

The husband who wonders what his wife wants with two new dresses, soon finds out it's two new hats.

The woman who is not interested in clothes is seldom interesting in clothes.

Many a girl wears clothes that show bad taste and good form at the same time.

The apparel oft proclaims the man—to be what he is not.

Women keep buying more and more clothes, and keep wearing them less and less.

Many a woman's clothes represent more dollars than sense.

The clothes that make the woman are the clothes that break the man.

Sports clothes nowadays are being worn louder and funnier.

CLOTHESHORSE

A clotheshorse is a woman whose clothes are her fortune and her husband's misfortune.

A clotheshorse never puts off till tomorrow what she can put on today.

A woman is never happy unless she has a lot of clothes she is not wearing.

Many a woman wears herself out shopping for clothes while her husband wears himself out paying for them.

A clotheshorse never seems to know the difference between body and soul and body and clothes.

A clotheshorse always wears her clothes out, but seldom more than once.

The extravagance of a clotheshorse often turns her husband into a workhorse.

A clotheshorse is another case where the cost of the package exceeds the value of the contents.

CLUB

I don't care to belong to a club that accepts people like me as members. —*Groucho Marx*

In every organization, factions speak louder than words.

Nowadays, when his wife talks too much, a man goes to his club; in primitive times, he just reached for it.

There's no place like home—which is why so many men join lodges.

What this country needs is an organization opposed to all organizations.

The reason cavemen used to knock women down with clubs was that there were no women's clubs in those days.

The world is full of odd fellows who don't belong to any lodge.

Clubwomen attend meetings to solve problems that wouldn't exist if women didn't leave home so much to attend meetings.

COAT

Many a man keeps on drinking till he hasn't a coat to his back or stomach.

There's only one thing that makes a man give a mink coat to a woman, and that's a woman.

The ambition of many a woman is to have as many coats as an onion.

When it comes to mink coats, some women will go to any lengths—half, three-quarters or full.

A fur coat is an outer garment that fattens the figure and slims the wallet.

The reason so many wives have mink coats is that men give in before women give up.

When a woman wears a new fur coat, she can hardly wait until the men she likes and the women she dislikes have seen her in it.

COCKTAIL

Cocktails have all the disagreeability without the utility of a disinfectant. —*Shane Leslie*

One martini is alright, two is too many, three is not enough. —*James Thurber*

Cocktail lounges are usually half lit to match the patrons.

A cocktail is a drink imbibed by people who don't like to eat on an empty stomach.

The most difficult thing about making a good martini is finding where the wife has put the jar of olives.

The martini was invented to teach men how to enjoy gin, and women how to enjoy olives.

At a cocktail party, the cocktails consist of one part whiskey and two parts gossip.

The only fishing through the ice that some men ever do is for the olive.

Nothing makes a woman look more beautiful than three cocktails in a man.

COED

In a coeducational college there is always a student body if you have a faculty for making love.

The coed who is poor in history may be very good on dates.

The coed who marries to escape school soon finds out that her education is just beginning.

A coed spends half her time pursuing a bachelor's degree, and the other half pursuing a bachelor.

A coed sometimes loves to learn but more often learns to love.

A coed considers her college education a success if she quits to get married.

Many a coed likes to marry before she graduates so as to have a sympathetic roommate at college.

An extravagant coed usually makes a poor mother—and an impoverished father.

Many a coed is eager to get married, especially if her parents disapprove.

To many a student the most appealing subject in college is a coed.

A coed is usually less interested in what she gets out of college than whom.

The coed who marries before she graduates has put the heart before the course.

The coed who gets married is merely transferring from one coeducational institution to another.

The more forward a coed is with college men, the more backward she is in her studies.

COFFEE

I like my coffee black as the devil, hot as hell, pure as an angel, and sweet as love.
— *Talleyrand*

If I were a woman, I'd wear coffee as a perfume.
— *John Van Druten*

Many a man dawdles away an hour over a cup of instant coffee.

Good coffee keeps more people awake than a bad conscience.

Coffee has to travel quite a distance to reach the United States, and much of it you meet is still weak from the trip.

Sometimes when you order coffee, half milk, you have to guess what the other half is.

Many a man can't sleep when he drinks coffee, but for most men it's the other way around: they can't drink coffee when they sleep.

The first requisite for a good cup of coffee in the morning is to get your wife out of bed.

A person has the right to complain of the coffee when he finds grounds for it in his cup.

Half the world's supply of coffee is consumed in the United States in spite of what some of us have to drink at breakfast.

Once you get a mouthful of very hot coffee, whatever you do next is going to be wrong.

Coffee is a stimulant; if you drink it at breakfast it will keep you awake all day.

Sweetening one's coffee is generally the first stirring event of the day.

COFFEE BREAK

Another appointed round that neither rain nor cold nor snow can halt is the coffee break.

The employee who is far behind in her work is probably far ahead on her coffee breaks.

There's no such thing as an unmixed blessing: whenever a company puts in a four-day week, the employees lose two coffee breaks.

Do the employees at a tea factory get a coffee break?

The Communist slogan "Workers, arise!" has come to mean in capitalist countries that it's time for the coffee break.

Coffee breaks are an evil: if they were eliminated entirely, people could retire several years earlier.

In some government offices there are so many coffee breaks that the employees can't sleep at their work.

You can always tell who the boss is: he's the one who watches the clock during the coffee break.

COFFIN

Have my coffin fit well around the shoulders.   — *Wilson Mizner*

The consumer's side of the coffin lid is never ostentatious.
— *Stanislaw J. Lec*

The nearest anyone comes to a conception of his own death is lying in a comfortable coffin listening to the flattering remarks of his mourners.
— *Finley Peter Dunne*

It's not the cough that carries you off, but the coffin they carry you off in.

COINCIDENCE

It is only in literature that coincidences seem unnatural.
— *Robert Lynd*

He is never lucky in the coincidence of his facts with the truth.   — *Winston Churchill*

COLD

There is only one way to treat a cold, and that is with contempt.
— *William Osler*

I wish it were possible to pull a cold, like an aching tooth.
— *Ed Howe*

I gargle with whiskey several times a day, and I haven't had a cold in years. — *W. C. Fields*

It's much more uncomfortable to have a cold in the head than an idea.   — *Jules Renard*

When we are suffering from a cold, it is surprising how much good advice we can get along without.

A cold would be more bearable if we didn't have to listen to all the advice on how to treat it.

The only thing some people do for a cold is sneeze.

An alcoholic's cure for a cold is not to feed it or starve it, but to drown it.

It takes about a week to cure a cold, but it cures itself in about seven days.

Why is it that only people who are not doctors know how to cure a cold?

Nothing draws two people together so much as both having colds at the same time.

Among the many remedies that won't cure a cold, the most common is advice.

A cold can be either positive or negative: sometimes the eyes have it, and sometimes the nose.

The only sure thing about a sure cure for a cold is that it isn't.

If a girl sneezes, she's catching cold; if she yawns, she getting cold.

It's surprising how many people everyone knows who have remedies that won't cure the common cold.

Many are cold, but few are frozen.

People who take cold baths in winter seldom have colds, but they have something worse—cold baths.

Some people are bothered by colds; their friends are forever telling them all about theirs.

The early bird catches a cold.

COLD WAR

The cold war is the truce that is stranger than fiction.

The cold war is certain to lead to peace—with or without people.

The only good thing about the cold war is that you learn a lot of geography.

The cold war allows the world neither to live in peace nor to rest in peace.

The cold war will never end until each side is ahead of the other in the arms race.

The cold war is a state of suspended hostilities that continues to plague too many, too much, too long.

During the cold war, states with conflicting ideologies smoke the pipe of peace, but without inhaling.

The cold war is the kind of war in which the shooting is replaced by the shouting.

As long as there is the cold war, there is peace, but on a wartime basis.

All that countries involved in the cold war see of the dove of peace is its bill.

The cold war is the kind of peace that gives the world no peace.

The cold war covers a short period of history made up of a long period of hysteria.

COLLECTION

Passing the buck is an evasion of responsibility, except when the collection plate comes around.

The man who puts a half dollar in the collection plate always expects a ten-dollar sermon.

A half dollar isn't supposed to be as good as a dollar, but it goes to church more often.

Liberality is beginning to be recognized in the churches, but it has not yet reached the contribution boxes.

Many a man puts a quarter in the collection plate and then complains that the church is cold.

It is important to give the Lord credit, but it is even more important to give Him cash.

Money is the root of all evil, and the contribution plate is intended to extract it.

A good example of a good-for-nothing is the churchgoer who doesn't contribute.

COLLEGE

College is wonderful because it takes the children away from home just as they reach the arguing stage.   — *Will Rogers*

I was a student-waiter at college who waited on the student-waiters—the lowest form of college life.   — *J. P. McEvoy*

My great-grandfather sent my grandfather to college at the age of thirteen when he was too young to dissipate.
    — *A. Lawrence Lowell*

A college teaches; a university both teaches and learns.
    — *Robert M. Hutchins*

Men may be born free; they cannot be born wise, and it is the duty of the university to make the free wise.   — *Adlai Stevenson*

The use of a university is to make young men as unlike their fathers as possible.
    — *Woodrow Wilson*

Hamilton College has turned out a good many fine young men— it turned me out.   —*Josh Billings*

I once knew a student who boasted that he had graduated from college without taking any course that was offered above the first floor.
                    —*Robert M. Hutchins*

A university is what a college becomes when the faculty loses interest in students.   —*John Ciardi*

A little learning is a dangerous thing, but at college it is the usual thing.

Money isn't everything, but without it college students would be out of touch with their parents.

To get into college nowadays, it's necessary for a student to have good grades, and for his father to have good credit.

College is the interlude of freedom a young man has between subjection to his mother and submission to his wife.

Some parents not only send their boy through college, but also his wife, baby and dog.

All college students pursue their studies, but some are further behind than others.

Some students go to college to learn to think, but most go to learn what the professors think.

The only thing a person is willing to pay for without getting is a college education.

How can we expect our children to get an education in college if they can't find a place to park their cars?

In every college there are some students who mistake a liberal education with a generous allowance.

Most college courses are alike: the notes of the professor become the notes of the students without passing through the minds of either.

Many a man spends the happiest years of his life as a freshman at college.

The young man who can raise enough money on his own to go to college these days doesn't really need any more education.

College students like to hear from home more often, even if it is only twenty-five dollars.

The greatest advantage of going to college is that you'll never regret you didn't.

A college is an athletic institution where a few courses are also offered for the benefit of the feeble-bodied.

Many a high school graduate plans to work his way through college—if his father can afford it.

Progress does not always mean improvement: observe the transition of a college student from freshman to sophomore.

Another thing that a young man learns at college is that he's terribly short of money.

There are two kinds of colleges —educational and coeducational.

Many a man who works his way through college later works his son's way through.

Half a loaf is better than not going to college at all.

There's one thing missing from every college curriculum—a course on what the students think they know.

Now is a good time for the colleges to try to work their way through some of the students.

Education is most important to men: you must either go to college, or start your own business so that you can hire men who did.

College never hurts a man, unless of course he is the collegian's father.

The three major problems for a college campus are parking for the faculty, athletics for the alumni, and sex for the students.

No one can study something for a year without learning anything, except a college student.

Another occupation that requires no training is writing for money: ask any man who has a son or daughter at college.

Of what use is a college education to high school graduates who already know everything?

A college student is a young man who goes through college and his father at the same time.

You can't expect first-class learning by students if they get second-class teaching by professors.

The less a young man gets out of college, the more he gets out of his father.

The freshman class always makes a senior feel that the university is going to the kids.

Sending your daughter to college is like sending your clothes to the laundry: you get out what you put in, but you hardly recognize it.

Two can live as cheaply as one—if the two are the parents and the one is their daughter at college.

Another disadvantage of going to college is that it slows up your education for four years.

Some students take up the arts in college, some take up the sciences, while others just take up space.

Because a college student is always broke, he never has any trouble finding something to write home about.

College is a fountain of knowledge where some students come to drink, some to sip, but most come just to gargle.

Another virtue of postgraduate courses is that they keep the boss' son out of the business for another few years.

A boy's college education is sometimes of real value; it cures his mother of bragging about him.

A college student is seldom as eager to get ahead in college as he is in traffic.

COLONIALISM

The touchiest part of a colonial policy is how to keep inferior peoples inferior.

Colonialism is a system under which a territory usually gets a raw deal in exchange for its raw materials.

COLOR

The enemy of all painting is the color gray. — *Delacroix*

The only time some women show their true colors is when they neglect to go to the beauty parlor.

An optimist notices the green lights, a pessimist notices the red, while the jaywalker is color-blind.

The good die young, but the old dye for various reasons.

Green is a soothing color, but not to the golfer who misses the hole by inches.

The world will forgive you for being blue, sometimes forgive you for being green, but it will never forgive you for being yellow.

There was once a poet who described the rainbow as having all the colors of the peacock.

On the road always keep your eyes on two things: red lights and green drivers.

Marriage is the difference between painting the town red and painting the back porch green.

Greenbacks are the only accessory that never clashes with the color scheme of a woman's costume.

COLUMBUS

Progress has so improved the world that if Columbus came back to earth today he'd think he was in hell.

Traveling on credit is not new: centuries ago Columbus took a trip on borrowed money.

America is still the land of opportunity; the only foreigner who didn't make any money here was Columbus.

Bestir yourself! Don't sit around waiting for Columbus to discover you.

If Columbus had turned back, nobody would have blamed him, but nobody would have remembered him either.

Columbus was the first young man to go West.

COLUMNIST

A newspaper is known by the columnists it keeps.
— *Irvin S. Cobb*

A newspaper columnist soon learns that he can usually print a blue story if he just changes copulate to osculate.
— *Earl Wilson*

Nowadays a girl can't go to bed with a man without some columnist writing that she's engaged to him.

In breaking the news to the public, many a columnist fractures the facts.

Half the world doesn't know how the other half lives, but it's not the fault of the columnists.

COMEDIAN

I don't want to run for office; there's already too many comedians in Washington. — *Will Rogers*

Being a monologuist is a lonely occupation: you stand on the stage talking to yourself, being overheard by audiences.
— *Fred Allen*

A comedian can only last till he takes himself serious, or until his audience takes him serious.
— *Will Rogers*

The test of a real comedian is whether you laugh at him before he opens his mouth.
— *George Jean Nathan*

A comedian is a person who knows a good thing when he says it.

Some comedians should stay out of television; they look better on radio.

Many a word spoken in jest is repeated, especially if spoken by a comedian.

Comedians nowadays are not getting better, but they are getting better paid.

A comedian says things funny; a wit says funny things.

It's hard to laugh at comedians if you're a comedian, especially if they're getting laughs.

A good comedian is worth his wit in gold.

There will always be more male comedians than women—women simply can't bear being laughed at.

A comedian's ambition is to be healthy, wealthy and wisecracking.

Some comedians will do almost anything to get laughs as long as they don't have to resort to good taste.

The comedian who loses half his writers becomes a half-wit.

Some comedians employ wry wit, while others resort to corn.

COMEDY

Radio and television sure are funny—all except the comedy programs. — *Fred Allen*

The most comic things of all are the things that are most worth doing—like making love.
— *Chesterton*

There is high comedy and low, and the higher you go the less loudly they laugh.
— *Peter De Vries*

All tragedies are finished by death; all comedies are ended by a marriage. — *Lord Byron*

Politicians do more funny things naturally than I can think of doing purposely. — *Will Rogers*

You can't have Falstaff and have him thin. — *Santayana*

COMFORT

People who want to live with ease, do what they ought, not what they please.

Money may not buy happiness, but with it you can be unhappy in comfort.

No man has ever been able to explain why a woman feels more comfortable in uncomfortable shoes than she does in comfortable ones.

A woman will wear anything new, no matter how uncomfortable; a man will wear anything comfortable, no matter how old.

Ego is what makes a man believe everybody is comfortable because he is.

A woman has passed the dangerous age as soon as she starts trying on a pair of shoes for comfort.

COMIC BOOK

Comic books comprise one of the most widespread forms of contemporary illiterature.

Today a tree, tomorrow a comic book.

Comic books are published for simple-natured children but are read by bloodthirsty kids.

COMIC STRIP

Some adults are so devoid of humor that they laugh at comic strips.

There are more comic strips on the beaches than in the newspapers.

Many more people would be well-informed on current events if they were included in comic strips.

A sense of humor is often a hardship, especially when a man has to explain the comic strips to his children.

COMMERCIAL

The quickest way to kill broadcasting would be to use it for direct advertising.
— *Herbert Hoover*

The worst thing about television are the sponsors who make the impossible programs possible.

Many a commercial gives you a headache while trying to sell you a remedy for it.

There's nothing more annoying to a sponsor than having people forget the brand but remember the tune of the commercial.

A commercial either insists you want a product you don't need, or need a product you don't want.

Seeing is believing, but not when you're looking at a television commercial.

Television is an advertising medium where the commercial urging you to save is followed by another urging you to borrow.

A commercial is a radio or television advertisement in which we are offered the opportunity of a lifetime every hour.

Thanks to television commercials, children now know that what a couple in a romantic embrace talk about is cigarettes, calories and cars.

The only thing in America that promises the people more than the politicians is a commercial.

Television commercials offer you relief from all ills, except the ills of commercials.

The purpose of a television commercial is to attract customers, but its practice is to distract them.

When you've got to go, you've got to go, and the best time to go is during the television commercial.

Television commercials wouldn't be so bad if they weren't so often.

A television sponsor is a man who watches the commercials and goes to the refrigerator during the show.

Advertising has so little to say about the world's most productive economy that it has to resort to singing commercials.

What this country needs even more than a good five-cent cigar is a good five-second commercial.

There are so many commercials on television that actors should be demanding equal time.

A commercial always seems to occupy the opening and closing quarter hours of a half-hour program.

Another trouble with the commercials on television is that too much tell goes with the vision.

COMMITTEE

A committee is usually a group of the unprepared, appointed by the unwilling, to do the unnecessary.

To get something done, a committee should consist of no more than three men, two of whom are absent.

The word *committee* is a noun of multitude that signifies many but does not signify much.

The best way to kill a good idea is to get a committee to work on it.

A committee consists of several men who cannot do a job in several hours as efficiently as one man can do it in one hour.

The man who shows up punctually at a committee meeting, is probably attending for the first time.

Committee work is like a soft chair—easy to get into, but hard to get out of.

A committee is a group of people appointed to find some innocent individual to do the work.

Marriage is a committee on ways and means where she has her way while he provides the means.

If Moses had been a committee, the Israelites would still be in Egypt.

A committee consists of a group of men that keeps minutes and wastes hours.

Some men can sit on a standing committee and still lie down on the job.

Committees have become so important nowadays that subcommittees have to be appointed to do the work.

COMMON

The greatest service we can do the common man is to abolish him and make all men uncommon. — *Norman Angell*

Nobody wants to be called common people, especially common people. — *Will Rogers*

God must hate the common people because He made them so common. — *Philip Wylie*

The only thing some couples have in common is that they both are.

COMMON SENSE

Nothing is more fairly distributed than common sense: no one thinks he needs more of it than he already has. — *Descartes*

Common sense is compelled to make its way without the enthusiasm of anyone. — *Ed Howe*

Common sense is not an issue in politics—it's an affliction. — *Will Rogers*

Common sense is not sense common to everyone, but sense in common things. — *William James*

I don't know why it is that the religious never ascribe common sense to God. — *Somerset Maugham*

He depended on his mother wit to get him out of any scrape his father ignorance had got him into. — *Strickland Gillilan*

There's only one kind of common sense but a thousand varieties of stupidity.

Common sense is usually lack of imagination, and imagination is usually lack of common sense.

The most uncommon form of intelligence is common sense.

Common sense is about the only article not being advertised.

A little common sense would prevent many divorces, and even more marriages.

COMMUNICATION

Every improvement in communication makes the bore more terrible. — *Frank Moore Colby*

The most popular of all intercommunication systems is the water cooler.

Much information comes from communication, and much communication comes from misinformation.

Now that world telephone and television transmission are a reality, the only communications problem left on earth is that between parents and teenagers.

The advantage of modern means of communication is that they enable you to worry about things in all parts of the world.

A communication addressed *To Whom It May Concern* usually gets to people to whom it doesn't concern.

The advance of science has enabled man to communicate at twice the speed of sound while he still acts at half the speed of sense.

COMMUNISM

When Stalin sneezed, it was considered by the Russians as a contribution to the science of Marxism-Leninism.   — *Tito*

I never agree with Communists or any other kind of kept men.
          — *Mencken*

A Communist is like a crocodile: when it opens its mouth you cannot tell whether it is trying to smile or preparing to eat you up.   — *Winston Churchill*

Communism, like any other revealed religion, is largely made up of prophecies.   — *Mencken*

Communism is a form of government under which every citizen at election time enjoys the privilege of voting Yes.

The iron curtain is a Communist barrier created so that half the world won't know how the other half lives.

Communism is a form of society where the less people have to eat, the more they have to swallow.

A Communist is a man who would rather be left than President.

Communism is a system of government under which it is impossible to lose an election bet.

All the world's a stage, with Communism trying to turn it into a puppet show.

In Communist lands people either sing in the same key or suffer behind the same lock.

People have certain freedoms under Communism, one of which is the freedom from the political burden of making up their minds.

If it weren't for the Communists, Communism would be more attractive.

Under a completely planned economy, when no ham is available, no eggs are available at the same time.

Democracy can learn some things from Communism: for example, when a politician is through, he is through.

Under Communism, the right to vote means to vote right

Communism is based on the principle that what people don't know about their government, doesn't hurt them.

An American Communist is a man who likes everything about Russia except the idea of going to live there.

COMMUTER

A commuter is one who spends his life in riding to and from his wife. — *E. B. White*

The patient commuter dawdles and catches the next train, whereas the impatient commuter rushes and misses the last one.

Many a commuter complains that the fast trains don't stop at his station, and that the slow ones stop at all the other stations.

There is only one sure way for a commuter to catch a train, and that is to miss the previous one.

Most of the men running for office are not politicians—they're commuters.

Many a married man who misses the last train home catches it.

COMPANY

Hearts that are delicate and kind, and tongues that are neither —these make the finest company in the world. — *Logan P. Smith*

In mixed company women practice a kind of visual short-hand that they later decode in detail in other women's company. — *Malcolm de Chazal*

After you have been married five years, there should always be someone to dinner.
— *E. V. Lucas*

In preferring the company of ladies to that of the bottle, I only exchange a headache for a heartache. — *James Kirke Paulding*

The company of women improves men's manners but impairs their morals. — *Montesquieu*

A man has to live with himself, and he should see to it that he always has good company.
— *Charles Evans Hughes*

He had no principles and was delightful company.
— *Mark Twain*

A man should think less of what he eats and more with whom he eats because no food is so satisfying as good company.
— *Montaigne*

I cannot spend an hour in anyone's company without getting the material to write a readable story about him. — *Somerset Maugham*

If a man is judged by the company he keeps, what about Judas?

Two are company—until they are made one.

Of course a man is known by the company he keeps—it would be rather strange if they didn't.

You spend an evening with some people, but invest it with others.

A man is known by the company he thinks nobody knows he's keeping.

When it is more profitable to talk than to listen, change your company.

A man is known by the company he keeps, and a company is known by the men it keeps.

The young man who prefers the company of other young men to that of girls is not always a homosexual—he may just be broke.

Never quarrel before company, and always remember that two is company.

A man is known by the company his wife keeps.

A man is broke by the company he keeps, especially if he keeps company.

Pleasant company is always accepted.

A gold digger is the kind of woman who doesn't care for a man's company unless he owns it.

There are two kinds of company: in one it is better to talk than to listen, in the other it is better to listen than to talk.

COMPARISON

All perception of truth is the perception of an analogy: we reason from our hands to our head. — *Thoreau*

Nothing is either good or bad but by comparison.

Everything is relative: to the radical a liberal is conservative, and to the reactionary a conservative is liberal.

When comparisons are odious, use superlatives.

Every woman should have two men in her life: a husband, and another man to compare him with.

Bad is called good when worse happens.

Compare what you want with what you have, and you'll be unhappy; compare what you deserve with what you have, and you'll be happy.

Behind every successful man there's a woman sneering that she knows a man who's more successful.

It is remarkable how little a man can live on, especially when compared with how much he wants.

COMPATIBLE

The idea of two people living together for 25 years without an argument suggests a lack of spirit only to be admired in a sheep. — *A. P. Herbert*

A compatible marriage is one where the man makes the living and the woman makes the living worthwhile.

Another compatible marriage is where the wife has her way when they agree, and the husband has her way when they disagree.

The art of getting along with a woman is understanding what she doesn't say.

The man who would rather play golf than eat should marry the woman who would rather play bridge than cook.

There's no better way to get along with a wife than to let her think she's having her own way —and then letting her have it.

A compatible marriage is usually one where the husband and wife have many faults in common.

The egotist who is always talking about himself should marry the gossip who is always talking about other people.

A compatible marriage is one in which the husband and wife are in perfect agreement about the divorce settlement.

The man to whom money isn't everything, should marry the woman to whom everything isn't money.

COMPENSATION

People demand freedom of speech as a compensation for the freedom of thought which they seldom use. — *Kierkegaard*

If I have praise I don't deserve, I say nothing and accept it to compensate for someone's else having had blame he doesn't deserve. — *Robert Frost*

There's compensation in everything: the man with a small mind, usually has a big mouth.

There's compensation in marriage too: when you have someone to share your troubles, you have twice as many troubles as when you were single.

One of the compensations of a fat woman is telling how she's going to lose it.

There is compensation in all things: the man who is short in funds, usually has a long face.

COMPETITION

The only competition worthy of a wise man is with himself. — *Washington Allston*

There is no resting place for an enterprise in a competitive economy. — *Alfred P. Sloan*

It's not trying to keep up with the Joneses that causes so much trouble—it's trying to pass them.

Honesty is the best policy because it has so little competition.

Some families always try to keep up with the Joneses, except when the Joneses are trying to keep up with them.

The most important competition of mankind is the human race between production and reproduction.

The reason why men who mind their own business succeed is that they have so little competition.

Nothing gets you into debt faster than trying to keep up with people who are already there.

Behind every successful man is a woman who is trying to keep up with the Joneses.

Marriage turns some women into partners, others into competitors.

No one has more trouble keeping up with the Joneses than old man Jones himself.

If you can't win, make the fellow ahead of you break the record.

If it's hard for you to keep up with the Joneses, just think how hard it must be for them to keep ahead.

Buying on time enables people to keep up with the people who keep up with the Joneses.

COMPLAINT

I believe in grumbling; it is the politest form of fighting known.
— Ed Howe

People that pay for things don't complain; it's the guy you give something to that you can't please. — Will Rogers

Every man feels the need of a good-natured woman to grumble to. — Ed Howe

Every man complains of his memory, but no man complains of his judgment.

All the world knocks a knocker.

Another place where you meet a cross-section of humanity is at a complaint desk.

The chronic complainer is a man whose like is seldom seen.

Don't complain that your wife doesn't make meals like mother used to make unless you make money like father used to make.

Have you ever noticed that a knocker is always outside the door?

The man who is always kicking seldom has a leg to stand on.

Behind every successful man is a woman complaining she has nothing to wear.

Don't complain about the traffic: if there were less cars on the road, it would be even harder to find a parking place.

The worst thing you can do to a chronic complainer is to deprive him of a grievance.

Some men are afraid that if they don't complain about their meals their wives might love them.

A chronic complainer gets all his exercise out of kicking.

The woman who says she can read her husband like a book, is always furnishing book reviews.

There is more kicking done with the tongue than with the foot.

Some men complain about everything, even about the noise when opportunity knocks.

Middle age is the period when the old complain to you about the young, and the young complain to you about the old.

You can't please some people: they complain when they don't get what's coming to them, and complain even more when they do.

Some women complain about everything: they go through life always demanding to see the manager.

The man who goes around complaining that the world is against him, is probably right.

If you can't bite, don't growl.

No one complains about the younger generation except those who no longer belong to it.

Some men have a den in their home, while others just growl all over the house.

COMPLEXION

Don't envy a good complexion —buy one!

Many a young girl gets an inferiority complex from an inferior complexion.

A woman's real complexion usually travels under false colors.

A woman will sometimes sacrifice everything to her complexion —even her complexion.

COMPLIMENT

If you can't get a compliment any other way, pay yourself one.
— Mark Twain

No one has ever been able to cash a compliment.   — Ed Howe

I have been complimented many times and they always embarrass me; I always feel that they have not said enough.
— Mark Twain

Ladies inclined to go fishing for compliments will find them commonly in shallow water.
— Bayard Taylor

The only chain that can bind love is an endless chain of compliments.   — Helen Rowland

Compliment some men, and they will consider that there was nothing else to say. — Ed Howe

You can't say anything complimentary to a woman that will surprise her.   — Ed Howe

Don't tell a woman she's pretty; tell her there's no other woman like her, and all roads will open to you.
— Jules Renard

The man who compliments nine women on their looks and the tenth on her cleverness makes but one mistake.

After a woman passes fifty, be careful how you compliment her; you are liable to overdo it.

Compliments please a woman more than flowers, and they cost a lot less.

Never compliment a woman on her intelligence unless she is very beautiful or very homely.

Woman is complementary to man but not always complimentary.

After paying you a compliment, some people look as if they were waiting for change.

A woman can remember a compliment a man paid her long after she has forgotten his name.

A compliment is sometimes a matter of fact, but more often a matter of tact.

The best bait when fishing for compliments is a compliment.

When a man compliments his wife, she should be flattered; when a woman compliments her husband, he should prepare for trouble.

The flatterer who gives a compliment gives nothing, and the woman who receives it gets less.

Never hesitate to flatter: the less truth there is in a compliment, the more readily is it believed.

COMPOSER

The public doesn't want new music; the main thing it demands of a composer is that he be dead.
— *Arthur Honegger*

Rossini would have been a great composer if his teacher had spanked him enough on his backside. — *Beethoven*

It isn't necessary to be tone deaf to write a popular song, but it helps.

If it must be Richard, I prefer Wagner; if it must be Strauss, I prefer Johann.

At the head of the list of modern American composers is the tranquilizer.

Our popular composers will stop at nothing: it's unbelievable what they will sell for a song.

COMPROMISE

A compromise is a settlement by which each side gets what neither side wanted.

The man who says he is willing to meet you halfway is usually a poor judge of distance.

Some men are such compromisers, even when they go to the dogs, they expect the dogs to meet them halfway.

When a husband and wife reach a compromise over the garden— she does it.

A compromise is the art of dividing a cake in such a way that each one thinks he is getting the biggest piece.

COMPUTER

The real danger is not that machines will begin to think like men, but that men will begin to think like machines.
— *Sydney J. Harris*

A computer is a marvelous machine as quick as a wink without having to think or taking a drink.

Computers will never replace office workers entirely until they learn how to spread gossip.

A computer can figure out all kinds of difficult problems, except the problem of how to pay for it.

The man who installs an electronic computer replaces the female sex with the neuter.

The computer of today is remarkably human, except that it hasn't learned yet to stop for coffee breaks.

Computers can figure out all kinds of problems, except the things in this world that just don't add up.

The computer saves man a lot of guesswork, but so does the bikini.

Modern computers are almost human, except that they haven't learned yet to swear, drink or gamble.

Office computers are calculating machines invented to replace calculating females.

Computers are fantastic: in a few minutes they can make a mistake so great that it would take many men many months to equal it.

Computers can solve all kinds of problems, except the unemployment problem they create.

Computers will never replace man entirely until they learn to laugh at the boss's jokes.

A small town is where the only computer is a sharp pencil.

A computer is almost human, except that it never blames its mistakes on other computers.

Computers will never be perfected until they can compute how much more than the estimate the job will cost.

CONCEIT

Conceit grows as naturally as the hair on one's head, but it takes longer to come out.
— *Thomas C. Haliburton*

Conceit may puff a man up, but it can never prop him up.
— *Ruskin*

Conceit is just as natural a thing to human minds as a center is to a circle. — *Dr. O. W. Holmes*

Swelled heads are so preoccupied with the few things they know that there is no room left for the innumerable things they don't know.   — *Bernard Shaw*

The greatest magnifying glasses in the world are a man's own eyes when they look upon his own person.   — *Alexander Pope*

Many a conceited young man has let his father's success go to his head. ·

Conceit is a strange disease: it makes everyone sick except the person who has it.

A swelled head seldom covers a broad mind.

I don't think I'm handsome—but what's my humble opinion against a mirror's?

A conceited man thinks he is complimenting his wife when he praises her husband.

Don't be conceited: even postage stamps become useless when they get stuck on themselves.

A swelled head always provides plenty of room for improvement.

Being conceited is the only satisfaction some men find in life.

Man is a conceited creature: when we're right we credit our judgment; when we're wrong we curse our luck.

When a man gets too big for his breeches, his head gets too big for his hat too.

Even the actor who is not conceited knows he has every reason to be.

The real test of financial success is getting ahead without getting a big one.

CONCERT

At a concert of amateur musicians it is difficult to tell whether the musicians are tuning their instruments or playing.

At concerts a musician often finds himself playing accompaniments to conversation.

People who have a lot to say shouldn't go to a concert to say it.

A concert is a performance during which all the musicians play, but only part of the audience talks.

CONCLUSION

A conclusion is the place where you got tired thinking.
— *Martin H. Fischer*

Jumping to conclusions seldom leads to happy landings.

A scandalmonger not only draws her own conclusions, but colors them as well.

The person who jumps at conclusions usually scares the best ones away.

If you keep both feet on the ground, you're less likely to jump at conclusions.

CONDUCTOR

Conductors must give suggestive signals to the orchestra, not choreography to the audience.
— *George Szell*

The conductor has the advantage of not seeing the audience.
— *André Kostelanetz*

A conductor should have the score in his head, not his head in the score.

A conductor is a man who would rather face the music than his audience.

Too many conductors get in the way of the music: instead of conducting the orchestra, they conduct the audience.

CONFERENCE

No grand idea was ever born in a conference, but a lot of foolish ideas have died there.
— *Scott Fitzgerald*

The executive who spends most of his time in conference is the one who interferes least with production.

Half the world doesn't know what the other half does in conference.

A conference is a meeting where many an executive shows his ability to think on his seat.

When a man goes into conference with his secretary, they probably put their heads together.

A conference is a meeting held to decide when the next meeting will take place.

The advantage of a conference is that it enables you to talk about the things you should be doing.

CONFESSION

Nothing spoils a confession like repentance. — *Anatole France*

Confession is good for the soul only in the sense that a tweed coat is good for dandruff.
— *Peter De Vries*

The worst of my actions and feelings do not seem to me so offensive as the cowardice of not daring to admit them.
— *Montaigne*

It is the confession, not the priest, that gives us absolution.
— *Oscar Wilde*

Honest confession is good for the soul, but bad for the reputation.

It is safest to tell your wife everything—everything she is liable to learn from someone else.

CONFIDENCE

I have great faith in fools— self-confidence my friends call it.
— *Edgar Allan Poe*

An egotist is a man who has even more confidence in himself than his wife has in her analyst.

Beware if your wife has too much confidence in you—she's probably spending this year the money she knows you're going to earn next year.

If you want a woman to believe an outrageous lie, tell it to her in strict confidence.

Confidence is that quiet, assured feeling you get just before you fall flat on your face.

Usually when the woman who is talking lowers her voice, the woman who is listening raises her eyebrows.

The only time some men confide their business troubles in their wives is when their wives buy something expensive.

Confidence is the feeling you have before you understand the situation.

Never share your confidence with a confidence man—you'll never get it back.

Many a patient has more confidence in a doctor than the doctor has in himself.

Confidence is keeping your chin up; overconfidence is sticking your neck out.

A confidence man first takes you in his confidence, and then takes you in.

If you worry about what people think of you, it's because you have more confidence in their opinion than you have in your own.

CONFORMITY

Most people can't understand how others can blow their noses differently than they do.
— *Turgenev*

In morals, always do as others do; in art, never. — *Jules Renard*

When people are free to do as they please, they usually imitate each other. — *Eric Hoffer*

It takes far more courage to violate a custom than a law.

CONFUSION

If we wish to make a new world, we have the materials ready—the first one too was made out of chaos. — *Robert Quillen*

The times are not merely out of joint—it's a compound fracture.

The world is so confusing nowadays, even your barber has trouble giving you all the answers.

Give a statistician some facts and figures, and he will draw his own confusions.

My mind's made up—don't confuse me with the facts.

CONGRESS

Ancient Rome declined because it had a Senate; now what's going to happen to us with both a Senate and a House? — *Will Rogers*

After a man has been in Congress, he rarely goes back to real work. — *Ed Howe*

Congress is really made up of children that never grow up.
— *Will Rogers*

Congress consists of one-third, more or less, scoundrels; two-thirds, more or less, idiots; and three-thirds, more or less, poltroons. — *Mencken*

A hundred years ago there wasn't such a thing as a stenographer—every Congressman could write then. — *Will Rogers*

Sitting in Congress is the privilege of the few; sitting on Congress is the prerogative of the many.

Congress is strange: a man gets up to speak and says nothing; nobody listens, and then everybody disagrees.

Congress would give the people what they wanted if the people knew what they wanted, and if Congress could give it to them.

Next time a man tells you talk is cheap, ask him if he knows how much a session of Congress costs.

Congress is a legislative body that runs the government like nobody's business.

A congressman is chosen by the people to spend a little of his time and a lot of their money.

Some men join the Navy and see the world; others join Congress.

Congress would be a better institution if it indulged in more frankness and less franking.

In Congress the majority governs, but the minority rules.

There are always too many Democratic congressmen, too many Republican congressmen, and never enough U.S. congressmen.

A congressman is far more extravagant in the House than he is at home.

No matter how short the session, Congress always has the necessary time to pass unnecessary legislation.

Some men serve one term in Congress, but most serve several

terms before they are pardoned by their constituents.

The little boy who goes to the store and forgets what his mother sent him for, will probably grow up to be a congressman.

Congressional debates are schemes for keeping the public from finding out what they are talking about.

Congress in session: Nothing ado about much.

The secret of many a congressman's income is a secret.

To a congressman, non-essential spending is the money that goes to another section of the country.

Congress doth make cowards of us all.

Some members of Congress ought to have their mouths taped instead of their speeches.

When a man runs for Congress, you're a friend; when he's elected, you're a constituent; when he's legislating, you're a taxpayer.

What this country needs is more ex-senators and ex-congressmen.

Every year Congress spends more money than all its members are worth.

The trouble with Congress is that so many of its members have a lot more on their minds than there's room for.

Congress adjourns for the Christmas holidays every year—

anything to make the people happy on Christmas.

Note to Congress: Sufficient unto the day is the drivel thereof.

Every day that Congress is not in session, the taxpayers save millions of dollars.

About the only time Congress conforms to the will of the people is when it decides to adjourn.

The members of Congress all row together in the same boat, but in different directions.

Congress is strong for economy, and usually borrows billions of dollars to achieve it.

It's a wise congressman who knows his own constituents, but it's a wiser constituency that knows its own congressman.

Nothing in life is certain, at least while Congress is in session.

A congressman steps into office by the suffrage of the people, and stays in office by their sufferance.

A congressman is usually more interested in House politics than his wife is in home economics.

Every two years the voters elect a brand-new House of Representatives to be run by the same old crowd.

No matter how many additional members Congress has, there will always be plenty of room for improvement.

Taxpayers are happy when Congress adjourns because con-gressmen then start to spend their own money.

Another thing that costs more than it's worth is Congress.

A congressional committee is made up of members of Congress carefully chosen to ignore some special problem.

Congress is a national body that tries everything else before finally giving up and doing the sensible thing.

Everything we have is taxed by Congress: our income, our property, and our patience.

CONSCIENCE

I have a New England conscience—I like to pay my bills on the second of the month.
— *Sinclair Lewis*

My conscience is more trouble and bother to me than anything else I started with. — *Mark Twain*

The voice of conscience has a difficult time making connections with the ears. — *Ed Howe*

Conscience is thoroughly well-bred, and soon leaves off talking to those who do not wish to hear it. — *Samuel Butler*

Invariably Gladstone earnestly consulted his conscience, and invariably his conscience earnestly gave him the convenient answer.
— *Bertrand Russell*

Conscience originated when the elderly father surrounded his wives and tools with a pious taboo against his son's desires.
— *Freud*

Conscience is a mother-in-law whose visit never ends. — *Mencken*

Conscience is what makes a boy tell his mother before his sister does.

Conscience is the playback of the still, small voice that warned you not to do it in the first place.

Next to death, the most infallible cure for a guilty conscience is success.

In every person's conscience there's a policeman who is usually off duty.

The reason conscience has a small, still voice is that it's often a small, still conscience.

More people would listen to their conscience if they could tell it what to say.

Your conscience doesn't really keep you from doing anything wrong; it merely keeps you from enjoying it.

Conscience is the still, small voice which we are always trying to convince that it was the other fellow's fault.

When you battle with your conscience and lose, you win.

Removing the conscience of some people would be only a minor operation.

The still, small voice of conscience probably gets that way from being overworked.

The man with a clear conscience probably has a poor memory.

Conscience is the still, small voice that tells us what others should do.

It's only a good person who can have a bad conscience.

The man whose conscience doesn't bother him probably has it very well trained.

Conscience is the small, still voice that tells you the Internal Revenue Service may check your income tax return.

Conscience is a voice from within that lots of people do without.

Conscience is the still, small voice which tells a candidate that what he is doing is likely to lose him votes.

The man with a clear conscience feels almost as good as the criminal with no conscience at all.

Conscience is the still, small voice which you never hear until you're caught doing something wrong.

There's nothing worse than to be born a scoundrel and be handicapped by a conscience.

Conscience doth make cowards of us all, but more often cowardice doth make us all conscientious.

Conscience is that still, small voice that tells you to leave it alone because someone's watching.

Sometimes the greatest help a conscience can get comes from cold feet.

A teen-ager would be more likely to listen to the voice of conscience if it were on his favorite channel.

Conscience is the still, small voice that you wish you could teach not to interrupt you.

CONSERVATIVE

Conservatism offers no redress for the present, and makes no preparation for the future.
— *Disraeli*

Old-fashioned Tories always are thunderstruck; that's how they live; indignation keeps them warm.
— *Stephen Leacock*

A conservative is a man who just sits and thinks, mostly sits.
— *Woodrow Wilson*

There are men so conservative that they believe nothing should be done for the first time.

A conservative is a man whose mind is always open to new ideas, provided they are the same as the old ones.

Many a man gets a reputation as a conservative merely because he is a slow thinker.

A conservative is a man who moves with the times, but only when the times are standing still.

A standpatter is one who fights for the status to remain quo.

Many a fear sticks a feather in his cap and calls himself a conservative.

A conservative is a man who thinks something is radically wrong with radicals.

A conservative believes in moving continually forward in the direction of the status quo.

CONSIDERATION

A man who won't lie to a woman has very little consideration for her feelings.

The best way to keep from stepping on the other fellow's toes is to put yourself in his shoes.

There's no one so considerate as the girl who goes abroad to study singing.

CONSISTENCY

Consistency requires you to be as ignorant today as you were a year ago.   — *Bernard Berenson*

Consistency is a jewel, but too much jewelry is vulgar.

Consistency is the only jewel found among more men than women.

CONSOLATION

A woman ought to be pretty to console her for being a woman at all.   — *Ed Howe*

A good wife is a man's consolation, and a bad one is his friend's consolation.

A wife is a great consolation, especially when a man comes home after his girl friend has run out on him.

A dear friend is always around when you need him; a mere acquaintance is always around when he needs you.

The only consolation parents get out of a juvenile delinquent is that he wasn't born twins.

Woman is man's solace, but if it wasn't for her he wouldn't need any solace.

The lazy man who hates to get up to go to work has one consolation: every day he's one day nearer to Social Security.

CONSTITUTION

Our Constitution protects aliens, drunks and U.S. senators.
— *Will Rogers*

The Constitution gives every American the inalienable right to make a damn fool of himself.
— *John Ciardi*

Some lawyers are clever enough to convince you that the Constitution is unconstitutional.

When a corrupt official hasn't a leg to stand on, he stands on his constitutional rights.

Many a government official who has sworn to uphold the Constitution, ends up by leaning on the Fifth Amendment.

Americans may be divided into three classes: those who are for the Constitution, those who are against it, and those who have read it.

The Constitution guarantees you the pursuit of happiness, but doesn't guarantee to run interference for you.

CONSUMER

We have no more right to consume happiness without producing it than to consume wealth without producing it.
— *Bernard Shaw*

The consumer is not a moron —she is your wife. — *David Ogilvy*

If the government was as afraid of disturbing the consumer as it is of disturbing business, this would be some democracy.
— *Kin Hubbard*

Consumer credit is something the consumer has to go into debt to create.

Statistics show that women spend 85 per cent of the consumer dollar, children 15 per cent, and men the rest.

CONTEMPT

When you are down and out, something always turns up—and it is usually the noses of your friends. — *Orson Welles*

An intellectual snob is a man who ignores the pretty girl beside him on the plane because he's contemptuous of the book she's reading.

The exclusiveness of some families is a fortunate thing for the neighbors.

Silent contempt is the noblest way a man can express himself—when the other fellow is bigger.

CONTENTMENT

Nothing contributes more to a person's peace of mind than having no opinions at all.
— *G. C. Lichtenberg*

My motto is: Contented with little, yet wishing for more.
— *Charles Lamb*

Better little with content than much with contention. — *Franklin*

Contentment is the art of keeping your tastes below your neighbor's income.

There are only two ways to be contented: one is liking what you do, and the other is doing what you like.

Be content with what you have, not with what you are.

There's nothing that can give you a little peace of mind like a lot of ignorance.

Contentment is the best of all riches—and it's not taxed.

Peace of mind lies in not wishing for things we don't have, but what else is there to wish for?

The man who is too busy to worry by day is probably too sleepy to worry at night.

Contentment is the smother of invention.

Most of us won't be contented with our lot until it's a lot more.

If you want peace of mind, keep on good terms with your neighbors, your wife, and your stomach.

The contented man is never poor; the discontented man, never rich.

Contentment is better than riches, but only if you have both.

Contentment is often the result of being too lazy to kick.

Peace of mind is the acid test of happiness as well as the placid test.

Contentment is not hard to attain, at least not for a person with a poor memory and no imagination.

The secret of contentment: when you haven't what you like, like what you have.

There's only one way to achieve peace of mind, and that is to co-operate with the inevitable.

CONTRACT

I got all the schooling an actress needs—that is, I learned to write enough to sign contracts.
— *Hermione Gingold*

Remember, in every lease the big print giveth and the small print taketh away.

Knowledge is what you get from reading the small print in a contract; experience is what you get from not reading it.

The older you get, the slower you read a contract.

A contract is an agreement where the size of the print tends to contract the more you read.

The fine print in a contract will give you a surprise if you read it, and an even greater surprise if you don't.

Don't take the will for the deed—get the deed.

Some documents are so evasive, you don't look for loopholes in the contract, but for a contract in the loopholes.

By the time you learn that you should always read the fine print, your eyes can no longer see it.

CONTRADICTION

Truth is polygonal: I never feel sure that I have got it until I have contradicted myself five or six times. — *John Ruskin*

History is full of contradictions: the loudspeaker, for example, was invented in an age that has nothing to say.

The person who never contradicts himself is probably in the cemetery.

Never contradict your wife— if you listen a short while, she will contradict herself.

Many a man thinks conversation is merely contradiction.

A bachelor is the only man who never contradicts his wife.

CONTRARY

Some folks are so contrary that if they fell in a river, they'd insist on floating upstream.
— *Josh Billings*

A woman is nice to you because she doesn't like you, or mean to you because she does.

Man is a perverse creature: in a bus, you can't get him to move to the back; in a church, you can't get him to move to the front.

If you let a woman think that you think she will, she won't; but if you let her think you think she won't, she will.

A husband often gets blamed because if he hadn't advised his wife to do it, she would have done it.

Some women are so contrary, they won't even do their husbands' bidding in a bridge game.

When a man takes his wife's advice, he probably wants to prove how wrong she is.

Some men go through life always pushing the door marked PULL.

CONTROL

Of the many kinds of remote control, a man's control of his wife is by far the remotest.
— *Olin Miller*

The girl who sings every time she's asked, has no control over her voice.

Liberty is letting you do as you please, but with controls over the other fellow.

The hardest things for a woman to control are in this order: her temper, her weight, and her children.

CONVENTION

Some men bring their wives gifts when returning from a convention; others have nothing to hide.

Going to a convention with your wife is like going on a hunting trip with the game warden.

A political convention is a battle between deals and ideals.

A convention is a meeting where the delegates always dress conventionally, but often act unconventionally.

Conventions too make strange bedfellows.

At political conventions the dark horse is always a sort of nightmare.

The badge of the delegate shows you whom he is for, but it does not show you what he is after.

A sales manager earns his living by being a slave to conventions.

At a political convention the delegates try to make hay while the favorite son shines.

CONVERSATION

I often have long conversations all by myself, and I am so clever that sometimes I don't understand a single word I am saying.
— *Oscar Wilde*

If other people are going to talk, conversation simply becomes impossible.
— *James McNeill Whistler*

Considering how foolishly people act and how pleasantly they prattle, it would be better for the world if they talked more and did less. — *Somerset Maugham*

Everything in marriage is of a passing nature except conversation, with most of the time being spent in it. — *Nietzsche*

A good conversationalist is not one who remembers what was said, but who says what someone wants to remember.
— *John Mason Brown*

The misfortune of Goldsmith in conversation is this: he goes on without knowing how he is to get off. — *Samuel Johnson*

The meaning doesn't matter if it's only idle chatter.
— *W. S. Gilbert*

When a person leaves your party pleased with his cleverness and himself, he is also pleased with you. — *La Bruyère*

Marriage is the permanent conversation between two people who talk over everything and everyone till death breaks the record.
— *Cyril Connolly*

Conversation would be vastly improved by the constant use of four simple words: *I do not know.*
— *André Maurois*

The wife who knows all about her husband's past never runs out of conversation.

Egotists are always confusing conceit with conversation.

Money talks, and it's the only conversation some people are interested in.

Conversation is 90 per cent talking and 10 per cent listening.

Marriage is a lifelong conversation in which a woman talks too much, and a man listens too little.

A starlet is the kind of girl who is interesting to converse with as long as she doesn't talk.

You don't have to be conversant with a subject to be able to converse about it.

It's all right to hold a conversation, but only if you let it go now and then.

Think twice before you speak, and the other fellow will monopolize the conversation.

Conversation is the art of hearing as well as being heard.

For a juicy conversation, three women are needed: two to do the talking, and one to be the subject.

The two cardinal sins of conversation are talkativeness and silence.

If the art of conversation is disappearing, why do you get so many busy signals on the telephone?

A conversation between women always concerns who, why, how, when and wear.

There are two kinds of women who are never at a loss for conversation: women who have babies, and women who haven't.

A gossip talks to you about others, a bore talks to you about himself, and a brilliant conversationalist talks to you about yourself.

Conversation is ruined by two kinds of people: the man who knows too much, and the man who knows too little.

The man who marries a woman because she is a good conversationalist will probably divorce her because she talks too much.

Conversation is a contest in which the first person to draw a breath is declared the listener.

Chatter is a form of conversation where much is spoken but little is said.

CONVICTION

Some men are just as firmly convinced of what they think as others are of what they know.
— *Aristotle*

If a judge followed his own convictions, he'd spend all of his life in jail.

The difference between an opinion and a conviction is that you hold one, while the other holds you.

By the time we arrive at middle age, we have settled on definite convictions, most of which are wrong.

When a wrangler convinces people to go along with his views, it is only because they hate arguments.

COOK

We may live without friends, we may live without books, but civilized man cannot live without cooks.   *— Owen Meredith*

Whoever heard of a man getting a divorce from a woman who was a good cook? *— Kin Hubbard*

No wonder we have so many diseases—look how many cooks we have.   *— Seneca*

Too many cooks spoil the broth—far too many.

The saddest thing in life is to marry a woman who looks like a cook—and isn't.

The man who claims he'd rather make love to his wife than eat is probably married to a poor cook.

Train up a cook in the way she should go, and when she is trained, she will.

A poor cook never uses an alibi; she merely keeps on claiming to be a good cook.

COOKBOOK

Even the finest of cookbooks is no substitute for the poorest of dinners.   *— Aldous Huxley*

While learning to cook, the average bride burns many things, including the cookbook.

Of all books, the cookbook has done most good for humanity— and the most harm.

What this country needs are more wives who are handier with the cookbook than with the checkbook.

What the modern bride doesn't know would fill a book—a cookbook.

COOKING

· The husband that uncomplainingly eats what's set before him may live more peacefully, but not as long.   *— Kin Hubbard*

A soupçon is a pinch of something that's always added, but never subtracted.   *— Arthur Baer*

The easier something's prepared, the less a husband likes it.
            — Kin Hubbard

A woman's way to a man's heart is through his stomach, but not by jumping down his throat.

Many foods that are well done are not done well.

Home cooking is something that far too many wives are not.

It's bad manners to talk with your mouth full, except when

you're praising your hostess' cooking.

Cuisine is another thing in whose name many crimes are committed.

Every husband praises his mother's cooking, but not his mother-in-law's.

Many a bride who cooks on an electric stove gives her husband gas pains.

Most women enjoy cooking, especially when it is done by the chef of a good restaurant.

Many a newlywed cooks just the way her husband had better like it.

The only thing some women cook successfully is their husbands' goose.

Many a wife does wonderful things with leftovers—she throws them out.

The only virtue in a mother-in-law's visit is that it improves a wife's cooking.

COOKOUT

An outdoor grill often cooks steaks rare and fingers well-done.

Where there's smoke there's fire, except when it's a cookout.

Progress is wonderful: it is only after we modernized the kitchen that the backyard cookout became popular.

The present generation requires ten times as much equipment for a cookout as our forefathers required to conquer the wilderness.

Why is it that our neighbor's barbecue always smells better than ours tastes?

In ancient times when meat was burnt outdoors it was a sacrifice; nowadays it is a cookout.

Summer is the season when a man thinks he can cook better on an outdoor grill than his wife can on an indoor stove.

There's nothing like progress: a generation ago only hobos went in for outdoor cooking.

CO-OPERATION

I never can understand how two men can write a book together; to me that's like three people getting together to have a baby. —*Evelyn Waugh*

No member of a crew is praised for the rugged individuality of his rowing. —*Emerson*

Co-operation is everything: freckles would make a nice coat of tan if they'd get together.

When a woman makes a fool out of a man, she seldom does it without his co-operation.

One man who works with you is worth a dozen men who work for you.

Co-operation is not an unmixed blessing: when snowflakes co-operate, they tie up traffic.

Marriage is a partnership in which two people co-operate for a common purpose against each other.

Some husbands are always co-operative: they are willing to mow the lawn in winter, and shovel snow in summer.

The man who is pulling his own weight never has any left over to throw around.

CORN

Hell hath no fury like a woman's corn.   — *Franklin P. Adams*

Corn is something discovered by Indians, distributed by farmers, distilled by moonshiners, and dispensed by comedians.

The best place to have a corn is on the bottom of your foot: nobody can step on it but you.

Corn is estimated out West by the foot, down South by the gallon, and on television by the hour.

A corn on the ear is worth two on the foot.

In Kentucky the corn is full of kernels, and the colonels are full of corn.

One man's corn is another man's bourbon.

Many a woman buys shoes as if she were trying to make two corns grow where only one grew before.

CORPORATION

A corporation is an ingenious device for obtaining individual profit without individual responsibility.

A man is judged by the company he keeps, especially in a proxy battle.

A corporation has all the powers and privileges of an individual: all it lacks is a conscience.

A man is known by the company he keeps—getting dividends from.

CORRECT

In infancy, our parents start correcting us; in adolescence, we start correcting them.

To err is human, and so is trying to avoid correcting it.

The proofreader is another man who corrects everybody's language but his own.

The hardest job a politician has is to find a way to correct a mistake without admitting he has made one.

Timing is everything: it's already too late to start correcting the children once they have started correcting you.

To err is human, but when the eraser wears out before the pencil, you're overdoing it.

A man never knows what he cannot do until he tries to undo what he did.

COSMETICS

Cosmetics are a powerful form of chemical warfare used by women in the battle of the sexes.

Beauty always comes from within—within jars, tubes and compacts.

Cosmetics are used by teen-agers to make them look older sooner, and by their mothers to make them look younger longer.

Without cosmetics, a girl can have a winning smile but a losing face.

Cosmetics are a woman's way to keep a man from reading between the lines.

The more work a woman does on her face, the less work she does around the house.

Many women are as pretty as they used to be, but it takes them much longer.

Beauty is less often skin deep than skin dope.

Another way in which a woman loses face is by misplacing her cosmetic kit.

Fashions may come and fashions may go but there's always a demand for cosmetics; women can't go wan forever.

No matter how you make up, your face wears off as the evening wears on.

Very few women shine in business—at least, not while they have their powder compacts handy.

Progress brings with it a growing appreciation of beauty: women in the middle ages use far more cosmetics than women in the Middle Ages.

A woman is as old as she looks until she puts her face on.

Beware the species of womankind that has more on the face than in the mind.

Cosmetics are what young women use to improve on Mother Nature, and what older women use to fool Father Time.

Face-saving was invented centuries ago; then along came the cosmetic industry and put it on a paying basis.

Cosmetics make a woman look old-fashioned when she doesn't use any.

Another reason why girls kiss and make up is that cosmetics wear off.

It always takes a woman longer to make up her face than her mind.

Men are vainer than women though they don't make-up—they think they don't need it.

COST

It's not what you pay a man but what he costs you that counts.
— *Will Rogers*

I have seen folks who had traveled all over the world, and all they could tell you was how much it had cost them.
— *Josh Billings*

All good things are cheap, all bad things very dear. — *Thoreau*

Strange is the procurement system of the Pentagon: a mouse grows into an elephant on a cost-plus-fixed-fee contract.

It doesn't cost very much to please a woman, but keeping her pleased is what breaks a man.

A husband's appreciation of his wife's clothes is usually confined to their cost.

In every business there is a constant struggle between the head and the overhead.

Time is money, especially when you're having the time of your life.

It costs more to amuse a child nowadays than it once did to educate his father.

If it's a small world, why does it cost so much to run it?

The best things in life are free, but it costs a lot of time and money before you find this out.

COST OF LIVING

How can wages ever meet high prices if they are always going in the same direction?

The easiest way to figure out the cost of living is to take your income and add 10 per cent.

Nowadays it's hard to bring your income up to your expenses, and even harder to bring your expenses down to your income.

All the talk about the high cost of living is just propaganda put out by people who eat.

Because the cost of living is so high, it would be wise for many a young man to postpone marriage until she is earning more.

No matter how high wages rise, the cost of living is always a few dollars above your income.

The high cost of living has not always been a conversation piece, but that was before money was invented.

The cost of living is much too high, and so is the cost of dying.

It costs twice as much to live as it did fifty years ago, but it's better to pay double now than to have paid half then.

Whatever goes up must come down, except the cost of living.

The rising cost of living makes the money you haven't got now worth less than the money you didn't have in the past.

Two can live as cheaply as one —large family used to.

The only trouble with the high standard of living is the high cost of living.

Between the high prices and the high taxes, is it any wonder many of us are always cleaned and pressed?

Despite its rising prices, the cost of living remains constant —all you've got.

If a month's bills were placed end to end, they would reach much farther than the paycheck.

If life is worth what it's costing nowadays, people were getting a real bargain in the good old days.

The cost of living doesn't seem to have much effect on its popularity.

The people should get increases when the cost of living goes up, and their congressmen should get increases when the cost of living goes down.

Everyone complains about the cost of living, but no one wants to stop living on account of the cost.

As the cost of living rises, all of us pay more for things we shouldn't buy.

At today's prices very few people can afford to be poor.

In the good old days two could live as cheaply as one; nowadays one can live as expensively as two.

As wages rise, so does the cost of living—thus, we all have to run faster to stay in the same place.

Living within your income these days leads to some mighty cramped quarters.

Some statistics are unreliable but those involving the cost of living are usually on the up and up.

COUGH

In England no one goes to the theater unless he or she has bronchitis.　　　　　　　*—James Agate*

Some people with bad coughs go to the doctor, but most go to the movies.

The art of acting consists chiefly in keeping the audience from coughing.

COUNT

For every woman who counts her blessings, there are a hundred women who count their calories.

Before you get angry at someone's faults, always count ten—ten of your own.

To the mathematician, if you can't count it, it doesn't count.

The centipede is so called not because it has a hundred feet but because the scientist who named it, couldn't count.

A countdown is a check-off seconds before a missile is blasted, or years after a woman of thirty has passed it.

A little girl counts on her fingers, while a big girl counts on her legs.

When angry with her husband, a wise woman always counts ten —but not over him.

Middle age is the time in life when a woman stops counting years, and starts counting calories.

The things that count most are the things you can't count.

The happy man counts his blessings; the unhappy one counts his cash.

COUNTERFEIT

A counterfeiter is the only man whose wife never complains that he doesn't make enough money.

Another man who is always forging his way ahead is the counterfeiter.

A counterfeiter is one who gets into trouble by carrying the do-it-yourself practice too far.

The counterfeiter is another man who makes money without earning it.

Money cannot buy love, or the law, or the respect of people—that is, counterfeit money.

The counterfeiter is a man who makes money in order to make money.

The counterfeiter is the only man whose problem is not how to make money but how to spend it.

You don't have to be in Congress to pass bad bills—there are also counterfeiters.

The counterfeiter who makes big money, should be careful not to make it too big.

The counterfeiter is the only man who is not allowed to make as much money as he can.

COUNTRY

To enjoy living in the country requires the mind of a philosopher, the feeling of an artist, the soul of a poet—and a good station wagon.

If fresh air is so healthy, why do most highway deaths take place in the country?

The land of milk and honey has its drawbacks: you can get kicked by a cow and stung by a bee.

The best part of living in the country is the people you don't meet.

COURAGE

The bitter part of discretion is valor.   —*Henry W. Nevinson*

Courage is almost a contradiction in terms: it means a strong desire to live taking the form of readiness to die.   —*Chesterton*

Courage is looking a saleslady straight in the eye and saying you'd like something a little cheaper.

There's only one thing more important in life than background, and that's backbone.

When we do a courageous thing it is heroic; when someone else does it, it is foolhardy.

Sometimes it takes less courage to die for a woman than to live with her.

A man may have more courage than a woman, but he doesn't get half the chance to show his backbone.

Everyone is in awe of the liontamer in a cage with half-a-dozen lions—everyone but a school bus driver.

A man has to have a lot of courage to admit that he hasn't any.

"If we had any guts, we'd get out of here," as one skeleton said to another in the medical laboratory.

Probably the reason the lions didn't eat Daniel was because most of him was grit and the rest backbone.

COURT

An appeal is when you ask one court to show its contempt for another court.
— *Finley Peter Dunne*

Courtroom: a place where Jesus Christ and Judas Iscariot would be equals, with the betting odds in favor of Judas. — *Mencken*

Our court dockets are so crowded today, it would be better to refer to it as the overdue process of law. — *Bill Vaughan*

The value of love is highest during courting days, but its cost is highest during days at court.

The man who goes to court without a lawyer has probably decided to tell the truth.

In court, wrangling between lawyers is nine points of the law.

Some men court, then marry, then go to court again.

A lawyer is always willing to go to court and spend your last cent to prove he's right.

The two chief reasons why it's hard to keep a courthouse clean are pigeons and politicians.

It's not only the neighbors who are trying to keep up with the Joneses; sometimes it's the process server.

He who courts and does not wed must sometimes go to court instead.

COURTSHIP

The fellow who waits to get married until he has enough money, isn't really in love.
— *Kin Hubbard*

The hardest problem of a girl's life is to find out why a man seems bored if she doesn't respond to him, and frightened if she does. — *Helen Rowland*

If a woman doesn't chase a man a little, she doesn't love him.

Men who do not make advances to women are apt to become victims to women who make advances to them.

Courtship begins with a man fishing for a girl, and ends with her making the catch.

Courtship is a romantic ship that's often washed up on the sea of matrimony.

It's difficult to finish with a girl with whom it was easy to begin.

The trouble with courtship is that some men don't know when

to stop, and others don't know when to go.

A girl often has a man eating out of her hand by keeping him at arm's length.

The ideal conditions for courtship are when the moon is out, and also her parents.

Faint heart ne'er won fair lady —without plenty of help on her part.

Courtship is the period when girls use their heads to make men lose theirs.

Courtship hasn't changed much in thousands of years; in ancient times a girl used to sit and listen to a lyre all evening.

In fishing for a husband, be sure to distinguish between a nibble and a bite.

Courtship is the period when a girl doesn't say all she means, and a man doesn't mean all he says.

Courtship is the period when most women try to break men of a bad habit—being bachelors.

There are three ways to win a wife: by audacity, tenacity, or mendacity.

He who courts and runs away, lives to court another day.

Courtship is the only game in which two people chase each other at the same time.

There are many long courtships because many a boyfriend spends so much money on her, he can't afford to get married.

Courtship is a game of hearts that was played in caveman days with clubs, but is now played with diamonds.

When a woman is being courted, her instinct tells her whether the man needs inducement or discouragement.

It's always easier to keep a man guessing than to keep him after he's stopped guessing.

Courtship is the period when a man pursues a girl who is running toward him.

When fishing for a husband, some girls don't mind what worm they'll go out with.

Courtship is the period when a woman resists a man's advances while she blocks his retreat.

COURTSHIP AND MARRIAGE

Before marriage, she tells him where to take her; after marriage, she tells him where to go.

Courtship is a short period of long kisses usually followed by a long period of short kisses.

Before marriage, he promises to tell her everything; after marriage, he finds out she already knows everything.

Until he's married, a man goes with a girl; after that, he's taken.

Before marriage, two's company and three's a crowd; after

marriage, two's company and three's a great relief.

Before marriage, he thinks they were made for each other; after marriage, she thinks about making alterations.

The short romantic period when a man is always calling a girl up is usually followed by a long period when she is always calling him down.

Before marriage, she misses a lot of meals to get him; after marriage, she makes a lot of meals to keep him.

Many a man spends his courtship telling a girl he is unworthy of her, and his married life trying to prove it.

Before marriage, a girl never knows when she will find her husband; after marriage, she never knows where.

During courtship, you are always saying foolish things; during marriage, you are always doing them.

Before marriage, a woman thinks of a man; after marriage, she thinks for him.

The girl who plays hard to get before marriage often becomes hard to take afterward.

When courtship is over, it is over; when marriage is over, it is just beginning.

Before marriage, he lies awake thinking of what she said; after marriage, he falls asleep before she finishes saying it.

Before marriage, he learns how to fondle her; after marriage, she learns how to handle him.

Sometimes a man spends so much on his girl friend, he finally marries her for his money.

Before marriage a girl promises to make him a good wife; after marriage she prefers to make him a better husband.

Before marriage, she doubles his joys; after marriage, she triples his expenses.

Courtship begins with a man seeking a girl's hand, and ends with her having him under her thumb.

Before marriage, she turns his head with her beauty; after marriage, she turns his stomach with her cooking.

During courtship, a woman tries to make a husband out of a man; during marriage, she tries to make a man out of a husband.

Before marriage, her parents wonder when he'll go home; after marriage, she wonders when he'll come home.

COW

All the really good ideas I ever had came to me while I was milking a cow.   – *Grant Wood*

Look at those cows and remember that the greatest scientists have never discovered how to turn grass into milk.
                    – *Michael I. Pupin*

Size isn't everything: a cow is big enough to catch a mouse, but she's never caught one yet.

Why shouldn't a cow be contented? It is all the time surrounded by a lot of high-priced meat.

Milk the cow, but don't pull off the udder.

COWARD

The coward is always telling you that discretion is the better part of valor.

The man who boasts that he never quarrels with his wife usually mistakes cowardice for chivalry.

Many a man who keeps out of trouble gets credit for a cool head when it's really cold feet.

The yellow streak in human nature is often brought out by the precious metal of the same color.

Marriage doth make cowards of us all.

A coward is one who faces anything difficult or dangerous by turning his back on it.

Cold feet are usually the result of burnt fingers.

Many a coward is considered brave because he was afraid to run away.

Silence isn't always golden: sometimes it is just plain yellow.

A coward is a fellow with cold feet who has sense enough to stay out of hot water.

Conscience gets a lot of credit that really belongs to cowardice.

The meek will inherit the earth, but only because they won't have the courage to refuse.

The coward is a man who lives in fear of his life, and in even greater fear of his wife.

A coward has a yellow streak, is always in a blue funk, and shows the white feather.

When you practice it, it's caution; when the other fellow does, it's cowardice.

CREATION

I sometimes think that God in creating man somewhat overestimated His ability. — *Oscar Wilde*

A subject for a great poet would be God's boredom after the seventh day of Creation.
— *Nietzsche*

Man is not the apex of Creation, but the ex-ape.

Man was made first so woman could claim she was an improvement on him.

The reason God made man after He made the other creatures was that He didn't want any advice while the work was going on.

God made bees and bees made honey; God made man, and man made money.

Man was created first; woman was a sort of recreation.

Did nature create man to show that she is big enough to make mistakes, or was it pure ignorance?

God made everything out of nothing, but man seems to make nothing out of everything.

Second thoughts are best: God created man, woman was an afterthought.

Woman was created last so she wouldn't have to wait for someone to talk to.

The world was created in six days, no Senate confirmation being necessary.

"O Lord, how you made me jump!" as the grasshopper said when it was created.

Man was created first, and woman has kept him waiting ever since.

CREDIT

Credit is a clever financial trick that enables us to spend what we haven't got.

Nowadays there are three classes: the haves, the have-nots, and the charge-its.

Getting things on credit is like getting them for nothing, and paying for them later is like throwing the money away.

When a man cannot get credit it's because he is not known, or because he is.

Many a motorist drives a time-payment car over a bond-financed highway on credit-card gas.

It's the woman who pays and pays, unless she has a charge account.

Free enterprise accounts for the millions of new cars being sold every year, but you also have to give the American public an enormous amount of credit.

Never put off till tomorrow the things you can buy today—tomorrow your credit may not be good.

Formerly people went without things to have money; nowadays they go without money to have things.

A charge account is the current way to get a shock at the beginning of every month.

Give a woman credit for anything nowadays, and she'll buy it.

Most families can use more credit than they are getting—and usually do.

Credit is what enables people to spend money they haven't earned, to buy things they don't need, to impress people they don't like.

Buying on time always makes the months shorter and the years longer.

A credit plan is a financial device to help the neighbors keep up with the Joneses, and the Joneses to keep up with themselves.

A smart man never gives his wife more credit than he can afford.

When some wives go shopping, they remind you of General Custer—the only word they use is "Charge."

The problem nowadays is not so much how to live within your income, but how to live within your credit.

Some women don't care how much money a man has as long as his credit is good.

Next to the man who invented taxes, the one who caused the most trouble in the world is the man who invented credit.

No woman ever seems to get out of breath running up a charge account.

Credit is what people need in order to buy what they don't need.

A man with a large family may not deserve a lot of credit but he certainly needs it.

Money isn't everything: there are also charge accounts, time payments, and credit cards.

If men should ever stop having faith in one another, we'll all have to start living within our incomes.

The man who can get credit the easiest is the man who needs it the least.

It's much easier to get credit for what you buy than for what you do.

CREDIT CARD

Man can't live on bread alone—he has to have credit cards.

Money used to be very popular before the invention of the credit card.

A credit card is a convenient device that saves you the trouble of counting your change.

Shakespeare paraphrased: He who steals my purse steals credit cards.

Nowadays it's not who wears the pants in the family, but who carries the credit cards.

Money isn't everything, but it's mighty handy when you've lost your credit cards.

The advantage a credit card has over money is that it can be used over and over again.

In childhood, a library card takes you to exotic, faraway places; in adulthood, a credit card does.

The credit card was invented to enable people to accumulate more debts more easily in more places.

The advantage of a credit card is that you don't know you are broke, at least not before the end of the month.

A credit card is a financial device that enables people who own more, to owe more.

The only thing you cannot buy nowadays with a credit card is money.

Jack Sprat could eat no fat, his wife could eat no lean—he forgot his credit card.

Money is the most popular medium of exchange—next to credit cards.

The greatest enemy of home cooking was the invention of the credit card.

There are many kinds of credit cards but they all have one thing in common: they run you into debt.

With a credit card, you don't need money; and with money, you don't need a credit card.

The only thing you can't buy nowadays with a credit card is experience.

A credit card adds to your credit, but adds even more to your creditors.

A batch of credit cards fattens a wallet before it thins it.

Money can't buy happiness—that's why we have credit cards.

You can trust a man who puts his cards on the table, especially if they are credit cards.

A credit card sometimes adds to the high cost of living, but more often to the cost of high living.

You can pay for everything nowadays with a credit card, except the monthly bills you run up with it.

CREDITOR

It is better to make friends with your creditors than to make creditors of your friends.

Oh, wad some power the giftie gie us to see our creditors before they see us.

It disappoints a man to return from his vacation and find that his long rest has done his creditors no good.

The man who avoids debt doesn't have to worry about avoiding creditors.

Some men are satisfied if they have all the money they want; others, if they have all the money their creditors want.

It is not only a man's sins, but his creditors who find him out.

Money talks, but the people who want their money talk the loudest.

Usually the people who have the most trouble keeping up with the Joneses are the Joneses' creditors.

Some people not only think the world owes them a living, but consider themselves preferred creditors.

Never put off till tomorrow the creditor who will wait till the day after.

A realist is one who realizes that his creditors are even more worried than he is.

CREMATION

He married an Anglo-Indian widow, and soon after published a pamphlet in favor of suttee.
— *George Meredith*

People who believe in cremation have grave doubts about death.

If tombstones told the truth, everybody would wish to be cremated.

CRIME

If England treats her criminals the way she has treated me, she doesn't deserve to have any.
— *Oscar Wilde*

Criminals do not die by the hands of the law: they die by the hands of other men.
— *Bernard Shaw*

It takes all sorts of people to make the underworld.
— *Don Marquis*

We don't seem able to check crime, so why not legalize it and then tax it out of business?
— *Will Rogers*

Crime doesn't pay: sooner or later every murderer gets a ticket for parking.

The way of the transgressor is hard—for the police to find out.

Crime doesn't pay, but only if you get caught.

It takes two to make a criminal: one individual and one society.

If crime doesn't pay, how come it is one of the biggest businesses in the United States?

There would be a great deal more crime if some people had more nerve.

Crimes will continue to be committed as long as those who do them aren't.

Crime doesn't pay—at least, not on television.

A police lineup is the only place where a man hates to be introduced to his audience.

The reason crime doesn't pay is that when it does, it is called by a more respectable name.

The only crime greater than writing a bad poem is writing a bad check.

In the underworld, money isn't the root of all evil, but evil is the root of all money.

Crime doesn't pay, but at least you are your own boss.

The battle against crime should begin in the high chair so as not to end in the electric chair.

The story of crime and punishment is not to be told in short sentences.

Crime doesn't pay—or wouldn't if the government ran it.

Poverty is no crime, but it's apt to count against you if you commit one.

Liberty isn't the only thing in whose name many crimes are

committed; there is also interior decoration.

In a television mystery, crime does not pay, except for the sponsor.

In the world of crime, the survival of the fittest is the survival of those who are fit for nothing else.

Crime doesn't pay, except for the writers of detective stories.

A public enemy is a hardened criminal toward whom we'd be better disposed if his father had been the last of his family.

CRISIS

If you can manage to stay scared all the time, you'll soon find that these international crises won't bother you at all.

During an emergency a person's presence of mind is often offset by absence of thought.

The man who knows history never lets an international crisis move him to hysteria.

Many a man living today is reluctant to shuffle off before he sees how civilization wriggles out of this one.

The best way for a husband to meet a marital crisis is with a firm hand—full of flowers.

CRITIC

A critic is a gong at a railroad crossing clanging loudly and vainly as the train goes by.
— *Christopher Morley*

A critic is a man created to praise greater men than himself, but he is never able to find them.
— *Richard Le Gallienne*

One of the first and most important things for a critic to learn is how to sleep undetected at the theater.   — *William Archer*

Nature fits all her children with something to do: he who would write and can't write, can surely review.   — *James Russell Lowell*

When I dislike what I see on the stage, I can be vastly amusing, but when I write about something I like, I am appallingly dull.
— *Max Beerbohm*

A dramatic critic is a man who leaves no turn unstoned.
— *Bernard Shaw*

This critic deserves more respect, the respect due to honest, hopeless, helpless imbecility.
— *John Ruskin*

A man must serve his time at every trade save censure—critics all are ready made.
— *Lord Byron*

Many a critic seems more like a committee framing resolutions than a man writing down what he thinks.   — *Frank Moore Colby*

The sheer complexity of writing a play always has dazzled me; in an effort to understand it, I became a critic. — *Kenneth Tynan*

The first man who objected to the general nakedness and advised his fellows to put on clothes, was the first critic. — *Edwin L. Godkin*

A critic is a man whose watch is five minutes ahead of other people's watches.   — *Sainte-Beuve*

Never answer a critic—unless he's right.   — *Bernard Baruch*

Since we cannot equal it, let us avenge ourselves by abusing it.
— *Montaigne*

A true critic hath one quality in common with a harlot, never to change his title or his nature.
— *Swift*

Show me a critic without prejudices, and I'll show you an arrested cretin.
— *George Jean Nathan*

I was so long writing my review that I never got around to reading the book.
— *Groucho Marx*

The caterpillar strips the blossoms, but the critic strips the tree of both caterpillars and blossoms.
— *Jean Paul Richter*

A television critic is forced to be literate about the illiterate, witty about the witless, and coherent about the incoherent.
— *John Crosby*

To literary critics a book is assumed to be guilty until it proves itself innocent.   — *Nelson Algren*

A critic is a man who knows the way but can't drive the car.
— *Kenneth Tynan*

The only critics worth reading are the critics who practice, and practice well, the art of which they write.   — *T. S. Eliot*

I have been aided by some censorious but able reviewers who were willing to take pains in order to inflict them.
— *Frank Moore Colby*

Has anybody ever seen a drama critic in the daytime? Of course not!—they come out after dark, up to no good.
— *P. G. Wodehouse*

I take no more notice of the wind that comes out of the mouths of critics than of the wind expelled from their backsides.
— *Da Vinci*

One battle doesn't make a campaign but critics treat one book, good or bad, like a whole war.
— *Hemingway*

The chief requisite for an art critic is the ability to find meanings in a painting which the artist didn't know were there.

Opportunity knocks but once, but you can't say the same for a critic.

Some critics have tried to do it and failed; others feel too damn superior even to try to do it.

A critic never knows his own limitations but always knows the limitations of others.

The artist knows beforehand what should be done; the critic knows afterward what should have been done.

There are two kinds of critics: some are necessary evils, others are evil necessities.

The critics arrived after the world was created.

One critic may not be an ass, but two are bound to be biassed.

An art critic uses big words because, if readers knew what he was talking about, they'd know he didn't know what he was talking about.

Most critics act on the principle that a writer is ruined by praise and saved by criticism.

A critic writes because he has to say something, not because he has something to say.

If a critic's work were done by a woman, it would be called nagging.

All the world's a stage, and all the players think they're first-rate drama critics.

What a critic lacks in appreciation, he more than makes up in depreciation.

A critic is a man who has no faults, but everyone he writes about has.

A drama critic sometimes finds things gripping, but more often things find him griping.

There are two kinds of critics: those who write what they don't know about, and those who don't know what they write about.

All the world's a stage, with most of us playing the critic's role.

The creator of literary works is no more responsible for his critics than a dog is for his fleas.

CRITICISM

The artists who want to be writers, read the reviews; the artists who want to write, don't.
— *Faulkner*

Impersonal criticism is like an impersonal fist fight or an impersonal marriage—and as successful. — *George Jean Nathan*

Express a mean opinion of yourself occasionally; it will show your friends that you know how to tell the truth.   — *Ed Howe*

I look upon book reviews as an infantile disease which new-born books are subject to.
— *G. C. Lichtenberg*

The main use of criticism is in showing what manner of man the critic is.   — *Frank Moore Colby*

I never give them hell; I just tell the truth and they think it is hell.   — *Harry S. Truman*

Dramatic criticism is the venom from contented rattlesnakes.
— *Percy Hammond*

I love criticism just so long as it's unqualified praise.
— *Noel Coward*

When I have to praise a writer, I usually do it by attacking his enemies.   — *Mencken*

Most drama criticism is written by persons who would rather be in bed.   — *Frank Moore Colby*

If criticism had any real power to harm, the skunk would have been extinct by now.
— *Fred Allen*

The man who is asked by an author what he thinks of his work is not obliged to speak the truth.
— *Samuel Johnson*

Reviewing has one advantage over suicide: in suicide you take it out of yourself; in reviewing you take it out of other people.
— *Bernard Shaw*

Anyone can be accurate and even profound, but it is damned hard work to make criticism charming.   — *Mencken*

One of the greatest creations of the human mind is the art of reviewing books without having to read them. — *G. C. Lichtenberg*

Drama criticism is an inhuman system that requires a man to talk like an Act of Congress.
— *Frank Moore Colby*

Newspaper reviews are often greater crimes than the crimes a newspaper reviews.

Criticism wouldn't be so hard to take if it weren't so often right.

Criticism is the art of writing about yourself while appearing to be writing about another man's work.

CROSSWORD PUZZLE

Our notion of a miracle man is the Welsh crossword puzzle champion. — *Franklin P. Adams*

The worst fate in the world is to be wrecked on a desert island with a crossword puzzle book and no pencil.

Many couples have been married for years and there's never been a crossword puzzle between them.

The man of few words is an asset everywhere, except when he is solving a crossword puzzle.

No one has more self-confidence than the person who does a crossword puzzle with a pen.

The habitual grouch is another crossword puzzle we can't solve.

The only time some married men get in the last word is when they finish a crossword puzzle.

It's called *crosswords* because husbands and wives often try to solve them together.

CROWD

Anything that makes a noise is satisfactory to a crowd.
— *Dickens*

Never follow the crowd if you want the crowd to follow you.

Summer is the season when people get out of the crowded city to get out on the crowded highway.

A crowd finds it easier to cheer than to think.

CRUELTY

Man's inhumanity to man makes countless thousands of dollars.

Many cruel things are done in the name of civilization, but if we didn't have civilization, we'd find some other excuse.

Man's inhumanity to man is human compared to woman's inhumanity to woman.

It's always the kindest husband that lets his wife have a divorce on grounds of extreme cruelty.

Man's inhumanity to man makes countless thousands do likewise.

CRUISE

During a cruise a man never runs out of money as fast as his wife runs out of clothes.

Behind every successful man is a woman who wants to go on another cruise.

A cruise does nothing for some people except to change the rings under their eyes from black to tan.

The passenger on a cruise who doesn't know port from starboard, should look at the label on the bottle.

A cruise sometimes puts you in the pink, but more often in the red.

CULTURE

The university will always exist as a community of persons pursuing culture, talking culture, thinking culture, above all criticizing culture.   — *Bernard Shaw*

Our modern culture is one in which nine-tenths of our intellectuals can't read any poetry.
     — *Randall Jarrell*

Culture is roughly anything we do and the monkeys don't.
     — *Lord Raglan*

Culture is one thing and varnish another.   — *Emerson*

The culture some men display on a date with a girl is all physical.

Some women are fond of culture, while others are fond of being thought to be fond of culture.

A well-rounded person is one who can entertain himself, entertain guests, and entertain ideas.

The only thing cultured about some women is a string of cultured pearls.

A culture hound is the kind of woman with the patience to sit through something which only a highbrow can enjoy.

CUNNING

Never try to outsmart a woman, unless you are another woman.   — *William Lyon Phelps*

Some women are as deep as the ocean and just as full of craft.

Life is a battle of wits, and many people have to fight it unarmed.

Beware of your wife when her lips drip honey; she's probably after a wad of your money.

The man who lives by his wits seldom finds life a joke.

A good way for a girl to get her man is to play her cards well; a better way is to play dumb.

The female of the species is more cunning than the male: she knows how to forgo her birthdays without forgoing the presents.

It's a clever husband who will buy his wife such fine china that she won't trust him with the dishes.

Never underestimate the purr of a woman.

On the sea of matrimony the craft is usually possessed by the wife.

The man who says you cannot take it with you, may be trying to take it from you.

It takes a clever man to know how to agree with his wife in such a way that she will change her mind.

It doesn't take a long while for a clever woman to get a husband; it takes only a little wile.

CURE

The cure for anything is salt water—sweat, tears, or the sea.
                    —Isak Dinesen

It is a pity that marriage is the only medicine that has so far been discovered to cure a love affair.   —Ed Howe

Medicines cure diseases, but only doctors can cure patients.
                    —Jung

I have a perfect cure for a sore throat—cut it. —Alfred Hitchcock

A fool will not only pay for a cure that does him no good, but he will write a testimonial that he was cured.   —Ed Howe

The man who doctors himself with the aid of medical books, runs the risk of dying of a typographical error.

Some remedies are worse than the disease, but the cure for poverty is not one of them.

If you are terribly in love, the best way to cure yourself is to run away—with the girl.

Time heals everything, but don't try sitting it out in a doctor's reception room.

There is nothing wrong with the younger generation that marriage and children won't cure.

The advantage of being poor is that a doctor will cure you faster.

CURIOSITY

Men are generally more anxious to find out why things are so than whether things are so.
                    —Montaigne

Curiosity is lying in wait for every secret.   —Emerson

A boy often passes from an early stage when he wants to know everything to a later stage when he wants to know next to nothing.   —Chesterton

We are all like Scheherazade's husband in that we want to know what happens next.
                    —E. M. Forster

A woman will spend half her days trying to find out something whose discovery will make her unhappy for the rest of her life.

If at first you don't succeed, pry, pry again.

The clever wife who reads her husband like a book, never inquires into earlier editions.

The most curious thing in the world is the woman who isn't.

Nobody's business is everybody's curiosity.

A woman in love always wants to know just where her man is when he's out of her sight.

Curiosity feeds on love; only a dog can love without asking questions.

Half the world doesn't know how the other half lives, but is always trying to find out.

More heads are turned by screeching brakes than pretty girls.

A woman doesn't need the right to open her husband's mail; all she needs is the curiosity.

There is some good in every heart, and some rubber in every neck.

Curiosity is the mother of window shades.

CURVE

Some girls have curves in places where other girls don't even have places.

Middle age is the time in life when a woman's curves turn into circles.

There would be fewer highway accidents if the only persons passing on curves were the judges of beauty contests.

Men who stick to the straight and narrow path are never led astray by curves.

A reckless driver often takes a curve at high speed, even when there isn't any curve.

A curved line is the loveliest distance between two points.

CUSTOM

Don't complain that things are not what they used to be; remember, this includes you.

Times change: it was once the custom to take a bath weekly and religion daily.

Fashions change with the times: women once wore bathing suits that were longer than their skirts are today.

Times change: formerly people used to get along without something if it cost too much.

CUSTOMER

Treat your customer as if she were your best girl, not your wife.

It's no problem to think what you'd like to say to a difficult customer—the problem is not saying it.

In politics, people are friends or enemies; in business, they are all customers.

Commercially speaking, some customers are easier to trim than a window.

The customer is always right, unless his bill is overdue.

CYNICISM

The power of accurate observation is commonly called cynicism by those who have not got it.
— *Bernard Shaw*

The only deadly sin I know of is cynicism. — *Henry L. Stimson*

A cynic is just a man who found out when he was about ten that there wasn't any Santa Claus, and he's still upset.
— *J. G. Cozzens*

A cynic sees little to admire in the world, while the world sees even less to admire in him.

There are some people who can see nothing good in this world without the aid of a mirror.

The cynic who doesn't believe in anything still wants you to believe him.

A cynic is a man who thinks courtship is the first in a series of steps leading to divorce.

A cynic is a man who knows everything and understands nothing.

The cynic who sneers at human nature is probably speaking from self-knowledge.

Only a cynic can see viruses in the milk of human kindness.

A cynic thinks it's right that divorce should cost more than marriage because it's worth more.

To the cynic, what is is no better than it ought to be.

DAMAGE

A suit for damages is always made several sizes too large.

What this country needs is a quick-drying cement that sets before a youngster can walk on it.

To the victor belong the spoils, but the spoils usually spoil the victor.

More harm is done to infants in infancy than to adults in adultery.

DANCE

I don't understand anything about the ballet; all I know is that during the intervals the ballerinas stink like horses. — *Chekhov*

When some men dance they're all feet, and when they stop they're all hands.

A choreographer is a dance creator who uses his head to give employment to other people's feet.

The only good thing about the new dances is that nobody knows when you make a mistake.

In dancing, the women usually know the steps and the men know the holds.

There's always room for a good man, except on a crowded dance floor.

The modern dance is no dance in the first place, and when you've finally learned it, it's not modern any more.

Many a girl who can't dance well makes up for it during inter-mission.

Dancing is the art of getting your feet out of the way faster than your partner can step on them.

Some girls love to dance, while others dance to love.

Some people grow old grace-fully; others take up the latest dance craze.

The girl who is too tired to run an errand for mother can wear out the huskiest man on the dance floor.

When some men are on a dance floor they never know what to do with their minds.

He who dances must pay the piper—also the waiter and the hat-check girl.

The woman who knows just what her husband is going to do next, probably isn't dancing with him.

Sometimes when you ask a woman to dance, she is on your feet in a moment.

Dancing is an indoor sport that resembles wrestling, except that no holds are barred.

Some men always rub people the wrong way; others never do, except when they are on a crowded dance floor.

Some of the modern dances are so lively, you have to exercise everything but discretion.

The hula-hula dance is simple: you put some grass on one hip, some more grass on the other hip, and then you rotate the crops.

Another thing that has devel-oped by leaps and bounds is the modern dance.

DANDY

I hate to see a man over-dressed: a man ought to look like he's put together by accident, not added up on purpose.
— *Christopher Morley*

A dandy is a show-off who turns a girl's head, and everyone else's stomach.

Many a man dresses to kill, but no one has the nerve to do it.

DANGER

Don't play for safety—it's the most dangerous thing in the world.
— *Hugh Walpole*

In this world there is always danger for those who are afraid of it.   — *Bernard Shaw*

This country has come to feel the same when Congress is in ses-sion as when the baby gets hold of a hammer.   — *Will Rogers*

If a little knowledge is dangerous, where is there the man who has so much as to be out of danger?   *— T. H. Huxley*

The most dangerous time to be right is when everyone else is wrong.

Driving while drunk is almost as dangerous nowadays as walking while sober.

A little knowledge is a dangerous thing, especially when your wife has it.

It is a dangerous politician who believes everything he says.

The two greatest hazards on the highway are drivers under twenty-five going over seventy, and drivers over seventy going under twenty-five.

The only thing more dangerous to a bachelor than a jealous husband is a single girl.

The dangerous age in man is when he has ceased being dangerous to anything but his own reputation.

A reckless driver endangers others in four ways—north, south, east and west.

The man who rocks the boat is seldom at the oars.

A little learning is a dangerous thing, and so is a little woman.

There are three great dangers to safe driving in America today: hic, hike and hug.

DARK

Love may be blind, but it certainly finds its way around in the dark.

When a girl's date tries to keep her in the dark, she doesn't remain long in the dark about his intentions.

The darker the parking place, the brighter the ideas a young man gets.

DATE

A date turns into trouble when both wait at the right time, but one waits at the wrong place.

Early to bed and early to rise, and your girl will go out with other guys.

A mother worries if her daughter comes home from a date too late—or too early.

When a girl goes out with a man who is old enough to be her father, he is probably rich enough to be her husband.

You will never find good lookers on blind dates.

A philanderer is the type of man who is not to be trysted.

The less men there are to go around, the more they go around.

Some young men are so slow, the girl feels like screaming; others are so fast she has to.

Going out with a man is sometimes like playing checkers: he makes a move, and then she jumps.

A good line is the shortest distance between two dates.

When a man breaks a date, he has to; when a girl does, she has two.

When you expect to meet a vision on a blind date, she usually turns out to be a sight.

Why is it that when a girl is old enough for her parents to let her go out alone, she doesn't?

Some girls are so good at figures, they can remember dates they never had.

When a middle-aged couple have to go somewhere, the woman's first thought is what to wear, and the man's is how to get out of it.

Dating is always a problem for women: the man who looks as if he might make a good husband, probably is.

If at first you don't succeed, date the boss's daughter.

There will always be new frontiers as long as there is a boy to ring the front doorbell on his first date.

A dumb girl will never turn a deaf ear to a blind date.

Many a girl breaks a date by going out with him.

DAVID AND GOLIATH

David should have killed Goliath with a harp.

— *Stanislaw J. Lec*

Guided missiles are nothing new: David killed the giant Goliath with one.

"Such a thing never entered my head before," as Goliath said when struck by the shot from David's sling.

DAY

One of these days is none of these days.

You can take a day off but you can't put it back.

What can you expect from a day that begins with having to get up in the morning?

Some playboys keep such late hours, the morning after is usually a day later.

After middle age the days go two at a time.

DAY AND NIGHT

The difference between wife and mistress is the difference between night and day.

— *Harry Hershfield*

Night falls but never breaks, and day breaks but never falls.

When men talk about the good old days they usually mean the nights.

The playboy's life is one swift round of activity—day in and night out.

Middle age is the period in life when a night out is followed by a day in.

Every night rolls on until stopped by the break of day.

DAYDREAM

If you have built castles in the air, that is where they should be; now put foundations under them.
— *Thoreau*

How many of our daydreams would darken into nightmares were there any danger of their coming true. — *Logan P. Smith*

The daydreamer is the only man who does most of his dreaming while he is awake.

Every schoolboy lets his mind wander, but only the truant follows it.

Castles in the air are all right as long as you don't step out of the door.

A daydreamer sleeps by night but dreams by day.

DEADBEAT

A deadbeat divides people into two classes: those to whom he owes money, and those who don't trust him.

The more people a deadboat knows, the more people he owes.

A deadbeat is the only man outside of Congress who is accustomed to ignore bills.

A deadbeat is always short of funds, but long on promises.

The man who will borrow and not pay back is probably too great a coward to steal.

A deadbeat doesn't care whose means he lives beyond.

The only man who is more anxious to get into debt than out of it is a deadbeat.

A deadbeat never pays as he goes, but goes anyway.

A deadbeat doesn't have to build anything at all to have the world beat a path to his door.

DEAF

A touch of deafness lightens one of life's heaviest chores—listening to bores. — *Ogden Nash*

In the kingdom of the deaf, the one-eared man is king.
— *Bernard Shaw*

Being hard-of-hearing is an affliction but it's not so bad as having to listen to some people.

Blessed are the hard-of-hearing for they shall miss much idle gossip.

Money talks, but it's hard of hearing when you call it.

You cannot convince a cynic that a department store doesn't hire only hard-of-hearing personnel for its complaint department.

DEATH

I am ready to meet my maker, but whether my maker is prepared for the great ordeal of meeting me is another matter.
— *Winston Churchill*

If some died and others did not, death would be a terrible affliction.
— *La Bruyère*

When a man dies, and his kin are glad of it, they say, "He is better off."
— *Ed Howe*

Homer is dead, Dante is dead, Shakespeare is dead, and I'm not feeling so well myself.
— *Artemus Ward*

Death has this consolation: it frees us from the thought of death.
— *Jules Renard*

He said he dislikes psychiatrists, keeps away from doctors, and would die before he would send for a mortician.
— *Don Marquis*

Most people would rather die than think: many do.
— *Bertrand Russell*

Death is a very dull, dreary affair, and my advice to you is to have nothing whatever to do with it.
— *Somerset Maugham*

Providence has placed death at the end of life in order to give people time to prepare for it.

In the good old days you lived until you died and not until you were just run over.

The good die young because only the young die good.

The one consolation of death is that it is also the end of your taxes.

The last thing a man wants to do is the last thing he does—die.

Many a man's death is due to a broken heart; if he hadn't broken a woman's heart, she wouldn't have shot him.

To the unbeliever, death is the end; to the believer, the beginning.

Many a man dies with his boots on—the accelerator.

Don't worry about getting older; when you stop getting older, you're dead.

The proof that the good die young is that infant mortality is steadily decreasing.

DEBT

The man who buys a car doesn't run into debt: he rides into it.
— *Carey Williams*

Some debts are fun when you are acquiring them, but none are fun when you set about retiring them.
— *Ogden Nash*

We often pay our debts not because it is only fair that we should, but to make future loans easier.
— *La Rochefoucauld*

A debtor is any person who has enough money to make the down payment.

The man who is long in debt is usually short in money.

Some people worry because they are in debt; others, because they can't even get in.

After a man works his way out of debt he draws a deep breath of satisfaction, and then goes into debt again.

The faster you run into debt, the more you get behind.

There's nothing as short as a short-term debt.

The first thing a man runs into when he buys a new car is—debt.

Some husbands can pay debts promptly, but most of us are good to our wives.

Another thing that leads people into debt is trying to keep up with people already there.

Nowadays it's a happy marriage when the couple are as deeply in love as they are in debt.

The people who put on the most style are often the ones who put off the most creditors.

When some men pay their debts they act as if they were conferring a great favor on their creditors.

Five credit cards, four youngsters, three meals a day, two cars, and a contented wife—why shouldn't I be in debt?

About the only thing you can acquire without money is debt.

The man who drives this year's car on next year's income is probably wearing last year's clothes.

Nowadays anyone who isn't in debt is probably underprivileged.

DECEIT

The worst of marriage is that it makes a woman believe that all other men are just as easy to fool.
— *Mencken*

When a person cannot deceive himself, the chances are against his being able to deceive other people. — *Mark Twain*

A sucker is born every minute, and two to trick him.
— *Wilson Mizner*

After a man is fifty, you can fool him by saying he is smart, but you can't fool him by saying he is handsome. — *Ed Howe*

What makes human society tolerable is that men are forever deceiving one another.
— *La Rochefoucauld*

Appearances are deceiving, but it's better to have them deceive for us than against us.

The cleverest kind of deception is practiced not by words but by silence.

The thing that smacks most of deceit is when two women kiss.

About the time a man thinks he has a woman fooled, she fools him by changing her mind.

Clothes make the man, and fake the woman.

If you fool people to get their money, that's fraud; if you fool them to get their votes, that's politics.

To deceive a deceiver is no deceit.

Beware of the woman who takes you in when you take her out.

The mind of a confidence man is like a flash of lightning—swift but crooked.

You can only fool some of the people some of the time because the rest of the time they are trying to fool you.

Nothing can be so deceptive as men's statistics, except women's figures.

DECISION

When I have made up my mind I always listen to reason because it can then do me no harm.
— *Oliver Goldsmith*

When a person tells you, "I'll think it over and let you know" —you know. — *Olin Miller*

All our final decisions are made in a state of mind that is not going to last. — *Marcel Proust*

Being married saves a man a lot of time making up his mind about things.

A decision is what an executive is forced to make when he can't get anyone to serve on a committee.

If you've made up your mind that you can't do it, you're absolutely right.

Where ignorance is bliss, 'tis folly for the courts to render decisions which the people can understand.

My decision is maybe—and that's final.

The average man often faces the hard problem of trying to decide which will cost less—to tell the truth or hire a lawyer.

When a man decides to marry, it is often the last decision he is allowed to make.

When a man says he hasn't made up his mind, he means he hasn't had a chance to ask his wife.

A woman's shopping trip consists of three parts: indecision, decision, change of decision.

It's a good idea to see if you're on firm ground before you put your foot down.

The usual decision a committee makes is to postpone making one.

Never trust a woman's final decision: it seldom agrees with the one that follows it.

There's nothing easier than making up your mind about some things, especially what you would do in the other fellow's place.

DECORATION

If interior decorators have such good taste, why hasn't one tried to furnish a place to look like a home?

You never know what you can do over till you try.

Nowadays when a woman furnishes her home in Early American style, it probably means she has paid for it in cash.

An interior decorator never hesitates to do things to your house he wouldn't dream of doing to his own.

DEDUCTION

One can infer what a man's wife is like from his opinions about women in general.
— *John Stuart Mill*

The income tax return allows many deductions, the most general one being that taxes are too high.

The principle behind the withholding tax is to permit the government to take more and more deductions from your pay until they catch up with it.

The taxpayer who is making out his income tax return always uses deductive reasoning.

In one respect at least we are better off than the next generation: a man's wages are still bigger than his tax deductions.

DEFEAT

Politics has become so expensive that it takes a lot of money even to be defeated.
— *Will Rogers*

The worst thing about defeat is the sympathy that goes with it.

A beaten candidate in politics never knows whether he has a defeat to live down or a moral victory to live up to.

You can't win: if the atom bomb doesn't get you, the income tax will.

Defeat always leaves a candidate puzzled: he doesn't know whether he lied too much or too little.

DEFENSE

The woman who cannot tell a lie in defense of her husband, is unworthy of the name of wife.
— *Elbert Hubbard*

The only defensible war is a war of defense.   — *Chesterton*

I will defend my opinion to the last drop of my ink.   — *Molière*

My father never raised his hand to any one of his children, except in self-defense.   — *Fred Allen*

The best defense is a good offense, and the more offensive the better.

Pity the poor lap dog: he's too small to defend himself from the constant kisses of his mistress.

The first lesson in the art of self-defense is to keep your glasses on.

The weaker the defense, the stronger the language.

There are only two things against which there is no adequate defense: the atom bomb and stupidity.

A pedestrian remains helpless until he gets a car like everyone else to defend himself.

A wife is always ready to defend her husband against anyone except herself.

So live that your friends can conscientiously defend you—but never have to.

DEFICIT

A deficit is the only thing you have left after you pay your taxes.

A deficit is what you have when you haven't as much as when you had nothing.

The government is the only organization that operates on a deficit and still makes money.

DEFINITION

Definitions would be good things if we did not use words to make them.   — *Rousseau*

What an endless amount of talk there would be in the world if people changed the names of things to definitions!
— *G. C. Lichtenberg*

We would all do a lot less talking if we only used words which we could define.

DEGREE

No one has ever passed so few examinations as I have and received so many degrees.
— *Winston Churchill*

I early learned that a Ph.D. thesis consists of transferring bones from one graveyard to another.   — *J. Frank Dobie*

You get an education by degrees, but degrees are not an education.

College girls nowadays go in for all sorts of degrees, but mostly they work for an M.R.S.

Don't worry about our crowded colleges: they'll all empty by degrees.

When something is a matter of degree, even though positive or superlative, it is still comparative.

Nothing disappoints a coed more than spending four years at college without having anything to show for it except a degree.

No college should be so large that its faculty members have more degrees than a thermometer.

At a wedding a man loses his bachelor's degree and a woman wins her master's.

The college that gets richer by degrees knows to whom to give the honorary ones.

Another thing this country needs is a college that gives a degree in common sense.

DELAY

What is time but the stuff delay is made of?   — *Thoreau*

By the street of By-and-By one arrives at the house of Never.

There's nothing easier than not being able to find time to do the things you don't want to do.

DELUSION

If it weren't for his delusions, many a man would go out of his mind.

The only work a goldbricker performs is laboring under the delusion that he is fooling the boss.

DEMAGOGUE

Demagogues are simply persons who promise in loud, ringing voices to solve the insoluble and unscrew the inscrutable.
          — *Mencken*

A demagogue is a person with whom we disagree as to which gang should mismanage the country.   — *Don Marquis*

A demagogue's mind is a beautiful mechanism: it can think anything he asks it to think.
          — *Mencken*

A demagogue is always more patriotic than the President.

A demagogue is a man who pretends to be behind the people in order to become their leader.

With a demagogue, it's government of the people, by the people, for the people, and to hell with the people.

A demagogue is a politician who rocks the boat and then alarms you about the dangerous storm at sea.

A demagogue is a man with strong lungs who always appeals to men with weak heads.

The man who has an important message for the world always wants to send it collect.

A demagogue has no use for the public unless the public is of some use to him.

A demagogue is a public speaker who tries to get a rise out of you when you're sitting down.

A demagogue is a man whose open mouth is always appealing to men with closed minds.

DEMOCRACY

Democracy is ever eager for rapid progress, and the only progress which can be rapid is progress downhill.   — *James Jeans*

Democracy is a word all public men use and none understand.
          — *Bernard Shaw*

The doctrine that the cure for the evils of democracy is more democracy is like saying that the cure of crime is more crime.
          — *Mencken*

Democracy is the hole in the stuffed shirt through which the sawdust slowly trickles.
          — *E. B. White*

If one man offers you democracy and another offers you a bag of grain, at what stage of starvation will you prefer the grain to a vote? — *Bertrand Russell*

Democracy reads well, but it doesn't act well. — *Bernard Shaw*

Democracy is the art and science of running the circus from the monkey cage. — *Mencken*

I have great faith in the people; as for their wisdom—well, Coca-Cola still outsells champagne. — *Adlai Stevenson*

Representative government should be something for us to support rather than something to support us. — *Irvin S. Cobb*

Democracy means not "I'm as good as you are" but "you're as good as I am." — *Theodore Parker*

We adore titles and heredities in our hearts and ridicule them with our mouths; this is our democratic privilege. — *Mark Twain*

Democracy is the theory that the common people know what they want, and deserve to get it good and hard. — *Mencken*

A fanatical belief in democracy makes democratic institutions impossible. — *Bertrand Russell*

If you want to understand democracy, spend less time in the library with Plato, and more time in the buses with people. — *Simeon Strunsky*

A democracy is a government in the hands of men of low birth, no property, and unskilled labor. — *Aristotle*

Democracy is the last refuge of cheap misgovernment. — *Bernard Shaw*

Democracy is only a dream: it should be put in the same category as Arcadia, Santa Claus and Heaven. — *Mencken*

Democracy is a form of government where you can always say what you like, and do what you're told.

Government of the people and for the people never seems to get along with the people.

Democracy is a ship of state whose officers try to steer a straight course in all directions.

The virtue of a free government is that the more freedom you have, the less government you need to have.

Democracy is a form of government whose citizens have complete freedom to choose which candidate they prefer to mess things up for them.

Some people are incorrigible; because we have a democracy they seem to think they are entitled to a voice in it.

Democracy is a slow process of stumbling to the right decision instead of going straight forward to the wrong one.

In a democracy you can speak your mind; the only difficulty is to get someone to listen.

Democracy is a form of political faith that the next bunch of politicians we elect will be an improvement.

Where there's a will there's a way, unless it's the will of the people.

Democracy is a form of government under which everyone has the freedom to elect officials to restrict his freedom.

Politicians would give the people what they wanted if the people knew what they wanted and the politicians were able to give it to them.

Democracy is a form of government in which the people often vote for someone different but seldom get something different.

Under a democratic form of government men are given freedom of speech, with women taking most of it.

The chief defect of a democracy is that only the political party out of office knows how to run the government.

Democracy is a form of government where every taxpayer has complete freedom in electing officials who have complete freedom in taxing him.

Popular government is still only a theory because no one has yet found a government that is popular.

Democracy is a form of government where you can say what you think even if you don't think.

There's nothing like democracy: it gives every man an equal right to feel superior.

Democracy is a process by which the people are free to choose the man who will get the blame.

In a democracy all men are equal, except that the President is more equal than anyone else.

Democracy is the worst form of government, except for all the other forms that have already been tried.

DENIAL

A fool will deny more in a single hour than a hundred philosophers have proved in a hundred years. — *Samuel Johnson*

After a woman reaches fifty, she is usually called upon to deny her weight as well as her age. — *Ed Howe*

Washington is the place where nobody believes a rumor until it has been officially denied.

DENTIST

If there's anything a dentist hates, it's a drooping mustache. — *Kin Hubbard*

You needn't go to war to test your courage—have your teeth fixed. — *Ed Howe*

Man has to go to the dentist to keep his teeth in good condition so that he won't have to go to the dentist. — *Ogden Nash*

It hurts just as much to have a tooth extracted as it does to have one pulled.

DEPARTMENT STORE

There are two kinds of department store customers: those with a charge account, and those of no account.

You can find almost anything in a department store nowadays, except the person who came shopping with you.

If some women had their way, department stores would have a department where they could complain about the complaint department.

DEPARTURE

My two duties with a parting guest are to see that he doesn't forget anything that is his and doesn't take anything that is mine.
— *A. N. Whitehead*

When I go abroad I always sail from Boston because it is such a pleasant place to get away from.
— *Oliver Herford*

She's afraid that if she leaves, she'll become the life of the party.
— *Groucho Marx*

A man never knows how to say good-by, a woman never knows when.   — *Helen Rowland*

Some guests spend most of the evening between the time they get up to say good-by and the time they leave.

The guest who does not part with kisses, should part with haste.

When in doubt, go home.

Don't talk about yourself: it will be done when you leave.

When women say good-by, it's usually much adieu about nothing.

The conversation of a bore is never interesting until he reaches the point—the point of departure.

No man goes before his time— unless the boss leaves early.

There's a great deal of difference between *go* and *let's go*.

The most unwelcome guest is the visitor who takes everything but leave.

Everyone knows how to say good-by, but not everyone knows when.

A man is judged by the company he keeps; a woman is judged by the company she has just left.

If a thing goes without saying, let it.

The hardest thing for some people to say in 25 words or less is *good-by*.

The only thing you enjoy about some people is their departure.

It's nice to see relatives get along, and the sooner some of them get along the better.

DEPENDENCE

A married man forms habits and becomes dependent on mar-

riage just as a sailor becomes dependent on the sea.
— *Bernard Shaw*

The man who is used to having things done for him, should go out and marry a widow with five children.

The disadvantage of being a man others can depend on, is that others too often do.

You can always depend on a friend—to give you a useless remedy for your cold.

Every one of us has at least one friend whom he can depend on—he's always around when he needs us.

What the world needs is a Declaration of Interdependence.

There's no justice: a citizen is allowed a tax deduction for every dependent except the most expensive one—the government.

Never depend on the other fellow—he may be depending on you.

DESCRIPTION

Description is always a bore, both to the describer and the describee.
— *Disraeli*

There are three things you cannot describe without using your hands: a spiral stairway, an accordion, and a woman's figure.

Then there was the angler who caught a fish so big, he dislocated both shoulders describing it.

A windbag is a man who can blow up a one-minute experience into a two-hour description.

There has never yet been a fisherman who could keep both hands in his pockets while describing the fish that got away.

When an author writes that a scene is indescribable, he usually spends pages describing it.

When a stranger identifies you from a friend's description, it's best that you don't hear the description.

DESERT

A desert is a dry, barren region where there is nothing to be heard but silence.

The man who can't save for a rainy day should move to the desert.

DESERVE

Most of us get what we deserve, but only those who are successful will admit it.

A woman thinks she doesn't get all the good things she deserves; her neighbors thinks she doesn't deserve all the good things she gets.

A confidence man often gets what he goes after, but seldom gets what's coming to him.

The woman who talks all day deserves a husband who snores all night.

People who complain they don't get all they deserve, don't realize how lucky they are.

DESIRE

The man's desire is for the woman; the woman's desire is for the desire of the man. — *Coleridge*

The stoical scheme of supplying our wants by lopping off our desires is like cutting off our feet when we want shoes.   — *Swift*

A girl's kisses leaves something to be desired—the rest of her.

When you see something desirable, you want it; that's why laws are made.

DESPERATION

When you get to the end of your rope, tie a knot and hang on.

It's better to keep your feet on the ground than your head in the clouds, especially when you're at the end of your rope.

DESSERT

The best part of dinner is the dessert, and it usually arrives when you can't eat any more.

The worst thing about a reducing diet is that you have to desert desserts.

DESTINATION

No man goes further than the man who doesn't know where he is going.   — *Oliver Cromwell*

To get anywhere, strike out for somewhere or you'll get nowhere.

People who wonder where the younger generation is headed should keep in mind where it came from.

Where does a man go when he wants to get away from himself?

Marriage is like politics: you go partly where you want to go, and partly where you're taken.

If the younger generation doesn't know where it is going, it must be following in its father's footsteps.

You may not know where the younger generation is headed, but you can be sure they'll get there in a car.

A man always has someone wondering where he's going: first his mother, then his wife, and finally his mourners.

It takes less time nowadays to reach your destination, but more money.

DETECTIVE

When a woman hires a detective to follow her husband, it's probably to learn what that other woman sees in him.

When a detective can't find the criminal, he is always sure to boast about the clues.

A sucker can usually locate a swindler even when the most skilled detectives are baffled.

DETOUR

All roads lead to Rome, and all detours lead to profanity.

Another thing a detour shows is that the shortest distance between two points is always being repaired.

The only profitable detour is the one around duty.

Driving has its traffic problems, but also its compensations: when the main highways are closed, the detours are always open.

The way to a man's heart may be through his stomach, but a pretty girl can always find a detour.

The test of a well-adjusted motorist is his ability to enjoy the scenery while on a detour.

Another thing that makes the world go round is a detour sign.

DEVIL

"You forget," said the devil with a chuckle, "that I have been evolving too."   —W. R. Inge

In giving the devil his due, you are liable to give yourself away.
                              —Ed Howe

Satan fell by the force of gravity: he took himself too seriously.
                              —Chesterton

In all systems of theology the devil figures as a male person.
                              —Don Marquis

There never was a devil who didn't advise people to keep out of hell.   —Ed Howe

When a man says, "Get thee behind me, Satan," he's probably ashamed to have even the devil see what he's up to.

We have done away with the devil these days because man can now be trusted to carry on the work himself.

When a man is between the devil and the deep blue sea, his fear of drowning generally triumphs.

Some people sell themselves to the devil; others rent themselves out by the day.

The devil always takes the hindmost—among men of little faith.

Satan never takes a vacation, probably because he's accustomed to the heat.

Get thee behind me, Satan, and push me along.

DIAGNOSIS

One finger in the throat and one finger in the rectum makes a good diagnostician.   —William Osler

Now and then even a good medical man mistakes a case of pneumonia for a broken leg.
                              —Mencken

One of the most common of all diseases is diagnosis.
                              —Karl Kraus

The doctor asks the patient what's wrong, and then the patient asks the doctor.

A diamond is the hardest substance known to man, especially if he's trying to get it back.

DIAMOND

Let us not be too particular: it is better to have old secondhand diamonds than none at all.
— *Mark Twain*

Money isn't everything—there's also diamonds.

The diamond is the hardest stone—to get.

When a girl is engaged, she is immediately put in solitaire confinement.

When your troubles seem endless, remember that a diamond is only a piece of coal that has been hard-pressed for a long time.

A diamond is the hardest substance known to man: it cannot only cut glass, but will even make an impression on a woman's heart.

A diamond will cut into anything, especially into a man's savings.

A girl never cares who casts the first stone at her as long as it's a diamond.

Too many girls believe that the chief foundation for true love is a large stone.

Diamonds are produced by great pressure—usually on the men who buy them.

DIARY

The life of every man is a diary in which he means to write one story but writes another.
— *James M. Barrie*

It's the good girls who keep diaries; the bad girls never have the time.   — *Tallulah Bankhead*

I never travel without my diary; one should always have something sensational to read in the train.
— *Oscar Wilde*

She is so sure of getting her own way, she could even write her diary in advance.

Hell hath no fury like the diary of a woman scorned.

The evolution of a new diary: double entry, single entry, blank.

Wars take longer nowadays because generals spend most of their time keeping diaries for future books.

Some people are such liars, they cannot even tell the truth in a diary.

DICTATION

After World War I millions of women cried "We will not be dictated to," and proceeded to become stenographers.
— *Chesterton*

When some executives dictate, their secretaries have to take a lot for grunted.

Another optimist is the man who marries his secretary and thinks he will continue to dictate to her.

DICTATOR

Every despot must have one disloyal subject to keep him sane.
— *Bernard Shaw*

All dictators are alike: they have control of everything—except their feelings.

Under dictatorship, the people in prison are always superior to the people who put them there.

The country that has only one man who can save it, is not worth saving.

In a democracy, you believe it or not; in a dictatorship, you believe it or else.

Under a dictatorship the people have to follow their leader when they should be chasing him instead.

A dictator's chief problem is keeping the stomachs of his subjects full while keeping their heads empty.

In a dictatorship, suppression is nine points of the law.

Dictators believe in only one liberty—the liberty to do away with all the other liberties.

Under dictatorship, free speech merely means the right to talk your head off.

DICTIONARY

There's no sense in reading a dictionary; if you've read one, you've read them all.

The dictionary is the only place where success comes before work.

In a domestic quarrel, words can wound, especially when your wife throws a dictionary at you.

The last words of Noah Webster probably were: zyme, zymosis and zymurgy.

Literature and vocabulary don't go together, otherwise the dictionary would be a literary masterpiece.

The man who doesn't know the meaning of the word *fail*, should buy a dictionary.

DIET

Dieting is a trying time when you stop eating food and start eating calories.

Women diet to retain their girlish figures or their boyish husbands.

Another thing many people get fed up with is a reducing diet.

Dieting is the period when you can eat as much as you like, but only of the foods you don't like.

Reducing diets show to what great lengths women will go so as not to go to great widths.

A diet is another thing a woman vows to stick to through thick and thin.

Nowadays dieting is more widespread than the women who follow it.

The only thing that's broken faster than a New Year's resolution is a reducing diet.

The best thing for a person on a diet to eat is—less.

In matters of dieting, a word to the wide is seldom sufficient.

Eat, drink and be merry for tomorrow ye diet.

There's nothing that will take the starch out of a person like a reducing diet.

A second week of a diet isn't too bad because by that time you're probably off it.

A reducing diet proves that the more you will, the less you weigh.

A diet is a selection of foods that makes other people lose weight.

More diets start in dress shops than in doctors' offices.

Dieting is sometimes a matter of health, but more often just a matter of form.

A reducing diet is a strange thing: the more you put it off, the more you put on.

Dieting is the period when the hours get longer and the portions get shorter.

You follow a reducing diet for days, but talk about it for months.

The trouble with dieting is that a pound of will power takes off only an ounce of weight.

The diet that reduces the stomach, usually swells the head.

You must keep your diet up if you want to keep your weight down.

There are two kinds of dieters: those who are always telling you what to eat, and those who are always telling you what not to eat.

What's the use of going on a diet on which you starve to death just to live longer?

Another effective diet consists of only four words: "No more, thank you."

Women on a diet lose weight not by talking about it, but by keeping their mouths shut.

Some women go on a diet, but most are merely wishful shrinkers.

Dieting is a losing proposition: you lose weight with difficulty but lose your temper with ease.

If you must diet, you are better off when you are on it.

The worst thing about a reducing diet is not watching your food, but watching everyone else's.

The only thing harder than sticking to a diet is keeping quiet about it.

If at first you don't recede, diet and diet again.

DIFFERENCE

All young men greatly exaggerate the difference between one young woman and another.
— *Bernard Shaw*

There is as much difference between us and ourselves as between us and others.   — *Montaigne*

We drink when we're not thirsty, and we make love all the time —that's all the difference there is between us and other animals.
— *Beaumarchais*

It makes all the difference whether you hear an insect in the bedroom or in the garden.
— *Robert Lynd*

What a lot of difference marriage makes—and what a lot of differences.

There's only about eighteen inches difference between a pat on the back and a kick in the pants.

Marriage is an institution that turns a lover who is different into a husband who is indifferent.

There is sometimes a great difference between a young man looking for a job and one looking for work.

The difference between us and other people is that their money looks bigger and their troubles smaller.

Anyone can tell right from wrong, but telling opportunity from temptation is much tougher.

The difference between a cow and a baby is that a cow drinks water to make milk while a baby drinks milk.

There's a big difference between having a good time and having time to be good.

Another difference between man and animals is that the animals are content with the horrors provided by nature.

The difference between gossip and news depends on whether you are telling it or hearing it.

The difference between an itch and an allergy is at least $25.

The difference between two men is usually a woman.

Wealth is the accumulated difference between our income and our outgo—and so is debt.

Another difference between husband and wife is when he says it's overdrawn, and she says it's underdeposited.

Another difference between death and taxes is that death is frequently painless.

It never occurs to some people that there's a big difference between giving advice and lending a hand.

Matrimony always creates differences: you settle down after you get married whereas you settle up before you get divorced.

The only difference between a rut and a grave is their dimensions.

DIFFERENT

There's nothing new under the sun, but always something different.

No two children are alike, especially if one is yours and the other isn't.

Like every other woman in the world, every woman thinks she's different from every other woman in the world.

If you want to be different nowadays, just act normal.

No two people are alike, and both are usually glad they aren't.

DIFFICULTY

There are two things you will never understand: one is a psychiatrist's statement, and the other is a railroad timetable.
— *Will Rogers*

There are two ways of meeting difficulties: you alter the difficulties, or you alter yourself meeting them.   — *Phyllis Bottome*

The difficulty with marriage is that we fall in love with a personality, but we must live with a character.   — *Peter De Vries*

Some men make difficulties, and difficulties make some men.

Life is a journey where you are always getting out of one difficulty to find yourself in another.

You can't take the boy out of some men—all through life they keep getting into jams.

We live in trying times: we must deliver the goods, yet not be caught with them.

The hardest way out of a difficulty is to look for an easy way out.

A woman's middle years are tough: that's the time when her children and her husband are at a difficult age.

DIGESTION

About the time you're successful enough to take two hours for lunch, the doctor limits you to a glass of milk.

The proof of the pudding is not in the eating, but in the digesting.

Some people are too busy worrying about their stomachs to give their food a chance to digest.

The poor man who cannot afford filet mignon is no worse off than the rich man who cannot digest it.

DIGNITY

She balanced her dignity on the tip of her nose. — *Heywood Broun*

When a person stands on his dignity, it's probably because he has a very insecure footing.

Dignity may command a lot of respect, but it can never make up for the fun it misses.

The most wonderful balancing act in America is Congress standing on its dignity.

There is nothing more dignified than a corpse.

One of the worst ways of trying to raise yourself above others is to stand on your dignity.

If you want to know how little your dignity is worth, take it to the pawnbroker.

The first thing in the human personality that dissolves in alcohol is dignity.

You may be a fine, upstanding, respectable citizen, but a slippery pavement doesn't care.

DIME

The nickel and the penny aren't of much value nowadays, but the dime makes a good screwdriver.

What this country needs is a good five-cent dime.

You can no longer make anyone feel like two cents—the minimum has gone up to a dime.

Nowadays the value of a dime is even smaller than its size.

The only money that goes as far today as it did a generation ago is the dime that rolls under the bed.

DINNER

At a dinner party we should eat wisely but not too well, and talk well but not too wisely.
— *Somerset Maugham*

It would be better if more people worked for their dinners, and fewer people dressed for them.
— *Will Rogers*

The husband who goes home and finds fault with dinner should take his wife out to a restaurant so she also can find fault.

Many a dinner conversation is a rehash of what's gone on before, and so is the dinner.

Never start an argument at a dinner table; the person who isn't hungry is sure to win.

At dinnertime, parents sit down to eat while their children sit down to continue eating.

A buffet dinner is one where the guests outnumber the chairs.

Educated women make the best wives: they may not be good cooks but they find more ways to explain why dinner isn't ready.

Behind every successful man is a woman—who keeps asking him when he'll come home for dinner.

In the old days dinnertime fitted in with father's return from work, and not with the children's television program.

DIPLOMA

A college diploma is often the receipt a young man gets for bills his father paid.

The best way to keep the wolf from the door is by means of a sheepskin.

DIPLOMACY

To say nothing, especially when speaking, is half the art of diplomacy. — *Will Durant*

The principle of give and take is the principle of diplomacy—give one and take ten.
— *Mark Twain*

A real diplomat is one who can cut his neighbor's throat without having his neighbor notice it.
— *Trygve Lie*

A diplomat is a fellow that lets you do all the talking while he gets what he wants.
— *Kin Hubbard*

In order to be a diplomat, one must speak a number of languages, including doubletalk.
— *Carey Williams*

"Frank and explicit" is the right line to take when you wish to conceal your own mind and confuse the minds of others.
— *Disraeli*

Diplomacy: the patriotic art of lying for one's country. — *Bierce*

A diplomatic language has a hundred ways of saying nothing but no way of saying something.
— *Will Rogers*

Diplomats are only useful in fair weather; when it rains, they drown in every raindrop.
— *De Gaulle*

Diplomacy is the art of diving into trouble without making a splash.

Ambassadors are appointed to turn our affairs of state into a state of affairs.

Diplomacy is the art of guided missives backed up by guided missiles.

Diplomacy is the art of keeping your shirt on while you are getting something off your chest.

Diplomacy is the art of being crafty, or the craft of being artful.

A diplomat is a man who uses his head without anyone suspecting it.

A diplomat is a man who tries never to stand between a dog and a lamppost.

Diplomacy is the fine art of telling half truths, or the finer art of telling half lies.

Another diplomat is the man who praises married life but remains single.

Diplomacy is the conduct of foreign affairs by men who indulge more in good feeding than in good feeling.

A diplomat always knows what to talk about, but doesn't always talk about what he knows.

Diplomacy is the art of taking both sides of a question—or neither.

A diplomat is a man who can hold his tongue in several languages.

Diplomacy is the art of saying "Nice doggie," until you can find a rock.

A good diplomat is one who can always make himself misunderstood.

Diplomacy is the art of handling a porcupine without disturbing the quills.

A diplomat is one who can put his foot down without stepping on someone else's toes.

The three chief requisites in the life of a diplomat are: self-control, protocol and alcohol.

A diplomat always has to watch his appease and accuse.

Secret diplomacy will never be ended until women are admitted to the diplomatic corps.

A diplomat is anyone who thinks twice before saying nothing.

DIRECTION

If you cry "Forward!" to a monk and a revolutionist, they will go in exactly opposite directions. — *Chekhov*

A man loses his sense of direction after four drinks; a woman loses hers after four kisses. — *Mencken*

The penguin flies backwards because he doesn't care to see where he's going; he wants to see where he's been. — *Fred Allen*

Some women drivers have such a poor sense of direction that they go the wrong way even on a two-way street.

Some men are like directional signs: they are always pointing in the right direction, but never go that way themselves.

Fear sometimes carries a man farther than courage, but not in the same direction.

A sense of direction is a great help in driving, except at a cloverleaf intersection.

It isn't enough to make sure you're on the right track; you must also make sure you're not going in the wrong direction.

When a woman says she is approaching middle age, she never tells you from which direction.

Even the best sense of direction can't keep a man from getting lost on an income tax form.

The time it takes to get between the top and the bottom depends on which way you are going.

When success turns a man's head, it always leaves him facing in the wrong direction.

When it comes to the parting of the ways, a diplomat goes both ways.

Paying as you go is all right, but first make sure you're going in the right direction.

DIRTY

What this country needs is a spot remover to remove the spots left by spot removers.

To the housewife on a rainy day, all men have feet of clay.

Some men may not leave footprints on the sands of time, but they certainly leave them everywhere else.

Many a mother worships the ground her son walks on—until he tracks it into the house.

DISADVANTAGE

Many a man works hard and saves money so that his sons won't have the disadvantages that made a man of their father.

You never realize that education has its disadvantages until you come across some nuisance who insists upon reading aloud.

The worst drawbacks of television are the poor reception of good programs, and the good reception of poor ones.

Science has put woman at a disadvantage: man can now travel faster than sound.

Another disadvantage of being a bachelor is that when things go wrong, he has only himself to blame.

A job is like marriage: after a while you stop noticing anything but its disadvantages.

DISAGREEMENT

Some women agree with their husbands in name only.

Domestic differences are reduced by having two television sets, two cars and two bathrooms, and by not having two opinions.

The art of conversation lies in the ability to disagree without being disagreeable.

Marital quarrels are always due to the same thing: the woman is right and her husband doesn't agree with her.

The man with whom nobody disagrees is probably very well informed—or else he's the boss.

What happens when an unimpeachable source disagrees with an unquestioned authority?

It takes two to make a marriage, or any other form of disagreement.

Always be tolerant with the person who disagrees with you; after all, he has a right to his stupid opinion.

DISAPPOINT

The biggest disappointments come to those who get what's coming to them.

It is better to marry a young girl and surprise her than to marry a widow and disappoint her.

Every time the President makes one appointment, he makes a dozen disappointments.

All things come to him who waits, especially disappointments.

The greatest disappointment in a golfer's life is when he does a hole in one without witnesses.

The man who is disappointed in love usually lives to be glad of it.

A woman is never so disappointed as when she asks a man to behave, and he does.

A bachelor is a man who is sometimes disappointed in love, but never in marriage.

DISARMAMENT

The notion that disarmament can put a stop to war is contradicted by the nearest dogfight.
— Bernard Shaw

If the arms race doesn't stop, the human race will.

A diplomat knows how to be disarming, especially when his country isn't.

To settle its differences the world ought to try heads or hearts instead of arms.

No disarmament plan is valid unless the signatories have the weapons to enforce it.

The first move toward obtaining permanent peace is to disarm —suspicion.

Complete world peace will never be attained so long as countries keep fighting over disarmament.

Disarmament is like a party: no one wants to arrive until everyone else is there.

DISBELIEF

A thing that nobody believes cannot be proved too often.
— Bernard Shaw

Never believe all you hear, unless you are stone deaf.

Seeing is not always believing; no matter how often you see some people, you seldom believe them.

There's only one thing worse than asking a woman her age, and that is to look incredulous when she tells it.

Even if a man could understand women, he still wouldn't believe it.

DISCIPLE

I am impelled for the first time to breathe a fervent prayer: Save me from my disciples.
— Oscar Wilde

Adherent: a follower who has yet not gotten all he expects.
— Bierce

There's no one like a disciple to expose our faults.
— Jules Renard

DISCIPLINE

The trouble with most children nowadays is that they get everything, except discipline.

When a father doesn't have the upper hand with his children, it is usually because he has failed to lower his.

It's a wise father that *no's* his own child.

A disciplinarian believes in clubs for teenagers, especially when other forms of punishment fail.

In bringing up children, it's better to raise your hand than your voice.

A disciplinarian can train his child to do almost anything, except to run into his arms when he comes home.

The parent who does not punish cannot persuade.

Discipline can accomplish wonders: many a wayward child is straightened out by being bent over.

A disciplinarian is a parent who has the courage of his restrictions.

There's nothing like parental discipline to bring up children, especially stern punishment.

DISCOVERY

The discovery of a new dish gives greater pleasure than the discovery of a new star.
— *Brillat-Savarin*

What is wanted is not the will to believe but the wish to find out, which is its exact opposite.
— *Bertrand Russell*

One of the advantages of being disorderly is that one is constantly making exciting discoveries.
— *A. A. Milne*

Things don't turn up, they must be turned up.

Some men get discovered, while others just get found out.

The good man who goes wrong is usually the bad man who has just been found out.

A wife is a creature who can look in the drawer of a dresser and find a man's handkerchief that isn't there.

It isn't what teenagers know that worries parents; it's how they found it out.

DISCRETION

Once a husband demanded virtue in a wife; now all he expects is discretion.

Your friend has a friend, and your friend's friend has a friend: be discreet.

Discretion is the better part of indiscretion.

The trouble with discretion is that it usually comes too late to do any good.

Discretion is when you are sure you are right, but still ask your wife.

A man never knows much until he is old, and then he is too discreet to tell it.

The age of discretion is reached when you have learned to close your eyes to a situation before someone else closes them for you.

It is easy for a man to be indiscreet in his talk, but only up to a pint.

DISCUSSION

I'll discuss anything—I like to go perhaps-ing around on all subjects.   — *Robert Frost*

Jaw-jaw is better than war-war.
— *Winston Churchill*

It is difficult to be emphatic when no one is emphatic on the other side.
— *Charles Dudley Warner*

Why is it that in political discussions your opponent never seems to realize that you have the better of the argument?

Many people are too busy discussing the new books to find time to read them.

Great minds discuss ideas, good minds discuss events, small minds discuss people.

Some women never talk about other women; they are too busy talking about themselves.

Usually, when your wife has something she wants to talk to you about, it's about something she doesn't have.

Of two evils, choose the one most likely to be talked about.

You can always tell whom a group of women are discussing if you know who left the room last.

When everybody talks about a man, it's a eulogy; when everybody talks about a woman, it's an elegy.

Some people have to talk about what they are going to do or they would have nothing to talk about.

Never exchange ideas with a fool because you're sure to get the worst of the bargain.

A wrangler always contributes more heat than light to a discussion.

DISEASE

The worst thing about being sick is having a disease you can't afford.

A hypochondriac never gets cured of any disease until he acquires another.

Love passes, but syphilis remains.

DISGUISE

When some men want to go somewhere incognito, they go sober.

During the hunting season, hunters would be safer if they disguised themselves as deer.

The reason opportunity is seldom recognized is that it usually comes disguised as hard work.

If poverty is a blessing in disguise, the disguise is perfect.

DISHONESTY

There's one way to find out if a man is honest: ask him; if he says yes, you know he is crooked.
— *Groucho Marx*

If all mankind were suddenly to practice honesty, many thousands of people would be sure to starve.   — *G. C. Lichtenberg*

Honesty pays, but it don't seem to pay enough to suit some people.
— *Kin Hubbard*

The penalty for dishonesty is the disgrace of dying rich.

Honesty is the best policy, but there are too few policy holders.

Some men never do anything crooked until they find themselves in straightened circumstances.

Half the world doesn't understand how the other half gets away with it.

Some are born good, some make good, and some are caught with the goods.

The only time some men are on the level is when they are sleeping.

The path of least resistance is what makes rivers crooked—and men.

DISHWASHING

No woman cares to live her life over again because that would mean millions of dishes to wash.

Another way to keep your teenage daughter out of hot water is to put dirty dishes in it.

The man who is tired out after his day's work at the office, should insist that his wife buy him a dishwasher.

The honeymoon is over when he stops helping her with the dishes, and starts doing them himself.

Breathes there a man with soul so dead who doesn't at least remove the apron before answering the doorbell?

Afterdinner speeches deal with many topics, the most controversial one being who will do the dishes.

There's nothing like a dish towel for wiping that contented look off a husband's face.

The man who is boss in his own home is not afraid to ask his wife to help him with the dishes.

You never hear of a man's being shot by his wife while doing the dishes.

Another way to avoid dishwashing is to have your husband eating out of your hand.

Many homes have dishwashers because most husbands would rather buy one than be one.

A teenager can always make her father happy by helping him with the dishes.

The best way to put the boss in a good humor is to do the dishes for her.

Many a man thinks he can dry his wife's tears with a dishcloth.

Love begins when she sinks into his arms, and ends with her arms in the sink.

The most convincing afterdinner speaker is the one who can talk his guests into helping with the dishes.

The hand that rocks the cradle is usually too busy washing dishes to bother about ruling the world.

Many a man who thinks he is marrying a cook soon finds that his wife has married a dishwasher.

The most popular afterdinner speech that any man can make is, "I'll wash the dishes."

If you save all the office gossip until after dinner you can get your wife to help you with the dishes.

DISILLUSION

There are two kinds of disillusioned women: those who have loved and lost, and those who have loved and married.

Disillusion is the scratch of the pin after you have pinned your faith on the wrong person.

The saddest disillusion of all is to go back and find your homesickness wasn't worthwhile.

The cynic who is disillusioned with life is probably disillusioned with married life.

Disillusion is commonly found in only three classes of people: unmarried women, unmarried men, and married couples.

There's no one so disillusioned as the girl who married because she was tired of working.

DISLIKE

If anyone dislikes you, you can overcome his dislike by asking him for any kind of information.
            — Ed Howe

I'm a controversial figure: my friends either dislike me or hate me.   — Oscar Levant

The reason women dislike one another is men.   — La Bruyère

There are three intolerable things in life—cold coffee, lukewarm champagne, and overexcited women.   — Orson Welles

If there's anything a grouch dislikes, it's one thing more than another.

There are some people you dislike when you first meet them, but when you get to know them, you loathe them.

Sometimes it is hard to tell whether a woman is nice to you because she doesn't like you, or mean to you because she does.

If you don't like what you're doing, the chances are no one else does.

The woman who never likes the looks of things, should have her eyes examined.

More often it's ill will that blows nobody any good.

Men dislike women who don't understand them, and women dislike men who do.

A neighbor is a person you don't know well enough to dislike, or a person you know too well to like.

A woman will try on dozens of hats before she finally chooses one her husband will dislike.

The man who repulses the sick, the poor and the unfortunate eventually becomes repulsive himself.

The man who never does anything he doesn't like, rarely likes anything he does.

DISMISS

Another man who is apt to be fired is the minor employee who acts like a big shot.

The man who talks by the yard and thinks by the inch should be removed by the foot.

The surest method of fire prevention is to marry the boss's daughter.

The employee who is fired with enthusiasm is seldom fired.

There's no accounting for love: many a girl cannnot put a man out of her mind even after he has put her out of his life.

DISOBEDIENCE

The man who doesn't expect his wife to obey him has probably been married before.

It's a wise father who knows his own child—will do everything he is told not to do.

You can always tell an eight-year-old, but you have to tell him more than once.

DISPLAY

He who displays too often his wife and his wallet is in danger of having both of them borrowed.
— *Franklin*

Knowledge is power, but the unnecessary display of it is weakness.

As she shows, so shall we peep.

This generation is no worse than the previous ones; it simply doesn't hide behind closed doors.

A woman's clothes should be so designed that she can be seen in the best of places.

If starlets covered up their figures, how could they display their emotions?

A woman is never happy unless she has a lot of clothes to leave off.

DISPOSITION

I always astonish strangers by my amiability because no human being could possibly be so disagreeable as they expect me to be.
— Bernard Shaw

I will not say that women have no character—they have a different one every day. — Heine

Another thing to save for a rainy day is a sweet disposition.

When a man gives up smoking, he always sustitutes something for the cigarettes—usually an irritable disposition.

Don't envy the husband whose wife has an even disposition—she may be always mad.

In the battle between a good disposition and a bad cold, the good is usually worsted.

Contentment sometimes depends on a person's position, but more often on his disposition.

Menial work brings out the disposition of people: some turn up their sleeves, some turn up their noses, while most don't turn up at all.

DISPROVE

Silence is one of the hardest things to refute. — Josh Billings

The man who listens to reason is usually thinking of some way to refute it.

DISSATISFACTION

A man who is not satisfied with a little, will be satisfied with nothing. — Epicurus

Many a man wonders why others find it so hard to please him since he is so easily pleased —with himself.

A human being is never satisfied: as a child he wants the moon, and as an adult he wants the earth.

Some men are always dissatisfied, especially when they get what they deserve.

We always hope for the best, and when we get it, want something better.

The poor are always dissatisfied because they can't get more money, and the rich because they can't keep more.

Most of us won't be contented with our lot until it's a lot more.

DISSIPATION

Young men who spend half their money on drink and horse racing ought to marry; they might as well be wasting it on their wives. — Finley Peter Dunne

Dark circles under the eyes are not made with a compass.
— Don Herold

A lot of people spend six days sowing wild oats, then go to church on Sunday and pray for a crop failure. — Fred Allen

Let us have wine and women, mirth and laughter—sermons and soda water the day after.
— *Lord Byron*

Burning the candle at both ends is the worst way of making both ends meet.

When his doctor orders a playboy to cut out wine, women and song, the first thing he cuts out is singing.

The future is never made any brighter by burning the candle at both ends.

The man who is old before his time must have had some time before he was old.

Dissipation adds life to your years while it subtracts years from your life.

When a man lives it up at night, he usually has to live it down in the morning.

Burning the candle at both ends makes it twice as hard to keep your wife in the dark.

Late to bed and early to rise will give you dark rings under the eyes.

Many a man looks as old as he does because he acts as young as he does.

DISTANCE

Going to the moon isn't very far; the greatest distance we have to cover still lies within us.
— *De Gaulle*

A girl is judged by the company she keeps—at a distance.

Cultivate reserve and keep your distance—especially from creditors.

Some distant relatives wouldn't be so annoying if they kept their distance.

Another poor judge of distance is the man who parks behind you.

The man who is going to the dogs usually overestimates the distance.

You cannot always tell from the speedometer how far a couple in a car have gone.

Many a man who travels by jet figures the distance of a flight not by the number of miles but by the number of martinis.

Modern transportation has made it more and more difficult to have distant relatives.

The man who is willing to meet you halfway, is probably a poor judge of distance.

Distance lends enchantment, but not when you run out of gas.

A girl's problem is how to keep her boyfriend at arms' length without letting him get any farther away.

A miss is as good as a mile, but some of them are better at two miles.

Another poor judge of distance is the family man who thinks he'll be able to make both ends meet.

Distance is a relative matter, until they find out that you've become rich.

The distance a person has to go to borrow trouble is getting shorter all the time.

The girl who looks better at a distance, never gets far enough away.

Some people are always looking for short cuts, even where the road is straight.

DISTRIBUTION

There are several ways in which to apportion the family income, all of them unsatisfactory.
— *Robert Benchley*

What a Communist he is—he would have an equal distribution of sin as well as property!
— *Oscar Wilde*

There are three things in life where an equal distribution will never be achieved: wealth, rain, and parking space.

Everybody favors an equal distribution of wealth, provided he gets more than he is getting now.

There is only one thing more widely distributed than experience, and that is ignorance.

A racehorse is a creature designed by God to redistribute wealth among mankind.

The three greatest means of redistributing wealth are taxes, wives and children.

DISTRUST

Never trust a man who speaks well of everybody.
— *John Churton Collins*

Men think women cannot be trusted too far; women think men cannot be trusted too near.

There are some people you shouldn't trust any farther than you can throw a bull by the tail.

Always distrust the neighbor who warns you against other neighbors.

There are only two occasions when a girl cannot trust a philanderer: one, when she's not with him; and two, when she is.

The woman who really should see an analyst, seldom does: she distrusts any man who keeps a couch in his office.

Never trust two kinds of persons: the superior who always finds fault with his inferior, and the inferior who never finds fault with his superior.

A vote of confidence is the first sign of distrust.

If a young man doesn't bring his girl home to Mother, it may be that he can't trust Dad.

DIVIDEND

If ignorance paid dividends, everyone would make a fortune in the stock market.

A man is known by the company he keeps—getting dividends from.

In the stock market a dividend is a certain per cent, per annum, perhaps.

An ulcer is the extra dividend you get while driving on the road to success.

When a man asks for five minutes of your time, he expects an extra ten minutes as a dividend.

DIVISION

Divorce changes a situation from united we stand to divided we can stand it better.

United we stand, divided we furnish headlines for the Communist press.

DIVORCE

Of course there is such a thing as love, or there wouldn't be so many divorces.   — Ed Howe

Many a woman would get a divorce if she could do it without making her husband happy.

The best thing about divorce is that it puts marriageable men back in circulation.

Divorces are sometimes caused by husbands having dinner with their secretaries, but more often by having breakfast with their wives.

The more you read the divorce news, the harder it is to tell who's whose in America.

Divorce is the only institution that has done more to promote peace in the world than the United Nations.

Sometimes it's that husband of hers that makes a woman want a divorce; but more often it's that husband that isn't hers.

Divorce suits are so called because nothing but a divorce seems to suit.

If men get the women they want, and women get the men they deserve, how do you explain the high rate of divorce?

Divorce is the price people pay for playing with matches.

Many a divorce suit is of the two-pants variety.

The difference between a co-respondent and a correspondent is just one letter.

Some women have so many divorces, they ought to have charge accounts at the courts.

The cause of many divorces is a miss understanding.

The present divorce rate is so high, bride and groom must have solemnly promised: Until debt do us part.

Divorce is a shipwreck on the sea of matrimony, always blamed on the mate.

Divorce is a marital dissolution that follows a mutual disillusion.

A divorce suit would not appeal so much to the newspapers if it were cleaned before being pressed.

Divorce is both a release and a relief, especially when a woman leaves a man's bed and boredom.

A divorcee first complains about her husband because she is unhappy, and then is unhappy because she has no husband to complain about.

Divorce is the key that opens the strongbox where the bonds of matrimony are kept under wedlock.

In some divorces the wife wants the custody of the children; in others, the custody of the money.

What many a man wants most to get out of marriage is to get out.

Two's company and three's a divorce.

Some women get divorces on the grounds of incompatibility; others, on just the first two syllables.

The wife who always has the last word often gets it as the divorcee.

There's only one thing more unreasonable than love at first sight, and that is divorce at first fight.

Divorce is a legal separation when a man stops bringing the money home to his wife and starts mailing it.

A divorce suit is often brought into court because the husband and wife are both trying to wear the pants.

The three chief causes of divorce are men, women, and marriage.

Some couples divorce because of a misunderstanding; others, because they understand each other too well.

DOCTOR

A physician who treats himself has a fool for a patient.
— *William Osler*

Taking a lady's hand gives her confidence in her physician.
— *William Osler*

The doctor is an enemy of God: he battles against death.
— *Camus*

A doctor is a healthy man who can't keep away from sick people.

When a patient is at death's door, it is the duty of his doctor to pull him through.

Nature cures, but the doctor sends the bill.

Another person who always knows what to do until the doctor comes is the doctor's wife.

A physician's fees are ill-gotten gains.

A doctor is the only salesman who always finds his clients in a moment of weakness.

Doctors should let the well enough alone.

The man who gets sick calls a doctor, but the man who becomes ill summons a physician.

For dieting, the best doctor is the one who lets you eat everything—as long as you pay your bill.

When a doctor doesn't know, he calls it a virus; when he does know but can't cure it, he calls it an allergy.

A doctor is a general practitioner who calls in a specialist to share the blame.

DOCTOR AND LAWYER

Some men are in the hands of a doctor or lawyer all the time.
— *Ed Howe*

Fond of doctors, little health; fond of lawyers, little wealth.

DOG

I have always thought of a dog lover as a dog that was in love with another dog. — *James Thurber*

The nose of the bulldog has been slanted backwards so that he can breathe without letting go.
— *Winston Churchill*

Money will buy a pretty good dog, but it won't buy the wag of his tail.   — *Josh Billings*

The dog has seldom pulled man up to his level of sagacity, but man has frequently dragged the dog down to his. — *James Thurber*

You may make a fool of yourself with a dog, and not only will he not scold you, but he will make a fool of himself too.
— *Samuel Butler*

A dog teaches a boy fidelity, perseverance, and to turn around three times before lying down.
— *Robert Benchley*

A mad dog neither drinks nor smokes, but that doesn't therefore make him a safe and pleasant companion.
— *Henry Cabot Lodge*

Every dog has its day, and I have had mine.   — *Bernard Shaw*

The dog has got more fun out of man than man has got out of the dog, for man is the more laughable of the two animals.
— *James Thurber*

If you're very wealthy, you ride to hounds; if you're very poor, you go to the dogs.

Every boy who has a dog should also have a mother, so the dog can be fed regularly.

A watchdog is a dog kept to guard your home, usually by sleeping where a burglar would awaken the household by falling over him.

The noblest of all dogs is the hot dog; it feeds the hand that bites it.

Every dog isn't a growler, and every growler isn't a dog.

A dog's bark may be worse than his bite, but everyone prefers his bark.

Never judge a dog's pedigree by the kind of books he does not chew.

The only two who can live as cheaply as one are a dog and a flea.

A dog can express more with his tail in minutes than his owner can express with his tongue in hours.

The reason a dog has so many friends is that he wags his tail instead of his tongue.

There is only one smartest dog in the world, and every boy has it.

A dog is a man's best friend, and vice versa.

You always sympathize with the underdog, except when the other dog is yours.

Every dog may have his day, but it's the puppies that have weak ends.

The ideal dog food would be a ration that tastes like a postman.

When a dog wags his tail and barks at the same time, how do you know which end to believe?

One reason a dog is such a comfort when you're downcast is that he doesn't ask to know why.

When some men go to the dogs, it's pretty tough on the dogs.

Every man gets mad when a dog bites him, whether the dog is mad or not.

Every boy should have two things: a dog, and a mother willing to let him have one.

It's no coincidence that man's best friend cannot talk.

Play safe: let sleeping dogs lie, and let lying dogs sleep.

A dog's bark may be worse than its bite, but it's never quite so personal.

If a dachshund's head you pat on Sunday, he'll wag his little tail on Monday.

If a dog could talk, he wouldn't long remain man's best friend.

DOGMATISM

Dogma does not mean the absence of thought, but the end of thought.   — *Chesterton*

Every dogma must have its day.

A dogmatic person always has concrete opinions—thoroughly mixed and permanently set.

There's only one thing that's certain in our uncertain world, and that's the dogmatist.

The more opinionated a girl is, the more likely she is to wind up talking to herself.

DOLLAR

Our problem is not what the dollar is worth at home or abroad —it's how to get hold of it, whatever it's worth. — *Will Rogers*

A dollar bill is like a secret: once broken, it is never a dollar again. — *Josh Billings*

A dollar weighs next to nothing, yet it can bend many a conscience.

The size of a dollar depends entirely upon how many more you have.

A greenback is a familiar form of paper money that's built more for speed than endurance.

A dollar saved is a dollar earned, but seldom vice versa.

Looks are deceiving: the dollar bill looks just the same as it did a generation ago.

A dollar is a strange thing: the farther it gets away from you, the bigger it looks.

The world is so full of a number of things, no wonder the almighty dollar has wings.

Size isn't everything: a ten-dollar bill is no bigger than a one.

In the good old days the dollar you didn't have used to buy four times as much.

The youngsters of today know the value of a dollar: that's why they have no respect for it.

The government ought to issue $2 bills: they're so handy for buying a dollar's worth of anything.

Another way you can make a dollar go farther these days is to buy a golf ball with it.

You can't go by mathematics: the dollar you borrow is never as big as the dollar you pay back.

In the past a person used to do much more for a dollar than he does today, and vice versa.

Dollars are not banked by those who are always depositing their quarters on easy chairs.

A dollar doesn't go far these days, except those that end up in outer space.

Isn't it about time to change the saying to a dollar for your thoughts?

DOMINATE

Some men are born to rule; others live with their in-laws.

The woman who has her husband eating out of her hand, must save a lot of dishwashing.

Formerly the test was who wore the pants in the family; nowadays it's who controls the electric blanket.

A woman is happily married when she has a husband who's scared to death of her.

A shower is given for a girl about to get married to symbolize the beginning of a reign.

Many a wife gains the upper hand by using her lower jaw.

A happy marriage must be based on mutual understanding: both must understand that she's the boss.

A man can't call his soul his own: the company tells him what to do, the union what not to do, and the wife what he'd better do.

The man whose wife has a will of her own is usually the sole beneficiary.

Marriage is an institution where he rules the roost, and she rules the rooster.

Give a woman an inch, and she wants to become the ruler.

There are only two types of wives: one has her husband under her thumb, the other has the upper hand.

DOOR

Don't ever slam a door: you might want to go back.
— *Don Herold*

When opportunity knocks, some people wait for it to break the door down and come in.

There's many a damn 'twixt the door and the jamb.

Television is another invention that has opened many doors but most of them are attached to refrigerators.

Some people push open the door of opportunity while others expect it to be opened by an electric eye.

More heads are turned by squeaky doors than by pretty girls.

DOUBT

In all affairs it's a healthy thing now and then to hang a question mark on the things you have long taken for granted.
— *Bertrand Russell*

I respect faith, but doubt is what gets you an education.
— *Wilson Mizner*

Test love as you would an egg: if there's any doubt about it, there's no doubt about it.

When in doubt, mind your own business.

There is no one as positive as a chronic skeptic—he is never in doubt about his doubts.

Nothing is so doubtful as uncertainty—except a dead-sure thing.

When in doubt, give advice.

Many a woman has doubts about her husband's love; she really doesn't think he loves half the other women he says he does.

The best way to keep a man is—in doubt.

When in doubt, be conventional.

DRAMA

One of my dramas enjoyed a continuous run of one successive night. — *Brander Matthews*

Our leading dramatic authors refuse to write a play dealing with an abnormal situation such as a married woman in love with her own husband.   — *Bernard Shaw*

A play should give you something to think about; when I understand a play the first time, I know it can't be much good.
— *T. S. Eliot*

I didn't like the play, but then I saw it under adverse conditions —the curtain was up.
— *Groucho Marx*

The most enjoyable moment in every play is immediately after the curtain goes up and before everybody starts coughing.

In a comedy nobody dies and everybody gets married; in a tragedy everybody dies and nobody gets married.

All plays are problem plays, the problem being to get the play produced.

Give a play a bad name, and there will be standing room only.

There's no such thing as a bad school play.

Many a play that comes to Broadway is a mystery play—the mystery is how it ever got to Broadway.

Some of the modern plays will be classics when Shakespeare is forgotten, but not before.

The center of the stage is where all good actors go when they die.

DREAM

The end of wisdom is to dream high enough not to lose the dream in the seeking of it. — *Faulkner*

Tell me whom you sleep with, and I will tell you whom you dream of.   — *Stanislaw J. Lec*

I had a wonderful dream last night—don't miss it.
— *Groucho Marx*

My life's dream has been a perpetual nightmare.   — *Voltaire*

People who insist on telling their dreams are among the terrors of the breakfast table.
— *Max Beerbohm*

There's only one thing rarer in sleep than to dream we are sleeping, and that is to dream we are dreaming.

It is a comfort to remember that if our dreams haven't come true, neither have our nightmares.

The only time a skeptic believes in dreams is when he's asleep.

A psychoanalyst believes in his own dreams when he's asleep, but in yours when he's awake.

An optimist expects his dreams to come true; a pessimist expects his nightmares to.

Many people who like to be referred to as dreamers are merely sleepers.

DRESS

Being a well-dressed man is a career, and no one who goes in for it has time for anything else.
— *Heywood Broun*

Women dress alike all over the world: they dress to be annoying to other women.
— *Elsa Schiaparelli*

Greek dress was in essence un-artistic; nothing should reveal the body but the body. — *Oscar Wilde*

Most women dress as if they had been a mouse in a previous incarnation, or hope to be one in the next. — *Edith Sitwell*

An apple tree in bloom puts to shame all the men and women that have attempted to dress since the world began.
— *Henry Ward Beecher*

The well-dressed man is he whose clothes you never notice.
— *Somerset Maugham*

Cavaliers and Puritans are interesting for their costumes and not for their convictions.
— *Oscar Wilde*

I'm a Hollywood writer; so I put on a sports jacket and take off my brain. — *Ben Hecht*

Half the world doesn't know why it takes the other half so long to dress.

The dress that makes one girl look slim, often makes others look round.

A man must have an awful lot of money to enable him to dress as well as his wife does.

The best-dressed woman usually arrives last with the least.

Why is it that the dress you don't like, always lasts the longest?

One woman's finery is the dress another woman wouldn't be caught dead in.

A rag is any dress a woman has to wear more than once.

Women don't dress to please men; if they did, they would dress a lot faster.

DRINKING

I've made it a rule never to drink by daylight, and never to refuse a drink after dark.
— *Mencken*

What we want is more drink and less words. — *Artemus Ward*

When I was younger, I made it a rule never to take strong drink before lunch, and now it is my rule never to do so before breakfast. — *Winston Churchill*

A man is a fool if he drinks before he reaches fifty, and a fool if he doesn't drink afterwards. — *Frank Lloyd Wright*

I don't drink: I don't like it— it makes me feel good.
— *Oscar Levant*

I drink exactly as much as I want—and one drink more.
— *Mencken*

Many a man drinks to make him forget the woman who is driving him to drink.

Some men can take a drink or leave it alone—for a few hours.

Beware of drinking: an alcoholic habit is as easy to swear off as it's hard to leave off.

There's only one thing worse than a drinking man, and that's a man who doesn't drink.

Before marriage, a man drinks for pleasure; after marriage, it's from sorrow.

Two can live as cheaply as one can drink.

There are two kinds of problem drinkers: those who never know when to stop, and those who never buy.

Some people drink to success, others to excess.

When a man drinks too much, he becomes tight; when a woman does, she becomes loose.

The girl who goes in for drinking is bound to meet many a Scotch-and-sofa man.

If you drink too much whiskey, you are under the influence; if you drink too much champagne, you are under the affluence.

One swallow doesn't make a summer, but it does break many a New Year's resolution.

Men always make passes at girls who drain glasses.

Some men would live strictly on a liquid diet if it weren't for pretzels and peanuts.

With some men it's love at first drink.

Drinking makes you feel like a new person, but makes you look like an old one.

Some people can handle their liquor, while others go off the handle.

Some men are always drinking —either to cure a cold or prevent one.

Drink often drives a man to misfortune, and misfortune often drives a man to drink.

The girl who marries a drinking man to reform him, will soon have her hands full as well as her husband.

Some men take to drink when their wives walk out on them; others, when their wives walk in on them.

Many a drinker's plans to stay on the wagon go a-rye.

When some men stop drinking, they save their friends a lot of money.

Love makes the world go round, and so does a good stiff drink.

When I don't feel well, I drink, and when I drink, I don't feel well.

Some men drink because it makes them feel bright, while others abstain because it makes them act foolish.

Some men get up with the lark, while others want a swallow the first thing in the morning.

Too much drinking injures a man internally, externally and eternally.

Drinking makes you lose your inhibitions and give exhibitions.

Some men are driven to drink, but most men walk to a bar.

Drinking doesn't drown your sorrows, it merely irrigates them.

In the good old days grandma's nightcap went on her head instead of to it.

Drinking to drown one's misery is putting a fire out with oil.

Some men drink to forget, some drink to be gay, while some drink to make other people interesting.

DRINKING AND DRIVING

Many a man who is drunk prefers to drive because he feels he is in no condition to walk.

People who insist on drinking before driving, are putting the quart before the hearse.

Most of those who are driven to drink, make the trip in the driver's seat.

The one for the road may be two for the cemetery.

There's only one thing worse than being driven to drink, and that's driving yourself home from it.

The motorist who has a few quick ones is bound to have a few close ones.

Some men never drink when they're driving—only when their wives are driving.

There are times when you should sit tight, but never attempt to drive in that condition.

No man should drive a car while intoxicated; it's hard enough to get the pedestrian you're after even when you're sober.

If you must drive after drinking, try driving a nail; the worst thing you'll hit will be your thumb.

DRIVE-IN THEATER

The only safe place to fall asleep at the wheel is in a drive-in theater.

Drive-in theater patrons are not discriminating: no matter how poor the movie, most of them love every minute of it.

More love scenes take place in cars at a drive-in theater than on its screen.

The honeymoon is over when the husband gets out of the car at a drive-in theater to wipe off the windshield.

A drive-in theater is the only place where it's possible for you to be run over on your way to the men's room.

DRIVING

If you drive too fast, you'll wreck the front of your car; if you drive too slow, you'll wreck the back of it.

Another man who lets the rest of the world go by is the man who drives his car at the legal speed.

There are only two kinds of drivers on the highways: the dependable and the expendable.

The average motorist is a careful driver; it's the fellow ahead who always stays too close.

It takes some people two weeks to learn to drive, while it takes others two cars.

The headless horseman was a myth, but the headless driver is a stark reality.

Drive carefully; don't insist on your rites.

Another thing that seldom turns out as it should is the car just ahead of you.

Safe driving at a moderate speed requires nothing more than self-control—and a strong rear bumper.

The man who doesn't know where he's going but is on his way, is probably just learning to drive.

If more motorists would drive right, more pedestrians would be left.

Drive toward others as you would have them drive toward you.

In driving, the car to watch is the car behind the car in front of you.

Most men are careful drivers: every time they have an accident, it's the other driver's fault.

The most difficult thing in learning to drive is how to get off a freeway.

Always drive as if your family were in the other car.

One of the hardest things to explain is why the driver in front of you is always traveling slower than you are.

Marriage changes a man: it enables him to keep both hands on the steering wheel when he drives.

The trouble with much driving is not the 100 horsepower under the hood, but the one asspower behind the wheel.

Everybody should learn to drive a car, especially those who sit behind the steering wheel.

Don't drive as if you owned the road; drive as if you owned the car.

Youngsters who cannot shift for themselves often drive cars that can.

People don't consider driving as work: if they did, they would slow down.

Another careful driver is the man who has just seen the motorist ahead being stopped by a state trooper.

If your wife wants to learn to drive, do not stand in her way.

A careful driver is probably the one who is still unfamiliar with the gadgets on his new car.

Drive like hell, and you'll get there.

He who stops to look each way will live to drive another day.

Half the world doesn't know how the other half lives—considering how the other half drives.

When approaching a school, watch out for children: they may be driving the car behind you.

Learning to drive is easy: go when it's green, stop when it turns red, and slow down when your instructor turns white.

Good driving is cooperative, not competitive; it is better to be outstripped than outlived.

DROPOUT

Many a freshman helps the college of his choice by becoming a dropout.

Another way to solve the school dropout problem is to make a high-school diploma a prerequisite for a driver's license.

A dropout never knows what kind of work he's out of because he has never learned a trade.

What you don't know doesn't hurt you, unless you're a dropout.

The chief problem in any retraining program for high-school dropouts is how to prevent the students from becoming dropouts from the dropout program.

A dropout is a youngster who will find it hard to earn a living because he refuses to learn a living.

Dropouts are a big problem in our schools, but drop-ins can sometimes be an even bigger problem in our homes.

If there's so much sex in the high schools, why are there so many dropouts?

Don't become a dropout: a little learning is a dangerous thing.

The trouble with school dropouts is not that they cannot see the handwriting on the wall, but that they cannot read it.

The only school that has no dropouts is the school of experience.

The juvenile delinquent who becomes a dropout usually gets into reform school without a scholarship.

DRUG

The young physician starts life with 20 drugs for each disease, and the old physician ends life with one drug for 20 diseases.
— *William Osler*

We have drugs to make women speak, but none to keep them silent. — *Anatole France*

Some of the latest wonder drugs are so powerful, you can't take them unless you're in perfect health.

They are called miracle drugs because they enable a doctor to turn the illnesses of his patients into a fur coat for his wife.

A miracle drug is any medicine you can get the children to take without screaming.

An old-timer is one who remembers when the wonder drugs

of the day were castor oil and camphor.

The most suitable gift for the man who has everything—a shot of antibiotics.

People shouldn't complain about the price of medicine: even the latest wonder drugs cost no more than the cheapest yacht.

They are called wonder drugs because you wonder if they will work.

DRUM

The job of a drummer is not so much to make good music as to drown out the bad.

A drum is the only toy you never give a child more than once.

Two heads are better than one, but only if you're a drum.

The first thing a child learns after he gets a drum is that he's never going to get another.

DUEL

The duel is one of the most dangerous institutions; since it is always fought in the open at daybreak, the combatants are sure to catch cold. — *Mark Twain*

Andrew Jackson fought duels when duels were duels, and not just the inconvenience of getting up before sunrise. — *Will Rogers*

A duel is the briefest of sports for it requires only two seconds to fight.

DULL

There are no uninteresting things; there are only uninterested people. — *Chesterton*

The conversation was dull, as it always is when we only say nice things about our neighbors. — *Choderlos de Laclos*

Early to rise and early to bed makes a male healthy and wealthy and dead. — *James Thurber*

Dullness is the coming of age of seriousness. — *Oscar Wilde*

The dullest conversationalist is the one who tells nothing but the truth.

Be it ever so humdrum, there's no place like home.

There are many things that are improper in the church, but dullness is not one of them.

A dullard is a person whose point of view isn't sharp enough to penetrate anything.

Some people are too good to be interesting.

Every now and then you meet a bore who is so dull that he can even put a cup of coffee to sleep.

DURATION

The only difference between love and insanity is in the duration of the disease.

Beware of being attached to animals: they don't last long

enough; beware of being attached to people: they last too long.

Some people are so careful that most of the products they buy outlast the payments.

Youth is when you think you'll live forever; middle age is when you wonder how you've lasted so long.

DUST

Man is made of dust, but woman thinks it's gold dust.

Most troubles are imaginary: what you think are huge clouds in the sky may be nothing more than dust on your eyelashes.

Man is nothing but dust, and he is always throwing it in someone's eyes.

When a bachelor opens the windows of his apartment, more dust blows out than in.

If man is made of dust, why don't some men ever dry up?

DUTY

In a free country it is the duty of writers to pay no attention to duty.   — *E. B. White*

He well remembered that he had a salary to receive, and only forgot that he had a duty to perform.   — *Edward Gibbon*

The first duty of a woman is to be pretty, the second is to be well-groomed, and the third is never to contradict.
        — *Somerset Maugham*

Do something every day that you don't want to do; this is the golden rule for acquiring the habit of doing your duty without pain.
        — *Mark Twain*

Duty: that which sternly impels us in the direction of profit, along the line of desire.   — *Bierce*

A moralist dwells on the happiness of duty; an immoralist on the duty of happiness.

Once a fixed idea of duty gets inside a narrow mind, it can never get out.

Half the world knows how the other half ought to live.

The trouble with many a man who stands up vigorously for his rights is that he falls down miserably on his duties.

The man who is all wool and a yard wide never shrinks from doing his duty.

No man ever becomes so lost to decency and righteousness that he cannot see another man's duty.

Intelligence is knowing what you ought to do; ability is knowing how you should do it; and virtue is not doing it.

The best way to get rid of your duties is to discharge them.

Every woman has two chief obligations: she should wear well and she should wear clothes well.

EAR

What a blessing it would be if we could open and shut our ears as easily as we open and shut our eyes! — *G. C. Lichtenberg*

A teenager is the only person who talks on the telephone long enough to have to change ears.

Be careful when you lend your ears to public speakers—they're inclined to keep them too long.

Don't get too involved in other people's problems; too many people first get you to lend an ear, and then proceed to chew it off.

EARLY

People who find it hard to get up early find it even harder to go to bed early.

Nowadays early to bed and early to rise probably means the television set isn't working.

The early birds gets the worm, and the early worm gets eaten.

Early to bed is a wise old saying, prized only after your hair starts graying.

You can't always judge by appearances: the early bird may have been up all night.

Early to bed and early to rise makes a man healthy (if he exercises), wealthy (if he strikes oil), and wise (if he studies hard).

Early marriages all too often prove that the early bird catches the worm.

Early to bed and early to rise makes you the kind party-givers despise.

If you're always early, you're a bird.

A few people get up bright and early, but most of us just get up early.

Early to bed and early to rise is the best way to read the morning paper in peace and quiet.

Early to bed and early to rise is the way of a girl before she gets wise.

If you must rise early, be sure you are a bird and not a worm.

Early to bed and early to rise— till you make enough money to do otherwise.

EARLY AND LATE

I'd rather be late for supper in this world tonight than be in some other world on time for breakfast in the morning.
— *Irvin S. Cobb*

Being a bachelor has its disadvantages: for one thing, he has to get up very early to make the money to stay up very late.

EARN

A lot of women are getting alimony who don't earn it.
— *Don Herold*

Mathematics is strange: many make thousands but not many make millions.

Society is made up of two classes: those who get more than they earn, and those who earn more than they get.

When a lot of credit goes with it, a little earning is a dangerous thing.

You can't tell from a man's clothes how much he makes: look at his wife.

If you earn $10,000 a year and your wife earns nothing, she's a dependent; but if she earns $10,000 and you earn nothing, you're a bum.

Marrying for money is the hardest way to earn it.

The only taxpayer who can keep what he earns is the one who cannot earn his keep.

EARN AND SPEND

There is only one thing for a man to do who is married to a woman who enjoys spending money, and that is to enjoy earning it.   — *Ed Howe*

Almost any man knows how to earn money but not one in a million knows how to spend it.
— *Thoreau*

O money, money, money! I often stop to wonder how thou canst go out so fast when thou comest in so slowly. — *Ogden Nash*

A woman thinks it's a man's duty to earn money, and hers to spend it.   — *Schopenhauer*

The man who earns a little, should spend a little less; the man who earns a lot, should spend a lot less.

It isn't what you earn that counts; it's what your wife doesn't spend.

Some men are great successes in making money, but failures in choosing ways to spend it.

When your outgo exceeds your income, your upkeep is your downfall.

When a woman spends more than her husband earns, is it extravagance in her or confidence in him?

It is hard to earn more than your wife can spend, but it is even harder to find such a wife.

Saving is a simple matter: you just make money faster than your family can spend it.

The trouble with marriage is that a man earns money five days a week while his wife spends money seven days a week.

Few of us belong in a high income bracket, but we make up for it by belonging in the high outgo.

Every wife likes a strong, silent man, especially one who is strong on making money and silent on the way she spends it.

A man's appearance shows how much he is earning, and his wife's appearance shows how much he is spending.

EARTH

I don't know if there are men on the moon, but if there are, they must be using this earth as their lunatic asylum.

— *Bernard Shaw*

Man makes a great fuss about this planet which is only a ball-bearing in the hub of the universe. — *Christopher Morley*

Many women want the earth, but they don't want it on their rugs.

The earth is one of the smallest stars in the universe, but the one with the biggest taxes.

The polar regions are not alike: there's all the difference in the world between them.

It's lucky for them that now isn't the time ordained for the meek to inherit the earth.

One half the world doesn't know why the other half doesn't get off the earth.

The earth is round, and the world is not square either.

The earth is a temporary lodging for the living, but a permanent residence for the dead.

The earth is a three-dimensional planet: longitude, latitude and platitude.

When the meek eventually inherit the earth, it will probably be in such a condition that nobody would have it.

Earthlings cannot get together with their fellow-inhabitants on earth, yet are trying to get together with inhabitants of other planets.

EASTER

Many women go to church regularly—they never miss an Easter.

Easter is the only time when it's perfectly safe to put all your eggs in one basket.

Too many women think Easter Sunday is Decoration Day.

There are always some church-goers whom the preacher doesn't remember from one Easter to the next.

EASY

The man who first called them easy payments was a poor judge of adjectives.

If we had our lives to live over again, we could make the same mistakes much more easily.

When the going seems somewhat easier, watch out—you may be going downhill.

Marriage is like any other job —it's much easier when you like your boss.

EATING

Women eat while they are talking; men talk while they are eating. — *Malcolm de Chazal*

He who does not mind his belly will hardly mind anything else. — *Samuel Johnson*

There ought to be some way to eat celery so it wouldn't sound like you were stepping on a basket. — *Kin Hubbard*

We are always reminded of our favorite reform after dinner: it's that people eat too much.
— *Ed Howe*

I have been a success: for sixty years I have eaten, and have avoided being eaten.
— *Logan P. Smith*

When it comes to eating, you can sometimes help yourself more by helping yourself less.
— *Richard Armour*

In eating corn on the cob or watermelon, you have a choice: you can be fastidious, or you can enjoy it. — *Olin Miller*

One half of what we eat enables us to live; the other half enables the doctor to live.

Many an infant is the spitting image of its mother, especially at feeding time.

If you want to get fat, don't eat fast; if you want to get thin, don't eat—fast.

Strenuous exercise is harmful after middle age, especially if you do it with a knife and fork.

The reason pediatricians eat so well is that children don't.

The trouble with a diet is that you don't eat what you like, and don't like what you eat.

Eating is important to both sexes, but to a woman it's where she eats, and to a man it's what.

Some live to eat, others eat to live, but most of us eat to reduce.

Two can live as cheaply as one—if one doesn't eat.

Be temperate in diet; our first parents ate themselves out of house and home.

The trouble with what just melts in your mouth is the way it bulges on you afterwards.

Children are always being told to eat more by parents who are always being told to eat less.

When a man eats with his knife, it's probably because his fork leaks.

Half of what we eat keeps us alive, and the other half kills us.

A glutton lives to eat, while a freeloader lives to eat out.

The married man who complains that he never gets a chance to open his mouth, must eat sooner or later.

The more second helpings a girl takes today, the fewer second glances she gets tomorrow.

Many doctors pay their food bills with the money from patients who have eaten too much.

Nature enables us to live from eating, and human nature enables us to die from overeating.

EATING AND DRINKING

The man who drinks like a fish, usually eats like a bird, and acts like an ass.

Overindulgence in drink gives a man a hangover, and overindulgence in food gives a woman an overhang.

It was woman who first tempted man to eat, but he took to drink on his own account thereafter.

ECCENTRIC

The man with a new idea is a crank until the idea succeeds.
— *Mark Twain*

There's no one so eccentric as the woman who prefers comfort to fashion.

Another eccentric is the man who is not only in favor of freedom, but even in favor of it for his opponents.

You seldom meet an eccentric character who has any.

We call a man eccentric if he keeps within his budget, carries no snapshots of his children, and drives slower than the speed limit.

An eccentric is a person who is too rich to be called a crackpot.

Another eccentric is the person who enjoys olives even when they are not served with gin and vermouth.

ECHO

The sound of a kiss is not so loud as that of a cannon, but its echo lasts a great deal longer.
— *Dr. O. W. Holmes*

When some people hear an echo, they think they originated the sound. — *Hemingway*

Don't be an echo: remember, though it's always an exact imitation, it never contributes anything new.

The girl who is the image of her father is probably the echo of her mother.

ECONOMICS

Practical men who believe themselves exempt from any intellectual influences, are usually the slaves of some defunct economist.
— *John Maynard Keynes*

Economics deals with the two great problems of life: how to make money, and how to get along without it.

Economics is a paradox: to have national prosperity we must spend, but to have individual prosperity we must save.

The man who wants inflation of his income, probably wants deflation of everything else.

Economics does not apply to the female of the species: a woman without principle always draws interest.

Another trouble with economics is that there are more ways to get into debt than there are ways to pay it off.

There's no such thing as an economic recession in some backward countries—they've never been prosperous enough to have one.

Economics is a paradoxical science: the national economy is worse off, the more there is of it.

Things always balance out: when someone gets something for nothing, someone else gets nothing for something.

ECONOMIST

An economist is a man who knows more about money than the people who have it.

When an economist doesn't know the answer, he changes the problem.

An economist can figure out complex problems of taxation and finance, but cannot straighten out his wife's household accounts.

Economists are always half right in their forecasts of better or worse conditions, but they are never sure which half it will be.

An economist is a man who writes a 100-page report concluding that in cold weather people use more fuel.

Economists tell us how we can get a rising standard of living, but not how we can keep up with it.

An economist is a man who knows how to throw the money he hasn't got after the money he never had.

An economist is one who watches the government running in the red, and concludes from it that the economic state of the nation must be rosy.

An economist is a person whose business it is to mind other people's business.

The difference between a moralist and an economist is that one wants people to be better while the other wants them to be better off.

An economist can explain why the cost of living keeps going up, but not why the value of human life keeps going down.

Economists would be more popular if they could show us how to attain a higher standard of living without a higher cost of living.

If all the nation's economists were laid end to end, they would point in all directions.

An economist is an expert who will know tomorrow why the things he predicted yesterday didn't happen today.

ECONOMY

I favor the policy of economy, not because I wish to save money, but because I wish to save people.   *— Calvin Coolidge*

Oh, marvelous are woman's ways, and most wonderful are her economies.   *— Gelett Burgess*

The love of money is the root of all virtue.   *— Bernard Shaw*

I would rather have my people laugh at my economies than weep for my extravagance.
  — Oscar II of Sweden

It is much easier to economize on luxuries than to luxuriate on economies.

Most women don't start economizing until they run out of money.

If you live within your income, you will get along without worry —and without a lot of other things too.

False economy is not spending money on a sunny day because you're saving it for a rainy day.

The trouble with most people's economy is that they don't save any money.

A woman's idea of economy is to stop all buying—except what she can get on credit.

It is easy to economize when you are broke.

The most comfortable way to economize is to travel with a good spender.

Many an extravagant woman thinks her husband is a miser when he is merely an economizer.

When a man has to economize, he always starts with his wife.

When we practice it, it's economy; when the other fellow does, it's stinginess.

Economy is a strange thing: it means buying the big size in a box of cereal, and the small size in a car.

Some women don't seem to know what economy is, except

when they put the candles on their birthday cake.

What this country needs is less economists and more economizers.

The man who is always practicing economy usually has a wife who is out of practice.

EDITOR

A great editor is a man of outstanding talent who owns 51 per cent of his newspaper's stock.
— Henry Watterson

An editor should have a pimp for a brother, so he'd have someone to look up to. *— Gene Fowler*

Some writers enclose a stamped, self-addressed envelope for the manuscript to come back in; this is too much of a temptation to the editor. *— Ring Lardner*

I became the editor of a weekly newspaper because I wanted to be my own particular kind of a damn fool.   *— William Allen White*

An editor is a man who knows what he wants, but doesn't know what it is.

A newspaper editor spends half his time putting things in the paper, and the other half keeping things out.

An editor is a man to whom the wastebasket is mightier than the pen.

An editor is one who separates the wheat from the chaff, and prints the chaff.

EDUCATION

Education is the period during which you are being instructed by somebody you do not know, about something you do not want to know. — *Chesterton*

Your education begins when what is called your education ends. — *Justice O. W. Holmes*

My idea of an educated person is one who can converse on one subject for more than two minutes. — *Robert A. Millikan*

The primary purpose of a liberal education is to make one's mind a pleasant place in which to spend one's leisure.
— *Sidney J. Harris*

In education we are striving not to teach youth to make a living, but to make a life.
— *William Allen White*

One of the benefits of a college education is to show a boy its little value. — *Emerson*

The chief object of education is not to learn things but to unlearn things. — *Chesterton*

He learned the arts of riding, fencing, gunnery, and how to scale a fortress—or a nunnery.
— *Lord Byron*

My father must have had some elementary education for he could read and write and keep accounts inaccurately. — *Bernard Shaw*

Without a gentle contempt for education, no gentleman's education is complete. — *Chesterton*

Sixty years ago I knew everything; now I know nothing; education is a progressive discovery of our own ignorance.
— *Will Durant*

Education is an admirable thing, but nothing that is worth knowing can be taught.
— *Oscar Wilde*

Anyone who has passed through a classical education and not been made a fool by it, has had a very narrow escape. — *Hazlitt*

If a man empties his purse into his head, no one can take it from him. — *Franklin*

There is one kind of co-education that everybody believes in— the co-education of teachers and students. — *John Dewey*

Education is too important to be left solely to the educators.
— *Francis Keppel*

An education is a wonderful thing; no college should be without one.

Educators that complain that America spends more on liquor than on education don't realize how much you can learn at cocktail parties.

Some men complete their education by going into business, but most men marry.

Education is the process of changing blissful ignorance into some other kind of ignorance.

A mother never realizes the full value of education until summer is over and the children go back to school.

Education never hurts a man, unless he marries the coed he meets at college.

The United States spends more than any other country on education, but then, we need it more.

If the cost of college tuition continues to rise, education will become as expensive as ignorance.

Education is what is left over after you have forgotten the facts.

The best time for a young man to marry is when his education is finished, or when he is ready for it to begin.

Education teaches a man how to speak, not how long or how often.

American schoolchildren are busy trying to keep up with their teachers who go to summer school trying to keep ahead of them.

The most widespread form of compulsory education is experience.

Adult education often begins with a teenage marriage.

Another thing an education should include is the knowledge of what to do with it.

To get a better education for your children nowadays, you have to pull a few wires—from the radio, the television and the record-player.

An educator is a man who educates other men to make more money than he does.

The aim of education should be to teach a person something about everything, and then everything about something.

There must be something wrong with education: there are so many more bright children than grown-ups.

As long as parents help children with their homework, there will always be adult education.

A college education doesn't make fools; it merely develops them.

Graduate study is a form of higher learning that enables a student to bore you with more intellectual details.

Educating a born fool is much like fertilizing a stone.

Another advantage of a good education is that it enables you to hide your ignorance.

Education begins when your father sends you to college, and is completed when you send your son there.

EFFICIENCY

It's pretty hard to be efficient without being obnoxious.
— *Kin Hubbard*

An efficiency expert is hired to spend his time figuring out how others should spend their time.

Every large corporation nowadays needs an efficiency expert to figure out how much time each executive can spend on the golf course.

An efficiency expert is a man who believes in economy at any cost.

No man ever convinced his wife that a pretty secretary is as efficient as a homely one.

An efficiency expert is a man hired to introduce short cuts in order to make more time to make out more reports.

A new broom sweeps clean, but the old one knows where the dirt is.

The test of efficiency is the length of time it takes you to find out when you're wrong.

An efficiency expert is one who waits to make up a foursome before going through a revolving door.

EFFORT

Men should not try to overstrain their goodness more than any other faculty. – *Samuel Butler*

If it required some effort to go from today to tomorrow, some people would always remain in yesterday.

In every office you'll find a man who always tries to do the best he can't.

You never know what you can do until you go broke trying.

If at first you don't succeed, try someone else.

Everything requires effort: the only thing you can achieve without it is failure.

Some men strive to leave footprints on the sands of time, while others strive even harder to cover up their tracks.

EGG

Hen eggs are more popular than duck eggs because a hen cackles to advertise her product.
– *Will Rogers*

It's quality that counts, not quantity: a fly lays more eggs than a hen.

If a man has the price he can get anything he wants and the way he wants it, except medium soft-boiled eggs.

The cock crows, but the hen lays the eggs.

What this country needs is an incubator that will lay eggs.

Feed a hen with mere thanks, and she'll lay you no eggs.

The first thing you learn in some home economics courses is that you don't open an egg with a can opener.

You can't unscramble an egg, unless it's a nest egg.

Another reason a hen lays an egg is that she cannot stand it up on end.

EGOTISM

His is the kind of egotism another man's egotism can't put up with.   — *Robert Frost*

Egotists do not see the world with themselves in it, but see themselves with the world around them.   — *Herbert Samuel*

What can you possibly add to a mind that's full, especially one that's full of itself?   — *Joubert*

An egotist always resents meeting another egotist as if he alone had the right to be one.
— *Jules Renard*

A reasonable amount of egotism is good for a man; it keeps him from brooding over the success of his friends.

An egotist is a man who thinks he is everything you think you are.

Egotism is the ability to see things in yourself that others cannot see.

An egotist is never sure whether he is part of the universe, or the universe is a part of him.

An egotist is a man whose self-importance makes his mind shrink while it makes his head swell.

An egotist is a man who thinks first of himself and then thinks of himself second.

We have a world of people to fall in love with, yet some people choose themselves.

An egotist is a man who thinks that if he hadn't been born, people would have wondered why.

The most intolerable thing about an egotist is that he talks about himself when you want to talk about yourself.

An egotist is a conceited person who thinks the worst thing that could happen to him would be if he were someone else.

Every man thinks he is smarter than others, but only the egotist says so.

An egotist has a distorted view of the world because of his I's.

The trouble with an egotist is that his egotism doesn't trouble him at all.

A swelled head inflated with ego usually rests on a stuffed shirt filled with its own importance.

There are two kinds of egotists: those who admit it, and the rest of us.

Egotism is the only disease where the patient feels well but his company feels sick.

An egotist is one who can hardly wait to hear what he's going to say about himself next.

When an egotist gets up in the morning and puts his pants on, he thinks the whole world is dressed.

Give the egotist his due: he never goes around talking about other people.

An egotist is one who is so wrapped up in himself that he pays no attention to us.

Egotism is the one thing nobody will forgive in others, and which everybody forgives in himself.

Egotism is deceiving: a man will think a pretty woman is smiling at him when she is really laughing at him.

The man who doesn't recognize the existence of a superior being may be an atheist, but he is more often an egotist.

You can always tell an egotist by the faraway look that comes into his eyes when the conversation turns to someone else.

EINSTEIN

Einstein made the real trouble: he announced in 1905 that there was no such thing as absolute rest; after that there never was.
— *Stephen Leacock*

Even Einstein had to rely for his time on his clock.
— *Stanislaw J. Lec*

Sit with a pretty girl for an hour, and it seems like a minute; sit on a hot stove for a minute, and it seems like an hour—that's relativity.   — *Einstein*

I think and think for months, for years; 99 times the conclusion is false, but the hundredth time I am right.   — *Einstein*

Einstein was right about the relativity of time: the minute

which a neighbor only has to visit, is usually longer than an hour.

Long before Einstein it was known that everything had four dimensions: length, breadth, thickness, and cost.

Einstein's theory of relativity, as practiced by Congressmen, simply means getting members of your family on the payroll.

Long before Einstein proved it, politicians were aware that there's no such thing as a straight line.

ELECTION

No matter who wins, the people are always worsted in an election.   — *Ed Howe*

Political elections are a good deal like marriages—there's no accounting for anyone's taste.
— *Will Rogers*

Both winning and losing candidates get a kick out of an election, but not in the same place.

After the election, the successful candidates start making molehills out of the mountains they erected.

There are two sides to every political question, but only one office.

After every election the American way is to unite behind the new administration—and blame everything on it.

An election is a political campaign where the candidates are always different, and the people usually indifferent.

Money talks, but campaign money is careful not to tell where it came from.

During election time the office-holder with a big sinecure becomes a little insecure.

The only race in which most people pick the winner is an election.

Another man who is convinced that history repeats itself is the candidate for re-election.

During a political campaign the air is full of speeches—and vice versa.

An election is a political campaign where the loser gets the boot, and the winner gets the booty.

Truth crushed to earth will rise again, but by that time the votes have already been counted.

An election is an important democratic process by which you are given a choice to decide who will spend your money.

The only consolation about an election is that only one of the candidates can get in.

An election is a conflict of interests disguised as a contest of principles.

An election is like a horserace: you can tell more about it after it's over.

Election is the time of year when candidates run for public office, and America becomes the land of promise.

A cynic isn't the only one who believes that everything said during an election by rival candidates about each other, is true.

ELECTRICITY

You cannot receive a shock unless you have an electric affinity for that which shocks you.

— *Thoreau*

Youngsters brighten up a home, but only because they never turn off the lights.

Knowledge is power but, no matter how much you know, you still can't run your electric appliances with it.

The greater the civilization, the more helpless man becomes when the electric power breaks down.

If it's an all-electric home, the chances are that everything in it is charged.

The modern home is equipped with electric appliances that can do anything you want done, except pay your electric bills.

ELECTRONICS

Electronics is the science that deals with machines that are smarter than the people who use them.

The marvels of electronics cannot be overestimated: it is now possible to hear the same commercial dozens of times.

What this country needs is a power mower that can be operated from an air-conditioned room.

ELEPHANT

They say the elephant never forgets, but what has he got to remember?

The only reason many American families don't own an elephant is that they've never been offered one on installment credit.

ELEVATOR

Living in an ivory tower has many disadvantages, one of which is the absence of elevator service.

If a man takes off his hat in an elevator nowadays, it means he has manners—or hair.

The reason many people don't climb the ladder of success is that they're waiting for the elevator.

ELOQUENCE

The finest eloquence is that which gets thing done.
— Lloyd George

Eloquence is what you think you have after a few martinis.

Eloquence is the art of saying as little as possible but making it sound as much as possible.

A public speaker usually gets very flowery when he starts going to seed.

No spellbinder is more eloquent than the woman who suffers in silence.

Some men electrify their audiences, others only gas them.

Many a public speaker can talk eloquently about nothing without previous preparation.

EMBARRASS

It's always embarrassing to run unexpectedly into a girl you used to be engaged to.
— P. G. Wodehouse

Breath is what a mother holds when her youngster starts telling a neighbor about some family incident.

Some people are temporarily embarrassed all the time.

Truth is stranger than fiction, and usually more embarrassing.

When children ask embarrassing questions, invention is the necessity of mother.

Parents are embarrassed when their children tell lies, and even more embarrassed when they tell the truth.

In embarrassing situations, women cry and men lie.

At eight, children often embarrass their parents; at eighteen, they are often embarrassed by them.

Always disguise your embarrassment: try to look like an owl when you have behaved like an ass.

Many an embarrassing moment wouldn't be so embarrassing if it only lasted a moment.

EMBEZZLE

The embezzler who wants to get away from it all, always takes a lot of it away with him.

An embezzler doesn't always get away with it even after he gets away with it.

When a bank cashier disappears without explanation, no explanation is needed.

The cashier who is short in the bank will probably be long in jail.

Another man who isn't as rich as he thinks he ought to be is the embezzler.

Many cashiers forget that banks should be cleaned out by cleaning women only.

EMOTION

It is easier to manufacture seven facts out of whole cloth than one emotion. – *Mark Twain*

He was white and shaken, like a dry martini. – *P. G. Wodehouse*

When a girl is noted for her warmth, it seldom comes from what she's wearing.

If at first you don't succeed, try a little ardor.

Small children constantly play on your emotions: they are either a lump in the throat or a pain in the neck.

EMPLOYMENT

Early to bed and early to rise probably indicates unskilled labor.
                            – *John Ciardi*

Too many employers are looking for men between the ages of 25 and 30 with 35 years' experience.

The employer generally gets the employee he deserves.

Formerly heaven protected the working girl; nowadays she also has a union, unemployment insurance, a pension plan and social security.

A good personnel manager hires only optimists in the sales division and only pessimists in the credit department.

Some married women have steady employment keeping their husbands at work.

More people are looking for positions than jobs, and more for jobs than work.

EMPTY

When a book and a head collide and there is a hollow sound, it is not always in the book.
                        – *G. C. Lichtenberg*

Unlike an empty head, an empty stomach doesn't let its owner rest until he fills it.

There's nothing as empty as an inflated balloon, except a stuffed shirt.

A fool empties his head every time he opens his mouth.

If all the perfect husbands in the world were brought together in one place, the place would be empty.

When the stomach is empty, the head will swallow anything.

At a cocktail party it may be hard to find a guest empty-handed, but it's easy to find one empty-headed.

ENCORE

Those who sing their own praises seldom receive an encore.

Play on a woman's vanity and you are sure to get an encore.

ENCOURAGE

Everyone needs encouragement; a pat on the back is good for a man's backbone.

The best thing a girl can give the man who has everything is—encouragement.

The wife who is always encouraging her do-it-yourself husband, never objects to his taking her out to dinner.

Encouragement is what a girl uses to make a slow man think he's a fast worker.

ENCYCLOPEDIA

A pest is a man who can talk like an encyclopedia—and does.
                    —Oliver Herford

Girls who try to be walking encyclopedias should remember that reference books are never taken out.

Every schoolchild should have an encyclopedia at home; it will help parents do the homework much faster.

A know-it-all can talk on all branches of knowledge like an encyclopedia—without ever opening one.

END

Supper, she used to say, was one of the four ends of man, and what the other three were she could never remember.
                    —Lytton Strachey

They were at their wits' end, and it hadn't taken them long to get there. —Desmond McCarthy

Marriage is often the end of a man's troubles—but which end?

There's a divinity that shapes our ends, but none to make them meet.

The Lord gave us two ends to use: success depends on which we choose—heads we win, tails we lose.

The good old days were an era when the day was done before the worker was.

When she says she'll think it over—it is!

Some of the happiest moments in life are when you get the last laugh, have the last word, and pay the last installment.

When a person's conversation bores you no end, it's because it hasn't any.

The trouble with an argument is that, after all is said and done, most people refuse to leave it that way.

Many can rise to the occasion, but few know when to sit down.

Just about the time you think you can make both ends meet, somebody comes along and moves the ends.

ENDURE

What makes a marriage last is for a man and a woman to continue to have things to argue about.   — *Rex Stout*

Bear it like a man, even if you feel it like an ass. — *Bernard Shaw*

Truth, in matters of religion, is simply the opinion that has survived.   — *Oscar Wilde*

To be enduring, a marriage should be endurable.

Even a cynic believes in enduring love if he doesn't have to endure it too long.

Some people find it hard to stand their own poverty; others find it even harder to stand their neighbor's prosperity.

Philosophy enables a man to endure anything, even his own philosophy.

ENEMY

You needn't love your enemy, but if you refrain from telling lies about him, you are doing well enough.   — *Ed Howe*

I'm lonesome; they are all dying; I have hardly a warm personal enemy left.   — *Whistler*

Everyone needs a warm personal enemy or two to keep him free from rust in the movable parts of his mind. — *Gene Fowler*

Life would not be worth living if we didn't keep our enemies.
— *Finley Peter Dunne*

After a few years of married life, a man and his wife are apt to be the sort of enemies that respect each other.   — *Don Marquis*

Nothing would more contribute to make a man wise than to have always an enemy in his view.
— *Halifax*

Many a young man is his own worst enemy, at least until he gets married.

A friend may become an enemy, but a relative is one from the start.

There is absolutely no hope for the man who is too lazy to acquire enemies.

Love your enemies—it will drive them crazy.

An enemy is sometimes made over politics, sometimes over money, but most often made overnight.

Speak well of your enemies; remember you made them.

The enemy is made up of human beings just like us—that's why they can't be trusted.

The only time a man is apt to follow the biblical injunction to love his enemies is when he is his own worst enemy.

We often admire a man for the enemies he has made, but not when we are included among them.

The one nice thing about having enemies is that they never borrow money from you.

To have peace of mind settle among your enemies; you always know what to expect of them.

It would be much easier if we were charged to love our enemies' enemies.

An enemy is a former friend you know well enough not to speak to.

ENERGY

The energy spent in struggling against the inevitable could often prevent it from becoming inevitable.

A live wire makes hay with the grass that grows under other people's feet.

There's a world of difference between the man who works up steam and the man who generates a fog.

A piece of candy gives you just enough energy to stretch your hand out for the next piece.

The trouble with go-getters is that they always do today what ought to be put off till tomorrow.

People do more talking than listening: under the law of gravity, it takes more energy to shut one's mouth than to open it.

ENGAGEMENT

There is an advantage to long engagements: the longer a man is engaged, the less time he has to be married.

Some engagements end happily, but in most cases the parties get married.

The engagement which is too short is usually followed by a marriage which is too long.

An engagement is an urge on the verge of a merge.

The proof that women can keep secrets is that a woman may be engaged for months before telling her fiancé about it.

Every girl likes to be engaged to a man, even if it is only in conversation.

There's a difference between an engagement and a date: the first leads to marriage and the other to divorce.

An engagement is the only period during which a girl is neither married nor single.

An engaged couple spend half the time breaking up, and the other half making up.

An engagement is a short period lacking in foresight, followed by a long period loaded with hindsight.

You can always tell that a couple is engaged if she has a ring and he's broke.

There's only one advantage to a long engagement: it gives her more time to look around for something better.

Another man who is looking for trouble and soon has it coming to him is a fiancé.

If a girl has any pride, she will break off her engagement when the man goes off and marries another girl.

The word *engagement* has two meanings: in war, it's a battle; in courtship, a surrender.

ENGLAND

There are only two classes in good society in England: the equestrian classes and the neurotic classes. — *Bernard Shaw*

If you want to eat well in England eat three breakfasts daily.
— *Somerset Maugham*

The British lion always rouses itself to fresh efforts by lashing itself with its tail. — *W. R. Inge*

Teach the English how to talk and the Irish how to listen—then society will be quite civilized.
— *Oscar Wilde*

Those comfortably padded lunatic asylums are known, euphemistically, as the stately homes of England. — *Virginia Woolf*

On the Continent people have good food; in England people have good table manners.
— *George Mikes*

England is the paradise of women, the purgatory of men, and the hell of horses.
— *John Florio*

England is an island entirely surrounded by hot water.

England has seldom been blockaded, but often blockheaded.

Britannia which once ruled the waves, now often waives the rules.

In England, saving for a rainy day and a vacation are usually the same thing.

ENGLISH

Our ancestors unhappily could bring over no English better than Shakespeare's.
— *James Russell Lowell*

I haven't been abroad in so long a time that I almost speak English without an accent.
— *Robert Benchley*

When we Americans are through with the English language it will look as if it had been run over by a musical comedy.
— *Finley Peter Dunne*

What does he know of English who only English knows?
— *James Thurber*

The world was made before the English language, and seemingly upon a different design.
— *Robert Louis Stevenson*

A lot of good English is wasted on a cue ball.

Next to money, English is the leading international language.

The English language is called our mother tongue because father seldom gets a chance to use it.

ENGLISHMAN

I hope we English will long maintain our *grand talent pour le silence*. — *Carlyle*

An Englishman's idea of God is another Englishman twelve feet tall. — *Grant Allen*

He was the worst kind of Englishman—he could not even cheat without being found out.
— *Norman Douglas*

If a playwright is funny, the English look for a serious message, and if he's serious, they look for the joke—that's the English sense of humor.
— *Sacha Guitry*

The Englishman is at his best on the golf links, and at his worst in the Cabinet.
— *Bernard Shaw*

Some people say there is a God, others say there is no God, but the Englishman thinks the truth lies somewhere in between.
— *Yeats*

An Englishman is content to say nothing when he has nothing to say. — *Samuel Johnson*

The English are like their own beer: froth at the top, dregs at the bottom, and excellent in the middle. — *Voltaire*

Not only is England an island, but every Englishman as well.
— *Novalis*

Contrary to popular belief, English women do not wear tweed nightgowns. — *Hermione Gingold*

Silence may be defined as a conversation with an Englishman.
— *Heine*

Once a foreigner, always a foreigner: he may become British, but he can never become English.
— *George Mikes*

It is the proud perpetual boast of the Englishman that he never brags. — *Wyndham Lewis*

It is possible to wear out an Englishman, but not an English suit. — *Al Capp*

The English are more silent than other nations, but less dumb.

ENJOYMENT

My mother had a great deal of trouble with me, but I think she enjoyed it. — *Mark Twain*

I don't think we enjoy other people's suffering; it isn't actually enjoyment, but we feel better for it. — *Finley Peter Dunne*

Some men seem to enjoy everything, except the good will of their neighbors.

Ecstasy is the delight experienced only in youth, but appreciated only in age.

A critic is a man who enjoys writing about things he doesn't enjoy.

Some girls can get all the men they like, while others like all the men they can get.

Never put off enjoyment because there's no time like the pleasant.

Many people never seem to enjoy a trip until it's over.

ENOUGH

Nobody has enough; nevertheless, some people have a great deal too much. — *Samuel Butler*

Nothing is enough for the man to whom enough is too little.
— *Epicurus*

When there's food for eight, there's enough for ten. — *Molière*

If all of us got all we wanted out of life, there wouldn't be enough left to go around.

Enough money always means more money than you have now.

When a woman says she's had enough, she hasn't; when a man says he's had enough, he's had too much.

Enough is what would satisfy us—if the neighbors didn't have any more.

ENTERPRISE

Initiative is doing the right thing without being told.
— *Elbert Hubbard*

A go-getter never has time to attend to other people's business because he always has more business than he can attend to.

All things come to him who goes after them.

What this country needs is less emphasis on free, and more on enterprise.

Enterprise may not be enough to get you to the top, but it will get you off the bottom.

All things come to him who waits—that's why the smart man hustles.

Enterprise means taking advantage not of things that happen but of things that do not happen.

ENTERTAIN

The man who doesn't entertain evil thoughts on sex, is probably letting them entertain him.

Television is superior to the movies as a form of entertainment: it enables more people to be bored at the same time.

The best way to entertain some people is to listen to them.

ENTHUSIASM

Acquire an enthusiasm; you can't be enthusiastic and unhappy at the same time.

The man who allows himself to be carried away with enthusiasm often has to walk back.

Enthusiasm is contagious, and so is the lack of it.

ENTRANCE

To make a long story short, there's nothing like the boss walking in.

The quickest of all conversation-stoppers is the sudden entrance of the person being talked about.

Another difference between men and women is that women always enter a room voice first.

The sudden entrance of a wife has made many a secretary change her position.

ENTRANCE AND EXIT

I prefer the sign NO ENTRANCE to the sign which says NO EXIT.
— *Stanislaw J. Lec*

A person enters a casino to get something for nothing, and exits when he gets nothing for something.

We dig our graves with our teeth, and the entrees are largely responsible for our exits.

Opportunity always looks more favorable on its way out than on its way in.

ENVY

Envy is the sincerest form of flattery. — *John Churton Collins*

Envy has no holidays.
— *Francis Bacon*

The only thing more certain than the hatred of enemies is the envy of friends.

It takes a smart politician to keep the note of envy out of his voice while accusing his opponent of fooling the public.

Man wants but little here below, but that little is what the other fellow has.

It's easy to understand why men should not envy women, but it's hard to understand why women should envy men.

When you make your mark in the world, watch out for the envious with erasers.

If envy were a disease, everyone would be sick.

EPIGRAM

You can cram a truth into an epigram; the truth, never.
— *Norman Douglas*

He would stab his best friend for the sake of writing an epigram on his tombstone.
— *Oscar Wilde*

The art of newspaper paragraphing is to stroke a platitude until it purrs like an epigram.
— *Don Marquis*

It is with epigrams as with other inventions: the best ones annoy us because we didn't think of them ourselves.
— G. C. Lichtenberg

Anyone can tell the truth, but only a few of us can make epigrams.   — Somerset Maugham

There's nothing so lively as a deadly epigram.

An epigram is a wisecrack that has lived long enough to acquire a reputation.

A good epigram is like a diamond: its sparkle comes from patient polishing.

An epigram is the marriage of wit and wisdom; a wisecrack, their divorce.

All epigrams exaggerate, including this one.

A dram of epigram is worth a ton of pun.

EPITAPH

I would have written of me on my stone: I had a lover's quarrel with the world.   — Robert Frost

There should be something said on tombstones about husbands having been good providers, and less about love.   — Ed Howe

Don't judge a book by its cover, or a person by his epitaph.

The good die young and, if epitaphs tell the truth, the bad live forever.

So live that no man who reads will laugh at the flowery praise in your epitaph.

If a man could do it over again, he still couldn't live up to his epitaph.

The proof that widows have better taste than married women is shown by the epitaph on their husbands' tombstones.

After reading the epitaphs in a cemetery, you wonder where they bury the sinners.

Heaven would be vastly overcrowded if people could get into it with their epitaphs as passports.

Many a tombstone inscription is a grave error.

EQUALITY

The only way women could have equal rights nowadays would be to surrender some.
— Burton Hillis

Equality of opportunity is an equal opportunity to prove unequal talents.   — Herbert Samuel

Among giants, try and be a dwarf; among dwarfs, try and be a giant; but among equals, try and be an equal.   — Stanislaw J. Lec

The law cannot make all men equal, but they are all equal before the law.   — Frederick Pollock

I don't look down upon royalty, the wealthy and the socially elect; they'd be just as good as anybody else if they had an equal chance.
— Will Rogers

Equality is what does not exist among equals. — *E. E. Cummings*

All men are created equal and endowed by their Creator with a mighty urge to become otherwise.

All men are equal, but it's what they're equal to that counts.

All men are born equal, but some of them outgrow it.

A feminist is a woman who wants equality more than she wants a man.

The only place where you can find equality is in the cemetery.

A good marriage is like a good handshake—there is no upper hand.

All men are equal, and the cynic thinks they are all equally bad.

In the polling booth as in the men's room, all men are peers.

The trouble with equality is that we all want to be equal with our superiors.

Many a man believes in equality so much that the success of others makes him miserable.

We are all created free and equal—free to try to become unequal.

Equality is another thing that people all over the world have always loved—to talk about.

The Founding Fathers said that all men are equal; they were probably afraid to say the same thing about women.

Equality is the principle that one man is as good as another, and often a great deal better.

All men are created free and equal, then they grow up and get married.

ESCAPE

Many a marriage hardly differs from prostitution, except being harder to escape from.
— *Bertrand Russell*

Open sesame—I want to get out.   — *Stanislaw J. Lec*

The man who lives to tell the tale spends the rest of his life talking about nothing else.

Nowadays the problem is not to escape from reality; it's to escape from the horrors of television.

Some movies are so bad, it is hard to believe they were ever released; they probably escaped.

ESTIMATE

Everyone should take a wife's estimate into account when forming an estimate of a man.
— *Balzac*

The man who thinks too much of himself usually thinks too little of others.

Many a husband thinks his wife is the most wonderful woman in the world, and that's not just his opinion—it's hers too.

The more we think of some people, the less we think of them.

A man is no greater than his wife's opinion of him.

Every estimate ought to include an estimate of how much more it will cost than the estimate.

The man who underestimates the world's greatness usually overestimates his own littleness.

Never underestimate the power of a woman—nor overestimate her age and weight.

ETIQUETTE

Etiquette means behaving yourself a little better than is absolutely essential. — *Will Cuppy*

Etiquette is the least important of all laws, but the one most observed. — *La Rochefoucauld*

Etiquette requires us to admire the human race. — *Mark Twain*

Etiquette is a code of conduct where, no matter what state the world is in, the most important problem is which fork to use.

A person can usually go much farther on good manners than on good morals.

Etiquette is the art of knowing the right way to do the wrong thing.

Many a man who is too proper to use a knife in his mouth, will not hesitate to use it in your back.

Etiquette disapproves of your talking with a full mouth, but not with a empty head.

EULOGY

We owe eulogies to the living, but pay them to the dead.

Men always get eulogies when they are dead, never when they are dead-broke.

A eulogy is the praise not of what a dead person has been, but what he should have been.

EVASION

I never made a mistake in my life; at least, never one that I couldn't explain away afterwards. — *Kipling*

If he dodges cars, he's a pedestrian; if he dodges taxes, he's a businessman; and if he dodges responsibility, he's a congressman.

The most popular form of hunting among civilized people is for a loophole.

When a politician is on the fence, the fence is really a hedge.

It's not what a man earns that counts, it's his income after tax evasion.

When a candidate wants to avoid the facts, he usually discusses great moral issues.

It is easy to dodge our responsibilities, but we cannot dodge the consequences of dodging our responsibilities.

A legislator spends half his time making laws, and the other half helping his friends evade them.

The social structure of America has two extremes: the tax dodgers and the taxi dodgers.

Some candidates are more straightforward than others, especially in dodging the issues.

No two issues are so far apart that a politician can't straddle them.

EVE

The first woman with a mind of her own was Eve, and look what happened to her.

If Eve had been a modern woman she would have looked around for a smaller leaf.

Second thoughts are best: woman was the second thought of the Creator.

The first woman was named Eve because her arrival brought an end to Adam's perfect day.

Eve wasn't extravagant in clothes because she had all the men in the world.

There was once a woman who never suspected her husband—her name was Eve.

Eve craved a fig leaf, and man has been paying expensive dress bills ever since.

Beware of women bearing gifts: remember Eve.

EVENING GOWN

A beautiful woman seductively dressed will never catch cold no matter how low cut her gown.
— *Nietzsche*

A woman considers her evening gown all the more becoming, the more it becomes less.

Lives there a man who is so abnormal that he can't be stirred by a low-cut formal?

Many an evening gown is not so much a dress as a slip cover.

A woman will starve herself to get into an evening gown, and her husband will starve himself to pay for it.

An evening gown should not only be attractive but also distractive.

An evening gown is a low-cut dress with a woman inside trying to get out or outside trying to get in.

If you cannot see why a woman wears a low-cut gown, she shouldn't.

Many an evening gown has no sleeves, no neck, no back, and the less said about the rest of it the better.

There are times when a woman shows a lot of backbone, as in her choice of an evening gown.

A plunging neckline is the only thing you can look down on and approve of at the same time.

An evening gown is one in which the wearer is head and shoulders above it.

Some women know how to get the most out of an evening gown while leaving the least in it.

Many an evening gown covers a warm heart—and that's about all.

Sometimes an evening gown looks as if the wearer had been poured into it—and hadn't set properly.

An evening gown is specially designed to help its wearer catch a man or a cold.

In these days of low-cut gowns, it takes a lot of will power to look a woman in the eye.

Many an evening gown has its neckline where its waistline ought to be.

A woman enjoys wearing an evening gown because it has just enough material to keep a man warm.

The more style there is to an evening gown, the less there is of anything else.

EVIDENCE

Reformers are in favor of suppressing everything, but politicians are in favor of suppressing nothing but the evidence.
— *Finley Peter Dunne*

Circumstantial evidence is like a blackberry which, when red or white, is really green.

Evidence is not always proof; some people who are a good deal in evidence don't prove much.

Learning by experience is good, but in the case of mushrooms and toadstools, hearsay evidence is better.

You can't always judge women by their clothes—there is seldom enough evidence.

EVIL

Wickedness is a myth invented by good people to account for the attractiveness of others.
— *Oscar Wilde*

All that is necessary for the triumph of evil is that good men do nothing. — *Edmund Burke*

There are a thousand hacking at the branches of evil to one who is striking at the root. — *Thoreau*

It may be that the world was created so that evil could exist.
— *Jules Renard*

I never wonder to see men wicked, but I often wonder to see them not ashamed. — *Swift*

Avoid the appearance of evil; it is harder to live down than evil.

Of two evils, choose the one you enjoy most.

A necessary evil is never necessay but always evil.

To the cynic, money isn't the root of all evil—evil is the root of all money.

There may be no rest for the wicked, but there is often arrest.

Of two evils, choose the prettier.

Speak no evil, see no evil, hear no evil—and you'll never be the life of the party.

Instead of choosing the lesser of two evils, choose the one you haven't tried before.

The wicked flee when no man pursueth, but they flee even faster when someone is after them.

Love of money is the root of half the evil in the world, and lack of money is the root of the other half.

The evil that men do makes them eligible for nomination to office.

Of two evils, pass up the first, and turn down the other.

A great evil is the number of people who are trying to get something for nothing, and a greater evil is the number of people who succeed.

EVOLUTION

All modern men are descended from a wormlike creature, but it shows more on some people.
— *Will Cuppy*

One touch of Darwin makes the whole world kin.
— *Bernard Shaw*

Some folks seem to have descended from the chimpanzee much later than others.
— *Kin Hubbard*

Evolution is like walking on a rolling barrel: the walker isn't so much interested in where the barrel is going as in keeping on top of it.   — *Robert Frost*

We are descended not only from monkeys, but also from monks.
— *Elbert Hubbard*

Man started out as one single cell and is now a social security number running into the millions.

The more you see of the opponents of evolution, the more you must admit that there has been no evolution.

The course of evolution: we came from monkeys and we go to the dogs.

Man has not entirely evolved from living in trees—his eyes still swing from limb to limb.

The theory of evolution is more concerned with what man descended from than with what he descends to.

Man has changed very little in the last thousand years—and every wife resents it.

A million years from now the earth will probably be peopled by creatures who will stoutly deny that they ever descended from man.

Believe it or not, every fool you meet is the end result of millions of years of evolution.

If evolution really worked, nature would have long ago produced pedestrians with wings.

Darwin didn't go far enough; some members of our species have started on the way back.

Thinking has developed man's brain, and not thinking has developed woman's intuition.

EXAGGERATION

She felt in italics and thought in capitals.   — *Henry James*

There's nothing wrong with the average person that a good psychiatrist can't exaggerate.

The fish you catch this year may not be as large as those you caught last year, but they will be by next year.

Be careful when you stretch the truth too far—it may snap back.

Nothing increases the size of the fish you caught more than the absence of witnesses.

The only time a woman will not exaggerate is when she is talking about her own age.

If fish were as big as the stories told about them, sardines would be sold in garages instead of tin cans.

The wife who makes a mountain out a molehill probably has a husband who makes a molehill out of a mountain.

Exaggeration always makes the truth more acceptable, and the lie less.

Most fish would be bigger if fishermen's arms were longer.

Another person who never has any need for a magnifying glass is the faultfinder.

Never exaggerate your faults—your friends will attend to that.

A fisherman's exaggerations make it easier to swallow a fish-bone than a fish story.

EXAMPLE

Virtuous men do good by setting themselves up as models before the public, but I do good by setting myself up as a warning.
                                    –Montaigne

A mare will no more take after its father and mother than a Congressman will take after a good example.   *–Will Rogers*

Setting a good example for your children takes all the fun out of middle age.

There's only one thing more contagious than the measles, and that's a good example.

Example is better than precept: your son will follow your footsteps sooner than follow your advice.

An ounce of example is worth a pound of advice.

A parent's hardest problem is how to teach his children good manners without having to set a good example.

When a man gets too old to set a bad example, he starts giving good advice.

The younger generation is more in need of models than critics.

Everyone has some useful purpose in life, even if it is only to serve as a horrible example.

Husbands who follow the example of Oedipus have wives who are wrecks.

Many a man sets a good example, but only when he has an audience.

EXCEPTION

Exceptions prove the rule—and wreck the family budget.
—*Olin Miller*

One can survive everything nowadays except death, and live down anything except a good reputation. —*Oscar Wilde*

To win back my youth there is nothing I wouldn't do, except to take exercise, get up early, or be a useful member of society.
—*Oscar Wilde*

Education teaches us the rules, while experience teaches us the exceptions.

EXCESS

To restrain people from excesses, just pass a law changing human nature, and make it retroactive to the Garden of Eden.
—*Bernard Shaw*

Wisdom has its excesses just like folly, and they should be equally restrained. —*Montaigne*

My advice to girls: first, don't smoke—to excess; second, don't drink—to excess; third; don't marry—to excess. —*Mark Twain*

The road to excess leads to the palace of wisdom. —*William Blake*

A word to the wise is not only sufficient, it is altogether too much.

Parents save for a rainy day their excess money; children, their excess energy.

The hardest thing in life is to know when you've had enough before you've had too much.

There are two kinds of people who shouldn't drink to excess: men and women.

Some people read too much, some people write too much, but everyone talks too much.

EXCHANGE

What a pity human beings can't exchange problems: everyone knows how to solve the other fellow's.

The rate of exchange on Christmas gifts will always be very high.

Discussion is an exchange of intelligence; argument is an exchange of ignorance.

Gossip is a medium of exchange where nothing is ever redeemed.

When in doubt about a gift, make it money: it's the easiest gift to exchange.

A fortune-hunter is a generous man who is willing to give his name in exchange for her money.

Giving up smoking is exchanging one bad habit for another, usually one pack of cigarettes for two of gum or three of mints.

The exchange of Christmas gifts ought to be reciprocal rather than retaliatory.

There's no such thing as a perfect gift for a woman, but the nearest thing to it is the gift she can exchange for something else.

EXCITEMENT

The man who is always trying to create a sensation will soon find that he can't even create a disturbance.   — *Josh Billings*

What is required is sight and insight—then you might add one more: excite.   — *Robert Frost*

A busybody rarely gets excited over anything until she realizes that it is none of her business.

Most of the excitement of life is hunting for some.

The man who loses his head easily never misses it.

EXCUSE

There is hardly any man so strict as not to vary a little from truth when he is to make an excuse.   — *Halifax*

We all find excuses instead of time for the things we don't want to do.

A bachelor is poor at making excuses—he never has to explain anything to a wife.

When it comes to excuses, the world is full of great inventors.

Children are always wasting time trying to convince their parents that it was someone else's fault.

A politician will find an excuse to get out of anything, except out of office.

You are young only once— after that you have to think up some other excuse.

A man's work lasts from sun to sun, but his excuses for staying late at the office are never done.

A lie by any other name would be just as poor an excuse.

The man who wants to do it finds a way; the man who doesn't finds an excuse.

There aren't nearly enough crutches in the world for all the lame excuses.

It's a mistake for a man to tell his wife a thing or two; he should tell her one and stick to it.

Some people are so full of excuses that they even have excuses for mistakes they haven't made yet.

Some men make good; others make good excuses.

There's no excuse for a human being who's full of excuses.

All men are skilled at making one thing or another, even if it is only at making excuses.

EXECUTIVE

It is a rare executive who doesn't wear out several suits to every pair of shoes.

There are two kinds of executives: one tries to get around him better men than himself; the other tries to get around better men than himself.

An executive is a man who is always annoying the hired help by asking them to do something.

The difference between a junior executive and a senior executive is sometimes a matter of age, but more often a matter of poundage.

A busy executive usually keeps his calendar, his wastebasket, and his liquor cabinet full.

A successful executive is one who delegates all responsibility, shifts all the blame, and appropriates all the credit.

Every executive should have two women: a secretary to take things down, and a wife to pick things up.

An executive is a man who talks golf in the office, and business on the golf course.

Some executives delegate authority, some farm out work, while most pass the buck.

An executive is a man employed to talk to visitors so that the other employees can get their work done.

It is easier for an executive to open the door of opportunity because he is in a key position.

EXERCISE

I have never taken any exercise except sleeping and resting.
— *Mark Twain*

Violent exercise is like a cold shower: you think it does you good because you feel better when you stop. — *Robert Quillen*

I never take any exercise—except for breathing.
— *Mary Garden*

Exercise should be avoided: if you are well, you don't need it, and if you are sick, you shouldn't take it.

Statistics show what really happens if you exercise daily—you die healthier.

You are middle-aged if you get most of your exercise watching the sports programs on television.

Those who do not find time for exercise will have to find time for illness.

The only drawback about exercise is that it makes you tired.

Even when you are pushing seventy, you still need more exercise.

We have all read about the value of exercise from the sedentary writer who sits in his chair exercising his typewriter.

Observe your dog: if he's fat, you're not getting enough exercise.

In youth, we can touch the toes without bending the knees; in middle age, we're lucky if we can touch the knees without bending the toes.

There's no better exercise for strengthening the heart than

reaching down and lifting people up.

Some people exercise by jumping to conclusions, some by side-stepping their responsibilities, but most people get it by running down their friends.

The exercise that does you the least good is patting yourself on the back.

Some people would never get any exercise at all if they didn't have to walk to their cars.

Taking bending exercises is the modern form of stooping to conquer.

Many a businessman doesn't need exercise; he burns up enough energy trying to keep his head above water.

EXHIBITIONIST

An exhibitionist is a girl who doesn't care what's showing as long as it isn't her slip.

A show-off is always trying to figure out how to wear the labels of her expensive clothes on the outside.

Some girls can't even wear an air of innocence without making it conspicuous.

When a show-off is forced to take a back seat, he always takes affront.

Some girls exhibit a generous nature; others show how generous nature has been to them.

A show-off is always trying to make an impression, but it's never the impression he is trying to make.

A show-off is always shown up in a showdown.

EXIT

It is easier to stay out than to get out.   —Mark Twain

One of the delights known to age, and beyond the grasp of youth, is that of Not Going.
                    —J. B. Priestley

On the new superhighways you see many unexpected sights, like the exit you are now too late to take.

A married man should think twice before going out for the evening: first, a reason for going out, and second, a reason for going out alone.

The man who steps aside in a bus for a lady, probably expects her to open up a path to the exit for him.

The trouble with some guests who stand up to go is that they think they have already gone.

Three-quarters of our population live in or near cities; the other quarter is on the highway looking for the exit.

EXPECT

A pinch of probably is worth a pound of perhaps.
                    —James Thurber

A thing long expected takes the form of the unexpected when at last it comes.   — *Mark Twain*

A road map in April is what a seed catalog is in March.

About the time a man is old enough to know better you can expect the worst.

You can't kiss a girl unexpectedly; the nearest you can come to it is to kiss her sooner than she thought you would.

Many people expect too much of marriage, and too much marriage is what they get.

Life expectancy is increasing: you can expect anything from life nowadays.

Sometimes the unexpected happens when you don't expect a person to come up to expectations.

Nowadays girls don't look for too much in a man—just someone to live with until the divorce.

Do a little more every day than you are expected to do, and soon you will be expected to do more.

Marriage is a condition in which no woman gets everything she expected, and no man expects everything he gets.

Blessed are those who expect nothing, for they shall never be disappointed.

EXPENSE

A married man seldom has any trouble meeting expenses—his wife introduces him to them.

Why is it that every time you make both ends meet, something breaks in the middle?

Many things can make a woman dearer to her husband, but the most common one is clothes.

Some women dress to please their husbands, while others never bother about the expense.

It never fails: when it is most difficult to meet expenses, you meet them everywhere.

EXPENSE ACCOUNT

A padded expense account is the softest part of a traveling salesman's job.

Eat, drink and be merry for tomorrow they may not be deductible.

An expense account is a device that enables a salesman to get his lunches, dinners and hangovers free.

You can eat your cake and put it on the expense account too.

An expense account is a tax deduction which allows a person to spend more on luxuries than on necessities.

The man who always reaches for the check is probably generous, sociable—and on an expense account.

An expense account permits us to squander our money instead of letting the government do it for us.

EXPENSIVE

You can't name anything that's more expensive than being good-natured.

Few things are more expensive than a girl who is free for the evening.

One of the few things women's clothes leave to the imagination is why they are so expensive.

The best things in life are free, but the trouble is that the next best are so expensive.

Talk is cheap, but not when money does it.

A thing of beauty is an expense forever.

Marriage turns the girl who is dear to your heart into a woman who is dear to your purse.

An expensive wife often makes a pensive husband.

EXPERIENCE

Experience is not what happens to a man; it is what a man does with what happens to him.
— *Aldous Huxley*

Experience teaches us only one thing at a time—and hardly that, in my case.   — *Mark Twain*

We learn from experience that we never learn from experience.
— *Bernard Shaw*

To most men, experience is like the stern lights of a ship which illumine only the track it has passed.   — *Coleridge*

Experience is the only thing most people get out of life.

Experience is the one thing you have plenty of when you're too old to get the job.

It's easier for a man with money to get experience because there are so many eager to help him.

Experience is the training that enables people to get along without education.

It's important to profit by your experience, but even more important to recover from it.

Experience stops us from making the same mistakes, but not from making a different one each time.

Experience is the only teacher that gives the test first and the lesson later.

There is no substitute for experience, but letting your wife do it is the next best thing.

Experience is an expensive form of knowledge which we let others have the benefit of for nothing.

The trouble with experience is that so few people are born with it.

Experience is another thing you get whether you want it or not.

Experience is what is bound to happen in everyone's experience.

When a man starts out to get something for nothing, he makes an expensive addition to his store of experience.

Experience teaches us what fools we used to be, but not what fools we are going to be.

Everyone prefers to learn certain things by personal experience, like the proverb that money does not bring happiness.

Experience is a wonderful thing: it enables you to recognize a mistake every time you repeat it.

Experience is a medicine of endless doses which you keep on taking all your life.

Learn by experience—preferably, other people's.

Experience is one of the few things in life you can't get on the easy payment plan.

A man becomes experienced by watching what happens to him when he isn't.

Experience is what happens to you while you are making other plans.

Experience is the best teacher, but the tuition is much too high.

To teenagers, a parent's experience is not the best teacher, but the worst preacher.

Experience has to be paid for; that's why divorce is more expensive than marriage.

There are no free scholarships to the School of Experience.

Experience enables us in the future to make the same mistakes much more easily.

Experience is like drawing without an eraser.

The trouble with experience is that it is always teaching you things you don't want to know.

Experience is a matter of knowing how much is too much.

Experience is a good school but it never gives you any vacations.

Some people have a natural talent for learning the least from the most experience.

Experience is the best method of acquiring knowledge because everyone gets individual instruction.

Man is an acquisitive creature: no matter how much experience he already has, he is always accumulating more.

Experience is the best teacher: it should be, considering how much it costs.

Some people speak from experience, while others, from experience, don't speak.

Experience is always worthwhile: if it doesn't keep you from making the same mistake twice, at least it keeps you from admitting it twice.

When a man with money meets a man with experience, the man

with the experience gets the money, and the man with the money gets the experience.

Experience teaches wisdom: the experienced husband has learned to think twice before saying nothing.

Experience comes with age—which is the time it does you the least good.

There's only one thing more painful than learning from experience, and that is not learning from experience.

The trouble with experience is that you never have it until after you need it.

EXPERIMENT

Anyone with an active mind lives on tentatives rather than tenets.   — *Robert Frost*

Never trust a girl who says she loves you more than anyone else in the world; it shows she has been experimenting.

Money may not buy happiness, but most of us are willing to make the experiment.

EXPERT

An expert is a man who has stopped thinking—he knows!
— *Frank Lloyd Wright*

The reputation of an expert is sometimes based on what he knows, but more often on what others don't know.

An expert is a man who takes something you already know and makes it sound confusing.

Some men do things, while others just sit around and become experts on how things should be done.

A connoisseur is easily pleased with the best of everything.

An expert is a man who always has a good reason for guessing wrong.

EXPLANATION

A little inaccuracy sometimes saves tons of explanations.   — *Saki*

Never explain: your friends will understand you, and your enemies will not believe you anyway.
— *Elbert Hubbard*

Why should we need any more light on poems than the light which radiates from the poems themselves?   — *T. S. Eliot*

I may have said the same thing before, but my explanation, I am sure, will always be different.   — *Oscar Wilde*

The first 40 years of life give us the text, the next 30 the commentary.   — *Schopenhauer*

The less you know about a subject, the longer it takes you to explain it.

An ounce of keeping your mouth shut is worth a pound of explanation.

When a politician makes an explanation, the explanation has to be explained.

There are some critics whom you can understand quite well until they start to explain what they mean.

Bores are all alike: their explanation is always longer than their information.

A know-it-all is always recognized by his ability to explain everything.

In America Congress makes the laws and the Supreme Court has to explain what they mean.

It usually takes less time to do a thing right than to explain why you didn't.

EXPOSURE

Every once in a while some fellow without a single bad habit gets caught.   — *Kin Hubbard*

Two things always tell on a woman: time, and her best friend.

The good man who goes wrong is really a bad man who has just been found out.

Man proposes and marriage exposes.

When fame comes to a person, it often comes in the form of an exposé.

Often it's the years that tell on a man, but more often it's the women.

The chief problem of fashion designers is how to show a lot of pretty clothes and a lot of pretty woman at the same time.

Every man has depths which have never been plumbed—until he runs for office.

Children are always spilling things—sometimes at home, but more often at the neighbors.

Nothing tells on a woman quite so fast as gossiping neighbors.

Some evening gowns show everything but good taste.

EXPRESSION

One's eyes are what one is, one's mouth is what one becomes.
— *Galsworthy*

It is one of the unwritten laws of French politeness that a long face is a breach of manners.
— *Richard Le Gallienne*

It is difficult to be emphatic when no one is emphatic on the other side.
— *Charles Dudley Warner*

When a thought is too weak to be expressed simply, simply drop it.   — *Vauvenargues*

Of all the things you wear, your expression is the most important.

A poker face enables a card player to conceal the kind of hand he has by the kind of face he hasn't.

A sourpuss never loses his gloomy expression, except when he has bad news to report.

Another way to tell whether a man is having a good time at a party is to watch the expression on his wife's face.

Many a person who has nothing wrong with him, doesn't let his face know about it.

When you see a woman with a vacant expression, she is probably thinking of herself.

Put a man or woman on a bedpan, and they'll always assume a dead-pan.

EXTINCTION

Becoming extinct is the perfect answer to everything, and I defy anybody to think of a better.
— *Will Cuppy*

If the world should blow itself up, the last audible voice would be that of an expert saying it can't be done. — *Peter Ustinov*

The dodo seems to have been invented for the sole purpose of becoming extinct, and that was all he was good for. — *Will Cuppy*

The reason life on other planets is extinct may be that their scientists were more advanced than ours.

Size isn't everything: the mammoth became extinct not because it was too big but because its brain was too small.

The woman who hesitates is not lost; she is extinct.

EXTRAVAGANCE

All decent people live beyond their incomes; those who aren't respectable live beyond other people's; a few gifted individuals manage to do both. — *Saki*

Extravagance is inevitable: the poor can't economize and the rich won't.

An extravagant girl makes a poor mother and a poorer father.

A woman is often a credit to a husband, but more often a debt.

Just as soon as people make enough money to live comfortably, they want to live extravagantly.

The only extravagance some wives have is that they like to spend money.

Extravagance is a form of excessive spending indulged in by your neighbors.

Extravagance is anything a husband spends money on which his wife can't use.

Don't tell your wife that she spends too much; you can never make enough for her to do so.

In this extravagant age, anyone who preaches economy might as well start by saving his breath.

Extravagance is a good trait in a boyfriend, but a bad one in a husband.

Many men fail in business because their wives have such extravagant husbands.

Two can live as cheaply as one, but only if the one is living it up.

Many a teenager has a way with money—her way and her parents' money.

EXTREME

Formerly the younger generation often went to extremes, but nowadays they often start from there.

Women's wear often goes to extremes, but seldom to extremities.

First husbands run to extremes: a widow's first husband is the best of men, and a divorcee's is the worst.

The woman who wears tight shoes at one extremity probably has a narrow understanding at the other.

A candidate is always opposed to the extreme right and extreme left, but always in favor of the extreme middle.

The problem of education tend to go to extremes: on one hand we have too many overcrowded schools, and on the other too many dropouts.

The woman who regards her trouble as extreme is probably having difficulty with her feet.

EYES

The faultfinder is a person who has one sharp eye for faults, and one blind eye for virtues.

Some people sleep with one eye open; others wake with both eyes shut.

In life, actions speak louder than words, but in love, the eyes do.

Genetics determines the color of her eyes, but it is jewels that light them up.

Drink to me only with thine eyes—it's cheaper that way.

Early to bed and early to rise, and you'll never show red in the whites of your eyes.

A bright eye indicates curiosity; a black eye, too much.

Alphabetically speaking, it's the eyes of a woman that disturb the ease of a man.

Another disadvantage of marrying a girl taller than you are is that you'll never see eye to eye.

FACE

Who sees the human face correctly: the photographer, the mirror or the painter?   — Picasso

If our faces were not alike, we couldn't distinguish man from the beast; if they were not different, we couldn't distinguish man from man.   — Montaigne

He might have brought an action against his countenance for libel and recovered heavy damages.   — *Dickens*

I have come to look on my face as a mask behind which the reality is the reality that it hides.
                    — *William Allen White*

It is the common wonder of all men how, among so many millions of faces, there should be one alike.   — *Sir Thomas Browne*

I never forget a face, but in your case I'll make an exception.
                    — *Groucho Marx*

When some people lose face, they feel worse but look better.

Nature gives you the face you have at 20; life gives you the face you have at 30; but the face you have at 40 is the one you made yourself.

When a girl hasn't a pretty face, it's a sign that she won't mind if you lie to her about it.

A woman's face is her fortune —or misfortune.

The more beautiful a girl's face, the less a man can tell you what clothes she has on.

Many a woman has the kind of face that grows on a man instead of the kind that should grow on a woman.

Woman is like a coin: prized according to face value.

You can't beat nature: the less hair you have to comb, the more face you have to wash.

The face that over cocktails seemed so sweet, is less alluring over shredded wheat.

A woman's face is her fortune only when it draws a lot of interest.

FACT

There is nothing stubborn about a fact; whenever it meets a fool it is ready to lay down its life for him.   — *Frank Moore Colby*

The greatest American superstition is belief in facts.
                    — *Hermann A. Keyserling*

A fact in science is not a mere fact, but an instance.
                    — *Bertrand Russell*

Value judgments are not to be established on the basis of facts —and that's a fact.
                    — *Joseph Wood Krutch*

To some lawyers all facts are created equal. — *Felix Frankfurter*

The surest way to spoil a good story is by sticking to the facts.

When a politician has no time to bother with the facts, he can always discuss great moral issues.

Get the facts, or the facts will get you.

As a matter of fact is an expression that precedes many an expression that isn't.

Facts and figures go together: the girl with a good figure soon learns the facts.

Nothing can be more disputed than an indisputable fact.

What is usually missing from a hot political argument are cold facts.

FADDIST

Nothing ruins the appetite like a speech on digestion by a food fanatic in the course of a meal.
— *Dr. Morris Fishbein*

Every now and then you meet a fresh-air fiend who is so healthy, it's sickening.

A food faddist is a person who is determined to be healthy even if it kills him.

A faddist is a person who is always giving up something new, and taking up something newer.

Nothing gives his friends more pleasure than when a health faddist becomes ill.

FAILURE

The woman who has been married and divorced a number of times reminds us of the man who is always failing in business.
— *Ed Howe*

The only time you mustn't fail is the last time you try.
— *Charles F. Kettering*

A man can fail many times, but he isn't a failure until he begins to blame somebody else.
— *John Burroughs*

A failure is a man who has blundered, but is not able to cash in on the experience.
— *Elbert Hubbard*

It sometimes happens that when a man fails in doing everything else well, he marries well.

If at first you don't succeed— forget it.

Don't despise the advice of the man who failed; he should be an authority on what not to do.

Every boy born in the United States has an equal chance of becoming a failure.

A has-been is anybody who was formerly somebody and is now nobody.

It's hard for us to see why we are not more successful, but easy to see why our friends are failures.

Many a man is a failure until he gets married, and then he has a fighting chance.

You can generally tell when a man isn't successful by the way he lies to make other people think he is.

Many a failure never gets his head above water because he never sticks his neck out.

The young man who thinks the world owes him a living becomes the old man who blames the world for his failure.

Failure is not falling down; it is remaining there when you have fallen.

Many a man seldom gives his wife credit for anything, except for the failure he is.

There are two chief ways to insure failure: always underrate your competition, and always overrate yourself.

There are two kinds of failures: those who thought and never did, and those who did and never thought.

Marriage is so often a failure because so many inexperienced men and women enter into it.

Fortune turns the man down who is always waiting for things to turn up.

It takes some people all their lives to become failures, while others achieve it in just a few years.

You may fail through laziness, you may fail through ignorance, but the surest way to fail is through a combination of both.

It's better to be a has-been than a never-was.

There are two kinds of failures: those who cannot do what they are told, and those who can do nothing else.

If at first you don't succeed, blame it on your wife.

The man who spends half his life telling what he's going to do, probably spends the other half explaining why he didn't do it.

The man who tries his hand at something and fails, should try using his head for a change.

FAIR

The nearest thing that any honest man can come to the thing called impartiality is to confess that he is partial.   *– Chesterton*

All's fair in love and war— and they are alike in other ways too.

Whoever named them the fair sex was a poor judge of justice.

Many a man plays a fair game of golf—but only if you watch him.

If you lean over backwards to be fair, it's harder for your enemies to knife you in the back.

FAITH

There are very few women who have as much faith in the Lord as a bride has in her husband.   *– Ed Howe*

I always prefer to believe the best of everybody—it saves so much trouble.   *– Rudyard Kipling*

It takes a lot more faith to live this life without faith than with it.   *– Peter De Vries*

It's fine to believe in ourselves, but we mustn't be too easily convinced.   *– Burton Hillis*

It's not dying for a faith that's so hard, it's living up to it.   *– Thackeray*

We have not lost faith, but we have transferred it from God to the medical profession.   *– Bernard Shaw*

Faith is something entirely possessed by children, and they don't know they have it.   *—Ed Howe*

Only a woman can believe in a man who she knows isn't to be believed.

About the time a girl loses her faith in fairy tales, she begins to believe in love.

Of course Americans trust in God—you can tell by the way they drive.

Faith is feminine: even the cynic who believes in nothing can find a girl who believes in him.

You cannot do much with faith, and you cannot do much without it.

FAITH, HOPE AND CHARITY

Every debtor thinks his creditor should be endowed with faith, hope and charity.

Applause at the beginning of a speech shows the audience has faith; in the middle, it shows their hope; and at the end, their charity.

The best things in life are three: faith, hope and charity.

Can Faith and Hope be called Sisters of Charity?

The man who puts too much faith and hope in a stock market tip will probably have to call for charity.

Many a play requires our faith, hope and charity: faith in the first act, hope in the second, and charity in the last.

And now abideth faith, hope and charity, these three; and the greatest of these is—a sense of humor.

St. Paul paraphrased: And now abideth faith, hope and deductible charity.

FALL

Some people stand for nothing because they fall for everything.

It would have been more convincing if the fall of man had been attributed to a banana instead of an apple.

The man who falls down gets up a lot faster than the man who lies down.

You may be a fine, upstanding citizen, but that seems to make no difference to a freshly waxed floor.

If you're made of the right material, a hard fall is bound to result in a high bounce.

When a man falls down his temper generally gets up before he does.

Don't worry when you stumble; remember, a worm is the only thing that can't fall down.

FALLOUT

Once upon a time a fallout was merely a lovers' quarrel.

An old-timer is one who remembers when the only fallout a man had to worry about was caused by a hairbrush.

Many a man's den is his fallout shelter: that's where he retreats when he and his wife fall out.

A family man is exposed to fallout every day—when he opens the hall closet.

FALSE

There are 869 different forms of lying, but only one of them has been squarely forbidden: Thou shalt not bear false witness against thy neighbor.   — *Mark Twain*

Nothing can be falser than a truism.

People who prize an antique for its beauty suddenly find it unsightly when it turns out to be a fake.

The only falsehood allowed a husband on his income tax return is to list himself as the head of his household.

FAME

The present condition of fame is merely fashion.   — *Chesterton*

Fame usually comes to those who are thinking about something else.   — *Dr. O. W. Holmes*

Being famous is like having a string of pearls given you: it's nice, but after a while it's only to wonder if they're real or cultured.
        — *Somerset Maugham*

By the time the French Academy elects a man to a seat, what he really needs is a bed.
        — *Jean Cocteau*

It isn't easy to live after death; it takes a lifetime.
        — *Stanislaw J. Lec*

Remember that the conquest of glory excels the glory of conquest.
        — *Da Vinci*

Fame: an embalmer trembling with stage fright.   — *Mencken*

The fame of great men ought to be judged always by the means they used to acquire it.
        — *La Rochefoucauld*

The first test of fame is to have a crazy person imagine he is you.

Before a man can wake up and find himself famous, he has to wake up and find himself.

Newspaper fame is a case of hero today and gone tomorrow.

Sometimes the pinnacle of fame and the height of folly are twin peaks.

Fame doesn't consist in waking, but in staying awake.

Footprints on the sands of time are not made by sitting down.

The man with the thirst for fame often finds it a long time between drinks.

Notoriety begins and popularity ends as soon as your enemies outnumber your friends.

The man who rests on his laurels will soon find that his laurels no longer rest on him.

The young man who leaves home to set the world on fire, usually has to come back for more matches.

The distance from obscurity to fame is much longer than from fame to obscurity.

Fame is more than wealth, but only if you have both.

Some people wake up and find themselves famous; others find themselves famous and then wake up.

Some men wake up and find themselves famous, while others stay up all night and become notorious.

People no longer leave footprints on the sands of time—they leave tire tracks.

The man who wakes up famous has not been asleep.

FAMILIAR

Nothing is wonderful when you get used to it.   — Ed Howe

He met every kind of person except the ordinary person; he knew everybody, so to speak, except everybody.   — Chesterton

Familiarity is the root of the closest friendships, as well as the intensest hatreds.   — Rivarol

When a man tells a girl she looks familiar, he probably wants to get the same way.

The trouble with marriage is familiarity: if husband and wife would treat each other like strangers, marriage would always be a success.

FAMILY

I would rather start a family than finish one.   — Don Marquis

A family is a unit composed not only of children but of men, women, an occasional animal, and the common cold.   — Ogden Nash

The family you come from isn't as important as the family you're going to have.   — Ring Lardner

If you cannot get rid of the family skeleton, you may as well make it dance.   — Bernard Shaw

A family is a form of government where the father is the chief executive, and the mother is the speaker of the house.

In a family where the parents do too much talking, the children probably do too little listening.

A family is where the father does the providing, the mother the deciding, and the children the overriding.

In the good old days, large families were the rule, not the exemptions.

The way of the transgressor is hard—on his family.

Money talks, and in some families it keeps up a running conversation.

A wife and children can be a great handicap, especially if you are not married.

The trouble with the family is that children grow out of childhood but parents never grow out of parenthood.

It takes a lot of money to raise a family, but a good deal more to support them after they are raised.

Some men are born lucky; others have large families.

Another thing that brings a family closer together is a small car.

Don't judge a man by his family—Cain belonged to a good one.

The average household consists of a father, mother, two children and a television repairman.

No family ever deserves the praise it gets from the girl who is about to marry into it.

You can always tell the family man: he's the one with his wallet full of snapshots.

A household is a battleground where the children always triumph unless both parents unite to defend themselves.

The thing most needed in the American home today is the family.

Most families don't want father burdened with money, so they relieve him of his burden.

Children keep a family together, especially when one can't get a babysitter.

In most families, while the youngsters are growing up, the grown-ups are growing out.

The family that stays together probably has only one car.

FAMILY TREE

Ancestors never boast of the descendants who boast of ancestors.   —Don Marquis

Don't try to trace your family tree too far back, or you'll find your ancestors still living in it.

Many a man makes a place in the sun for himself by taking refuge in the shadow of the family tree.

A family tree is like riding in a train backwards: it shows you where you came from, but not where you're going.

The first thing a social climber wants is a family tree.

Why pay money to have your family tree traced; just go into politics and your opponents will do it for you.

Money doesn't grow on trees, but it grows on many family trees.

Man is nothing more than the temporary quarters where his ancestors rest for a while on their way to become his descendants.

The woman who boasts she is a descendant from a great family is probably still descending.

FANATIC

A fanatic is a man who does what he thinks the Lord would do if only He knew the facts of the case. — *Finley Peter Dunne*

One cannot suppress the fanatic —he will be on hand to do his worst for every cause.
— *Frank Moore Colby*

Fanaticism is the gravest danger there is: I might almost say that I was fanatical against fanaticism. — *Bertrand Russell*

The worst vice of the fanatic is his sincerity. — *Oscar Wilde*

A fanatic always exhausts your patience before he exhausts his subject.

A fanatic is another person who goes through life with a closed mind and an open mouth.

A fanatic is a person who can never get his cause off his mind, or his mind off his cause.

Another person who is hard to listen to, but easy to talk about is the fanatic.

A fanatic always has to change his audience because he never wants to change the subject.

FARMER

A good farmer is nothing more than a handy man with a sense of humus. — *E. B. White*

Don't go in for farming unless you want to vegetate.

There are three kinds of farming: extensive, intensive, and pretensive.

The man with the hoe never gets as far as the man with the hokum.

The advantage of living on a farm is that cows and chickens don't come in and urge you to play bridge when you'd rather read.

A farmer is always raising things, but never as much as the middleman.

All it takes to be a successful farmer these days is faith, hope and parity.

A gentleman farmer never dirties himself with the soil or soils himself with the dirt.

In some places they raise more corn to feed more hogs to buy more land to raise more corn to feed more hogs.

What the farmer really needs is a car that will eat oats.

It isn't the farmer that lives on the fat of the land; it's the fat of the land that lives on the farmer.

If you work hard and long enough on a farm, you can make a fortune—if you strike oil on it.

Politics makes strange bedfellows—also strange authorities on the farm problem.

A gentleman farmer is one who has time to read all the government literature on farming.

FASHION

Ten years before its time, a fashion is indecent; ten years after, it is hideous; but a century after, it is romantic.
— *James Laver*

Her frocks come from Paris, but she wears them with a strong English accent. — *Saki*

Fashions are the only induced epidemics, proving that epidemics can be induced by tradesmen.
— *Bernard Shaw*

He who goes against the fashion is himself its slave.
— *Logan P. Smith*

Fashion by any other name would be just as ridiculous.

A fashion plate is a woman who knows clothes inside out, or who knows nothing outside clothes.

The reason men's suits look the same year after year is that most men are wearing the same ones.

Fashion is the reason why women don't dress true to form.

There's nothing new under the sun, but there's always something new over the daughter.

Every time a wife convinces her husband that women are the intellectual equals of men, along comes the latest fashion.

If you think the fashions of today are ridiculous, take another look into the family album.

Many a man smiles at his wife for slavishly following the fashions in dress while he is slavishly following the fashions in thought.

If you save it for nine years, it will be back in fashion.

A fashion plate is a woman of fashion who is followed by the woman who follows the fashion.

Another optimist is the man who expects the rising hemline in women's fashions to meet the dropping neckline.

The most attractive thing about the latest fashion is that it won't last.

It's the men who pay the bills who are the real slaves to fashion.

All men are created equal, but necklines, waistlines and hemlines show that women are not.

Women follow the fashions because they want to look different or because they want to look the same.

A fashion plate always gets away with murder while her husband faces the charges.

Many things are expensive because they are fashionable, and fashionable because they are expensive.

The women who are the first to wear the latest fashions are usually the ones who shouldn't.

Fashions are never just right: some dresses start too late, others end too early.

You can never tell what a woman will do next because, just

when you've got her all figured
out, the style changes.

A thing of beauty is a joy—
until the style changes.

Evolution of women's styles:
sleeveless, backless, shameless.

Fashion is for women without
taste just as etiquette is for people without breeding.

A fashion plate usually has
what it takes to wear the latest
fashions—a rich husband.

FASHION DESIGNER

A fashion designer creates new
fashions from the old ones as
soon as they are old enough.

The only man who can fool all
the women all the time is a fashion designer.

A fashion designer is busy designing new fashions for women
while nature is busy designing
women in the same old shape.

The reason women's fashions
are always changing is that designers don't like to make the
same mistake twice.

Fashion designers rarely design
sensible clothes for women because men are insensible to sensible clothes.

FAST AND SLOW

Half the motorists can't drive
fast enough to please their girl-
friends, while the other half can't
drive slow enough to appease
their wives.   — *Bill Vaughan*

Slow husbands generally make
fast wives.

The man who claims he never
drives too fast, always slows down
when he sees a state trooper.

Quick lunches make slow funeral processions.

FATE

Fate weaves the darkness, which
is perhaps why she weaves so
badly.   — *Max Beerbohm*

Destiny: a tyrant's authority for
crime, and a fool's excuse for
failure.   — *Bierce*

We make our own fortunes and
we call them fate.   — *Disraeli*

Men heap together the mistakes
of their lives and create a monster they call destiny.   — *Hobbes*

There is a destiny that shapes
our ends rough, hew them as we
will.   — *Frank Harris*

Fate is the irony that permits
us to kill time before time kills
us.

This is man's fate: to add to his
weight, and subtract from his
pate.

It does no harm to believe in
fate if you act as if you did not.

FATHER

The fundamental defect of
fathers is that they want their
children to be a credit to them.
         — *Bertrand Russell*

Paternity is a career imposed on you without any inquiry into your fitness. — *Adlai Stevenson*

You can't sell a slave in America, so your father is just a blessing, not a commodity.

A father is sometimes the master in his own home, but more often merely the paymaster.

No one is more helpless than a new-born father.

An expectant father suddenly stops giving his friends advice on how to raise their children.

The hardest task of being a father is not having several little mouths to feed, but having one big mouth to heed.

A father is the parent who is busy doing his children's homework while they are busy watching television.

Many a father spends part of his time keeping the wolf from his door, and the rest of the time keeping the wolf from his daughter.

A father is a banker provided by nature.

There's one thing you must give fathers credit for: they always go through the suffering of childbirth without an anesthetic.

The price many a father has to pay to get his daughter off his hands it to put her husband on his feet.

FATHER AND SON

Every father expects his boy to do the things he wouldn't do when he was young. — *Kin Hubbard*

The worst waste of breath, next to playing a saxophone, is advising a son. — *Kin Hubbard*

A man never knows how to be a son until he has become a father.

By the time a man realizes that his father was usually right, he has a son who thinks he's usually wrong.

A young man's success in life often depends on his selection of a father.

At five years of age your son is your master, at ten your slave, at fifteen your double, and after that your friend or foe.

It is not unusual for a son to fill his father's shoes—also his socks and shirts.

It never occurs to a boy of eighteen that he will some day be as dumb as his father.

So live that you are the man your son thought you were before he became an adolescent.

The old-fashioned father who was eager to put his shoulder to the wheel, now has a son who can't wait to put his hands on it.

A boy's best friend is his father, and if he gets up early or stays up late he may get to see him.

The worst misfortune that can happen to an ordinary man is to have an extraordinary father.

Most fathers want their sons to have things they never had, like A's on their report cards.

A chip off the old block often destroys the symmetry of the family tree.

Watch out that the footsteps your son follows are not those you think you've covered up.

No wonder a father has mixed feelings when his son goes off to college: while he loses a son, he gains a car.

A father usually believes in heredity until his son starts acting like a damn fool.

Adolescence is the period when your son is not what you thought he was, and he thinks you are not what he thought you were.

It's bad to be a bachelor, but even worse to be a bachelor's son.

FATHER'S DAY

Father's Day is the day in June when father remembers he hasn't yet paid the bills for Mother's Day.

Father's Day and Mother's Day are alike, except that on Father's Day you buy a much cheaper gift.

FAULT

I like a friend better for having faults that one can talk about.
— *Hazlitt*

His only fault is that he has none. — *Pliny*

Don't tell your friends their social faults: they will cure the fault and never forgive you.
— *Logan P. Smith*

We criticize our neighbor's faults, less to correct them than to show that we do not have them. — *La Rochefoucauld*

If you could see all a man's weak points, you'd think he had the measles. — *Ed Howe*

It is well that there is no one without a fault for he would not have a friend in the world.
— *Hazlitt*

People who have no faults are terrible; there is no way of taking advantage of them.
— *Anatole France*

The woman who hasn't many faults generally makes the most of those she has.

Faultfinders are all alike: they demand very much in others, but are satisfied with very little in themselves.

Everyone finds fault with the man who finds fault with everyone.

Another thing a husband doesn't have to remember is his own faults; his wife is sure to keep reminding him of them.

The best way to look at a woman's faults is to shut your eyes.

Rare is the person who can weigh the faults of others without putting his thumb on the scales.

A man will sometimes own up to a dozen faults in order to hide one.

A woman never knows her worst fault until she quarrels with her best friend.

When a fault gets the better of a man, it is usually his own fault.

A faultfinder never hesitates to criticize his own faults—but only when he sees them in others.

Finding fault is the most common type of unskilled labor.

Fault is one of the easiest things to find, and yet many people keep on looking for it.

Nature didn't make us perfect, so she did the next best thing— she made us blind to our faults.

Why can't our neighbors do as we do, and shut their eyes to our faults?

It takes only ten minutes to find in others the faults we cannot discover in ourselves in a lifetime.

The first faults are theirs who commit them; the second, theirs who permit them.

The faults of others are like headlights of an approaching car —they always seem more glaring than our own.

The worst fault of some people is telling other people theirs.

If you acknowledge your faults, you deprive your friends of the pleasure of pointing them out.

A bachelor is the only man who never finds out how many faults he has.

A faultfinder never learns that while we all have our faults, we prefer to be our own faultfinders.

Don't be critical: the man everyone likes usually likes everyone.

We are never blamed for having faults, but for having faults different from those who blame us.

It is easier to look over a person's faults than to overlook them.

To a faultfinder, the world is made up of only two kinds of people: those with bad faults, and those with good faults.

Don't criticize your husband's faults; it it weren't for them, he might have married a better wife.

FAVOR

There's nothing that binds one to a woman like the benefits one confers on her.
— *Somerset Maugham*

To accept a favor from a friend is to confer one.
— *John Churton Collins*

Never let your inferiors do you a favor—it will be extremely costly. — *Mencken*

The man has no occasion to hate me—I can't recall that I ever did him a favor. — *Disraeli*

Never claim as a right what you can ask as a favor.
— *John Churton Collins*

If you do a favor, forget it; if you receive one, remember it.

The first one to ask a favor is usually the last one to remember it.

Never put off till tomorrow the favor someone is willing to do for you today.

Most people are anxious to do a favor for those who don't need it.

There is only one thing worse than favors forgotten, and that is favors remembered—by the giver.

Do some men a favor and they are so grateful, they come back for more.

A good friend never forgets a favor, especially if he did it.

Always receive a favor in such a way that the giver wishes he had done you a greater one.

Do a man a favor once, and he may be grateful; repeat the favor, and he'll think you owe it to him.

If you do someone a favor, he'll always remember you—when he needs another favor.

FAVORITE

Every mother and every mother country has a favorite child.
— *Stephen Leacock*

In my mother's eye I was a 10-month child, better baked than the others, more glazed and crispier by staying in the oven longer.
— *Sartre*

A mother loves the child who became the thief or murderer more than the one who became the priest.
— *Faulkner*

The old-fashioned wife knew what her husband's favorite dishes were, but the modern wife knows what restaurants serve them.

FAVORITISM

Nepotism: appointing your grandmother to office for the good of the party.
— *Bierce*

If at first you do succeed, it's probably your father's business.

There would be many more successful men if more bosses had marriageable daughters.

FEAR

There's nothing I'm afraid of liked scared people. — *Robert Frost*

Tell us your phobias, and we will tell you what you are afraid of.
— *Robert Benchley*

The man who fears suffering is already suffering from what he fears.
— *Montaigne*

No girl who is afraid to stay home alone in the evening should ever get married. — *Ed Howe*

Those who lack the courage will always find a philosophy to justify it.
— *Camus*

The one thing in the world I am most afraid of is fear.
— *Montaigne*

Too many children are afraid of the dark, and too many adults are afraid of the light.

Why is it that a man who is scared of his wife will not hesitate to race a locomotive to a crossing?

The man who doesn't know the meaning of the word *fear* probably doesn't know many other words either.

A woman is the only thing I'm afraid of that I know won't hurt me.

A good scare is usually worth more to a person than good advice.

Do right, and fear no man; don't write, and fear no woman.

FEELING

All the reasons of a man cannot outweigh a single feeling of a woman.   — *Voltaire*

The feeling of friendship is like being comfortably filled with roast beef; of love, like being enlivened with champagne.
— *Samuel Johnson*

A good way to perk up your spirits whenever you're downcast is to think back over the persons you might have married.

A man is as young as he feels, but seldom as important.

A girl slaps a man's face, not to hurt his feelings, but to stop them.

Petting is popular everywhere probably because it creates a lot of good feeling.

A man is as young as he feels after trying to prove it.

Most people during middle age feel just as young as ever, but only once in a while.

FEET

The man with both feet on the ground usually takes orders from the man with both feet on the desk.

Many a married man suffers from cold feet, but they are not always his own.

A wife soon discovers that her husband has feet of clay, especially when he starts putting them on the sofa.

A foot on the brake is worth two in the grave.

The only time a woman admits she has big feet is when she hasn't.

Give a chiropodist an inch, and he will take a foot.

Some are born with cold feet, some acquire cold feet, and others have cold feet thrust upon them.

When a woman is dressed to kill, her feet are usually the first victims.

The young man who stands on his own two feet has probably failed his driving test.

If you put your best foot forward you won't step on someone else's toes.

The man who has one foot in the grave should be mighty glad he was born a biped.

Many a man who hoped to gain a foothold on success has wound up being a chiropodist.

FENCE

The back fence is the shortest distance between two gossips.

Politics consists of three sides: our side, the wrong side, and a fence.

A fence is a barrier used by neighbors to gossip over, with much to be said on both sides.

FERTILIZER

If a professional gardener were to enter the Garden of Eden, he would sniff and exclaim, "What marvelous humus!" — *Karel Capek*

Money is like manure: if you spread it around, it does a world of good; but if you pile it up, it stinks to high heaven.

Many candidates think that the way to get grassroots support is to spread around a lot of fertilizer.

The best fertilizer for the amateur gardener is the chemical that kills all plant growth, leaving him lots of leisure for other things.

FICKLE

Changeable women are more endurable than monotonous ones; they are sometimes murdered but seldom deserted. — *Bernard Shaw*

We criticize the fickleness of women when we are the victims; we find it charming when we are the objects.   — *Desnoyers*

No wonder women are changeable—they have to play smart to get a job, and play dumb to get a man.

It's really the men who are changeable; that's why many a wife who loves her husband one week can't stand him the next.

Never try to change a woman's mind; just wait awhile and she'll do it herself.

A woman is a fickle creature who is always rearranging her face, her figure and her furniture.

Every woman is a fickle creature; she demands feminine rights or masculine chivalry, whichever suits her needs at the moment.

A scatterbrain is always changing her mind even though she has no mind to change.

The man who writes about women should always reserve the right to laugh at his ideas of the day before.

The only thing that changes sides more often than a windshield wiper is a fickle woman.

The woman who is constantly changing her mind doesn't do so to improve it.

A woman's mind is like a time-table—subject to change without notice.

In a fickle woman, change is a permanent quality.

FICTION

People who write fiction, if they had not taken it up, might have become very successful liars.
— *Hemingway*

Stories, like whiskey, must be allowed to mature in the cask.
— *Seán O'Faoláin*

There's less fiction being read today than ever before, especially pure fiction.

The most imaginative fiction being written today is the income tax return.

FIDELITY

An ideal wife is one who remains faithful to you but tries to be just as charming as if she weren't. — *Sacha Guitry*

There's a great difference between being constant in love and constantly in love.

Constancy in a woman is a nuisance—when you've ceased to love her.

The husband who remains affectionate and faithful has probably had the same pretty secretary for a long time.

Men in love with themselves never waiver in their devotion.

FIGHT

Fighting is essentially a masculine idea; a woman's weapon is her tongue. — *Hermione Gingold*

Let him that is without stone among you cast the first thing he can lay his hands on.
— *Robert Frost*

One of the heaviest burdens a person can carry is a chip on his shoulder. — *Olin Miller*

You cannot love a thing without wanting to fight for it.
— *Chesterton*

The underdog often starts the fight, and occasionally the upper dog deserves to win. — *Ed Howe*

Some men can't seem to be able to live with their wives without fighting—at least, not happily.

If you do not like to get into a fight, avoid arguments with pacifists.

Never kick a man when he's down, unless you're sure he's not going to get up again.

He who fights and runs away, lives.

Men fight with their fists, women with their tears.

Many a belligerent man is a failure before he gets married, and then has a fighting chance.

It takes three people to engineer a fight: two to make it, and one to run for the police.

When words fail, try a punch on the jaw.

The man who avoids fighting is not always a coward—he may be a bachelor.

Two wrongs don't make a right, but they often make a fight.

Many a stranger gets into a street brawl in order to avoid being shot as an innocent bystander.

Divorce is the refuge of those who refuse to fight it out to the bitter end.

FIGURE

I have everything I had twenty years ago, only it's all a little bit lower.   — *Gypsy Rose Lee*

The man whose weekly salary runs into four figures probably has a wife and three daughters.

Some young men have a head for figures, but all young men have an eye for them.

Figures don't lie, but liars figure.

The woman who nibbles on things every hour soon develops an hourglass figure.

There's a considerable difference between a figure of one million dollars and a million-dollar figure.

The director of the budget is the only Washington official who can cut a ridiculous figure without being laughed at.

If you wonder what your wife does with all the grocery money, stand sideways and look at yourself in the mirror.

When a woman meets a man who looks her straight in the eyes, she'd better do something about her figure.

It isn't the color or cut of a woman's clothes that attract men, but the contour.

Figures don't lie, except political figures.

If a girl won't look after her figure, neither will a man.

A woman's age remains a youthful figure long after she herself has lost it.

The woman with an hourglass figure today is the woman with an hour-and-a-half-glass figure tomorrow.

There's safety in numbers, but there's danger in figures.

You can prove anything by figures, like showing that a motorist does sixty miles an hour even if he drives only six minutes.

It's better for a girl to be well formed than well informed.

By the time a man gets to the point where he can buy his wife clothes at a fancy figure, she no longer has one.

When an elderly man has a youthful figure, he doesn't want his wife to see him with her.

FIGURE 308 FINGER

Figures don't lie, unless they are women's.

Some women keep their youthful figures; others not only keep them, but double them.

A pretty woman who attracts widespread attention is never widespread.

FIGURE OF SPEECH

Heaven help us from the devil and from metaphors!   *— Heine*

A good example of a figure of speech is when you hear of a woman being speechless.

During an election campaign the statistics voiced by candidates are usually unreliable figures of speech.

FINANCE

High finance isn't burglary or obtaining money by false pretenses, but rather a judicious selection from the best features of those fine arts.
— Finley Peter Dunne

Alexander Hamilton originated the put and take system in our national treasury: the taxpayers put it in, and the politicians take it out.   *— Will Rogers*

Finance in one easy lesson: the more money you get, the more money you need.

You should spend the first half and the second half letting your money work for you.

Nowadays you can't live on love—without refinancing.

A financial analyst thinks he sees the forest clearly, but keeps bumping into the trees.

The Constitution guarantees you the pursuit of happiness, but doesn't guarantee to finance the chase.

About the time you catch up with the Joneses, they start to refinance.

When one optimist finances another optimist, guess which one becomes a pessimist?

International finance is the art of borrowing on the strength of what you already owe.

A loan company is a place where you can borrow enough money to get you completely out of debt.

Many a woman's idea of finance is very simple: when you owe debts, just borrow enough to pay them.

How can the millions of people employed in the auto industry make a living out of something nobody has paid for?

A finance company never puts off till tomorrow who can be dunned today.

FINGER

All your fingernails grow with inconvenient speed except the broken one.   *— Ogden Nash*

The first handshake in life is the greatest of all: the clasp of an infant around the finger of a parent.

People who are always pointing fingers, rarely hold out their hands.

The girl who dates a confirmed bachelor can never put her finger on anything definite, or put anything definite on her finger.

Keep your fingers away from a power saw—it doesn't know you need them.

If you want to drive in a nail without smashing your fingers, hold the hammer in both hands.

When you point your finger accusingly at someone else, remember, you've got three fingers pointing at yourself.

It's hard for the man who slips a ring on a girl's finger to avoid winding up under her thumb.

FINGERPRINT

The finger of God never leaves the same fingerprint.
— *Stanislaw J. Lec*

So live your life that your autograph will be wanted, not your fingerprints.

Small children mark up a home with more fingerprints than are kept by the FBI.

Man is a creature of puzzling values: he admires those who leave footprints on the sands of time, but not those who leave fingerprints.

The more children's fingerprints there are in a home, the fewer there are on police records.

FINISH

In war as in love, to bring matters to a close, you must get close together. — *Napoleon*

A fast finish for a car is lacquer, but a faster finish is liquor.

No man is complete until he is married—and then he is finished.

If you want a real lasting finish put on your car, try beating the train to the railroad crossing.

FIRE

I don't approve of open fires: you can't think, or talk, or even make love in front of a fireplace—all you can do is stare at it. — *Rex Stout*

The burned child shuns the fire —until the next day.
— *Mark Twain*

The college student who wants to set the world on fire was probably the schoolboy who wanted to set the schoolhouse on fire.

Many a fire is caused by friction between the insurance policy and the mortgage.

The best way to make a fire with two sticks is to be sure that one of them is a match.

What is it about a fire that makes it so eager to start in a forest and so reluctant to start in a fireplace?

By the time you have money to burn, the fire has gone out.

Civilization began with man's discovery of fire in the world and will probably end with his setting the world on fire.

The person who says, "Where there's smoke, there's fire," never owned a fireplace.

Always fight fire with fire, but not if you're a fireman.

Love is the only fire against which there is no insurance.

Nothing is more cozy and restful than a warm, crackling fire in the living room, but only if you have a fireplace.

FIRST

A young man with his first smoke makes himself sick; a young man with his first love makes others sick.

Which came first—the caterpillar or the butterfly?

Which came first—the ant or the picnic?

Which came first—the sun or the shadow?

Girls believe in love at first sight, men believe in it at first opportunity.

FISH

A fish drowns in the air.
— *G. C. Lichtenberg*

The life of fishes is ova before it begins.

You can't tell: maybe a fish goes home and lies about the size of the man he got away from.

Very few fish can close their eyes, but then the sea is never dusty.

How lucky it is that a fish doesn't cackle every time it lays an egg!

The only opportunity a fish has to take a shower bath is to jump up when it rains.

Even a fish won't get caught if it keeps its mouth shut.

FISHING

Fishing seems to be the favorite form of loafing. — *Ed Howe*

All you need to be a fisherman is patience and a worm.
— *Herb Shriner*

Has it ever struck you that the trouts bite best on the Sabbath —God's creatures tempting decent fishermen? — *James M. Barrie*

Fishing seems to be divided, like sex, into three unequal parts: an-

ticipation and recollection and, in between, actual performance.
— *Arnold Gingrich*

The only time a fisherman tells the truth is when he calls another fisherman a liar.

More big fish have been caught with words than with hook, line and sinker.

Nothing grows faster than a fish between the time he nibbles and the time he gets away.

Only a fisherman thinks it's worth spending one hundred dollars for a fishing outfit to catch one dollar's worth of fish.

A thoughtful wife has the meat and potatoes ready when her husband comes home from a fishing trip.

Fish is supposed to be good for the brain, but fishing is even better for the imagination.

Sometimes a fisherman doesn't catch anything until he gets home.

A fisherman first lies in wait for a fish, and then lies in weight after landing it.

To some wives, a fishing rod is a pole with a worm at each end.

An angler always hopes to catch a fish so big that he won't have to lie about it.

An angler is a man who has fish lying about him, or who is lying about fish.

All men are divided into three classes: fish, fishermen and bait.

Fish may be bought if they can't be caught.

If there were no fish there would be a lot less lying.

Some men, in telling a fish story, will go to any length.

The art of fishing is sitting still for a long time until you don't catch anything.

The best weather for fishing is the weather when they are caught.

If all the big fish that got away were in the sea, there wouldn't be any room for the water.

There are better fish stories in the sea than ever came out of it.

The best way to catch a fish is by worming your way into its confidence.

When you go fishing, if you'll throw out your hook without baiting it, you won't be disturbed.

Another reason many a man goes fishing is that his wife won't let him drink at home.

The way some fishermen catch fish is by the tale.

Why is it that fish usually take their vacation the same time as fishermen?

Talk, if you must, of the ones that got away, but not of the one that didn't.

Some men catch fish; others merely feed them.

FIT

A man buys shoes to fit his feet;
a woman, to fit the occasion.

A woman is likely to keep trying on shoes till the salesman has
a fit.

In the Orient clothes do not
make the man—they do not even
fit him.

The woman who is shopping
for shoes has no sense for the
fitness of things.

Middle age is the time in life
when your clothes don't fit, but
it's you who need the alterations.

By the time a man can afford
a little foreign sports car, he cannot fit into it.

It's the price of the dress a
woman buys, and not the fit, that
makes a husband throw one.

FLAG

A citizen of the United States
is protected by the American flag
in every country, except the
United States.

The man who is always waving
the flag, usually waives what it
stands for.

FLATTERY

It is possible to be below flattery as well as above it.
                          —Macaulay

I love flattery: it's much better
for me than whiskey, and not so
hard on the liver.   —Joyce Cary

A man who flatters a woman
hopes either to find her a fool
or to make her one.
                —Samuel Richardson

When you honestly say you
hate all kinds of flattery, you are
really saying that you don't know
all kinds.   —G. C. Lichtenberg

Just praise is only a debt, but
flattery is a present.
                    —Samuel Johnson

Love of flattery in most men
proceeds from the mean opinion
they have of themselves, but in
women it proceeds from the contrary.   —Swift

Always let your flattery be seen
through, for what really flatters
a man is that you think him
worth flattering.   —Bernard Shaw

We all claim to dislike flattery,
but what we really dislike is the
way in which we are flattered.
                —La Rochefoucauld

The best way to get someone
to listen to reason is to mix some
flattery with it.

When a man boasts that he
understands women, you can be
sure that some woman has been
flattering him.

The woman who pays no at-
tention to flattery is either deaf
or dead.

There's nothing like a little flattery to make a woman respect
your judgment.

To him who hath shall be given—flattery.

No matter how flat your conversation, a woman likes to have it flatter.

Nobody flatters a flatterer.

A little flattery now and then makes husbands out of single men.

The flatterer makes believe to see us as we see ourselves.

Flattery is not fattening, though it inflates your ego and gives you a swelled head.

Flattery proves that the more we lie to others, the more they like us.

How much flattery a woman can absorb before bursting is still undecided because no woman has ever reached the bursting point.

Flattery is the art of patting a person on the back in order to turn his head.

Faint praise ne'er won fair lady.

The way to a man's heart is through his stomach, but a much easier way is through flattery.

When a woman says, "You flatter me"—do so.

Flattery is another thing that never hurts a man unless he inhales.

A woman's idea of flattery is the exaggerated compliments men pay to other women.

An egotist never knows when he is being flattered.

A flatterer never hesitates to tell you what he doesn't think of you.

Some men distrust people who flatter them, and dislike those who don't.

Flattery is the art of saying the right thing for the wrong reason.

To keep friends, always give your candied opinion.

If a man tells a woman she is beautiful, she will overlook most of his other lies.

Flattery is the best cure for a stiff neck because there are few heads it won't turn.

Flattery seldom falls flat.

If you cannot praise a woman's looks, you can at least call her intelligent.

You can flatter any man by telling him he's the kind of man who can't be flattered.

Believe half of what you hear, and less than half if it's flattery.

When you come home inexcusably late and your wife gives you a dirty look, the best thing to apply is soft soap.

Flattery is the fine art of telling a person just what he thinks of himself.

The reason flattery makes people feel good is because they know they deserve it.

Flattery is a two-way street: tell a man how smart he is, and he'll soon be praising your intelligence.

A woman wants someone else to flatter her; a man can flatter himself.

Flattery is something you say to another and which you both know is not true.

FLEA

If you go long enough without a bath, even the fleas will let you alone. — *Ernie Pyle*

The fate of the flea is that all of his children will eventually go to the dogs.

Great fleas have little fleas upon their backs to bite 'em, and little fleas have smaller fleas, and so *ad infinitum*.

The only two who can live as cheaply as one are a dog and a flea.

FLIGHT

If a woman once makes up her mind to marry a man, nothing but instant flight can save him. — *Somerset Maugham*

In love, a man is victorious only when he runs away. — *Napoleon*

He who fights and runs away may live to run another day.

Running is good for the figure, especially when running from danger.

FLIRTATION

Flirting is the gentle art of making a man feel pleased with himself. — *Helen Rowland*

All women are flirts, but some are restrained by shyness, and others by sense. — *La Rochefoucauld*

The greatest miracle of love is the reformation of a flirt. — *La Rochefoucauld*

A flirt is the only woman who goes out of a man's life without slamming the door.

A flirt fools some of the men all of the time, and all of the men some of the time, but not all of the men all of the time.

A flirt is a tempting female who is less coy than decoy.

A flirt makes some men forget they're married, and makes others remember it only too well.

When a flirt fishes for a man, she fishes merely for the sport.

A flirt is usually less anxious to catch a man than to catch his eye.

Many a sincere flirtation ends in a faithless marriage.

The reason some girls never learn to flirt is that they can do it best without learning.

A flirt is always using her eyes to attract a husband, but seldom her own.

A flirt says things with her face and figure that other girls waste time putting into words.

A flirt may not always be equal to the occasion, but she is always equal to the occasional.

What married life needs is more wives who flirt with their own husbands, and less who flirt with other women's.

When a flirt turns around to look at a man, it's only to see if he has turned around to look at her.

When it comes to throwing herself at a man, many a flirt is quite an athlete.

When a flirt walks, she makes eyes at men with her whole figure.

Flirtation originated with a young woman who was too impatient to wait for an introduction.

The flirt is no stronger than her weakest wink.

In fishing for a man, a flirt seldom knows where to draw the line.

A flirt spends her time making temporary male friends, but permanent female enemies.

A flirt may not think of men all the time, but when she thinks, she thinks of men.

A flirt is a woman whose favorite man is always the next one.

FLOOD

There's only one thing worse than a flooded basement, and that's a flooded attic.

A woman is a flood of loveliness—dam her.

FLORIDA

The trouble with Florida is that you run into so many people you thought you'd escaped.
— *Kin Hubbard*

In winter when the days get horrider, we long for Florider.
— *Bill Vaughan*

All's fair in love and war— and in Florida weather reports.

Florida for climate, New York for company.

The native of Florida who saves up for a rainy day is a traitor.

Miami Beach is a winter resort where it sometimes gets so cold the temperature falls below the hotel rates.

It never freezes in Florida, at least not until you've bought an orange grove.

Where does a doctor in Florida send his patients to recuperate?

Florida weather isn't unusual; it's unbelievable.

Florida is the favorite place for Americans who like to summer in the winter.

FLOWER

Whatever a man's age, he can reduce it several years by putting a bright-colored flower in his buttonhole.
— *Mark Twain*

Botany is not a science; it is the art of insulting flowers in Greek and Latin. — *Alphonse Karr*

Hawaii is the only place I know where they put flowers on you while you are alive. — *Will Rogers*

A daisy may tell her you love her, but it takes an orchid to prove it.

Some men say it with flowers; others try to unsay it with them.

He who throws bouquets at himself need lose no sleep over the florist's bill.

Some girls get orchids; others get forget-me-notes.

The only man who profits by the husbands who have lost arguments with their wives is the florist.

A botanist knows all about flowers, and a florist knows all about the prices he can get people to pay for them.

Every married man soon learns that there are some things you cannot say with flowers.

Botany is the only thing about flowers that coeds dislike.

People who live in glass houses should raise flowers.

Another advantage of amateur gardening is that it enables a man to raise beautiful flowers without having to learn how to spell them.

Say it with flowers, but don't throw bouquets at yourself.

You have to be dead before some people will say it with flowers.

A man brings his wife flowers when he wants her to remember an event—or to forget one.

When a sick florist goes to the hospital, what do you send him?

To the floriculturist, every flower he grows is more beautiful than it looks, and more fragrant than it smells.

Talk is cheap, but not if you say it with flowers.

FLY

The hand is quicker than the eye is, but somewhat slower than the fly is. — *Richard Armour*

The fly that doesn't want to be swatted is safest on the fly-swatter. — *G. C. Lichtenberg*

Nothing makes a bald-headed man so mad as a fly that doesn't know when it has had enough.

The only fly that's popular is at the end of a fishing line.

Of course, you can catch more flies with honey than with vinegar, but who needs flies?

It is better to have the fly in the ointment than in the jam.

The fly is a peculiar insect that walks on the ceiling and shakes hands with its hind legs.

FOLKSONG

A folksong is like a woman: you can recognize one, but you can't explain it. — *Burl Ives*

A folksong is a song that nobody has written. — *Mark Twain*

Formerly a folksong became popular without being recorded; nowadays its popularity is due to someone's criminal record.

The trouble with many folksingers is that they sing through the nose by ear.

There are two kinds of folksingers: those who can sing and won't, and those who can't sing and do.

What this country needs are less folksingers who can carry a guitar, and more who can carry a tune.

Many a folksinger sings with feeling, but doesn't always feel as bad as he sounds.

FOLLOW

At a gesture from Sarah Bernhardt, I would follow her to the ends of the earth—with my wife. — *Jules Renard*

In America the people are supposed to follow their President, while their President is supposed to follow the people.

As long as a man follows the races, he is bound to be behind.

Many a man follows his bent till he goes broke.

Modern times have created a new kind of genius: the man who can follow a do-it-yourself sheet of instructions.

FOOD

To a man with an empty stomach, food is God. — *Gandhi*

Getting enough to eat, and then getting rid of it, are two of the great problems of life. — *Ed Howe*

The truffle is not really an aphrodisiac, but it may make the man more amiable and the woman more amorous.
 — *Brillat-Savarin*

The more food there is in the world, the more fools will be fed.
 — *Frank Moore Colby*

Tell me what you eat, and I'll tell you what you are.
 — *Brillat-Savarin*

Food is an edible substance occasionally found in reducing diets.

Leftovers are a kind of food that are here today—and here tomorrow.

It isn't the travel that's broadening—it's all that rich foreign food.

Mankind is divided into two classes: those who are looking for food, and those who are looking for an appetite.

The only food that never goes up in price is food for thought.

The best way to serve leftovers is to someone else.

Instant foods have made it possible for the housewife to spend less time preparing dinner than to get the family to the table.

The best thing you can say about gravy is that it has no bones.

Nutrition is an inexact science: it cannot explain how teen-agers manage to thrive on hamburgers and Coke.

A refrigerator is a place where you store leftovers until they are ready to be thrown out.

Some wives serve only those foods which are low in calories and high in trading stamps.

FOOL

There are more fools in the world than there are people.
— *Heine*

There is one fool at least in every married couple.
— *Henry Fielding*

You must play the fool a little if you don't want to be thought completely a fool.   — *Montaigne*

The man who doesn't recognize a fool when he sees one, is one himself.   — *Baltasar Gracián*

You never know what a fool you can be till life gives you the chance.   — *Eden Phillpotts*

Most fools think they are only ignorant.   — *Franklin*

A man may be a fool and not know it, but not if he is married.
— *Mencken*

There's no fool like an old fool who marries a young fool.

The world would be a pleasanter place if there weren't so many fools in it, but it would be harder to make a living.

There is no fool like the fool who thinks he is fooling you.

It's bad enough to act like a fool, but it's even worse when you're not acting.

There's no fool like an old fool, except an older fool.

Nature makes some men fools all of the time, but women make all men fools some of the time.

A fool and his money are soon parted, but seldom by another fool.

Every human being knows a fool when he sees one, but not when he is one.

Never call a person who disagrees with you a fool, nor agree with him when he calls himself one.

For every woman who makes a fool out of some man, there's another woman who makes a man out of some fool.

There's no fool like an old fool; if you don't believe it, ask any young fool.

In all this foolish world no creature is so perfect a fool as a woman—excepting always a man.

If you must be a fool, be one while you're young: it's better to cause grief to parents than to children.

There's only one man wise enough to give advice on how to handle women, and that's the fool.

A man must first make a fool of himself, before he can let a girl do the job.

There's no fool like an old fool —unless he's got money.

The world is full of fools, and there's always one more than you think.

A fool tells a woman he understands her; a bigger fool tries to prove it.

When a man wants to make a fool of himself, he usually gets some woman to help him.

There's no fool like an old fool —you just can't beat experience.

If a man doesn't make a fool of himself over a woman before he's 30, he's fairly safe until he's 60.

The man who is not as big a fool as he used to be, may be getting smarter, but he is more likely getting thinner.

What fools these mortals think other mortals be!

When nature neglects to make a fool out of a man, it gives some woman the chance.

It is better to keep your mouth shut and be thought a fool than to open it and remove all doubt.

There's no fool like an old fool who tries to act like a young fool.

Money doesn't make a fool out of a girl as often as a girl makes money out of a fool.

In the old days every small town had its village idiot; nowadays he just doesn't stand out from the rest.

No woman makes a fool out of a man; she merely directs the performance.

If a fool and his money are soon parted, who got yours?

We call a man a fool when he doesn't think as we think he should think.

No one is perfect, except the man who makes a perfect fool of himself.

Every girl feels that she might just as well make a fool out of a man as to let some other girl do it.

FOOLISH

Since Adam and Eve ate the apple, man has never refrained from any folly of which he was capable.   —*Bertrand Russell*

The foolishness of the simple is delightful, only the foolishness of the wise is exasperating.

— *Santayana*

An act of folly isn't foolish when you know it for the folly it is. — *Logan P. Smith*

Foolish fashions are as contagious as diseases.

— *La Rochefoucauld*

Every man has his follies, and oftentimes they are the most interesting things he has got.

— *Josh Billings*

If others had not been foolish, we should be so. — *William Blake*

There's no one so foolish as the husband who tells his wife everything, except the wife who believes everything her husband tells her.

Some people are born silly, some acquire silliness, and others fall in love.

Life is just one foolish thing after another, and love is just two foolish things after each other.

The sanest remarks of some people would be too foolish for a popular song.

It is folly to be foolish.

When in love try not to say foolish things; if you succeed, you are not in love.

FOOLPROOF

A reckless driver is the proof that a fool is seldom foolproof long.

Calling anything foolproof seems to take a lot for granted.

Some things are fireproof, many things are waterproof, but no things are foolproof.

FOOTBALL

Football is all very well as a game for rough girls, but it is hardly suitable for delicate boys.

— *Oscar Wilde*

College football would be more interesting if the faculty played instead of the students—there would be a great increase in broken arms, legs and necks.

— *Mencken*

An atheist is one who watches a Notre Dame-Southern Methodist University football game and doesn't care who wins.

Everything has its virtues: even a losing football team acts as a powerful deterrent on betting alumni.

There's only one thing more brutal than a football game, and that's the price of the tickets.

Football is a game for strong people: anyone who can sit for hours on a cold seat, eating peanuts, can't be a weakling.

The worst thing about football is that none of the cheerleaders ever gets injured.

A forward pass is never successful until it is in the hands of a receiver.

The football season is the only time of the year when girls whistle at men in sweaters.

A ticket scalper is a man who enables you to see one football game for the price of five.

Boys go four years to college because it takes about that long to develop an all-American football player.

Football disproves the law of evolution: the fittest don't always survive.

Many a man who spends thousands of dollars on his son's college education, gets only a quarterback.

About the only college students who can't see football games are the players.

One thing no alumni will stand for is a college football team that plays like a bunch of amateurs.

Football, not baseball, is our national pass time.

The toughest problems a football coach faces are defensive linebackers and offensive alumni.

A football game is where the spectators have four quarters to finish a fifth.

College football players seldom have trouble with running and kicking, but often have trouble with passing.

All men are born free, but football men are more likely to get through college that way.

The good old days were when a football game was something that got people outdoors.

FOOTNOTE

A scholar, when you let him into a poem, can never take a step without leaving a footnote.
— *Frank Moore Colby*

When you get to the footnote at the bottom of the page, like as not all you find is *ibid*.
— *Frank Sullivan*

FOREIGN AFFAIRS

A foreign secretary is forever poised between a cliché and an indiscretion. — *Harold Macmillan*

The big powers should declare definitely where they stand—and on whom.

Our foreign relations are perfect strangers to most of us.

There are two kinds of foreign policy: one is to speak softly and carry a big stick; the other is to speak loudly and carry a flyswatter.

The trouble with the Near East is that it's too near, and with the Far East that it isn't far enough.

Our foreign policy is neither good nor bad, but fair to meddling.

Honesty is the best policy, but not the best foreign policy.

Foreign affairs is a subject of great interest to Americans, and even greater interest when their sons reach draft age.

American foreign policy seems to be to speak softly and carry a big stick—of candy.

The deal which small nations get from big ones is usually from the bottom of the pact.

Foreign policy is a course of action which the party in power claims is highly successful but for which the opposition is to blame.

What this world needs is more foreign policies based on the theory that half aloof is better than none.

The trouble with America's foreign relations is that so many of them are broke.

FOREIGN AID

Foreign aid proves that though charity begins at home, it usually ends abroad.

The American tourist is amazed at the Taj Mahal, but even more amazed that it was built before foreign aid.

Many a foreign country would like China to leave them alone, and would also like America to leave them a loan.

Taxpayers would be more willing to support their government if their government were less willing to support other governments.

The trouble with America's foreign aid is that it's mostly an endowment policy.

The purpose of foreign aid should not be to support the rest of the world in the style to which we are accustomed.

A skillful diplomat is one who knows how to refuse foreign aid without being deprived of it.

America's foreign-aid policy is based on our having the highest standard of giving in the world.

Foreign aid is a popular refreshment made in America and consumed abroad.

Atlas carried the world on his shoulders, but Uncle Sam is trying to outdo him by carrying it with his hands in his pockets.

The trouble with foreign aid is that it enables too many countries to live beyond our means.

America was formerly isolationist, and it still plays a loan hand.

America's foreign-aid policy is an open book—an open checkbook.

Heaven help us if we discover that other planets are inhabited —think of the increase in our foreign aid.

Foreign aid is a form of foreign trade by which American dollars are exchanged for ill will.

FOREIGNER

Half the trouble with modern man is that he is educated to

understand foreign languages and misunderstand foreigners.

— Chesterton

Most people can be at ease in a foreign country only when they are disparaging the inhabitants.

— George Orwell

The United Nations is a good idea, but it's a pity they have to have so many foreigners in it.

FORESIGHT

Some people can see the trouble so far ahead that there is always some in sight.

The problem is not whether you can see the handwriting on the wall, but whether you can read it.

FORESIGHT AND HINDSIGHT

The old see better behind than the young before.

If a man's foresight was as good as his hindsight, he'd be better off by a damn sight.

There's many a forward look in a backward glance.

Hindsight is good, foresight is better, but second sight is best of all.

The only thing that enables a person to look forward behind him is a rear-view mirror.

If the hindsight of some women were as good as their foresight, they wouldn't be wearing slacks.

FORGERY

A forger gets into trouble not because he doesn't hold his tongue, but because he doesn't hold his pen.

Imitation is the sincerest form of flattery, except when it's forgery.

Most people appreciate the value of an honored name, but most of all the forger.

FORGET

The man who cannot forget himself is easily forgotten by others.

Elephants and headwaiters never forget.

When a man drinks to forget, the only thing he forgets is when to stop.

A wife is never too old to learn that she knows a lot of things she ought to forget.

Never forget a friend, especially if he owes you money.

It isn't how much you learn that makes you educated; it's how little you forget.

The person who goes on a vacation to forget things, doesn't find out until he opens his luggage whether he has.

Advice to psychiatrists: In treating cases of amnesia, collect the fee in advance.

Life would be more pleasant if we could forget our troubles just as easily as we forget our blessings.

FORGIVE

The secret of forgiving everything is to understand nothing.
— *Bernard Shaw*

Once a woman has forgiven her man, she must not reheat his sins for breakfast.
— *Marlene Dietrich*

A woman who can't forgive should never have more than a nodding acquaintance with a man.
— *Ed Howe*

People will sometimes forgive you the good you have done them, but seldom the harm they have done you.
— *Somerset Maugham*

Always forgive your enemies —nothing annoys them so much.
— *Oscar Wilde*

I believe in the forgiveness of sin and the redemption of ignorance.
— *Adlai Stevenson*

I can pardon everyone's mistakes but my own.
— *Marcus Porcius Cato*

Some people forgive their enemies; others even forgive their friends.

To err is human; to forgive, unusual.

Nowadays the quality of mercy is not only strained, but also tenderized, sterilized, and homogenized.

A woman will forgive a man anything except his failure to ask to be forgiven.

Some people can forgive anything in a friend, except success.

Give, and your wife will forgive.

Forgiveness is the fragance the violet dashes on the heel that crushes it.

Too many people find it's easier to pray for forgiveness than to fight temptation.

Any woman will forgive a man who marries for money, provided it's not her money.

FORGIVE AND FORGET

Women forgive injuries, but never forget slights.
— *Thomas C. Haliburton*

If everybody remembered the past, nobody would ever forgive anybody. — *Robert Lynd*

A woman may promise to forgive and forget, but she will never promise to forget she has forgiven.

Forgive your enemies, of course, but don't forget them.

Another thing you should always forgive and forget in a friend is his advice.

There are two types of people: those who are more for getting, and those who are more for giving.

FORTUNE HUNTER

A fortune hunter is a considerate man who doesn't let money stand between a girl and her happiness.

During inflation when the value of the dollar drops, the man who marries for money gets cheated.

A fortune hunter is a man with cheap ideals but expensive tastes.

The man who marries for money doesn't marry for better or worse—he marries for more or less.

A fortune hunter is looking for a golden wedding fifty years ahead of time.

Many a man seeks to marry a rich girl so that his wife may have everything she wants.

A fortune hunter is another man who is willing to go through fire for a girl, but only if she has money to burn.

Some men are interested in the bonds of matrimony only if they pay big dividends.

When a fortune hunter takes a girl for better or for worse, it's better for him and worse for her.

Many a bachelor never marries until he meets the right amount.

The fortune hunter always marries for love—love of money.

The man who marries for money soon discovers that that's the hardest way to earn it.

A fortune hunter is a man without any dollars who is trying to find a rich woman without any sense.

FORTUNETELLER

A fortuneteller always foretells a bright future for others in order to make a brighter future for herself.

Religion gives faith, and the church gives hope, but nothing deceives like a horoscope.

A fortuneteller tells an unmarried woman there's a man in her future, and tells a married woman there's a future in her man.

FRANCE

What I gained by being in France was learning to be better satisfied with my own country.
— *Samuel Johnson*

Every Frenchman wants to enjoy one or more privileges; that's the way he shows his passion for equality.   — *De Gaulle*

How can anyone govern a nation that has 246 different kinds of cheese?   — *De Gaulle*

FRANK

Why should I be ashamed to describe what nature is not ashamed to create?   — *Aretino*

The man who insists on telling others what he likes, should be prepared to hear what he doesn't like.   — *Terence*

A man that should call everything by its right name would hardly pass the streets without being knocked down as a common enemy.   *—Halifax*

Frank and explicit—that is the right line to take when you wish to conceal your own mind and confuse the minds of others.
—Disraeli

We want all our friends to tell us our bad qualities; it is only the particular ass that does so whom we can't tolerate.
—William James

If people would say just what they think for a single minute, society would overturn.
—Sainte-Beuve

When a man asks you what you think of him, fool him and give him your honest opinion.

Husbands should be frank and tell their wives everything, and wives should be generous and believe it.

We all like our friends to be perfectly frank—about other people.

The most disagreeable trait of some people is that they say so many things that are so.

There will always be two kinds of people: those who say what they think, and those who keep their friends.

Never give anyone frank advice until you're out of reach.

The person who says just what he thinks, will soon get just what he deserves.

Candor does not mean that you must always be upright, downright and forthright.

There is no one so tactless as the man who says what everyone else is thinking.

There's nothing like frankness if you want to create your own lack of opportunities.

It is the blunt man who makes the sharpest comments.

Think twice before you speak, especially if you intend to say what you really think.

The man who says what he thinks is sometimes fearless, sometimes artless, but always friendless.

The outspoken woman is usually the kind who always tells the truth no matter how much it hurts—the other woman.

The person who always says what he thinks, doesn't always think.

FREE

If the best things in life are free, why are the next-best things so expensive?

The best things in life are free, but only because the tax experts haven't yet figured out a solution.

When you get something for nothing, the donor usually expects to collect.

The man who thinks the best things in life are free, just hasn't been caught yet.

A lot of happiness is overlooked because it doesn't cost anything.

The best things in life are free —and so are the worst men.

Nothing is really free in life, and even death is not free—it costs our life.

If the best things in life are free, why is the family budget so hard to balance?

FREEDOM

Freedom rings where opinions clash. — *Adlai Stevenson*

The basic test of freedom is perhaps less in what we are free to do than in what we are free not to do. — *Eric Hoffer*

The trouble with fighting for human freedom is that you have to spend much of your life defending sons-of-bitches. — *Mencken*

Freedom is not an ideal, it is not even a protection, if it means nothing more than the freedom to stagnate. — *Adlai Stevenson*

Men fight for freedom; then they begin to accumulate laws to take it away from themselves.

When there's more freedom for mankind, the women will have it.

Creating all men free and equal isn't enough; some means must be devised to keep them free and equal.

In America everybody has more or less freedom—more before marriage and less afterward.

No one can enjoy freedom unless he is willing to surrender some part of it.

The man who wants to think, speak and act just as he pleases, should have himself committed to a mental institution.

The United States has always been a free country where every man can do as his wife pleases.

FREE SPEECH

People demand freedom of speech to make up for the freedom of thought which they avoid. — *Kierkegaard*

Every man has a right to be heard, but no man has the right to strangle democracy with a single set of vocal chords. — *Adlai Stevenson*

Why shouldn't speech be free: very little of it is worth anything.

Many a person excerises his right to free speech by indulging in loose talk.

Some people's idea of freedom of speech is the right to insult the President with impunity.

Free speech is a wonderful thing: we'd hate to have to pay to hear some public speakers.

The Founding Fathers who introduced freedom of speech hadn't the remotest idea of what would be said today.

Freedom not to listen is sometimes even more precious a right than freedom of speech.

What this country needs is more free speech worth listening to.

At no time is freedom of speech more precious than when a man hits his thumb with a hammer.

The right of every person to speak freely includes the bore who should halve his say.

There's an important difference between free speech and cheap talk.

Free speech is a wonderful thing, but some people are too free with their speeches.

Many a woman regards free speech not as a right but as a continuous obligation.

FRENCH

The French language is a piano without a pedal.   — *Gide*

In Paris they simply stared when I spoke to them in French; I never did succeed in making those idiots understand their own language.   — *Mark Twain*

France was long a despotism tempered by epigrams.   — *Carlyle*

An American who speaks French can only be understood by other Americans who have also just arrived in Paris.   — *Fred Allen*

When Frenchmen reach the age when they believe in God for the second time, they become very agreeable.
— *G. C. Lichtenberg*

Ici on parle français is written over the gates of hell.
— *Benjamin Jowett*

I have a native land, and it's the French language.   — *Camus*

In France, only the impossible is admired.   — *Napoleon*

Frenchmen have a peculiar sense of humor; Americans find this out when they try to talk to them in French.

All languages are illogical: in French, for example, *feminin* is masculine.

When an American goes to Paris, he seldom has as much trouble with his French as the French do.

There's no one so affected as the American woman who talks to her French poodle in French.

The American tourist in Paris usually speaks just enough French to make himself misunderstood.

FREUD

Yesterday I was very irritable; you should have been here so as to wish you weren't.   — *Freud*

Freud was way off base in considering sex the fundamental motivation: the ruling passion in men is minding each other's business.   — *Robert Frost*

It was Freud who taught us that the secrets we keep best are those we keep from ourselves.

FRIEND

Everyone's friend is no one's.
— *Schopenhauer*

To find a friend one must close one eye—to keep him, two.
— *Norman Douglas*

If one of my friends happens to die, I drive down to St. James's Coffee House, and bring home a new one.
— *Horace Walpole*

One friend in a lifetime is much; two are many; three are hardly possible. — *Henry Adams*

There are a good many fools who call me a friend, and also a good many friends who call me a fool. — *Chesterton*

A friend in power is a friend lost. — *Henry Adams*

Mme. de Staël is such a good friend, she would throw all her friends into the river for the pleasure of fishing them out.
— *Talleyrand*

One's friends are that part of the human race with which one can be human. — *Santayana*

A friend is a present which you give yourself.
— *R. L. Stevenson*

There are people whom one should like very well to drop, and would not wish to be dropped by. — *Samuel Johnson*

It's what people don't know about each other that makes them such good friends.

Some friends are a habit, others a luxury.

To keep friends, treat them kindly; to kill friends, treat them often.

A true friend remains a friend even when you don't deserve to have a friend.

It is surprising how many friends a man has until he needs one.

If a false friend is one who stabs you in the back, is a true friend one who stabs you in the front?

There are three kinds of friends: best friends, guest friends, and pest friends.

A true friend laughs at your stories even when they're not so good, and sympathizes with your troubles even when they're not so bad.

If at first you don't succeed, you'll probably have more friends.

Old friends are best: where can you find a new friend that has stood by you as long as the old ones have?

If a friend won't lend you fifty dollars, he's probably a close friend.

No man ever knows whether two women are friends because they like each other or because they dislike each other.

A true friend will see you through when others see that you are through.

Everyone has two kinds of friends: those who are around when you need them, and those who are around when they need you.

How can you have friends if you don't let people impose upon you?

Some people have a large circle of friends, while others have only friends they like.

You can always tell a real friend: when you've made a fool of yourself, he doesn't feel you've done a permanent job.

You can't use your friends and have them too.

Those who think alike don't make the best friends: people who move in parallel lines can never get together.

The best time to make friends is before you need them.

When your friends know you too well, it sometimes means they don't know you any longer.

A friend is a person who runs interference for you in your pursuit of happiness.

The man who is always his own best friend has few others.

A friend not in need is a friend indeed.

A man's hair and teeth are his best friends, but even the best of friends will fall out.

When you lose a friend by lending him some money, you get the best of the bargain.

A true friend walks in when the rest of the world walks out.

A friend is always delighted at your success, provided it doesn't exceed his own.

FRIEND AND ENEMY

It takes your enemy and your friend, working together, to hurt you: the one to slander you, and the other to bring you the news.
— *Mark Twain*

No friendship is as intimate as that of girl for girl, and no enmity as intense as that of woman for woman.
— *Walter Savage Landor*

The beauty of enmity is insecurity; the beauty of friendship is in security. — *Robert Frost*

The art of dealing with one's enemies is an art no less necessary than knowing how to appreciate one's friends.
— *Truman Capote*

He treats his enemies as if they might someday become his friends, and his friends as if they might become his enemies.
— *Napoleon*

May God defend me from my friends; I can defend myself from my enemies. — *Voltaire*

To affirm that a vicious man is only his own enemy is about as wise as to affirm that a virtuous man is only his own friend.
— *C. C. Colton*

Life is an eternal battle between a man and his enemies, or between a woman and her friends.

The man who has trouble keeping his friends has no trouble keeping his enemies.

Another way of making enemies is to talk to your friends as only a friend should.

Everyone needs a bitter enemy and a firm friend: the bitter enemy to tell him his faults, and the firm friend to tell everyone else.

A man's best friend is his dog, and his worst enemy, his dogma.

A man will always remember his enemies, but he will sometimes forget his friends.

In politics it is often safer to have a clever enemy than a foolish friend.

Another way to get rid of an enemy is to turn him into a friend.

You make more enemies by what you say than friends by what you do.

An enemy may be worse than a friend, but at least he never gives you any advice.

There's only one person who can do you more harm than an enemy with the worst intentions, and that's a friend with the best.

Money may not buy you more friends, but it does attract a better class of enemies.

Never tell your friends anything you don't want your enemies to know.

FRIENDSHIP

Women give nothing to friendship except what they borrow from love.   — *Chamfort*

The pleasure found in friendship as in love comes more from the things we don't know about others than from the things we know.   — *La Rochefoucauld*

Friendship is an arrangement by which we undertake to exchange small favors for big ones.   — *Montesquieu*

One of the rewards of a good friendship is an almost total ignorance of your friend's secrets.   — *Ben Hecht*

Thy friendship oft has made my heart to ache; do be my enemy—for friendship's sake.   — *William Blake*

Friendship is almost always the union of a part of one mind with a part of another: people are friends in spots.   — *Santayana*

It is a mark of friendship to imagine the worst possible things about a friend.   — *Ben Hecht*

A man's friendships are invalidated by his marriage, but they are also no less invalidated by the marriage of his friends.   — *Samuel Butler*

No one can ruin friendships as fast as the woman who says

things even before she has thought of them.

Friendship is possible only because people do not say to your face the things they say behind your back.

Friendship is like a bank account: you cannot continue to draw on it without making deposits.

The best way to keep friendships from breaking is not to drop them.

FRUSTRATION

Every writer is a frustrated actor who recites his lines in the hidden auditorium of his skull.
— *Rod Serling*

Frustration is the difference between what you are and what you think you are.

There's nothing so frustrating to a woman as having a juicy bit of gossip about another woman who is on the same party line.

The most frustrating of all life's ups and downs is keeping appearances up and expenses down.

FUN

What a terrible time people have trying to have a good time!
— *Ed Howe*

There is danger, destruction, torment—what more do we need to make us merry?
— *Bernard Shaw*

A woman wants men to have a good time in a woman's way.
— *Ed Howe*

A little nonsense then and now is relished by the highest brow.

The angels that fear to tread where fools rush in must miss a lot of fun.

Having fun is like buying life insurance: the older you get, the more it costs.

The average husband wishes he had as much fun when he is out as his wife thinks he has.

We don't stop having fun when we're old; we're old when we stop having fun.

Time is money, especially a good time.

A fun-loving girl is usually a fund-loving girl as well.

Eat, drink, and be merry, for tomorrow you may not be able to afford it.

The trouble with fun is that it often ends up as trouble.

If youth really were wise it would miss most of its fun.

FUNERAL

A funeral eulogy is a belated plea for the defense delivered after the evidence is all in.
— *Irvin S. Cobb*

I did not attend his funeral, but I wrote a nice letter saying I approved it. — *Mark Twain*

What bereaved people need is a little comic relief, and this is why funerals are so farcical.
— *Bernard Shaw*

We usually meet all our relatives only at funerals where someone always observes, "Too bad we can't get together more often."
— *Sam Levenson*

Some people look as if they were walking around to save funeral expenses.

Time and tide take man for a ride.

Some men never head a procession until they're dead.

If the cost of funerals continues to go up, some people will be better off alive.

Funerals are very expensive; that's why people rarely have them until the last minute.

Some people never come up to the front of the church unless escorted by pallbearers.

The last lap of a joy ride is usually made in a hearse.

No matter how famous a man is, the size of his funeral depends partly on the weather.

Everything comes to him who waits, including the hearse.

FUNNY

When a thing is funny, search it for a hidden truth.
— *Bernard Shaw*

The only way to amuse some people is to slip and fall on an icy pavement.   — *Ed Howe*

There's nothing funnier than a fellow who isn't funny trying to be funny.   — *David Sarnoff*

Politicians do more funny things naturally than I can think of doing purposely.   — *Will Rogers*

Every man is funny if he loses his hat and has to run after it.
— *Chesterton*

Women's fashions do not have to go out of style before they look funny.

The funniest thing in the world is usually your boss's joke.

It is his sense of humor that enables a practical joker to see the funny side of things that have no funny side.

There's only one thing funnier than a man crying over his wife's troubles, and that's a woman laughing at her husband's jokes.

FURNITURE

Furniture is another thing that wives like to push around.

If you want to see a house full of antique furniture, visit a family with money; if you want to see a house full of old furniture, visit a family with kids.

What this country needs is early American furniture that can be bought at early American prices.

No man likes a wife who is constantly pushing furniture around, especially when he is in it.

New furniture often becomes antique before it's fully paid for.

There are three kinds of furniture: antique, modern and comfortable.

FURS

Behind every successful man is a woman who wanted a mink.

It's strange how many animals are killed to dress the girl that's dressed to kill.

The thing that keeps men broke is not the wolf at the door but the mink in the window.

There are more fur-bearing animals in the city than in the woods.

The nicest thing about being a mink is that you can hang around a beautiful woman long after you're dead.

A fur coat is made from the hides of many animals—and one husband.

Many a girl gets a mink the same way a mink does.

Lots of animals would still be wearing their fur coats if it weren't for installment credit.

Some women believe that since a mere worm can give silk, a mature man ought to be able to give mink.

It's hard to keep a mink wife on a muskrat salary.

Every woman believes that man was intended to be a fur-bearing animal.

When a woman wears a new dress, her friends want to know where she got it; when she wears a new mink coat, they want to know how.

Most fur coats come from the male animal.

Some husbands are so stingy, they think no one in the world needs a mink except a mink.

Faint heart ne'er won fur, lady.

There's no one like a gold digger to bring out the animal in a man—especially the mink.

The forbearing wife is rarely the fur-bearing one.

The girl who wants to bring out the mink in a man must first bring out the wolf.

Some women look smart in a new mink coat, some look elegant, while others just look guilty.

The only females who are indifferent to mink coats are minks.

FUTURE

The trouble with our times is that the future is not what it used to be.   *—Paul Valéry*

The future is hidden even from the men who make it.
—Anatole France

Time enough to think of the future when you haven't any future to think of. — *Bernard Shaw*

Never worry about the future —it never becomes serious until it is the present.

There's one good thing about the future: it never lasts.

The worst thing about the future is that it gets here faster than it used to.

What the future has in store for you depends largely on what you place in store for the future.

The man who thinks most of the future is generally the man who has no future to think of.

A few men make the future, while the rest wait for the future to make them.

The man who is always saving up for the future will probably not be there when the future arrives.

A woman worries about the future before she gets a husband; a man worries about it after he gets a wife.

When the fools are all dead, the rest of the world will get along very well without us.

There is no future in any job; the future lies in the man who holds the job.

GADABOUT

There's only one thing worse than the husband who never comes home, and that's the wife who never stays home.

A gadabout is a woman whose place is in the home—of some other woman.

A gadabout is a roaming creature who looks for a husband before marriage, and whose husband looks for her afterward.

Many a woman marries in order to have a home to get away from.

GAMBLING

A gambler is nothing but a man who makes his living out of hope. — *William Bolitho*

The better the gambler, the worse the man.
— *Publilius Syrus*

An habitual gambler never gives up and never gives in even when his money gives out.

Don't gamble unless you can afford to lose, and if you can afford to lose, you don't have to gamble.

You get out of anything just what you put into it, except in the case of slot machines.

Gamblers are people who usually leave everything to chance— and usually leave everything.

Two can live as cheaply as one can gamble.

Marriage is a gambol, spelled g-a-m-b-l-e.

The only person who can afford to gamble is the pauper.

Americans spend billions of dollars a year on games of chance —including weddings.

Another way to prevent your husband from gambling is for you to spend it first.

Always sympathize with the underdog, but never bet on him.

A gambler would rather win a dollar on a bet than earn ten.

You can always find an illegal gambling joint somewhere—if you know the wrong people.

A gambler doesn't always know where his next dollar is coming from, but he always knows where it is going to.

Marriage is the only form of gambling favored by all the clergy.

There is no fun in gambling unless you are betting more than you should.

A dog is man's best friend, especially after you have bet on a horse.

Money can be lost in more ways than won.

The best throw of the dice is to throw them away.

GAME

Men may trifle with their business and their politics, but they never trifle with their games.
— *Bernard Shaw*

It is in games that many men discover their paradise.
— *Robert Lynd*

A well-adjusted person is one who can play golf and bridge as if they were games.

If you watch a game, it's fun; if you play it, it's recreation; if you work at it, it's golf.

What some people enjoy most about table tennis is stepping on the ball.

GARAGE

Walking isn't a lost art—how else can one get to the garage?

An American is a motorist who spends a lot of money for a garage, and then parks his car outside.

The chief purpose of the garage built in the split-level house is to store the junk that formerly cluttered up the attic.

Many a home is ruined by the husband backing horses, and many a garage by the wife backing cars.

The hardest spot to find a parking place is usually in a one-car garage.

Many a home is nothing more than a garage with a bedroom, bathroom and kitchen attached.

In the good old days, when a teen-ager went into the garage, he came out with a lawnmower.

Within walking distance means in the suburbs no farther than the garage.

GARDEN

People who think they can run the earth should begin with a small garden.

We all go back to the soil eventually, but only the gardener does it while he's still alive.

The best thing about gardening is that if you put it off long enough, it won't be necessary.

Many a man gets a good deal of pleasure out of his garden—mostly out of it.

The chief objection to gardening is that by the time your back gets used to it, your enthusiasm is gone.

The best way to raise a successful garden is by trowel and error.

All gardeners know better than other gardeners.

Nothing discourages an amateur gardener like watching his family eat the entire garden at one meal.

About all the amateur gardener gets for his pains is liniment.

Gardening is good for the waistline, but the trouble is that it's even better for the appetite.

The best garden club is a hoe handle.

In the spring many an amateur gardener has her husband under her green thumb.

A garden is a thing of beauty and a job forever.

As ye sow, so shall ye reap, unless of course you are an amateur gardener.

A gardener is a woman who loves flowers, or a man who hates weeds.

Gardening is one of the earliest symptoms of lumbago.

Many a man has given up gardening after finding that the only thing that can be raised on his land is taxes.

The less help you have in your garden, the more it belongs to you.

If you don't grow your own vegetables, it helps to praise the crop in your neighbor's garden.

Another thing an amateur gardener grows is round-shouldered.

Don't make the garden too big if your wife tires easily.

Gardening is largely a painstaking matter, usually in the small of the back.

GARLIC

There's no such thing as a little garlic.   —*Arthur Baer*

Garlic makes a man wink, drink and stink. —*Thomas Nashe*

Only a French chef can add garlic to a dish and enter it in the flower show. — *Arthur Baer*

If you want to hide the smell of fish on pots and pans, rub them with garlic.

Garlic is good for flavoring food, but what is good for garlic?

The only thing stronger than a mother's love is a garlic breath.

GAS STATION

The only explanation for the high price of gasoline is that the earth has begun to charge storage.

A gas station is a place where you sometimes fill the car, but more often drain the kids.

There are so many gas stations now that you can fuel all of the people all of the time.

GENERAL

I don't mind when a private fails to salute me, but he must never forget to salute a second lieutenant.
— *General John J. Pershing*

The best service a retired general can perform is to turn in his tongue along with his suit.
— *General Omar Bradley*

At the age of four with paper hats and wooden swords we are all generals—only some of us never grow out of it.
— *Peter Ustinov*

The main object of the army is to promote the generals' welfare.

GENERALIZATION

Generalizations are generally wrong. — *Mary Wortley Montagu*

General propositions do not decide concrete cases.
— *Justice O. W. Holmes*

My mind seems to have become a kind of machine for grinding general laws out of large collections of facts. — *Charles Darwin*

One of the perils of a great war is that it revives the passionate faith of the common man in generalizations. — *Robert Lynd*

The chief end of man is to frame general propositions, and no general proposition is worth a damn. — *Justice O. W. Holmes*

All generalizations are false, including this one.

The narrower the mind, the broader the statement.

GENEROUS

When a man is generous, the last one to find it out is his wife.

The test of generosity is not how much you give, but how much you have left.

A woman's idea of generosity is to keep nothing to herself.

A woman doesn't go to church to show off her new clothes; she goes to show everybody what a generous husband she has.

When a man is generous to a fault, it is never one of his wife's.

Women are so generous, they just love giving each other away.

GENIUS

The world wants geniuses, but it wants them to behave just like other people. — *George Moore*

I don't want to be a genius—I have enough problems just trying to be a man. — *Camus*

Everyone is a genius at least once a year; a real genius has his original ideas closer together. — *G. C. Lichtenberg*

God is constantly at work creating great geniuses to pull the common people up. — *Goethe*

I can't tell you if genius is hereditary because heaven has granted me no offspring. — *Whistler*

Great geniuses have the shortest biographies—their cousins can tell you nothing about them. — *Emerson*

A man who is a genius and doesn't know it, isn't. — *Stanislaw J. Lec*

Do not pity the unsuccessful lover of a woman of genius; save your sympathy for the man who marries her. — *Don Marquis*

There is in genius itself an unconscious activity; nay, that is the genius in the man of genius. — *Coleridge*

The world has a standing pique against genius. — *Hazlitt*

Genius might be described as a supreme capacity for getting its possessors into trouble of all kinds. — *Samuel Butler*

Every man of genius is considerably helped by being dead. — *Robert Lynd*

Geniuses are like ocean liners: they should never meet. — *Louis Aragon*

The secret of genius is known only to those aphorists who have none.

The man who leaves footprints on the sands of time never wears expensive shoes.

Every family should have several children, so that if one is a genius, there will be others to support him.

Everybody in an art colony is a genius—without having any.

Genius is the capacity for taking infinite pains—and giving even more.

For every young man with a spark of genius, there are a hundred with spark-plug trouble.

A genius is a crackpot until he hits the jackpot.

A genius is the man of tomorrow who is paid today with the wages of yesterday.

Every child is a genius up to the age of six.

The original sin of every man of genius is the sin of being original.

GENIUS AND TALENT

When I had to fill in a census paper, I gave my profession as genius and my infirmity as talent.
— *Oscar Wilde*

Men of genius do not excel in any profession because they labor in it, but they labor in it because they excel. — *Hazlitt*

Genius learns from nature, talent from books. — *Josh Billings*

You've got a talent for genius.
— *O. Henry*

Genius does what it must, and talent does what it can.
— *Owen Meredith*

How many young geniuses we have known, and none but ourselves will ever hear of them for want in them of a little talent.
— *Emerson*

The relation of genius to talent is the same as that of instinct to reason. — *Jules Renard*

I put all my genius into my life; I put only my talent into my works. — *Oscar Wilde*

Genius never writes about men of talent, but men of talent always write about men of genius.

Talent seeks to be something, genius seeks to be someone.

Talent comes from the inside and is shaped by the outside; genius comes from the inside and shapes the outside.

Talent is the infinite capacity for imitating genius.

Talent is what you have; genius is what you are.

Another difference between talent and genius is that talent gets paid.

Talent is what you possess, genius is what possesses you.

It takes a genius to recognize his own lack of talent.

The mark of talent is to do the possible with ease; the mark of genius is to do the impossible with difficulty.

Talent is keeping in step with the crowd; genius is keeping in step with yourself.

Talent is often mistaken for genius, especially by the man who has it.

It takes genius to move mountains, but talent can always throw a bluff.

Talent does things tolerably well, genius does them intolerably better.

Genius is what it must be, talent what it can be, and the majority of us what we shouldn't be.

Talent is full of thoughts, genius is full of thought.

GENTLEMAN

A man becomes a gentleman the moment the betting odds on his word of honor pass 3 to 2.
—*Mencken*

I can make a lord, but only God Almighty can make a gentleman. —*James I of England*

Being a gentleman is hiding your manners. —*Ed Howe*

When an Englishman is totally incapable of doing any work whatsoever, he describes himself in the income-tax form as a gentleman. —*Robert Lynd*

The man who is always talking about being a gentleman, never is one. —*Robert S. Surtees*

If a man is a gentleman, he knows quite enough; and if he's not a gentleman, whatever he knows is bad for him.
—*Oscar Wilde*

A gentleman is one who doesn't get fresh until the second date.

A gentleman never contradicts a woman, often out of courtesy but more often out of cowardice.

A gentleman is a man who, when his wife drops something, pushes it to where she can pick it up more easily.

It's a fine thing to be a gentleman, but it's always a handicap in an argument.

It takes three generations to make a gentleman, but you get two generations off for good behavior.

A gentleman is one who never swears at his wife when ladies are present.

To be born a gentleman is an accident; to die one is an achievement.

A gentleman is a man who holds the door open while his wife carries in the groceries.

A gentleman is one who, when he invites a girl up to see his etchings, shows her his etchings.

You can always tell a gentleman in a bus: he's the one who gives a lady a headstart in the race for a seat.

It's hard for a girl to know sometimes if a man is a perfect gentleman or just not interested.

A gentleman will always give up his seat to a lady—when he is about to get off the bus.

GEOGRAPHY

Ohio is the farthest west of the East, and the farthest north of the South. —*Louis Bromfield*

The trouble with geographies is that they are never published in loose-leaf editions.

Before marriage, he tells her she's all the world to him; after marriage, he learns a lot about geography.

A showgirl usually has an interesting history and an even more interesting geography.

GEOLOGY

If the Middle Ages had exploited the earth's surface as we are doing, we probably wouldn't be on it now. —*Jakob Burckhardt*

A geologist is a man who buries himself in the study of the earth before he is buried in it.

Geology teaches us that Mother Earth is as successful in concealing her age as any of her daughters.

GERMAN

In the German language the fish is a he, the scales are she, and the fishwife it.
—*Mark Twain*

The German either licks your boots, or shoves his naked backside in your face.
—*Winston Churchill*

What are the English and French to think of the language of our philosophers when we Germans don't understand it.
—*Goethe*

He was a German by marriage —each of his parents had married a German.
—*Strickland Gillilan*

GHOST

I have seen too many ghosts to believe in them. —*Coleridge*

Some people go to mediums to bring them into contact with the spirit world, but most go to bartenders.

The man who hasn't a ghost of a chance is probably out of spirits.

GHOSTWRITER

In heaven we will all be ghost writers, if we write at all.
—*Robert Frost*

A ghostwriter is the spirit that moves a man who would otherwise have nothing to say.

The ambition of every ghostwriter is to have another ghostwriter ghostwrite for him.

GIFT

In buying presents, give a girl something she can wear, and a boy something he can eat.
—*Ed Howe*

The art of giving presents is to give something which others cannot buy for themselves.
—*A. A. Milne*

To receive a present in the right spirit, even when you have none to give in return, is to give one in return. —*Leigh Hunt*

A talented wife seldom appreciates her husband as much as a gifted one.

A box of candy means friendship, a bunch of flowers means love, but a diamond means business.

Many a woman tolerates a man's presence for the sake of his presents.

'Tis better to have loved and lost than never to have loved at all—better for the florist and the jeweler.

What you are is God's gift to you; what you make of yourself is your gift to God.

Even when a woman knows it's the thought and not the size of the gift that counts, she wishes he would think big.

You can't tell whether a marriage is a failure or not till you've seen the wedding presents.

When a man promises his wife a gift, he feels as generous as if he were really going to give it to her.

In courtship we enjoy not so much the gift of the lover as the love of the giver.

You never realize how fortunate you are until you enter a gift shop and see some of the things your friends might have given you.

The man of rare gifts makes a poor husband.

A bride's present to the groom usually consists of several maiden aunts, numerous cousins, and a mother-in-law.

What do you give to the man who has everything, or to the woman who returns everything?

Presents make the heart grow fonder.

No woman is wholly convinced that a man really loves her until

he buys her something she doesn't need at a price he can't afford.

All the world loves a lover, except of course when you have to buy him a wedding gift.

A gold digger remembers a man's gift long after she has forgotten his name.

Ever since Eve gave Adam the apple, there's always been trouble between the sexes about gifts.

The best gifts we get are from those who have nothing to give but themselves.

People seldom think alike until it comes to buying wedding presents.

For her birthday a clever man will buy for his wife—shoes for the baby, grass seed for the front lawn, or seat covers for the car.

It's hard to know what to give the man who has everything, and even harder, the woman who wants everything.

GIRDLE

The only kind of girls who model girdles are the ones who don't need them.

Figures don't lie—unless they're wearing girdles.

A girdle is a device to make a woman slimmer on the outside than she is on the inside.

Fashions may come and fashions may go, but girdles will always be around.

The only exercise some women get is struggling into and out of a tight girdle.

There's a destiny that shapes our ends, but most women put more faith in a girdle.

Women wear girdles out of instinct; they have a natural desire to be squeezed.

GIRL

I am fond of children—except boys.   — *Lewis Carroll*

Females refer to themselves as girls, especially after they reach middle age.

The modern girl may have her little weaknesses but she isn't effeminate.

The child is father to the man, except when the child is a girl.

A miss in your car is better than a miss in your carburetor.

On a date, a good girl is good but a bad girl is better.

The modern girl is usually underdeveloped and overexposed.

Girls are pretty, generally speaking; and they are pretty generally speaking.

The girl who is easy to get is usually hard to take.

The modern girl wants to go with every Tom, Dick and marry.

GIVE

We hear a great deal about the Lord loving cheerful givers; we wonder where He finds them.
          — *Ed Howe*

It is better to give than to lend, and it costs about the same.

If your husband gives you everything you ask for, it means only one thing—you're not asking for enough.

We make a living by what we get, but make a life by what we give.

Why is it that you keep something for many years, and then give it away only a few weeks before you need it?

GIVE AND TAKE

Blessed are those who can give without remembering, and take without forgetting.
          — *Elizabeth Bibesco*

As it is more blessed to give than receive, so it must be more blessed to receive than to give back.   — *Robert Frost*

A good example of give and take is to take pains to give pleasure.

Many judges hand out sentences as if it were more blessed to give than to receive.

Government is a system of give and take where the taxpayer gives and the tax collector takes.

The man who takes and never gives, may last for years but never lives.

Marriage is a matter of give and take; so what your husband doesn't give you, you have to take.

Advice is like a physic—easy to give but hard to take.

GLAMOUR

Glamour is what makes a man ask for your telephone number, and a woman ask for the name of your dressmaker. — *Lilly Daché*

A glamour girl is a thing of beauty and an expense forever.

Glamour is something that evaporates when the sweater is a little too large.

A glamour girl is one who looks good enough to eat and dresses with taste.

A glamorous creature has the kind of figure that men give the once-over twice.

There's something glamorous about every woman, especially when there are a few drinks in a man.

A glamorous creature finds it easier to defend her virtue among men than her reputation among women.

GLASSES

Some people look intelligent when they wear glasses, but it's only an optical illusion.

Glasses can change your personality completely—if you empty them often enough.

Rose-colored glasses are seldom bifocal.

Some people get glasses because of too many headaches, while others get headaches because of too many glasses.

When a man makes passes at girls who wear glasses, it's probably due to their frames.

He never has his glasses changed, except when they don't hold enough.

What this country needs is a pair of sunglasses that can protect a man from the glare of his wife.

You're never old until the gleam in your eye comes from the sun hitting your bifocals.

There's a great deal of difference between using glasses over or under the nose.

If your eyes trouble you and you see spots in front of them, get glasses; you'll see the spots much better.

Most people look better without their glasses, and some look better without yours.

If you have difficulty finding where you put your glasses, a good trick is to leave them just where you empty them.

When a man stops looking at pretty women, he probably needs bifocals.

Nature is wonderful: millions of years ago she didn't know we were going to wear glasses, yet look at the way she placed our ears.

Men seldom make passes at girls who wear glasses, unless they are contact lenses.

Many a man who fell in love at first sight, now wishes he had started wearing glasses sooner.

GLOVES

There are two kinds of women: the careless type who lose their gloves, and the careful type who lose only one.

Nowadays a nonconformist is one who keeps gloves in the glove compartment of his car.

GLUTTONY

To a glutton life's chief necessities are food, clothing, food, shelter and food.

A glutton is a person with poor tastes to whom everything tastes good.

A glutton is always eating when he is not hungry, or is always hungry when he is not eating.

A glutton is one who likes to diet on all kinds of food.

A glutton's greedy sense of taste shows little sense but lots of waist.

A glutton is one who would sooner die than diet.

All gluttons have one thing in common: they don't believe in eating on an empty stomach.

A glutton is a man who eats as if he were fattening himself up for the market.

To the glutton, every dish that's served is merely an appetizer.

A glutton is one whose mind is always on his stomach, and whose stomach is always on his mind.

When it comes to food a glutton will stomach anything, except a diet.

A hog is never blamed for being a hog, unless he's a man.

A glutton is a man with eating habits crude who's always in the mood for food.

GOD

You must believe in God in spite of what the clergy say.
            —Benjamin Jowett

It is easy to understand God as long as you don't try to explain Him.   *—Joubert*

It's God—I'd have known Him by Blake's picture anywhere.
                —Robert Frost

If God has created us in his image, we have more than returned the compliment. *—Voltaire*

God does not believe in our God.   *—Jules Renard*

I am not concerned whether God is on my side or not, but I am concerned whether I am on God's side. — *Lincoln*

I cannot believe in a God who wants to be praised all the time. — *Nietzsche*

I know not which is the more childish—to deny God, or to define Him. — *Samuel Butler*

God created man in his own image, says the Bible; philosophers reverse the process: they create God in theirs.

— *G. C. Lichtenberg*

God give me strength not to trust in God! — *Sinclair Lewis*

O Mighty God, I believe! As to Monsieur the Son, and Madame his mother, that is another matter! — *Voltaire*

Beware of the man whose God is in the skies. — *Bernard Shaw*

If there is a God, atheism must seem to Him as less of an insult than religion. — *Goncourt*

When we know what God is, we shall be gods ourselves. — *Bernard Shaw*

Creator: a comedian whose audience is afraid to laugh. — *Mencken*

God is beginning to resemble not a ruler but the last fading smile of a Cheshire cat. — *Julian Huxley*

Proving the existence of God while standing on one leg is not the same thing as thanking God while praying on both knees. — *Kierkegaard*

There cannot be a God because, if there were one, I could not believe that I was not He. — *Nietzsche*

As a man Christ was glorious; as God, one asks, "Was that all He could do?" — *Jules Renard*

I cannot imagine how the clockwork of the universe can exist without a clockmaker. — *Voltaire*

God is subtle, but he is not malicious. — *Einstein*

If the average man is made in God's image, then such a man as Beethoven or Aristotle is plainly superior to God. — *Mencken*

Impiety: your irreverence toward my deity. — *Bierce*

Is there a God? God only knows.

God is not without sin—He created the world.

GOD AND DEVIL

Satan hasn't a single salaried helper; the Opposition employ a million. — *Mark Twain*

God and the devil are an effort after specialization and division of labor. — *Samuel Butler*

GOD AND MAN

We love the Lord, of course, but we often wonder what He finds to love in us. — *Ed Howe*

All the errors and incompetencies of the Creator reach their climax in man. — *Mencken*

We must be greater than God, for we have to undo His injustice. — *Jules Renard*

The Lord loves everyone, but most men are more particular than the Lord.

GOLD

The golden age only comes to men when they have forgotten gold. — *Chesterton*

If silence is golden, a lot of people are off the gold standard.

To increase the value of gold, have it handled by a dentist.

The only golden thing that some women dislike is silence.

Then there was the unfortunate prospector who went searching for oil and kept finding nothing but gold.

Silence may not be golden, but it is always worth its weight in gold.

GOLDEN RULE

Alter the golden rule: what you do not like done to yourself, do not do to others. — *William Osler*

Do unto the other fellow the way he'd like to do unto you— and do it first. — *Edward N. Westcott*

Don't do for others what you wouldn't think of asking them to do for you. — *Josh Billings*

The exception proves the rule, especially the Golden Rule.

Judge your fellow men by the golden rule, not by the gold standard.

Do not do unto others what they will not do for themselves.

Act according to the Golden Rule, but always act as if it's your move.

Sometimes it seems that we may have also buried at Fort Knox the golden rule.

The golden rule also applies to night drivers: dim unto others as you would have them dim unto you.

GOLF

I've seen lifelong friends drift apart over golf just because one could play better, but the other counted better. — *Stephen Leacock*

I regard golf as an expensive way of playing marbles. — *Chesterton*

Rail-splitting produced an immortal President in Lincoln, but golf hasn't produced even a good A-1 Congressman. — *Will Rogers*

It is almost impossible to remember how tragic a place the world is when one is playing golf. — *Robert Lynd*

Find a man with both feet firmly on the ground, and you've found a man about to make a difficult putt. — *Fletcher Knebel*

Many a husband has a secret craving to use his golf clubs in a way the manufacturer didn't intend.

The man who takes up golf to get his mind off his work, soon takes up work to get his mind off golf.

Golf is a game in which the slowest people in the world are those in front of you, and the fastest are those behind.

The best thing that can be said about golf is that it isn't compulsory.

Many a golfer prefers a golf cart to a caddy because it cannot count, criticize—or laugh.

There are three ways to improve your golf game: take lessons, practice constantly—or start cheating.

Only a remarkable man can live down a hole in one.

Another good thing about golf is that you can be a pedestrian without being run over.

There's nothing like golf to build a man up physically and mentally so that he can play more golf.

There's no game like golf: you go out with three strangers, play eighteen holes, and return with three enemies.

An amateur golfer is one who addresses the ball twice—before and after swinging.

Teach your wife to play golf, and she'll never hit anything; teach her to drive a car, and she'll never miss.

Many a man whose doctor advised him to play golf, has an instructor who advises him to quit.

The trouble with some golfers is that they stand too close to the ball—after they hit it.

In life, a man's honesty is often his handicap: in golf, a man's handicap is often his honesty.

Making a hole in one isn't so wonderful—look at all the exercise you miss.

The secret of good golf is to hit the ball hard, straight, and not too often.

Golf originated as a Scotch game, but now it is often played with rye.

Golf isn't so much a game as a passionate faith that you can hit it a mile next time.

Greater love hath no man than this—that he give up his golf for his wife.

Many a woman is a fair golf player: she goes around in a couple of hundred strokes and a couple of thousand words.

Golf is a five-mile walk punctuated by disappointments.

In primitive society, when native tribes beat the ground with clubs and yell, it is called witchcraft; in civilized society it is called golf.

In golf, nothing counts like your opponent.

Sometimes a golfer makes such a wild shot that when he finally finds the ball, he has lost the course.

Some men play golf for the exercise only; others play a good game.

Many an executive who is run down should lay off golf for a while and put in a good day's work at the office.

The way some men play golf, they'd be better off in church on Sundays.

The man who blames fate for other accidents, feels personally responsible when he makes a hole in one.

Golf was once a rich man's sport, but it now has millions of poor players.

Another thing to be thankful for is that many people do their worst driving on golf courses.

Many a man goes out to play golf feeling fit as a fiddle, and comes home tight as a drum.

There are less men today in the country plowing the fields with plows than with niblicks and mashies.

A beginner's golf game is improving when he is able to hit the ball in one.

The consolation for the loser in golf is that he gets more practice and exercise than the winner: he gets to hit the ball more times.

A long Sunday drive can be a pleasure, but only if the ball stays on the fairway.

A golfer is a man who keeps his elbows straight for eighteen holes, but bends it on the nineteenth.

Many an executive talks golf all morning at the office, and business all afternoon on the golf course.

The best way to get a man to dig in a garden would be to call it a sand trap.

Golf develops a beginner's self-control, but caddying for a beginner develops it even more.

As soon as a businessman takes up golf, he becomes an executive.

The man who never falls asleep in church on Sunday is probably out on the golf course.

A golf club may be a driver, a mashie or a putter, but a golf ball is a golf ball no matter how you putt it.

GOOD

The best is the enemy of the good.
— *Voltaire*

In the United States, doing good has come to be, like patriotism, a favorite device of persons with something to sell. *— Mencken*

When we are happy we are always good, but when we are good we are not always happy. *— Oscar Wilde*

There is so much goodness in real life—do let us keep it out of our books. *— Norman Douglas*

If I knew that a man was coming to my house with the conscious design of doing me good, I should run for my life. *— Thoreau*

It's better to do good than well, and then maybe you'll do good as well. *— Robert Frost*

Most men who want to do good, want it done at the expense of others. *— Ed Howe*

It is better to be beautiful than to be good, but it is better to be good than to be ugly. *— Oscar Wilde*

Men have a singular desire to be good without being good for anything. *— Thoreau*

Hunt for the good points in the other fellow; remember, he has to do the same in your case.

Just because a man is as good as his word doesn't mean that he is any good.

People who tell you something for your own good, never seem to have anything good to tell you.

The good men do sometimes lives after them, but no one is interested in it.

The do-gooder who is very good for the world is usually no good for his wife.

You can't keep a good man good.

The good die young; that's why we meet so few of them among adults.

There must be a lot of good in selfish people because they have never let any of it come out.

No one likes to be caught in the act, except the person who is doing good.

Do good, and never mind to whom.

A Pollyanna sees good in everyone, probably because she doesn't see so good.

It would be a better world if women were all as good as they look, and men as good as they seem.

Some people go about doing good, others just go about.

When a man and woman marry they take each other for better or for worse, but not for good.

A man is as good as the woman he's with.

Do you give your child an allowance every day for being a good boy, or do you want him to be good for nothing?

Being told things are for our own good never does us any.

The good who do not die young get over it.

Before marriage, a man thinks nothing is good enough for her; after marriage, he still thinks nothing is good enough for her.

No man is as good as his wife says her first husband was.

GOOD AND EVIL

The first lesson of history is the good of evil. — *Emerson*

The goodness of some people is the worst thing about them.
— *Ed Howe*

I have met so many good people that I have almost lost my faith in the wickedness of mankind. — *Will Durant*

Love what's lovable and hate what's hateable—it takes brains to see the difference. — *Robert Frost*

God does not like people to be too good; he likes them neither too good nor too bad.
— *Samuel Butler*

We should expect the best and the worst from mankind, just as we do from the weather.
— *Vauvenargues*

The man who has never done any harm will never do any good.
— *Bernard Shaw*

He was as evil, vicious and degenerate as any fellow in Paris, but otherwise the most wonderful fellow in the world.   — *Rabelais*

In the past you had to apologize for your bad deeds; nowadays you have to apologize for your good ones.   — *Camus*

It's from their having stood contrasted that good and bad so long have lasted.   — *Robert Frost*

You do something evil if you do nothing good.

To say the good die young is a standing invitation for the small boy to be bad.

Life too often presents us with a choice of evils rather than goods.

Show me a man who never says anything really bad about anyone, and I'll show you a man who never does anything really good for anyone.

A man is as good as he has to be, and a woman as bad as she dares.

To many people the choice between good and evil is the choice between what they want to do and what they ought to do.

In literature as in life, men and women are not good or bad, but good and bad.

The world is made up of people who are good and bad: the good decide which is which.

To a bachelor one woman is as good as another, if not better, while one wife is as bad as another, if not worse.

Many a preacher spends so much time condemning evil that he has no time left to do good.

There's so much good in the worst of us, and so much bad in the best of us, that it's hardly fit for any of us to talk about the rest of us.

GOSSIP

Half the evil in the world is gossip started by good people.
— *Ed Howe*

Of every ten persons who talk about you, nine will say something bad, and the tenth will say something good in a bad way.
— *Rivarol*

When a man tells you what people are saying about you, tell him what people are saying about him—that will immediately take his mind off your troubles.
— *Ed Howe*

A gossip can't be telling the truth all the time—there simply is not that much truth.

A gossip is anybody who is not too busy to be a busybody.

The gossip deserves credit for choosing someone more interesting than herself to talk about.

Gossip is a form of malicious talk indulged in by other people.

There's only one thing worse than the woman who gossips, and that's the woman who never knows any.

A gossip is a woman with a mouthful eager to give others an earful.

Many a woman never puts off till tomorrow the gossip she can spread today.

A gossip spends half her time talking to her neighbors about others, and the other half talking to others about her neighbors.

Some gossip is too good to be true.

What a wife doesn't know doesn't hurt her, but it does give her friends something to talk about.

There's no fun listening to gossip unless you believe it.

A little gossip goes a long way.

In spreading gossip, the female of the species is much faster than the mail.

Cars do not run down nearly so many people as gossips do.

A gossip is a woman whose mouth continues to work long after her conscience has ceased to function.

Gossip is like spinach: it all boils down to very little.

Some women tell all they know, while others tell a great deal more.

A gossip is a woman who talks so much that her supply of truth gives out before she gets through.

Some things go without saying, but gossip isn't one of them.

Remember, anyone who will gossip with you, will not hesitate to gossip about you.

Gossip is the only sound that travels faster than sound.

When two women get together, they have each other to talk to, but they still need another to talk about.

Not every woman repeats gossip—someone has to start it.

The reason a gossip can't wait to spread scandal is that she may find out it isn't true.

The woman who doesn't gossip has no friends to speak of.

History repeats itself, but the neighbors repeat it when it's your personal history.

A gossip loves to discuss the events of the day, friend by friend.

Get a gossip wound up, and she will run someone down.

Even when a gossip doesn't believe it all, she tells it all.

There are two sides to every story—until the gossips get hold of it.

We hate to repeat gossip, but what else can you do with it?

A clam is the only thing with a big mouth that doesn't talk about the neighbors.

GOVERNMENT

My experience in government is that when things are non-controversial and beautifully coordinated, there is not much going on. *—John F. Kennedy*

A government is the only known vessel that leaks from the top. *—James Reston*

Government is too big and important to be left to the politicians. *—Chester Bowles*

The punishment which the wise suffer who refuse to take part in the government, is to live under the government of worse men. *—Emerson*

The government is not one bit better than the government we got for one third the money twenty years ago. *—Will Rogers*

One of the things we have to be thankful for is that we don't get as much government as we pay for. *—Charles F. Kettering*

Govern a great nation as you would cook a small fish—don't overdo it. *—Confucius*

Our form of government is best described by calling it a government by the chairmen of the Standing Committees of Congress. *—Woodrow Wilson*

If anyone at all is to have the privilege of lying, the rulers of the state should be such persons. *—Plato*

The machinery of government would not work if it were not allowed a little play in its joints. *—Justice O. W. Holmes*

Every decent man is ashamed of the government he lives under.
— *Mencken*

I will govern according to the common weal, but not according to the common will.
— *James I of England*

Good government cannot exist side by side with bad politics: the best government is the best politics.   — *Adlai Stevenson*

To rule is easy, to govern difficult.   — *Goethe*

It is astonishing with how little wisdom mankind can be governed, when that little wisdom is its own.   — *W. R. Inge*

The government is mainly an expensive organization to regulate evildoers and tax those who behave.   — *Ed Howe*

To govern is always to choose among disadvantages.
— *De Gaulle*

The form of government that is most suitable to the artist is no government at all.
— *Oscar Wilde*

Under good government, we should be ashamed of poverty; under bad government, we should be ashamed of wealth.
— *Confucius*

Every government faces the problem of how to get people to pay taxes they can't afford, for services they don't need.

The men who have wisdom enough to understand our government, have the wisdom to stay clear of it.

No matter how much it costs to run the country, it wouldn't cost any less to let it walk.

There are two classes that don't know what the people want: the people's representatives and the people.

Our government will never be overthrown—there's far too much of it.

There are only three types of government: those that break heads, those that count heads, and those that use heads.

What this country needs is a return to popular government at popular prices.

You can't escape it—you either work for the government, or work for persons who work for the government.

Laws do not govern—lawyers do.

It is every citizen's duty to support his government, but not necessarily in the style to which it has been accustomed.

The trouble is not that the government makes us work for posterity, but that it insists on being paid by us.

No government is as good as it says it is, or as bad as the opposition says it is.

There are two forms of government: the short form and the long form.

You can't please everyone: some people are displeased with the government when it does nothing, while others are displeased when it does something.

Congress favors a stable government, judging from the amount of stalling it does.

Another trouble with government is that it seems to think the individual owes it a living.

There are three kinds of government: those with too much overhead, those with too much underhand, and those with both.

There's only one ship that never slows down in a fog, and that is the ship of state.

GOVERNMENT AND BUSINESS

The business of government is to keep the government out of business—that is, unless business needs government aid.
— Will Rogers

The government is the only partner in a business enterprise that is privileged to share the profits without having to share the losses.

The directors of private institutions always want more business in government and less government in business.

GRADUATION

The thing that surprises the college graduate most when he gets out in the world is to find out how much uneducated people know.

The college student is apt to find that the beginning comes after the commencement is past.

Experience is the only school from which no one every graduates.

The ideal gift for the high-school or college graduate is a job.

Okay college graduate: here's the world; it's all yours—take it away and don't bring it back.

GRAMMAR

The basis of most of the world's troubles are matters of grammar. — Montaigne

Damn the subjunctive!—it brings all our writers to shame.
— Mark Twain

The adjective is the worst enemy of the noun even though it agrees in gender, number and case. — Voltaire

Is there anything more charming than a thoroughly defective verb? — Norman Douglas

Even kings must obey the laws of grammar. — Molière

I would prefer a phrase that was easy and unaffected to a phrase that was grammatical.
— Somerset Maugham

Syntax must be bad, having both sin and tax in it.
— Will Rogers

The subjunctive mood is in its death throes, and the best thing to do is to put it out of its misery.
— *Somerset Maugham*

An illiterate person makes grammatical errors even in his dreams.

A grammarian always has more trouble with his relatives than with his relative pronouns.

When money talks, nobody notices what grammar it uses.

Another ungrammatical creature is the owl that always hoots *to who* instead of *to whom*.

A grammarian is one who thinks it is more important to write correctly than to write well.

GRANDCHILDREN

By the time most of us can really afford to have children, we are having grandchildren.

The nice thing about grandchildren is that you aren't too busy supporting them to have time to enjoy them.

Grandchildren don't make a man feel old; what does is the realization that he's married to a grandmother.

GRANDPARENTS

When grandparents enter the door, discipline flies out the window.
— *Ogden Nash*

A married daughter with children puts you in danger of being catalogued as a first edition.
— *Warwick Deeping*

You often meet grandparents who bore you about their grandchildren, but never vice versa.

Many a child is spoiled because you can't spank his grandmother.

Grandparents are people who are overindulgent, overanxious and over fifty.

The grandmother of today has something that the grandmother of the past didn't have—blonde hair.

A grandmother is a woman who used to sit up with her children, and now sits up with her children's children.

If you think spanking is not necessary, the chances are you're a grandparent.

By the time a couple can afford to go out evenings, they have to babysit with the grandchildren.

GRASS

Don't envy your neighbor whose grass is greener—his water bill is higher too.

The man who refuses to submit to his wife is often brought to his knees by crabgrass.

The curious thing about grass is that it grows greener on the other side of the fence, but grows faster on your side.

There's something perverse about grass: it refuses to grow on your lawn but thrives in the cracks of your sidewalk.

When spring comes, can crabgrass be far behind?

If the grass next door is greener, your neighbor has probably plowed more greenbacks into it.

Happiness lies in your own backyard, but it is often hidden by the crabgrass.

The last man to let the grass grow under his feet is often the first to have it grow over his head.

Nothing is certain but death and taxes—and crabgrass.

Another thing you can make from grass is butter: all you need is a cow and a churn.

Winter is the only cure so far discovered for crabgrass.

Grass grows by inches and dies by feet.

Give crabgrass an inch, and it will take a yard.

GRATITUDE

I feel a very unusual sensation —if it is not indigestion, I think it must be gratitude. – Disraeli

A man is occasionally thankful when he says "Thank you."
– George Eliot

In this world of sin and sorrow there is always something to be thankful for; as for me, I rejoice that I am not a Republican.
– Mencken

Nothing tires a man more than to be grateful all the time.
– Ed Howe

Children are grateful to Santa Claus for filling their stockings with toys; why aren't their parents grateful to God for filling theirs with legs?   – Chesterton

If you can't be thankful for what you have, be thankful for what you have—escaped.

Politicians are skilled at creating every kind of debt, except a debt of gratitude.

If your wife doesn't treat you as she should, be thankful.

Gratitude is the feeling that people who have done you favors in the past are obliged to continue doing you favors in the future.

If we stopped to think more, we would stop to thank more.

This age of the atomic bomb is the first time in history that a person can be thankful that he's around to be thankful.

Of all human feelings, gratitude has the shortest memory.

A man's gratitude is always greatest just before you do him a favor.

Everyone has something to be thankful for: even the man who

can't pay his debts can be thankful he isn't one of his creditors.

GRAVE

In our attempts to cover the ground quickly, the ground is apt to cover us.
— *Herbert Beerbohm Tree*

The grave is still the best shelter against the storms of destiny.
— *G. C. Lichtenberg*

The paths of glory lead but to the grave—also the paths of ignominy, profligacy and skullduggery.
— *Fred Allen*

Many a wife sends her husband to an early grave with a series of little digs.

A foot on the brake is worth two in the grave.

The man who is buried in thought naturally has a grave appearance.

So far it's been the other way around: the earth has inherited the meek.

GRAVITY

The two things that will never be abolished are the law of gravity and the gravity of the law.

The law of gravity is the only law that operates without favoritism, without graft, and without delay.

A good comedian obeys the law of gravity: he never laughs at his own jokes.

The law of gravity doesn't always work: it is usually easier to pick up a girl than it is to drop her.

GREAT

People do not become great by doing great things; they do great thing because they are great.
— *Bernard Shaw*

The defects of great men are the consolation of dunces.
— *Isaac D'Israeli*

I like to admire great men, but only those whose writings I do not understand.   — *G. C. Lichtenberg*

It's great to be great, but it's greater to be human.
— *Will Rogers*

There is the great man who makes every man feel small, but the really great man is the man who makes every man feel great.
— *Chesterton*

Great men are those who profit the most from the fewest mistakes.   — *Ed Howe*

A great man is always willing to be little.   — *Emerson*

We are both great men, but I have succeeded better than he has in keeping it a secret.   — *Bill Nye*

There's no way to be great except by trying to be great.
— *Camus*

Some men are born great, some achieve greatness, and some have greatness thrust upon them by their press agents.

Money makes fools of great people, and it makes great people of fools.

When an egotist wants to be in the presence of true greatness, he goes off by himself.

Some men are born great, some achieve greatness, and some just grate upon you.

GREED

To be clever enough to get a great deal of money, one must be stupid enough to want it.
— *Chesterton*

There are some men who, in a fifty-fifty proposition, insist on getting the hyphen too.

The greedy man is pretty sure to get what he wants—but not enough of it.

Greed enables a person to buy the things money can buy while losing the things money cannot buy.

The girl who never got enough dolls often grows up into the woman who cannot get enough dollars.

The man to whom money is the best of friends, usually aims to make as many friends as possible.

One man's cupidity is another man's stupidity.

When a man has more money than he needs, he still feels he needs more money than he has.

Once upon a time money swore solemnly that nobody who did not love money, should have it.

GREETING

January is the month we extend good wishes to our friends, and the rest are months when the good wishes are not fulfilled.
— *G. C. Lichtenberg*

When you ask some people how they are, they expect you to listen to the details.

A chilly reception doesn't cool one off on a hot day.

Now and then you meet a man with such a cordial handclasp and such a friendly personality, you know he hasn't any money.

A hypochondriac always takes advantage of the situation when you ask "How are you?"

When a woman greets another with an icy smile, she usually follows it up with a few well-frozen words.

GREETING CARD

Sentiment has no place in business, unless, of course, you're in the greeting-card business.

Another person who never fails to send you a get-well card is your creditor.

What this country needs is a greeting card informing the receiver that you are not going to send him any more greeting cards.

Life is a card game during the first half of which we get birthday cards, and during the second half get-well cards.

GROUCH

Only the man who has achieved success can afford to be as irritable at the office as he is at home.

A sourpuss is a person whose face looks as if it has worn out before his body.

A grouch is the kind of man who spreads good cheer wherever he doesn't go.

A sourpuss always sets the corners of his mouth at twenty minutes past eight.

A grouch is a man who has lost heart and has to depend wholly on his liver.

A sourpuss is one who always looks as if he had just been cut out of someone's will.

A grouch is always unpleasant, even when you catch him off-guard.

A sourpuss is a peevish person who never wipes his opinion off his face.

A grouch is never satisfied unless he is dissatisfied.

A sourpuss is the kind of man who would look unhappy even if he wasn't married.

A grouch always looks as if he were weaned on a pickle.

A sourpuss looks as if life isn't worth living, but acts as if it isn't worth leaving.

GROWTH

Every man must do his own growing, no matter how tall his grandfather was.

Why do the extraordinary sons whom mothers are always praising become the ordinary husbands whom wives are always blaming?

There's only one thing that can keep growing without nourishment, and that's the human ego.

If you think you're too old for growing pains, try gardening.

Children should eat and get big while they are little so that they won't be little when they get big.

While children are growing vertically, their parents are usually growing horizontally.

How quickly children grow up: you no longer get through sitting up with them than you're sitting up for them.

Some people grow richer, some grow wiser, but most just grow older.

There's nothing wrong with the younger generation that the older generation didn't outgrow.

GUARANTEE

Get double security from your relatives.   —*Ed Howe*

The Constitution guarantees you the pursuit of happiness, but doesn't guarantee that you will catch up with it.

Mighty few products sold with a lifetime guarantee last as long as you last.

The Constitution guarantees free speech; it does not guarantee listeners.

GUARD

You don't set a fox to watching the chickens just because he has a lot of experience in the hen house.   — Harry S. Truman

Any time a man can't come and settle with you without bringing his lawyer—look out for him.
— Will Rogers

The virtue of a man is not to be measured by what he does while his wife is watching.
— Francis Bacon

A watched kettle never boils, and a watched toaster never pops.

The woman who has to watch her waistline is lucky: she has it right out in front of her where she can see it.

Eternal vigilance is the price of liberty, but how can we watch all of the politicians all of the time?

GUEST

To be an ideal guest, stay at home.   — Ed Howe

After you have been married five years, there should always be someone to dinner. — E. V. Lucas

One of the chief advantages of marriage is that you can hand over to your wife a guest you can't stand.   — G. C. Lichtenberg

A husband's job is to keep talking to unexpected guests at the front gate while his wife straightens out the living room.

Of all guests, the most unwelcome are those who try to make both weekends meet.

Don't put all your eggs in one basket, or all your whiskey in one guest.

It's what the guests say after they leave that really counts.

It's better to let your husband bring a friend home to dinner than to have a friend bring your husband home after dinner.

There are two kinds of guests: those who come *after* dinner, and those who come after *dinner*.

It's easy for a guest to be more pleasant than he really is, but not if he stays longer than a weekend.

Some people own their own homes; others have company most of the time.

GUIDE

Most of the trouble in this world is due to someone's attempt to let his conscience be your guide.

Child guidance is what parents get from their children nowadays.

If you let your conscience be your guide, you'll miss the most exciting places.

GUILT

Every man is guilty of all the good he didn't do.   — *Voltaire*

There are two sides to every question, especially the judge's "Are you guilty or not guilty?"

The law considers every man innocent until he is found guilty, but his wife doesn't.

Silence is not always golden; sometimes it's guilt.

When money talks, it usually says "Not guilty."

HABIT

The unfortunate thing about this world is that good habits are so much easier to give up than bad ones.   — *Somerset Maugham*

The chains of habit are too weak to be felt until they are too strong to be broken.
    — *Samuel Johnson*

A man knows even less about his reading habits than he does about his sex habits.
    — *Norman Cousins*

Habit is habit, and not to be flung out of the window by any man, but coaxed downstairs a step at a time.   — *Mark Twain*

The second half of a man's life is made up of nothing but the habits acquired during the first half.   — *Dostoevski*

First we make our habits, and then our habits make us.

Giving up a bad habit usually brings on a worse one—that of bragging about it.

Some women marry for love, some for money, and others from force of habit.

A man seems to inherit all sorts of habits, except making money.

Some men are regular in their habits, but their habits are irregular.

It is easier to acquire two good habits than to break off one bad one.

If you don't own a riding habit, you should acquire a walking habit.

Love makes marriage possible, and habit makes it endurable.

The oldest habit some people have is telling you how young they are.

Another good habit is the practice of correcting your bad habits.

Habit is often mistaken for loyalty.

A man spends the first half of his life learning habits that shorten the other half.

Marriage is an institution where two people constantly try to change each other's habits.

HAIR

A woman with her hair turned up always looks as if she were going some place—either to the opera or the shower bath.
— *Orson Welles*

A number of things are good for gray hair, but the best one is a sensible head.

Beware the woman who starts stroking your hair—she's probably after your scalp.

The man who doesn't comb his hair looks best with a chrysanthemum in his buttonhole.

When a woman worries too much about getting gray, she sometimes turns blond overnight.

Another good way to keep your hair from falling out is to knot it on the inside.

The man who worries about his hair getting thin, would worry much more if it were getting fat.

There's nothing rarer than hearing a person admit that his gray hair isn't premature.

A woman's head is often turned by flattery, but more often by tinting.

If your hair starts to trouble you, don't worry; it will come out all right.

Middle age is the period when a woman's hair starts turning from gray to black.

The woman who can't do anything with her hair, could do even less without it.

A hair in the head is worth two in the brush.

Having your gray hair dyed doesn't do away with the worries that caused it.

The best way to avoid falling hair is to jump out of the way.

The good die young, and the old dye for various reasons.

As long as gray hairs can be counted, they don't count.

Both sexes have their hair problems: with women it's tint, with men 'tain't.

The only thing that can stop falling hair is a floor.

Breathes there a child who doesn't ponder why Dad gets gray and Mom gets blonder?

HAIRCUT

If you can do nothing else toward beautifying the community in which you live, you can at least get your hair cut.

If you want a thing to be well done, do it yourself—unless you want a haircut.

Some men, after they get a haircut, always hear better.

Every now and then you see an offbeat character who looks as if he cuts his hair with pinking shears.

Many a man who seems weighed down with care really needs nothing but a haircut.

Economics makes no sense: no matter how much or how little hair you have, the price of a haircut is the same.

HAIRDO

Another thing about women is that they can be persuaded to do anything with their hair, except leave it alone.

In many a beauty parlor the talk alone is enough to curl your hair.

Hair tinting is more popular than ever: many a girl is out to get a boyfriend or dye trying.

If men were less interested in feminine hairdos, women would be more interested in what's in their heads than what's on them.

The best way to get your husband to appreciate your old hairdo is to get a new one.

Don't tell a teen-ager that her hair looks like a mop; she probably doesn't know what a mop is.

Some hairdos look as if they had been arranged in front of an electric fan.

What this country needs are less extreme hairdos and more sensible *hair don'ts*.

A hairdo on a woman's head is even more changeable than what's on her mind.

HALO

What after all is a halo?—It's only one more thing to clean.
— *Christopher Fry*

A halo has only to fall a few inches to become a noose.

The man with a swelled head often mistakes it for a halo.

Many a woman could take a great weight off her mind if she discarded her halo.

Beware the reformed sinner: he usually exchanges the circles under his eyes for one over his head.

HAMLET

Hamlet has been played by 5,000 actors—no wonder he is crazy.
— *Mencken*

Are the commentators on Hamlet really mad, or only pretending to be?
— *Oscar Wilde*

The way actors play Hamlet, it is easy to see why Ophelia should go and drown herself.

Shakespeare murdered Hamlet, and a great many Hamlets have murdered Shakespeare.

Hamlet is the tragedy of tackling a family problem too soon after college.

HAND

It takes all kinds of people to make the world: right-handed, left-handed and underhanded.

A bachelor always knows how to hold a woman's hand so that she doesn't get a grip on him.

The man whose right hand always knows what his left hand is doing is probably a juggler.

Getting married is very much like a game of cards: it depends a good deal on what kind of a hand you hold.

Housewives can keep their hands smooth and lovely by putting two things into the dishwater —their husbands' hands.

The first and still the best do-it-yourself kit consists of your own pair of hands.

No matter what the stakes, card playing is still cheap compared with the other well-known game where you hold hands.

You can't trust some people; if you lend them a hand, be sure you get it back.

HANDBAG

If you're a man, you can't take it with you; if you're a woman, you can always put it in your handbag.

In the past woman needed an attic; today she has a handbag.

There's a place for everything, especially in a woman's handbag.

A thorough man can get to the bottom of almost anything, except a woman's handbag.

Nothing surprises a man more than when his wife finds what she wants on her first dive into her handbag.

The contents of a woman's handbag are the best proof that money isn't everything.

HANDWRITING

Whoever wrote that, writes a hand like a foot.   —Swift

Graphologists find it easier to analyze some people's handwriting than to read it.

When a man sees the handwriting on the wall, there's probably a child in the family.

Graphology enables us to analyze all kinds of handwriting, except the handwriting on the wall.

HANDYMAN

An old handyman with experience knows almost as much as a young handyman thinks he knows.

Many a husband can fix anything a handyman can, and often for less than twice the money.

HANGING

A man who is unhappy in love should hang himself not from the nearest tree, but around the neck of the nearest woman.
                    —Jean Renoir

If the desire to kill and the opportunity to kill always came together, who would escape hanging?   —Mark Twain

No man is so good as not to deserve hanging ten times over were he to submit all his thoughts and actions to the laws.

– Montaigne

Never saw off the branch you are on, unless you are being hanged from it. *– Stanislaw J. Lec*

We'll shape a noose for the last king from the intestines of the last priest. *– Diderot*

Beware when your lawyer promises he will get you a suspended sentence—you may be hanged.

HANGOVER

You pay for the liquor; the hangover is free.

A hangover is when everything you poured down your throat has gone to your head.

The best cure for a hangover is to drink black coffee the night before instead of the morning after.

The higher a man feels in the evening, the lower he feels in the morning.

The best thing to take for a hangover is whiskey the night before.

The morning after is generally caused by a lovely Eve.

The hangover you get the morning after comes from not using your head the night before.

Early to bed and early to rise, and your head will not feel seven times its own size.

You're getting old when you worry about the morning after before the night before.

Two heads are better than one, unless you have a hangover.

No one gets a hangover from other people's drinking.

A hangover is where, having lost your head the night before, you wake up with two heads the morning after.

Eat, drink and be merry for tomorrow ye die—or wish ye were dead.

HAPPEN

Some people make things happen, some watch things happen, while others wonder what has happened.

Some men tell their wives everything that happens; others tell them a lot of things that never happen.

There is nothing trivial if you love the person to whom it happens.

A news commentator spends his time explaining what would happen if something which isn't likely to happen should happen.

The know-it-all always knows what to do until it happens to him.

A premonition is the strange feeling you get that something is going to happen, but only after it has happened.

Different women have sexual relations in different ways: some let it happen, others help it happen.

HAPPINESS

To be without some of the things you want is an indispensable part of happiness.
— *Bertrand Russell*

It is hard to be happier than other people because we always believe others to be happier than they are. — *Montesquieu*

The only really happy folk are married women and single men.
— *Mencken*

Most of us believe in trying to make other people happy only if they can be happy in ways which we approve. — *Robert Lynd*

Happiness makes up in height for what it lacks in length.
— *Robert Frost*

Happiness isn't something you experience; it's something you remember. — *Oscar Levant*

Ask yourself whether you are happy, and you cease to be so.
— *John Stuart Mill*

Happiness isn't everything: a hog is always happier than a man, and bacteria are always happier than hogs. — *Mencken*

Most folks are about as happy as they make up their minds to be. — *Lincoln*

Happiness grows at our own firesides, and is not to be picked in strangers' gardens.
— *Douglas Jerrold*

If you ever find happiness by hunting for it, you will find it as the old woman did her spectacles —safe on her nose all the time.
— *Josh Billings*

Happiness is the interval between periods of unhappiness.
— *Don Marquis*

Every man is thoroughly happy twice in his life: just after he has met his first love, and just after he has left his last one.
— *Mencken*

If you would make a man happy, do not add to his possessions but subtract from his desires. — *Seneca*

A person is never happy except at the price of some ignorance.
— *Anatole France*

Happiness comes fleetingly now and then to those who have learned to do without it, and to them only. — *Don Marquis*

The happiest people seem to be those who have no particular reason for being happy except that they are. — *W. R. Inge*

The happiest periods in a man's life are his boyhood and about ten years from now.

Happiness consists of filling a child's stomach, a woman's wardrobe, and a man's wallet.

If ignorance is bliss, why isn't the world happier?

The greatest essentials of happiness are something to do, something to love, and something to hope for.

A man is usually as happy as he wishes his neighbors to be.

Wealth doesn't bring happiness, and poverty doesn't bring it either—what on earth is a man to do?

When you make two people really happy, one of them is probably you.

A woman is happy when she gets the man she wants; a woman is happier when she gets the man every other woman wants.

Marital happiness sometimes depends upon the person you marry, and sometimes upon the person you didn't marry.

Happiness is a way station between too much and too little.

If it weren't for our troubles we'd never be able to appreciate happiness.

The happy rich and the happy poor are both possible, but not the happy mean.

You'll be happy if you stop worrying because you're not.

Happiness is what everyone is in pursuit of, though no one knows where it is.

The secret of happiness lies in keeping on good terms with everyone and everything, especially your conscience, your wife and your stomach.

The conviction of the rich that the poor are happy is no more foolish than the conviction of the poor that the rich are.

The happiest man on earth is the one who never knows it.

Happiness is the ability to avoid letting your troubles bother you any more than they bother your friends.

Happiness consists of not longing for the things that make us happy.

The secret of happiness is learning to accept the impossible, do without the indispensable, and bear the intolerable.

Money can't buy happiness, but it helps you to look for it in many more places.

It's better to marry the man you can be happy with than the man you can't be happy without.

Some people spread happiness wherever they go; others, whenever they go.

Happiness is like jam: it's hard to spread even a little without getting some on yourself.

Do something daily to make others happy, even if it's only to leave them alone.

Happiness is a large pitcher of martinis, a thick juicy steak, and a big hungry dog to eat the steak so it doesn't go to waste.

Some marriages are happy because a husband adores his wife; others, because he adorns her.

The modern formula for happiness seems to be doing and buying things we cannot afford.

A man never knows what real happiness is until he gets married, and then it's too late.

There is no happiness in the world, so we might just as well be happy without it.

HARMONY

They who are all things to their neighbors cease to be anything to themselves.   *—Norman Douglas*

Most of us would get along better if we followed the advice we give to others.

The only time two women are in perfect accord is when they both hate the same woman.

They would get along better if the father treated his son as a guest, and the son treated his father as a host.

Married life is like the harmony of a great orchestra: the brass predominates.

Many a husband finds it impossible to bring harmony into his home life unless he plays second fiddle.

Keep the peace at home: there is little comfort in pointing out that your wife is a bigger fool than her husband.

The lost chord in the harmony of the United Nations is accord.

HARVARD

About all some men accomplish in life is to send a son to Harvard.   *—Ed Howe*

Each year 25 percent of the freshman class at Harvard enjoy the first so much that they repeat it.   *—A. Lawrence Lowell*

Every boy born in Boston has to go to Harvard, but if he knows the right people he can get out of it.   *—Fred Allen*

You can always tell a Harvard man, but you cannot tell him much.

HASTE

Though I am always in haste, I am never in a hurry.
—John Wesley

When a woman dresses in a hurry, she always looks it.
—Ed Howe

No man who is in a hurry is quite civilized.   *—Will Durant*

Some couples marry in haste because each is afraid the other will back out.

Haste makes waste—and dented fenders.

Some people are always in a hurry, even when they don't know where they're going.

The person who in the pursuit of happiness is in a hurry, is liable to pass it right by.

Marry in haste, and you'll have more trouble than a soap opera.

The man who hasn't time to stop at a railroad crossing, always finds time to attend the funeral.

What's the use of hurrying when there's a perfectly good day coming tomorrow that hasn't even been touched?

A hasty remark sometimes gets a man in trouble, especially at an auction.

The man who never has enough time to do a job properly always has enough time to do it over again.

HAT

She had a passion for hats, none of which returned her affection.   — *Storm Jameson*

The difference between a man and a woman buying a hat is about three hours.

Why is it that a hat that looks pretty on a girl who can't afford it, is always bought by a stout dowager who can?

Milliners never seem to have any difficulty discovering geometrical shapes wholly unknown to mathematicians.

Blessed are the poor: a poor woman pays three dollars instead of twenty-five for a three-dollar hat.

Some men think women's hats are funny; others have to pay for them.

Something is better than nothing, except the hats women buy that do something for them.

When a woman's hat is attractive, some hat designer has probably made a mistake.

Summer is the season when the men who have not been wearing felt hats all winter change to not wearing straw hats.

Charity covers a multitude of sins, but hats cover more sinners.

A woman will try on many hats before she finds one that's ridiculous enough to buy.

Hat designers are expert in creating a wide variety of women's hats, all of which husbands thoroughly dislike.

Fashions may come and fashions may go, but women's hats that look ridiculous go on forever.

Another person to whom two heads are better than one is the milliner.

One nice thing about spending an evening at home is that you don't have to redeem your hat after it's over.

A candidate needs four hats: one to cover his head with, another to throw into the ring, a third to pass around, and finally one to talk through.

You can quickly stop your husband from laughing at your new hat—just tell him what you paid for it.

A milliner is a magician who can make a hat become a woman.

Any woman with a foolish hat looks like a big enough fool to wear that kind of a hat.

A hat designer's success usually goes to her customer's head.

Husbands never seem to realize that no hat that looks like a hat would ever be bought by a woman.

HATE

There must be something good about a man who hates dogs and children.   *– W. C. Fields*

I hate them which hate God, but I don't find God sufficiently hating them which hate me.
                        – Samuel Butler

In politics, a community of hatred is almost always the foundation of friendship. *– Tocqueville*

It is better to be hated for what you are than to be loved for what you are not.   *– Gide*

It does not matter much what a man hates provided he hates something.   *– Samuel Butler*

Although some couples have been married for years, they still feel the same; they can't stand each other.

Some men have two pet hates: they hate to get up to eat, and they hate to stop eating to sleep.

A man will always hate another man who tells the same lies he does.

Before marriage many a man is humbly grateful; after marriage he is grumbly hateful.

HEAD

If you leave the smallest corner of your head vacant for a moment, other people's opinions will rush in from all quarters.
                        – Bernard Shaw

Some men don't worry about getting ahead; they do very well without one.

Some people have heads like doorknobs—anybody can turn them.

The man who loses his head is the last one to miss it.

The greatest mistake of the head is in growing too big for the hat.

A woman usually attaches more importance to what's on her head than to what's in it.

Two heads are better than one, but not when they are soreheads.

We have a head on us for the same reason a pin has: to keep us from going too far.

A woman's head on a man's shoulder often achieves more than his does.

The man who goes through life looking for something soft, can always find it under his hat.

The emptier the head, the harder it is to fill.

A man's head is turned by beauty; a woman's, by flattery.

The head never begins to swell until the mind stops growing.

Take a lesson from the woodpecker: it always uses its head when working.

The chief end of man is the one with the head on it.

The greatest undeveloped territory in the world usually lies under your hat.

HEADACHE

Never have a headache on the same day as your husband; but if you do, be sure to mention it first.   — *E. V. Lucas*

Losing your head will not prevent your getting headaches.

When you have a headache, you can always go to your medicine cabinet and find an empty aspirin bottle.

HEAD AND HEART

Your heart leads you into scrapes from which your head has to extricate you.   — *Ed Howe*

A sensible woman should be guided by her head when taking a husband, and by her heart when taking a lover. — *Ninon de Lenclos*

Some people feel with their heads and think with their hearts.
                    — *G. C. Lichtenberg*

The heart is forever making the head its fool. — *La Rochefoucauld*

The man who is said to have his heart in the right place is apt to have something wrong with his head.   — *Ed Howe*

Many a man must first lose his head before he can find his heart.
                        — *Nietzsche*

A woman's head is always influenced by her heart, but a man's heart is always influenced by his head.   — *Countess of Blessington*

The best rule for friendship is to keep your heart a little softer than your head.

To handle yourself, use your head more; to handle others, use your heart more.

When a man loses his heart, his head has to do double work.

The woman without a heart always makes a fool of the man without a head.

Always use both head and heart: it isn't enough to have a heart of gold—so has a hard-boiled egg.

The young man who loses his heart is apt to lose his head as well.

There is no better combination than a hard head and a soft heart.

HEALTH

The best way to keep healthy is to eat what you don't want, drink what you don't like, and do what you'd rather not.

Health is something that makes you feel it's a fine day when it isn't.

You can tell how healthy a man is by what he takes two at a time—stairs or pills.

There are many roads to health, but the principal ones are the allopaths, the homeopaths, and the osteopaths.

Youth thinks nothing of health, and age thinks of nothing but.

Your health depends more on the number of years that have passed over your head than on the number of colds that have passed through it.

The picture of health requires a happy frame of mind.

The hypochondriac spends so much time worrying about his health that he has no time left to enjoy it.

HEALTH AND SICKNESS

If I had my way, I'd make health catching instead of disease.
— *Robert G. Ingersoll*

There is no blessing like health, especially when you are sick.

No one gets as much pleasure out of good health as some people do out of minor ailments.

Healthy people have one thing in common: they always give advice to the sick.

Everything depends on the point of view: to a virus, health is a form of disease.

HEALTH AND WEALTH

Money cannot buy health, but I'd settle for a diamond-studded wheelchair.   — *Dorothy Parker*

Another good rule that won't work both ways is the saying that health makes wealth.

The relative value of health and wealth depends on which one you've lost.

Money cannot buy health, but it can buy furs for the doctor's wife.

HEAR

The world doesn't hear what a father says to his children, but posterity will. — *Jean Paul Richter*

Hearin' is one thing and listenin' is another.
— *William F. De Morgan*

What you hear never sounds half as important as what you overhear.

If you want to hear everything, keep both eyes open.

Money talks, but most of us can't keep it long enough to hear what it says.

HEARING AID

One of the best hearing aids a man can have is an attentive wife.   — Groucho Marx

The woman who never hears any gossip needs a hearing aid.

Some people refuse to wear a hearing aid because they already hear more than they can understand.

Pity the woman who must wait until her husband's hearing aid is repaired before she can continue telling him what she thinks of him.

HEART

As the arteries grow hard, the heart grows soft.   — Mencken

Two things are bad for the heart—running up stairs and running down people.
          — Bernard Baruch

A man's heart may have a secret sanctuary where only one woman may enter, but it is full of little anterooms which are seldom vacant.   — Helen Rowland

After giving a man the key to her heart, a woman usually changes the look the next day.
          — Sainte-Beuve

The way to a man's heart is through his stomach, but the way to a woman's heart is a buy-path.

The man who puts his heart into his work has very little of it left to bring home to his family.

Don't worry about your heart: it will last you all your life.

Never worry about your heart till it stops beating.

You never forget a love affair because it is something you learn by heart.

Never put your heart into matters concerning money, nor your money into matters concerning your heart.

Once a girl's heart is broken she spends the rest of her life distributing the pieces.

You cannot steal a woman's heart without an accomplice.

The best cure for a broken heart is to get it broken again.

HEAT

It was so hot today, the only thing I could do all afternoon was to lie on my bed and read Jeans's Dynamical Theory of Gases.
          — J. Robert Oppenheimer

Many a woman wears an evening gown that keeps everybody warm but her.

Marriage usually begins with warm hearts and ends with hot heads.

Spring is the season when you turn on the heat the day after you turned it off for the year.

Many a heated argument between man and wife is due to an old flame.

It isn't the heat, it's the people who keep reminding us about the humidity.

HEAVEN

If you're not allowed to laugh in heaven, I don't want to go there.   — *Martin Luther*

The main object of religion is not to get a man into heaven, but to get heaven into him.
    — *Thomas Hardy*

The surprising thing about heaven is that it remains a heaven with so many different women living under the same roof.
    — *Ed Howe*

What a pity that the only way to heaven is in a hearse!
    — *Stanislaw J. Lec*

If I have any beliefs about immortality, it is that certain dogs I have known will go to heaven, and very, very few persons.
    — *James Thurber*

Probably no invention came more easily to man than when he thought up heaven.
    — *G. C. Lichtenberg*

The few men who have managed to reach heaven must be terribly spoiled by this time.
    — *Ed Howe*

A lawyer's dream of heaven: every man reclaimed his property at the resurrection, and each tried to recover it from all his forefathers.   — *Samuel Butler*

My idea of heaven is to sit and listen to the music of Victor Herbert.   — *Andrew Carnegie*

I would give part of my life to know what the average weather is like is heaven.
    — *G. C. Lichtenberg*

On earth there is no heaven, but there are pieces of it.
    — *Jules Renard*

There are lots of good women who, when they get to heaven, will watch to see if the Lord goes out nights.   — *Ed Howe*

There's no marrying in heaven; that's why it's heaven.

Heaven must be an awful place if it is peopled only by those saintly souls whose company bores us here below.

Heaven is sure to be not quite exclusive enough to suit some people.

Heaven lies about us in our infancy, and we lie about heaven the rest of our lives.

You cannot enter the kingdom of God without election, subjection, and inspection; otherwise, it's rejection.

A lot of people will be unhappy in heaven when they find out they can't institute any reforms there.

No one really knows what you wear in heaven, but it's probably an expression of surprise at seeing who's there.

Some people want to go to heaven for the same reason they want to go to California—their relatives are there.

Heaven doesn't appeal very much to a man whose daughter is taking harp lessons.

Many people wouldn't want to go to heaven if they couldn't send back picture postcards.

He who finds nothing of heaven on earth would find nothing but earth in heaven.

To a movie star heaven is a land where everything that your press agent says about you comes true.

There will be lots of people in heaven just as surprised to see you there as you will be to see them.

There aren't many men who could get to heaven on passports signed by their wives.

The preacher who praises the beauty and pleasure of heaven, seems in no greater hurry to go there than anyone else.

A girl's idea of heaven is a place where there are no other girls.

HEAVEN AND HELL

There is no such place as heaven: the people made hell out of it long ago. *— Ed Howe*

Many might go to heaven with half the labor they go to hell.
— Ben Jonson

Heaven and hell are one place, and we all go there: to those who are prepared, it is heaven; to those who are not, it is hell.
— Lincoln Steffens

I don't like to commit myself about heaven and hell—you see, I have friends in both places.
— Mark Twain

The wicked often work harder to go to hell than the righteous do to enter heaven.
— Josh Billings

Men have feverishly conceived a heaven only to find it insipid, and a hell to find it ridiculous.
— Santayana

When I think of the number of disagreeable people that I know who have gone to a better world, I am sure hell won't be so bad at all. *— Mark Twain*

To be in hell is to drift; to be in heaven is to steer.
— Bernard Shaw

One of the pleasures of heaven must be reading the weather reports from hell.

Nowadays the right and left of politics have replaced the above and below of religion.

When a man dies, his widow can only hope he's gone where she knows he hasn't.

One man's idea of hell is to be forced to remain in another man's idea of heaven.

Another way in which marriage resembles suicide is that you don't know whether it will land you in heaven or hell.

Man no longer believes that he will go to heaven—that's the hell of it.

Where marriage is the entrance to hell by way of heaven, divorce is the entrance to heaven by way of hell.

Hades is the polite word for hell, but there is no polite word for heaven.

All reformers probably go to hell because there's no need for them in heaven.

If the road to hell is paved with good intentions, is the road to heaven paved with bad ones?

The experience of man proves that heaven and hell exist within himself, but he lets his mind tell him they exist outside.

You must keep straight to go to heaven, but you must take a wrong turn first to go to hell.

Heaven for climate, and hell for company.

HEEL

Some men look down at the heel, others look up at the thigh.

In the footprints on the sands of time some people leave only the marks of a heel.

When a man looks down at the heel, there's usually a trim ankle above it.

HEIGHT

A man's stature is measured by what he does with what he has.

A man is the right height only when he is bigger than any insult hurled at him.

There's no limit to the heights a man can attain by remaining on the level.

HEIRESS

Heiresses are never jilted.
— *George Meredith*

An heiress is the only woman whose money talks more than she does.

Nothing improves a woman's looks like inheriting a fortune.

An heiress is a woman so wealthy that she can buy all the things she doesn't want.

HELL

There may be some doubt about a hell beyond the grave but there is no doubt about there being one on this side of it.
— *Ed Howe*

I never give them hell; I just tell the truth, and they think it's hell. — *Harry S. Truman*

All heck may break loose over the air, but not hell, because the network censor does not acknowledge the existence of hell.
— *Fred Allen*

Hell hath no music like a woman playing second fiddle.
— *John Patrick*

Hell is a place where a man is visited by a good many of his kin.
— *Ed Howe*

Hell is a special favor reserved only for those who have given it to others on earth.

How do you know that this life isn't another world's hell?

Hell hath no fury like a woman scorned, and it also has many other discomforts of home.

The only place where a pessimist has nothing worse to look forward to is hell.

If there is no hell, a good many preachers are obtaining money under false pretenses.

If husbands went everywhere their wives told them to go, there would be fewer divorces and more widows.

A good preacher tries to keep you out of hell, and tries to keep the hell out of you.

If the sun is too hot to be inhabited, how about hell?

Some women will follow a man to hell, but the majority prefer to send him there alone.

Nobody really believes in a hell, except for his neighbors.

It's hard to pity those who are in hell, for they had such a good time getting there.

Hell is for two classes of people: those who will do anything, and those who won't do anything.

There are no marriages in hell; they've got enough hell without them.

Where do people in hell tell one another to go?

Hell is filled with Americans who drop quarters in the collection plate and deduct dollars from the income tax.

He kept extra money in a copy of Dante's *Inferno* so he would always know the answer to "Now where in hell did I put the money?"

If people are not afraid of hell as they used to be, it's because familiarity breeds contempt.

Strange that the man who has money to burn cannot take it with him!

The man who thinks there is no hell has probably never married.

Cold-blooded people who want to warm up should go to hell.

HELP

Never befriend the oppressed unless you are prepared to take on the oppressor. *— Ogden Nash*

Give me the ready hand rather than the ready tongue.
— Garibaldi

It isn't the sissy men who help women most, but the rough, capable ones who can be caught and trained. *— Ed Howe*

It is not by sitting still at a grand distance and calling the human race *larvae* that men are to be helped. *— Emerson*

God help the honest; the dishonest always help themselves.

Some friends are always ready to give you moral support, especially when you need financial aid.

There are many times when you cannot get help, but there is never a time when you cannot give it.

Now is the time for all good parties to come to the aid of man.

God help those who do not help themselves!

Some friends are so glad to help you out of trouble that they are always willing to help you into some to prove it.

The man who is looking for a helping hand can always find one —attached to his arm.

Knowing what to say helps a little; knowing what not to say helps more.

When you need advice, everyone is ready to help you; when you need help, everyone is ready to advise you.

Every little bit helps, but it only helps a little bit.

Heaven help those who help others to help themselves.

A real friend never gets in your way, unless you happen to be on the way down.

There's a difference between asking the Lord for help, and expecting Him to do the whole job Himself.

Go to friends for advice, to women for sympathy, to strangers for charity, and to relatives for nothing.

If you do not ask their help, all men are good-natured.

A helpmate is the mate who sometimes helps her husband make money, but more often helps him spend it.

"Every little bit helps," as the gull said when it pissed into the sea.

The only people you should try to get even with are those who have helped you.

Ask not what your country can do for you: if it does, you are sure to be taxed for it.

One way to help others is to keep out of their way.

The fate of a sucker is to be often in need of succor.

HEN

If you cut off a chicken's head, you increase its activity but not its longevity.

The hen is immortal; her son will never set.

Nowadays the riddle is not why does the chicken cross the road, but how?

HENPECKED HUSBAND

A henpecked husband is one whose wife insists upon running everything, and then bawls him out for making her bear the burden.
— *Robert Quillen*

A henpecked husband is a man who is treated by his wife like a wife.

The man who won't admit he's henpecked, probably smokes a big cigar while washing the dishes.

The man who is afraid to think for himself usually chooses the wrong woman to think for him.

A henpecked husband is a man who consults his better half instead of his better judgment.

Many a wife wouldn't act like a man if her husband acted more like one.

A henpecked husband suffers in silence in a home where there's very little of it.

The only time a weakling ever puts his foot down is when his wife has finished vacuuming under it.

A henpecked husband is a domestic animal trained to wash up and dry up, but never to act up.

Many a man is so dominated by his wife that he is even afraid to get a divorce.

A henpecked husband prefers a son to a daughter so he can help him with the dishes.

If you want your wife to keep her trap shut, don't act like a mouse.

A henpecked husband is the only species of worm that's afraid to turn.

Marriage makes a difference: the man about town sometimes becomes the mouse around the house.

A henpecked husband always seems to have made a poorer marriage than his wife.

Some men are afraid to marry; others don't know what fear is until after they marry.

Marriage brings out the animal in some men, usually the chicken.

Some husbands are so henpecked, they are even afraid to talk back to other men's wives.

HEREDITY

Heredity runs in our family.
— *Don Marquis*

Varicose veins are the result of an improper collection of grandparents.
— *William Osler*

Heredity is the transmission of unpleasant characteristics from the other side of the family.

Heredity is transmitted by both parents: many a girl is the picture of her father and the sound track of her mother.

Like father, like son: the infant who tries to get his toes into his mouth, probably has a father who is also trying to make ends meet.

Heredity is something you believe in if you have a very bright child.

Heredity is what sets the parents of a teen-ager wondering about each other.

HEREDITY AND ENVIRONMENT

With a good heredity, nature deals you a fine hand at cards; and with a good environment, you learn to play the hand well.
— *Walter C. Alvarez*

Life isn't what heredity and environment do with us, but what we do with them.

Man is the control experiment of heredity and environment; and since his heredity controls him, he tries to control his environment.

Heredity is when you wind up with your mother's complexion; environment is when you wind up with your father's car.

HERMIT

A hermit is simply a person to whom civilization has failed to adjust itself. — *Will Rogers*

A hermit may get away by himself, but he cannot get away from himself.

A hermit believes in doing without others as he would have others do without him.

A hermit behaves as if the proper way to live is to quit living.

HERO

The main thing about being a hero is to know when to die.
— *Will Rogers*

Every man is a hero except those who have valets.
— *Finley Peter Dunne*

Heroes are sometimes created out of the scantiest materials, such as the apple William Tell never shot or the flag Barbara Frietchie never waved.
— *Gerald W. Johnson*

Every bachelor is a hero to some married women. — *Mencken*

A boy doesn't have to go to war to be a hero; he can say he doesn't like pie when he sees there isn't enough to go around.
— *Ed Howe*

We can't all be heroes because someone has to sit on the curb and clap as they go by.
— *Will Rogers*

The hero is a man who has fought impressively for a cause of which we approve.
— *Dumas Malone*

Show me a hero and I will write you a tragedy.
— *Scott Fitzgerald*

No man is a hero to his wife's lawyer.

A bragger never realizes how heroic he is until he tells about it the next day.

Many a coward is acclaimed a hero simply because he ran the wrong way.

No author is a hero to his proofreader.

History is a record of the mess created in the world by its heroes.

Teen-age talk is mostly idol gossip.

Many a hero is a man who didn't have the courage to be a coward.

The best thing that youngsters who join a fan club can do, is to beat their hero on the head with it.

HEROINE

A woman is not a heroine just because she is dying for a man.

Some men are attracted only to the woman who is promiscuous enough to be the heroine of a bestseller.

No man is a hero to his valet, and no woman a heroine to her maid.

HESITATION

He who hesitates is lost—or married.

He who hesitates is the one who doesn't pick up the dinner check.

He who hesitates is worse than lost: he is miles away from the next cloverleaf.

He who hesitates is lost—and so is his parking place.

He who hesitates is lost, but she who hesitates is won.

HIDE

It is often easier to hide something than to hide the fact that you are hiding something.
— *G. C. Lichtenberg*

If a man is foolish enough to reveal his thoughts, the least he can do is conceal his whereabouts. — *E. B. White*

When I think of us human beings, it seems to me that we have a lot of nerve to make fun of the ostrich. — *Heywood Broun*

Look wise, say nothing, and grunt: speech was given to conceal thought. — *William Osler*

You can always tell a fool, unless he's hiding inside you.

Architects cover their mistakes with ivy, doctors with earth, and brides with sauce.

Burying your head in the sand only makes a sensitive part of your anatomy more vulnerable.

Whitewash often covers a thing, but seldom covers it up.

A woman will readily reveal her age only when she wishes to conceal it.

You can always tell the know-it-all: he doesn't know enough to conceal what he doesn't know.

The attitude of Congress toward hidden taxes is not to do away with them, but just to hide them better.

It is surprising how much some women can tell about themselves without telling anything.

HIGH

When some men aspire high, they never get any further than the height of folly.

More and more people nowadays are concerned with the higher things in life, especially prices and wages.

HIGHBROW

A highbrow is a man who has found something more interesting than women.   — *Edgar Wallace*

Eggheads of the world unite: you have nothing to lose but your yolks.   — *Adlai Stevenson*

An egghead is a man who has a lot in his head but nothing on it.   — *Adlai Stevenson*

A highbrow is one who checks a book out of the library that no one else has checked out in years.

A low neckline attracts every kind of man except a highbrow.

A highbrow is a man who does not understand everything he knows.

An egghead is a learned person who has no difficulty making an easy thing difficult.

The woman who is a highbrow may have plenty of knowledge, but doesn't always have enough wisdom to conceal it.

A highbrow is a person who can use the word *whom* without feeling self-conscious.

A highbrow is one who talks to you about things he doesn't understand but expects you to.

HINDSIGHT

If you look back too much, you will soon be heading that way.

Hindsight is the ability to see an opportunity, but only after you've missed it.

A rear-view mirror is the only thing that enables a person to have hindsight before the event.

After the unexpected has happened, there is always someone who knew it would.

Most of us know just what we should have done yesterday tomorrow.

The average man has excellent vision, but it is mostly hindsight.

Hindsight enables us to see what we should have done, but not before we've made fools of ourselves.

HINT

The thicker the skull, the sharper the hint must be to penetrate it.

The neurotic who always takes a hint when it is not intended, should marry the bore who never takes a hint when it is intended.

Broad hints are usually wasted on narrow-minded people.

The only thing a woman can throw with accuracy is a hint.

HISTORY

God cannot alter the past, but historians can. — *Samuel Butler*

History repeats itself, and that's one of the things that's wrong with history. — *Clarence Darrow*

History is a nightmare from which I am trying to awake.
— *James Joyce*

History is nothing but a pack of tricks that we play upon the dead. — *Voltaire*

When Herodotus found himself short on facts, he didn't hesitate to use imagination, which may be why he is called the first historian.
— *John F. Kennedy*

The first requisite in a historian is to have no ability to invent.
— *Stendhal*

I have written too much history to have any faith in it; and if anyone thinks I'm wrong, I'm inclined to agree with him.
— *Harry S. Truman*

We learn from history that we learn nothing from history.
— *Bernard Shaw*

The only form of fiction in which real characters are not out of place is history.
— *Oscar Wilde*

History is simply a piece of paper covered with print; the main thing is still to make history, not to write it. — *Bismarck*

History is rather interesting when it repeats itself, historians are not. — *Philip Guedalla*

The secret of historical composition is to know what to neglect.
— *James Bryce*

History is always written wrong, and so always needs to be rewritten. — *Santayana*

There is such a thing as too much history, and we are having it. — *Robert Nathan*

Italy had a Renaissance, Germany had a Reformation, but France had a Voltaire.
— *Will Durant*

What is history but a fable agreed upon? — *Napoleon*

History supplies little more than a list of people who have helped themselves with the property of others. — *Voltaire*

History is the science of what never happens twice.
— *Paul Valéry*

The historian must have some conception of how men who are not historians behave.
— *E. M. Forster*

History is little more than the register of the crimes, follies, and misfortunes of mankind.
— *Edward Gibbon*

History would be a wonderful thing—if it were only true.
— *Tolstoy*

We can learn little from history unless we first realize that she does not repeat herself.
— *Harold Nicolson*

Ignorance is the first requisite of the historian.
— *Lytton Strachey*

Historian: an unsuccessful novelist. — *Mencken*

The men who make history have no time to write it.
— *Metternich*

A historian is one who avoids small mistakes of fact while on his way to great errors of interpretation.

History repeats itself, historians repeat one another.

A historian is a person whose job it is to spread news that's long out of date.

Three types of men have shaped the course of history: kings, generals and historians.

For the sake of posterity, let's hope the history being made today won't repeat itself.

History teaches us the mistakes we are going to make.

If we were to speak only well of the dead, history would be even falser than it is now.

What this country needs are cheaper ways of making history.

History repeats itself, but only when the unexpected happens.

Nothing makes you feel older than the discovery that your children's history lessons are what you studied as current events.

For a faithful picture of past history you need a time exposure.

History repeats itself, but we wish it would repeat itself at longer intervals.

Accidents make history—and also historians.

Many college students like to believe that the study of history is a thing of the past.

After you have heard two eyewitness accounts of an accident, you begin to wonder about history.

There's a lot of history that isn't fit to repeat itself.

Nowadays adults are making history faster than the children are learning it at school.

History is an account of past events explaining how other nations have always been wrong.

History repeats itself, especially in matters that shouldn't have happened in the first place.

HOARSE

No woman is ever so hoarse that she cannot talk about it.

Some women talk so much, their husbands get hoarse listening to them.

The rich man has acute laryngitis, but the poor man has a sore throat.

When a woman is hoarse, it's probably because her husband came home very late the night before.

Nothing frightens a chatterbox out of her wits so much as the thought of getting laryngitis.

HOBBY

My personal hobbies are reading, listening to music, and silence.
— *Edith Sitwell*

One woman's hobby is another woman's hubby.

If you have it, it's a hobby; if your boss has it, it's an avocation.

The way to a man's wallet is through his hobby.

Among the fastest-growing hobbies nowadays are photography, stamp-collecting and bank robbery.

Your favorite pastime is a hobby, the other man's is an obsession.

Tie yourself to a hobby and you'll never be at a loose end.

The best thing about a hobby is that it gives you something to do while you're worrying.

Everyone should have a hobby of some kind even if it's only criticizing the government.

Hobbies are a great help in keeping people from becoming neurotic, but what about the people they live with?

HOLD

Don't take the bull by the horns, take him by the tail; then you can let go when you want to.
— *Josh Billings*

You are sure to hold a man as long as you make him want to hold you.

Before marriage, when a man holds a girl's hand, it's love; after marriage, it's self-defense.

The man who can't hold his liquor usually can't hold his wife either.

A shrew is a woman with a hold over her spouse, but no hold over her speech.

Before marriage, a girl has to kiss a man to hold him; after marriage, she has to hold him to kiss him.

HOLE

The first time some men do any deep thinking is when they find themselves in a hole.

The difference between golf and life is that in golf you try to get into a hole, whereas in life you don't have to try.

A hole is nothing at all, but you can break your neck in it.

Many a man tries to dig himself out of a financial hole by making the hole bigger.

The only job where you start at the top is digging a hole.

HOLIDAY

A good holiday is one spent among people whose notions of time are vaguer than yours.
— *J. B. Priestley*

It is the day after the holiday when a holiday is most needed.

There are three classes of holiday motorists: those who go to the country, those who go to the beach, and those who go to the hospital.

The man who looks half dead should take a holiday—or has.

After the Christmas holidays most of us are way behind on our bills, but way ahead on our calories.

How wonderful holidays would be if there wasn't the day after!

Memorial Day is a day set aside to decorate old graves of soldiers and to dig new ones for reckless drivers.

HOLLYWOOD

There's genius, genius everywhere in Hollywood—now if only there were some talent!
— *Henri Bernstein*

The only way to avoid Hollywood is to live there.
— *Igor Stravinsky*

Strip away the phony tinsel of Hollywood and you find the real tinsel underneath. — *Oscar Levant*

Hollywood is the land of yes-men and acqui-yes girls.
— *Dorothy Parker*

Hollywood may be thickly populated, but to me it's still a bewilderness. — *Cedric Hardwicke*

Over in Hollywood they almost made a great picture, but they caught it in time.
— *Wilson Mizner*

The trouble with Hollywood is that it looks at the world through gross-colored glasses.

Marry in Hollywood and repeat indefinitely.

Hollywood is the place where many writers go to earn the money to go somewhere else.

The best acting in Hollywood is done by the stars congratulating the Academy Award winners.

Hollywood is the place where they put beautiful frames in pictures.

Hollywood is divided into two classes: those who own swimming pools, and those who can't keep their heads above water.

Hollywood is a place where you live happily and get married ever afterward.

HOME

We shape our dwellings, and afterwards our dwellings shape us.
— *Winston Churchill*

Home was quite a place when people stayed there.
— *E. B. White*

Home life is no more natural to us than a cage is to a cockatoo. — *Bernard Shaw*

The worst feeling in the world is the homesickness that comes over a man occasionally when he is at home. — *Ed Howe*

Of the home economists we have met in our lifetime, all had one trait in common: not one of them was at home.
— *E. B. White*

A married couple should never quarrel in public—what have they got a home for?

There's always a woman telling you when you have to be home—first your mother, then your wife, and then your babysitter.

There's no place like home, especially if you haven't the money to go out.

Home is where everybody has the right to talk, and nobody bothers to listen.

The best way to keep teenagers at home is to make home pleasant—and keep the car keys.

There are two kinds of women: those who make a home for a man, and those who make a man for a home.

There's no place like home, and many a man is glad of it.

Home is where the mortgage is.

The wife who is perfectly at home in art, music and literature is probably at home everywhere —except at home.

A man's home is his wife's castle.

There's no place like home, once in a while.

A true cosmopolitan is a man who is at home even when he's away from home.

Home is where the heart is, and the car isn't.

The only way some men can get away from their families is to stay at home.

There's no place like home— thank God!

The trouble these days is not so much in being found out as in being found in.

The rich spend more money on their homes, while the poor spend more time in theirs.

Home is where the husband runs the show, but the wife writes the script.

Time change: the modern house is full of plants and the garden full of furniture.

There's no place like home, which is why so many husbands go out nights.

A man's home is his castle, or so it seems when he has to pay the taxes on it.

Home is the place where everything sooner or later wears out, including your nerves.

All that keeps some families from having a home of their own is a popular teen-age daughter.

There's no place like home—except Florida, Mexico and Europe.

Many a man stays out late at night because he has no wife to go home to—or because he has.

Home is where you slip in the bathtub and break your neck.

Three corners of a home rest upon the wife, and the fourth upon the husband.

There's no place like home, especially when you're looking for trouble.

All men are not homeless, but some are home less than others.

Home is the only place where a man can do as he pleases—when his wife's away.

The question isn't why men leave home but why they ever go there in the first place.

There's no place like home—when you are not invited anywhere.

To a do-it-yourselfer, a man's home is not his castle, but his project.

Home is where you go when you're tired of being polite to people.

One of the few good things you can say about home is that you can always go there without making a reservation.

There would be far fewer divorces if more people felt at home at home.

The modern home is a place to go to get ready to go somewhere else.

There's no place like home—while the car is being repaired.

Some men are never at home long enough to get homesick.

HOMEWORK

Half the parents who do their children's homework for them shouldn't; the other half can't.

When it comes to homework, most schoolchildren like to do nothing better.

'Tis better to have loved and lost than to spend your evenings doing your children's homework.

Homework is one of the few things a child is punished not for doing, but for not doing.

Nowadays many a mother doesn't dare to help her children with their homework for fear they'll find out how little she knows.

Get a good education while you're young; it will come in handy when you have to help your children with their homework.

When it comes to doing homework, some children prefer to dilly while others prefer to dally.

Homework sometimes shows how much children don't know, but more often how much their parents don't know.

A lazy schoolboy lets his father do his homework, but a bright one helps his father with it.

When a teen-ager is watching television, listening to her record-player, and talking on the phone, she is probably doing her homework.

If it takes parents so long to do their children's grade school homework, what will parents do when their children get to high school?

HOMOSEXUALITY

Homosexuality will become a more fashionable device than fornication.   — *Smollett*

If we were all homosexuals there would soon be no homosexuals.

A homosexual is less dangerous than other men: you can trust him anywhere with a woman.

Another man who doesn't believe in mixed marriages is the homosexual.

A homosexual is the only man who ever meets a man he would like to marry if he were a woman.

Homosexuals have been guilty of the same offenses committed by heterosexuals, except for the population explosion.

A homosexual should never marry: he and his wife might fall in love with the same man.

Where there's no difference between the sexes, there's a great difference in love.

A homosexual is a man who believes in vice versa.

Among homosexuals, when boy meets girl no one knows which is which.

A homosexual is sometimes a man to a woman, but more often a woman to a man.

What a homosexual doesn't like about the opposite sex is that it is so opposite.

A man is judged by his peers, a homosexual by his queers.

Homosexuals are men to whom men are the opposite sex.

Homosexuality is a philosophy of behavior based on *a posteriori* experience.

HONESTY

Honesty is a good thing, but it is not profitable to its possessor unless it is kept under control.
            — *Don Marquis*

We must make the world honest before we can honestly say to our children that honesty is the best policy.   — *Bernard Shaw*

No man is born perpendicular, although many men are born upright.
— *E. B. White*

Honesty is the best policy—when there is money in it.
— *Mark Twain*

Some persons are likable in spite of their unswerving integrity.
— *Don Marquis*

I have not observed men's honesty to increase with their riches.
— *Jefferson*

Honesty is the best policy—for poor people.

Does the man who is as honest as the day is long, become less and less honest every day in the fall?

No man knows if honesty is the best policy unless he has tried both.

Honesty pays—and dishonesty gets paid.

Honesty is not the best policy; it is merely the safest.

Honesty is still the best policy, but nowadays there are less policyholders than there used to be.

A lot of people are as honest as the day is long, but when it gets dark—look out!

Honesty is the best policy, but not the best politics.

HONEYMOON

She said he proposed something on their wedding night her own brother wouldn't have suggested.
— *James Thurber*

Every bride likes to take her husband with her on her honeymoon.

The honeymoon is over as soon as the bride removes her wedding ring from the dishwater.

A honeymoon is the period when a man treats a new wife like a new car.

The honeymoon is over when he phones he'll be late again for dinner, and she has already left a note that it's in the refrigerator.

What becomes of the honeymoon when it goes into eclipse?

The honeymoon is over when your wife starts to complain about the noise you make preparing your own breakfast.

The honeymoon is the only period when a woman isn't trying to reform her husband.

The honeymoon is over when she starts wondering what happened to the man she married, and he starts wondering what happened to the girl he didn't.

A husband may forget where he went on his honeymoon, but he never forgets why.

The honeymoon is over when he stops helping her with the dishes—and starts doing them himself.

There's only one way to avoid lovers' quarrels on a honeymoon, and that is for the bride and groom to spend it in different places.

When the honeymoon is over a man discovers his wife isn't an angel, so he quits posing as a saint.

A honeymoon is the period before he takes her off a pedestal and puts her on a budget.

Another reason why the honeymoon is the period of greatest happiness during marriage is the absence of in-laws.

The honeymoon is over the first time she says, "You'll do nothing of the kind!"

People take shorter honeymoons nowadays, but they take them more often.

The honeymoon is over when she stops lowering her eyes and starts raising her voice.

Some newlyweds quarrel on their honeymoon but most couples don't settle down to married life so quickly.

The honeymoon is over when the bride who took her husband for better or for worse, starts taking him for granted.

HONOR

Because he didn't ask for titles and honors but only for immense wealth, these other things came to him also.   — *Saki*

Your word can never be as good as your bond because your memory can never be as trustworthy as your honor.
— *Bernard Shaw*

Reverence: the spiritual attitude of a man to a God and a dog to a man.   — *Bierce*

It is better to deserve honors and not have them than to have them and not deserve them.
— *Mark Twain*

There's honor among thieves— at least, until they begin to deal with lawyers.

Less is sometimes more: honor is more than honors.

There's no such thing as honor among thieves; they are just as bad as other people.

HOPE

We should not expect something for nothing but we all do, and call it hope.   — *Ed Howe*

The natural flights of the human mind are not from pleasure to pleasure, but from hope to hope.
— *Samuel Johnson*

Hope is the only thing that is not taxed today.
— *Lord Birkenhead*

Every cloud has a silver lining, but it is sometimes a little difficult to get it to the mint.
— *Don Marquis*

Hope is generally a wrong guide though it is very good company by the way.   — *Halifax*

Every man knows better than he hopes. — *Ed Howe*

We hope for the best, and if we get it we hope for something better.

Hope is a great blessing, but if it weren't for hope none of us would ever be disappointed.

Hope springs eternal in the human breast, but it often summers elsewhere.

Mothers hope their sons will be what they once thought their husbands were.

There are no hopeless situations; there are only people who have grown hopeless about them.

HORN

Take a lesson from the rhinoceros: he never blows his own horn.

The way a man honks his horn while waiting for her, shows whether or not they are married.

The fellow who blows his own horn the loudest is probably in the biggest fog.

The man who blows his own horn never has more than one appreciative listener.

In a traffic jam, nothing is more used than a horn—and nothing is more useless.

The man who continually blows his own horn usually stays at the little end.

The candidate who tries to solve the country's problems by blowing his own horn, probably tries to untangle a traffic jam the same way.

HORSE

The only time a horse gets scared nowadays is when he meets another horse. — *Will Rogers*

I'd horsewhip you if I had a horse. — *Groucho Marx*

Men who have a great deal to do with horses seem to demoralize faster than the horses do.
— *Josh Billings*

Isn't it wonderful how much work a horse will do without feeling the need for alcoholic stimulants?

A racehorse is the only creature that can take thousands of people for a ride at the same time.

Horses are what more people bet on than get on.

In pitching horseshoes, the first rule is to remove the horse.

Formerly when you wanted a horse to stand still, you tied him to a hitching post; nowadays, you first place a bet on him.

Never put the cart before the horse—unless you're backing up.

More people place a bet on a horse than a harness.

Times change: in the old days no one asked how many miles a horse did on a bundle of hay.

Nowadays you have to go to the race track if you want to see what a horse looks like.

The horse is a friend of man —until you start betting on him.

Pity the man whose first wife was a clotheshorse, and whose second is a nag.

No horse can go as fast as your money does when you bet on him.

It's a wise horse that knows its own fodder.

HORSEBACK RIDING

Riding a horse makes gentlemen of some and grooms of others.   — Cervantes

Before riding your first horse, you can't imagine that anything filled with hay can be so hard.

The best thing for the inside of a man is the outside of a horse.

Learning to ride a horse can be difficult: the animal is uncomfortable in the middle, and dangerous at both ends.

Some horses are so polite that when they come to a fence, they stop and let you go over first.

There's nothing like your first horseback ride to make you feel better off.

The woman who takes up horseback riding to reduce, quickly takes several pounds off —off the horse.

HORSE RACE

Horseplaying makes no sense: the jockeys get the ride, the horses get the exercise, the bookmakers get the money, and the horseplayers get the headaches.
                    — Fred Allen

We cannot expect to have an honest horse race until we have an honest human race.

Winning a lot of money at the race track is possible, even probable, but only if you're a fast horse.

The man who goes to the race track in a liberal frame of mind often leaves it with a strong feeling of race prejudice.

The fastest way to squander money is to put it on fast horses who aren't quite fast enough.

In horse racing, there is nothing so uncertain as a sure thing.

If 50,000 people ran daily at a race track, not one horse would attend.

Many a man refuses to work today because he expects to win at the races tomorrow.

Man never loses faith: thousands of children who lose their trust in Santa Claus grow up and play the horses.

Betting on the horses is getting nothing for something.

If you bet on a horse on the nose, it's ten to one he has sinus trouble.

Many race horses are given peculiar names, especially if they don't finish among the first three.

Lots of things run into money, except the horses you bet on.

Money makes the mare go, but not if it's bet on her.

Mine was not only the last horse in the race, but also the last race in the horse.

The man who plays the horses is a gambler pure and simple, especially simple.

Experience is the best teacher, but when it comes to horse racing, some people go on taking postgraduate courses all their lives.

HORSE SENSE

Horse sense is what a horse has that keeps him from betting on people.   *— W. C. Fields*

There is just as much horse sense as ever, but the horses have most of it.

The high rate of automobile accidents proves that most of the horse sense of the good old days belonged to the horse.

Things have come to a hell of a pass when a man with horse sense acts like an ass.

The horse had one advantage over the car: it had enough horse sense to be afraid of the car.

The less horse sense a wife has, the more she nags her husband.

The careful driver is the one who realizes that horsepower is always safer when mixed with horse sense.

HOSIERY

The first lesson a child learns at his mother's knee nowadays is to be careful of her stockings.

Only a woman can rave over a pair of sheer stockings when they're empty.

The trouble with women is that they'd rather mend your ways than your socks.

What this country needs is something to make hoes as attractive as hose.

Another mystery is why a girl's legs in nylon look sexy while a man's legs merely look soxy.

In women's hosiery, what's sheer today is gone tomorrow.

HOSPITAL

What some people don't know about driving would fill a hospital.

If you want to meet the most daring motorists alive, visit the hospital.

A hospital is a place where the patients want to get better, and the nurses want to get better paid.

No patient should leave a hospital until he's strong enough to face the cashier.

A hospital is the place where the night nurse wakes you up to give you a sleeping pill.

HOST

One of the duties of a hostess is to serve as a procuress.
    — *Proust*

Macbeth and Lady Macbeth stand out as the supreme type of all that a host and hostess should not be. — *Max Beerbohm*

A host doesn't mind his guests' shortcomings nearly as much as their long stayings.

You can always tell the host at a cocktail party: he's the one who keeps looking at his watch.

Female guests should never be better dressed than the hostess, and male guests should never be better informed than the host.

A good test of a hostess is the people she invites; a better test is the people she doesn't.

Every man is a hero in his own home—until all the guests have gone.

The trouble with giving a cocktail party is that when it gets boring, you're the only one who can't leave.

HOTEL

No hotel can offer you all the comforts of home, but neither can it offer you all the arguments.

A hotel is a place whose owner offers you a room in which to retire at a price which enables him to.

Husbands are never satisfied: they are always looking for home atmosphere in a hotel, and hotel service at home.

The best motels with vacancies are the ones you passed fifty miles back.

HOUSE

There are only two kinds of houses on the market: the kind you don't want, and the kind you can't afford.

Some houses are built to last; others are built to sell.

One way to bring the outdoors into your living room is by a picture window; another is by your children's shoes.

The trouble with a dream house is that it costs twice as much as you dreamed it would.

It may take a heap o' livin' to make a house a home, but before that it takes a heap o' borrowin'.

A GI home is the government's revenge against a soldier for not re-enlisting.

Some of the new modern houses have wall-to-wall carpeting, wall-to-wall windows, and back-to-the-wall financing.

What it takes to make a house look lived in is children.

A house may be too small for one family, but it can never be big enough for two.

Marriage is a trick to make a housekeeper think she is a householder.

Many a man would be more contented with his lot if he had a house on it.

The advantage of buying a new house is that you get all the modern inconveniences.

There's more fun remodeling an old house than building a new one, and the cost is no more than twice as much.

HOUSEKEEPING

Every girl can keep house better than her mother till she tries.   — *Thomas Fuller*

A mother spends half her time doing things, and the other half keeping her children from undoing them.

More and more married women are working nowadays, some of them even at home.

Some women are good housekeepers; others try not to overwork their vacuum cleaners.

Housekeeping is a form of unpleasant work to which a husband patiently gives the best years of his wife.

The only job where the work is steady but the pay isn't is housework.

Housework merely tires a woman, but it ruins a man.

All work and no pay makes a housewife.

Home is where mother knows best—until daughter takes a course in home economics.

Some husbands are reasonable; others want their wives to do the housework for twenty years and still look like the girls they married.

When a housewife has nothing to do, she still has something to do.

Some husbands help most with the housecleaning when they stay away from home.

A happy household is one where the wife helps her husband with the housework.

It is sometimes better to do your own housekeeping than to worry so much about your maid not showing up.

Housework is what a woman does that nobody notices unless she hasn't done it.

Woman's work is never done, probably because she can't get off the telephone long enough to do it.

Keeping house is like threading beads on a string with no knot at the end.

HUMAN NATURE

There is a great deal of human nature in people. — *Mark Twain*

It is human nature to think wisely and act foolishly.
— *Anatole France*

There's about as much human nature in some folks as there is in others, if not more.
— *Edward N. Westcott*

You *can* change human nature, but you can't change the man who says you can't.

Man has now conquered almost every dangerous thing in nature, except human nature.

Human nature consists of 90 per cent giving advice, and 10 per cent lending a helping hand.

It is human nature to wonder how so many incompetent men succeed where we can't.

The best time to study human nature is when you are alone.

Don't expect too much from human nature: remember, man is made up of pounds of muscle but only ounces of brain.

The man who has a good opinion of himself is probably a poor judge of human nature.

It is human nature to do whatever human nature does.

Human nature often goes contrary to nature: for example, women and trees bare their limbs in opposite seasons.

The noblest quality of a human being is being human.

HUMAN RACE

The chief obstacle to the progress of the human race is the human race.
— *Don Marquis*

The human race—to which so many of my readers belong.
— *Chesterton*

If I could get my membership fee back, I'd resign from the human race.
— *Fred Allen*

Humanity, I love you because when you're hard up, you pawn your intelligence to buy a drink.
— *E. E. Cummings*

The human race is composed of two groups: number one, yourself; and number two, all the others.

Discussions about the human race seldom make sense because there are so few impartial outsiders.

Some reformers worry about the human race as if they belonged to it.

Men and women chasing each other is what makes the human race.

There's only one thing more unpredictable than a horse race, and that's the human race.

The human race wouldn't be so difficult if it didn't have to keep up with its neighbors and its creditors at the same time.

Half of mankind is a little lower than the angels, and the other half is a little higher than the apes.

The difference between the sexes is what perpetuates the human race, and the similarity between them is what preserves it.

The pursuit of happiness is what makes the human race.

Nowadays the human race is usually a race for a parking place.

There's always one race that a bookmaker is sure to make a profit on, and that is the human race.

The human race is over a million years old, but it never seems to act its age.

The human race is a race to determine whether man makes an end of war before war makes an end of man.

HUMILITY

I feel coming on me a strange disease—humility.
— *Frank Lloyd Wright*

Whenever he met a great man he grovelled before him and my-lorded him as only a free-born Englishman can do. — *Thackeray*

Humility is not renunciation of pride but the substitution of one pride for another. — *Eric Hoffer*

It is God, not man, who should be humble when he reflects upon the indifferent job he has made of a human being.
— *Somerset Maugham*

What do you do when humility leads to still greater glory?

Strong-willed women don't always marry meek men; they just get that way.

Humility is the embarrassment you feel when you tell people how wonderful you are.

HUMOR

My method is to take the utmost trouble to find the right thing to say, and then to say it with the utmost levity.
— *Bernard Shaw*

The humorist runs with the hare, the satirist hunts with the hounds. — *Ronald A. Knox*

The chief difference between American humor and English humour is the way they spell it.
— *William Cole*

The field of humor is crowded only when Congress is in session.
— *Will Rogers*

Humor has been analyzed with great success by any number of people who haven't written any.
— *Henry Morgan*

Good taste and humor are a contradiction in terms, like a chaste whore.
— *Malcolm Muggeridge*

Humor is falling downstairs, if you do it in the act of warning your wife not to.
— *Kenneth Bird*

Humor is merely tragedy standing on its head with its pants torn. — *Irvin S. Cobb*

If at the close of business each evening, I myself can understand what I've written, I feel the day hasn't been totally wasted.

—S. J. Perelman

If I studied all my life, I couldn't think up half the number of funny things passed in one session of Congress.

—Will Rogers

The satirist shoots to kill while the humorist brings his prey back alive, and eventually releases him again for another chance.

—Peter De Vries

A woman may have a witty tongue or a stinging pen but she will never laugh at her own individual shortcomings.

—Irvin S. Cobb

As our government deteriorates, our humor increases.

—Will Rogers

Humor must both teach and preach if it would live forever; by forever I mean 30 years.

—Mark Twain

Many a gagwriter is nothing more than an exhumerist.

If you want your children to appreciate your ancient jokes, tell them they're folk humor.

It is good to understand humor, better to enjoy it, and best to understand and enjoy it.

HUNGER

An actor should skip a couple of meals before doing a love scene; hunger and love produce the same look on a man's face.

—José Ferrer

Society is a mass of people who get hungry at the same time.

The man who tries to live by his wits soon finds out that hunger is a terrible thing.

Hunger is the best sauce, but it should be taken with something.

Empty stomachs are wiser than empty heads—they talk only once in a while.

The trouble with table manners is that they were invented by people who were never very hungry.

HUNTING

The fascination of shooting as a sport depends on whether you are at the right or the wrong end of the gun.

—P. G. Wodehouse

When people go hunting in this vicinity, about all they find to shoot at are signs reading: NO HUNTING ALLOWED ON THESE PREMISES.   *—Ed Howe*

Before marriage, every girl is a hunter, but not every one is a trapper.

A hunter is a sportsman who cannot afford to be loaded because his gun is.

All that some hunters ever bag is their trousers.

A pointer is a hunting dog that's a man's best friend but an animal's worst enemy.

If lions painted, there would be many more pictures of lions killing men than men killing lions.

A big game hunter always kills more flies than animals.

HUSBAND

The husband who wants a happy marriage should learn to keep his mouth shut and his checkbook open. — *Groucho Marx*

American husbands are the best in the world; no other husbands are so generous to their wives, or can be so easily divorced.
— *Elinor Glyn*

Husbands never become good; they merely become proficient.
— *Mencken*

A first husband is the best of men to a widow, the worst of men to a divorcee.

Some women have good husbands; others married the men they wanted.

The best husbands aren't caught, they're made.

A husband is seldom as smart as his mother thinks, nor as dumb as his mother-in-law says.

A husband is the only relative who contests his wife's will while she's alive.

Colleges are full of young men who would make good first husbands.

A married man is a bachelor whose luck finally ran out.

A husband is a lover whose face is unshaved, pants unpressed, and stomach out of order.

Many a first husband shows a great deal more sense than the second by dying.

A husband is a man who has made one mistake, but keeps learning from it all his life.

It's a terrible thing to lose a husband; you know what you've lost, but you never know what you'll get the next time.

A movie star is known by the husbands she doesn't keep.

A good husband is not one without faults, but one with some faults that are not as bad as some others.

There are two kinds of husbands: those who never talk back to their wives, and those who listen in an aggravating manner.

A married man's socks are mended by his wife, and his manners are mended by his daughter.

Married men make the best husbands.

Most men would rather be the second husband of a widow than her first.

The best husband is the one who is always puttering around

the house; he doesn't have much opportunity to get into mischief.

A woman never knows what kind of a husband she doesn't want until she marries him.

Many a woman thinks she can do nothing without a husband, and when she gets one she finds she can do nothing with him.

Some husbands pay their debts promptly, while others are good to their wives.

A married man's fate: hooked, booked, cooked.

There's only one thing worse than a husband who never comes home, and that's a husband who hangs around the house all the time.

Marriage turns the man who thinks he knows women into a man who doesn't know what to think.

In choosing a husband all women are interested in the physical, but some are more interested in the fiscal.

Husbands are like fires: they go out when unattended.

Every married man can name one woman who has a wonderful husband.

Being a husband is like any other job—it helps if you like the boss.

A good husband is merely a good son grown up.

A husband is a man who has lost his liberty in the pursuit of happiness.

HUSBAND AND WIFE

A man should be taller, older, heavier, uglier and hoarser than his wife.   – Ed Howe

No husband can ever know as much about himself as his wife thinks she knows about him.

Every father knows that money talks mostly in the mother tongue.

Marriage is a partnership where no matter how good a husband is, his wife is still the better half.

A man and his wife are one, one too many sometimes.

In most families, husband and wife tend to think alike, with the wife always having the last think.

What every wife wants to know: how the other half lives.

There are two sides to every man: the side his wife knows, and the side he thinks she doesn't know.

Many a married woman leads a double life—hers and his.

The faults of wives are many, husbands have only two—everything they say, and everything they do.

A wife remembers when and where she got married, while a husband forgets why.

After all is said and done, it's usually the wife who has said it, and the husband who has done it.

Husbands have more problems than wives—for one thing, they have to put up with wives.

One wife is just as good as another, if not better; and one husband is just as bad as another, if not worse.

Many a husband doesn't speak to his wife for a long time, but his turn will eventually come.

It is surprising that there aren't many more successful men—what with all the advice from their wives.

Woman works in the absence of man, and man rests in the presence of woman.

Some husbands would be happier if they had married other women; other husbands, if their wives had married other men.

A happy wife sometimes has the best husband, but more often makes the best of the husband she has.

Some husbands would like to get women back into the kitchen; others would be content if they could only get them back into the home.

What every do-it-yourself husband has is a do-it-now wife.

The divorce rate wouldn't be so high if there were fewer married couples and more husbands and wives.

The husband who talks but little usually has a wife who does little but talk.

To make your husband happy, treat him like a dog: give him plenty of affection and a loose leash.

A woman should understand her husband more than she loves him; a man should love his wife more than he understands her.

Many a woman would make a better wife if she stopped trying to make her man a better husband.

HYPOCHONDRIAC

A hypochondriac talks so much about her troubles that no one troubles much about her talk.

When two hypochondriacs meet, they first exchange greetings and then symptoms.

Another type of woman who is a problem to which there is no solution is the hypochondriac.

A hypochondriac is one who can't leave being well enough alone.

Hypochondria is an illness where the more you think, the more you think you need a doctor.

A hypochondriac is an unpleasant person who is always telling us her troubles before we can tell her ours.

No doctor can break a hypochondriac of the habit of not feeling well.

A hypochondriac is a sick woman whose affliction is a healthy imagination.

A hypochondriac always broods over her health, but never hatches a remedy.

I used to tell my troubles to everyone I knew, and the more I told my troubles the more my troubles grew.

A hypochrondriac can get more talk out of a minor pain than others can get out of a major operation.

A hypochondriac is the man who stays at home when he's the only one in the office without a cold.

A hypochondriac is a woman who feels well only when she feels ill.

A hypochondriac is always suffering from an habitual lack of ailments.

A hypochondriac spends half her time talking about illnesses she hasn't got, and the other half not listening to her friends talk about illnesses they have got.

When two hypochondriacs meet, which one tells the other about his troubles?

A hypochondriac is a woman who is always sure to have some ailment in mind.

A hypochondriac can suffer in a hundred different ways, but never in silence.

A hypochondriac is a woman who goes through life always on her deathbed.

The hypochondriac who is always telling about his troubles performs a valuable service: he keeps other people from thinking about their own.

A hypochondriac is a man with an infinite capacity for finding pains.

The hypochondriac gives herself all kinds of ailments while she gives others only a pain in the neck.

HYPOCRISY

A hypocrite is a person who—but who isn't?   *—Don Marquis*

He is the kind of politician who would cut down a redwood tree, then mount the stump and make a speech for conservation.
—Adlai Stevenson

Hypocrisy is the parents' first duty.   *—Bernard Shaw*

If it were not for the intellectual snobs who pay, the arts would perish with their starving practitioners—let us thank heaven for hypocrisy. *—Aldous Huxley*

Never to talk about yourself is a refined form of hypocrisy.
—Nietzsche

There is always a type of man who says he loves his fellowmen, and expects to make a living at it.
—Ed Howe

Where there is no religion, hypocrisy becomes good taste.
                    — *Bernard Shaw*

Hypocrisy is the homage that politics pays to principle.

A hypocrite is a person who isn't himself on Sundays.

If the world despises a hypocrite, what must they think of him in heaven?

A hypocrite is an animal that walks upright but seldom talks that way.

A hypocrite pats you on the back in front of your face, and slaps you in the face behind your back.

The best time to deal with a hypocrite is when he isn't himself.

A hypocrite always practices what he preaches—against.

A hypocrite always seems to be a person of probity until you begin to probe.

It is often only a short step from the hypercritical to the hypocritical.

ICE

Ice sometimes makes you slip, but more often it is what's mixed with it.

Don't be misled by a woman's tears: nothing weeps more copiously than a cake of ice.

Nothing is impossible: you can even carry water in a sieve—if you wait till it freezes.

IDEA

The value of an idea has nothing whatever to do with the sincerity of the man who expresses it.   — *Oscar Wilde*

It takes a wonderful brain and exquisite senses to produce a few stupid ideas.   — *Santayana*

Why do we call our generous ideas illusions, and the mean ones truth?   — *Edith Wharton*

The trouble with most of us is we swallow political ideas before they're ripe, and they don't agree with us. — *Finley Peter Dunne*

All of our ideas come from the natural world: trees equal umbrellas.
                    — *Wallace Stevens*

I like to be the midwife of confused and painful ideas which are struggling to reach the light of day.   — *Bernard Berenson*

In a war of ideas, it is the people who get killed.
                    — *Stanislaw J. Lec*

Ideas won't keep: something must be done about them.
                    — *A. N. Whitehead*

For an idea ever to be fashionable is ominous, since it must afterwards be always old-fashioned.   — *Santayana*

An idea that is not dangerous is unworthy of being called an idea at all.   — *Oscar Wilde*

When an idea gets into an empty head it has the time of its life.

It's a good idea to exchange ideas, and sometimes a better one to change them.

Ideas are like children: there are none so wonderful as your own.

Never judge an idea by the words it wears.

Some people express an idea; others send it by slow freight.

The way to convert yourself to an idea is to talk someone else into believing it.

A swelled head never gets that way by letting ideas soak into it.

Ideas die quickly in some heads because they can't stand the solitary confinement.

The smaller the idea, the bigger the words to express it.

Do not undertake vast projects with half-vast ideas.

The man whose head you cannot get a new idea into is usually the same man whose head you cannot get an old idea out of.

IDEAL

The idealist cannot be reformed: if he is driven out of his heaven, he makes an ideal out of his hell.   — *Nietzsche*

An idealist is one who, on noticing that a rose smells better than a cabbage, concludes that it will also make better soup.
— *Mencken*

The ideal man should always say much more than he means, and always mean much more than he says.   — *Oscar Wilde*

Idealism is the noble toga that political gentlemen drape over their will to power.
— *Aldous Huxley*

An idealist is a more dangerous animal than the Philistine just as a man is a more dangerous animal than a sheep. — *Bernard Shaw*

When people cease to reflect, they become idealists.
— *Norman Douglas*

Living with a dog is easy—like living with an idealist. — *Mencken*

Living up to ideals is like doing everyday work with your Sunday clothes on.   — *Ed Howe*

An ideal husband is one who thinks his wife's headache is as important as his own ulcer.

We are an idealistic people, and we'll make any sacrifice for a cause so long as it won't hurt business.

No man marries his ideal because, while he is looking for the ideal woman, she is looking for the ideal man.

If some people lived up to their ideals, they would be stooping.

The quickest way to lose an ideal is to marry it.

An idealist finds it almost as hard to live up to his ideals as to pay his debts.

An idealist tries to shape the world to his wishes instead of trying to shape his wishes to the world.

The ideal husband is one who never quarrels, never gambles—and never marries.

Idealism increases in direct proportion to one's distance from the problem.

A man sometimes ceases to be a girl's ideal when he marries her, but more often when he marries another girl.

What this country needs is to realize the ideal and to idealize the real.

Many a woman who marries her ideal soon discovers that he's her ordeal.

We build our ideals and they in turn build us.

Ideals are very valuable—except for use.

To remain a woman's ideal, a man must die a bachelor.

The man who claims he has high ideals will probably stand by them as long as it pays.

Many a girl has an ideal boy friend, but no woman has an ideal husband.

The young man who starts out trying to save the world usually ends up learning to save his breath.

Why is it that when a woman marries the ideal man, he never turns out to be a perfect husband?

A visionary is an impractical person whose thoughts are based on ideals in a world whose actions are based on deals.

IDLE

You must have been warned against letting the golden hours slip by, but some of them are golden only because we let them slip by.   *—James M. Barrie*

If you go to sleep while loafing, how are you going to know you are loafing?   *—Don Marquis*

If a loafer isn't a nuisance to you, it's a sign that you're a bit of a loafer yourself.   *—Ed Howe*

As peace is the end of war, so to be idle is the ultimate purpose of the busy.
                     —Samuel Johnson

It is better to have loafed and lost than never to have loafed at all.   *—James Thurber*

Whoever named it idle curiosity was a poor judge of idleness.

The man with nothing to do always gives it his personal attention.

Hard work never killed anybody, but for that matter neither did loafing.

The worst thing about time-wasters is that so much of the time they waste doesn't belong to them.

An idler is a man whose life's work is to avoid it.

Doing nothing is the most tiresome job in the world because you can't stop and rest.

There is no fun in having nothing to do; the fun is in having lots to do and not doing it.

Killing time is not murder—it's suicide.

It is said that nothing is impossible, yet there are lots of people doing nothing every day.

The man who does nothing usually does somebody.

In an idler's life there is nothing doing every minute.

A person with an hour to kill usually wants to kill it with someone who can't spare a minute.

If work is a virtue, too many employees are living in sin.

You don't have to be bored at not doing anything; it depends on what you're not doing.

The idler is a man who is always glad to be laid off, especially when compensation sets in.

IGNORANCE

The less I know about a subject, the more confidence I have, and the more new light I throw on it.   — Mark Twain

It wasn't until quite late in life that I discovered how easy it is to say "I don't know."
— Somerset Maugham

In the future the so-called Dark Ages will perhaps be lengthened to include our own.
— G. C. Lichtenberg

When ignorance gets started, it knows no bounds.   — Will Rogers

Every now and then you meet a man whose ignorance is encyclopedic.   — Stanislaw J. Lec

Lots of folks don't know when they're well off, but ten times as many don't know when they're not well off.   — Kin Hubbard

A man must have a certain amount of intelligent ignorance to get anywhere.
— Charles F. Kettering

To be ignorant of one's ignorance is the malady of the ignorant.   — Bronson Alcott

God will not have any human being know what will sell, nor even when anyone is going to die, nor even whether or not it is going to rain.   — Samuel Butler

I do not believe in the collective wisdom of individual ignorance.   — Carlyle

I would rather have my own ignorance than another man's knowledge because I have got so much more of it.   — Mark Twain

Most ignorance is vincible ignorance: we don't know because we don't want to know.
— *Aldous Huxley*

There is a preschool ignorance that precedes knowledge and a postgraduate ignorance that follows it.   — *Montaigne*

It's what a man doesn't know about a girl that makes him fall in love with her.

Ignorance has its virtues: without it there would be mighty little conversation.

When money talks, it doesn't always know what it's talking about.

No wonder we are ignorant: the man who knows it all has the hardest time trying to tell it to someone.

There's nothing new under the sun, but there are lots of old things we don't know.

What you don't know doesn't hurt you, but it amuses a lot of people.

The husband who doesn't tell his wife everything probably thinks that what she doesn't know won't hurt him.

The ignorance that is bliss is the ignorance of the man who thinks he knows it all.

You can't underestimate the ignorance of some people.

There are few things nowadays more expensive than education, and one of them is ignorance.

Just as soon as we discover that ignorance is bliss, it isn't.

Ignorance of the law is no excuse, and neither is the ignorance of the lawmakers.

A man doesn't know what he knows until he knows what he doesn't know.

When a man doesn't know what he's talking about, he's probably talking about women.

Ignorance is bliss, but not when you're a dropout.

IGNORE

The art of being wise is the art of knowing what to overlook.
— *William James*

Many problems disappear if you ignore them long enough, like snow and adolescence.

Success depends less on the advice you take than on the advice you ignore.

The first half of our lives is spent ignoring our parents's advice, and the second half in trying to keep our children from ignoring ours.

Television brings the family into the same room so that they can ignore each other close together.

The confidential doctor-patient relationship is best exemplified when the doctor ignores the patient's symptoms and the patient ignores the doctor's bills.

Women never refer to their age until it would be wiser to ignore it.

In some shops you have to wait on yourself; in others they hire salesladies to ignore you.

Anyone can put off an unpleasant duty, but it takes a real strong-willed man to ignore it completely.

ILLEGIBLE

I can always find plenty of women to sleep with, but the woman really hard for me to find is a typist who can read my writing.   – *Thomas Wolfe*

I would rather scribble over again what I have written than take the trouble to decipher it.
      – *Montaigne*

The advantage of an illegible handwriting is that it covers up many a mistake in spelling.

When a physician makes his mark, it's usually illegible.

ILLITERATE

The illiterate who cannot read or write was probably born that way.

There are almost five million illiterates in the United States, excluding those who write comic books.

Illiteracy has its advantages: you can never be misinformed through reading.

All men are created free and equal—and illiterate.

Many a man makes his mark in the world, especially if he is illiterate.

The chief advantage of being illiterate is that it saves you from reading some terrible kinds of literature.

ILLUSION

Everything is an illusion, including this notion.
     – *Stanislaw J. Lec*

It is respectable to have no illusions, and safe, and profitable —and dull.   – *Joseph Conrad*

The one person who has more illusions than the dreamer is the man of action.   – *Oscar Wilde*

There are optical illusions in time as well as space.   – *Proust*

Self-deception is the illusion of the person who believes that he has no illusions.

The worst thing about love is that it creates illusions without making provision for their future upkeep.

IMAGINATION

You cannot depend on your eyes when your imagination is out of focus.   – *Mark Twain*

With the high cost of living, all the poor man has left is his

imagination, and television has taken that away from him.
— *Fred Allen*

After a man passes sixty, his mischief is mainly in his head.
— *Ed Howe*

There is nothing more terrible than imagination without taste.
— *Goethe*

Were it not for imagination, a man would be as happy in the arms of a chambermaid as of a duchess. — *Samuel Johnson*

Every man is a hero to his imagination.

The best motorist drives with imagination: he imagines his family is in the car.

The girl who thinks she has broken her heart has only sprained her imagination.

Poets all have imagination because they imagine people are going to read their poems.

The play of imagination is a great help in the work of imagination.

Woman's chief asset is man's imagination.

Imagination is that admirable quality in ourselves which is objectionable falsehood in others.

There's only one thing that appeals to the imagination more than the love of art, and that is the art of love.

Truth is stranger than fiction, and also harder to make up.

Imagination is what makes you think you are having a wonderful time when you are only spending money.

Many an imaginative man falls in love with a homely girl because she is so beautiful.

There is no greater bore than the man who has so much common sense that he has no imagination.

The length of a man's kiss usually depends on the breadth of his imagination.

There's no one so imaginative as a mother: she really believes that her children are as smart as she tells people they are.

Many a girl who elopes wishes later that she had merely let her imagination run away with her.

That thing that women's fashions leave to the imagination is what makes them so expensive.

IMITATION

When people are free to do as they please, they usually imitate each other. — *Eric Hoffer*

The only good imitations are those that poke fun at bad originals. — *La Rochefoucauld*

To copy others is necessary, but to copy oneself is pathetic.
— *Picasso*

The grape gains its purple tinge by looking at another grape.
— *Juvenal*

The worst thing about a good book is that it is always imitated by a lot of bad ones.
— *G. C. Lichtenberg*

The man who has the most imitators is the one with the inimitable style.

The poor imitate the rich and grow poorer; the rich imitate the poor and grow richer.

Imitation is the flattest form of sincerity.

Children are natural mimics who act like their parents in spite of every effort to teach them good manners.

It is the real thing that has to prove its identity; the clever imitation will pass without question anywhere.

Imitation of another is limitation of oneself.

Try to be like an ancient Greek in words and a Roman in deeds.

Many a man ought to be locked up for impersonating a human being.

IMMIGRATION

Remember always that all of us are descended from immigrants.
— *Franklin D. Roosevelt*

All men have been emigrants or the sons of emigrants since Adam and Eve left Eden.

People who believe in restricted immigration believe that the worst is yet to come.

Many an American whose ancestors came over on the Mayflower is lucky—there were no immigration laws then.

IMMORAL

I wonder why murder is considered less immoral than fornication in literature. — *George Moore*

Immorality is the morality of those who are having a better time. — *Mencken*

She has neither character nor morals: imagine what a sweet and compliant morsel she will make.
— *Choderlos de Laclos*

The modern novel is true to life: its characters have a rigid code of immorals.

A pessimist is a man who thinks all women are immoral and an optimist hopes it is true.

IMMORTALITY

The average man does not know what to do with this life, yet wants another one which will last forever. — *Anatole France*

The first requisite for immortality is death. — *Stanislaw J. Lec*

The best argument I know for an immortal life is the existence of a man who deserves one.
— *William James*

Without the hope of an afterlife, this life is not even worth the effort of getting dressed in the morning. — *Bismarck*

Immortality is the condition of a dead man who doesn't believe that he is dead. — *Mencken*

Those who have produced immortal works have done so without knowing how or why.
— *Hazlitt*

Immortality is the power to influence others after others can no longer influence you.

Immortality is when a man is dead but his words are alive.

The man of the hour is seldom the man of eternity.

IMPARTIAL

I cannot undertake to be impartial as between the fire brigade and the fire. — *Winston Churchill*

The man who can see both sides doesn't have a chance in an argument.

A wise man is impartial, not neutral; a fool is neutral, not impartial.

IMPATIENCE

Impatience is a state of annoyance when your head is in a hurry but the rest of you keeps it waiting.

There's no one so impatient as the man whose wife keeps telling him for an hour that she'll be ready in a minute.

Don't be impatient: remember, you can't warm your hands by burning your fingers.

The most important thing about bringing up children is knowing when to lose your patience.

The less patience a person has, the more he loses it.

If you want to learn patience, borrow money: no man is impatient with his creditors.

IMPORTANCE

When everyone is somebody, then no one's anybody.
— *W. S. Gilbert*

The longer you live, the less importance you attach to things, and the less importance you also attach to importance. — *Jean Rostand*

There is nothing that you and I make so many blunders about, and the world so few, as the actual amount of our importance.
— *Josh Billings*

The man of talent seeks to be important; the man of genius seeks to do the important.

Money is important because it enables you to buy the things that are more important than money.

Landing a man on the moon isn't nearly as important to a girl as landing a man on the earth.

If you make your job important, it will probably return the favor.

At twenty a man attaches too much importance to how she looks, and at forty to how she cooks.

Money may not be the most important thing in the world, but it's way ahead of whatever is in second place.

IMPOSSIBLE

Nothing nowadays is impossible, except some people.

Nothing is impossible to the man who does not have to do it himself.

The difficult we do at once, the impossible takes a little longer.

The only virtue in attempting the impossible is that, if you fail, you've got an excellent excuse.

The difference between a bachelor and a married man is that one longs for the impossible and the other has married her.

They said it couldn't be done; so he tackled it with a smile and found—it couldn't be done.

Nothing is impossible, except getting your name off a mailing list.

The word *impossible* is peculiar because if you examine it closely, you'll find that most of it is *possible*.

IMPRESSION

The person who uses a lot of big words isn't trying to inform you; he's trying to impress you.
— *Olin Miller*

The worst piece of luck that can happen to a busy man is to make a favorable impression on a bore.
— *Ed Howe*

Some people are impressed only when they are suppressed.

Before you put your best foot forward, make sure you know which one it is.

First impressions are often lasting, especially when they are made by car bumpers.

A smart aleck knows everything, except how to make a good impression.

Always put your best foot forward, but be careful not to trip over it.

It is always wrong to strike a woman, but not if you strike her fancy.

Trying to make an impression usually ends up in making merely an impression of trying.

Always try to put your best foot forward, especially when you haven't a leg to stand on.

To impress people favorably, let them impress you.

Always put your best foot forward, but don't do it inch by inch.

IMPROPER

Impropriety is the soul of wit.
— *Somerset Maugham*

Truth is stranger than fiction— and more decent.

If some persons preached what they practiced, they would have to be censored.

The proper study of mankind is man, the improper study is woman.

The impropriety of yesterday is the fashion of today.

An oldtimer is one who remembers when the only improper things one learned at school were the improper fractions.

The man whose behavior leaves his wife speechless has hit upon something priceless.

IMPROVEMENT

I cannot say whether things will get better if they change; what I can say is they must change if they are to get better.
— G. C. Lichtenberg

As nations improve, so do their gods.   — G. C. Lichtenberg

Sometimes when a woman makes a fool out of a man, it's an improvement.

Most people strive to be better off, but few strive to be better.

Whiskey improves with age, but age doesn't improve with whiskey.

People who make the best of things seldom try to make them any better.

You can always tell the kind of book that will improve your mind: you begin to yawn after reading a few pages.

The best way to better your lot is to do a lot better.

In learning to drive, you are improving as long as you don't take a turn for the worse.

A congressman often betters himself by winning his job, and often betters the country by losing it.

Nothing improves a man's driving like being followed by a police car.

The trouble is that everyone today wants to get to the Promised Land without going through the Wilderness.

In Congress, it's never too late to amend.

A teen-ager's driving is improving when his father merely has to have the car repaired instead of replaced.

The woman who can read her husband like a book always wants to edit him.

The movie star who improves a great deal has probably been marrying a better grade of man every year.

Nowadays we are getting better foods from the farmers and better products from the manufacturers —why then can't we get better weather from the weather bureau?

IMPUDENCE

Nothing is so impudent as success, unless it be those she favors.
— James Robinson Planché

Gall is what enables a man, sitting in a bus, to flirt with a woman who is standing.

Man may not live by bread alone, but many people live chiefly on crust.

Insolence is the art of keeping your manners fresh instead of your mind.

The man who has plenty of cheek probably has a fat head too.

IMPULSE

If I ever marry, it will be on a sudden impulse—as a man shoots himself.   — Mencken

Obey some impulses, but make other impulses obey you.

If you must act on the spur of the moment, do so only after a long period of premeditation.

The trouble with a teen-ager is that she seldom obeys anything but her impulse.

An impulsive wife always wants her husband to follow her advice, especially when she has no logical reason for it.

INABILITY

I do not know upon what subject he will next employ his versatile incapacity.
— A. E. Housman

You never know what you cannot do until you try.

Many men come to grief from having too much confidence in their own inability.

By the time you are old enough to understand women, you are too old to do anything about it.

Some husbands are very versatile—they can't do anything.

What some of us need most is a good, swift kick in the seat of our can'ts.

INCOME

There are few sorrows in which a good income is of no avail.
— Logan P. Smith

Many a man doesn't live within his income because he can't afford it.

The ideal income is a thousand dollars a day—and expenses.

A wife can usually live within her husband's income, provided he has another one for himself.

The man who has more income than he needs is usually married to the woman who needs more income than he has.

The two most important things about your income are—make it first, and then make it last.

Many a man can't live within his income because his wife can't live within her credit.

The taxpayer wouldn't mind the government's living beyond its income if it wasn't also living beyond his.

Some wives want a husband to be a breadwinner, but most expect him to be a bakery.

The woman who doesn't complain about having to live within her husband's income is probably an heiress.

Courtship is another thing whose outcome depends on the income.

People who live within their income are really trying to hold back prosperity.

Most of us could live quite comfortably, and even save a little, on the money we tell others we make.

Behind every man who lives within his income is a wife who doesn't.

INCOME TAX

I make a fortune from criticizing the policy of the government, and then hand it over to the government in taxes to keep it going.   *– Bernard Shaw*

There will always be two classes of people who don't like to pay income taxes: men and women.

There's nothing like the income tax to make you realize how much you don't have to be thankful for.

The only expense nowadays that you can't charge to your credit card is your income tax.

Providence giveth and the income tax taketh away.

A tax exemption is a government incentive allowing children to contribute to the support of their parents.

After saving enough money to pay his income tax, many a man has to borrow some to live on.

Another thing about the income tax—what you don't owe won't hurt you.

Income taxes could be a lot worse; suppose we had to pay on what we think we're worth.

The income tax is a neat plan devised to clean you out of your filthy lucre.

No one knows who figured out the meager amount of tax exemptions for wife and children, but it must have been a bachelor.

Time, tide and the tax collector wait for no man.

A withholding tax is the only part of a man's wages that a wife can't lay her hands on.

A fool and his money are soon parted, but the rest of us wait to be taxed.

The withholding tax is a trick devised by the government to prevent you from spending all you earn.

Every child is as good as gold, at least at income tax time.

Early to bed and early to rise, and you'll be in a tax bracket up to the skies.

Congress seems to have overlooked nothing, except a tax on our income taxes.

An income tax form taxes the citizen's ingenuity while the government takes everything else.

INCOME TAX RETURN

The income tax is an annual game in which the taxpayer fills a government return while the government empties his pockets.

Preparing an income tax return is like a girl preparing to go to the beach: you take off as much as the law allows.

The more an income tax form taxes your brains, the less it taxes your income.

The income tax form is the only blank that's loaded.

Making out an income tax is a lesson in mathematics: addition, division, multiplication and extraction.

Income tax forms are generally filed, but more often chiseled.

Despite all attempts to simplify it, there's nothing more taxing than filling out an Internal Revenue form.

Two and two always make four, except when figuring out your tax deductions for charity.

It takes more brains to make out an income tax return than it does to make the income itself.

When making out your income tax, remember that it's better to give than to deceive.

INCOMPATIBLE

Marriage is an eternal battle between the feminine love for interior decoration and the masculine love for comfort.

Many a man who was born to command makes the mistake of marrying the woman who was born to countermand.

The woman who spends money like water often has a husband who is watertight.

Another incompatible couple is the season of the year and its weather.

The man who forgets things he ought to remember is probably married to the woman who remembers things she ought to forget.

Another incompatible couple is the one where the wife's vote cancels out the husband's.

Marriage is the process of choosing the right woman with whom to be incompatible.

Some couples can't get along together because they have nothing in common to quarrel about.

Another type of incompatibility is the marriage between a man old enough to know better and a girl not quite old enough.

A common form of incompatibility is the marriage of a man with a bus income to a taxicab wife.

INDECISIVE

Once I make up my mind, I'm full of indecision. — *Oscar Levant*

They are decided only to be undecided, resolved to be irresolute, adamant for drift, solid for fluidity, all powerful for impotence. — *Winston Churchill*

The man who cannot make up his mind is probably torn between vice and versa.

Nothing makes a person so indecisive as having to choose from a tray of French pastry.

Many a poor worm doesn't know which way to turn.

The man who doesn't know whether he will or not, is probably a man of *might*.

INDEPENDENCE

The value of money is that with it we can tell any man to go to the devil.
— *Somerset Maugham*

Some husbands assert their independence by refusing to wear an apron while doing the dishes.

Almost all politicians are married men, which explains why a candidate rarely runs as an independent.

INDEPENDENCE DAY

We have killed more people celebrating Independence Day than we lost fighting for it.
— *Will Rogers*

What distinguishes Independence Day from all other days is that then both orators and artillerymen shoot blank cartridges.
— *John Burroughs*

We celebrate the Fourth of July by festive fireworks, colorful parades, and a fantastic weekend of traffic deaths.

Independence Day is the day married men celebrate something they once had.

Some men celebrate the Fourth of July by buying a fifth on the third.

INDIFFERENCE

Indifference to poetry is one of the most conspicuous characteristics of the human race.
— *Robert Lynd*

Nothing matters to the man who says nothing matters.
— *Lin Yutang*

The worst sin toward our fellow creatures is not to hate them, but to be indifferent to them; that's the essence of inhumanity.
— *Bernard Shaw*

By the time we are old enough not to care what anyone says about us, no one does.

You can't divorce your wife because she's indifferent, unless she's in different men's beds.

Nonchalance is the art of looking like an owl when you have acted like an ass.

If a girl seems cold at first, brace up; chills are often followed by fever.

A hypochondriac is never aware that other people are no more interested in her troubles than she is in theirs.

We wouldn't worry about what people think of us if we knew how seldom they do.

Worry kills more people than work, and to be on the safe side, some men do neither.

INDIGESTION

The proof of the pudding is not in the eating, but in the repeating.

Food isn't the only thing that causes indigestion: you can also get it from eating crow and swallowing your pride.

There's nothing worse for a man than dyspepsia, especially when his wife has it.

The quickest way to get indigestion is to eat something when something's eating you.

Woman's inhumanity to man makes countless dyspeptics.

Indigestion is the incompatibility between a man's stomach and his wife's cooking.

A dyspeptic is a man whose favorite pastime is indigestion.

A dyspeptic is the only man who can eat his cake and have it too.

Many people think they have a grievance when it's only indigestion.

The worst indigestion is that which comes from having to eat your own words.

The only thing digestible about some doughnuts is the hole.

A sourpuss doesn't have to have indigestion to look as if he had.

Some men are born dyspeptic, some achieve dyspepsia, and others eat their wives' cooking.

INDISCRETION

It's almost got so you can't speak the truth without committing an indiscretion.
— *Kin Hubbard*

Discretion may be the better part of valor, but indiscretion is usually the better part of love.

Nowadays many a woman reaches the age of discretion without achieving it.

INDISPENSABLE

Make yourself indispensable, and you'll move up; act as if you're indispensable, and you'll move out.

A man works hard all year convincing his boss he's indispensable so he can get a few weeks' vacation to prove he isn't.

Everything is relative: you're expendable when you ask for a raise, but indispensable when you ask for a day off.

INDIVIDUALISM

The best things and best people rise out of their separateness; I'm against a homogenized society because I want the cream to rise.
— *Robert Frost*

The majority of people display their individuality most in the kind of fool they become.
— *Ed Howe*

Whenever two people meet there are really six people present: each man as he sees himself, as the other person sees him, and as he really is. — *William James*

No bird soars too high if he soars with his own wings.
— *William Blake*

Everyone would like to behave like a pagan, with everyone else behaving like a Christian.
— *Camus*

There are only two ways to preserve your freedom and individuality: saying *no*, and living alone. — *Chamfort*

It takes more than age to make a personage out of a person.

The man who doesn't care what others think is generally found at the top of the ladder or at the bottom.

An individualist is a man who doesn't care for the government, and doesn't want the government to take care of him.

Many a man refuses to do the things he dislikes so that he can work himself to death doing the things he likes.

INDULGENCE

If you want to see what children can do, you must stop giving them things.
— *Norman Douglas*

We should be inclined to pay more attention to the wisdom of the old if they showed greater indulgence to the follies of the young. — *Hazlitt*

Spoil the rod and spare the child. — *William Dean Howells*

The woman who has an indulgent husband should see that he doesn't indulge too much.

Children would learn to write sooner if they were allowed to do so on wet cement.

Permissive parents take the pleasure out of childhood: they deprive their children of the joy of disobedience.

The child who gets all he wants usually grows into the man who gets all he deserves.

A brat is a child whose parents sail on the sea of matrimony without ever using a paddle.

Many a teen-ager has a father to tell him what to do, and a mother who does it for him.

You can do two things to make your wife happy: first, let her think she's having her own way, and second, let her have it.

Give a pig and a boy everything they want, and you'll get a good pig and a bad boy.

Many a brat whose parents can't get away with a parking ticket gets away with murder.

A woman can always make a fool out of her husband by just letting him have his own way.

The permissive mother believes her child should be allowed to do as he wants, even if he doesn't want to.

INERTIA

The way to be nothing is to do nothing.   – Ed Howe

Sitting still and wishing makes no person great; the good Lord sends the fishing, but you must dig the bait.

Success comes to the man who does today what you were thinking of doing tomorrow.

It isn't enough to be on the right track; you're liable to get run over if you just stay there.

When day is done, be sure that something else has also been.

Some people are like wheelbarrows: they stand still unless someone pushes them.

More people would get to the top if someone discovered a way to sit down and slide uphill.

INFANT CARE

One of the most important things to remember about infant care is: Never change diapers in midstream.   – Don Marquis

The secret of infant care lies in keeping one end full and the other end dry.

Training a young child is always a matter of pot luck.

A bottle-fed baby has at least one advantage: it doesn't have cigarette ashes constantly flicked in his face.

INFATUATION

Infatuation is a mental state when a man is out of his mind because there's a woman in it.

Infatuation is what makes an intelligent man look foolish to a foolish girl who looks intelligent to him.

Infatuation is a disease usually cured by marriage.

Marriage based on infatuation is an attempt to make a short story long.

Infatuation begins when you find your dream girl, and ends when she turns into a nightmare.

Infatuation is a state of mind which has nothing to do with the mind.

Infatuation begins with illusion on one side, and ends with disillusion on both.

First she sweeps him off his feet, then he has her on his hands.

Infatuation is a state of mind when a man shows great ingenuity in making a fool of himself.

Infatuation is the only kind of fire which is never covered by insurance.

Infatuation makes a man act pathetic, especially when the girl acts apathetic.

INFERIOR

Remember, no one can make you feel inferior without your consent.   *—Eleanor Roosevelt*

The trouble with an inferiority complex is that the people who ought to have it, never do.

The philosopher is physically inferior to prehistoric man, but it is better to be inferior than prehistoric.

Never tell your girl you are unworthy of her—she'll find it out herself soon enough.

When a snob develops an inferiority complex, he starts thinking he is no better than anyone else.

If science hadn't proved it, it would be hard to believe that man has descended from an inferior animal.

An inferiority complex is the exaggerated feeling a person has of his own unimportance.

We should be patient with our inferiors; they are ourselves of yesterday.

An inferiority complex is the only trait which enables us to see ourselves as others see us.

Rare is the man who acquires a feeling of inferiority before he develops it normally with marriage.

There's nothing so rare as a truck driver with an inferiority complex.

The woman who tries to associate with her inferiors always has trouble finding them.

INFERIOR AND SUPERIOR

Hollywood is the town where inferior people have a way of making superior people feel inferior.   *—Dudley Field Malone*

No man can ever end with being superior who will not begin with being inferior. *—Sydney Smith*

A superior person won't look down on you; an inferior person can't.

People of superior intelligence have no choice but to vote for people of inferior intelligence to govern them.

Why does the person with an inferiority complex always feel so superior?

Some people look down on those whom they think inferior; others look down on those who think they are superior.

An awareness of his own superiority has kept many a man in an inferior position.

Superior men seldom feel superior, and inferior men seldom feel inferior.

INFIDELITY

The lover thinks of possessing his mistress more often than her husband thinks of guarding his wife. — *Stendhal*

Love will never be ideal until man recovers from the illusion that he can be just a little bit faithful or a little bit married.
— *Helen Rowland*

After a man is married he has the legal right to deceive only one woman. — *Ed Howe*

All the world loves a lover—except the husband.

Some women are seldom faithful to their husbands; others are faithful lots of times.

First it's boy meets girl, and then it's man cheats wife.

The proof of the pudding is in the eating, and the proof of the marriage is in the cheating.

Marriage often changes a man's taste: many a man likes all married women except his wife.

The infidelity of a wife is usually a triangle, the infidelity of a husband, a hexagon.

The two ages of man: when he wants to be faithful and is not, and when he wants to be faithless and cannot.

Men are generally true to their first love; that's why many wives are so unhappy.

Many a woman has an educated husband who knows everything —and suspects nothing.

Many a man finds true happiness in marriage, but only because his wife doesn't watch him too closely.

So live that you will never have to urge your wife to be a good sport about it.

When a married man is too good to be true, he probably isn't.

Behind every married man there's a woman—and she often catches him too.

An extramarital affair is often a game not worth the scandal.

INFLATION

A dollar saved is a quarter earned. — *John Ciardi*

One good thing about inflation is that the fellow who forgets his change nowadays doesn't lose half as much as he used to.
— *Kin Hubbard*

Inflation is the process of shrinking a dollar bill without reducing its size.

The average American wants inflation of his income and deflation of everything else.

Everything seems to go up in price nowadays—except money.

During inflation even the Joneses have a hard time keeping up with themselves.

Inflation is the period when it's easier to earn money than to earn a living.

The cost of living is constantly rising because the luxuries of yesterday become the necessities of today.

Inflation affects everything, including the wages of sin.

There's one consolation in inflation: the money you haven't got isn't worth as much as it used to be.

It's not the original high prices that hurt, it's the upcreep.

One of the benefits of inflation is that kids can no longer get sick on a nickel's worth of candy.

During inflation, conversation consists of two things: what's going on, and what's going up.

Because the best things in life are free, we have to make up for the loss by raising the prices of the second best.

Inflation wouldn't be so bad if prices wouldn't keep rising.

Why is it that, as farmers are constantly producing more with less labor, the price of food keeps going up?

The only good thing you can say for inflation is that the high prices prevent you from buying more things that you don't need.

Many a man remains a bachelor because two can't live as cheaply as once.

Inflation never seems to bother Congress: if it gets too high, they always solve it by raising their own salaries.

Inflation is being broke with a lot of money in your pocket.

At today's high prices, you are lucky if you can make one end meet.

Inflation is what makes people pay more while they live on less.

By the time you acquire a nest egg, inflation has turned it into chicken feed.

Inflation is the period when the standard of living continues to rise until the people can't afford it.

The worst thing about history is that every time it repeats itself the price goes up.

It isn't so much that during inflation your money goes only half as far, but that it gets there twice as fast.

The danger with creeping inflation is that it doesn't always continue to creep but sometimes stands up and runs.

If the cost of living continues to rise, newlyweds may have to do without some of the things their parents could never afford.

During inflation the two-dollar lunch you have been paying three dollars for goes up to four dollars.

Inflation is the only thing people are down on that's on the up and up.

INFLUENCE

He has one of those terribly weak natures that are not susceptible to influence.
— *Oscar Wilde*

Women make us poets, children make us philosophers.
— *Malcolm de Chazal*

In most law courts a man is assumed guilty until he is proven influential.

A woman is more influenced by what she suspects than by what she is told.

You can't carry weight with others by putting your thumb on the scales.

If you think you have influence, try ordering someone else's dog around.

It isn't what you know, it's whom you know.

When a woman really loves a man, he can make her do anything she wants to do.

A live wire is never dead, especially if he has connections.

INFORMATION

A great part of the information I have was acquired by looking up something and finding something else on the way.
— *Franklin P. Adams*

When a man has anything to tell in this world, the difficulty is not to make him tell it, but to prevent him from telling it.
— *Bernard Shaw*

Every general wishes he had more information before he goes into battle, but each crisis you go into is on insufficient information.
— *Robert Frost*

A man who tells nothing or who tells all will equally have nothing told him. — *Chesterfield*

You can always tell a well-informed man: his views are the same as yours.

A cheap way to keep up with the Joneses is to listen to their children's conversation.

Everybody belongs to one of two classes: those who always know more than they tell, and those who always tell more than they know.

Never give an informative book to a conceited man—he knows too much already.

An executive knows something about everything, an expert knows everything about something, and the switchboard operator knows everything.

There's no man so well-informed as the man whose wife has just told him what she thinks of him.

There are three reasons for acquiring information: some people want to know it, some want to use it, but most want to tell it.

INGRATITUDE

The best definition of man is: an ungrateful biped. — *Dostoevski*

If you don't think this is a thankless world, try picking out a hat for your wife.

INHERITANCE

We pay for the mistakes of our ancestors, and it seems only fair that they should leave us the money to pay with.
— *Don Marquis*

Poverty is often overcome by will power, especially when it's a matter of inheritance.

A good man leaves an inheritance to his son, and a good lawyer takes it away from him.

No matter how poor a person is, he is sure to inherit something, even if it is only some relatives.

It's just as well that the meek will inherit the earth; no one else would stand for the inheritance tax.

Where wealth is inherited, dollars are often divorced from sense.

The man who makes no will makes lawyers his heirs.

It's just as well that you can't come back and see what they've done with what you couldn't take with you.

A beneficiary is a person who can take it from you because you cannot take it with you.

The meek will probably be pushed off the earth long before they get a chance to inherit it.

Many a lawyer attempts to split hairs in his attempts to split heirs.

Life wouldn't be half so tough if we could also inherit experience.

A fool and her money are soon courted.

The trouble with wealth is that it's usually handed down instead of handed out.

If people would leave their legacies to their lawyers, it would save a lot of time.

The meek shall inherit the earth, but only after the aggressive have plundered the riches thereof.

INJURY

The marks you receive in the school of experience are mostly bruises.

To nourish a grievance, feed it on vitamin X which contains vanity, jealousy, and pride.

If you jump at conclusions, you'll suffer contusions.

Nothing in the world beats a good wife—except a bad husband.

INJUSTICE

A book might be written on the injustice of the just.

—Anthony Hope

There's no such thing as injustice—a trial will convince you.

Half of mankind's evils are due to the injustices of human nature, and the other half to the human nature of injustice.

Equity follows the law, but seldom overtakes it.

IN-LAWS

Lowbrows suffer from mothers-in-law, highbrows from daughters-in-law. *—Chekhov*

As long as men don't outlaw women, women will in-law them.

A son-in-law is what every girl hopes her mother will have.

If you want to know how old a woman is, ask her sister-in-law.

A man shouldn't be judged by the company he keeps, especially if they are his in-laws.

It's not the by-laws of marriage that cause most domestic troubles —it's the in-laws.

There never was a mother-in-law who remembered that she was once a daughter-in-law.

The young man who wasn't good enough for our daughter always turns out to be the father of the smartest grandchildren in the world.

As troublemakers, few outlaws can beat in-laws.

INNOCENCE

It's too bad that a girl can't get married without dragging some innocent man to the altar with her.

Early to bed and early to rise is the way of a girl before she gets wise.

The law assumes you are innocent until proved guilty, but the public doesn't.

INSANITY

The main difference between men and women is that men are lunatics and women are idiots.

—Rebecca West

When a man goes crazy, his wife is the first to know it and the last to admit it. *—Ed Howe*

We do not have to visit a madhouse to find disordered minds; our planet is the mental institution of the universe. *—Goethe*

The man who cannot believe his senses, and the man who cannot believe anything else, are both insane. *—Chesterton*

When we remember we are all mad, the mysteries disappear and life stands explained.

—Mark Twain

We don't call a man mad who believes that he eats his God, but we do call him mad if he believes he is Jesus Christ. *—Helvétius*

There's only one difference between a madman and me: I am not mad.   — *Dali*

Insanity is hereditary: you can get it from your children.
                    — *Sam Levenson*

We want a few mad people now—see where the sane ones have landed us.   — *Bernard Shaw*

Some men are born insane, some achieve insanity, and some go in for psychoanalysis.

Insanity is different from love, but it's sometimes hard to tell the difference.

The man who is crazy about his wife may be sane enough away from her.

You step over the borderline of sanity not when you start talking to yourself, but when you start to listen.

The female of the species is no crazier than the male.

Sooner or later every man is crazy to get married, but only the bachelor realizes it in time.

There are more men than women in mental hospitals, which just goes to show who's driving who crazy.

If you think you are mentally ill, you are not; if you think everyone else is, you are.

The real difference between people is not sanity and insanity, but more or less insanity.

Whom the gods would employ, they first make mad.

INSINCERITY

Few men speak humbly of humility, modestly of modesty, skeptically of skepticism.   — *Pascal*

Marriage always requires the greatest understanding of the art of insincerity between two human beings.   — *Vicki Baum*

I am not sincere, not even when I say I am not.
                    — *Jules Renard*

Every man alone is sincere: at the entrance of a second person, hypocrisy begins.   — *Emerson*

A woman often means the bitter things she says to a man, but seldom the sweet things she says to a woman.

INSOMNIA

The best cure for insomnia is to get a lot of sleep.
                    — *W. C. Fields*

An insomniac sometimes lies awake nights, but more often lies about lying awake nights.

You haven't a bad case of insomnia unless you can't even sleep when it's time to get up.

The worst form of insomnia is when you can't even sleep on the job.

An insomniac is either asleep with one eye open, or awake with both eyes shut.

Why is it that people who are troubled with insomnia are generally so proud of it?

Insomnia is sometimes caused by an upset stomach, but more often by an upset wife.

What you don't worry about gives someone else insomnia.

An insomniac finds it hard to fall asleep at night, and even harder to stay awake by day.

Insomnia is one of the ailments conveyed to man from dogs; some people get it from the dog next door.

Every insomniac wishes he could fall asleep as easily as his foot does.

Is the insomniac one who is wide awake because he can't sleep, or one who can't sleep because he is wide awake?

An insomniac is one who sleeps better with a pill than with a pillow.

People who have insomnia lie awake all night for an hour.

Whiskey may not cure your insomnia, but it makes you more content to stay awake.

Every cloud has a silver lining: the man with insomnia doesn't keep others awake with his snoring.

An insomniac is a man who is unable to sleep or who, when he does sleep, dreams that he is awake.

INSPIRATION

A woman is constantly inspiring a man to do great things, and then preventing him from accomplishing them. *— Oscar Wilde*

Inspiration is a trick that poets have invented to give themselves importance. *— Jean Anouilh*

I don't know anything about inspiration because I don't know what inspiration is; I've heard about it, but I never saw it.
— Faulkner

Work sometimes comes from inspiration, but more often inspiration comes from work.

The usual way of a woman to inspire her husband to bigger things is to run up bigger bills.

INSTALLMENT CREDIT

Installment credit has made buying easier, but paying harder.

A credit plan is a system under which you continue to pay and pay, time and time, again and again.

You can sell anything by installment credit; all you have to do is make the payments far enough apart.

Half the world doesn't know how many things the other half is making time payments on.

Installment buying is popular because it enables you to live within your income as well as beyond your means.

Installment credit is a clever scheme that enables you to buy all the things you can't afford.

The haves are those who have money, while the have-nots are those who have everything that can be bought on time payments.

Installment credit is a financial trick to enable you to go through life buying things with money you haven't got.

With time payments we don't need a five-day week as much as we need a five-week month.

The reason installment credit is so universal is that it enables you to spend your salary before you draw it.

Some of the hardest things to keep up are the easy payments.

Installment credit is a plan that enables you to buy things on convenient payments that fall due at inconvenient times.

Time is money, especially for the person who buys on time.

Ever since the introduction of installment credit plans, people have been wishing they could afford to live the way they are living.

The difficulty is not in buying on time—it's paying on time.

Installment credit has revolutionized society: never have so many people lived so well so far behind before.

The disadvantage of installment buying is that by the time you are sick and tired of it, you own it.

Installment credit is a financial trick to enable you to spend money you haven't got at prices you can't afford for things you don't need.

Some people who buy on time don't seem to know when time leaves off and eternity begins.

Installment credit makes the months shorter and the years longer.

INSTRUCTION

We have not had the three R's in America, but the six R's: remedial reading, remedial 'riting, and remedial 'rithmetic.
— *Robert M. Hutchins*

The man I meet with is not often so instructive as the silence he breaks. — *Thoreau*

Instruction is what a mother gets when she listens in on a group of teen-agers discussing their parents.

He who is not taught by his parents will be taught by the world.

If at first you don't succeed, try reading the directions.

INSULT

If you can't ignore an insult, top it; if you can't top it, laugh it off; and if you can't laugh it off, it's probably deserved.
— *Russell Lynes*

The best way to procure insults is to submit to them.
— *Hazlitt*

There are two insults no human being will endure: that he has no sense of humor, and that he has never known trouble.
— *Sinclair Lewis*

It is an insult to one's morals to be called fast, and an insult to one's intelligence to be called slow.

INSURANCE

Honesty is the best policy without general coverage.
— *John Ciardi*

There is no one with endurance like the man who sells insurance.

Insurance companies are never alarmed by the young man who intends to set the world on fire.

Insurance is the business of protecting you against everything, except the insurance agent.

People who live in glass houses should take out insurance.

What really hurt Humpty Dumpty wasn't that he had a bad fall, but that he had recently let his accident insurance lapse.

Nothing separates the men from the boys like the cost of automobile insurance.

An insurance policy is an agreement made up of words that are too big to understand, and type that is too small to read.

A man never realizes the value of his home until he has occasion to collect the fire insurance.

Accidents will happen, unless you have an accident policy.

INTELLECTUAL

An intellectual is a man who takes more words than necessary to tell more than he knows.
— *Adlai Stevenson*

A large section of the intelligentsia seems wholly devoid of intelligence. — *Chesterton*

There are two kinds of people: the intelligentsia and the rest of us; the intelligentsia does the classifying.

Every college is full of intellectuals who seem to be out of practice.

The intelligentsia are persons whose education and intelligence are seldom on speaking terms.

INTELLIGENCE

If an animal does something, we call it instinct; if we do the same thing for the same reason, we call it intelligence.
— *Will Cuppy*

There is no such thing as an underestimate of average intelligence. — *Henry Adams*

Yes, I'm optimistic; maybe in a million years people will be as intelligent as horses. — *Don Herold*

You never know how intelligent some people are until they tell you.

Many a man would reach a greater height if he had more depth.

The three most important events of human life have nothing to do with intelligence: birth, marriage and death.

There are two types of smart women: the highbrows and the low necks.

No man is half as intelligent as he wants some woman to think he is.

The less intelligence you claim, the more intelligence people will give you credit for.

When you hire people who are smarter than you are, you prove you are smarter than they are.

People who claim that the average man has the intelligence of a fourteen-year-old always exclude themselves.

You can always tell an intelligent man: he's the one whom we can convince that our way of thinking is right.

A man's intelligence is seldom questioned as long as he can keep his tongue from trying to prove it.

What's the use of man's superior intelligence if it doesn't keep him out of marriage and other troubles?

Intelligence is what a man looks for in a woman after he has looked at everything else.

INTELLIGENCE TEST

What this country needs is an intelligence test for people who give them.

An intelligence test is an examination that attempts to fathom the depths of a person's ignorance.

The best intelligence test is what we do with our leisure.

An intelligence test is a series of problems intended to test your ability to acquire and retain misinformation.

So far no intelligence test has ever been devised to equal matrimony.

An intelligence test sometimes shows a man how smart he would have been not to have taken it.

What this country needs is an intelligence test for congressional candidates.

Where ignorance is bliss, 'tis foolish to take an intelligence test.

INTENTION

The worst work is always done with the best intentions.
— *Oscar Wilde*

Good intentions usually last as long as the remorse which gives them birth.

A do-gooder gets credit for good intentions everywhere except in a bank.

The road to hell is paved with the good intentions of friends and the bad intentions of enemies.

Good intentions, like good eggs, soon spoil unless they are hatched.

The hardest task of a girl's life is to prove to a man that his intentions are really serious.

A person is hard up indeed who cannot get credit even for good intentions.

A girl doesn't have to watch the speedometer to know what her boy friend is driving at.

The path to success is not paved with good intentions, but with good intentions that are carried out.

INTEREST

It is a cursed evil to any man to become as absorbed in any subject as I am in mine.   — *Darwin*

The average man is more interested in a woman who is interested in him than he is in a woman with beautiful legs.
— *Marlene Dietrich*

A man's interest in the world is only the overflow from his interest in himself. — *Bernard Shaw*

I don't believe in principle, but I do in interest.
— *James Russell Lowell*

A man's interest in a woman must have some other reason since he can get all the talk he wants from other men.

By the time a young man realizes how much he owes his parents, some girl comes along and gets most of the interest.

Newspapers play up the doings of rich people, it being only natural that money should draw interest.

It took a genius to invent money, and an even greater genius to think up interest.

You eat better on ten per cent, but you sleep better on five.

Women and money are very much alike: if you don't keep them busy they lose interest.

Another sure way of letting your money draw interest is to have a lot of poor relatives.

Money rules the world: when Romeo loses his capital, Juliet loses her interest.

INTERESTING

Every man has his follies, and they are often the most interesting things he has got.
— *Josh Billings*

The first of all democratic doctrines is that all men are interesting.   — *Chesterton*

There are no uninteresting things; there are only uninterested people.   — *Chesterton*

A clever girl is always interested in whatever interests the man she's interested in.

The most trying of all social duties is to appear interested in the things that don't interest you.

It's not what we tell people about ourselves that interests them; it's what we could tell them and don't.

A woman's idea of an interesting man is one who will sit and listen to her talk.

Money talks, but seldom enough to bore us.

It takes two to make a quarrel, and three to make it interesting.

The secret of the man who is universally interesting is that he is universally interested.

Your troubles are not interesting unless you are rich.

There is nothing so interesting in this world as your own affairs, except other people's affairs.

If money really talked it might make interesting remarks about the people who have it.

INTERFERE

People who hope they don't intrude are always the ones who do.

If you interfere between man and wife, remember this: they will be friends again but you won't.

If you want the world to beat a path to your door, just try to take a nap some Sunday afternoon.

INTERNATIONAL

One nation's common sense is another nation's high blood pressure. —*E. B. White*

Let us never negotiate out of fear, but let us never fear to negotiate. —*John F. Kennedy*

We cannot negotiate with those who say, "What's mine is mine, what's yours is negotiable." —*John F. Kennedy*

There's only one man in a million who understands the international situation, and you meet him everywhere.

Civilized nations are always being shocked at the uncivilized behavior of other civilized nations.

Life is a dance, and international relations a square dance: countries are always changing partners.

Remember, having a preference for your own country does not require your having a prejudice against others.

The international situation is more confusing than ever: by the time you know where you stand, your feet hurt.

An international conference is a meeting to decide where the next meeting is to be held.

The only international language is the one which money talks.

INTERPRETATION

There's more fuss and nonsense about interpreting interpretations than interpreting things.
— *Montaigne*

When a man starts thinking his wife doesn't understand him, the interpreter he chooses is usually a pretty girl.

The interpreter is one who translates a language he doesn't understand into another language he can't speak.

INTERRUPTION

It is a matter of life and death for married people to interrupt each other's stories, for if they did not, they would burst.
— *Logan P. Smith*

To be really enjoyed, sleep, health and wealth must be interrupted.   — *Jean Paul Richter*

The quickest way to make a long story short is by interrupting.

A bore is always talking during the interruption of other people.

Some women are forever interrupting; they don't enter a conversation, they invade it.

A bachelor is one who can describe his symptoms to the doctor without having his wife interrupt.

There's only one thing harder than threading a sewing machine with the motor running, and that's getting a word in edgewise with some people.

Some women gab so much, you couldn't get a word in even if you folded it in two.

Some women never let ideas interrupt the easy flow of their conversation.

You can sit through your favorite television program and have a telephone too.

The man who is always interrupting, listens faster than you can talk to him.

Nothing will break up an ordinary conversation quicker than for someone to drop into it an intelligent remark.

Many a woman is offended if her husband talks while she is interrupting.

What this country needs are less people who interrupt conversations, and more people who interrupt interrupters.

When your work speaks well for you, don't interrupt.

The woman who is always interrupting a man's conversation, is already married—or never will be.

It is bad manners to interrupt a person when he's talking, especially when he's praising you.

Never interrupt a man who is telling a funny story; you may be cutting his jocular vein.

INTERVIEW

A famous person is always surprised to discover what he said when he reads about it in the press.

The average reporter is as accurate as the average man he interviews.

There's nothing like being a celebrity: interviewers will quote you on subjects you know nothing about.

You seldom learn a statesman's views from his interviews.

Many a famous man's wit is due to his having been interviewed by a bright reporter.

INTOLERANCE

Intolerance is a form of egotism, and to condemn egotism intolerantly is to share it.
— *Santayana*

The closed mind, if closed long enough, can be opened by nothing short of dynamite.
— *Gerald W. Johnson*

Intolerance is a matter of being down on something you are not up on.

A bigot always surprises you by the many things he doesn't learn from experience.

The intolerant person always seems to be positive in the negative.

INTOXICATION

Alcohol, taken in sufficient quantities, produces all the effects of intoxication. — *Oscar Wilde*

I never worry about being driven to drink; I just worry about being driven home.
— *W. C. Fields*

No man is smart enough to be funny when he is drunk.
— *Ed Howe*

I know some people who are constantly drunk on books as other men are drunk on whiskey or religion. — *Mencken*

People can't tell us apart, we stagger so much alike.
— *Finley Peter Dunne*

I've been asked if I ever get the d.t.s; I don't know; it's hard to tell where Hollywood ends and the d.t.s begin. — *W. C. Fields*

I always know when a man is drunk, even when I'm drunk myself. — *Norman Douglas*

A drunkard in the gutter is exactly where he ought to be.
— *William Graham Sumner*

It is only the man who is drunk who ever volunteers the information that he is sober.

When drunk, men often say sensible things which sound foolish to them when sober.

Before marriage, he's intoxicated by her beauty; after marriage, he's a reformed drunkard.

Another odd thing about a drunkard is that he can approach you from several directions at once.

Many a woman never knows where her husband is after midnight—and neither does he.

Though a fifth will go into three with none left over, there may be one to carry.

The man who is tight in many places soon finds himself in many tight places.

Few people can stand up as well after they have been drinking sitting down as they can sit after drinking standing up.

As soon as some men finish a quart, they start a quartet.

If he's rich, they call him a playboy; if he's poor, they call him a drunk.

Some people have a veneer that comes off easily with a little alcohol.

The man who claims he knows his capacity for alcohol, usually gets drunk before he reaches it.

INTRODUCTION

The best thing to do when you meet an irresistible talker is to introduce him to an immovable bore.

The person who is always finding fault never seems to have been introduced to himself.

The most common family name in America is Houyhnhnm; you are introduced to them everywhere.

We would all need introductions if we could see ourselves as others see us.

INTUITION

A woman uses her intelligence to find reasons to support her intuition. — Chesterton

If a woman's intuition is so reliable, why does she have to ask so many questions?

Intuition is what enables a wife who knows less than her husband, to understand more.

Feminine intuition operates more on the instant than on the instinct.

A woman's intuition may not be scientific, but it's the best of all lie detectors.

In some women, intuition is like a sixth sense; in others, a sick sense.

An ounce of intuition is worth a pound of tuition.

A woman's intuition always seems to work at its worst when she's driving a car.

Intuition is a suspicious instinct that makes a woman distrust the man she trusts.

Feminine intuition is what enables a woman to guess wrong more often than a man.

A woman's intuition enables her to guess everything but the truth, and to discover everything but the facts.

Intuition is what leads a woman to contradict her husband before he says anything.

A woman's intuition is an instinct that helps her jump at once to the wrong conclusion.

With feminine intuition the presence of suspicion makes up for the absence of facts.

Intuition is a sixth sense possessed by people who show no sign of the other five.

A woman's intuition tells her in a flash that she is right, especially when she is wrong.

Intuition is what enables a woman to size up a situation in a flash of misunderstanding.

To a woman, an ounce of eavesdropping is worth a pound of intuition.

A woman's intuition is uncanny: it enables her to tell that her husband is lying, even when he is telling the truth.

Feminine intuition is nothing more than a wife's ability to read between the lies.

INVENTION

People think of the inventor as a screwball, but no one asks the inventor what he thinks of other people.   *— Charles F. Kettering*

The universe is full of magical things patiently waiting for our wits to grow sharper.
     — Eden Phillpotts

I can forgive Alfred Nobel for having invented dynamite, but only a fiend in human form could have invented the Nobel Prize.   *— Bernard Shaw*

The printing press and gunpowder were invented at the same time, and it's a question which has done more for the human race.   *— Finley Peter Dunne*

The greatest invention of the nineteenth century was the invention of the method of invention.
     — A. N. Whitehead

We owe to the Middle Ages the two worst inventions of humanity—gunpowder and romantic love.   *— André Maurois*

What this country needs is less inventions, and more mechanics to service those we already have.

Necessity is the mother of invention, and she certainly has some queer children.

An inventor is a man who prefers to get ahead by monkeying rather than aping.

If necessity is the mother of invention, how do all the unnecessary gadgets get invented?

A man in love always acts as if he invented it.

Necessity may have been the mother of invention, but today invention is the mother of necessities.

The road to war is paved with good inventions.

Necessity is the mother of invention, and reward is its father.

Fortunately the wheel was invented before the car, otherwise the scraping noise would be terrible.

If necessity is the mother of invention, she must be worried about having so many children that won't work.

INVESTIGATION

The four branches of government are: the executive, the legislative, the judicial, and the investigative.

A small business is one that has never been investigated by a congressional committee.

INVESTMENT

The principal interest of an investor should be the principal and not the interest.

Too bad you can't invest in taxes—they are the only thing sure to go up.

An investor should be more interested in the return of his money than in the return on his money.

The patient man realizes a profit on his investment whereas the only thing the impatient man realizes is his mistake.

Marriage is an investment, with the mother-in-law putting her two cents in.

When someone tries to get you to invest money in a good buy, make him spell out the term.

With some people you spend an evening, with others you invest it.

The wise investor in stocks or mutual funds always seeks outcome rather than income.

INVITATION

When a woman refuses an invitation by saying that acceptance would be an imposition, that settles it—she is getting ready to accept.
                    —Ed Howe

The only man who is really free is the one who can turn down an invitation to dinner without giving any excuse.
                    —Jules Renard

Nothing is more irritating than not being invited to a party you wouldn't be caught dead at.
                    —Bill Vaughan

Some people are never invited out more than once because they don't accept invitations; others because they do.

Marriages start out in disappointment: more people are invited to the church than to the reception.

Virtue is its own reward: the man who says good things is invited out more often than the man who does good things.

A fool and his money are invited places.

Many a party is given for the pleasure of not inviting someone.

If you must invite a chatterbox, try to dilute her with company.

All things come to him who waits, including an invitation to his girl friend's wedding.

IQ

The IQ is often less important in education than the *I Will*.

Don't let a woman's conversation mislead you: there may be more to her than meets the IQ.

Your IQ shows you are not what you think you are, but what you think, you are.

Watching most television programs makes you wish you had a lower IQ.

Some men never know when they've had enough to drink; others stop when they've reached their intelligent quota.

IRISH

The Irish are a fair people— they never speak well of one another.   — *Samuel Johnson*

Ireland is a country in which the probable never happens and the impossible always does.
— *John P. Mahaffey*

I believe that I am the only Irishman who has ever been in the National Gallery of Ireland, except the officials.
— *Bernard Shaw*

I am allergic to all Irish wit, charm and humor not provided by myself.   — *Denis W. Brogan*

There is nothing wrong with Ireland except that it is Irish, and there is nothing wrong with England except that it is not Irish.
— *Bernard Shaw*

God is good to the Irish, but no one else is, not even the Irish.
— *Austin O'Malley*

I showed my appreciation of my native land in the usual Irish way by getting out of it as soon as I possibly could.
— *Bernard Shaw*

An Irishman is never at peace except when he is fighting.

IRONY

When a cynic marries, it is his ironic fate to be henpecked.
— *Kierkegaard*

One of my old formulas is to be an enthusiast in the front part of your heart and ironical in the back.   — *Justice O. W. Holmes*

Another of life's ironies is that it creates so many more poor nephews than rich uncles.

The irony of fate is that by the time you can afford the steaks, you haven't the teeth to chew them.

Life usually gives a man money to burn after the fire has gone out.

The irony of life is that by the time your ship comes in, you're too old to enjoy the cruise.

When you buy a suit with two pairs of pants, and then burn a hole in the coat—that's life.

ITALY

Italians go to ruin usually in three ways: women, gambling and farming—my family chose the slowest one. —*Pope John XXIII*

In Italy, the whole country is a theater, and the worst actors are on the stage.

—*Bernard Shaw*

JAYWALKER

A jaywalker is one who reaches the obituary column before he reaches the other side of the street.

When a jaywalker sends his children through college, it's usually on the proceeds of his life insurance.

A jaywalker is often prone to be careless, and when he is careless, he is often prone.

Life is what you make it, but for the jaywalker it's if he makes it.

A jaywalker is usually covered by social security, but seldom receives its retirement benefits.

Another man who always dies with his boots on is the jaywalker.

For that rundown feeling, try jaywalking.

A jaywalker is an impatient pedestrian on his way to become a patient.

One of the best methods to prevent the oncome of old age is jaywalking.

A jaywalker is a man on his way to become a statistic.

The best thing a jaywalker can hope for is to be injured only slightly.

A jaywalker is a foolhardy individual who prefers to die without the aid of a doctor.

A jaywalker seldom looks where he's going, probably because he's in an ambulance.

The only hazard motorists have never been able to eliminate is the jaywalker.

Let the jaywalker beware: a car is now within the reach of every man.

The jaywalker may be wrong, but he doesn't deserve a death sentence.

Another person who deserves to get what's coming to him is the jaywalker.

The jaywalker who is not in good running condition should watch out for the car that is.

The advantage of a one-way street is that the jaywalker knows from which direction he is going to be knocked down.

A jaywalker can always choose what street to rush across, but not what hospital to be rushed to.

What a jaywalker needs these days more than laws is wings, and what is more, he often gets them.

The jaywalker never has the right of way, except when he's in the ambulance.

Every now and then a jaywalker makes a mistake and crosses with the green light.

JAZZ

There are just two kinds of jazz: good and bad.
— *Eddie Condon*

Jazz tickles your muscles, symphonies stretch your soul.
— *Paul Whiteman*

Jazz is so syncopated, you can't always tell what classical composer it was stolen from.

There's only one good kind of jazz player—the one who knows when to quit.

If music is the language of the soul, jazz must be the curse words.

Modern jazz may be here to stay, but it can never replace the old-fashioned earache.

JEALOUSY

The way to hold a husband is to keep him a little jealous; the way to lose him is to keep him a little more jealous. — *Mencken*

Jealousy is always born with love, but doesn't always die with it. — *La Rochefoucauld*

To be jealous is to love people as if you hated them.

The man who is stuck on himself seldom has any cause for jealousy.

The jealous woman who feels she knows her husband like a book always tries to keep him out of circulation.

A wife is seldom interested in what her husband is saying unless he's saying it to another woman.

Jealousy is the blister on the heel of matrimony.

A little jealousy now and then, improves the marriage of many men.

Why does the man who hasn't kissed his wife in years, resent the man who does?

Next to the atom bomb, the greatest explosion is set off by an old flame.

JEWELRY

Kissing your hand may make you feel very, very good, but a diamond bracelet lasts forever.
— *Anita Loos*

Some women wear so much jewelry, it's hard to tell whether they belong to the mineral or animal kingdom.

Jewelers hate to see women spend so much of their money on fleeting things like food and drink.

It takes all the fun out of a bracelet if you have to buy it yourself.

An African with a ring in her nose is a savage, but an American with a pearl in her ear is civilized.

A woman sometimes buys jewelry to satisfy a need, but more often to gratify a greed.

JILT

It's comparatively easy to leave a woman, but it's very hard to be left by one. — *Thackeray*

If you're rejected by one woman, don't try to win another —quit while you're ahead.

It is hard for a man to put out of his mind the woman who has put him out of her mind.

JOB

I don't want any fellow who has a job to work for me; what I want is a fellow whom a job has. — *Charles F. Kettering*

To the modern girl a job is only a bridge of sighs between school and marriage.
— *Fannie Hurst*

The difference between a job and a career is the difference between 40 and 60 hours a week.
— *Robert Frost*

Whenever you are asked if you can do a job, tell 'em, "Certainly, I can!"—and get busy and find out how to do it.
— *Theodore Roosevelt*

If a girl can't get a good job, she should get a husband with a good job.

Times have changed: in the old days a job was the first thing you went steady with.

The softer the job, the harder it is to get.

There are many kinds of jobs where girls can meet men, but only the air hostess meets them when they're strapped down.

The best man for the job is often a woman.

When poverty comes in at the door, love should go out and get a job.

Early to bed and early to rise, especially for those who can't get a job with better hours.

Too many people quit looking for work when they find a job.

Many a man holds both day and night jobs so he can drive from one to the other in a more expensive car.

Two can live as cheaply as one —if they both have good jobs.

When a man picks a soft job, he usually expects to lie down on it later.

Never send a boy to do a man's job—send a woman.

JOHNSON, SAMUEL

I could never make up my mind whether Boswell did not invent Johnson. — *Bernard Shaw*

If Dr. Johnson were to make little fishes talk, they would talk like whales. — *Oliver Goldsmith*

It is pleasanter to read Boswell's record of the conversations than it ever was to listen to Dr. Johnson. — *Somerset Maugham*

During the Samuel Johnson days they had big men enjoying small talk; today we have small men enjoying big talk.
— *Fred Allen*

Sam Johnson is hardly a name for a great writer.
— *Bernard Shaw*

JOKE

From the silence which prevails, I conclude he has been making a joke.
— *Richard Brinsley Sheridan*

Whenever my great command of the sublime threatens to induce solemnity of mind in my audience, I at once introduce a joke.
— *Bernard Shaw*

Times change: the farmer's daughter now tells jokes about the traveling salesman.
— *Carey Williams*

You can read philosophy by yourself if you want to, but you must share a joke with someone else. — *Robert Louis Stevenson*

They smiled at the joke not because they were amused, but because they wished to show respect for old age.
— *Strickland Gillilan*

Funny stories run riot in our social life, and often turn a pleasant dinner into an agonized competition. — *Stephen Leacock*

When my jokes are explained to her, and she has leisure to reflect upon them, she laughs very heartily. — *Sydney Smith*

There are only a few original jokes, and most of them are in Congress. — *Will Rogers*

If you've heard this story before, don't stop me, because I'd like to hear it again.
— *Groucho Marx*

Forgive, O Lord, my little jokes on Thee, and I'll forgive Thy great big joke on me.
— *Robert Frost*

The jest dulls its point when he who tells it is the first to laugh. — *Schiller*

Too many a word spoken in jest spoils the joke.

The trouble with telling a good story is that it is sure to remind some listener of a poor one.

Some people remember jokes, others dismember them.

The same old joke then and now is seldom relished by one's frau.

There are only seven original jokes, the first of which is "I am through with girls forever."

The average man is proof enough that a woman can take a joke.

When you laugh at the boss's joke, it doesn't prove you have a sense of humor, but it does prove you have sense.

Laugh and the world laughs with you, unless you laugh at your own joke.

The man who has a favorite joke should be required by law to keep a list of the people he has already told it to.

To be okay and not passé, a joke today must be risqué.

When telling a joke, make it short; otherwise you give the listener time to think of one to tell you.

The good die young, but not if they are jokes.

When a husband's jokes seem funny to his wife, it's a sign she's had too much to drink.

There's only one bore more tiresome than the man who tells old jokes, and that's the one who tells original ones.

He who laughs last probably intended to tell the same joke himself.

If Adam came back to earth, the only thing he would recognize would be the jokes.

JONAH

It required effort once for the whale to swallow Jonah, and it requires effort now to swallow the story.

Jonah proved that you can't keep a good man down.

When you get cheated by a shark, think of Jonah: he was completely taken in by a whale.

"That's a clear case of prophet and loss," as the sailors said when they tossed Jonah overboard.

JOURNALISM

If a newspaper prints a sex crime, it's smut, but when the New York Times prints it, it's a sociological study.
— Adolph S. Ochs

Journalists do not live by words alone, although sometimes they have to eat them.
— Adlai Stevenson

Half my lifetime I have earned my living by selling words, and I hope thoughts.
— Winston Churchill

Journalism is unreadable, and literature is unread. — Oscar Wilde

Many a good newspaper story has been ruined by oververification.
— James Gordon Bennett

Journalism is now conducted like any other business—as sensibly as the office of any moderately fraudulent financier.
— Chesterton

Journalism is the ability to meet the challenge of filling space.
— Rebecca West

Trying to determine what is going on in the world by reading the newspapers is like trying to tell time by watching the second hand of a clock. — Ben Hecht

Journalism consists in buying white paper at two cents a pound and selling it at ten cents a pound. — Charles A. Dana

If Christ came back to earth now he would not attack the high priests, but the low journalists.
— *Kierkegaard*

Journalism is a profession whose idea of news is to devote several pages to sports and only one paragraph to education.

JUDGE

It is impossible to obtain absolute unbiased judges without appointing Hottentots who can neither read nor write. — *Mencken*

A judge is an official who administers justice in a few words but many sentences.

All judges judge, but not all have judgment.

Judges without conviction are the most generous in handing it out.

A judge is a man who ends a sentence with a sentence.

JUDGMENT

We should all be obliged to appear before a board every five years, and justify our existence to its satisfaction on pain of liquidation. — *Bernard Shaw*

The very last thing that men think they've got the most of, they've got the least of, and that is judgment. — *Josh Billings*

Next to good judgment, diamonds and pearls are the rarest things in the world. — *La Bruyère*

Good judgment comes from experience, and experience comes from bad judgment.

Never judge women or gifts by what they are wrapped up in.

A man is judged by his deeds, a woman by her misdeeds.

Never judge by appearances, but always remember that you will be judged by them.

Any man can prove he has good judgment by saying you have.

A person's better judgment never tells him anything until after he's gone and made a fool of himself.

We judge others by their actions; we judge ourselves by our motives.

Never judge a man by his purse, but by his personality.

A good way to judge a man is by what he says, a better way is by what he does, and the best way is by what he gives.

A man is judged by his peers, a critic by his cheers, jeers and sneers.

The snap judgments of impulsive people are easily unfastened.

The best way to prove that you have good judgment is by not relying upon it alone.

Some people seem to be waiting for Judgment Day before they'll start using it.

Don't judge a man by what he stands for, but by what he stands up for.

The man who questions his wife's judgment should never forget whom she married.

JUNE

June is the month when, if you're not wedding, you're weeding.

June is the month when the kids get out of school and into your hair.

June is the month of brides: the other eleven are devoted to divorcees.

JURY

A jury too often has at least one member who is more ready to hang the panel than the traitor. — *Lincoln*

Jury: a group of twelve men who, having lied to the judge about their hearing, health and business engagements, have failed to fool him. — *Mencken*

When everybody acquires an education how are you going to pick a jury?

Every woman juror tries conscientiously to decide the case according to the law and the evidence—and her intuition.

The prouder a man is of his citizenship, the more he dodges jury duty.

Few men like to serve on a jury, except in a bathing beauty contest.

Many are called but few are chosen—for a jury.

Every American believes in trial by jury—until he is called to serve on one.

Most women dislike jury duty because it's all listening.

JUSTICE

Justice is justice though it's always delayed and finally done only by mistake. — *Bernard Shaw*

Children are innocent and love justice, while most adults are wicked and prefer mercy.

— *Chesterton*

Justice is what takes a man's part when injustice would take his all.

Justice usually triumphs in spite of all the publicity issued to support it.

If there really was such a thing as justice, it would bring us our just rewards, and bring our neighbor his just deserts.

Justice is like any other woman: she's always worrying about what the scales are going to show.

All things come to him who waits—even justice.

If you always please to do what is just, you will not always do just what you please.

Only fools and knaves are likely to get justice, probably because they are the only ones ever tried by a court and jury of their peers.

JUVENILE DELINQUENCY

When your neighbor's child goes wrong, he's a juvenile delinquent; when yours does, he's just passing through a phase.

A juvenile delinquent is a youngster who has been given a free hand, but not in the proper place.

If life were lived backward from old age to youth, there would be much more juvenile delinquency.

A juvenile delinquent is a juvenile who should have been punished more, or a delinquent who should have been punished less.

A juvenile delinquent sometimes tries to do right, but only because he thinks it is wrong.

Time cures everything: give a juvenile delinquent enough time, and the delinquent will no longer be a juvenile.

Many a son who is sweet during infancy starts to ferment during childhood.

The solution to the problem of juvenile delinquency lies in taking juveniles off the streets at night— and also their parents.

The juvenile delinquent often takes after his parents in many disrespects.

Adults always seem to blame juvenile delinquency on everything but heredity.

A juvenile delinquent is merely misguided if you're the parent, but really murderous if you're the victim.

Juvenile delinquency often starts in the high chair and ends in the electric chair.

Every juvenile delinquent feels insecure, but not half as insecure as the rest of his neighborhood.

Juvenile delinquency is sometimes a case of adolescents acting like their parents, but more often reacting to them.

An oldtimer is one who remembers when a juvenile delinquent was a youngster returning from the woodshed.

A juvenile delinquent is a minor who creates a major problem.

Some youngsters are so retarded, they don't become juvenile delinquents until they're in their twenties.

Parents of delinquent juveniles never seem to know why their children grew up to be juvenile delinquents.

A juvenile delinquent is a youngster who is very good at being no good.

The age of delinquency begins when youngsters start doing what their parents are doing.

The problem of juvenile delinquency would be less of a problem if parents devoted more time to their children's problems.

Juvenile delinquency is created by a society that ties up its dogs but lets its children run around loose.

KANGAROO

God must have made some parts of creation for sheer fun—how else would you account for the kangaroo?   — *Chesterton*

The largest species of grasshopper known to man is the kangaroo.

The only female that knows everything she has in her bag without looking is a kangaroo.

KEY

Never judge a man by the number of keys on his key ring.

The sensible thing would be to provide opportunity with a door key.

The key to a woman's heart often hangs on a ring.

Because hard work is the key to success, many men prefer to pick the lock.

Strange how the key to a girl's heart so often fits a Cadillac too.

KILL

Some men are alive simply because it is against the law to kill them.   — *Ed Howe*

Man has always been more successful in doing away with his fellow man than in getting rid of rats, flies and mosquitoes.

If drinking kills people, and smoking kills people, and gluttony kills people, what kills all those people who live right?

When man kills more animals than men, we call it hunting; when man kills more men than animals, we call it war.

In a civilized nation you will always find societies for the humane killing of animals, but not for the humane killing of people.

KINDNESS

I have found men more kind than I expected, and less just.
    — *Samuel Johnson*

One can always be kind to people about whom one cares nothing.   — *Oscar Wilde*

When you go in search of the milk of human kindness, don't take along a pail.

Some men are so kind to their wives, they are more like neighbors than husbands.

The kindness planned for tomorrow doesn't count today.

The milk of human kindness is sometimes skimmed, sometimes condensed, but most often evaporated.

KING

My subjects and I have come to an agreement: they may say

what they please, and I may do
what I please.
                    — *Frederick the Great*

The right kind of monarchy is
one where everybody goes about
with the permanent conviction
that the king can do no wrong.
                    — *Chesterton*

If my ancestors were not reg-
icides, it was not because they
weren't ready and willing—only a
king never came their way.
                    — *Finley Peter Dunne*

KISS

Where words cease, music begins, and where music ceases,
kissing begins. — *Norman Douglas*

A kiss can be a comma, a question mark or an exclamation
point.   — *Mistinguette*

I am in favor of preserving the
French habit of kissing ladies'
hands—after all, one must start
somewhere.   — *Sacha Guitry*

Few men know how to kiss
well; fortunately, I've always had
time to teach them.
                    — *Mae West*

A kiss is an operation, cunningly devised, for the mutual
stoppage of speech at a moment
when words are utterly superfluous.   — *Oliver Herford*

The first kiss is stolen by the
man; the last is begged by the
woman.   — *Mencken*

Formerly a kiss used to follow
a nice evening, but nowadays a
nice evening follows a kiss.

When a man tells you your
kisses are intoxicating, watch out:
he is probably mixing his drinks.

The honeymoon is over when
the kiss that was a temptation becomes an obligation.

If you are in doubt whether to
kiss a pretty girl or not, give her
the benefit of the doubt.

Don't wait to know her better
to kiss her; kiss her, and you'll
know her better.

Any man who can drive safely
while kissing a pretty girl, is simply not giving the kiss the attention it deserves.

Every time some men plant a
kiss they expect to reap a harvest.

The girl who shuts her eyes
when she is being kissed, keeps
them open when some other girl
is.

At twenty, a kiss is an experiment, at forty a sentiment, and
after that a compliment.

If your wife kisses you when
you get home, is it affection or
inspection?

A kiss that speaks volumes is
seldom a first edition.

Lots of things have been started
by kisses, especially young things.

The man who kisses every girl
he meets gets a lot of rebuffs—
also a lot of kisses.

A kiss is not enough for one,
just enough for two, and too
much for three.

It's a good idea to kiss the children good night, if you don't mind waiting up for them.

Some girls blush when they are kissed, and some swear; but the worst are those who laugh.

The trouble with girls who are highbrows is that they would rather be osculated than kissed.

KITCHEN

Give me a kitchen full of utensils and a stock of unprepared food, and I would starve.
— *Montaigne*

My one culinary talent lies in thinking up new and palatable ways of opening tin cans.
— *Will Cuppy*

Some women will go anywhere for dinner, except to the kitchen.

In one respect the old-fashioned kitchens were superior to the modern ones—they had old-fashioned housewives in them.

Another way to get your wife to spend more time in the kitchen is to put an extension phone there.

There's nothing like a wife's know-how in the kitchen, or a husband's know-where.

In some homes men congregate in the kitchen because it is the only place they can get away from the women.

No home is complete without a man, but every kitchen is.

Half the accidents happen in the kitchen, and usually the husband has to eat them.

Nowadays less things are thought out in the kitchen than thawed out.

A kitchen is the place where tea is kept in a cocoa jar labeled COFFEE.

KITTENISH

The kittenish woman is usually about 50, looks like 40, acts like 30, and talks like 20.

There's no one so kittenish as the middle-aged woman who pretends to be young by acting childish.

A kittenish woman tries to act in the present as she used to feel in the past.

Even if a kittenish woman were twice as young as she tries to be, she wouldn't be half as young as she thinks she is.

Nothing is so irritating as to come home feeling dog tired, only to find your wife acting kittenish.

A kittenish woman never looks younger than she is, but always acts younger than she looks.

KLEPTOMANIAC

Kleptomania is a mental illness whose victim is always taking something for it.

A kleptomaniac is a woman with a weakness for shoplifting but with a constitution of steal.

A shoplifter seems to think that the best things in life are free.

A kleptomaniac is a woman who seizes a good thing when she sees it.

KNEE

In the good old days when a man courted a girl he was on his knees; nowadays she's on his.

The man who remembers what he learned at his mother's knee, was probably bent over it.

When a man is on his knees proposing to a girl, he may as well say his prayers.

The trouble with many an adolescent is that he learned little at his mother's knee, and even less across his father's.

A youngster starts out in life learning things at his mother's knee, especially how to watch out for her cigarette ashes.

KNOT

Children and lunatics cut the Gordian knot which the poet spends his life trying to untie.
— *Jean Cocteau*

To some husbands, the marriage tie is simply a forget-me-knot.

When a woman becomes untidy, the marriage knot becomes untied.

It takes an extraordinary mastery of language to describe any kind of knot without using your hands.

Marriage isn't merely a knot— it's a knot on a noose.

When the marriage knot becomes untied, it's the children who are left at loose ends.

KNOW-IT-ALL

There are scores of thousands of human insects who are ready at a moment's notice to reveal the will of God on every possible subject.
— *Bernard Shaw*

What hindered Thomas Aquinas but the delusion that he knew everything without observing anything! — *Houston S. Chamberlain*

A know-it-all is a man who never opens his mouth without subtracting from the sum of human knowledge.

A word to the wise is sufficient, but not to the wiseacre.

When two know-it-alls get together, why do they always disagree?

Knowledge is power, but not for the man who knows it all.

A know-it-all is a man whose wide range of information is always based on a narrow acquaintance with facts.

The man who knows it all doesn't because he doesn't know what others think of him.

What a man knows is always less than what he doesn't know, unless he's a know-it-all.

Some men know all the answers, but no man knows all the questions.

The know-it-all seldom meets his intellectual equal, and never his superior.

A wiseacre thinks he knows it all until some woman comes along and begins to educate him.

The only person who knows less about more things than a smart aleck is the know-it-all.

The man who thinks he knows everything always irritates those of us who do.

The know-it-all never learns anything because he knows too much already.

A know-it-all knows everything except one thing: he doesn't know how much he doesn't know.

A know-it-all is always obnoxious, especially when he's right.

You can always tell a know-it-all: he knows the answer even before he understands the question.

KNOWLEDGE

What man knows is everywhere at war with what he wants.
— *Joseph Wood Krutch*

It is better to know nothing than to know what ain't so.
— *Josh Billings*

It is a great nuisance that knowledge can only be acquired by hard work.
— *Somerset Maugham*

Knowledge is power, but only if a man knows what facts not to bother about.   — *Robert Lynd*

Man's business here is to know for the sake of living, not to live for the sake of knowing.
— *Frederic Harrison*

We are here and it is now: further than that all human knowledge is moonshine.   — *Mencken*

No person ever knew so much that was so little to the purpose as Macaulay.   — *Mencken*

I am not young enough to know everything.
— *James M. Barrie*

He not only overflowed with learning, but stood in the slop.
— *Sydney Smith*

A little knowledge is a dangerous thing, but we must take that risk because a little is as much as our biggest heads can hold.
— *Bernard Shaw*

Knowledge is a polite word for dead but not buried imagination.
— *E. E. Cummings*

The world is full of ignorant people who don't know what you have just found out.

It is not how much we know that counts, but how much we know than nobody else knows.

A little learning is a dangerous thing—almost as dangerous as a lot of ignorance.

You don't have to be listed in *Who's Who* to know what's what.

No one knows as much at eighty as he thinks he knows at eighteen.

Knowledge doesn't pay—it's what you do with your knowledge that pays.

The man who knows how will always have a job; the man who knows why will always be his boss.

A little learning is a dangerous thing, but only to the person who mistakes it for a lot.

An intelligent man knows everything, a shrewd man knows everyone.

It is not enough to know what not to say; it is also necessary to know how and when not to say it.

Many a person has a lot of knowledge, but doesn't let it go to his head.

The wise man knows a little, but the wiseacre knows it all.

Learning without wisdom is like a load of books on an ass's back.

There is very little difference between the man who knows it all and the man who knows nothing.

Some people know a lot more when you try to tell them something than when you ask them something.

Life is an eternal struggle where know-how is good, know-when is better, and know-whom is best.

Why is it that the man who knows how to do everything, never does?

A little learning is a dangerous thing, but not when the other fellow doesn't know any more than you do.

Everybody knows more than somebody, but nobody knows more than everybody.

A wise man acquires knowledge even from those who have none themselves.

Beware of the man who knows too much, especially if it happens to be yourself.

A little knowledge is a dangerous thing, especially when a child brings home a poor report card.

LABOR AND MANAGEMENT

Collective bargaining is a form of negotiation where management bargains and labor tries to collect.

Management believes that constant wage increases should be a capital offense.

Capital and labor should be one, but which one?

Matrimony is another union whose members always have trouble with management.

LABORSAVER

Of all laborsaving devices in the home, there's nothing like a wife.

Procrastination is the greatest laborsaving device ever invented.

The virtue of a laborsaving device is that it gives you more time so you can worry about more things.

Many a man labors at two jobs in order to pay for the laborsaving appliances at home.

Of all the laborsaving devices available in gardening, there's nothing that beats a bad back.

Civilization creates so many laborsaving devices that man has to resort to an exercising device to keep him physically fit.

The best laborsaving device for women will always be a generous husband with lots of money.

LABOR UNION

God needed only six days to create the world—but then, that was before labor unions.

In union there is strength, and in unions even more strength.

Featherbedding is based on the principle that, if it takes one man to do a job in one hour, it should take two men two hours.

A labor union believes that the laborer is worthy of his hire, and the higher the better.

Featherbedding is the practice of doing less, having more time to do it in, and getting more pay for not doing it.

The state of the Union largely depends on the state of the unions.

LADDER

Many a man gets to the top of the ladder, and then finds out it has been leaning against the wrong wall.

Fortune's ladder has no top: no man ever stopped climbing for want of another rung.

Many a wife has helped her husband to the top of the ladder, and then decided the picture would look better on the opposite wall.

The man who is afraid to walk under a ladder will probably never get to the top of it.

When a man is climbing the ladder of success, it is probably steadied by a woman who believes in him.

LADY

In the theater a hero is one who believes that all women are ladies; a villain, one who believes that all ladies are women.
— *George Jean Nathan*

A lady is nothing very specific: one man's lady is another man's woman; sometimes, one man's lady is another man's wife.
— *Russell Lynes*

Your dress should be tight enough to show you're a woman, and loose enough to show you're a lady.

A lady is a woman with a good memory: she always remembers others, yet never forgets herself.

Abigail Adams, the wife of John Adams, was the first second lady of the land before she became the second first lady.

LAKE

It's a crime to catch a fish in some lakes, and a miracle in others.

A fisherman will often spend hours on a lake doing nothing because his wife won't let him do it at home.

LANDLORD

A landlord is a man whose promises are no better than his premises.

The average landlord thinks children are all right in their place, but not in his place.

A landlord is without honor even in his own building.

Tenants often take a holiday, but rent never does, which is one reason why the landlord is richer than his tenant.

The average landlord has a heart as big as his kitchenette.

An oldtimer is one who remembers when you got the land-lord to fix anything by just threatening to move.

LANGUAGE

Colleges which teach the dead languages as if they were buried, teach the living ones as if they were dead. — *Frank Moore Colby*

America is the only country left where we teach languages so that no pupil can speak them. — *John Erskine*

I have often wished that there were a language in which it would be impossible to tell a lie. — *G. C. Lichtenberg*

Because everyone uses language to talk, everyone thinks he can talk about language. — *Goethe*

A gifted person ought to learn English (barring spelling and pronouncing) in thirty hours, French in thirty days, and German in thirty years. — *Mark Twain*

There's only one language that no one speaks like a native— Esperanto.

Next to sex, language is the most important form of intercourse practiced by man.

Some people use language to express thought, some to conceal thought, but most use it to replace thought.

There are between two thousand and three thousand languages spoken throughout the world, not including that spoken by teen-agers.

Language is supposed to be a vehicle of thought, but all too often it is just an empty car full of gas.

The most famous dead languages are Latin, Greek and the King's English.

No one has a better command of the language than the man who knows just when to talk and when to shut up.

Man is the only animal that hasn't an international language.

LAP

If a dog jumps up into your lap, it is because he is fond of you; if a cat does, it is because your lap is warmer.
— *A. N. Whitehead*

The trouble with the lap of luxury is that it's usually covered up by a paunch.

The only ambition a napkin has is to get off a diner's lap and play on the floor.

A child reared in the lap of luxury is seldom turned over on it.

Many a girl covers more than one lap in the race to the altar.

The optimist says we are living in the lap of luxury, while the pessimist fears it may be the last lap.

There are some girls who have been on everybody's lap except their own.

The secretary who works for a rich boss often finds herself in the lap of luxury.

LAS VEGAS

Las Vegas is a popular resort where you find the best entertainers and the worst gamblers.

Las Vegas is the proof that yesterday's winning of the West was easier than today's winning in the West.

Many a man who goes to Las Vegas to get away from it all soon finds that Las Vegas gets it all away from him.

Las Vegas is the place where one triumph leads to another, and you soon find yourself hopelessly in debt.

There's safety in numbers, except when you're in Las Vegas.

Las Vegas is a resort whose two chief sources of income are seven and eleven.

LATE

People who are late are often so much jollier than the people who have to wait for them.
— *E. V. Lucas*

Man came first, and woman has been late ever since.

Pity the poor male: from eight to eighty he always has to explain to some woman why he didn't come home earlier.

Some women are absolutely reliable: you can always depend

upon their being just about an hour late.

Of all things that are better late than never, going to bed ranks first.

With men punctuality is a business, with women a past-time.

When a married man gets home late at night he doesn't know what he is letting himself in for.

Timetables are important in traveling: without them you'd never know how late trains and planes are.

To a night owl, it's always better late than never.

Late hours are bad for one, but good for two.

The time, the place, and the girl are seldom found together because the girl is usually an hour late.

If your wife no longer cares how late you come home, it's later than you think.

The latest thing in clothes is usually the woman you're waiting for.

The widow feels superior to the spinster because even a husband is better *late* than never.

A man is judged by the company he keeps, a woman by how late she keeps company.

Bachelors believe two things never come too late—death and marriage.

The latest way to dress for a party is a woman's.

In business, better late than never; in marriage, better never than late.

Why can't a woman get ready on time?—she gets everything else that way.

A statistician is a man who can estimate exactly how late his wife is going to be.

LATIN AND GREEK

Greek scholars are privileged men: few of them know Greek, and none of them know anything else.   — *Bernard Shaw*

Roman literature is Greek literature written in Latin.
          — *Treitschke*

Of all intellectual snobs, the worst is the woman who writes her shopping list in Latin.

Latin and Greek are not dead languages—they are immortal languages.

To many a high school student the greatest accomplishment of the ancient Romans was their ability to speak Latin.

LAUGHTER

If you don't learn to laugh at trouble, you won't have anything to laugh at when you're old.
          — *Ed Howe*

You grow up the day you have your first real laugh—at yourself.
          — *Ethel Barrymore*

Since I have had the full use of my reason, nobody has ever heard me laugh.   —*Chesterfield*

People learn while they laugh, but very few of them know that they are learning.
— *Frank Moore Colby*

Only in this world do we laugh: in hell, it won't be possible; and in heaven, it won't be proper.
— *Jules Renard*

Men have been wise in different modes, but they have always laughed the same way.
— *Samuel Johnson*

The salvation of the world depends on the men whose laughter destroys the fool instead of encouraging him. — *Bernard Shaw*

The most thoroughly wasted of all days is that on which one has not laughed.   — *Chamfort*

The church to which I belong is where the oftener you laugh the better, because by laughter only can you destroy evil without malice.   — *Bernard Shaw*

We do not stop laughing because we grow old; we grow old because we stop laughing.

You might as well laugh at yourself once in a while—everyone else does.

Another of life's unsolved mysteries is what youngsters are always giggling about.

Half the world doesn't see how the other half can see anything funny in what it laughs at.

It's better to be laughed at for not being married than to be unable to laugh because you are.

A laugh a day keeps the psychiatrist away.

In youth, it is most important to know when not to laugh; in age, when to.

An employee sometimes laughs at the boss's joke because he lacks a sense of humor, but more often because he lacks a sense of security.

Laugh and the world laughs with you; cry—and the world laughs harder.

The optimist laughs to forget; the pessimist forgets to laugh.

He who laughs last didn't get the joke at first.

Laugh a little more at your own troubles and a little less at your neighbors'.

The only medicine that needs no prescription, has no unpleasant taste, and costs no money is laughter.

Man is the only animal that laughs at himself, and he has plenty of reason to.

Laughter will never disappear from the face of the earth as long as women follow the latest fashions.

The man who laughs last is usually sitting behind a tall person in the theater.

Many people will laugh at the drop of a hat, especially if the man is still in it.

You can test a person's sense of humor by what he laughs at, and his sense of values by what he doesn't laugh at.

There's nothing so hollow as the laugh of the man who intended to tell the story himself.

The man who can laugh at himself never runs out of things he can laugh at.

He laughs best whose laugh lasts.

There's nothing that more thoroughly cures a girl of the giggles than to get married and raise a family.

LAUNDRY

Everything comes out in the wash, especially the buttons.

Marriage is the most expensive way for a man to get his laundry done free.

What this country needs is a washing machine with an attachment that will sew the buttons back on.

LAW

I care not who makes the laws of a nation if I can get out an injunction. — *Finley Peter Dunne*

American legal science is now on its own legs, and careth not a damn for either English precedent or ordinary common sense.
— *Mencken*

The best way to get a bad law repealed is to enforce it strictly.
— *Lincoln*

Laws are made to trouble people, and the more trouble they make, the longer they stay on the statute books.
— *Finley Peter Dunne*

You can't legislate intelligence and common sense into people.
— *Will Rogers*

I learned law so well, the day I graduated I sued the college, won the case, and got my tuition back.   — *Fred Allen*

In law, nothing is certain but the expense.   — *Samuel Butler*

Appeal: in law, to put the dice into the box for another throw.
— *Bierce*

Lawlessness in many modern matters seems to be the principal effect of law.   — *Chesterton*

It is much easier to write a good play than to make a good law, and there are not a hundred men in the world who can write a good play.   — *Bernard Shaw*

When the government puts teeth into a law, they are not always wisdom teeth.

Congress can pass laws to keep people from doing anything, except to prevent a man from making a fool of himself.

Necessity knows no law, and the man who practices law seldom knows necessity.

Everyone says our country has too many laws, yet everybody

knows of another law that ought to be passed.

In many a home the man's word is law, but it's one of those laws that's never enforced.

In the United States, Congress makes the laws, the Supreme Court interprets them, the President executes them, and the citizens disobey them.

Suppression is nine points of the law.

Ignorance of the law is no excuse, unless you can afford to hire a good lawyer.

In the old days there was one law for the rich and one for the poor: nowadays there are millions of laws for everyone.

Every time Congress makes a mistake, a new law is born.

Almost every law on the statute books is preceded by years of talk in the legislature, and followed by years of talk in the courts.

Possession is nine points of the law, and lawyers' fees are the other ninety-one points.

When better laws are made, Americans will break them.

The portion of the law usually found unconstitutional is the teeth.

LAWN

A good time to mow your lawn is when your neighbor's child is practicing on the piano.

If you want to enjoy your lawn more, think of your weeds as plants and your dandelions as flowers.

The boundary line between two properties is never so clean-cut as when your neighbor cuts his lawn.

Making two blades of grass grow where only one grew before is fine, provided they grow only half as high.

There's no better lawn than the one which shows a narrow path worn in the direction of the neighbors.

In the spring the suburbanite looks at his lawn and hopes that the plot will thicken.

Some neighbors are generous, while others allow you to use their lawn mower as long as you don't take it out of their garden.

You spend half your spare time making a lawn grow so fast that you have to spend the other half cutting it down.

Mowing a lawn is real hard work, especially when a man has to make a boy do it.

Some people take care of their lawns; others go in for a color scheme of green spots on a brown background.

Never mind about that mousetrap; just plant grass seed and see how quickly the world beats a path to your door.

A power mower is a small vehicle that gives the least mileage —only one yard to the gallon.

Many a man buys a lawn mower to keep the grass from growing under his neighbor's feet.

LAWSUIT

A lawsuit is a machine which you go into as a pig and come out of as a sausage. — *Bierce*

No man admits he is a physical wreck, except in a lawsuit for damages.

Truth ₊is stranger than fiction, especially in lawsuits.

Lawsuits are getting to be so costly as to make honesty the best policy.

It takes a lot of suits to keep a lawyer well dressed.

Never go to law: if you win you lose, and if you lose you're lost.

Just think of the endless litigation that will arise when the meek inherit the earth!

We will never know all the possibilities of argument until one lawyer is allowed to appear on both sides of the case.

Look before you leap—into litigation.

The way to win a lawsuit is to have a good case, a good lawyer, and good luck.

When an irresistible force meets an immovable body, there's usually a lawyer who will take the case.

It's better to take things into consideration than to take them into court.

Ignorance of the law prevents a lawyer from winning your case, but not from collecting his fee.

Circumstances alter cases, especially legal cases.

LAWYER

You cannot live without lawyers, and certainly you cannot die without them. — *Joseph H. Choate*

I used to be a lawyer, but now I am a reformed character.
— *Woodrow Wilson*

The minute you read something that you can't understand, you can almost be sure it was drawn up by a lawyer. — *Will Rogers*

I don't want a lawyer to tell me what I cannot do; I hire him to tell me how to do what I want to do. — *J. P. Morgan*

Lawyers, I suppose, were children once. — *Charles Lamb*

It is the trade of lawyers to question everything, yield nothing, and to talk by the hour.
— *Jefferson*

Lawyer: one who protects us against robberies by taking away the temptation. — *Mencken*

Lawyers make a living out of trying to figure out what other lawyers have written.
— *Will Rogers*

A lawyer is a man who prevents someone else from getting your money.

There are two kinds of lawyers: those who know the law, and those who know the judge.

A lawyer is a man who gets two people to strip for a fight, and then runs off with their clothes.

Some men inherit money, some earn it, and some are lawyers.

A law firm is successful when it has more clients than partners.

A lawyer is paid partly for what he knows, but mostly for what you don't.

If a young lawyer doesn't have clients, he doesn't eat; if he does have clients, he doesn't sleep.

Lawyers who take a keen interest in a case often take the principal too.

A small town that can't support one lawyer can always support two.

A lawyer is a man who profits by your experience.

When some couples get married, their lawyers live happily ever after.

Man's inhumanity to man makes countless thousands of lawyers.

Lawyers sometimes tell the truth—they will do anything to win a case.

Practice makes perfect, but with lawyers it is more likely to make them rich.

If there were no bad people, there would be no good lawyers.

Money talks, but big money doesn't—it hires a staff of lawyers.

The lawyer who has never yet lost a case, is probably just out of law school.

Honesty is the best policy, because good lawyers come high.

The doctors of law don't seem to be able to effect a cure.

Ignorance of the law excuses no man—from practicing it.

A lawyer's profession requires that when he reads a book, he should quote from it.

Lawyers help those who help themselves.

LAZY

He has decided to go to work until he can find something better.
— *Kin Hubbard*

Laziness is nothing more than the habit of resting before you get tired.   — *Jules Renard*

The lazier a man is, the more he is going to do tomorrow.

Man is by nature lazy, so God gave us children to make us get up early.

Lazy men are much maligned: they are perfectly willing to work provided it doesn't involve effort, exertion, labor or toil.

A goldbricker is a pest who knows best how to rest with zest.

Laziness travels so slowly, poverty soon overtakes it.

Many a man's ambition is to become the foreman so he can get paid for watching other people work.

A lazy man's wife is generally the power behind the drone.

Some men never go to work for a living until they have given everything else a fair trial.

An idler always finds it hard to start but easy to stop.

Every now and then one meets a man who is so lazy that he finds even loafing hard work.

Some men are lazy; others suffer from voluntary inertia.

A lazy man is always judged by what he doesn't.

If you have a tough job to do and want to find out the easiest way to do it, give it to a lazy man and watch him do it.

The trouble with the world is that laziness is seldom curable and never fatal.

Many men are too lazy to work, but some are even too lazy to fish.

The lazy man claims he is too heavy for light work and too light for heavy work.

When laziness attacks a woman, it always avoids her tongue.

The only time a lazy man ever succeeds is when he tries to do nothing.

LEADER

The nation will find it very hard to look up to the leaders who are keeping their ears to the ground.   — *Winston Churchill*

A wise statesman follows the people, especially if he is their leader.

Only one man in a thousand is a leader of men; the others are followers of women.

There are two kinds of leaders: those who are interested in the flock, and those who are interested in the fleece.

Nearly all born leaders of men are women.

LEAF

The man who said that work well done never needs doing over, has never raked leaves.

When turning over a new leaf, see that it is not a loose leaf.

Most of the leaves that are turned over on New Year's Eve start to fall before spring.

When raking the leaves in the fall, why are there so many thousands more than the trees bore in the summer?

"Half a leaf is better than none," as Eve said to Adam.

In the fall we all enjoy autumn leaves, especially when autumn leaves them on other people's lawns.

LEAP YEAR

Women have three years to hope in; the fourth, they leap into the open.   — *Samuel Hoffenstein*

Leap year is when February has a day that's even rarer than a day in June.

Every year is leap year for the pedestrian.

LEARN

I am always ready to learn, but I do not always like being taught.   — *Winston Churchill*

We should always continue to learn, but we should not always continue our education.
                    — *Montaigne*

A man learns to skate by staggering about making a fool of himself; indeed, he progresses in all things by making a fool of himself.   — *Bernard Shaw*

Never learn to do anything: if you don't learn, you'll always find someone else to do it for you.
                    — *Mark Twain*

I have learned a good deal from my own talk.
                    — *Thomas C. Haliburton*

Men never learn anything about women, but they have a lot of fun trying.   — *Olin Miller*

I didn't really begin to learn anything until after I had finished my studies.   — *Anatole France*

I learned more from the first stupid woman who fell in love with me than ever my brains taught me.   — *Bernard Shaw*

If I had learned education, I would not have had time to learn anything else.
                    — *Cornelius Vanderbilt*

Man learns in two ways: by doing, and by being done.

You learn more by letting the other fellow tell you what he knows than by your telling him what you know.

You are never too old to learn —to make new mistakes.

The learning process is simply a matter of progressing from cocksure ignorance to thoughtful uncertainty.

We should live and learn, but by the time we've learned, it's too late to live.

The man who is too old to learn today was the child who was too young to learn yesterday.

The man who can learn from his own mistakes, will always be learning something.

The man who knows it all has lots to learn.

Nowadays students must learn a lot of things they don't really want to know—and so do their teachers.

It takes a baby about two years to learn to talk, and about seventy years to learn to keep his mouth shut.

It's never too late to learn—and it's never too early either.

Learn from everyone: what to do from this one, what not to do from that one.

Only a woman can learn from a man things he himself didn't know he knew.

Do all your learning while you're young, for when you get older nobody can tell you anything.

No one is too old to learn, which is why so many people keep putting it off.

The best way to remain young mentally is not to learn anything after you graduate.

It's what a man learns after he knows it all that counts.

Too many people hold the view that if they learn how, they will have to do it.

You are never too old to learn some new way to act like a fool.

LECTURE

When audiences come to see us authors lecture, it is in the hope that we'll be funnier to look at than to read.   – Sinclair Lewis

My last American tour consisted of inflicting no less than ninety lectures on people who never did me any harm.
– Chesterton

All Americans lecture—I suppose it is something in their climate.   – Oscar Wilde

Many a lecture begins at eight o'clock sharp and ends at ten o'clock dull.

A lecturer often makes you feel dumb at one end and numb at the other.

Some lecturers talk in their sleep, but most talk in other people's sleep.

The lecturer who is full of his subject is usually very slow in emptying himself.

Dry lectures never satisfy a thirst for knowledge.

Lecturers should remember that the capacity of the mind to absorb is limited to what the seat can endure.

Another optimist is the woman who starts putting on her shoes when the lecturer says, "And now in conclusion—"

LEGISLATURE

Our state legislatures are unpredictable: you never know what they are going to tax next.

The legislature is the only school where the recesses are always longer than the sessions.

A legislature is an elected body that consists of a few figures followed by many zeros.

All state legislatures are alike: their members act as if they were elected to bring disorder out of chaos.

Every legislature continues to make new laws even though we already have more than we can break.

A state legislature is another place full of sound and fury, signifying nothing.

Another thing that needs much more pruning and much less grafting is our legislatures.

LEGS

If a man has good legs, the rest of the body will follow; and if a girl has good legs, man will follow.   — *Rudolf Friml*

A girl's face may be her fortune, but it's her legs that draw the interest.

One part of a domestic triangle is generally a curved leg.

While civilized man is giving up the use of his legs, civilized woman still finds a good use for hers.

Of two evils, choose the one with the better-looking legs.

LEISURE

We give up leisure in order that we may have leisure, just as we go to war in order that we may have peace.   — *Aristotle*

What is liberty? Leisure. What is leisure? Liberty.
        — *Bernard Shaw*

There's enough leisure for everybody but the wrong people have it.

The real problem of your leisure is how to keep others from using it.

There's always plenty of time, but only when you don't need it.

Another thing that always keeps going up is the cost of leisure.

The time you enjoy wasting is not wasted time.

We spend half our lives trying to find something to do with the time we have saved rushing through the other half.

Leisure is the time you spend on jobs you don't get paid for.

A man should be judged by what he does, a woman by what she does when she doesn't have anything to do.

Marry in haste, and you'll never have any leisure to repent in.

Increased leisure is no virtue: in the old days a man used to get drunk and beat his wife; nowadays he has time to do that and also watch television.

We invent laborsaving devices to enable us to save time so that we may acquire leisure in which to waste time.

LEND

Don't depend on your rich relatives: few of them will ever lend you anything except moral support.

How times have changed: in the old days it was much harder getting a loan than paying it back.

A friend in need is one who will ask for a loan of a hundred and settle for fifty.

You can always make a loan at a bank if you can show sufficient evidence that you don't need it.

The man who writes the bank's advertising is not the one who makes the loans.

LENT

The only thing some people give up for Lent is their New Year's resolutions.

People who find Lent passing most slowly are those who try hardest to keep it.

When a vegetarian keeps Lent strictly, ought he to eat meat three times a day?

LESSON

I get a great lesson out of golf —it takes the conceit out of me.
— *John D. Rockefeller*

The great secret of life is to learn lessons, not to teach them.
— *Thomas C. Haliburton*

History repeats itself, probably because we are so slow to learn its lessons.

To err is human, especially when you haven't prepared your lesson.

Memory is a mental process that enables us to forget a lesson in half the time it takes to learn it.

Experience is a teacher who never tells you in advance what your next lesson is to be.

Nothing is more frustrating to a youngster than to study the wrong lesson and learn something he wasn't required to learn.

LETTER

Many a woman writes a letter just for the sake of the P.S.!
— *Sacha Guitry*

For God's sake, don't give up writing to me simply because I don't write to you. — *Robert Frost*

Letter-writing is the only device for combining solitude and good company.   — *Lord Byron*

If you want to know your true opinion of someone, watch the effect produced in you by the first sight of a letter from him.
— *Schopenhauer*

The best letters of our time are those that can never be published.   — *Virginia Woolf*

This letter wouldn't have been so long, but I haven't the time to make it shorter.   — *Pascal*

Since letters are made up of words, how can words be made up of letters?

Some of us get letters after our names, but more of us get letters after our money.

It's better that your wife find a letter in your pocket that you forgot to mail than one you forgot to destroy.

If you leave a letter unopened long enough, it answers itself.

College boys don't write letters to their dads, they write requisitions.

The only thing which is neither literate nor illiterate is the small boy's first letter home from camp.

It's always easier to make out what a woman says in her letters than to make out what she means.

Many a woman wouldn't dream of opening a letter addressed to her husband, unless it's marked *Personal.*

It's against the law to send threatening letters through the mails, except when the Internal Revenue Service does it.

Some celebrities always answer their fan mail—even anonymous letters.

The only letters worth keeping are those that should never have been written.

A woman always adds a postscript to her letter: she's bound to have the last word even if she has to write it herself.

Many an executive has a secretary who slits his letters open in the office, and a wife who steams them open at home.

You write letters when you have something special to say, or when you have nothing special to do.

Christmas is the season when a smart child writes a letter to Santa Claus, but a smarter child writes one to Grandma.

The most common way of beginning a letter is to say that there is nothing to write about.

Getting a letter from a daughter at college sends some mothers to the dictionary, but most to the checkbook.

It is just as foolish to destroy a compromising letter as it is to write one.

LEVEL

Many a man who prides himself on being level-headed doesn't know how low the level is.

In an angry dispute each person descends to the other person's level.

LIAR

The best liar is he who makes the smallest amount of lying go the longest way. *— Samuel Butler*

I admire liars, but surely not liars so clumsy they cannot fool even themselves. *— Mencken*

Liar: (a) one who pretends to be very good; (b) one who pretends to be very bad. — *Mencken*

Honesty is the best policy, unless of course you are an exceptionally good liar.

A pathological liar has a minimum capacity for veracity or a maximum capacity for mendacity.

There are more liars in this country than you would believe.

It isn't necessary to call a man a liar: if he is, he knows it; and if he isn't a liar, he isn't a man.

We are all liars: even they who never lie to others, lie to themselves.

A pathological liar can always be expected to tell you where the truth lies.

All men are liars, but some are not found out until after they are married.

A liar's worst misfortune is not that no one believes him, but that he can't believe anyone else.

If there were no listeners, there would be no liars.

There's only one person who can lie more brazenly than a pathological liar, and that's another pathological liar.

Two liars are company, three are a crowd, and four or more a chamber of commerce.

A clever liar gives details, but the cleverest one doesn't.

To a liar, truth is more of a stranger than fiction.

The only person to whom nothing is impossible is the pathological liar.

Some people are liars; others merely tell the truth in such a way that nobody recognizes it.

To be a successful liar one must have either a bad character or a good memory.

Don't believe a liar even if you know he's telling the truth.

You can always tell when a pathological liar is telling the truth—his lips are not moving.

LIBEL

The trouble with libel is that the victim is liable to sue.

Many a bottle sells by its label, and many a book by its libel.

LIBERAL

Though I believe in liberalism, I find it difficult to believe in liberals. — *Chesterton*

A liberal is a man who leaves the room when the fight begins. — *Heywood Broun*

I can remember way back when a liberal was one who was generous with his own money. — *Will Rogers*

Another way to get a liberal education nowadays is to have a liberal father.

LIBERAL AND CONSERVATIVE

The liberal is a man who wants to tax the conservative's money.

A conservative believes in the present what liberals forced on the world in the past.

LIBERTY

The only liberty an inferior man really cherishes is the liberty to quit work, stretch out in the sun, and scratch himself.
— *Mencken*

Experience teaches us to be most on our guard to protect liberty when the government's purposes are beneficent.
— *Louis D. Brandeis*

Liberty is the only thing you cannot have unless you give it to others. — *William Allen White*

Liberty is being free from the things we don't like in order to be slaves of the things we do like.
— *Ernest Benn*

Liberty doesn't work as well in practice as it does in speeches.
— *Will Rogers*

If none were to have liberty but those who understand what it is, there would not be many free men in the world. — *Halifax*

I believe in only one thing: liberty; but I do not believe in liberty enough to want to force it upon anyone. — *Mencken*

One man's liberty ends where another man's nose begins.

Oh, Liberty! what liberties are taken in thy name!

It's not the liberty we have, but the liberties we take, that cause most of the trouble.

LIBRARY

Never lend books—nobody ever returns them; the only books I have in my library are those which people have lent me.
— *Anatole France*

I have now a library of nearly 900 volumes, over 700 of which I wrote myself. — *Thoreau*

No place affords a more striking conviction of the vanity of human hopes than a public library. — *Samuel Johnson*

Just the omission of Jane Austen's books alone would make a fairly good library out of a library that hadn't a book in it.
— *Mark Twain*

A person's library consists of all the books he has that no one wants to borrow.

There are too many books in every public library, and not enough people to dust them.

To maintain your library intact, buy three copies of every book: one to show, one to loan, and one to read.

The only source from which you can't keep books that you have borrowed is the public library.

There are thousands of books in the public library, but the one you want to read is always out.

LIES

One man lies in his words and gets a bad reputation; another in his manners and enjoys a good one. — *Thoreau*

Carlyle said, "A lie cannot live"; it shows he did not know how to tell them. — *Mark Twain*

A man finds it awfully hard to lie to the woman he loves— the first time. — *Helen Rowland*

It takes a wise man to handle a lie; a fool had better remain honest. — *Norman Douglas*

A man comes to believe in the end the lies he tells about himself to himself. — *Bernard Shaw*

Pretending that you believe a liar is also a lie.
— *Arthur Schnitzler*

Women have a hard enough time in this world: telling them the truth would be too cruel.
— *Mencken*

Heaven lies about us in our infancy, and everybody else when we grow up.

Actions lie louder than words.

Half the world doesn't know how much the other half lies about it.

If at first you're not believed, lie, lie again.

Children learn to lie from parents who teach them to say they don't want a second portion of ice cream.

Some people have a habit of lying, while others do very well without the habit.

Permit your child to tell white lies, and he will grow up color-blind.

A lie is an abomination unto the Lord, and an ever-present help in time of trouble.

Money talks, but it doesn't always tell the truth.

With politicians the lie is as much a part of speech as the noun and verb.

Children learn to lie by watching grownups who pretend they don't.

Some women find it hard to tell a lie; others can tell it as soon as their husbands open their mouths.

Opportunities lie at every hand, and so do a lot of people.

Another difference between golf and politics is that in golf you cannot improve your lie.

One good lie requires another.

It is not considered lying if you lie only when complimenting a woman.

The perjurer's mother probably told white lies.

Quote of the Week

It is better to be able to appreciate things you cannot have than to have things you cannot appreciate.

Evan Esar

Quote of the Week

It is better to be able to appreciate things you cannot have than to have things you cannot appreciate.

Evan Esar

Tell your child to lie for you, and he will learn to lie to you.

Not every husband lies to his wife—some men prevaricate.

The man who says he tells no lies is telling one.

Much of the lying done by men should be blamed on women: they insist on asking questions.

LIFE

Life is painting a picture, not doing a sum.
— *Justice O. W. Holmes*

With him life was at best an uncertain game, and he recognized the usual percentage in favor of the dealer. — *Bret Harte*

Life is a hospital in which every patient wants to change his bed for another's. — *Baudelaire*

It is impossible to cheat life; there are no answers to the problems of life in the back of the book. — *Kierkegaard*

He has spent his life best who has enjoyed it most; God will take care that we do not enjoy it any more than is good for us.
— *Samuel Butler*

Life seems to be divided into two periods: in the first we indulge, in the second we preach.
— *Will Durant*

We are here to add what we can to life, not to get what we can from it. — *William Osler*

Life does not cease to be funny when people die any more than

it ceases to be serious when people laugh. — *Bernard Shaw*

The best use of life is to spend it for something that outlasts life.
— *William James*

Life is very simple: it merely consists in learning how to accept the impossible, how to do without the indispensable, how to endure the insupportable.
— *Kathleen Norris*

Life is a dead-end street.
— *Mencken*

The second half of a man's life is made up of nothing but the habits he has acquired during the first half. — *Dostoevski*

Life is a crowded superhighway with bewildering cloverleaf exits on which a man is liable to find himself speeding back in the direction he came. — *Peter De Vries*

As I grow to understand life less and less, I learn to love it more and more. — *Jules Renard*

Many people who spend their time mourning over the brevity of life, could make it seem longer if they did a little more work.
— *Don Marquis*

Life is an infant that must be rocked in its cradle until it falls asleep. — *Voltaire*

It is not true that life is one damn thing after another: it's one damn thing over and over.
— *Edna St. Vincent Millay*

If only we could live two lives: the first in which to make one's mistakes, and the second in which to profit by them.

— *D. H. Lawrence*

Life consists not in holding good cards, but in playing well those you do hold. — *Josh Billings*

The life of man in this world is like the life of a fly in a room filled with a hundred boys, each armed with a flyswatter.

— *Mencken*

Life is a matter about which we are lost if we reason either too much or too little.

— *Samuel Butler*

Life is not fate but fatal.

When a person puts his best foot forward and gets it stepped on—that's life.

Life is a trivial comedy made up of important tragedies.

You get out of life just what you put into it—minus taxes.

The first part of our lives we spend time making money, and the second part we spend money killing time.

Life is so uncertain, half of it is *if*.

Man can live without air for seconds, without water for days, without food for weeks, and without ideas for years.

Life is what you make it, until a new group of elected representatives makes it worse.

You come into the world with nothing, and the purpose of your life is to make something out of nothing.

Take care of your life—without it, you're dead.

Life is a course that finally leaves you breathless from running around in circles trying to make ends meet.

About the time we learn how to make the most of life, most of it is gone.

Life is generally made up of three things: pretense, suspense, and expense.

During the first half of our lives, laughter comes after tears; during the second half, tears come after laughter.

Life is no laughing matter, except to the man who can laugh at his troubles.

By the yard, life is hard; by the inch, life's a cinch.

Life is a constant struggle to make ends meet, starting with the efforts of an infant to get his toes into his mouth.

Scientists are trying to produce life in the laboratory, but it shouldn't be difficult if the laboratory assistant is pretty and willing.

Life isn't all beer and skittles; few of us have touched a skittle in years.

You can't do anything about the length of your life, but you can do something about its width and depth.

Living a double life will get you nowhere twice as fast.

Life used to be one thing after another, but the pace is so fast nowadays that the things overlap.

The man who believes life is what you make it, usually marries the woman who believes life is what you make.

LIFE AND DEATH

There are few things easier than to live badly and die well.
— Oscar Wilde

A hundred years ago we were much smarter; then you lived until you died and not until you were just run over. — Will Rogers

By the time a man is ready to die, he is fit to live. — Ed Howe

Why are we so fond of a life that begins with a cry and ends with a groan?
— Mary, Countess of Warwick

There is nothing terrible in life for the man who realizes that there is nothing terrible in death.
— Epicurus

Life is a misadventure that we terminate on the shoulders of six strange men whose only objective is to make a hole in one with you. — Fred Allen

The life of the dead consists in being present in the minds of the living. — Cicero

Every man dies, but not every man has lived.

Since death is at the end of life, we are all moving in the wrong direction.

The first thing a man takes in life is his milk, and the last thing is his bier.

No one cheers his own birth, and no one mourns his own death.

Many a gourmand dies from good living.

Many a man lives like a dog and expects to be buried like a Christian.

Life is a matter of giving up one thing after another; death, a matter of giving up giving up.

We throw flowers at the dead, and mud at the living.

Eventually we all break even: we bring nothing into the world when we are born, and we take nothing out of it when we die.

Doctors say that people are living too fast, and traffic statistics show they are dying the same way.

At the end of life you can't take it with you, but during life everyone tries to take it from you.

LIFEGUARD

If clothes make the man, why are lifeguards so popular?

The best way to get even with a lifeguard is to go to his beach and drown yourself.

LIFE INSURANCE

Probably a widower enjoys a second wife as much as a widow enjoys her husband's life insurance.   — Ed Howe

A successful salesman of insurance makes life easy for his wife, and even easier for other men's widows.

Men show their egotism in the value they put on their lives when they take out insurance.

Honesty is the best policy, but life insurance is even better for the widow.

Where there's life insurance, there's hope.

Some men work themselves to death trying to keep up their life insurance.

Life insurance is the only game in which you have to die to win.

Life insurance is a form of prevision today so that there will be provision tomorrow.

There's only one thing worse than losing one's husband and that is not being able to collect the insurance.

Wives sometimes object to life insurance, but widows never do.

LIGHT

Many a man has fallen in love with a girl in a light so dim, he would not have chosen a suit by it.   — Maurice Chevalier

There are two kinds of light —the glow that illumines, and the glare that obscures.
    — James Thurber

All books will become light in proportion as you find light in them.   — Mortimer J. Adler

If you want your husband to continue being the light of your life, don't let him go out too often.

If children brighten up a home, it's probably because they never turn off the lights.

An optimist sees a light where there is none, and a pessimist always tried to put it out.

Let your light so shine before men that they cannot see what is going on behind it.

The man who burns the candle at both ends has the satisfaction of a good bright light for a little while anyway.

Most men object to the speed of light—it arrives too early in the morning.

Some night drivers scare the daylights out of you with their night lights.

By the time parents stop objecting because their children don't turn out the lights, they start objecting because they do.

The light a gossip throws on her neighbors is always a reflection.

The honeymoon is over when a man starts turning out the lights for economic rather than romantic reasons.

LIGHT AND DARK

Make light of your troubles; if not, keep them dark.

A woman is happy as long as she can keep her hair light and her past dark.

No darkness exceeds that which follows the sudden withdrawal of the limelight.

Dark secrets are the ones that soonest come to light.

LIGHTNING

Lightning never strikes twice in the same place—once is enough.

The Lord takes care of his own, but church trustees still put lightning rods on the steeple.

Spare the rod—and you'll get struck by lightning.

Lightning never strikes twice in the same place because, after it's hit, the same place isn't there any more.

LIKENESS

Nothing makes men more alike than putting dress suits on them.
— Will Rogers

Never try to make anyone like you: you know, and God knows, that one of you is enough.
— Emerson

A nation is never as uniform as it looks when it is put into uniform. — Arnulf Overland

Man thinks no two women are alike, but woman knows no one woman is alike. — Alfred Austin

A woman's clothing mustn't look too much like what everyone is wearing or like what no one is wearing.

When a mother says, "He's just like his father," is she praising or criticizing?

Every generation consists of people born about the same time, making the same mistakes.

If at first you don't succeed, relax; you're just like the rest of us.

All women are different before marriage, after which they are all alike.

Teen-agers always show their desire to be different by dressing alike.

Women are all the same—they all want to be different.

It's a wise child that resembles its rich relatives.

All men are alike—which is probably the reason why the mother of the bride always cries at the wedding.

To want a change in government is like biting another lemon to see which is the sweeter.

Money isn't everything: it's just a reasonable facsimile of same.

All women are alike, except that some are more alike than others.

Birds of a feather: the woman who is always telling about the men she could have married, and the man who is always telling about the fish that got away.

The woman who says all men are alike should marry the man who says he understands women.

LIMIT

The chief difference between intelligence and stupidity is that intelligence has its limits.

There is a limit to everything, except the number of untrue things people will believe.

There are only two things that have no limits: outer space, and the things a wife wants.

Be hopeful of a man whose limitations are not yet known; maybe he won't reach them.

There's no limit to the different things people would do—if they were you.

LINCOLN

It never occurs to politicians that Lincoln is worth imitating as well as quoting.

Lincoln used to split rails, but the only thing the modern politician splits is his infinitives.

Lincoln wasn't a handsome man, but he certainly looks good on a five-dollar bill.

Lincoln split logs; the modern politician merely rolls them.

LINE

A straight line is the shortest distance between two points, but only when you're sober.

A good line is the shortest distance between two dates.

Middle age is the period when a man's hairline goes back and his waistline goes forward.

When a man can read a girl like a book, he's usually poring over her lines.

There's a line on the ocean where you lose a day when you cross it; there's a line on the highway where you can do much better.

In order to keep a man in tow a girl should have a good line.

All a woman needs to be successful are two good lines: one a man can listen to, and the other he can look at.

LINGERIE

Women aren't embarrassed when they buy men's pajamas, but a man buying a nightgown acts as though he were dealing with a dope peddler.

— *Jimmy Cannon*

A lost soul is the man shopping for his wife in the lingerie department.

LINGUIST

Their oldest son was a disappointment to them; they wanted him to be a linguist, and then he became a Trappist monk.
— *Saki*

A linguist is a talented person who can make mistakes in more than one language.

A woman's ability to speak several languages is often combined with her inability to hold her tongue even in one.

A linguist is anyone who can make himself misunderstood in more than one language.

LIPSTICK

High school is a time when the girls start putting on lipstick, and the boys start wiping it off.

So live that if there is lipstick on your face, the neighbors will have no doubt who put it there.

A change of lipstick now and then is relished by the best of men.

There are some women who feel more undressed in public without their lipstick than without their clothes.

Any man with lipstick on his forehead is slipping.

Her hair may be of spun gold, her eyes mysterious pools of azure—but she can leave an awful mess on a cocktail glass.

When a girl makes up her lips it is usually to a man's taste.

Another difference between the sexes is that the male prefers to get his lipstick secondhand.

The trouble with lipstick is that it doesn't.

Many a husband wonders how his wife can keep her mouth still long enough to put on lipstick.

Kissing a girl always leaves its mark on a man.

If it is so hard for women to keep lipstick on, why is it so hard for men to get it off?

LIQUOR

You can have too much champagne to drink, but you can never have enough.   — *Elmer Rice*

Malt does more than Milton can to justify God's ways to man.
— *A. E. Housman*

What contemptible scoundrel stole the cork from my lunch?
— *W. C. Fields*

Claret is the liquor for boys, port for men, but he who aspires to be a hero must drink brandy.
— *Samuel Johnson*

Man wants but little drink below, but wants that little strong.
— *Dr. O. W. Holmes*

I exercise self-control, and never touch any beverage stronger than gin before breakfast.
— *W. C. Fields*

God made yeast as well as dough, and loves fermentation just as dearly as he loves vegetation.
— *Emerson*

Take that liquor away; I never touch strong drink; I like it too well to fool with it.
— *T. J. (Stonewall) Jackson*

The cost of living has gone up another dollar a quart.
— *W. C. Fields*

Liquor works two ways: it will either put you on top of the world, or under the table.

A liquor store is where they collect taxes for the government and also sell liquor.

Absinthe makes the heart grow fonder, and the breath grow stronger.

In the Caribbean, all roads lead to rum.

Liquor should not be given to the man who is given to liquor.

Alcoholic beverages consumed by Americans every year run into staggering figures.

There are two ways to get ahead in this country: one is to sell liquor, and the other is to drink it.

Liquor doesn't deteriorate with age, but the man who drinks too much of it does.

Get the best of liquor, but don't let liquor get the best of you.

It takes two pts. to make a qt., but authorities differ on how many it takes to make a gal.

The necessities of life cost several times as much as they used to, and often they are hardly fit to drink.

Liquor is an insidious habit: you start out by drinking now and then, and very soon you are drinking more now than you did then.

A little liquor makes you lose your inhibitions, a lot makes you give exhibitions.

LISTEN

A good listener is usually thinking about something else.
— *Kin Hubbard*

Look out for the fellow who lets you do all the talking.
— *Kin Hubbard*

A good listener is not only popular everywhere, but after a while he knows something.

The trouble with most people is that they listen with their mouths.

Some men are naturally good listeners; others get married and have to be.

Instead of listening to what is being said to them, many people are already listening to what they are going to say.

A first-class listener is a woman's best friend.

Most of us listen to other people's troubles just for the chance to get back at them with our own.

If you believe what you hear, you're probably eavesdropping.

You can always tell the sexes apart even when both are wearing pants: the one listening is the man.

Women like a strong silent man because they think he is listening.

Some wives will do anything their husbands say—except listen to them.

To the bore, a good listener is the most enjoyable of dumb animals.

Television is hardest on those who have to listen to those who listen to it.

A good listener is sometimes a man with nothing to say, and sometimes a woman with a sore throat.

Many husbands learn to listen, but few listen to learn.

LITERATURE

There is a great discovery still to be made in literature—that of paying literary men by the quantity they do not write. —*Carlyle*

Literature is the art of writing something that will be read twice. —*Cyril Connolly*

Literature has nothing to do with usefulness; the most useful place in any house is the toilet. —*Théophile Gautier*

We are all apprentices in a craft where no one ever becomes a master. —*Hemingway*

To be learned in literature is such a different thing from liking it. —*Frank Moore Colby*

Only those things are beautiful which are inspired by madness and written by reason. —*Gide*

My main reason for adopting literature as a profession was that, as the author is never seen by his clients, he need not dress respectably. —*Bernard Shaw*

Literature is an odd occupation: the less you write, the better it must be. —*Jules Renard*

Literature is news that stays news. —*Ezra Pound*

If I was a light of literature at all, it was of the very lightest kind. —*Samuel Butler*

It is one of the functions of literature to turn truisms into truths. —*Chesterton*

A species living under the threat of obliteration is bound to produce obliterature—and that's what we are producing. —*James Thurber*

Satire lies about literary men while they live, and eulogy lies about them when they die. —*Voltaire*

There is nothing like literature: I lose a cow, I write about her death, and my writing pays me enough to buy another cow. —*Jules Renard*

I knew a great deal of English literature by heart long before I could really get it into my head. —*Chesterton*

A sequel is an admission that you've been reduced to imitating yourself. — *Don Marquis*

My definition of literature would be just this: words that have become deeds.
— *Robert Frost*

H. L. Mencken suffers from the hallucination that he is H. L. Mencken—there is no cure for a disease of that magnitude.
— *Maxwell Bodenheim*

Of all the enemies of literature, success is the most insidious.
— *Cyril Connolly*

One must have a heart of stone to read the death of Little Nell by Dickens without laughing.
— *Oscar Wilde*

Writing is the only profession where no one considers you ridiculous if you earn no money.
— *Jules Renard*

Sherwood Anderson never tried to please anybody—he considered it everybody's duty to please him.
— *Ben Hecht*

As a writer, George Meredith mastered everything except language; as a novelist, he can do everything except tell a story.
— *Oscar Wilde*

Modern literature is so outspoken, it uses words you cannot even find in the dictionary.

All that glitters is not gold, nor all that litters, literature.

There are three kinds of literature: prose, poetry and love-letters.

You can tell a man's taste in literature by his judgment in knowing what not to read.

Where there are so many books, there must be some literature.

LIVING

We never live, we are always going to live. — *Voltaire*

The man who thinks the world owes him a living soon finds that the world pays its debt in the penitentiary.
— *William Graham Sumner*

In this age when it is said of a man, he knows how to live, it may be implied he is not very honest. — *Halifax*

The only way to live is to love like a fool when you're young, and work like the devil when you're old. — *Voltaire*

There are three ingredients in the good life: learning, earning and yearning.
— *Christopher Morley*

You should live so that when you die, God is in your debt.
— *Bernard Shaw*

I am indebted to my father for living, but to my teacher for living well. — *Alexander the Great*

You can always live on less when you have more to live for.

Even when a man has nothing to live on, he still lives on.

Half the world doesn't know with whom the other half lives.

The more livings a man can earn, the more he has to for others.

The reason so many people don't live within their incomes is that they don't consider that living.

One half the world doesn't know how the other half lives, and neither does the other half.

The man who thinks he can live without others, is mistaken; the man who thinks others cannot live without him, is even more mistaken.

Many a man who has too much to live on, has too little to live for.

Half the world doesn't know how; the other half lives.

The world is full of men making good livings but poor lives.

A good liver and a bad liver often go together.

Half the world doesn't know why the other half lives.

'Tis better to have lived and loved than never to have lived at all.

The trouble nowadays is that it is much easier to make money than it is to make a living.

Half the world knows how the other half ought to live.

There are only two ways to make a living: working for it and working someone for it.

LOBSTER

The more you eat of a lobster, the more you leave on your plate.

Lobster is eaten by some people for flavor, by some for nourishment, but by most for exercise.

A lobster never comes ashore without great risk of getting into hot water.

LOGIC

Logic is the art of going wrong with confidence.
                —Joseph Wood Krutch

Logic is like the sword: those who appeal to it shall perish by it.   *—Samuel Butler*

It took a million years to develop man's ability to reason, but it takes only a few minutes of feminine logic to destroy it.

Against logic there is no armor like ignorance.

A lot of time is wasted expecting woman to be logical.

Few of us ever test our powers of deduction, except when filling out an income tax form.

Love laughs more often at logic than at locksmiths.

Feminine logic is irrational, irrelevant, irresponsible—and irrefutable.

Logic will never learn that life seldom follows the script.

There is nothing in real life that's strictly logical, least of all the logician.

Logic is what a woman doesn't use when she tells her husband they ought to be thankful they have the means to live beyond.

LONDON

You can do anything you please in London so long as you don't do it on the street.
— *Mrs. Patrick Campbell*

The Londoner who saves up for a rainy day must be kept pretty busy.

London is a great city, but it would be even a greater city if it had a roof over it.

A London fog is often so thick that you can't even see what the weather is like.

When a Londoner looks as if he has a suntan, it's probably rust.

LONELY

Language has created the word *loneliness* to express the pain of being alone, and the word *solitude* to express the glory of being alone. — *Paul Tillich*

Early to rise and early to bed makes a girl healthy but socially dead.

Another person who is sure to be alone is the motorist who finds himself going the wrong way on a one-way street.

The girl who falls in love with herself will find herself alone with her sweetheart forever after.

The survival of the fittest is going to make some man very lonesome some day.

The bigger the city, the lonelier you can feel, especially when you stand in the rain and try to hail a cab.

LONGEVITY

No male can beat a female in the long run because they have it over us in sheer, damn longevity. — *James Thurber*

It's true that women live longer than men—especially widows.

The best way to prolong life sometimes is to throw up your hands.

The reason women live longer than men is because they get more pleasure out of feeling miserable.

The secret of living to a ripe old age is very simple: all you have to do is to go on living.

Life expectancy depends less on the star you were born under than on the color of the traffic light when you cross the street.

Women live longer than men, but that's only fair because they have much more to say.

Many a man lives to be ninety, but liquor and women finally get him.

Recipe for a long life: Be careful not to exceed the feed limit.

The only group of people who seem to have discovered the secret of long life are rich relatives.

For every man who lives to be seventy, there are three women, but by that time it's too late.

The average life span of a woman is constantly increasing, thus enabling her to stay twenty-nine much longer.

Life expectancy is steadily increasing, probably to enable us to complete the time payments.

No wonder women live longer than men—look how long they remain girls.

Many a man lives to a ripe old age because he never wastes any energy resisting temptation.

Man is an illogical creature who wishes for long life but never for old age.

It's not true that married men live longer than unmarried men—it just seems longer.

LOOK

No man is ever too old to look at a woman, and no woman is ever too fat to hope that he will look. — *Mencken*

A woman is as old as she looks to a man who likes to look at her. — *Finley Peter Dunne*

There are three kinds of women: those you look away from, those you look up to, and those you look around at.

A woman can say more in a look than a man can in a book.

If you want to get on, look ahead; if you want to get across, look both ways.

When a man stops looking at a pretty girl, it's either because his wife has appeared, or the girl has disappeared.

Youth looks ahead, old age looks back, while middle age just looks tired.

Nothing robs a man of his good looks like a hurriedly drawn shade.

The better a woman looks, the longer a man does.

When woman most looks as if she didn't know you were looking, she most certainly does.

A woman is as young as she looks, unless another woman is doing the looking.

A woman looks another woman up and down to see what she is wearing; a man looks a woman up and down to see what she is clothing.

The cure for love at first sight is to take a second look.

It's better for a woman to be looked over than to be overlooked.

A woman is as old as she looks; a man is old when he stops looking.

LOSE

The way to love anything is to realize that it might be lost.
— *Chesterton*

It's the good loser who finally loses out. — *Kin Hubbard*

Lose an hour in the morning, and you will spend all day looking for it. — *Richard Whately*

Many a man has been saved from losing lots of money by not having it.

There's only one thing a woman can lose and never know it's gone —her beauty.

A good loser is all right, but it isn't so much fun to beat him.

Some women lose things, but most women merely put them in a safe place and then forget the place.

No fat man is ever unhappy about losing 100 pounds, unless she's a beautiful blonde.

It is better to have loved and lost than never to have lost at all.

When some women grow old they lose their looks; others are not so lucky.

LOT

The only time a man is contented with his lot is when he's buried in it.

It is only when you are ready to buy a house that you discover that a lot is really not much.

Be contented with your lot, especially if it's a corner one.

LOUD

If you can hear whispering tenors, they're too loud.
— *Groucho Marx*

There's nothing wrong in having nothing to say as long as you are not saying it out loud.

Many a man misses opportunity when it knocks because he is knocking louder.

There are still some homes where children are seen and not heard, but that's only because the television is turned on very loud.

When hush money talks, it is vociferous.

In every dispute a man talks louder when he's wrong than when he's right.

LOVE

Love is merely the exchange of two illusions and the contact of two skins. — *Chamfort*

Love is an irresistible desire to be irresistibly desired.
— *Robert Frost*

To fall in love is to believe in a religion whose God is fallible.
— *Jorge Luís Borges*

No woman ever falls in love with a man unless she has a better opinion of him than he deserves.
— *Ed Howe*

Love is the wisdom of the fool, and the folly of the wise.
— *Samuel Johnson*

As soon as you cannot keep anything from a woman, you love her.   — *Paul Géraldy*

Love's blindness consists oftener in seeing what is not there than in seeing what is. — *Peter De Vries*

A man's love thrives far better on the stimulant of suspense than on the anesthetic of memory.
— *Helen Rowland*

You don't love a woman for what she says, but love what she says because you love her.
— *André Maurois*

It is better to love two too many than one too few.
— *Sir John Harington*

In their first passions, women love the lover; in the others, they love love.   — *La Rochefoucauld*

Men as a rule love with their eyes, but women with their ears.
— *Oscar Wilde*

The love that lasts the longest is the love that is never returned.
— *Somerset Maugham*

In the cuisine of love there are flavors for all tastes—else ugly women would never be sought after.   — *James G. Huneker*

The realist always falls in love with a girl he has grown up with, the romanticist with a girl from "off somewhere."   — *Robert Frost*

Love is like an hourglass, with the heart filling up as the brain empties.   — *Jules Renard*

Man makes love by braggadocio, and woman makes love by listening.   — *Mencken*

It is just as hard to live with the person we love as to love the person we live with.
— *Jean Rostand*

Many people in love can be sure of being admired when they are not admirable and praised when they are not praiseworthy.
— *Bertrand Russell*

Love is the emotion that a woman always feels for a poodle, and sometimes for a man.
— *George Jean Nathan*

First love is a kind of vaccination that immunizes a man from catching the disease a second time.
— *Balzac*

In order to be happy one should not know love's passion, but only love's pleasure.   — *Helvétius*

Love has the power of making you believe what you would normally treat with the deepest suspicion.   — *Mirabeau*

Love does not consist in gazing at each other but in looking outward together in the same direction.   — *Antoine de Saint-Exupéry*

A man may be said to love most truly that woman in whose company he can feel drowsy in comfort.   — *George Jean Nathan*

Love is the word used to label the sexual excitement of the young, the habituation of the middle-aged, and the mutual dependence of the old.   — *John Ciardi*

Love often leads to marriage—and almost as often to divorce.

It would be a happier world if love were as easy to keep as it is to make.

Love at first sight saves a lot of time and money.

Love is the last and most serious of the diseases of childhood.

Love usually begins by deceiving oneself, and usually ends by deceiving the other person.

People fall in love, but they have to climb out.

It's a good thing that love is blind, otherwise it would see too much.

The love of man for woman, or of woman for God, is not always mutual.

When love dies of starvation, it is usually the man's fault; when it dies of suffocation, it is always the woman's.

Half the fun of being in love is the worry of it.

When a man is in love for the first time he thinks he invented it.

Love is a mental disorder that makes a girl eager to give up seven hours in an office to slave fourteen hours in a house.

The game of love cannot be played with the cards on the table.

Some girls believe in love at first sight; others believe in waiting until he hangs up his hat and coat.

Falling in love is awfully simple, but falling out is simply awful.

You don't make love—it makes you.

A man first realizes he loves a girl when he begins to get mad at people who say she's stupid or homely.

Many people believe in love at first sight, but many more believe in love at first.

It is easier to love in spite of faults than because of virtues.

A girl can always tell when she's in love and usually does.

Love is a state of mind that begins when you think life can't be any better, and ends when you think life can't be any worse.

Every woman has to love something, even if it is only a man.

It's easy to understand love at first sight, but how explain love after two people have been looking at each other for years?

Woman loves to be loved, man just loves.

Love is like a mushroom: you can never tell whether it's the real thing until it's too late.

Love is the feeling that flatters your ego while it flattens your wallet.

If love is blind, how can there be love at first sight?

Love is a romantic feeling that wakens your sense of honor while it weakens your sense of humor.

Love is what makes the world go round—when it should be asleep.

When two people cannot see too much of each other nor too little of other people, they're in love.

Love makes time pass, and time makes love pass.

Advice to persons who have fallen in love: Fall out.

Some men fall in love with a girl at first sight; others love her the first time they lay hands on her.

LOVE AND MARRIAGE

Where there's marriage without love, there will be love without marriage.   — *Franklin*

Before marriage, a man declares he would lay down his life to serve you; after marriage, he won't even lay down his paper to talk to you. — *Helen Rowland*

Love is one long sweet dream, and marriage is the alarm clock.

Many a happy marriage is due to the fact that they both are in love with the same woman.

Love is a matter of give and take, marriage a matter of misgive and mistake.

Before marriage, a woman is a man's aspiration; after marriage, she's his exasperation.

If a girl loves a man very much, she'll marry him in spite of her parents' urging.

Few men marry their first love, and fewer marry their last.

The course of true love never runs smooth—it usually leads to marriage.

Love is blind, and marriage is an eye opener.

Occasionally you meet a man who thinks it is better to have loved and married than never to have loved at all.

In love, a woman knows her heart; in marriage, her mind.

Before marriage, he sees a halo on her head; after marriage, an expensive hat.

Every woman marries for love, even if it's only love of money.

Some men fall in love, but they get out of it by marrying the girl.

A lot of love is wasted before marriage that could be put to good use after marriage.

A man always retains tender thoughts of his first love, unless of course he marries her.

A happy man marries the girl he loves, but a happier man loves the girl he marries.

Before marriage, a woman raves over a man; after marriage, she raves at him.

Love can usually survive everything but marriage.

The cure for love is marriage, and the cure for marriage is love again.

Before marriage, a girl dotes on a man; after marriage, she finds herself joined to an antidote.

A good example of hot and cold may be found in the case of the lover who becomes a husband.

Love laughs at locksmiths, but not at locks—at least, not at wedlock.

Marriage is all very well, but to a bachelor it seems like carrying love a little too far.

Before marriage, a man yearns for a woman; after marriage, the y is silent.

LOVE AND MONEY

Any girl can live on love—if he's wealthy.

Kisses may be the language of love, but money still does the talking.

Money cannot buy love, but it can put you in a good bargaining position.

There would be more cases of love at first sight if more men knew that the girl had money.

Many a woman loves a man chiefly for himself, and only for his money up to a certain point —the decimal point.

The man who loves a girl more than words can tell should let money do the talking.

Money cannot buy love, but it makes shopping for it a lot easier.

The heart strings of some women always follow a man's purse strings.

LOVE LETTER

What a foolish love letter the other man writes!   – Ed Howe

At 24 I wrote a love letter that brought an indignant husband onto my hands and damn nigh saddled me with his idiotic wife.
– Mencken

Love letters should be written in invisible ink and mailed in the wastebasket.

A love letter begins by your not knowing what you are going to say, and ends by your not knowing what you have said.

It doesn't take much skill to write a love letter, but it takes considerable skill to get it back.

Love letters should always be dictated to a secretary.

It takes a clever man to write a good love letter, but only a fool would write it.

You don't know how convincing your love letters are until your wife intercepts one.

All the world loves a lover, but it laughs when they get hold of his love letters.

LOVER

All the world loves a lover, but it usually runs away from him when he talks.
— *Frank Moore Colby*

Every lover is a liar.
— *Ed Howe*

All the world loves a lover, but not while the love-making is going on. — *Kin Hubbard*

A lover who reasons is no lover.
— *Norman Douglas*

As lovers, men are inclined to be general practitioners rather than specialists. — *Helen Rowland*

All the world loves a lover, except sometimes the one that's all the world to him.
— *Finley Peter Dunne*

A foolish girl may make a lover a husband, but it takes a clever woman to keep a husband a lover. — *Ed Howe*

When a woman ceases to be mistress of herself she is likely to become the mistress of a man.
— *James G. Huneker*

How wonderful is that woman who continues to be a husband's sweetheart all her life—her own husband's!

There are only two kinds of lovers: the supremely happy and the supremely miserable.

All the world loves a lover—except the husband.

The usual way a woman loses an ardent admirer is by marrying him.

If men were the great lovers they think they are, women wouldn't have time for anything else.

All the world loves a lover—he never complains about the price.

All the world loves a lover, except those who are waiting to use the phone.

Many husbands who were super-lovers before marriage turn out to be merely supper-lovers afterward.

The girl who is always a bridesmaid but never a bride, probably has a confirmed bachelor as her fiancé.

Many a lover's quarrel is due to her wanting a big wedding and his wanting to break the engagement.

Promiscuous women are all alike: they prefer to have many lovers in one year to one lover for many years.

The mark of a great lover is mostly lipstick.

LOW

A low voice is an excellent thing in a woman—also a low hat.

The value of the dollar can never fall so low as the means some people adopt to get it.

One of the few virtues of being overweight is that it prevents you from stooping to anything low.

LUCK

I believe in luck: how else can you explain the success of those you dislike?   — *Jean Cocteau*

If a man who cannot count finds a four-leaf clover, is he lucky?   — *Stanislaw J. Lec*

It's the mark of an inexperienced man not to believe in luck.   — *Joseph Conrad*

Some people have good luck that they can't boast about—the good luck of not yet being found out.   — *Ed Howe*

The only sure thing about luck is that it will change. — *Bret Harte*

The less luck a man has, the more he believes in it.

People with luck usually turn out to have manufactured most of it themselves.

It's the good luck of other people that makes us dissatisfied with our own.

Lady Luck is the kind of a dame who smiles on a few of us, but laughs at the rest of us.

When a woman's first husband is the nicest of all, it's beginner's luck.

The man who depends on luck will soon have nothing else to depend on.

When he hasn't had hard luck for some time, a pessimist feels he hasn't had any luck at all.

A horseshoe is a symbol of good luck even though you cannot make both ends meet.

When an ambitious man finds a four-leaf clover, it usually means that he will have good luck.

If you want to depress your friends, tell them about some good luck you've had.

There are three kinds of people: those who have good luck, those who have bad luck, and those who have no luck at all.

A little more drive, a little more pluck, a little more work— that's luck.

There's only one kind of luck that can be trusted, and that's the good luck to be born with sense.

Luck is the corner where preparation meets opportunity.

Good luck will often follow the man who doesn't include it in his plan.

A lucky man needs no advice.

Success is all a matter of luck —ask any failure.

When the average husband sees the kind of man most women marry, he realizes how fortunate his wife is.

LUXURY

Never economize on luxuries.
    — *Angela Thirkell*

A luxury item is one that takes more time to sell than to make.

The *etc.*'s have cost mankind more than all the other luxuries combined.

A luxury is something you do not need, but cannot get along without.

A divorce decree costs more than a marriage license, but luxuries always cost more.

People used to go without luxuries to have money in the bank; nowadays they go without money in the bank to have luxuries.

How to get rich: manufacture something people want but don't need.

The trouble with living in the lap of luxury is that you never know when luxury is going to stand up.

Nowadays the poor can enjoy the luxuries of the rich—the payments just take longer.

Luxuries are what the man who is living within his income is probably living without.

LUXURY AND NECESSITY

The world was made for the poor man: every dollar will buy more necessities than it will buy luxuries.   — *Ed Howe*

There's nothing like a down payment to turn a luxury into a necessity.

We still have a few necessities we can get along without before parting with any of our luxuries.

If your neighbor has it, a luxury immediately becomes a necessity.

Feminine logic is what makes a woman give up necessities that are useless in order to buy luxuries that are essential.

Times change: cars are now regarded as necessities and children as luxuries.

If the necessities of life keep on increasing in price, it will soon be cheaper to live on the luxuries.

The worst thing about experiencing luxuries is that once you do, they become necessities.

Money is what we spend for luxuries and owe for necessities.

Take care of the luxuries, and the necessities will take care of themselves.

The good old days were those when a luxury didn't become a necessity just because you happened to want it.

There, little luxury, don't you cry; you'll be a necessity by and by.

There would be less complaint if the high cost of living deprived us of necessities instead of luxuries.

Another drawback of living in the suburbs is that the neighbors make your necessities too luxurious and your luxuries too necessary.

MACHINE

Machines are getting better and better, while man is getting worse and worse. — *Earnest A. Hooton*

One machine can do the work of 50 ordinary men, but no machine can do the work of one extraordinary man.
— *Elbert Hubbard*

The pencil sharpener is about as far as I have ever got in operating a complicated piece of machinery with any success.
— *Robert Benchley*

As machines get to be more and more like men, men will come to be more like machines.
— *Joseph Wood Krutch*

Businessmen are divided into two classes: those who have machines, and those who are.

Man is the only calculating machine so far invented that can reproduce itself.

The modern boy is machine-minded and can run almost anything, except an errand.

In the good old days, you needed less machinery to run a large farm than you need today to run a small farmhouse.

Man's mastery of the machine has finally been perfected—until something happens to the machine.

Some machines create unemployment, while others like political machines create employment.

The human body is a machine that's seldom in as good a working condition as the machines it operates.

MAGAZINE

Reading some magazines makes one wonder what the editor rejected.

In the old days woman's place was in the home; now it's on a magazine cover.

Times change: the women's magazines now feature articles that would have been too daring for the men's magazines a generation ago.

The three Fs of women's magazines: Food, Fashion and Family.

MAGIC

Money is a form of magic: it turns a long, lanky girl who has it into a tall, stately creature.

A magician is a man who cannot earn an honest living unless he practices all sorts of tricks on people.

Nowadays it doesn't take a magician to make a dollar look like a dime.

MAIL

The United States has the greatest variety of postage stamps, but they all taste the same.

If the world is getting smaller, why do they keep raising the postal rates?

It's strange how fast mail trucks drive on the streets and how long it takes a check to reach you.

Many a second-rate manuscript is mailed as first-class matter.

MAILING LIST

The prenatal period is the only time in a person's life when his name cannot be found on a mailing list.

Some people have their names perpetuated in stone or cast in bronze, but most of us are on mailing lists.

A wastebasket must embitter a circular that has crossed the country in a plane.

Opportunity doesn't knock at your door any more; now you're on its mailing list.

A man is never really down and out until his name is crossed off the sucker lists.

MAJORITY

Whenever you find that you are on the side of the majority, it is time to reform.
— *Mark Twain*

Marriage is a two-party system in which one of the parties acts as if she has the majority vote.

Every American knows that you don't have to fool all the people all the time, but only a majority.

Congress is a legislative body where a working majority is seldom a majority working.

MAJORITY AND MINORITY

The minority is sometimes right, the majority always wrong.
— *Bernard Shaw*

In a democracy the majority rules, but the minority tries to show the majority how.

An intelligent minority never stays that way after it becomes a majority.

Progress is a compliant majority queueing up behind a militant minority.

If women become more active in politics, Congress will be composed of a majority, a minority and a sorority.

MAN

The proof that man is the noblest of all creatures is that no other creature has ever denied it.
— *G. C. Lichtenberg*

Advice to young writers who want to get ahead: Don't write about Man, write about a man.
— *E. B. White*

The greatest nuisance to mankind is man. — *Samuel Butler*

Man is a biped, but fifty men are not a centipede. — *Chesterton*

Man begins where nature ends; nature and man can never be friends.   — *Thomas Hardy*

Men are queer animals—a mixture of horse-nervousness, ass-stubbornness and camel-malice.
          — *Thomas H. Huxley*

Man is nature's sole mistake.
          — *W. S. Gilbert*

The supercilious silliness of this poor wingless bird is cosmically comical and stellarly absurd.
          — *Don Marquis*

Man is the only creature that refuses to be what he is. — *Camus*

Each human being is a more complex structure than any social system to which he belongs.
          — *A. N. Whitehead*

Man thinks he amounts to a great deal, but to a flea or mosquito a human being is merely something good to eat.
          — *Don Marquis*

Man is nothing in relation to the universe, and everything in relation to nothing—he is in the middle between extremes. — *Pascal*

Man is God's highest present development: he is the latest thing in God.   — *Samuel Butler*

Man is the only animal that laughs and weeps because he is the only animal that is struck by the difference between what things are and what they ought to be.   — *Hazlitt*

Man is the only animal that can make a beast of himself.

Man is a creature great enough to split the atom and mean enough to split hairs.

The only thing on earth that would induce some girls to marry is—a man.

It takes two women to raise one male—his mother and his wife.

Man is the only animal that eats when he is not hungry and drinks when he is not thirsty.

The reason man is the more general term is that man embraces woman.

Man is the only creature that succeeds in improving on nature, especially on its cruelties.

When a male is born, his mother gets the flowers; when he marries, his bride gets the compliments; and when he dies, his wife gets the insurance.

Men generally fall into three classes: the handsome, the clever, and the majority.

Man is the most imperfect of all creatures: that's why he can't live without drugstores, barbershops, and beauty parlors.

Man is the only animal that thinks, but he is not what he thinks he is.

MAN AND WOMAN

Men are more interesting than women, but women are more fascinating.   — *James Thurber*

The trouble in the world is nearly all due to the fact that one-half the people are men, and the other half, women.

— *Ed Howe*

A tranquil woman can go on sewing longer than an angry man can go on fuming.

— *Bernard Shaw*

Man without woman would be as stupid a game as playing checkers alone.   — *Josh Billings*

What man sees in love is woman, what woman sees in man is love.   — *Arsène Houssaye*

One law for the woman and another for the man, or a skirt for the woman and a pair of breeches for the man, is unnatural.

— *Bernard Shaw*

To women, love is an occupation; to men, a preoccupation.

— *Lionel Strachey*

Women go to extremes: they are either better or worse than men.   — *La Bruyère*

Of the two lots, the woman's lot of perpetual motherhood, and the man's of perpetual babyhood, I prefer the man's.

— *Bernard Shaw*

Man wants a great deal here below, and woman even more.

— *James Thurber*

A man criticizes his enemies behind their backs; a woman, her friends.

Women think about love more than men, and men think about women more than love.

Man is the head, and woman his headache.

Women talk among themselves about other people; men talk to other people about themselves.

When a woman has a love affair she goes into ecstasies; a man goes into details.

A woman always remembers the man who wanted to marry her, while a man never forgets the woman who didn't.

Nothing so unmans a man as a woman.

Judge a man by the way he acts when he loses money; a woman by the way she acts when she gets it.

A woman will say she's shopping when she hasn't bought a thing, and a man will say he's fishing when he hasn't caught a thing.

Life is full of troubles, and most of them are man-maid.

The trouble with men is that they're too much alike, and the trouble with women is that they aren't.

A man likes to feel he is loved, a woman likes to be told.

Most men read too much to be wise, and most women talk too much to be beautiful.

Every man has his price, and every woman her figure.

Men are better off than women: for one thing, men marry later; for another, they die earlier.

A man gets what he wants by acting smart; a woman, by playing dumb.

Woman accepts man for the sake of marriage, and man accepts marriage for the sake of woman.

A man is known by what he does, a woman by what she doesn't do.

Men would rather be liked than listened to; women would rather be listened to than liked.

A woman knows the value of love, but a man only knows its cost.

Every man ought to have three women: a secretary for office work, a blonde for romance, and a wife when the others are not around.

Women talk more than men because woman's work is never dumb.

All women like to be loved, and all men love to be liked.

The only thing worse than the man who knows it all is the woman who tells it all.

What you say to a man goes in one ear and out the other; what you say to a woman goes in one ear and out over the phone.

The wisest of men are fools about women, but the most foolish woman is wise to men.

Of what value is it to man to get shorter working hours if he doesn't reduce woman's spending hours?

If you don't understand women, you are either a bachelor or a husband or a divorced man.

A man is as old as he looks before shaving, and a woman is as old as she looks after washing her face.

MANAGE

There's nothing so exhausting as the management of men, except the management of women.

— Disraeli

The great requisite for the prosperous management of ordinary business is the want of imagination.

— Hazlitt

Except during the nine months before he draws his first breath, no man manages his affairs as well as a tree does.

— Bernard Shaw

You never know what you can make do till you try.

Every man wishes his wife would manage him with less friction.

Why is it that the smallest amount a woman can possibly manage on is usually the largest amount her husband can possibly give her?

Any fool can run the world, but it takes an intelligent man to run his own business.

Husbands are easy to handle; to succeed, just keep on crying.

There's only one way to handle a woman, but no man yet has discovered what it is.

More diplomacy is required in managing a servant than in dealing with the affairs of state.

The woman who gets on with other women's husbands probably doesn't get on with her own.

A wise wife soon learns to manage her husband, but a wise husband never tries to manage his wife.

The views expressed by husbands at home are not necessarily those of the management.

Why is it that the husband who cannot manage his own household always knows how the President should run the country?

What a pity it is that nobody knows how to manage a wife, except a bachelor!

MANAGEMENT

Management is known by the company it keeps.

The first syllable is far more important than the second in management.

MANNERS

Manners are especially the need of the plain; the pretty can get away with anything.
— *Evelyn Waugh*

Good manners are made up of petty sacrifices. — *Emerson*

There are bad manners everywhere, but an aristocracy is bad manners organized. — *Henry James*

To succeed in the world it is not enough to be stupid, you must also be well-mannered. — *Voltaire*

A wise man saves his good manners for disaster; a fool practices them when they are useless.
— *Ben Hecht*

We sometimes meet an original gentleman who, if manners had not existed, would have invented them. — *Emerson*

Men reserve their most cordial manners for their friends, women reserve them for their enemies.

The newly rich have more comforts, but the newly poor have better manners.

Cultivate good manners, and you'll be mistaken for a doorman.

The keynote of good breeding is B natural.

Good manners are like good digestion: if you don't notice them, they are all right.

Never treat a guest like a member of the family—treat him with courtesy.

Some men operate on the theory that you don't need road manners if you drive a five-ton truck.

Children usually face the problem of learning good table manners without seeing any.

Breeding isn't everything, but it's lots of fun.

MAP

What this country needs is a road map a woman driver can follow.

A road map tells a motorist everything he needs to know, except how to fold it up again.

The man who crosses his bridges before he gets to them is probably following a road map.

On a motor trip there's nothing more exasperating than your wife when she's driving, except when she's reading the map.

Seldom does a man show as much originality as when he is folding a road map.

It is usually harder for a motorist to fold a road map than for his wife to read it.

A treasure map of the United States is a chart showing which highways don't have toll booths.

A road map is the only place where motorists will find all the roads free from traffic lights, traffic jams and traffic cops.

He travels fastest who knows how to fold up a road map quickly.

MARK

It is much easier to make a mark in politics than to erase one.

Remember that while you are marking time, time is also marking you.

The only place where some people leave their mark in this world is on someone else's fender.

Gossip is like mud thrown against a clean wall: it may not stick but it leaves a mark.

About the only kind of a mark some people make in the world is an easy mark.

MARRIAGE

The bonds of matrimony are like any other bonds—they mature slowly.   —Peter De Vries

No matter how happily a woman may be married, it always pleases her to discover that there is a nice man who wishes she were not.   —Mencken

It takes two to make marriage a success and only one a failure.
—Herbert Samuel

The great secret of successful marriage is to treat all disasters as incidents, and none of the incidents as disasters.
—Harold Nicolson

Marriage is like paying an endless visit in your worst clothes.
—J. B. Priestley

Never get married while you're going to college; it's hard to get a start if a prospective employer find you've already made one mistake.   —Kin Hubbard

A happy marriage is a long conversation that seems all too short.   — *André Maurois*

Getting married, like getting hanged, is a great deal less dreadful than it has been made out.
— *Mencken*

Marriage is the most licentious of human institutions—that is the secret of its popularity.
— *Bernard Shaw*

The trouble with wedlock is that there's not enough wed and too much lock.
— *Christopher Morley*

Marriages would be as happy if they were made by the Lord Chancellor without the parties having any choice in the matter. — *Samuel Johnson*

It's no disgrace for a woman to make a mistake in marrying —every woman does it.
— *Ed Howe*

I am to be married within three days—married past redemption.
— *John Dryden*

Those who marry late are best pleased with their children; and those who marry early, with their partners.   — *Samuel Johnson*

If it hadn't been for my wife, I couldn't have stood married life.
— *Don Herold*

He marries best who puts it off until it is too late. — *Mencken*

If there is such a thing as a good marriage, it is because it resembles friendship rather than love.   — *Montaigne*

No compass has ever been invented for the high seas of matrimony.   — *Heine*

No wonder there are so many unhappy marriages: the best man never gets the bride.

Every girl waits for the right man to come along, but in the meantime she gets married.

To a woman at 18 marriage is an adventure, at 22 a career, at 30 a goal, and at 40 a haven.

Married life wouldn't be so bad if men and women were as anxious to stay married as they are to get married.

Marriage is singular: you add one and one and make one.

Marriage is a union where the husband's dues for the rights of membership amount to his whole take-home pay.

Marriage is for women only— a man should have nothing to do with it.

Marriage is a feminine plot to add to a man's responsibilities and subtract from his rights.

Matrimony is a process that turns a woman from an attraction into a distraction.

No woman ever reaches thirty without having been asked to marry—at least by her parents.

Married life is a mistake: first he talks, then she talks, then the neighbors talk.

A fool and his money are soon married.

To many a girl all that marriage means is a roof over her head and a man under her thumb.

Some people marry for love, some for money, but most for a short time.

Money isn't the root of all evil —matrimony is.

The only thing worse than marrying a man to reform him is marrying a woman to educate her.

Marriage is a gamble—that's why we speak of winning a husband or wife.

Marriage is a committee of two on ways and means, with the right to add to their number.

Marriage is an unfailing method of turning an ardent admirer into a carping critic.

The trouble with matrimony is not with the institution, it's with the personnel.

There are only two kinds of married couples: the compatible and combatable.

Married life is like sitting in the bathtub: once you get used to it, it's not so hot.

Fools rush in where bachelors fear to wed.

There's only one way to make a happy marriage, and most husbands and wives would like to know what it is.

Married life isn't so bad—at least, after you get to be a trusty.

The aim of marriage should be to give the best years of your life to the spouse who makes them the best.

Whoever said marriage is a fifty-fifty proposition doesn't know the half of it.

Matrimony is a popular form of disagreement where the husband thinks the wife should spend less, and the wife thinks the husband should earn more.

Matrimony is the most effective reducing diet yet discovered for a swelled head.

The woman who laughs up her sleeve ought to marry the man who talks through his hat.

Marriage is an endless conversation in which the more the wife talks, the less the husband listens.

Marriage is like a cafeteria: you pick out something good-looking and pay later.

Matrimony is the only state of conflict where the battles take place after the war has been won.

To the young, marriage is a heaven; to the old, a haven.

Marriage is an investment that always pays dividends, but only if you pay interest.

It is better to marry a man without money than to marry money without a man.

Two fools make a moron, two morons make an imbecile, two imbeciles make an idiot, and two idiots make a marriage.

In order to have a good spouse, you have to be one.

Matrimony is a matter of ups and downs: keeping appearances up and expenses down.

Marriage is an institution where a man and woman share the same bedlam and board.

The man who has been married many years knows more about marriage than the man who has been married many times.

Don't get married on a shoestring or you may find it hard to stay tied.

Marriage is a continuous process of getting used to things you hadn't expected.

The man who marries well seldom has a wife who does.

Marriage is a game where the husband tries to be as fast on the deposit as his wife is on the draw.

MARRIAGE AND DIVORCE

A woman who has been married and divorced a number of times reminds us of the man who is always failing in business.
– Ed Howe

I guess about the only way to stop divorce is to stop marriage.
– Will Rogers

Marriage begins when two people say "I do," and ends when they don't.

Some marriages are failures; others result in divorce before they have a chance to be failures.

Woman's approval of divorce is one of her cunning ways to make marriage more alluring.

When a marriage ends in divorce, it is merely another fight that hasn't gone the distance.

Divorce is so easy nowadays that no one need hesitate about getting married.

Some people marry happily, some acquire happiness after marriage, while others get divorced and have happiness thrust upon them.

Girls used to be asked to name the day; now they're asked to name the lawyer.

Marriage represents a cross section of humanity, while divorce represents a very cross section.

Courtship is when she selects him, marriage is when she suspects him, divorce is when she rejects him.

Another reason for so many divorces is that too many girls are getting married before they are able to support a husband.

The two happiest moments in the lives of a married couple is when the clergyman marries them and the judge divorces them.

Before the marriage, she has sex appeal; before the divorce, ex-appeal.

It's not uncommon for slight acquaintances to get married, but a couple really have to know each other to get divorced.

Marry for love and you divorce for money; marry for money and you divorce for love.

Divorce keeps married people from staying married, and marriage keeps divorced people from staying divorced.

Marriage is often due to lack of judgment, divorce to lack of patience, and remarriage to lack of memory.

Insanity is grounds for divorce in some states, but grounds for marriage in all.

It's impossible to keep a movie star's marriage secret because news of the divorce is certain to leak out.

The woman who marries a man for his money will probably divorce him for the same reason.

There are two periods in life when a man thinks very seriously about marriage: before the wedding, and before the divorce.

One marriage in every three ends in divorce, while the other two fight it out to the bitter end.

Many marriages are first announced, then denounced, and finally renounced.

The high rate of marriages that crack up proves that marriage is not what it's cracked up to be.

Marriage sometimes breaks up the beautiful friendship that resumes with divorce.

Marriage always begins with a small payment to a minister and often ends with a large payment to a lawyer.

Marriage opens the gates of heaven and lets you in, divorce opens the gates of hell and lets you out.

A divorce suit always costs more than a wedding gown.

Love is a matter of chance, marriage a matter of money, and divorce a matter of course.

The frequency of divorce shows that women are fools to marry—but who else can a man marry?

The happiness of the first day of marriage is only exceeded by the happiness of the first day of divorce.

It has almost reached the point where marriage is considered sufficient grounds for divorce.

A movie star considers his marriage a success if no alimony is asked at the divorce.

MARRIAGE LICENSE

The secret of many a man's success is application—for a marriage license.   —*Burton Hillis*

A marriage license is a hunting permit that entitles you to one dear at a time.

The best place to find optimists is at a marriage license bureau.

Husband-hunting is the only sport in which the animal that gets caught has to buy a license.

The trouble with a marriage license is that it doesn't expire every year as other licenses do.

A marriage license is a document always recorded in black and white in order not to show its true colors.

A marriage license is the only license which is taken out after the hunt is over.

It isn't the cost of the marriage license but the weekly payments of your entire salary afterward.

Divorces have become so prevalent, it would save a lot of trouble if every marriage license had a divorce coupon attached.

A marriage license is a certificate that gives a woman the legal right to drive a man.

MARS

Man is an earthling who is feverishly planning to get to Mars before this planet is destroyed.

The first proof that our men have reached Mars will come when we are notified that their luggage has been sent to Venus.

If the Martians ever come to earth, how will they know which are the people and which are the pets?

The reason it's taking so long to get a man on Mars is that it's uphill all the way.

MARTYR

He who dies a martyr proves that he wasn't a knave, but doesn't prove that he wasn't a fool.
— *C. C. Colton*

It's not dying for a faith that's hard—it's living up to it.
—*Thackeray*

To die for an idea is to set a rather high price upon guesswork. — *Anatole France*

Let others wear the martyr's crown; I am not worthy of this honor. — *Erasmus*

A thing is not necessarily true because a man dies for it.
— *Oscar Wilde*

Martyrdom is the only way in which a man can become famous without ability. — *Bernard Shaw*

A martyr is a man who loses his head by sticking his neck out.

There's only one person who suffers more than a martyr, and that's the husband who has to listen to her.

You judge a man by the way he lives, a martyr by the way he dies.

MASSAGE

Massage is a method of pounding the hides of people who are anxious to hide their pounds.

Massage is a treatment designed to take weight off a person, but mostly off the person giving it.

MASTER OF CEREMONIES

A master of ceremonies is a man who introduces a celebrity by telling you he needs no introduction.

An emcee's introduction is like a bathing suit: it calls attention to the subject, but makes no attempt to cover it.

A master of ceremonies tells you what's coming next, but doesn't tell you how to avoid it.

MATCH

No man is a match for a woman, except with a poker and a hobnailed pair of boots—and not always even then.
— Bernard Shaw

After a woman reaches a certain age she feels that almost any man is a match for her.

After the wedding many a woman finds out that a good match is nothing but a stick with a head on it.

Matrimony is a match that often catches fire by friction with a mother-in-law.

If a girl makes a good match, all her relatives will beat a path to her door.

A fool with money to burn soon meets his match.

MATE

Where either the husband or wife has married the wrong mate, both have married the wrong mates.

Marriage is a voyage on the sea of matrimony where a man's mate usually becomes the captain.

A movie star is an actress who is always mating new mistakes.

MATERIALISM

Those who are of the opinion that money will do everything, may very well be suspected to do everything for money.   — Halifax

Love is the greatest thing in this world, yet nine out of ten people are after money.

Money doesn't mean everything in this world, but somehow everything in this world seems to mean money.

To the materialist, money matters are the only things that do.

When it is a question of money, all people are of the same religion.

The person who pursues the things only money can buy, soon loses the things money cannot buy.

Materialism is the belief that if there are other things in life besides money, it takes money to buy them.

Rare is the man who gets a lot of money without letting a lot of money get him.

Money isn't everything, but what isn't it?

MATHEMATICS

Mathematics may be defined as the subject in which we never know what we are talking about, nor whether what we are saying is true.   — *Bertrand Russell*

You propound a complicated mathematical problem: give me a slate and half an hour's time, and I can produce a wrong answer.
— *Bernard Shaw*

It is easier to square the circle than to get round a mathematician.   — *Augustus De Morgan*

One of the chiefest triumphs of modern mathematics consists in having discovered what mathematics really is.
— *Bertrand Russell*

The only place where a dollar is still worth one hundred cents today is in the problems in an arithmetic book.

In mathematics, fractions speak louder than words.

You can't always go by arithmetic: lending a person ten dollars for one week is not the same as lending him one dollar for ten weeks.

When you long for the good old days of your youth, just think of algebra.

Mathematics is no guide in family matters: it cannot explain what happens to a man if his wife is his better half and he marries twice.

A woman doesn't need to know arithmetic—she can always charge it.

Arithmetically speaking, rabbits multiply faster than adders add.

MATURITY

The immature man wants to die nobly for a cause, while the mature man wants to live humbly for one.   — *Wilhelm Stekel*

A mature wife is one who knows everything—and still doesn't get a divorce.

Maturity is the age at which you begin to realize there are more things you don't know than you do.

An adolescent is growing up when he stops wanting to go out with girls and wants to stay home with them.

A man never grows up until his mother stops worrying about him.

Another test of maturity is the ability to get more satisfaction from keeping a secret than from passing it on.

The adult who is always blowing up has stopped growing up.

A girl becomes a woman when she stops looking for the ideal man and starts looking for a husband.

A boy becomes a man when he stops asking his father for money and requests a loan.

The first time a girl complains that she has nothing to wear, she changes from girlhood into womanhood.

A mature person is one who has changed his wishful thinking into thoughtful wishing.

To separate the men from the boys, bring on the girls.

By the time a woman is mature enough to choose a proper mate, she has already been married for years.

MEANING

You can never tell what a woman doesn't mean until she has spoken.

Poets and babies are wonderful creatures, mostly because no one can understand what they say.

No man says all he means, and no woman means all she says.

If a woman meant what she said, she wouldn't say it.

He who laughs last has found a double meaning.

There's no telling what a woman will say till she says it, and then there's no telling half the time what she means.

MEANNESS

There are a lot of mean, stingy-souled people who wouldn't lie to help a friend. — Don Marquis

Some men are so mean that when they attend a ball game, they want to see the home team beaten. — Ed Howe

There are so many more mean men than good that a good man is always under suspicion.
— Ed Howe

With some people, the means justify the end; with others, the end justifies the meanness.

The meaner a man is, the harder it is to make him feel mean.

There's nothing meaner than a sadist, except a soft-hearted drama critic.

MEANS

Take care of the means, and the end will take care of itself.
— Gandhi

The means some people take to get ahead in this world will probably put them behind in the next.

The two chief means of acquiring success are elbow grease and soft soap.

MEASUREMENTS

In a beauty contest a girl's measurements never include her head size.

A tape measure is a device used to measure the acting talent of movie stars.

A woman's ideal measurements are 36–24–36—forward or backward.

You can't go by measurements: as long as a man wants to slip his arm around her waist, a woman is still slim.

Many a woman is a perfect 36–24–36, give or take a few inches here and there.

A woman's measurements are a set of three figures used to describe one figure.

An actress in straightened circumstances is probably one whose measurements are 36–36–36.

MEAT

I am a great eater of beef, and I believe that does harm to my wit. — *Shakespeare*

Meat prices have got many a family into a perpetual stew.

It's tough to pay a dollar a pound for meat, but it's tougher if you pay less.

The consumer doesn't object to the people who raise meat but to the people who raise meat prices.

One man's meat is another man's high cost of living.

Most lamb is sheep at any price, but venison is always deer.

MEDDLING

How happily some people would live if they would only mind other people's business as little as they mind their own!
 — *G. C. Lichtenberg*

One of the hardest things about the business of life is minding your own.

Half the world doesn't know how the other half lives—and it's none of its business.

Some men never seem to learn where their business ends and someone else's business begins.

The man who doesn't mind his own business rarely has a business of his own to mind.

Everybody's business is nobody's business, except the busybody's.

Make someone happy—mind your own business.

A person should spend half his time minding his own business, and the other half letting other people's alone.

To the gossip, the woman who minds her own business is narrow-minded.

MEDICAL

Soap and water and common sense are the best disinfectants.
 — *William Osler*

There is nothing so sickening as to leaf through a medical dictionary. — *Jules Renard*

It's surprising how many medical authorities you can find over bridge tables.

Medicine is a science, acquiring a medical practice an art.

The practice of medicine has advanced so much in recent years that it is now impossible for a doctor not to find something wrong with you.

The most difficult task of the medical profession is to train patients to become sick during office hours only.

A bacteriologist is a man whose conversations always start with the germ of an idea.

Another good thing about Medicare is that it enables us to have diseases which would otherwise be beyond our means.

Most of us are born with medical assistance, and most of us die the same way.

MEDICINE

One of the first duties of a physician is to educate the masses not to take medicine. — *William Osler*

I don't know much about medicine, but I know what I like.
— *S. J. Perelman*

The worst thing about medicine is that one kind makes another necessary. — *Elbert Hubbard*

There ain't much fun in medicine, but there's a good deal of medicine in fun.   — *Josh Billings*

One of the chief objects of medicine is to save us from the natural consequences of our vices and follies.   — *Mencken*

The surest way to get your youngster to take his medicine is to label the bottle *Poison* and hide it.

Preachers who declare the world is losing faith should consider the number of reducing nostrums on the market.

The best medicine for rheumatism is to give thanks that it isn't the gout.

MEDIOCRITY

Only a mediocre person is always at his best.
— *Somerset Maugham*

Mediocrity is merit to the mediocre.   — *Joubert*

Mediocrities can explain everything, and are surprised at nothing.   — *Delacroix*

MEET

It's lucky for some of the women that all of the men don't want the rest of the women.

We all meet a good many people who never meet us.

Sooner or later every woman meets the right man, but it's usually after she's married.

If you have difficulty meeting new people, try picking up the wrong ball on the golf course.

Lifelong friends seldom meet.

Another thing that makes a woman suddenly feel old is meeting a bald man who used to go to school with her.

Running into debt isn't too bad; it's running into creditors that's so upsetting.

A fool and his money are soon parted, but how did they get together in the first place?

MEETING

Before marriage, there's a meeting of minds; after marriage, she takes charge of the meeting.

It's better to have loved and lost—you don't have to attend PTA meetings.

The members of Congress are duty bound to meet but not to get together.

There's always something good in a PTA meeting, even if it only gives parents and teachers a chance to sympathize with one another.

MEMORY

Every man's memory is his private literature. — *Aldous Huxley*

Many a man fails to become a thinker only because his memory is too good. — *Nietzsche*

Nothing fixes a thing so intensely in the memory as the wish to forget it. — *Montaigne*

Creditors have better memories than debtors. — *Franklin*

Everyone complains of his memory, no one of his judgment. — *La Rochefoucauld*

Writing things down is the best secret of a good memory.

People are usually better than their memories: it is easier to forgive than to forget.

There are three kinds of memory: good, bad, and convenient.

If you don't think people have short memories, just ask someone what you've accomplished.

The best memory expert is a woman who has once been told another woman's right age.

Why is it that memory enables us to remember the favors we do for others, but not the favors others do for us?

It takes more than a good memory to have good memories.

Memory is what tells a man his wedding anniversary was yesterday.

A good memory test is to recall all the kind things you have said about your neighbors.

Memory is what makes you wonder what you've forgotten to do.

When a man starts to lose his memory, the best thing he can do is to forget about it.

There's only one way to improve your memory, and that's to lengthen it.

A fault-finder is a person with a bad memory who never remembers the good, or with a good memory who always remembers the bad.

A memory expert remembers everything, including many things he ought to forget.

Some people have wonderful memories: they can't remember what they worried about yesterday.

Never trust your memory: it makes you forget a favor in a few days, while it helps you remember an injury for years.

A good way to cure a bad memory is by lending small sums to your friends.

A man with a terrible memory forgets everything, a woman with a terrible memory remembers everything.

Some people have such good memories, they can remember when they were so young that they couldn't remember anything.

MENU

When a menu has practically everything on it, it should be replaced by a clean one.

If you cannot pronounce the name of the dish on the menu, you probably cannot afford it.

A la carte: you get what you can; table d'hôte: you take what you get.

The bigger the menu, the smaller the portions.

A chef is a head cook with a limited number of dishes but an unlimited number of names for them.

Some restaurants call the bill of fare a menu, and some call the menu a bill of fare.

MERCENARY

It's not right to marry a man for his money, but sometimes that's the only way a girl can get it.

We would all get on comfortably without money if only other people weren't mad about it.

Some women take a man for better or for worse, while others take him for everything.

No husband can ever give his wife all the money she wants—there simply isn't that much money.

The woman who runs her hands through a man's hair probably hopes to run them later through his money.

When money talks, some women don't miss a word.

If a girl really likes a man, money doesn't matter—unless, of course, he doesn't have any.

Some women take a man for what he is; others, for what he has.

MESSAGE

A great writer's nonsense is sure to drive his commentators mad looking for a message.
– *Frank Moore Colby*

You can send a message around the world in less than a second but it takes years to get it through the human skull.
– *Charles F. Kettering*

MIDDLE

I'm not a middle-of-the-roader because in the middle of the road is the worst place to drive.
– *Robert Frost*

There is no such thing as a happy medium: everyone is either praised or criticized too much.

The working farmer is usually lean; it's the middleman who develops the middle.

A middle-of-the-roader is like a pair of socks—neither right nor left.

MIDDLE AGE

Middle age is the time when a man is always thinking that in a week or two he will feel just as good as ever.   – *Don Marquis*

Middle age is a time of life that a man first notices in his wife.   – *Richard Armour*

Another sign of middle age is when you want to see how long your car will last instead of how fast it will go.

When men reach middle age, they get sadder and wiser; when women do, they get sadder and wider.

Middle age is when we can do just as much as ever, but would rather not.

Middle age is the period in a man's life when he has more on his mind, but less on his head.

Another problem during middle age is keeping your daughter in college while keeping yourself out of debt.

A middle-aged woman always finds it is easier to take years off her age than inches off her waist.

Middle age is the period when too much food and too little sleep make a person thick and tired.

Middle age is when you don't care where you go just so long as you're home by ten.

You've reached middle age when it is the doctor who warns you to slow down instead of the police.

Middle age is the time of life when a man is grounded for several days after flying high for just one night.

Middle age is the time in life when one keeps putting back the time when middle age sets in.

The worst thing about middle age is that you outgrow it.

Middle age is the period when you are too young to get on Social Security, and too old to get another job.

Middle age is when your memory is shorter but your experience longer, and your vitality is lower but your forehead higher.

A man's feelings for women begin to turn to thoughts when he reaches fifty.

Middle age is when you can do everything you used to do, but not until tomorrow.

Middle age is the time in life when the narrow waist and the broad mind begin to change places.

A woman has reached middle age when the only pinches she gets come from girdles and shoes.

Middle age is the time in life when you are either married or singular.

Middle age is an indefinite time in life that always starts years earlier for the other fellow.

Another thing about middle-age spread is that it brings people closer together.

Middle age is the time in life when you need more horsepower and less exhaust.

Middle age is the time in life when you're old enough to know better, but young enough to keep on doing it.

Many a middle-aged man continues to think he is as good as he never was.

Middle age is when a man your own age looks much older than you think you look.

Middle age is the period when a man must keep fit as a fiddle or look like a bass viol.

By the time a man is ready to admit he's middle-aged, he's already past it.

Middle age is the time in life when a woman's age remains the same while she grows older.

Middle age is the time in life when you stop criticizing the older generation and start criticizing the younger one.

Act your age, especially during middle age: don't go all out or you'll end up all in.

Middle age is the period when most women don't mind telling you their age—at least partly.

Middle age is the time in life when many a man grows old from having young ideas.

Life begins at forty, and so do double chins and wrinkles.

Middle age is the period when the middle-aged seem to you much younger than they used to be.

Middle age is the period when a woman subtracts from her age but adds to her weight.

Middle age is the time in life when you lose your punch, but gain a paunch.

Another sign of middle age is when you begin to think that women's fashions are crazier than ever.

Middle age is the time in life when you act like 18 one night, and feel like 118 the morning after.

Middle age is an interlude between two periods: when time marches on, and when time runs out.

About the time a man begins to get thin on the top, his wife begins to get fat on the bottom.

Middle age is the time in life when it takes you longer to rest than it does to get tired.

Middle age is the time in life when work begins to be a lot less fun, and fun begins to be a lot more work.

MILK

Man should go out of this world as he came in—chiefly on milk.　　　— *William Osler*

My illness is due to my doctor's insistence that I drink milk, a whitish fluid they force down helpless babies.　　　— *W. C. Fields*

If you must cry over spilt milk, condense it.

It's not hard to learn how to milk a cow if you begin with a calf.

Farmers know how to milk the cows, while politicians know how to milk the farmers.

Instead of crying over spilt milk, an opportunist lets the cat out of the bag.

Dairy slogan: Drinka pinta milka day.

MILLENNIUM

I believe that the millennium will get here some day, but I could compile quite a list of persons who will have to go first.
　　　— *Don Marquis*

The lion and the lamb will lie down together when the lamb hasn't anything the lion wants.

The millennium is not a biblical fiction; it has merely been indefinitely postponed.

The real millennium will come when the pedestrian and the motorist shall lie down together.

MILLIONAIRE

A man who makes a million dollars is just as well off as if he were rich.　　　— *John Jacob Astor*

It is easier for a man to be good for a million than for a million to be good for a man.

When a millionaire's money talks, it usually talks about more money.

The only difference between a millionaire and the rest of us is that while he's working on his second million, we're working on our first.

Many a woman's dream is to make a millionaire out of a multi-millionaire.

Some men don't marry until they find the one girl in a million; others won't until they find the one girl with a million.

No married man can understand why every bachelor isn't a millionaire.

Only a millionaire can afford to buy all the advertised products we can't afford to be without.

If there's one thing better than marrying a millionaire, it's divorcing him.

The man who claims that poverty and hard work are good for character is usually a millionaire.

A multimillionaire is the only man whose wife finds it hard to live beyond her husband's income.

A millionaire is a man with the most relatives.

The person who minds nobody's business but his own is probably a millionaire.

A millionaire is a man who gathers a fortune he doesn't need to leave to people who don't deserve it.

The man with a million is seldom as happy as the man who feels like a million.

Money doesn't always bring happiness: a man with ten million dollars is no happier than a man with nine million.

Nowadays in order to live like a millionaire you have to be a multimillionaire.

When a girl marries a millionaire, all her relatives beat a path to her door.

Not every man wants to be a millionaire; many are content just to live like one.

The only thing better than marrying a millionaire with a big heart is marrying one with a weak heart.

Many a woman doesn't care whether the man she dates is rich or poor—as long as he is a millionaire.

A millionaire is the only person who receives letters from second cousins.

MIND

An open mind is all very well, but it ought not to be so open that there's no keeping anything in or out.   *— Samuel Butler*

Reasoning with a child is fine, if you can reach the child's reason without destroying your own.
— John Mason Brown

When he had to use his mind, he felt like a right-handed person who has to use his left.
— G. C. Lichtenberg

The mind of man operates like a crab on the shore crawling backward in search of the Atlantic Ocean, and missing it. *— Mencken*

The open mind never acts.
— *Bernard Shaw*

I have a prodigious quantity of mind; it takes me as much as a week sometimes to make it up.   — *Mark Twain*

The mind is hindered by too little education—and by too much.   — *Pascal*

I have found that no exertion of the legs can bring two minds much nearer to one another.
— *Thoreau*

It requires a very unusual mind to undertake the analysis of the obvious.   — *A. N. Whitehead*

My mind is a one-track road, and can only run one train of thought at a time.
— *Woodrow Wilson*

A girl sometimes attracts a man by her mind, but more often by what she doesn't mind.

Man's reason for existence is the existence of his reason.

The wise husband learns to read his wife's mind, but doesn't try to understand it.

There are two kinds of fools: mindful and mindless.

The man who doesn't know his own mind hasn't missed much.

A scold never speaks her whole mind but only gives you a piece of it.

A frame of mind is about all some people have of it.

It's good to let your mind go blank occasionally, but only if you turn the sound off too.

When her mind wanders, a scatterbrain never has far to go.

It is a woman's privilege to change her mind, but her practice to change her husband's mind.

If a cluttered desk is the sign of a cluttered brain, what is the significance of an empty desk?

The best kind of mind is that which minds its own business.

The objection to an open mind is that convictions get out as often as new ideas get in.

Many a married couple are just two minds without a single thought.

If travel broadens the mind, some people must be nailed to the ground.

When a man changes his mind as much as a woman, he is probably married to her.

Know your own mind: don't let a flood of emotion wreck your train of thought.

Many a man who thinks he is broad-minded is merely thick-headed.

If a woman cannot make up her mind, how can she always be changing it?

The man who has half a mind to get married, should do it— that's all it takes.

When husband and wife are of one mind, it's not hard to guess whose.

MIND AND MATTER

Women represent the triumph of matter over mind, just as men represent the triumph of mind over morals. — *Oscar Wilde*

There is no difference between mind and matter: mind is matter —gray matter.

Many a host pays no attention to the seating of his dinner guests because those who matter don't mind, and those who mind don't matter.

MINING

People who try to get rich from mining, often put more into the ground than they take out of it. — *Bernard Baruch*

The man who discovers a uranium mine can rest comfortably on his ores.

MINORITY

If a man is in a minority of one, we lock him up.
— *Justice O. W. Holmes*

Another oppressed minority that deserves redress is the man who has a wife and two teen-age daughters.

A perfect example of minority rule is a baby in the house.

MIRACLE

I believe in the possibility of a lasting marriage because I still believe in miracles. — *Sacha Guitry*

Miracles sometimes occur, but one has to work terribly hard for them. — *Chaim Weizmann*

The only thing still old-fashioned enough to reject miracles is the new theology. — *Chesterton*

There is nothing more impressive than a miracle, except the credulity that can take it at par.
— *Mark Twain*

In Israel, in order to be a realist, you must believe in miracles.
— *David Ben-Gurion*

Miracles do happen: there are some married couples who have a joint bank account and no arguments.

MIRROR

Woman serves as a looking glass possessing the magic powers of reflecting the figure of man at twice its natural size. — *Virginia Woolf*

The acid test for a woman is to walk past a mirror without looking into it.

If we could see ourselves as others see us, few mirrors would be sold.

A mirror is the only thing not afraid to talk back to a woman.

The mirror shows everyone his best and his worst enemy.

Beauty is in the eye of the beholder, especially when a vain creature looks in the mirror.

A woman will look into a mirror any time, except when she's about to pull out of a parking place.

A mirror shows a man his tie, but a woman her years.

No man has the nerve to tell a woman what her mirror sometimes tells her.

In the search for beauty, a mirror is more useful than a microscope.

The person who is looking for faults should look in a mirror.

What your mirror tells you is probably right because it's the result of reflection.

What this country needs is a new type of mirror that will grow more charitable with the years.

An egotist never seems to find fault with a mirror.

If you want to see how you look asleep, stand in front of a mirror with your eyes shut.

MISANTHROPY

If a man isn't a misanthrope by the time he reaches forty, he never loved mankind. — *Chamfort*

There is always one person whom a misanthrope doesn't hate.

A misanthrope believes that there are only two kinds of good people: the dead and the unborn.

The punishment of the misanthrope is that he is forced to live in a world full of people.

The more a misanthrope has to do with people, the more he appreciates animals.

The misanthrope thinks the world is all right for a visit, but hates to live there.

To the misanthrope all men are equal—equally bad.

A misanthrope distrusts people who flatter him, and dislikes people who don't.

A misanthrope has little faith in mankind and even less in womankind.

All misanthropes are alike in their dislike of people.

A misanthrope is all right in his place, but his place hasn't been dug yet.

A misanthrope should never marry, because he won't enjoy it, and besides, he shouldn't reproduce himself.

MISBEHAVIOR

You never know what a three-year-old youngster is going to do next, thank goodness!

Stop worrying about what Junior will do when he grows up— better go see what he's up to now.

Beyond all human aid is the bad boy who is not even good just before Christmas.

A brat is a child who behaves like your own but belongs to your neighbor.

There's one lucky thing about spoiled children: we never have them in our own family.

MISER

The happiest miser on earth is the man who saves up every friend he can make.
— *Robert E. Sherwood*

A miser is one who accumulates money as fast as others accumulate clothes hangers.

A miser begins by saving up for a rainy day, and ends by saving up for the rainy days of his heirs.

A miser is the proof that not every fool and his money are soon parted.

A miser is even more economical than the man who is too economical.

A miser is a poor wretch who has nothing but money.

Every man serves a useful purpose: a miser, for example, makes a wonderful ancestor.

A miser is known by the money he keeps.

Nowadays it seems that the miser is the only one who lives within his means.

A tightward may be a great success in making money, but is a terrible failure in spending it.

The miser is another man who can't seem to distinguish between his need and his greed.

You can always tell a miser: he upsets himself a dollar's worth when he loses a dime.

A miser thinks no more of a dollar than other men think of their lives.

MISERY

Fate often puts all the materials of happiness into a man's hands just to see how miserable he can make himself with them.
— *Don Marquis*

I sometimes try to be miserable that I may do more work.
— *William Blake*

Misery loves company, but can't bear competition.   — *Josh Billings*

Nature has made man miserable enough, yet he makes himself even more miserable by human nature.
— *Montaigne*

Misery loves company, but company doesn't reciprocate.

When a wife feels miserable after a quarrel, she runs home to mother; when she wants her husband to feel miserable, she remains at home.

Misery loves company, but it's better to have arthritis in one leg than in both.

Every family manages to bear up under a great tragedy, but how many can stand the water being turned off for a few hours?

MISFORTUNE

Calamities are of two kinds: misfortunes to ourselves, and good fortune to others. — *Bierce*

I consider you unfortunate because you have never been unfortunate. — *Seneca*

Misfortune: the kind of fortune that never misses. — *Bierce*

If all our misfortunes were lumped together, with everyone forced to take an equal share, people would be glad to take back their own. — *Socrates*

Marriage, twins and other misfortunes never come singly.

Take it easy: if you go too fast, you'll catch up with misfortune; if you go too slow, misfortune will catch up with you.

Fortune knocks but once at any man's door, but misfortune has much more patience.

Man does not understand woman—that is his misfortune; woman understands man—that is also his misfortune.

When misfortune comes, take it like a man—blame it on your wife.

If it weren't for the misfortune of others, life would be absolutely unbearable.

MISINFORMATION

The surest way to convey misinformation is often to tell the strict truth. — *Mark Twain*

The disadvantage of being a good listener is that you acquire a great deal of misinformation.

You can always tell the smart-aleck: he takes every opportunity to show off his wide range of misinformation.

The most common way to receive misinformation is through the five senses.

Events are moving so fast nowadays that it's hard to keep up-to-date on our misinformation.

MISQUOTATION

Next to the originator of a good sentence is the first misquoter of it.

When some men cite the Scriptures, their quotations are wholly original.

When you see yourself quoted in print and you're sorry you said it, it suddenly becomes a misquotation.

Another advantage of education is that it enables you to misquote Shakespeare.

About the only thing that cannot be misquoted is silence.

MISSILE

A guided missile is an object that goes faster than sound, and almost as fast as money.

Missiles have made our world smaller, but our worries bigger.

An old-timer is the married man who can remember when the only guided missiles were dishes.

Guided missiles were invented by scientists to help politicians who are always promising us the moon.

Only a misguided world would go in for atomic guided missiles.

MISSIONARY

Missionaries are the divinely provided food for destitute and underfed cannibals. — *Oscar Wilde*

Missionaries are going to reform the world whether it wants to or not. — *Will Rogers*

If you want to make your money go as far as possible, give it to foreign missions.

Some men approve of missionaries because it rids the country of a lot of reformers.

A missionary is a person who teaches cannibals to say grace before they eat him.

Don't pity the missionary: suppose his task was to convert the heathen at home.

A missionary is one who loves the Almighty more than the almighty dollar.

The more clothes the missionaries put on uncivilized women, the more clothes civilized women take off.

A missionary sometimes reforms a cannibal by giving him religion, but more often by giving him indigestion.

MISTAKE

Lord, deliver me from the man who never makes a mistake, and also from the man who makes the same mistake twice.
— *Dr. William J. Mayo*

The man who has never made a mistake will never make anything else. — *Bernard Shaw*

There's many a mistake made on purpose.
— *Thomas C. Haliburton*

Things are seldom what they seem: that's why people mistake education for intelligence, wealth for happiness, and sex for love.

We call a person a fool when he makes mistakes that are different from the ones we make.

The successful man makes mistakes just like the failure, but he usually makes them when no one is looking.

When a fellow needs a friend he often makes a mistake and takes a wife.

Older people don't make as many mistakes as younger ones even though they've had more experience.

A do-it-yourselfer is always busy in his spare time making repairs, making furniture, and making mistakes.

Of all the mistakes a man can make with women, the greatest

is that of having nothing to do with them.

Since we all learn from our mistakes, why don't we make those from which we can learn most?

To err is human, but only when we ourselves make the mistake.

There's really no need for you to remember your mistakes since your wife will always remember them.

The man who never makes a mistake takes his orders from one who does.

A common mistake for married people to make is to think they couldn't have done any worse.

Consider yourself lucky: suppose your errors were published every day like those of a ball player.

There are two kinds of people who make mistakes: those who won't admit them, and those who call them experience.

The greatest mistake in life is to be in constant fear that you will make one.

We all make mistakes, but luckily we don't always marry them.

Learn from the mistakes of others—you can never live long enough to make them all yourself.

The best way to tell a woman's age is—a mistake.

You're never too old to learn how to make new mistakes.

Experience is what enables you to recognize a mistake after you make it again.

The man who claims he never makes a mistake has a wife who did.

The man who makes a mistake and then makes an excuse for it, is making two mistakes.

All some people learn from experience is that they made another mistake.

To err is human, but anybody can make a mistake.

The only place where you can find people who haven't made a mistake in years is the cemetery.

A man who commits a mistake and doesn't correct it, is committing another mistake.

All men make mistakes, but husbands find out about them sooner.

If experience is the best teacher, how is it that its students never stop making mistakes?

If you don't learn from your mistakes, there's no sense making them.

MISUNDERSTAND

No one can misunderstand a boy like his own mother.
—*Norman Douglas*

It is one of those things that are always misunderstood because they have been too often explained.
—*Chesterton*

It takes two to make a marriage, or any other form of misunderstanding.

You have to live with a woman to really misunderstand her.

What this world needs is the peace that passeth all misunderstanding.

The man who thinks marriage is a 50-50 proposition understands neither women nor fractions.

Many a married man gets into trouble through a miss-understanding.

The wife who complains of being misunderstood is probably unintelligible.

MODEL

An artist's model sometimes quits her job because the artist doesn't know where to draw the line.

Even when he has a model wife, a husband cannot help looking over the later models.

A model is the girl who shapes her career around a good figure.

A model house is easy to build, but where can you find a model family to live in it?

There's no one more unpopular with men than the model husband.

A good painter seldom makes a model husband but often has a model wife.

A house is not a home, and there's also a big difference between a model house and a model home.

An artist's model achieves success only after years of attireless effort.

A model husband is one who is smart enough to earn a lot of money, and foolish enough to give it all to his wife.

Fashion models are always so slim, they make a faminine appeal.

MODERATION

I believe about work as I believe about drink: it should be used in moderation.
    — George Jean Nathan

It's a sure sign of mediocrity always to be moderate with praise.
    — Vauvenargues

Moderation is a fatal thing: nothing succeeds like excess.
    — Oscar Wilde

Temperate temperance is best; intemperate temperance injures the cause of temperance.
    — Mark Twain

MODERN

Nothing is so dangerous as being too modern: one is apt to grow old-fashioned quite suddenly.
    — Oscar Wilde

The modern girl is afraid of nothing except a stack of dirty dishes.

Nowadays the girl who is up to date is probably up to anything.

Nothing modernizes a home so completely as an advertisement offering it for sale.

Modern art is like modern woman: you'll never enjoy it if you try to understand it.

The last thing a woman wants to be up to date in is her age.

MODESTY

The English instinctively admire any man who has no talent and is modest about it. — *James Agate*

Modesty died when clothes were born. — *Mark Twain*

I have often wished I had the time to cultivate modesty, but I am too busy thinking about myself. — *Edith Sitwell*

It is easy for a somebody to be modest, but it is difficult to be modest when one is a nobody. — *Jules Renard*

Modesty is the only sure bait when you angle for praise. — *Chesterton*

It is strange that modesty is the rule for women when what they most value in men is boldness. — *Ninon de Lenclos*

The man who is ostentatious of his modesty is twin to the statue that wears a fig leaf. — *Mark Twain*

Modesty is the art of encouraging people to find out for themselves how wonderful you are.

Everyone has plenty to be modest about, especially the man who is never modest.

Excessive modesty has ruined more kidneys than excessive liquor.

Modesty is the practice of withholding from others the high opinion you hold of yourself.

MONEY

Money is like a sixth sense, and you can't make use of the other five without it. — *Somerset Maugham*

The chief value of money lies in the fact that one lives in a world in which it is overestimated. — *Mencken*

When a man says money can do anything, that settles it—he hasn't any. — *Ed Howe*

I find it more trouble to take care of money than to get it. — *Montaigne*

I'm tired of love, I'm still more tired of rhyme, but money gives me pleasure all the time. — *Hilaire Belloc*

Where I was brought up we never talked about money because there was never enough to furnish a topic of conversation. — *Mark Twain*

Money would be more enjoyable if it took people as long to spend it as it does to earn it. — *Ed Howe*

The gods are those who either have money or do not want it.
— *Samuel Butler*

A man is seldom so harmlessly occupied as when he is making money.   — *Samuel Johnson*

Money is a commodity that is constantly changing hands—and people.

The chief advantage of having money is that you don't have to worry about not having it.

Money is not the root of all evil—no money is.

Money may be a curse, but you can always find someone to take the curse off you.

Money talks, but not when it's a small amount.

Money isn't everything, but it's mighty handy if you don't have a credit card.

There are more things in life to worry about than just money—how to get hold of it, for example.

Money doesn't go very far these days, or come very near.

Taking it with you isn't nearly so important as making it last until you're ready to go.

Money isn't everything; in fact, after the tax collector gets through, money isn't anything.

Every wife likes her husband to have something tender about him, especially legal tender.

Money is the route of all evil.

Money isn't everything—for one thing, it isn't plentiful.

Rich or poor, it's nice to have money.

Money can't buy everything—poverty, for example.

Money is a good thing, but you have to waste a lot of time making it.

There are two types of people: those who cannot make it, and those who cannot keep it.

Regardless of finance, inflation or taxation, the real problem always turns out to be money.

Those who have money, have trouble about it; those who have none, have trouble without it.

Money isn't everything, but subtract it from some people and there's nothing left.

Money always talks most when a man marries it.

The love of some one else's money is the root of all evil.

The success of some men in acquiring money is due to the success of other men in letting go of it.

Money isn't everything; usually, it isn't even enough.

What this country needs is not more money, but more people who have some of it.

There are more important things in life than a little money, and one of them is a lot of money.

Money talks, but it doesn't always talk sense.

If you want to know what God thinks of money, look at some of the people he gives it to.

Money isn't everything; sometimes it isn't even 99 per cent.

You can't take it with you, but where on earth can you go without it?

One man's money burns a hole in another man's pocket.

Money isn't everything, but it's way ahead of any of its competitors.

The mint makes it first, and it's up to us to make it last.

Money may not buy everything, but it's a great consolation until you have everything.

Money is what things run into, and people run out of.

A man making money is like a bee making honey; he can make it, but they won't let him keep it.

The trouble is not that you cannot take it with you, but that you cannot even keep it while you're here.

MONKEY

Man descended from monkeys, and monkeys descended from trees.

If man sprang from the monkeys, he ought to spring once more and make it a safe distance.

The question is not whether man descended from the monkey, but when he is going to stop descending.

MONOGAMY

I am a strict monogamist: it is 20 years since I last went to bed with two women at once, and then I was in my cups and not myself.
— Mencken

Love is the effort a man makes to be satisfied with only one woman. — Paul Géraldy

The Western custom sanctions only one wife and hardly any mistresses. — Saki

I'm not a real movie star—I still got the same wife I started out with nearly 28 years ago.
— Will Rogers

In the future the woman who sticks to one man will be regarded as a monomaniac.

Most men believe in monogamy because enough is enough.

Monogamy is a custom established to protect men who are incapable of protecting themselves.

Today the one-man woman is found only in a one-horse town.

The marriages of movie stars may best be described as serial monogamy.

MONTHS

March is the homeowner's month: it's time to put away the

snow shovel, but not yet time to get out the lawn mower.

If you want to avoid domestic strife, don't marry in January—and that goes for the other months too.

July is the month when mothers are again reminded why school-teachers need long summer vacations.

September is the month when amateur gardeners put off till October the chores they should have finished in August.

It's unwise to eat oysters in any month without an R or lobsters in any month without a vowel.

The best month to get married in is Octembruary.

MOOD

Good humor is one of the best articles of dress one can wear in society.   — Thackeray

Whenever a man encounters a woman in a mood he doesn't understand, he wants to know if she is tired. — George Jean Nathan

What I value more than all things is good humor.   — Jefferson

Some men always go home hoping to find their wives in a different humor.

Most letters of reference are excellent because you get them when the company is in good humor over getting rid of you.

A battle-ax is a woman of moods—usually the imperative mood.

One way to put the boss in a good humor is to do the dishes for her.

MOON

Everyone is a moon and has a dark side which he never shows to anybody.   — Mark Twain

The advantage of sending a man to the moon is that it would reduce by one the number of crackpots on earth.   — Harlow Shapley

Many a man who dreams of taking a trip to the moon should first visit his neighbors.

The distance to the moon was once measured in miles, but now it's in dollars.

In the good old days you could promise your child the moon without having to buy him a space suit.

In the good old days the only thing that jumped over the moon was the cow.

Soon a man from the earth will be able to go around the moon as easily as the man in the moon goes around the earth.

Some of today's youngsters who cry for the moon will probably grow up and get it.

The meek will inherit the earth, but only after the courageous ones have taken off for the moon.

Politicians have always promised the moon, but in the past no one believed them.

The first spaceman to orbit the earth was the man in the moon.

In the past the moon was an inspiration to lovers and poets; in the future it will be just another airport.

It wasn't until life on earth became too dangerous that men began to fly to the moon.

As time passes it becomes easier to get to the moon while it becomes harder to stay on the earth.

Putting a man on the moon used to tax our imagination, but nowadays it merely taxes our income.

The man in the moon is a distant creature who is probably wondering why everyone has suddenly become so anxious to visit him.

MORALIST

Moral luminaries are those who forgo ordinary pleasures and find compensation in interfering with the pleasures of others.
— *Bertrand Russell*

A moralist never seems to run out of ideas on what other people ought to do.

A moralist is one who wants you to live your life his way.

A moralist always overlooks the difference between what he is and what he wants you to be.

A moralist is someone who always knows better than you do what's bad for you.

A moralist believes that virtue is its own reward, and that people people should be good for nothing.

A moralist is a person whose conscience is always on his conscience.

MORALITY

What is moral is what you feel good after, and what is immoral is what you feel bad after.
— *Hemingway*

Morality is the theory that every human act must be either right or wrong, and that 99 per cent of them are wrong.
— *Mencken*

Bourgeois morality is largely a system of making cheap virtues a cloak for expensive vices.
— *Bernard Shaw*

Morality is the custom of one's country: cannibalism is moral in a cannibal country. — *Samuel Butler*

Go into the street and give one man a lecture on morality and another a shilling, and see which will respect you most.
— *Samuel Johnson*

All of us would gladly accept the advice of our moral superiors —the difficulty is to find any.

Another thing a person can't keep on an empty stomach is principles.

The morals of the country are getting better: when a government official wants to make money nowadays, he resigns.

Good morals are nobler than good manners, but not so popular.

You can never tell about a girl's morals—and you shouldn't.

MORTGAGE

A small house is better than a large mortgage.

Be there ever so many payments, there's no place like home.

If you have an urge to write something that will live forever, sign a mortgage.

Homes are built to provide a little security for a family, and a lot of security for the bank that holds the mortgage.

Some men are known by their deeds, others by their mortgages.

If medical science continues to prolong human life, some of us may eventually pay off the mortgage.

The only way some people can get out of debt is by refinancing the mortgage on their house.

By the time a family pays off the mortgage for a home in the suburbs, the home isn't home, and the suburbs aren't suburbs.

Every man should have a home: you can never tell when you might want to mortgage it to buy something else.

You can always find a bank to finance your new home with your interest in mind.

The disadvantage of buying a new house is not the wall-to-wall carpeting, nor the wall-to-wall windows—it's the back-to-the-wall financing.

MOSQUITO

If we walk in the woods, we must feed mosquitoes. —*Emerson*

Take a lesson from the mosquito: he never waits for an opening—he makes one.

A human being is the most popular blood donor for mosquitoes.

Mosquitoes are free from one vice at least: they can't stand cigarette smoke.

If nature is so wonderful, why didn't she make the mosquito a vegetarian?

The mosquito puts more clothes on people than modesty.

The mosquito is like a child: when he stops making a noise you know he's getting into something.

The trouble with a screened porch is that the mosquitoes can't get out.

Consider the mosquito: he doesn't say much, yet always carries his point.

The only ones who appreciate girls with fat legs are mosquitoes.

Even a mosquito doesn't get a slap on the back until he starts working.

There's always one more mosquito.

MOTHER

The hand that rules the cradle rocks the world. — *Peter De Vries*

She ought never to have been a mother, but she'll make a rare mother-in-law. — *Samuel Butler*

Every mother worries that some scheming female will capture her son, and that no scheming male will capture her daughter.

Nowadays many a girl is as old as her mother looks.

A mother is a housewife whose idea of leisure is the free time she has to indulge in other domestic chores.

Maternity is a fine thing—especially in a woman.

To the mother of young children, there's a time and place for everything, except rest.

God could not be everywhere, so he made mothers.

Every mother hopes her daughter will get a better husband than she did, but she knows her son will never get as good a wife as his father did.

There is nothing like the joy of motherhood, especially when all the children are in bed.

In all kinds of weather, for a doting mother the son always shines.

MOTHER AND DAUGHTER

A fluent tongue is the only thing a mother doesn't like her daughter to resemble her in.
— *Richard Brinsley Sheridan*

The teen-ager who tries to look older than she is, probably has a mother who tries to look younger than she is.

Where do mothers learn all the things they tell their daughters not to do?

You're getting old when you see a girl who looks like someone you used to know, and it turns out to be her daughter.

When a mother finally decides to give her daughter some advice, the mother usually learns plenty.

Mother knows best—until daughter becomes a teen-ager.

The mother who can easily remember her first kiss probably has a daughter who can hardly remember her first husband.

What mother used to call sin, daughter now calls experience.

A teen-ager would like to add to her age the years that her mother subtracts from her own.

The old-fashioned girl who didn't dare hold her boy friend's hand now has a daughter who doesn't dare let go of it.

It takes two to make a marriage: a young girl and an anxious mother.

MOTHER AND GRANDMOTHER

Just about the time she thinks her work is done, a mother becomes a grandmother.

Sometimes a wife goes home to mother only to find that mother has gone home to grandmother.

It's such a grand thing to be the mother of a mother that the world calls her a grandmother.

When a woman has stopped bragging about how smart her children are, it's because she has started bragging about how smart her grandchildren are.

MOTHER-IN-LAW

I know a mother-in-law who sleeps with her glasses on, the better to see her son-in-law suffer in her dreams. — *Ernest Coquelin*

The awe and dread with which the savage contemplates his mother-in-law are amongst the most familiar facts of anthropology.
— *James G. Frazer*

A mother-in-law dies only when another devil is needed in hell.
— *Rabelais*

If you must choose between living with your mother-in-law and blowing out your brains, don't hesitate—blow out hers.
— *Victorien Sardou*

To a mother-in-law, there's nothing easier to find than fault, and nothing harder to keep than still.

A mother-in-law seldom seems to know where mother-love ends and meddling begins.

A man's mother-in-law is a relative, and always on his wife's side.

If you've never heard a mother-in-law joke, she probably has no sense of humor.

A mother-in-law is the only thing that talks louder than money.

Every wife believes there are two sides to every question—her own and her mother-in-law's.

A mother-in-law is the only law under which you are assumed to be guilty until proved innocent.

It's not how often your mother-in-law visits you that counts, it's how long she stays.

A young man cannot be too careful in his choice of a mother-in-law.

A mother-in-law is the matrimonial kin that gets under your skin.

Every cloud has a silver lining: when you get a divorce, you also get rid of your mother-in-law.

Marry in haste and repent at your mother-in-law's.

A visiting mother-in-law usually takes everything but the trip back home.

Behind every successful man is a surprised woman—his mother-in-law.

A husband always prefers his wife's mother-in-law to his own.

The man who says nothing is impossible, has probably never lived with his mother-in-law.

Love is blind, but your mother-in-law isn't.

A man is a daredevil to his mother before marriage, but a doormat to his mother-in-law thereafter.

Faint heart ne'er won a mother-in-law.

When a woman acquiesces to her daughter's marriage to a man she dislikes, it is probably because she is looking forward to becoming his mother-in-law.

An ill-humored mother-in-law is no laughing mater.

If you tell your mother-in-law that the house is too small for all three of you to live in, she'll raise the roof.

A mother-in-law is an arbitrator who always favors one side in a dispute.

The bride who criticizes her husband's mother is eventually punished by becoming a mother-in-law herself.

No man is a hero to his mother-in-law.

Absence makes the heart grow fonder, unless it's your mother-in-law.

When two prospective mothers-in-law meet, each is suspicious of what the other is unloading.

The mother who thinks very much of a husband for her daughter before marriage is the mother-in-law who thinks very little of him afterward.

There are two kinds of mothers-in-law: the mother-in-love and the mother-in-awe.

The worst evil of remarriage is breaking in a new mother-in-law.

If mothers-in-law were as bad as they are painted, they would have retaliated long ago with a stream of son-in-law jokes.

A mother-in-law occupies the most important position in marriage, relatively speaking.

MOTHER'S DAY

No man would dare say a bad word against Mother's Day in public, or a good word for it in private. —*Alistair Cooke*

Americans devote one day of the year to mothers, and an entire week to pickles.

Another Mother's Day that's authentic but not authorized is the day school reopens in September.

Mother's Day is a holiday celebrated by letting mother cook a bigger dinner than on any other Sunday.

There's nothing unusual about a man giving presents to another man's wife, especially on Mother's Day.

MOTION

Why does an oak grow taller and live longer than a man? Because it does not waste its energy moving from one spot to another.
— Bernard Shaw

A good example of slow motion is a woman entering her thirties.

The advice to keep your feet on the ground does not mean to keep them from moving.

Another thing that keeps our country on the move is the great number of NO PARKING signs.

There's no one so eccentric as the inventor whose perpetual notion is to discover perpetual motion.

A man in a swivel chair can go around a lot without getting anywhere.

There are three types of people: those who are immovable, those who are movable, and those who move.

There's no such thing as perpetual motion, but the next thing to it is the family upstairs.

MOUNTAIN

A gossip usually makes a mountain out of a molehill by adding some dirt.

Faith may move mountains, but it takes work to tunnel them.

Send your mother-in-law on a trip to the mountains: she'll find something at last she can't walk over.

MOUSE

A woman is generally afraid of a mouse, but not if she has promised to love, honor, and obey him.

Church mice aren't poor—they wear fur coats.

If a man is afraid of his wife, he's not a man but a mouse; and if his wife is afraid of him, he must also be a mouse.

MOUSETRAP

In baiting a mousetrap with cheese, always leave room for the mouse.
— Saki

One of the simple but genuine pleasures in life is getting up in the morning and hurrying to a mousetrap you set the night before.
— Kin Hubbard

If a man builds a better mousetrap than his neighbor, the chances are he will catch mice.

If a man makes a better mousetrap, the tax collector will beat a path to his door.

If a man makes a better mousetrap than his neighbor, his neighbor will borrow it.

You don't have to build a better mousetrap for the world to beat a path to your door—just neglect to pay your bills.

MOUTH

Her mouth costs her nothing, for she never opens it but at others' expense.   — Franklin

A very big secret can get out of a very little mouth.

Newlyweds soon discover that though two hearts may beat as one, two mouths continue to eat separately.

Some people think without speaking; others never know what their mouths are going to say next.

At the end of the evening many a woman is so tired, she can hardly keep her mouth open.

The closest friend is always the one with the closest mouth.

The human mouth is a wonderful thing: it starts working the moment you are born and never stops until you stand up to speak in public.

Another good time to keep your mouth shut is when you are in deep water.

Many things are opened by mistake, but none so often as the mouth.

If you keep your mouth shut, you'll never put your foot in it.

There is one gap we can all close with profit—the one between the nose and the chin.

Think twice before you speak, and you'll never get a chance to open your mouth.

The surest way to keep people from jumping down your throat is to keep your mouth shut.

The trouble with many women is that they approach all problems with an open mouth.

MOVIE STAR

A movie actor's house is a series of movie sets, and he wears clothes that are hard to distinguish from his costumes.   — Mencken

In Hollywood a starlet is the name for any woman under thirty who is not actively employed in a brothel.   — Ben Hecht

The marriages of a movie star last almost as long as other women's honeymoons.

A movie star doesn't care to live in the institution of marriage, but prefers to make frequent visits.

Don't expect a movie star to be a good cook: she is more interested in plots and plans than in pots and pans.

A starlet is a young movie actress who has been married only once.

A movie star is usually wedded to her profession but divorced from her husband.

A movie star's life is a series of marriages alternating with divorces, or vice versa.

Some stars are heavenly bodies, but most stars have them.

The starlet who is trying to make it to the top always wears clothes that don't.

Many a starlet is so thrilled with her first marriage, she can hardly wait for the next.

How do movie stars spend their time between husbands?

A movie star always marries her first love—also her second, third and fourth.

When a starlet is going places, it's probably with the producer.

A starlet is a young movie star who will probably make a glamorous wife for half a dozen men.

A movie star spends her time between pictures getting married or divorced.

A movie star is a beautiful bubble that's constantly being blown up by a press agent.

No woman can be a successful movie star unless she's happily married now and then.

A movie star is a woman who has a weakness for wedding cake.

Among movie stars, love is the shortest distance between two marriages.

A movie star's background is never as important as her foreground.

A movie star is an actress who lives happily and gets married forever after.

The married life of a movie star is usually a little bit of matrimony and a lot of bitter acrimony.

Movie stars are romantic creatures: they are always going away on honeymoons instead of vacations.

A starlet is a young actress whose first movie usually lasts longer than her first marriage.

MUD

No mud can soil us but the mud we throw.
— *James Russell Lowell*

There's only one thing that profits more from mud-slinging than the laundry business, and that's politics.

Mud thrown is ground lost.

MULE

The female of the species is more dangerous than the mule.

Some women become nags because their husbands behave like mules.

Mules are stubborn, but man has will power.

MURDER

Female murderers get sheaves of offers of marriage.
— *Bernard Shaw*

A man has only to murder a series of wives to become known

to millions of people who have never heard of Homer.
— *Robert Lynd*

As long as there are writers of mystery novels, there will be new ways of murdering people.

A television mystery is a detective story where the sponsor gets away with murder.

Murder is the only sure method yet discovered of preventing your victim from identifying you.

Bluebeard had a way with women, and then did away with them.

In most murder cases there is usually no clue to the whereabouts of the police.

What this country needs are more self-made men and fewer self-made widows.

MUSCLE

Muscles come and go; flab lasts.
— *Bill Vaughan*

The heart is a muscle: when you think you're in love, you're really muscle-bound.

MUSIC

In music one must think with the heart and feel with the brain.
— *George Szell*

The English may not like music but they absolutely love the sound it makes.   — *Thomas Beecham*

After silence, that which comes nearest to expressing the inexpressible is music.   — *Aldous Huxley*

Unperformed music is like a cake in the oven—not fully baked.
— *Isaac Stern*

The music critic, Huneker, could never quite make up his mind about a new symphony until he had seen the composer's mistress.
— *Mencken*

My music is best understood by children and animals.
— *Igor Stravinsky*

The noises made by musical maniacs should be audible to themselves only.   — *Bernard Shaw*

As we grow older we find our admiration increasing for the girl who can't play without the music she has left at home.   — *Ed Howe*

There are more bad musicians than there is bad music.
— *Isaac Stern*

Musical people always want one to be perfectly dumb at the very moment when one is longing to be absolutely deaf.   — *Oscar Wilde*

Good music penetrates the ear with facility and quits the memory with difficulty. — *Thomas Beecham*

Either heaven or hell has continuous background music piped in; which one you think it is tells a lot about your personality.
— *Bill Vaughan*

Music is the only language in which you cannot say a mean or sarcastic thing.   — *John Erskine*

The sonatas of Mozart are unique: they are too easy for children, and too difficult for artists.
— *Artur Schnabel*

The more you love music, the more music you love.
— *Abram Chasins*

Sweet popular music is claptrap in the main, and the main is where it belongs. — *Peter De Vries*

Making music is like making love: the act is always the same, but each time it's different.
— *Artur Rubinstein*

The contemporary artist expresses his feelings through the music, instead of filtering the music through his feelings.
— *Isaac Stern*

During adolescence the music you enjoy is good music no matter how bad it is.

So far the greatest martial music ever written is the wedding march.

The difference between classical and popular music is the difference between antique and antic.

Good musicians execute their music but bad ones murder it.

Marriage brings music into a man's life—he learns to play second fiddle at home.

Some girls are music lovers, while others can love without it.

Classical music is music without words, modern music is music without music.

Some performers take pains with their music, others give them.

Music is another woman who talks charmingly and says nothing.

MUSICAL INSTRUMENTS

The chief objection to playing wind instruments is that it prolongs the life of the player beyond all reasonable limits.
— *Bernard Shaw*

It's easy to play any musical instrument: all you have to do is touch the right key at the right time, and the instrument will play by itself. — *Johann Sebastian Bach*

Bagpipes are one of the hardest instruments to play, and also one of the hardest to listen to.

No one should be allowed to play a saxophone until he knows how.

The radio cannot be classed as a musical instrument, though there are a lot of musicians practicing on it.

Playing an accordion in this world won't qualify you for playing a harp in the next.

Anyone who says that he enjoys bagpipe music will lie about other things too.

Another good thing about playing the mandolin is that you don't have to be in tune.

What some people enjoy most about a harp is that its strings break.

The only music typically American is that made by the mocking bird, the saxophone, and the cash register.

No matter how well you play the bagpipes, it always sounds as if you were practicing.

The evil that men do lives after them: the saxophone was invented a century ago.

MYSTERY

Women are one of the Almighty's enigmas to prove to men that he knows more than they do.
— *Ellen Glasgow*

The way a miss can fool a mister is a mystery.

If you believe in God, evil is a mystery; if you don't believe in God, goodness is a mystery.

There's only one thing more inexplicable than love, and that is marriage.

A sermon should make mysteries plain instead of making plain things mysteries.

The greatest mystery in the literary world is why financial writers have to earn a living by writing.

MYSTICISM

Mysticism is the connecting link between paganism and Christianity. — *Baudelaire*

Mysticism is not religion, but a religious disease. — *Santayana*

MYTH

Myth is nothing more than ancient gossip. — *Stanislaw J. Lec*

History is facts which become lies in the end; legends are lies which become history in the end.
— *Jean Cocteau*

A man convinced against his will is of the same opinion still; a woman convinced against her will is a myth.

NAG

Men nag their wives for what they do, woman nag their husbands for what they don't do.

A nag is a woman whose ability to remember is only exceeded by her inability to forget.

A nag never seems to have enough horse sense to bridle her tongue.

A woman nags a man until he does everything she wants him to, and then despises him because he has no mind of his own.

NAIVE

Oh, what a tangled web do parents weave when they think that their children are naïve.
— *Ogden Nash*

Only the most naïve woman would think her friends think she looks as young as they say she does.

No one is as naïve as the man who, when he is being taken, thinks he is going places.

An unsophisticated girl doesn't know all there is to *no*.

The people who fall for everything probably stand for nothing.

NAME

Nicknames stick to people, and the most ridiculous are the most adhesive. — *Thomas C. Haliburton*

The average girl at 18 starts out to make a name for herself, but decides at 20 that some man's will do.   — *Ed Howe*

It is hard for me to remember names; if I live long enough, I shall no doubt forget my own.
      — *Montaigne*

Of all eloquence a nickname is the most concise, of all arguments the most unanswerable. — *Hazlitt*

Every man's first name is more important than his last, until he becomes famous.   — *Camus*

People who address you as buddy or pal are not being over-friendly—they've just forgotten your name.

Why did the man who puts everything in his wife's name give her his name in the first place?

If you think civilized people no longer take advantage of the weak and unprotected, just look at the names they give to helpless infants.

A hamburger by any other name costs twice as much.

Love is a funny feeling: it makes a young man want to call a girl by his last name.

Some parents have difficulty deciding on a name for the new baby, while others have rich relatives.

A reckless driver is called a lot of names before he is finally called "the deceased."

It's much easier to get your name into the telephone directory than into Who's Who, but it costs a lot more.

When a girl marries she not only takes a man's name but everything else he has.

Give a book a bad name, and it becomes a movie.

The girl who shuts her eyes when she kisses a man is probably trying to remember his name.

There's nothing girls enjoy more than dropping names, especially their maiden names.

A namedropper is the only person who talks about others more than he does about himself.

Another man who never does business in his wife's name is the bachelor.

There are certain types of girls that men like to give their names to—but not their right names.

Parents who give their sons fancy names should also give them boxing lessons.

Ordinary things are called by such long names in the social sciences that you always think something else is being discussed.

Flour by any other name would smell as wheat.

Movie stars never adopt their husbands' names because it isn't worthwhile for such a short time.

NAPOLEON

Napoleon did supremely well many things that it was supremely ill to do. — *Herbert Samuel*

Size isn't everything: if Napoleon were living today he couldn't get a job as a doorman.

In the nineteenth century only one man thought he was Napoleon; in the twentieth century there are thousands who think so.

NATION

When abroad, I never criticize the government of my own country, but I make up for it when I come home. — *Winston Churchill*

Nationalism is an infantile disease, it is the measles of mankind.
— *Einstein*

Nations are like men: they love that which flatters their passions even more than that which serves their interests. — *Tocqueville*

Every nation ridicules other nations, and all are right.
— *Schopenhauer*

A nation is born Stoic, dies Epicurean. — *Will Durant*

Nationalism and rationalism seldom go together.

The world is made up of two kinds of nations: in one, it's *believe it or not;* in the other, it's *believe it or else.*

No nation is truly civilized until it reaches the point where nothing can be done without first being financed.

NATIONAL DEBT

The national debt is a deficit planned to teach the next generation the value of money by making them pay it off.

The man who yells for the government to balance the budget is probably paying installments on all sorts of things.

Blessed are the young, for they shall inherit the national debt.

What a pity that posterity is not around to see the wonderful things we are doing with its money!

America's faith in the future is best shown by the huge debt she expects the next generation to pay off.

The federal budget is based on the owe-as-you-go plan.

A budget is something that the government can't seem to do without, and can't seem to live within.

The government deficit is the difference between the amount of money the government spends and the amount it has the nerve to collect.

The next generation must pay off the huge national debt, which probably explains why a baby yells when it's born.

The national debt proves that America is less a government of checks and balances and more a government of checks than balances.

In civilized society every generation pays the debts of the last generation by issuing bonds payable by the next generation.

The national debt is really a public debt that the private citizen has to pay.

Times change: few economists today believe that the national debt is what keeps the government from being fiscally fit.

NATURE

Nature is an infinite sphere whose center is everywhere and whose circumference is nowhere.
— *Pascal*

How beautifully nature arranges everything: as soon as a child enters the world, it finds a mother ready to take care of it.

The danger is not what nature will do with man, but what man will do with nature.

Self-preservation is the first law of nature, with lying a close second.

There are times when there's nothing so unnatural as nature.

NEAT

Be careless in your dress if you will, but keep a tidy soul.
— *Mark Twain*

Neat people who go about furiously tidying things appall me; the neatest places I know are museums, stuffed with dead things.
— *St. John Ervine*

Many a woman would be more spick if she had less span.

Before the younger generation starts to straighten up the world, it ought to straighten up its rooms.

NECESSITY

Necessity is the mother of invention, especially the invention of lies.

Business was invented to supply the needs of the people; the needs of the people now exist for the sake of business.

One more thing this country needs is less needs.

A friend in need is a friend you don't need.

Most families can afford to be without the wonderful household necessities no family can afford to be without.

Man is a creature who has endless needs, but who never needs as much as he wants.

Necessity is the mother of invention, but to many a necessity is the mother of tension.

Think of the countless things we can't do without that haven't been invented yet.

Necessity knows no law, not even a mother-in-law.

It's the things she does not need that a woman needs to make her happy.

What this country needs are fewer people who know what this country needs.

Necessity is often the mother of invention, but more often she is childless.

A man is usually thrown on his own resources when he hasn't any.

A friend in need is what most of us have.

The tempo of life is growing faster: formerly when a college student needed money, he wrote home; nowadays he calls collect.

NEEDLE

Nowadays it's not as difficult to find a needle in a haystack as it is to find one in a girl's hand.

Any man will testify that a camel can pass through the eye of a needle much more easily than thread will.

About all that the modern girl knows about a needle is that you have to change it on a record player.

There's only one thing that's harder to find than a needle in a haystack, and that's a clam in clam chowder.

NEGLECT

If you feel neglected by your family, think of Whistler's father.

Hard work is often due to the piling up of the easy things you neglected to do.

Some women neglect their children, others hire nurses to do it.

NEIGHBOR

Love your neighbor, but be careful of your neighborhood.
— *John Hay*

We make our friends, we make our enemies, but God makes our next-door neighbor. — *Chesterton*

A man's best friend is seldom his neighbor. — *Ed Howe*

One could live on next to nothing if one's neighbors would live on less.

A neighbor will spend an hour talking at a door because she hasn't time to come in.

The difference between you and your neighbor is that you don't tell half of what you know, while he doesn't know half of what he tells.

The man who wants to know himself should make his neighbors angry.

Opportunity knocks but once, which shows it has little in common with the neighbors.

It would be much easier to love our neighbors as ourselves if they would only do things the way we do.

People who live in glass houses make the most interesting neighbors.

A good neighbor is one who neither looks down on you nor keeps up with you.

Neighbors are people who buy things they don't need with money they haven't earned to keep up with the Joneses they don't like.

A good neighbor is one who smiles at you over the back fence, but never climbs it.

Being a good neighbor has never yet stopped a person from having disagreeable thoughts about his neighbors.

The wise man moves next door to a family whose income is less than his.

Many people spend more time trying to make their neighbors good than in trying to make themselves good neighbors.

The only people who listen to both sides of an argument are the neighbors.

It wouldn't be so hard to love our neighbors as ourselves if we didn't dislike them so much.

A good neighbor is one who lets his grass grow as high as yours.

For every neighbor who tries to keep up with the Joneses, there's another neighbor who thinks what the Joneses have is not good enough for her.

Love thy neighbor, but do not make love to her.

Even the most forgetful of neighbors always remembers to send your children home at the hour arranged, and usually a little earlier.

The reason most of us can't save money is the neighbors—they're always buying something we can't afford.

Some neighbors will borrow everything from you, except your troubles.

Love is blind, but the neighbors aren't.

NERVOUS

Many a man gets a reputation for being energetic when he's merely nervous.

A girl isn't nervous when a man proposes—that's when she stops being nervous.

A man is old when girls get on his nerves instead of his lap.

If worry makes you so nervous that your hand shakes, learn to play a guitar.

It's easier to live with 200 pounds of curves than with 100 pounds of nerves.

The shortest cut to a nervous breakdown is to spend half your time keeping your mind on your work, and the other half keeping your work on your mind.

Nervousness is the price you pay for being like a racehorse instead of a cow.

The woman who is high strung is probably out of tune most of the time.

NEUROTIC

I used to talk to myself even before I went to Hollywood, but after I got there I found that I was answering myself back.
— *Irvin S. Cobb*

A neurotic is usually a woman who prefers a psychiatrist's couch to a double bed.

The female of the species is more neurotic than the male.

A neurotic never puts off till tomorrow the worrying she can do today.

One of the most common types of neurotic is the mother who, when her child refuses to eat, gets indigestion.

It's easy to entertain a neurotic: all you have to do is sit down and listen.

A neurotic never likes to suffer in silence because that takes all the pleasure out of it.

An emotional trauma is a state of mind precipitated by an accident, stimulated by an attorney, perpetuated by greed, and cured by a verdict.

Everybody is a little neurotic; nowadays you can't be normal if you aren't.

The compulsive neurotic never puts off till tomorrow, not even the things that shouldn't be done at all.

Neurotics worry about things that didn't happen in the past instead of worrying like normal people about things that won't happen in the future.

The difference is that a neurotic doesn't answer the telephone when it rings, while a psychotic answers it when it doesn't ring.

A neurotic builds castles in the air, a psychotic lives in them, and the psychiatrist collects the rent.

A psychotic thinks that two plus three equals six; a neurotic knows that two plus three equals five, but worries about it.

NEW

There is nothing new in the world except the history you do not know. — *Harry S. Truman*

We must beware of needless innovations, especially when guided by logic.
— *Winston Churchill*

The two most engaging powers of an author are to make new things familiar, and familiar things new. — *Thackeray*

When a husband opens the door to help his wife into the car, he has probably just acquired one or the other.

There's nothing new under the sun: nothing happens to you that hasn't already happened to someone else.

NEWLYWEDS

The first mean thing a newly married man does is to notice the pretty girls again.   — *Ed Howe*

A man finds himself seven years older the day after his marriage.
— *Francis Bacon*

A newlywed usually sleeps like a baby until he gets one.

A newlywed is a man who hasn't brought a friend home to dinner yet.

A new groom sweeps clean— and also washes dishes.

When newlyweds feather their nest, it's always their parents who have been plucked.

The first resolve of every newlywed couple is to be true to the last.

A bride becomes a wife when she stops raising her eyebrows and starts raising the roof.

Newlyweds always have a plan for the future, but it's mostly a credit plan.

The woman who thinks her husband is perfectly wonderful has probably just been married.

Formerly the groom worried about her first biscuits; nowadays the bride worries about his first cookout.

The way most newlyweds feather their nests is with down payments.

There are few things young newlyweds find harder to bear than to set up housekeeping without color television.

Newlyweds make the best customers: they don't remember what prices used to be.

Newlyweds prove that two can live as cheaply as one—on parents.

NEWS

What the good Lord lets happen, I am not ashamed to print in my paper.   — *Charles A. Dana*

News is anything that causes a woman to say, "My goodness!"
— *Mark Twain*

News that makes the headlines is always bad news.
— *Marquis Childs*

The dull period in the life of an event is when it ceases to be news and has not yet begun to be history.   — *Thomas Hardy*

No one knows what is news of importance until a century later.
— *Nietzsche*

News is history shot on the wing.   — *Gene Fowler*

We all want to get the news objectively, impartially, and from our own point of view.
— *Bill Vaughan*

Not all the news that's fit to print is fit to read.

The evil that men do—makes work for reporters.

If a dog bites a man it's not news, unless he's a newspaper editor.

No news is good news, except in a newspaper.

The world isn't growing worse —it's only that the news coverage is growing better.

All the news that's fit to print means not all the truth is in't.

A small town is a place where the news circulates before the newspaper does.

The worst thing about world news today is that we not only read it in the newspapers and hear it on the radio but we also see it over television.

If a man bites a dog, that's news; but if a dog bites a newspaperman, that's good news.

Don't draw any conclusions from the news: when it looks as if the news can't possibly get any worse, it usually does.

The most interesting item in the newspaper is the one your wife cut out before you saw it.

To most readers, the three favorite kinds of news are: the amatory, the inflammatory, and the defamatory.

NEWSPAPER

I read about eight newspapers a day; when I'm in a town with only one newspaper, I read it eight times.　　　— *Will Rogers*

Newspapers have degenerated: they may now be absolutely relied upon.　　　— *Oscar Wilde*

If words were invented to conceal thought, newspapers are a great improvement on a bad invention.　　　— *Thoreau*

Everybody's business is the newspaper's business.

Be good and you'll be happy, but you won't get your name in the newspapers.

You can't appreciate a standard-size newspaper until you try to wrap up a pair of shoes in a tabloid.

The course of true love never runs in the newspapers.

A newspaper's function is to enable a reader to worry about things in all parts of the world.

Life could be worse: suppose the Sunday papers were published daily?

A newspaper is a window to the world, but a window shade to the universe.

The bare truth in newspapers does not always get proper coverage.

A newspaper reports all sorts of events, including misfortunes like deaths and marriages.

A newspaper is a circulating library with high blood pressure.

NEW YEAR'S

The usual way to ring out the New Year is to drink out the old one.

New Year's Day starts out by making both ends of the years meet.

On New Year's Eve, the old year ends with people mixing drinks, and the new year begins with drinks mixing people.

The best thing to give up in a New Year's resolution is to give up giving up.

Many a man who celebrates the arrival of the new year should celebrate instead the survival of the old.

New Year's resolutions should be taken with a grain of salt— and two aspirins.

On New Year's Eve we first ring out the old, then ring in the new, and finally are ready to be wrung out ourselves.

One swallow doesn't make a summer, but it often breaks a New Year's resolution.

NEW YORK

New York: homes, homes everywhere, and not a place to live.   — *Don Herold*

New Yorkers are nice about giving you street directions—in fact, they seem quite proud of knowing where they are themselves.
    — *Katharine Brush*

I like New York too much to get any work done in it.
    — *Louis Bromfield*

New York is the one densely inhabited locality, with the possible exception of hell, that hasn't a trace of pride.   — *Irvin S. Cobb*

Work in New York is something they pad out the time with between booze parties.
    — *Don Marquis*

It is ridiculous to set a detective story in New York City— New York City is itself a detective story.   — *Agatha Christie*

New York is where you can get the best cheap meal and the lousiest expensive meal in the country.
    — *Robert C. Weaver*

In six days God created heaven and earth, but New York is still unfinished.

New Yorkers rush around by day to save time which they will waste at night.

The Indians had the right idea: they got rid of Manhattan before they had to pay taxes on it.

When a New Yorker is in a hurry, he doesn't take a taxi—he walks.

If you don't understand New York, all you have to do is think of it as the largest small town in the United States.

The first thing that strikes a stranger in New York is a car.

Some people commute to New York, others writhe in the subway.

America is full of yokels, and many of them have never been outside New York.

Traffic is so slow in New York that the taxi meters run faster than the taxicabs.

NICKEL

What this country needs is a good five-cent nickel.

About the only thing a nickel is good for nowadays is to make change for a quarter.

A nickel goes much farther than it used to: you have to carry it around for days before you can find something it will buy.

If you think children don't know the value of money, try giving one a nickel.

The nickel is a coin that remains the same size while the thing it buys gets smaller.

NIGHT

Life doesn't begin at forty, but night life usually does.

A night owl is a man who doesn't give a hoot how late he gets home.

NIGHT CLUB

One of the pleasures of a night club is to sit around watching the entertainers make lots of money.

It is never too late to visit another night club.

Another thing about a night club is that the waitresses are more appetizing than the food.

A nightclub is a place where the entertainer must be able to talk louder than his audience.

A night club is the only place still open by the time some wives finish dressing.

NO

No is no negative in a woman's mouth.　　*—Sir Philip Sidney*

When you say *no* to a woman, you must follow it with an explanation.　　*—Ed Howe*

It's a good thing I wasn't born a girl because I never could say *no*.
　　—Warren G. Harding

A petition is a list of people who didn't have the courage to say *no*.

Even a disobedient child will take *no! No! NO!* for an answer.

You don't have to say *no;* you can always take the matter under advisement.

Mothers always object to their teenage daughters using four-letter words—especially *nope*.

If you must say *no,* don't say it fortissimo.

Two negatives make an affirmative, except with a woman when it takes only one.

Many a wife simply doesn't understand her husband, especially when he says *no*.

Many a man and woman lived happily ever after—she said *no*.

The woman who *no*'s men, probably knows men.

It's easier for a girl to say *no* than to mean it.

Many a girl has a slight impediment in her speech: she can't say *no*.

The language barrier that's easiest to overcome is a woman's *no*.

NOAH

I don't believe Noah could have rounded up all the animals in one herd without the skunk causing a stampede.   *— Will Rogers*

Such is the human race: often it does seem such a pity that Noah and his party didn't miss the boat.   *— Mark Twain*

Majorities mean nothing: during the Flood only one man knew enough to get out of the rain.

Noah didn't wait for his ship to come in—he built one.

If Noah had been younger when he put two of everything into the ark, he would have included two blondes, two brunettes and two redheads.

The longest biblical reign was Noah's during the Flood.

Why didn't Noah swat those two flies when he had the chance?

NOISE

Everybody has their taste in noises as well as in other matters.   *— Jane Austen*

Noise is a stench in the ear, and the chief product of civilization.   *— Bierce*

The proof that Americans are a tolerant people is that the inventor of the juke box died a natural death.

What a terrible din there would be if we all made as much noise when things go right as we do when things go wrong!

To multiply a noise by one thousand, make it at two o'clock in the morning.

If everybody thought before they spoke, there wouldn't be enough noise in the world to scare a bird.

You can't be a howling success simply by howling.

A crying youngster is a problem: you have to give it a drum or a horn or a whistle to keep it quiet.

Next to the atom bomb, the loudest noise in the world is the first rattle in your new car.

NON-CONFORMITY

How conventional all you unconventional people are!   *— Bernard Shaw*

Be a non-conformist: the man who follows the crowd will never be followed by the crowd.

Bohemians always show their wish to be different by dressing alike.

Non-conformity is often merely a form of conformity in reverse.

NONSENSE

Forgive me my nonsense as I also forgive the nonsense of those who think they talk sense.
— *Robert Frost*

A man who talks a great deal, talks a great deal of nonsense; and a man who talks very little, hardly ever talks sense.
— *Hilaire Belloc*

A word to the wise is not sufficient: if it doesn't make any sense.   — *James Thurber*

When a mathematical or philosophical author writes with a misty profundity, he is talking nonsense.
— *A. N. Whitehead*

Nonsense is the sixth sense that makes you disbelieve the other five.

Sufficient unto the day is the drivel thereof.

NOSE

When I want heavy headwork, I always choose a man with a long nose.   — *Napoleon*

Notice that the nose was formed to wear spectacles: thus we wear spectacles.   — *Voltaire*

Plastic surgeons can do almost anything with a nose, except keep it out of other people's business.

Cyrano was the only man in history who could keep a cigar lit while taking a shower.

Most men are easily led by the nose—that's why girls use perfume.

By keeping his nose to the grindstone, a workhorse enables his children to turn up theirs.

Nature invented the nose for breathing and smelling, but human nature added a new use: sticking it into other people's business.

The lip can slip, the eye can lie, but the nose knows.

The nose is another thing that should be seen and not heard.

NOSTALGIA

When you finally visit your boyhood town, you find it wasn't the old home you longed for, but your boyhood.

Some men retain nostalgic memories of their first love, but most men marry them.

Nostalgia is the longing to go back to the good old days when you were neither good nor old.

NOTICE

There's a difference between beauty and charm: a beautiful woman is one I notice, a charming woman is one who notices me.
— *John Erskine*

The first thing a flirt notices about a man is if her husband is around.

Some men look women right in the eye, while some look at other things women like them to notice.

It is easier for a woman to suffer in silence if she knows someone is watching.

The neighbors in an apartment house never notice you—until you do something you'd rather they didn't notice.

A man never notices what his wife wears, but notices what other women wear: when a man knows what's in the package, he doesn't care how it's wrapped.

A flirt always notices a man in such a way that he notices her.

NOVEL

I can't understand why a person will take a year to write a novel when he can easily buy one for a few dollars.   — *Fred Allen*

Begin with an individual and you find you have created a type; begin with a type and you find you have created—nothing.
                — *Scott Fitzgerald*

The modern novel is an outspoken brand of literature in which a spade is called a spade, and so is everything else.

In the old-fashioned novel, the heroine married the right man in the last chapter; in the modern novel, she marries the wrong one in the first.

In the old-fashioned novel the hero didn't kiss the heroine until the last page; now he kisses her on the dust jacket.

A woman will sometimes start reading a novel because she likes the way it ends.

The modern novel is a blend of the erotic, the neurotic and the tommyrotic.

The great American novel has never been written but it's constantly being advertised.

Many a novel begins in a light vein and ends by becoming varicose.

Novels are all alike: you put down an interesting one with pleasure as well as a dull one.

Victorian writers considered sex a novel idea, and so do modern writers.

It's not true that the modern novel is here to stay—friends are always borrowing it.

An old-timer is a person who remembers when the most shocking novels contained asterisks.

Most novels are overwritten: there's too much space between the covers.

NOVELIST

I did not begin to write novels until I had forgotten all I had learned at school and college.
                — *Galsworthy*

Henry James would have been vastly improved as a novelist by a few whiffs from the Chicago stockyards.   *— Mencken*

The novelist is dead in the man who has become aware of the triviality of human affairs.
— Somerset Maugham

A novelist is the only writer who can make a name without a style, which is only one more reason for not bothering with the novel.   *— Robert Frost*

As artists, women novelists are rot, but as providers they are oil wells—they gush.
— Dorothy Parker

To write about writers is the novelist's confession that his arteries are hardening.
— Francis Hackett

A novelist must preserve a child-like belief in the importance of things which common sense considers of no great consequence.
— Somerset Maugham

NUDE

Clothes make the man; naked people have little or no influence in society.   *— Mark Twain*

The only ones who seem to object to nudity are those who haven't tried it yet. *— Irvin S. Cobb*

As long as people will pay admission to a theater to see a naked body rather than a naked mind, the drama will languish.
— Bernard Shaw

When you are trying to arrive at the proper estimate of a man, look at him in the nude. *— Seneca*

Some civilized women would lose half their charm without dress, and some would lose it all.
— Mark Twain

Women are born naked and spend most of their time trying to get back to their original state.

The female of the species is interested in clothes, but more interesting out of them.

The apparel off proclaims the woman.

The movies are a form of entertainment whose chief problem is to uncover new talent.

NUDIST

The trouble with a nudist camp is that it leaves nothing to the imagination.

Clothes make the man, except in a nudist colony.

Another advantage of a nudist camp is that you don't have to sit around for hours in a wet bathing suit after swimming.

In a nudist colony, a person's face doesn't matter.

Another reason why a man goes to a nudist camp is that his wife can't tell him what to wear.

Another man you don't catch with his pants down is a nudist.

The reason some women will never be nudists is that they can never decide what not to wear.

Let's not criticize the nudists—remember, they were born that way.

Two can live as cheaply as one, but only if both are nudists on a diet.

NUMBER

Men are like numbers: they acquire their importance from their position. — *Napoleon*

A philanderer always tries to get a girl's number before she gets his.

When a politician tries to do the greatest good for the greatest number, the greatest number is usually number one.

Life is a process of acquiring more and more numbers until one's number is up.

If you think there's safety in numbers, try playing roulette.

An adding machine is a typewriter that writes nothing but numbers.

NURSE

After two days in the hospital, I took a turn for the nurse.
— *W. C. Fields*

A woman must nurse something, even if it's only a grievance.

A nurse always checks the patients' pulses, and sometimes their impulses.

OBEDIENCE

Any man can be a good mate on the sea of matrimony: all he has to do is obey his captain's orders.

For every man who cannot do as he's told, there's another who cannot do anything else.

Parents who expect juvenile obedience, should never surrender to expedience.

There are two kinds of men: those who do what their wives tell them, and those who never marry.

At a wedding ceremony the bride promises to obey because she prefers not to make a scene.

One of the first things one notices in a backward country is the way children obey their parents.

Women are more docile than men: a wife will always obey her husband when he tells her to do as she wishes.

OBITUARY

There's no bad publicity, except an obituary notice.
— *Brendan Behan*

According to obituary notices, a mean and useless citizen never dies.

It's not the loss of life that makes death bitter—it's the obituaries.

A good way to get your name in the newspapers is to walk across the street reading one.

Dead men tell no tales, but their obituaries often do.

OBJECTION

Nothing will ever be attempted if all possible objections must first be overcome.   — *Samuel Johnson*

Man's ojection to love is that it dies hard; woman's, that when it is dead, it stays dead.   — *Mencken*

You can't always tell how much a girl wants you to kiss her by the strenuous objection she sets up.

No man objects to his wife calling him a fool; what he objects to is her taking an hour to do so.

There's nothing so objectionable as flattery, especially when it's directed at a person you dislike.

A girl doesn't object to being intimate; what she objects to is having you think she doesn't.

The one great objection to most fools is that they have no money to part with.

A witness in court swears to tell the truth but every time he tries, some lawyer objects.

A woman's *no* is no proof of her objection.

OBSCENITY

Nothing risqué, nothing gained.
    — *Alexander Woollcott*

Obscenity is whatever happens to shock some elderly and ignorant magistrate. — *Bertrand Russell*

Sir Robert Walpole said he always talked bawdy at his table because in that all his company could join.   — *Samuel Johnson*

Some of my plays were for many years under the ban of censorship for their obscenity, and they are now disparaged as old-fashioned and prudish.
    — *Bernard Shaw*

Damn all expurgated books; the dirtiest book of all is the expurgated book.   — *Walt Whitman*

Obscenity can be found in every book except the telephone directory.   — *Bernard Shaw*

The woman who used to blush when she heard an off-color story now has a granddaughter who memorizes it.

Most men enjoy a funny story providing it's off-color; most women enjoy an off-color story providing it's funny.

OBSESSION

When you have found out the prevailing passion of any man, remember never to trust him where that passion is concerned.
    — *Chesterfield*

A man may dwell so long upon a thought that it may take him prisoner.   — *Halifax*

An obsession is an idea which you must get out of your mind if you are not to go out of your mind.

The train of thought of an obsessed person always runs on a single track.

OBSOLESCENCE

The genius of American technology lies in building things to last twenty years and making them obsolete in two.

Obsolescence is what happens to your car once it is fully paid for.

Planned obsolescence is being introduced nowadays into everything, except war.

OBSTACLE

The course of true anything never does run smooth.
— *Samuel Butler*

If it weren't for obstacles, we'd never know whether we really want something or merely think we do.

The obstacles of life are intended to make us better, not bitter.

Most of the stumbling blocks men complain about are under their hats.

Money talks, but many a man has an impediment in his speech.

People lose sight of the hurdles when they jump at conclusions.

Obstacles are the stumbling blocks that often become the steppingstones to success.

OCEAN

The ocean is a body of water occupying about two-thirds of a world made for man—who has no gills.   — *Bierce*

No one would ever have crossed the ocean if he could have gotten off the ship in a storm.

Marriage is described as the sea of matrimony because husbands and wives are ever ready to sail into each other.

Now that man can barely keep his head above water, he has begun to show an intense interest in oceanography.

An oceanographer is a scientist to whom the sea's bottom is even more important than the moon's behind.

OFFENSIVE

You can be a rank insider as well as a rank outsider.
— *Robert Frost*

Never call a man a fool: he may be foolish enough to resent it.

A word to the wise is—resented.

OFFICE

Benchley and I had an office in the old *Life* magazine that was so tiny, if it were an inch smaller it would have been adultery.
— *Dorothy Parker*

A man who has no office to go to is a trial of which you can have no conception.
— *Bernard Shaw*

In some businesses, the office force is like one big family—nobody is congenial.

The man who gets to the office after nine o'clock is either an executive or will never be one.

In some offices 60 seconds make one minute, and 180 minutes make one lunch hour.

Office hours are the hours during which an office is normally open for gossip.

It isn't enough for a stenographer to write the words in shorthand correctly; she should also be able to spell them on the typewriter.

Many a girl marries and continues to go to work so she can afford clothes to wear to the office.

An office boy starts as an office boy and works up; a secretary starts as a secretary and works.

The first thing a girl learns at a new job is which men around the office are still single.

OFFICIAL

There are two kinds of public officials: those who do all they can for the office, and those who do the office for all they can.

An office-holder often does the greater part of his work before he gets the job.

Many an office-holder is sworn in one year, and cussed out the next.

A political appointee usually gets his post after someone else gets the gate.

When a public official loses his reputation, he finds the kind that really belongs to him.

Every citizen knows how a thing should be done, except the officials in charge of the job.

A public official can fool some of the people all of the time, and all of the people some of the time, but not his private secretary.

OFFICIALESE

Officialese is a form of government writing where you can understand the words, but not the sentences.

There are two kinds of officialese: one is hard to understand, and the other is easy to misunderstand.

A bureaucrat is a man who talks English but writes in officialese.

OIL

It's one thing to pour oil on troubled waters, but what do you pour on troubled oil?

In Texas, when a girl marries well, the well is usually oil.

When a girl worships the ground a man walks on, it's probably covered with oil wells.

OLD AGE

The tragedy of old age is not that one is old, but that one is not young.
                                    — Oscar Wilde

The sign of old age is to extol the past at the expense of the present.   — *Sydney Smith*

You aren't really old until nothing is fun enough to make you forget the weather.   — *Robert Quillen*

The first proof of old age is when you think that other people aren't having the fun you had.   — *Christopher Morley*

Senescence begins and middle age ends the day your descendants outnumber your friends.   — *Ogden Nash*

I'm 65 and I guess that puts me in with the geriatrics, but if there were 15 months in every year, I'd only be 48.   — *James Thurber*

It's good to reach a hale and hearty old age except for seeing your children become depressingly middleaged.

A man is old when his dreams about girls are reruns.

Another objection to old age is that there's not much of a future in it.

The trouble with old age is that it comes when we are too old to enjoy it.

A man at sixty begins to realize that his grandfather was not so old when he died at eighty.

A woman seldom gets old enough to admit she is that old.

A senior citizen is one who remembers when a senior citizen was called an old-timer.

You can't win: the only people who are not troubled with illness in old age, are those who are not troubled with old age.

An old man is a man who is ten years older than you are.

The trouble with most of us is that when we're old enough to know better, we're too old to want to.

To the old, no folks are old.

The conceited woman is never old, the unhappy woman too soon, and the wise woman at the right time.

You're never too old to learn, but that's what makes you old.

Old age is like everything else: to make a success of it, you've got to start young.

Calling a man a sexagenarian sounds like flattery.

The irony of life is that by the time you are old enough to know your way around, you are not going anywhere.

A man is old when he begins to hide his age; a woman, when she begins to tell hers.

Old age is the period when you begin to smile at things you used to laugh at.

Geriatrics is the science that attempts to solve the age-old problem of old age.

Another sign of age is when you feel like the morning after the night before—and you haven't even been anywhere.

It's not how old you are, but how you are old.

The first sign of old age is reluctance to commit suicide when the home team loses.

OLD-FASHIONED

There's an element of truth in every idea that lasts long enough to be called corny. — *Irving Berlin*

A teenager finds it hard to believe that some day he'll be as old-fashioned as his father.

Nowadays a woman is old-fashioned if she tries to make one husband last a lifetime.

An adolescent is always apologizing to his friends for having such old-fashioned parents.

ONION

It takes all the conceit out of the onion when you cook it.
— *John Burroughs*

Life is like an onion: you peel it off one layer at a time, and sometimes you weep. — *Carl Sandburg*

A pessimist remembers that the lily belongs to the onion family; an optimist, that the onion belongs to the lily family.

If you munch a sprig of parsley, you needn't eat your onions sparsely.

An apple a day keeps the doctor away, but an onion a day keeps everyone away.

OPEN

Keep an open mind, but don't keep it too open or people will throw a lot of rubbish into it.

An open mind helps a man understand a woman, an open wallet helps a woman understand a man.

It is good to have an open mind, but be sure it is not open at both ends.

If you've given up trying to pry something open, tell a youngster not to touch it.

Minds are like parachutes—they function only when open.

OPEN AND SHUT

The object of opening the mind, as of opening the mouth, is to shut it again on something solid.
— *Chesterton*

One hand opened in charity is worth two closed in prayer.

Many an open mind should be closed for repairs.

OPERA

The trouble with opera is that there's always too much singing.
— *Debussy*

All operatic triumphs resemble each other; it is the failures that differ. — *James G. Huneker*

If an opera cannot be played by an organ-grinder, it is not going to achieve immortality.
— *Thomas Beecham*

No good opera plot can be sensible for people do not sing when they are feeling sensible.
— *W. H. Auden*

One can't judge Wagner's opera *Lohengrin* after a first hearing, and I certainly don't intend hearing it a second time. — *Rossini*

Nobody really sings in an opera —they just make loud noises.
— *Galli-Curci*

I would rather sing grand opera than listen to it. — *Don Herold*

Opera: a play representing life in another world whose inhabitants have no speech but song, no motions but gestures, and no postures but attitudes. — *Bierce*

When an opera star sings her head off, she usually improves her appearance. — *Victor Borge*

Anything that is too stupid to be spoken, is sung. — *Voltaire*

The trouble with opera in the United States is that it is trying to sell caviar to a hamburger-eating country. — *Helen Traubel*

A prima donna's idea of a conceited person is anyone who isn't thinking about her.

What an opera singer needs most is size—a big voice, a big chest and a big mouth.

When some opera singers perform it, *Il Trovatore* becomes very ill.

Millions of dollars are spent on the opera which could be used in abolishing it.

OPERATION

The epithet *beautiful* is used by surgeons to describe operations which their patients describe as ghastly. — *Bernard Shaw*

An antivivisectionist is one who gags at a guinea-pig but swallows a baby. — *Mencken*

No one really gets over his operation till he stops talking about it.

Operations have become so common that you can hardly turn yours into a conversation piece nowadays, except when it's fatal.

If an operation is performed right, you walk; if performed wrong, you ride.

Some doctors operate on a patient just in the nick of time—a few hours later and the patient would have recovered.

To the surgeon who collects the bill in advance, every operation is a success.

An operation often enables the patient to live, but more often enables the surgeon to live.

A major operation is the kind where the patient has to borrow money to pay for it.

Not every operation is necessary, unless of course the surgeon needs more money.

There's no one so frustrating to a surgeon as the patient who recovers just before he has a chance to operate.

Before undergoing an operation, arrange your business affairs—you may live.

When some surgeons operate, they open you up and remove your bank account.

OPINION

I have views on most matters, and I am as willing as a politician to change most of them.
— *James Agate*

"That was excellently observed," say I when I read a passage in another where his opinion agrees with mine. — *Swift*

All sensitive men are of the same opinion about women, and no sensible man ever says what that opinion is. — *Samuel Butler*

Like all weak men, he laid exaggerated stress on not changing one's mind. — *Somerset Maugham*

Don't judge a man by his opinions, but by what his opinions have made him. — *G. C. Lichtenberg*

When I say "everybody says so," I mean I say so. — *Ed Howe*

With effervescing opinions, the quickest way to let them get flat is to let them get exposed to the air. — *Justice O. W. Holmes*

No one can have a higher opinion of him than I have—and I think he is a dirty little beast.
— *W. S. Gilbert*

Always listen to the opinion of others; it probably won't do you any good, but it will them.

Many a man forms his opinions only after submitting them to his preconceived ideas.

A wise man never tries to change a woman's opinion because he can never be quite sure what it is.

If your liver is out of order, your opinion is likely to be so.

You can always tell a well-informed man—his views are the same as yours.

A fool and his opinions are soon parted.

The man who never changes his opinions never corrects his mistakes.

Any man can find out what a girl thinks of him by marrying her.

How do I know what I think until I hear what I say?

With time a man will probably change all his opinions, except his opinion of himself.

When a man changes his mind as often as a woman does, he's probably married to her.

Some people base their opinions on fact, others bias them on prejudice.

Some people never change their opinion because it's been in the family for generations.

Some people never have opinions of their own but wear whatever happens to be in style.

OPPORTUNIST

When an opportunist sees the world going to the dogs, he starts selling dog food.

Opportunities lie on every hand, and so do opportunists.

An opportunist never casts his bread upon the waters unless he is sure the tide is coming in.

An opportunist never does anyone any harm unless he can do himself some good.

An opportunist never goes back on a friend as long as he can use him to advantage.

Opportunity knocks only once, but not opportunists.

An opportunist is a man who always tries to land on someone else's feet.

OPPORTUNITY

The three most important factors in making love are: first, opportunity; second, opportunity; third, opportunity. — *Montaigne*

A wise man will make more opportunities than he finds.
— *Francis Bacon*

I despise making the most of one's time: half the pleasures of life consist of the opportunities one has neglected.
— *Justice O. W. Holmes*

About the only way you can grasp an opportunity nowadays is by making a down payment.

Because this is a land of opportunity many a married man gets into trouble.

Opportunity knocks but once, but some people knock at every opportunity.

Many an opportunity is lost while a man is busy bewailing his lost opportunities.

Man's importunity is woman's opportunity.

Many a man misses opportunity when it knocks because he is out somewhere looking for four-leaf clovers.

Opportunity would have to advertise to get the attention of some people.

One man's outing is another man's inning.

Opportunity always seems to be where you were, never where you are.

There's no use going back for a lost opportunity—someone else has already found it.

Opportunity doesn't knock for people who don't give a rap.

It isn't enough to grasp an opportunity: you must do something more than just stand still and hold onto it.

Opportunities are like eggs: they come one at a time.

Opportunity knocks but once— that's why it has a better reputation than other knockers.

For a man, opportunity comes with a knock; for a woman, it comes with a ring.

What this country needs are equal opportunities for more people, and more people who are equal to them.

Opportunities are never lost; if you won't grasp them, another will.

The older you get, the longer it takes you to reach the door when opportunity knocks.

The secret of success is making hay with the grass that grows under other people's feet.

OPPOSITE

I owe my success to having listened respectfully to the very best advice, and then going away and doing the exact opposite.
— *Chesterton*

Doing just the opposite is also a form of imitation.
— *G. C. Lichtenberg*

Almost every wise saying has an opposite one, no less wise, to balance it. — *Santayana*

Opposites attract, like sloe gin and fast women.

Pleasure and pain are opposites: when you share grief, you decrease it; when you share joy, you increase it.

They are called the opposite sex because, when you think you have fooled them, it is just the opposite.

Some mothers-in-law are mean and bad-tempered; others are just the opposite: bad-tempered and mean.

Women are called the opposite sex because they never seem to agree with their husbands.

Opposites attract—that's why so many men are attracted to girls with money.

OPPOSITION

Any man can stand up to his opponents; give me the man who can stand up to his friends.
— *Gladstone*

Sometimes a man's wife won't let him marry the girl he likes— women are so unreasonable.
— *James G. Huneker*

Treating your adversary with respect is giving him an advantage to which he is not entitled.
— *Samuel Johnson*

Before marriage, she's his opposite; after marriage, his opposition.

Man proposes, and a mother-in-law opposes.

Opposition breeds success: you cannot light a match on a bar of soap.

Factions speak louder than words.

OPTIMISM

I hate the pollyanna pest who says that all is for the best.
— *Franklin P. Adams*

An optimist is a man who has never had much experience.
— *Don Marquis*

Being an optimist after you've got everything you want, doesn't count. — *Kin Hubbard*

Optimism: the world is the best of all possible worlds, and everything in it is a necessary evil.
— *F. H. Bradley*

The place where optimism flourishes most is the lunatic asylum.
— *Havelock Ellis*

Many optimists in the world don't own a thousand dollars, and because of their optimism never will. — *Ed Howe*

The habit of looking on the bright side of every event is worth more than a thousand pounds a year. — *Samuel Johnson*

An optimist is a fellow who believes what's going to be, will be postponed. — *Kin Hubbard*

An optimist is a man who tells you to cheer up when things are going his way.

Optimism is a state of mind that believes matrimony will be cheaper than the courtship.

Another optimist is the woman who thinks the man she is about to marry is better than the one she has just divorced.

Optimism is the belief that even when worst comes to worst, it won't be so bad.

A pollyanna is a woman accustomed to look at things with her eyes shut.

Another optimist is a man who hasn't yet read the morning newspaper.

Only an optimist can still look forward to the day when two can live as cheaply as one.

An optimist is the man who is always able to laugh at your troubles.

An optimist feels kindly toward everyone because he hasn't been cheated yet.

Another optimist is the middle-aged man who thinks that the cleaners have been shrinking the waistband of his trousers.

An optimist always seems to have the right feelings for the wrong reasons.

Remember the teakettle: when it's up to its neck in hot water, it sings.

An optimist is a man who spends his last dollar to buy a new billfold.

Another optimist is the man who tells you what a fool he used to be.

It's a good plan when you get the worst of it, to make the best of it.

Optimism is a great help in achieving success, or getting along without it.

The optimist has had unexpected expenses every month of his life, yet he doesn't expect to have any during the coming months.

OPTIMISM AND PESSIMISM

There is no sadder sight than a young pessimist, except an old optimist.   —*Mark Twain*

A pessimist is a person who has had to listen to too many optimists.   —*Don Marquis*

The old European culture could take pessimism lightly; the new American culture can only take optimism heavily.   —*Chesterton*

The optimist proclaims that we live in the best of all possible worlds, and the pessimist fears this is true.   —*J. B. Cabell*

Life is a telescope with the optimist looking through one end, and the pessimist through the other.

In time of trouble, the pessimist gets more pleasure out of his pessimism than the optimist out of his optimism.

An optimist is a man who looks forward to marriage, and a pessimist is a married optimist.

While the optimist is looking for the silver lining, the pessimist often finds gold.

The optimist finds fault with the pessimist, and the pessimist finds fault with everything else.

Most optimism comes from too little experience, and most pessimism from too much.

The optimist lets opportunity knock, while the pessimist does the knocking himself.

A pessimist asks you if there is milk in the pitcher; an optimist asks you to pass the cream.

If it wasn't for the optimist, the pessimist wouldn't know how happy he isn't.

The pessimist feels he is carrying that weight of the world on his shoulders; the optimist feels he is sitting on top of it.

The pessimist is more often right, the optimist more often happy.

If a man is a pessimist before forty, he knows too much; if he is an optimist after forty, he knows too little.

Love is responsible for most of the optimists, and marriage for most of the pessimists.

The optimist consoles himself that things could be worse; the pessimist just waits a while, and sure enough they are.

The world is in a state of ferment, with the optimist expecting the outcome to be champagne, and the pessimist fearing it will be vinegar.

The optimist says his glass is half full, while the pessimist says his is half empty.

A pessimist is an optimist on his way home from the race track.

The optimist sees an opportunity in every calamity; the pessimist sees a calamity in every opportunity.

ORCHESTRA

I don't hire women for my orchestra because if they're pretty, they distract my musicians, and if they're not, they distract me.
— *Thomas Beecham*

The genius of orchestra conductors is nonsense: the best conductor is the sergeant-major of a military band.   — *Igor Stravinsky*

There are two golden rules for an orchestra: they must begin together and end together; the public doesn't give a damn what goes on between.   — *Thomas Beecham*

If you can't face the music, you'll never get to lead the band.

Never blow your own horn— unless you're in an orchestra.

ORDER

Order leads to all the virtues, but what leads to order?
— *G. C. Lichtenberg*

Order is heaven's first law, but earth's last achievement.

Order may be heaven's first law, but it was disorder that produced earth's first lawyer.

ORIGINAL

What the world calls originality is only an unaccustomed method of tickling it.   — *Bernard Shaw*

I am chiefly original in my willingness to admit my ignorance.
— *Jules Renard*

He has left off reading altogether, to the great improvement of his originality. — *Charles Lamb*

Many a man has only one original idea, and that is that he's a great man.

Originality is rare: most of us know a good thing as soon as the other fellow sees it.

Originality is the fine art of remembering what you hear but forgetting where you heard it.

The only thing original in some men is original sin.

If you wish to be considered original, all you have to do is to repeat clever things to people who have never heard them before.

When a schoolboy has original ideas, they are usually confined to spelling.

Some teenagers show their originality in art, some in music, but most show it in building a sandwich.

Don't expect anything original from an echo.

ORPHAN

Adam and Eve had no parents, but they were not orphans.

When a small boy is left an orphan, he never knows what to do with it.

Some people who say "Our Father" on Sunday, go around the rest of the week acting like orphans.

ORTHODOXY

If you go to church and like the singing better than the preaching, that's not orthodox.
— *Ed Howe*

In all the welter of inconsistent and incompatible heresies, the one and only unpardonable heresy is orthodoxy. — *Chesterton*

Orthodoxy is my doxy, heterodoxy is another man's doxy.
— *William Warburton*

Beware of the fundamentalist who thinks it necessary to make a hell of this world so that we may enjoy heaven in the next.

OVERTIME

Matrimony is the only profession that permits a woman to work sixteen hours a day without overtime.

Time is money, especially overtime.

Procrastination may be the thief of time, but it breeds time-and-a-half.

OVERWEIGHT

I don't do anything to keep my weight down because it's my weight that's keeping me down.
— *Irvin S. Cobb*

Each year it grows harder to make ends meet—the ends I refer to are hands and feet.
— *Richard Armour*

From the day she weighs 140, the chief excitement of a woman's life is in spotting women who are fatter than she is. — *Helen Rowland*

A fat person lives shorter but eats longer. — *Stanislaw J. Lec*

No person is really fat: he is either too heavy for his height, or too short for his weight.

Fat men are usually good-natured because good-natured men are usually fat.

There are compensations for overweight women: men do not suspect them, and women do not fear them as competition.

Another thing which a man is the first to notice in a friend but the last to notice in himself is overweight.

No one should try to do two things at the same time, including the woman who puts on weight and shorts.

It's not how much you gain between Christmas and New Year's that counts, it's how much you gain between New Year's and Christmas.

The most discouraging thing about middle age is all those years going to waist.

The day is made brighter when you accidentally meet an old friend who is just a little plumper than yourself.

When a man gets too fat to conceal his weight, he starts to boast about it.

Overweight is sometimes caused by glands, but more often by

muscles that enable you to reach for second helpings.

The more we overeat, the harder it is for us to get close to the table.

Statistics on the number of people who are overweight are bound to be round figures.

The woman who is overweight cannot only dish it out, but can eat it all herself.

Overweight shortens life, probably on the principle that God summons you after you've eaten your allotted share.

The trouble with what melts in your mouth is the way it bulges lower down.

Overweight is usually the result of living from hand to mouth, from hand to mouth, from hand to mouth.

A fat man has an advantage over other men because he knows exactly where his cigarette ashes are going to land.

OWE

Don't go around saying the world owes you a living: the world owes you nothing, it was here first.   — Mark Twain

A man first owes it to himself to become successful—and then he owes it to the Internal Revenue Service.

The world owes every man a living—the kind he earns.

The ambition of every deadbeat is to owe money to as many people as he doesn't owe.

Many a man who is nothing boasts that all he is he owes to his mother.

Many a man finds that the living the world owes him is the most difficult of all debts to collect.

The United States is a wonderful country where the people owe a great deal to their government, especially on April 15th.

There's plenty of money around; the trouble is, everyone owes it to everyone else.

What you don't know won't hurt you, and neither will what you don't owe.

What with time payments, charge accounts and credit cards, about all you can do with money nowadays is to owe it.

The man who says he owes everything to his wife seldom pays it back.

OYSTER

He was a bold man that first ate an oyster.   — Swift

It took millions of years to evolve man from the oyster, but it takes only a few seconds to transfer the oyster into a man.

Consider the oyster: with a little grit it can produce a pearl of great value.

An oyster never gets stewed except during the R months.

An optimist looks at an oyster and expects a pearl; a pessimist looks at an oyster and expects ptomaine poisoning.

PACKAGE

Women should be thankful that the laws requiring truth in packaging don't apply to them.
— *Olin Miller*

One of the nicest gifts you can give a woman is one that comes wrapped in mink.

Christmas gifts come in beautiful wrappings, and the most beautiful of all is a happy family all wrapped up in one another.

PAIN

It is much easier to stand a pain than to stand an itch.

In youth the absence of pleasure is pain, in old age the absence of pain is pleasure.

The advantage of a late marriage is that it doesn't draw out the agony so long.

When a man is in pain, the pain is in him.

It's better to have a backache from working about the garden than a headache from worrying about the rest of the earth.

A malingerer is a shirker with an infinite capacity for faking pains.

PAINT

The most common way of removing paint is to sit on it.

The paint on the walls never looks the same to the landlord and the tenant.

A woman is seldom as bad as she is painted or a man as good as he is whitewashed.

Children brighten up a home, often with every color in their paint sets.

PAINTING

Painting is easy when you don't know how, but very difficult when you do.
— *Degas*

A painting in a museum hears more ridiculous opinions than anything else in the world.
— *Goncourt*

Can it be that the painters make John the Baptist a Spaniard in Madrid and an Irishman in Dublin?
— *Mark Twain*

There is pictorial license just as there is poetic license.
— *Delacroix*

Whistler is one of the greatest masters of painting in my opinion, and in this opinion Whistler himself entirely concurs.
— *Oscar Wilde*

It does not matter how badly you paint so long as you don't paint badly like other people.
— *George Moore*

If more than ten percent of the population likes a painting it should be burned, for it must be bad. — *Bernard Shaw*

Some painters transform the sun into a yellow spot, others transform a yellow spot into the sun. — *Picasso*

You always have to mar a picture a little in order to finish it. — *Delacroix*

Painting is the art of protecting flat surfaces from the weather and exposing them to the critic. — *Bierce*

Good painting is like good cooking: it can be tasted, but not explained. — *Vlaminck*

What a vanity is painting which is admired for its similarity in appearance to things whose originals are not admired! — *Pascal*

A painter leaves his emotions behind him for posterity to share. — *Augustus John*

Painting is an intermediate somewhat between a thought and a thing. — *Sydney Smith*

Every successful art gallery is based on the principle that it is far more important to sell a picture than to paint it.

The time when an abstract painter should stop painting is right before he begins.

Some painters are so talented that they can take the most beautiful landscape and in a few minutes transform it into something unrecognizable.

The worse the painting, the more pretentious the title.

An abstract painting is like a woman: you'll never get to like it if you try to understand it.

No one knows what many contemporary paintings represent other than a little labor.

Some modern artists fling paint at a canvas, wipe their brushes off with a rag, and then exhibit the rag.

Abstract painting is a form of art which has to be seen to be depreciated.

It takes art to paint a picture, but craft to sell it.

PAJAMAS

A man who has his initials on his pajamas must be uncertain of himself; surely he ought to know who he is by bedtime. — *Christopher Morley*

He was as helpless as a man when the drawstrings of his pajamas snap inside the hem. — *Christopher Morley*

Pajamas are a sleeping garment usually placed near the bed of newlyweds in case of fire.

When a small boy has nothing in his pockets, he's probably in his pajamas.

PANTS

What would women say if men changed the length of their trousers every year? — *Lady Astor*

If God intended for women to wear slacks, he would have constructed them differently.
— *Emily Post*

I never made any money until I took off my pants. — *Sally Rand*

The man who wears the pants in his house generally wears an apron over them right after dinner.

Talked about behind their backs are women bigger than their slacks.

Once upon a time when people wore blue jeans, they worked.

Slacks are not for you intended unless you are diminuended.

If there's no money in the pockets, what difference does it make who wears the pants in the family?

If some women knew how wonderful they look in slacks, they'd wear skirts.

The woman who looks bad in slacks and worse in jeans will probably be found wearing shorts.

The only thing slacks do for some women is enable them to put their feet on the desk.

A woman takes to wearing pants when she won't wear short dresses any shorter nor long dresses any longer.

A girl who wears slacks may be well-bred without being well-reared.

When a woman wears the pants in the family, the man often looks around for another skirt.

No one can put more into something than it can hold, except a woman in slacks.

Never judge a man by his appearance: the man who is most crooked usually has the straightest crease in his trousers.

Overweight women who are partial to slacks should practice discretion and not turn their backs.

When both men and women wear blue jeans, the over-all effect is always different.

When Shakespeare wrote that there's a divinity that shapes our ends, women didn't wear slacks.

With women wearing pants as well as men, why is it that you never hear of a man going through his wife's pockets?

There's nothing like a pair of slacks to expose the stern facts about a woman.

Women who bulge when wearing slacks should not indulge in daily snacks.

PAR

In golf, when you score below par, it's skill; when your opponent does, it's luck.

It's a wise stock that knows its own par.

Golf is the only game where your score depreciates by going above par.

PARADE

If they really want to honor the soldiers, why don't they let them sit in the stands and have the people march by? — *Will Rogers*

The trouble with walking in a parade is that life seems so dull and colorless afterward.
— *Kin Hubbard*

PARADOX

Bernard Shaw was a master of paradox, but more often its slave.
— *Herbert Samuel*

I prefer to be a man of paradox than a man of prejudice.
— *Rousseau*

Life is a paradox: you are more likely to get somewhere if you keep both feet on the ground.

Success is paradoxical: most men get to the top by going to the bottom of things.

PARASITE

A hanger-on is ever ready to take your part though he'd prefer to take your all.

The only asset of a parasite is his claim that the world owes him a living.

You can always depend on a hanger-on to depend on others.

PARENTS

Some people seem compelled by unkind fate to parental servitude for life. — *Samuel Butler*

There are times when parenthood seems nothing but feeding the mouth that bites you.
— *Peter De Vries*

To have a child is no more creditable than to have rheumatism—and no more discreditable.
— *Mencken*

You can always be sure of maternity, but you cannot always be sure of paternity.

Parenthood is a gradual process that turns a bright son of fourteen into a foolish father at forty.

Many problem children go by the name of parents.

A parent is one who treats an adolescent like a child, yet expects him to act like an adult.

The generation that criticizes the younger generation is always the one that raised it.

We get our parents when they are too old for us to change their habits.

It's very hard for rich parents not to be poor parents.

Parents are people who always think their chidren would behave much better if they didn't play with the brats next door.

There's only one thing worse than a doting parent, and that's a don'ting one.

Most parents begin by giving in, and end by giving up.

Formerly it used to take more patience to make a good parent; nowadays it takes more money.

Parents never seem to understand why their neighbors' children should be so destructive while their own are merely mischievous.

PARENTS AND CHILDREN

A father is always a Republican toward his son, and a mother is always a Democrat.
— *Robert Frost*

Children aren't happy with nothing to ignore, and that's what parents were created for.
— *Ogden Nash*

I don't know who are the best people to educate the young, but I know that parents are the worst.
— *William Morris*

Every child keeps hoping his parents will eventually run out of advice.

The first step in the art of being a parent consists in sleeping when the baby isn't looking.

Parents are the last people on earth who ought to have children.

The Lord certainly knew what He was doing when He gave small children to young couples.

You never know how much time has passed over your head until your children begin telling you instead of asking you.

Children leave their parents one by one, usually to return two by two.

What this country needs is a new child labor law to keep children from working—their parents to death.

There are no illegitimate children—there are only illegitimate parents.

How times have changed: a century ago minding one's children didn't mean obeying them.

Politicians who were born of poor but honest parents usually have children who were not.

Parents are all alike: first they try to get him to walk and talk, and then they try to get him to sit down and shut up.

A man can learn many things from his children until they grow old enough to know as little as he does.

The quickest way to get people to talk about their children is to talk about yours.

Parents who are lucky in their children usually have children who are lucky in their parents.

It's too bad God didn't give us our neighbors' children since these are the only ones we know how to raise.

Every parent wishes he knew as much as his children think he does, or as much as his children think they do.

If you don't want your children to hear what you're saying, pretend you're talking to them.

The worst thing about growing old is having to listen to a lot of advice from one's children.

Children are usually happier than their parents because they don't have children of their own to put up with.

The best way for a father to bring up his children is to love their mother.

Parents are inconsistent: first they want their youngsters home early because they're children, and later, because they're not children.

Children bring their parents closer together—usually in self-defense.

Parents are people who bring up children in expectation, and grandparents are people who bring them up in conversation.

Two can live as cheaply as one —on parents.

Many a parent wishes the schools would do a better job of bringing up her children.

Young couples want to start out where their parents are now, which is what keeps their parents where they are now.

PARIS

When God creates a beautiful woman in Paris, the devil retaliates with a fool to support her.
— Barbey d'Aurevilly

They call it the Latin Quarter because nobody there speaks Latin and nobody has a quarter.
— Will Rogers

London smells of petrol, burnt grass and tallow, thus differing from Paris where to these are added the smell of powder, coffee and cheese.
— Karel Capek

French fashion and American capital makes Paris the fashion capital of the world.

Paris is where the American tourist speaks French and then explains it in English.

PARKING

The only place where you can park as long as you want to, you don't want to.

Drive carefully: the life you save may belong to a pedestrian on his way to remove his car from the parking place you're looking for.

There would be less trouble finding a parking place if more people practiced birth control.

Two out of every three cars are driven by men, and one of them usually gets to the parking place before you do.

A parking place is a space that suddenly disappears while you are making a U-turn.

The grass is always greener on the other side of the fence, and the parking place is always available on the other side of the street.

Many a woman driver is content to park within easy walking distance from the curb.

In the old days people used to drive in the park; nowadays, they park in the drive.

Timing is everything, especially in finding a parking place.

An old-timer is one who remembers when the only problem about parking was getting the girl to consent to it.

America is a nation that adds every year a hundred new cars for every new parking place.

The main trouble with the straight and narrow path is that there's no place to park.

If you think this is a free country, just try to park your car somewhere.

In ancient times, there was the dog in the manger; nowadays there's the man who parks in the middle of a two-car parking space.

The early bird not only gets the worm but also gets the parking place before you do.

He who hesitates is not lost— he merely loses the parking place.

Men who fail to pass their drivers' tests usually wind up as parking-lot attendants.

When a man says it's a small world, he's probably looking for a place to park his car.

Why is it that the parking space that's available is usually only a few inches short?

What this country needs is a radar screen for cars which will detect the nearest parking place.

Einstein's theory that space is solid applies to parking space.

The time a motorist saves on a superhighway getting to a city he loses in that city by looking for a place to park.

There's only one sure way to find a parking place: get there before the other fellow does.

When you're driving it's always your wife who is the first to see a parking place, but only after you've passed it.

All the world loves a lover, probably because he always parks where he won't block traffic.

There are plenty of parking places everywhere, but the trouble is that they are already taken.

The used car is not so much of a problem as the used parking space.

Another advantage of a shorter workweek is that it would give a man more time to find a place to park.

The three most common types of parking are: illegal, double, and no!

Virtue has its own reward: you can generally find parking space near a church.

Another optimist is the man who can hand his car over to a parking-lot attendant without looking back.

If the city would put all the fire hydrants together, there would be much more parking space.

PARKING METER

The bigger the car, the more you get for your money in a parking meter.

The American way of solving its parking problem is by adding millions of parking meters every year, but mighty few parking places.

You cannot live on borrowed time, except when it's left on a parking meter.

Putting a coin in the parking meter is about the only exercise a motorist gets these days.

A parking meter is a device invented to make parking a little easier and make time pass a lot faster.

A woman driver can seldom figure out which of the three parking meters to put her coin in.

There are few greater satisfactions left in a motorist's life than parking on what is left of the other fellow's time.

A parking meter is a device that forces a car owner to make time payments forever.

For a parking lot, it's pay-as-you-go; for a parking meter, it's pay-as-you-come.

PARKING TICKET

A parking ticket is like a wife: no man complains about it until he has got one of his own.

Crime doesn't pay: sooner or later every criminal gets a ticket for parking.

The windshield wiper was invented to give the police a handy place to put parking tickets.

Another thing that comes to him who waits is an overtime parking ticket.

PARLIAMENT

Prime Ministers are wedded to the truth, but like other wedded couples, they sometimes live apart.
— *Saki*

The House of Lords is like a glass of champagne that has stood for five days.   — *Clement Attlee*

The lords temporal say nothing, the lords spiritual have nothing to say, and the House of Commons has nothing to say and says it.   — *Oscar Wilde*

The House of Lords is the British Outer Mongolia for retired politicians.
— *Anthony Wedgwood Benn*

The House of Commons is made up of hundreds of men all thinking a great deal of themselves and very little of each other.

PARROT

In the kingdom of the birds, the parrot is the best talker—and the worst flier.   —*Orville Wright*

A parrot's speech is like a baby's—intelligible only to its owner.

A parrot is a queer bird that goes in for swearing, but draws the line at drinking and smoking.

The parrot is another creature that does a lot of talking when it has nothing to say.

PARTNER

An optimist and pessimist make the best partnership because one sees the profits while the other sees the risks.

Marriage is an equal partnership where he makes the money and she makes the decisions.

Every business has a silent partner nowadays—the government.

Matrimony consists of a continual series of disagreements because it is the only partnership where nothing is put in writing.

When two partners in a business always agree, one of them is unnecessary.

It is easier for a man and woman to get along harmoniously as life partners as long as they avoid being bridge partners.

Marriage is a partnership where ten percent is what you make it and ninety percent is how you take it.

Marriage is a partnership, with the husband acting as the silent partner.

PARTY

Giving a party is like having a baby—its conception is more fun than its completion, and once you've begun it's impossible to stop.   —*Jan Struther*

The cocktail party is a cheap and convenient means of mixing drinks and bores.   —*Shane Leslie*

The talk becomes more interesting at some parties after some parties have left.

At a cocktail party the problem is not to get people to talk but to get them to listen.

Misery loves company, but happiness throws more parties.

At a cocktail party, the amount divulged usually depends on the amount indulged.

Why is it that at a party the ones who want to leave early and the ones who want to stay late are always married to each other?

They sometimes run out of drinks at a cocktail party but never out of talk.

The best thing to do with party leftovers is never to invite them again.

At a cocktail party glasses are upset, liquor spilled, names dropped, and reputations overturned.

The life of the party sometimes spins yarns but more often spawns yawns.

A cocktail party consists of men and women standing around in circles discussing men and women running around in triangles.

There's nothing worse than a dull party: it can be a fete worse than death.

A cocktail party is a holding operation: everyone holds a cocktail, a canapé and a conversation all at the same time.

Some parties begin once the ice is broken, and don't end until the furniture is too.

One of the pleasures of giving a party is having it over.

At a cocktail party half the people haven't enough wit to talk well, and the other half haven't enough wisdom to keep still.

After the one who is the life of the party passes out, everybody begins to have a good time.

People get together at a cocktail party to hear a few good things said about themselves, and a lot of bad things said about others.

A cocktail party is where you meet a lot of people who drink so much, you can't remember their names.

There is nothing so unbearable as a wild party at your neighbor's —unless you are there.

The three great American parties are the Democratic, the Republican, and the cocktail.

To give a party on the q.t., don't get more than one qt.

A cocktail party is where some guests eat the olives, some chew the cherries, while most spill the beans.

A fool and his money are soon partying.

At a cocktail party half the people don't know how much they've had, and the other half don't know how much they've said.

A discouraging glare from the wife has saved many a man from becoming the life of the party.

At a cocktail party half the guests open their mouths to talk too much, and the other half open their mouths to drink too much.

There are two kinds of wild parties: those you can never forget, and those you can't even remember.

At a cocktail party, the person who comes to drink causes less trouble than the one who comes to listen.

PASS

Anybody at all could get a passing mark with me; let life flunk 'em—I wouldn't. *– Robert Frost*

Keeping up with the Joneses is bad enough, but passing them on a hill is worse.

There is usually very little difference between passing the buck and passing a resolution.

At the race track you usually bet on a horse who has been trained to let other horses pass him.

Too many young men who have passed their driving tests think they can pass anything.

Whatever else it fails to pass, Congress always passes the buck.

An adolescent becomes an adult when he thinks it is more important to pass an exam than to pass the car ahead.

One advantage of traveling on the straight and narrow path is that no one is trying to pass you.

An old man looks back at what's past, a young man looks back at what's passing.

There are three chief periods in American history: the passing of the buffalo, the passing of the Indian, and the passing of the buck.

No man ever traveled to fame on a pass.

PASSION

Passion makes idiots of the cleverest men, and makes the biggest idiots clever.
— *La Rochefoucauld*

In her first passion woman loves her lover, in all the others all she loves is love. — *Lord Byron*

Unless a woman has amorous heart, she is a dull companion.
— *Samuel Johnson*

To be in a passion you good may do, but no good if a passion be in you. — *William Blake*

The chaste woman who teases is worse than a streetwalker.
— *James G. Huneker*

Love that begins at forty goes like sixty.

Passion is that funny feeling that drives a man to bite a girl's neck because she has beautiful legs.

If at first you don't succeed, girls, try a little ardor.

PAST

No man is rich enough to buy back his past. — *Oscar Wilde*

Events in the past may be roughly divided into those which probably never happened and those which do not matter.
— *W. R. Inge*

The thing most women dread about their past is its length.

There are two occasions when a man's past life is brought up before him: when he is drowning, and when he quarrels with his wife.

In the good old days they also used to speak about the good old days.

Half the pleasure of recalling the past lies in the editing.

The proof that women like to live in the past is that they remain for years at twenty-nine.

The good old days were the days when all this country needed was a good five-cent cigar.

The oftener you look back, the sooner you won't get ahead.

A man can sometimes tell by looking at a girl what kind of a past she is going to have.

The best thing about the good old days is that they cannot come back.

Living in the past has only one thing in its favor—it's cheaper.

An old-timer is one who remembers the five-cent cigar but forgets the ten-hour workday.

The man who longs for the good old days should try reading this book by an oil lamp.

A girl with a past always likes to bury it in some man's arms.

Mankind profits from its past, but not from its past mistakes.

PAST AND FUTURE

We can pay our debt to the past by putting the future in debt to ourselves.   — *John Buchan*

I like the dreams of the future better than the history of the past.
                          — *Jefferson*

There is only one tragedy in a woman's life: her past is always her lover, and her future invariably her husband. — *Oscar Wilde*

A European goes to New York and Chicago and sees the future; when he goes to Asia he sees the past.   — *Bertrand Russell*

If newlyweds could only read the future, many of them would make posterity a thing of the past.

The future is the past come home to roost.

Many a man goes into politics with a fine future, and comes out with a terrible past.

May the happiest days of your past be the saddest days of your future.

The girl with a future avoids the man with a past.

PAST AND PRESENT

Every father talks about the good old days while telling his children how much better they have it nowadays.

We think more of the future of our children than of the past of our parents.

The hardest job for a has-been is getting people interested in the present in what he was in the past.

When the girl of today pets, it's not like mother used to mate.

In the old days, people would hear their neighbors' troubles;

nowadays with television, they hear the whole world's troubles.

Times change: formerly the day was done before we were.

In the past all you had to do was keep up with the neighbors; nowadays you must also keep up with the payments.

PAST, PRESENT AND FUTURE

The trouble with our times is that the future is not what it used to be.   — *Paul Valéry*

Life lives less in the present than in the future always, and less in both together than in the past.
                              — *Robert Frost*

There is no time like the present—except the last two thousand years and maybe the next ten.

Historians tell us the past, economists tell us the future—only the present is beyond human understanding.

The present is the period when the future pauses for a short while before becoming the past.

Some girls like a man with a past, some like a man with a future, but all girls go for a man with a present.

A happy future is a present earned in the past.

Experience is what we possess in the present to keep us from repeating the past in the future.

The present was once the future from which we expected so much in the past.

The present generation is lucky: everything that's wrong is due to the previous generation and will have to be paid for by the next generation.

You cannot change the past, but you can ruin the present by worrying about the future.

PATENT

No one is so credulous as a little child, except an inventor taking out a patent.

The Patent Office is the mother-in-law of invention.

If a man builds a better mousetrap than his neighbor, the world will beat him out of his patent.

PATIENCE

It takes a man twenty-five years to learn to be married; it's a wonder women have the patience to wait for it.
        — *Clarence Budington Kelland*

A woman who has never seen her husband fishing, doesn't know what a patient man she has married.   — *Ed Howe*

Adopt the pace of nature: her secret is patience.   — *Emerson*

You must first have a lot of patience to learn to have patience.
                — *Stanislaw J. Lec*

Patience: a minor form of despair, disguised as a virtue.

— *Bierce*

Patience is a wonderful thing, especially in a creditor.

Patience is sometimes considered a virtue when it is merely a case of not knowing what to do.

Never become irritable while waiting for someone; if you are patient, you'll find that you can wait much faster.

The time when patience is most needed is when it is exhausted.

You can learn many things from your children—for example, how much patience you have.

Every woman thinks every other woman's husband is more patient than her own.

No matter how little patience you have with the mistakes of others, you always have lots of patience with your own.

The secret of patience is doing something else in the meantime.

There would be fewer divorces if husbands showed as much patience at home as they do while waiting for a fish to bite.

The trouble with a bore is that he is endowed with more patience than his listeners.

A mother's patience is never really put to the test until the television set breaks down during a rainy weekend.

PATIENT

The patient is never out of danger as long as the doctor continues to make visits.

The patient who is emotionally disturbed has probably just got his bill.

A jaywalker is often a patient for a few months because he wouldn't be patient for a few seconds.

Half the doctors don't know how the other half lose their patients.

In every hospital there are more male patients than patient males.

PATRIOTISM

I never felt the call to be an expatriate, but I hold it to be the inalienable right of anybody to go to hell in his own way.

— *Robert Frost*

I should like my country well enough if it were not for my countrymen.   — *Horace Walpole*

Intellectually I know America is no better than any other country, but emotionally I know she is better than any other country.

— *Sinclair Lewis*

Every man loves and admires his own country because it produced him.   — *Lord Lytton*

The man who loves other countries as much as he loves his own is like the man who loves other women as much as he loves his own wife.   — *Theodore Roosevelt*

Patriotism has less to do with a state than with a state of mind.

Patriotism is not the last refuge of a scoundrel—it's the first.

The patriot who is always ready to shed his last drop of blood for his country, is mighty particular about the first drop.

Chauvinists are all alike: they all talk a red, white and blue streak.

A genuine patriot should at all times be ready to die for his country, even though it costs him his life.

Many a man thinks he does his duty when he does his country.

If you believe in "My country, right or wrong," you must also believe in "My country, right or left."

When a patriotic employee wants a raise, it's because he wants the government to benefit from the extra tax on his salary.

PATRONAGE

We need in politics men who have something to give, not men who have something to get.
— *Bernard Baruch*

To the victors belong the spoils, and also the privilege of fighting over them.

Patronage is made up of many who are looking for jobs, but few who are looking for work.

Most of the rottenness of politics comes from the spoils system.

PAY

It is difficult to get a man to understand something when his salary depends upon his not understanding it.   — *Upton Sinclair*

Love's labor is the poorest paid of all.   — *Kin Hubbard*

Many a man is willing to do an honest day's work, but only if he can get a week's pay for it.

A dollar a word to the wise is sufficient.

The pay-as-you-go is a misnomer—after you pay, where can you go?

People are paid not for what they know, but for what they do with what they know.

The reason the bride's parents pay for the wedding is that the groom has already paid for the courtship.

It's always the woman who pays, but it's the man whose money she pays with.

If you pay as you go, you probably won't have enough money to come back.

Always pay debts and compliments, and you are sure to succeed.

Beware of places you don't have to pay to get into—you will probably have to pay to get out.

It's the woman who pays and pays because she's the only one at home when the bill collector calls.

If some folks were compelled to pay as they go, they would stay.

PAYMENT

The real test of a modern product is whether it lasts longer than the payments on it.

The world is so full of a number of things that it's hard to keep up with the payments.

The man who has everything probably needs one more thing: help with his payments.

The most common form of car sickness nowadays is the feeling you get every month when the payment falls due.

Wealthy people miss one of the great thrills in life—paying the last installment.

There's only one thing harder than a diamond, and that's making the payments on it.

A television set with ultra-high frequency probably refers to the payments.

You don't have to be reckless to lose control of your car—you can forget to keep up the payments.

PEACE

What a mess we are in now—peace has been declared.
                    — Napoleon

We are going to have peace even if we have to fight for it.
        — Dwight D. Eisenhower

Some members of Congress would best promote the country's peace by holding their own.
        — George D. Prentice

Gone are those pleasant nineteenth-century days when a country could remain neutral and at peace just by saying it wanted to.
            — William Shirer

War will never cease until babies begin to come into the world with larger cerebrums and smaller adrenal glands.
                    — Mencken

I do not want the peace which passeth understanding, I want the understanding which bringeth peace.   — Helen Keller

Universal peace sounds ridiculous to the head of an average family.   — Kin Hubbard

In his steadfast pursuit of world peace, man has always stuck to his guns.

The more we strive for peace on earth, the more it seems that the dove of peace is a bird of paradise.

The world should make peace first, and then should make it last.

The best argument for everlasting peace is that it would enable us to finish paying for past wars.

We will never have universal peace until each nation is satisfied with the piece it has.

Peace is a period set aside between wars to enable the generals to write their books.

Another way to end war is for soldiers to demand the same pay for fighting as other fighters get.

There is no way to cut the pattern of peace without having a few scraps left over.

What the world craves is the peace that passeth all misunderstanding.

Peace is a morbid condition where there is a surplus of civilians which war seeks to correct.

A child's idea of peace on earth is to beat a drum and blow a horn.

Man is learning to live peacefully in outer space and at the bottom of the sea, but not yet on earth between.

Blessed are the peacemakers, for they shall never be unemployed.

PEARL

Don't cast pearls before swine —that is, cultured pearls.

Give a man enough rope, and he'll hang himself; give a woman enough rope, and she'll want pearls on it.

PEDESTRIAN

The law usually gives the pedestrian the right of way, but makes no provision for flowers.

Man's inhumanity to man makes thousands hesitate at the curb.

The man who doesn't drive a car doesn't know what he's missing but knows what's missing him.

The pedestrian who jumps to a conclusion probably wasn't moving fast enough.

A pedestrian is a person walking or lying in the street.

The only man who never leaves his car keys in his other suit is the pedestrian.

There are three persons to every car, and they are always in front of it at street crossings.

It's strange that a motorist never remembers he used to be a pedestrian.

If all the pedestrians were laid end to end, they would greatly simplify the task of the reckless driver.

Another traffic hazard which motorists keep trying to get rid of is the pedestrian.

A pedestrian is a man whose wife beats him to the garage.

You always see more game when you haven't a gun, and more pedestrians when you haven't a car.

A pedestrian has rights, but usually they are only the last rites.

You can dodge some of the drivers all the time, and all the drivers some of the time, but you can't dodge all the drivers all the time.

A pedestrian is always safe when he has the right of way—as long as he doesn't try to exercise it.

Pedestrians live longer these days—provided they are rushed at once to the hospital.

The more patient pedestrians, the fewer pedestrian patients.

It requires no polls to learn what the man in the street is thinking—it's how to get across it safely.

Statistics show that the general run of pedestrians is a little too slow.

If evolution works, it will eventually produce a pedestrian who can jump two ways at once.

A pedestrian is one who is sure there is still a gallon of gas left in the tank when the gauge points to empty.

PENALTY

The penalty for getting the woman you want is that you must keep her.   — *Lionel Strachey*

Nowadays a citizen can hardly distinguish between a tax and a fine, except that the fine is generally much lighter.   — *Chesterton*

Baldness and overweight are the penalties of time: too many men in middle age come out on top after pushing their way to the front.

The penalty of success is to be bored by the attentions of people who formerly snubbed you.

When a man pays all the taxes he owes, he feels he is being fined for his honesty.

PENNY

A penny is something we see every day but never look at.
— *Stephen Potter*

Another thing you can still get for a penny is your incorrect weight.

A penny saved is a penny plus interest earned.

Save your pennies and the sales tax will take care of them.

The only thing a penny is good for nowadays is to offer it for a person's thoughts.

A penny saved is a penny earned—so what?

The sales tax was devised to prevent the penny from becoming obsolete.

PENSION

The pension too is mightier than the sword.

The proof that we are a peace-loving nation is that we seldom pay pensions for more than three wars at a time.

PERFECT

Have no fear of perfection— you'll never reach it.   — Dali

We are none of us infallible— not even the youngest of us.
— Benjamin Jowett

American women expect to find in their husbands a perfection that English women only hope to find in their butlers.
— Somerset Maugham

The artist who aims at perfection in everything achieves it in nothing.   — Delacroix

The husband who expects his wife to be perfect also expects her to understand why he isn't.

The only perfect people are those we do not know.

A perfect husband is one whose wife doesn't start to reform him right away.

The closest to perfection a person ever comes is when he fills out a job application form.

A perfectionist is a person with an exasperating aptitude for exactitude.

Nobody can be perfect unless he admits his faults, but if he has faults how can he be perfect?

None of the men who would make perfect husbands are married yet.

The more perfect a man is, the more women try to altar him.

A perfectionist is a person who takes great pains, and gives even greater pains to others.

It is only the perfect fool who won't marry until he finds the perfect woman.

Trifles make perfection, but perfection is no trifle.

A perfectionist is one whose pursuit of perfection often leads him to make a perfect nuisance of himself.

The only perfect husbands are other women's.

No one is perfect, except the man your wife could have married.

Perfection is a mixed blessing: an imperfect friend is preferable to a perfect stranger.

God help the man who won't marry until he finds the perfect woman, and God help the woman if he finds her!

Nothing is ever right to the perfectionist because everything has to be.

It takes a second marriage for a man to discover there is only one perfect husband—his wife's first mate.

PERFUME

For me a woman who wears no perfume has no future.
— Paul Valéry

Why is the name of a perfume always more alluring than its odor?

Perfume is a fragrance used by a woman to make a man imagine that two can live as cheaply as one.

Many a woman wastes good perfume on a man who orders hamburger with raw onions.

Perfumes should be used with caution: the girl with a perfume often lures the man without a cent.

Perfume is so expensive that you have to pay for it through the nose.

Virtue makes sense, but not the names of scents.

Perfume is an alluring liquid commonly used by women to brainwash men into marriage.

PERMANENT

There's nothing so permanent as a temporary tax.

What many a man dislikes most about married life is its permanence.

PERSEVERANCE

One of the first principles of perseverance is to know when to stop persevering. – *Carolyn Wells*

Big shots are only little shots who keep shooting.
– *Christopher Morley*

When I was young I observed that nine out of every ten things I did were failures, so I did ten times more work. – *Bernard Shaw*

Importunity knocks at the door oftener than his brother Op.

Don't stop trying: remember, it is always the last key that opens the lock.

The difference between perseverance and obstinacy is that one comes from a strong will, and the other from a strong won't.

When the going gets tough, the tough keep going.

Morale is the condition when your hands and feet keep on working while your head says it can't be done.

Opportunity knocks but once; trouble is more persistent.

Never give up: the mighty oak was once a little nut that held its ground.

PERSONALITY

Some persons are likeable in spite of their unswerving integrity.
– *Don Marquis*

Some people will hold anything except their tongues, keep anything except their word, and lose nothing except their patience.
– *C. C. Colton*

We are none of us all of a piece: more than one person dwells within us, often in uneasy companionship with his fellows.
– *Somerset Maugham*

Personality is the name we give to our little collection of queer habits.

A personage is what you are, a personality is what you have.

The man with personality plus is often everything else minus.

Time and tide make everyone a Jekyll or a Hyde.

You never know a man at all if you've met him only when his wife is around.

Some people get credit for having a nice personality when they are merely proud of their teeth.

The test of personality is: if you were someone else, could you stand yourself?

The woman who is overweight often has more person than personality.

PERSUADE

The man who can make others laugh obtains more votes for a bill than the man who forces them to think. — *Malcolm de Chazal*

A man in the wrong may more easily be convinced than one half right. — *Emerson*

One of the best ways to persuade others is with your ears— by listening to them.
— *Dean Rusk*

Nothing pleases a woman so much as to be coaxed to do something she wants to do.

Why is it that you convince a man, but persuade a woman?

Marriage obligates every husband to give his wife as much money as she can wheedle out of him.

Convince a woman against her will, and she will have no opinion still.

She's so persuasive that she once persuaded a very persuasive fellow out of being so persuasive.

PESSIMISM

My pessimism extends to the point of even suspecting the sincerity of other pessimists.
— *Jean Rostand*

A pessimist is seldom as tired of the world as the world is of him.

The pessimist is the only man who doesn't expect to be better off next year.

A pessimist is a man who doesn't choose the lesser of two evils, but both.

Even when a pessimist gets the best of it, he makes the worst of it.

There's no one with so gloomy an outlook as the pessimist who dreads the evil day when things get better.

A pessimist avoids looking at the bright side of things out of fear of getting eyestrain.

Some pessimists worry that things will never get back to normal; others, that things are already there.

A pessimist nowadays is a man who really knows what's going on.

Pessimists are all alike: they are always good for bad news.

A pessimist hesitates to pick up a four-leaf clover out of fear that it might turn out to be poison ivy.

With all the misfortune in the world today, if the pessimists aren't happy now, they never will be.

This is the best of all possible worlds—for the pessimists.

The pessimist wouldn't be happy even if he knew he was going to be buried in a solid gold coffin.

The pessimist can't enjoy his health today because he may be sick tomorrow.

The pessimist always expects misfortune, yet wants to continue living to enjoy more of it.

A pessimist is a man who looks both ways before crossing a one-way street.

A pessimist enjoys having something to worry about because, if he didn't have anything to worry about, he'd be even more worried.

The pessimist believes things are as bad as they can be, yet always expects them to get worse.

There is nothing like happiness for making a pessimist unhappy.

You can always tell a pessimist: he is constantly changing one form of worry for another.

Why should a pessimist worry about the world when the world doesn't worry about him?

The pessimist always does better today than he expects to do tomorrow.

A pessimist is one who, regardless of the present, is disappointed in the future.

A pessimist may have his faults but his ideas about fishing are generally accurate.

A pessimist is a gloomy person who passes all his days in constant expectation of the unexpected.

All you have to do to be a pessimist is to look at things as they are.

A pessimist always thinks the world is against him—and he is probably right.

A pessimist not only expects the worst, but makes the worst of it when it happens.

PEST

The greatest nuisance to mankind is man.   —*Samuel Butler*

Of all the unbearable nuisances, the ignoramus that has traveled is the worst.
—*Kin Hubbard*

I'm 42 around the chest, 42 around the waist, 96 around the golf course, and a nuisance around the house.
—*Groucho Marx*

A pest is a person who is as hard to like as a disappointment.

A nuisance is objectionable not because he is imperfect but because he is impossible.

A pest never goes where he is told until he dies.

There's no greater nuisance to busy people than the man who doesn't know how to waste time alone.

A friend in need is a damned nuisance.

PETS

To some people the best pet is not the dog that adores you, but the cat that ignores you.

It's nice for children to have pets—until the pets start having children.

A man likes to have a dog to worship him, a woman likes to have a dog to worship.

There's no excuse for the woman who kisses her dog—even a dog has some rights.

PETTING

Whoever named it necking was a poor judge of anatomy.
— *Groucho Marx*

Marriage has put an end to more necking and petting than parents ever have.

Petting brings two young people so close together that they can't see anything wrong with each other.

A fool and his money are soon petted.

Who remembers the old days when couples talked a while before they started necking?

The man who likes to pet always has his hands full.

A little petting now and then is why we have the married men.

When a girl holds a man's hands in the dark, it's either love —or necessary.

There's nothing new under the sun, and it's the same old goings on under the moon too.

Men who pet and tell are not half as bad as those who pet and exaggerate.

Petting is a form of passion which shows how a man feels about a woman.

In the battle of the sexes neither side can ever win because they always end up neck and neck.

The most amusing girl to spend an evening with is the one who has a lot of pet theories.

The man who is hungry for love eats with his hands.

Some women don't mind leading a dog's life as long as they get petted once in a while.

Petting may never be fatal, but it has put an end to many a bachelor.

Nowadays the girl who doesn't go in for petting probably goes out for it.

The art of petting is making advances.

Petting is the art of doing the wrong thing at the right time.

You'll find many dangerous curves and many stop signals, but if you follow the signs, you'll be surprised at how far you can get —with her.

Petting is a sport that lasts until one of the parties gives in, gives out or gives up.

The girl who loses her heart to a man loves to have him search for it.

PHILANDERER

A philanderer is one who considers every blonde a golden opportunity.

A philanderer likes to have his hands on a girl, but not a girl on his hands.

He who loves and runs away may live to love another day.

When a philanderer becomes a sexagenarian, he is probably in his second wolfhood.

A philanderer has two problems: one is to get the woman, and the other is to get rid of her.

Philanderer's motto: If at first you don't succeed, try another girl.

A philanderer is a man who often comes to work from a different direction.

The man who is interested in robbing the cradle is probably not interested in filling it.

A philanderer is always making love without love.

With a philanderer, love at first sight is about as long as it lasts.

A philanderer is like a dry cleaner: he works fast and leaves no ring.

Many a philanderer keeps on chasing women long after he's forgotten why.

It's hard for an old rake to turn over a new leaf.

A philanderer not only makes a study of women but takes up postgraduate work.

All philanderers are alike: they treat women as sequels.

A wolf is a two-legged creature who imitates his four-legged namesake—though he loses his teeth, he never loses his inclinations.

A philanderer is a man who picks up your chick instead of your check.

When a rake gives up sex, it's because sex has already given him up.

A philanderer is a man who is bad at being good, and good at being bad.

PHILANTHROPY

Take egotism out, and you would castrate the benefactors.

— *Emerson*

Philanthropy is the refuge of rich people who wish to annoy their fellow creatures.
— *Oscar Wilde*

Philanthropy proves that though money is the root of all evil, it is also the route of much good.

Money talks, but it rarely gives itself away.

A philanthropist is a generous man whose relatives hate him.

Philanthropy is based on the principle that it's better to give than to receive—as long as it's tax deductible.

Charitable organizations also cover a multitude of sins.

Philanthropy eases the conscience of the rich more often than it eases the condition of the poor.

A philanthropist is a rich man who is well informed on income tax deductions.

In philanthropy, benefactions speak louder than words.

A philanthropist is always ready to help suffering humanity, except those unfortunates he happens to know.

PHILOSOPHER

Philosophers before Kant had a tremendous advantage over philosophers after Kant in that they didn't have to spend years studying Kant. — *Bertrand Russell*

Any two philosophers can tell each other all they know in two hours. — *Justice O. W. Holmes*

Any man can be a philosopher if he only thinks enough about his own foolishness. — *Ed Howe*

A philosopher is a fool who torments himself while he is alive in order to be famous after he is dead. — *Jean D'Alembert*

There is only one thing a philosopher can be relied on to do, and that is to contradict other philosophers. — *William James*

In the schools of antiquity philosophers aspired to impart wisdom; in modern colleges our humbler aim is to teach subjects. — *A. N. Whitehead*

If you wish to understand a philosopher, do not ask what he says, but find out what he wants. — *Nietzsche*

Most philosophers are poor, so most of them give the poor the best of it. — *Ed Howe*

There was never yet a philosopher that could endure the toothache patiently. — *Shakespeare*

Philosophers want to know what the world is all about, but the world doesn't want to know what philosophers are all about.

Not all philosophers are married men, but all married men become philosophers.

The trouble with a philosopher is that he is always less interested in the means of life than in its meaning.

A philosopher is a thinker who thinks there is nothing so important as thinking.

Philosophers are so highly educated that they can take the simplest thing and quickly turn it into something unintelligible.

Only one philosopher in history had a perfect alibi for doing nothing, and his name was I. Kant.

Life may teach a philosopher to think, but thinking never teaches him to live.

A philosopher can always see both sides of a question, but no answer.

A philosopher is a man whose words you understand, but not the substance.

Formerly we really had philosophers; nowadays we merely have professors of philosophy.

The trouble with philosophers is not that they raise fundamental questions, but that they try to answer them.

When a philosopher makes a mistake, no one knows the difference.

PHILOSOPHY

Whenever I have nothing particular to say, I find myself plunging into cosmic philosophy.
— *Don Marquis*

Some would reject every philosophy, but that rejection is itself a philosophy.
— *Herbert Samuel*

It's easy to build a philosophy —it doesn't have to run.
— *Charles F. Kettering*

Philosophy consists very largely of one philosopher arguing that all others are jackasses.
— *Mencken*

Hegel set out his philosophy with so much obscurity that people thought it must be profound.
— *Bertrand Russell*

Women do none of the philosophizing, and have all the philosophy.
— *Don Herold*

Philosophy: a route of many roads leading from nowhere to nothing.
— *Bierce*

Metaphysics is almost always an attempt to prove the incredible by an appeal to the unintelligible.
— *Mencken*

Philosophy is an unusually ingenious attempt to think fallaciously.
— *Bertrand Russell*

What we call philosophy today is a complicated method of avoiding all the important problems of life.
— *Kenneth Rexroth*

Philosophy teaches us to bear with equanimity the misfortunes of others.
— *Oscar Wilde*

I would rather be wrong with Plato than right with the followers of Pythagoras.
— *Cicero*

The business of philosophy is to show that we are not fools for doing what we do.
— *Justice O. W. Holmes*

The thing called philosophy has existed a long time, and is excellent, except that it won't work.
— *Ed Howe*

It is more important that a philosophy be truly reasonable than that it be reasonably true.

Philosophy is usually about all a philosopher has.

The chief use of philosophy is that it enables us to put up with the uselessness of philosophy.

If there is any philosophy in a man, marriage will bring it out.

PHOTOGRAPHY

The trouble with photographing beautiful women is that you never get into the dark room until after they've gone.   — *Yussef Karsh*

I've posed nude for a photographer in the manner of Rodin's *Thinker,* but I merely looked constipated.   — *Bernard Shaw*

Folks that become prominent and don't take a good photograph are certainly up against it.
        — *Kin Hubbard*

Another nice thing about children is that they never carry snapshots of their parents in their pockets.

One way to see yourself as others see you is to get a passport photograph.

There's only one person quicker on the draw than a cowboy in a Western, and that's a woman with her grandchildren's photographs in her handbag.

A wedding picture is expressly taken to give the grandchildren of the bride and groom something to laugh at.

No man is a hero to a passport photographer.

It's not only the pessimist who takes the worst view of everything—there's also the poor photographer.

When a girl complains that her photographs don't do her justice, it's probably because they look like her.

If you look like your passport photograph, you need the trip.

Mathew Brady covered the entire Civil War with fewer photographs than are taken at the average church wedding nowadays.

The secret of posing for photographs is to know how to let go of your face.

The man who coined the phrase *pretty as a picture* had evidently never seen a passport photograph.

When a woman complains that her photographs don't do her justice, what she wants is not justice, but mercy.

If people looked like their passport photos, no one would be well enough to travel abroad.

PIANO

Most pianos are harmless things if people would only let them alone.

The reason children dislike learning to play the piano is that it's all work and no play.

The worst thing about a piano is that you can also sing while you play it.

An upright piano is often a downright nuisance.

Don't sell people short; you can always find someone ready to carry the stool when there's a piano to be moved.

The child who is forced to study piano may still grow up to love good music.

PICASSO

The world today doesn't make sense, so why should I paint pictures that do?   *— Picasso*

I don't own any of my own paintings because a Picasso original costs several thousand dollars —it's a luxury I can't afford.
                    — Picasso

If my husband ever met a woman on the street who looked like the women in his paintings, he would faint.
          — Mrs. Pablo Picasso

A picture is worth a thousand words, especially if the picture is by Picasso.

There are three kinds of people in the world: those who like Picasso, those who dislike Picasso, and those who never heard of Picasso.

PICKPOCKET

Pickpockets prefer to follow a trade where the take-home pay is never reduced by withholding taxes.

A pickpocket is a person who has the world at his fingertips.

PICNIC

A boy's good time at a picnic begins with getting lost from his mother.   *— Ed Howe*

A Sunday picnic with the kids is usually no picnic.

The ideal place for a picnic is somewhere else.

The person who really enjoys a picnic is the one who can't go at the last minute.

Nothing improves the weather like calling off a picnic.

The best part of a picnic is its postponement.

The best place for a picnic is always just a little further on.

The only thing some people save for a rainy day is a picnic.

At picnics people have their outings while ants have their innings.

When eating sandwiches on a picnic, remember that the seeds in raspberry jam never wiggle.

PICTURE

Pictures must not be too picturesque.   *— Emerson*

The first picture was the outline of a man's shadow cast by the sun upon a wall. — *Da Vinci*

A picture used to be worth a thousand words—then came television.

Movie stars are always appearing in pictures—sometimes in films, sometimes in wedding photos.

Watch out for the girl who's pretty as a picture—you may be the man she's out to frame.

Pictures are often hung on walls to decorate homes, but more often to cover up holes and soiled spots.

PIE

The better a pie tastes, the worse it is for you. — *Ed Howe*

The proof of the pie is in the amount of the crust that is eaten.

Pie isn't really fattening, at least not the way it's cut at some restaurants.

What kind of homes do the homemade pies you buy in restaurants come from?

When you don't know what kind of pie it is, it's mince.

An apple pie without some cheese is like a kiss without the squeeze.

Mathematics is more reliable than economics: while pi remains the same, pie keeps going up all the time.

PIG

The only sure way to make money with a pen is to raise hogs.

The reason a young pig eats so much is that he wants to be a hog.

The stockyard is the only place where you can see more hams than on television.

Don't be a hog: the only time a hog helps the community is when he dies.

PILGRIM

That stern and rockbound coast felt like an amateur when it saw how grim were the Pilgrims who landed on it. — *Don Marquis*

I'm glad my ancestors arrived on the Mayflower, but I'm gladder still that there are nine generations between us.
— *William Lyon Phelps*

Most of us know when and where the Pilgrims landed, but few of us know why.

It would have been much better if Plymouth Rock had landed on the Pilgrims.

PILL

I drink brandy every morning, and take pills every night.
— *Swift*

The bitterest pill is the one you take when you have to swallow your own medicine.

The fellow who invented pills was a very talented fellow, but the man who first sugar-coated them was a genius.

PIN

We have a head on us for the same reason that a pin has: to keep us from going too far.

No man knows how a woman can hold dozens of pins in her mouth, no matter how much he practices on shad.

A woman's life cycle: safety pins, fraternity pins, hair pins, diamond pins, safety pins.

Many a coed gets a fraternity pin even before she gets a sorority pin.

Goodness isn't everything: no man has as many points as a pin cushion.

Two heads are better than one, but not if they're on the same pin.

PIONEER

The pioneer who fought for his liberties now has descendants who take them.

American pioneers in their covered wagons endured many hardships while traveling westward into the setting sun, the worst being their lack of sunglasses.

A pioneer is a man whose annual property tax now exceeds what he originally paid for the place.

If they had to figure out all those clover-leaf intersections, our pioneer forefathers would never have reached the West.

PITY

Pity the meek, for they shall inherit the earth. — Don Marquis

Self-pity is a terrible thing, but who is going to pity you if you don't do it yourself?

Pity is akin to love, but a mighty poor relation.

One always feels sorry for the man who has to live with the woman who always feels sorry for herself.

The person who is always pitying himself seldom has much else to do.

PLACE

Have a place for everything and keep the thing somewhere else; this is not a piece of advice, it is merely a custom. — Mark Twain

I'd rather have them say "There he goes" than "Here he lies." — Don Marquis

Nobody likes to be put in his place, and nobody likes to be out of place.

All things come to him who waits, but not if he waits in the wrong place.

Woman's place nowadays seems to be either in the supermarket or the beauty parlor.

A wife works on the theory that you can find whatever you want when you don't want it by looking where it wouldn't be if you did want it.

An usherette is a girl who gets paid to put a man in his place.

A lovely young thing in your fond embrace is better than two in some other place.

Both preachers and realtors tell you the best place to be is elsewhere, but they don't agree on the place.

There's a place for everything, but the trouble is most of us can't find the place.

Instead of putting others in their place, try putting yourself in their place.

The trouble with being able to read a woman like a book is that you're liable to forget your place.

Be it ever so humble, there's no place like somewhere else.

PLAGIARISM

Immature artists imitate; mature artists steal.   — *Lionel Trilling*

About the most originality that any writer can hope to achieve honestly is to steal with good judgment.   — *Josh Billings*

All work and no plagiarism makes a dull speech.

Plagiarism is taking the ideas or writings of another and making them worse.

Modern music is usually played so fast that it's hard to tell what classical composer it was stolen from.

If plagiarism is a sin, then many a sermon is sinful.

PLAN

The man who leaves nothing to chance will do few things badly, but he will do very few things.
— *Halifax*

We, the tail of the universe, don't know what its head is planning.   — *G. C. Lichtenberg*

What is holding America back is not planned obsolescence but unplanned parenthood.

Either plan less or do more.

The man who is always busy planning things for tomorrow is usually too busy to do anything today.

Life is what happens to us while we are making other plans.

You don't have to plan to fail; all you have to do is fail to plan.

PLATITUDE

In the beginning was the word, in the end the platitude.
— *Stanlislaw J. Lec*

Platitude: an idea (a) that is admitted to be true by everyone, and (b) that is not true.
— *Mencken*

It is one of the functions of literature to turn truisms into truths. — *Chesterton*

In modern life nothing produces such an effect as a good platitude—it makes the whole world kin. — *Oscar Wilde*

Platitude: all that is mortal of a departed truth. — *Bierce*

A platitude is a verbal garment used by people to cover their intellectual nakedness.

Some politicians seek public office without fanfare, but most adopt a fighting platitude.

Platitudes are epigrams without a sense of humor.

The man who remarks that it goes without saying, goes right ahead and says it anyway.

Beware the public speaker who spreads lassitude through his aptitude for platitude.

There will always be international crises, and there will always be statesmen who will solve them by platitudes.

PLATONIC LOVE

Platonic love is love from the neck up. — *Thyra Samter Winslow*

Of course Platonic love is possible, but only between husband and wife.

In Platonic love, a lovely friend never turns into a friendly lover.

PLAY

We don't stop playing because we grow old, we grow old because we stop playing. — *Herbert Spencer*

A clever mother gets her children ready and out to play at the neighbors before the neighbor's children can reach her home.

A man is as young as he feels after playing with children.

Parents can never understand why children always want to play with bad children instead of with good ones.

When a girl becomes playful, watch out: she probably means business.

If your mother let you play with everything in the house, you had a good time, but you have no heirlooms.

The man who loses all the time may be a good sport, but he's a bad player.

PLAYBOY

A playboy is sometimes a clever man, but more often a dame fool.

The life of a playboy is one continuous round of wine, women, and s'long.

A playboy is a man whose fortune always depends on his choice of a father.

A playboy finds business no pleasure because pleasure is his business.

A playboy usually combines the talent for spending money with the talent for not making it.

A playboy is a man whose energies are mostly miss-directed.

A playboy usually owes all he is to his mother, and all he has to his father.

A playboy always likes the girl he goes out with to be just as she is: single if she's single, and married if she's married.

A playboy spends his money like water, but not on water.

Sooner or later every playboy reaches the age when he chases girls only if it's downhill.

The playboy who doesn't really know what he wants in life is usually willing to pay any price for it.

A playboy spends his time lengthening his nights and shortening his days.

A playboy squanders a large amount of money that his father has, or a large amount of his father's money that he has.

A playboy usually spends part of his money on liquor, part of it on women, and the rest foolishly.

PLAYWRIGHT

Every playwright should try acting, just as every judge should spend some weeks in jail to find out what he is handing out to others.   — *E. M. Remarque*

At dramatic rehearsals, the only author that's better than an absent one is a dead one.
— *George S. Kaufman*

The secret of playwriting can be given in two maxims: stick to the point, and whenever you can, cut.   — *Somerset Maugham*

Often as he sneered at Plato, Aristotle never called him a playwright.   — *Max Beerbohm*

Writing a play is a bit more difficult than writing recipes telling how to write plays.
— *Don Marquis*

The playwright of today likes to believe that he is throwing light upon his time, when his time is actually throwing light upon him.   — *James Thurber*

Many a young man who wants to become a playwright badly realizes his ambition: he becomes a bad playwright.

Fools write plays that angels love to back.

A playwright is a man who stands in the back of the theater on opening night and wishes he were dead.

PLEASANT

Be nice to people until you make a million; after that, people will be nice to you.

The reason fat people are generally good-natured is that it takes them so long to get mad clear through.

Be pretty if you can, be witty if you must, but be agreeable if it kills you.

It pays to be nice to people you meet on the way up for they are the same people you meet on the way down.

It would be a great world if we were always as pleasant as we sometimes are.

When some people look pleasant, the effort they are making shows right through.

If you want to say something pleasant to someone, write it; if you want to write something unpleasant to someone, say it.

PLEASE

Those who live to please, must please to live.
— *John Churton Collins*

If you wish people to think well of you, don't speak well of yourself.   — *Pascal*

If you want to please women, tell them what you wouldn't want other men to tell your wife.
— *Jules Renard*

He that can please nobody is not so much to be pitied as he that nobody can please.
— *C. C. Colton*

The person who is willing to do anything to please everybody is a universally and deservedly despised person.   — *Bernard Shaw*

You may say what you please, but it is better to say what pleases other people.

If women were as hard to please before marriage as after, most men would still be bachelors.

The woman who doesn't know if her husband is hard to please has probably never tried.

A man likes you for what he thinks you are; a woman for what you think she is.

If you let your children do anything they please, eventually you won't be pleased by anything they do.

The women who dress to please men seldom dress to please the men who foot the bills.

There are two kinds of women: the few who can get any man they like, and the many who like any man they can get.

The person who always does as he pleases seldom pleases.

The woman who claims she can marry anybody she pleases evidently doesn't please anybody.

PLEASURE

No man is a hypocrite in his pleasures.   — *Samuel Johnson*

I do not believe in doing for pleasure things that I do not like to do.   — *Don Herold*

Women who surrender without knowing how to resist are nothing but pleasure machines.
— *Choderlos de Laclos*

That man is richest whose pleasures are the cheapest.
— *Thoreau*

When pleasure is the business of life, it ceases to be pleasure.
— *Thomas C. Haliburton*

Anticipating pleasure is also a pleasure.   — *Schiller*

A pleasure is none the less a pleasure because it does not please forever.   — *Somerset Maugham*

It is not pleasure that makes life worth living; it is life that makes pleasure worth having.
— *Bernard Shaw*

Only three things in my life I've really liked to do: shooting, writing and making love.
— *Hemingway*

Pleasure should be a mixed dish: one part taking, and two parts giving.

Women get more pleasure out of life than men because women get pleasure also out of feeling miserable.

It's always a great pleasure to be missed by someone—if you're there to enjoy it.

Some people don't leave the primrose path until they have lilies in their hands.

A playboy devotes himself to pleasure regardless of expense; a spendthrift devotes himself to expense regardless of pleasure.

One of the chief pleasures of middle age is looking back at the people you didn't marry.

The greatest of all pleasure is the pleasure of giving pleasure.

The primrose path is kept in good condition because there are always plenty of travelers to pay its upkeep.

Some people go to a lot of trouble getting pleasure, while others get a lot of pleasure making trouble.

A killjoy is a person who gets his pleasure by keeping others from getting theirs.

PLOT

Many an author gets a plot for a new novel from the screen version of his last one.

Reading the book before seeing the movie always makes it more difficult to guess the plot.

The friendship of two women is always a plot against a third.

POCKET

Feel for others—in your pocket.
— *Charles H. Spurgeon*

Some women don't care what kind of clothes a man wears as long as his pockets are well-lined.

Another suit that wears out sooner at the pockets than anywhere else is a lawsuit.

Many a man loses a lot of money through the hole in the top of his pocket.

Many a man's empty pockets are due to his wife's fondness for change.

Some women pick their husbands' clothes, others just pick their pockets.

Some men start in life without a cent in their pockets, others start in life without pockets.

You can't take it with you—a shroud has no pockets.

POET

Poets die in different ways: most of them do not die into the grave, but into business or criticism.　　— *Robert Frost*

The poet occupies a position halfway between that of a saint and Balaam's ass.

— *Coventry Patmore*

Petrarch was a sing-song love poet who deserved his Laura better than his laurels.　— *Chesterfield*

It is the business of reviewers to watch poets, not of poets to watch reviewers.　　　— *Hazlitt*

Poets are terribly sensitive people, and one of the things they are most sensitive about is cash.

— *Robert Penn Warren*

Modern poets write against business, but all of us write for money.　　　— *Robert Frost*

Every English poet should master the rules of grammar before he attempts to bend or break them.　　　— *Robert Graves*

Poets are prophets whose prophesying never comes true.

— *Ed Howe*

A poet should be treated with leniency and, even when damned, should be damned with respect.

— *Edgar Allan Poe*

A poet is a man who puts up a ladder to a star and climbs it while playing a violin. — *Goncourt*

A poet is a person who thinks there is something special about a poet and about his loving one unattainable woman. — *Robert Frost*

I'd rather be a great bad poet than a bad good poet.

— *Ogden Nash*

Perhaps the saddest lot that can befall mortal man is to be the husband of a lady poet.

— *George Jean Nathan*

My quarrel with poets is not that they are unclear, but that they are too diligent.

— *E. B. White*

The bad poet is usually unconscious where he ought to be conscious, and conscious where he ought to be unconscious.

— *T. S. Eliot*

Both T. S. Eliot and I like to play, but I like to play euchre, while he likes to play Eucharist.

— *Robert Frost*

A poet more than thirty years old is simply an overgrown child.

— *Mencken*

It seems that God took away the minds of poets that they might better express His.

— *Socrates*

Poets are almost always bald when they get to be about forty.

— *John Masefield*

Pope's more ambitious works may be defined as careless thinking carefully versified.
— *James Russell Lowell*

An unromantic poet is a self-contradiction, like the democratic aristocrat that reads the *Atlantic Monthly*.   — *Robert Frost*

Today's poet has less trouble making himself heard than making himself plain.
— *Louis Untermeyer*

A poet is a man who cannot afford to say it with flowers, but says it instead with flowery language.

Nobody ever knows a poet is alive until he is dead.

A professional poet nowadays is always poor, though he is not always a poor poet.

Poets are born, not made; that's why there are so many of them.

A poet is a man to whom a statue is erected after he has died in poverty and neglect.

Many a modern poet doesn't understand what he has written, but expects the reader to.

Poets are born, not paid.

POETRY

There's no money in poetry, but then there's no poetry in money either.   — *Robert Graves*

All bad poetry springs from genuine feeling.   — *Oscar Wilde*

Poetry is like fish: if it's fresh, it's good; if it's stale, it's bad; and if you're not certain, try it on the cat.   — *Osbert Sitwell*

The writers of free verse got their idea from incorrect proof pages.   — *Robert Frost*

The real difficulty about writing poetry is filling up the other twenty-three hours of the day.
— *Virgil Thomson*

I don't like to boast, but I have probably skipped more poetry than any other person of my age and weight in this country.
— *Will Cuppy*

Poetry is what Milton saw when he went blind.   — *Don Marquis*

If left to its own tendencies, I believe poetry would exclude everything but love and the moon.
— *Robert Frost*

Ignorance is one of the sources of poetry.   — *Wallace Stevens*

How these authors magnify their office—one dishonest plumber does more harm than a hundred poetasters!   — *Augustine Birrell*

Their poems resemble a glass of tepid lemonade in which a couple of teaspoonfuls of Matthew Arnold have been dissolved.
— *Edith Sitwell*

Poetry provides the one permissible way of saying one thing and meaning another. — *Robert Frost*

Poetry is the opening and closing of a door, leaving those who

look through to guess about what was seen during a moment.
— *Carl Sandburg*

His poetry possesses all possible virtues and only one fault: it is dead. — *Heine*

Once in a while I meet someone who has read me; it did him good—I mean it served him right.
— *Robert Frost*

The business of the poet is not to hold a cracked mirror up to nature. — *Oliver St. John Gogarty*

The ear is the only true writer and the only true reader of poetry. — *Robert Frost*

No *vers* is *libre* for the man who wants to do a good job.
— *T. S. Eliot*

There are three kinds of limericks: limericks when ladies are present, limericks when ladies are absent but clergymen are present, and limericks. — *Don Marquis*

If it were not for poetry, few men would ever fall in love.
— *La Rochefoucauld*

Both the old idea of rhymed verse turned out to measure, and the new idea of free verse turned out to grass, are equally erroneous. — *Stephen Leacock*

When I feel physically as if the top of my head were taken off —that is poetry.
— *Emily Dickinson*

Poetry is a search for syllables to shoot at the barriers of the unknowable.
— *Carl Sandburg*

Poetry has never brought me in enough to buy shoestrings.
— *Wordsworth*

There are two ways of disliking poetry: one way is to dislike it, the other is to read Pope.
— *Oscar Wilde*

The only really difficult thing about a poem is the critic's explanation of it.
— *Frank Moore Colby*

A true sonnet goes eight lines and then takes a turn for better or worse, and goes six or eight lines more. — *Robert Frost*

Poetry is the achievement of the synthesis of hyacinths and biscuits. — *Carl Sandburg*

In a poem the words should be as pleasing to the ear as the meaning is to the mind.
— *Marianne Moore*

All that is worth remembering of life is the poetry of it. — *Hazlitt*

Tell them I Am, Jehovah said; and I have taken that as a command to iamb and not write free verse. — *Robert Frost*

I like to think of poetry as statements made on the way to the grave. — *Dylan Thomas*

What stimulates me to write a poem is that I have got something inside me that I want to get rid of—it is almost a kind of defecation. — *T. S. Eliot*

A beautiful line of verse has twelve feet, and two wings.
— *Jules Renard*

Poetry is a way of taking life by the throat.   — *Robert Frost*

With the so-called modern poets, a dislocated world demands a dislocated poem to describe it.
— *Oliver St. John Gogarty*

Poetry is the impish attempt to paint the color of the wind.
— *Maxwell Bodenheim*

Poetry is better understood in the verse of the artist than in the prose of the critic.
— *Matthew Arnold*

How about a movement to steer all the free versifiers to a country as free in name as Liberia?
— *Robert Frost*

You will not find poetry anywhere unless you bring some of it with you.   — *Joubert*

Poetry is boned with ideas, nerved and blooded with emotions, all held together by the delicate, tough skin of words.
— *Paul Engle*

Poets untie writing and then tie it up again differently.
— *Jean Cocteau*

Like a piece of ice on a hot stove, a poem must ride on its own melting.   — *Robert Frost*

Think you if Laura has been Petrarch's wife, he would have written sonnets all his life?
— *Lord Byron*

The chief difficulty with modern poetry is not so much the poetry itself as what is written about it.
— *Louis Untermeyer*

If poetry comes not as naturally as the leaves to a tree, it had better not come at all.
— *John Keats*

There ain't nothing so easy to write as poetry—if you know how.   — *Josh Billings*

Poetry is a series of explanations of life, fading into horizons two swift for explanations.
— *Carl Sandburg*

When a man ceases to write poetry, he has probably married the girl.

There's more truth than poetry in some poetry.

The evil that men do lives after them, the good is oft interred in their poems.

Poetry is a gift; maybe that's why you can't sell it.

The Constitution protects free speech, but only the American sense of humor protects free verse.

If you can understand it, it's verse; if you can't understand it, it's poetry.

Poetry is a language that tells us something which cannot be said.

A poem is a composition in verse whose writer can't make dollars out of it, and whose reader can't make sense out of it.

Even when some poets put all their brains into poetry, it comes out as blank verse.

POINT OF VIEW

We have but to change the point of view and the greatest action looks mean.   — *Thackeray*

A beautiful girl can get almost anything—except your point of view.

The other man's word is an opinion, yours is truth, and your wife's is law.

A slap in the face is the shortest distance between two points of view.

There are two sides to every question, and every marriage proves it.

The trouble with an all-around person is that he has no particular point of view.

There are two sides to every question—as long as it doesn't concern us personally.

A youngster thinks children are always right, teachers sometimes, and parents never.

Your point of view is everything: the pond is an ocean to a tadpole.

There are three sides to every argument: your side, the other person's side, and to hell with it.

Many a man has so narrow a point of view that it slips right through the facts.

The older you get, the more lawless the younger generation becomes.

There are two sides to every question, unless your wife holds one of them.

POISE

One woman's poise is another woman's poison.

Poise is the ability to be ill at ease inconspicuously.

Poise is the presence of mind to continue talking while the other person picks up the check.

POISON

When you consider what a chance women have to poison their husbands, it's a wonder there isn't more of it done.
      — *Kin Hubbard*

There's one thing in favor of drinking poison: it never becomes a habit.

If you are overweight, potatoes and pies are a kind of poison—avoirdupoison.

One man's mate is another man's poison.

POKER

People would be surprised to know how much I learned about prayer from playing poker.
      — *Mary Austin*

It is my firm conviction that there are not and never have been any great women poker players.   — *Heywood Broun*

Poker was played in Biblical times: Noah had a full house, and Solomon held at least four queens.

The man who loses at poker and still keeps on playing will never lack for friends.

Poker makes many a poor player poorer.

In poker, the best way to conceal your hand is with your face.

Poker is a matter of good judgment if you win, but bad luck if you lose.

POLICE

It takes vice to hunt vice— that accounts for policemen.
— *Finley Peter Dunne*

The husband of a policewoman often takes the law into his own hands.

Highway police are state troopers specially trained to examine drivers' licenses.

What the police department doesn't know would fill a jail.

POLITE

During a long and varied career as a bachelor, I have noticed that marriage is the death of politeness between a man and a woman.
— *Arnold Bennett*

Make a woman mad, and she is no more polite than a man.
— *Ed Howe*

One of the greatest victories you can gain over a man is to beat him at politeness. — *Josh Billings*

Politeness is good nature regulated by good sense.
— *Sydney Smith*

Politeness is like an air cushion: there may be nothing in it, but it eases our jolts wonderfully.
— *Samuel Johnson*

Some folks are too polite to be up to any good. — *Kin Hubbard*

A man should be as polite all the time as a candidate is just before election. — *Ed Howe*

Politeness is the art of choosing among your thoughts.
— *Madame de Staël*

Nobody loses anything by being polite but there are a lot of people who are afraid to take the risk.

Girls like a man to be gentle but not necessarily a gentleman.

Courtesy is the art of treating the other fellow as if he were as important as he thinks he is.

The disadvantage of being nearsighted is that a man is in danger of mistaking his wife for another woman and being polite to her.

The less a man knows about you, the politer he is.

At a finishing school a girl spends a few years learning how to behave in polite society, and the rest of her life trying to find it.

About the only thing ever lost by politeness is a seat in a crowded bus.

You can always tell a polite driver: he sounds his horn before he forces you off the road.

Courtesy is contagious—let's start an epidemic.

POLITICAL ECONOMY

The trouble with political economy is that it is often more political than economy.

Political economy are two words that should be divorced on the grounds of incompatibility.

A popular form of political economy is paying the least amount of graft for the greatest number of favors.

POLITICAL PARTY

The more you observe politics, the more you've got to admit that each party is worse than the other.
                        — Will Rogers

I will make a bargain with the Republicans: if they will stop telling lies about Democrats, we will stop telling the truth about them.
                        — Adlai Stevenson

Ignorance makes most men go into a political party, and shame keeps them from getting out of it.
                        — Halifax

I am not a member of any organized party—I am a Democrat.
                        — Will Rogers

I like Republicans, have grown up with them, worked with them, and would trust them with anything in the world, except public office.   — Adlai Stevenson

The best political party is but a kind of conspiracy against the rest of the nation.   — Halifax

Take a Democrat and a Republican, and keep them both out of office, and I bet they turn out to be useful citizens.
                        — Will Rogers

Damn your principles! Stick to your party.   — Disraeli

I never said all Democrats were saloonkeepers; what I said was that all saloonkeepers were Democrats.   — Horace Greeley

At every election the Republicans contend that now is the time for all good Democrats to come to the aid of the Republican party.
                        — Adlai Stevenson

The best political setup is the two-party system—otherwise whom could the outs blame for the state of affairs?

Some politicians are self-made, but most are machine-made.

Americans are an easygoing people who never stay mad long enough to get a third party well organized.

In politics, if you're against it, it's a machine; if you're for it, it's a party.

A political party is another thing selected for us by our parents or our husbands.

The only men whose political opinions differ widely now are those who belong to the same party.

When is the time for all good men to come to the aid of both parties?

What's the use of a third party when the country doesn't know what to do with the two parties it has now?

Men first make a political machine, and then the political machine makes them.

Another reason why we don't believe in a third party is that it was a third party that ruined things in the Garden of Eden.

There's a difference between Democrats and Republicans, but you'd never know it from watching Congress.

POLITICIAN

Since a politician never believes what he says, he is always astonished when others do.
— *De Gaulle*

Politicians are the same the world over: they promise to build a bridge even where there is no river. — *Nikita Khrushchev*

There's nothing as shortsighted as a politician, unless it's a delegation of them. — *Will Rogers*

America is the only country where you can go on the air and kid politicians, and where politicians go on the air and kid the people. — *Groucho Marx*

There are some politicians who, if their constituents were cannibals, would promise them missionaries for dinner. — *Mencken*

A politician is an arse upon which everyone has sat except a man. — *E. E. Cummings*

Half our politicians wouldn't be where they are except for opposing crime, and the other half wouldn't be where they are except for supporting it. — *Bergen Evans*

Most politicians keep principles only as a horse dealer keeps horses. — *W. R. Inge*

He is absolutely unique—he is the only politician I ever met who had learned anything from experience. — *Bernard Shaw*

The smarter the politician, the more things he believes, and the less he believes any of them. — *Mencken*

A politician sometimes knows the right thing, sometimes does the right thing, but most often just says the right thing.

A successful politician is one who knows how to get into the public eye without irritating it.

The cheaper the politician, the more he costs the country.

Many a politician who's been appointed acts as if he's been anointed.

Sometimes it's hard to tell which is thicker, a politician's skin or his skull.

A politician spends half his time making promises, and the other half making excuses.

The worst thing about political jokes is that some of them get elected.

A politician is seldom either a gentleman or a scholar, but often combines the worst of each.

Politician's motto: When in danger or in doubt, run in circles, yell and shout.

Give a politician a free hand, and he'll put it in your pocket.

A politician is the only man who opens his mouth more often than his wife does.

A politician should not write when he can talk, and should not talk when he can nod his head.

When in trouble, bad politicians go to good lawyers.

Half the politicians with money want power, and half the politicians with power want money.

A politician's talent for making promises is surpassed only by his talent for not keeping them.

It's unfortunate that a mere ninety percent of the politicians give the other ten percent a bad name.

A politician listens to the people in order to know, not what to do, but what to say.

The best way to make a politician see the light is to make him feel the heat.

A lot of politicians need platforms because they haven't a leg to stand on.

Most politicians have been trite and found wanting.

Some politicians work for the people, while most politicians work for the people whom the people work for.

Politicians are bought, not made.

There are two sides to every question, and a good politician takes both.

Half the politicians point with pride to the same things the other half view with alarm.

Every politician has his price, especially those who are worthless.

A politician is a man who shakes your hand before election, and your confidence after.

You sometimes meet a politician who is nice to you even if you can't do anything for him.

POLITICIAN AND STATESMAN

A statesman is in politics because he has money, a politician has money because he is in politics.

A statesman is a politician with whom you agree, a politician is a statesman with whom you disagree.

A statesman leaves footprints on the sands of time, while a politician leaves pussyfoot prints.

The difference between the statesman and the politician is that one acts on principle while the other acts on self-interest.

It is difficult for a politician to be a statesman, especially if he doesn't belong to our party.

A statesman lives to serve his country well, a politician serves it to live well.

A statesman thinks he belongs to the state, a politician thinks the state belongs to him.

Politicics is the art of promise; statesmanship, the art of compromise.

If he shears the sheep, he's a statesman; if he skins them, a politician.

POLITICS

Politics is the science of how who gets what, when and why.
    — *Sidney Hillman*

The difficulty with businessmen entering politics after they have had a successful business career is that they want to start at the top.   — *Harry S. Truman*

Politics is too serious a matter to be left to the politicians.
    — *De Gaulle*

What is politics but persuading the public to vote for this, and support that, and endure these, for the promise of those?
    — *Gilbert Highet*

Politics makes estranged bedfellows.   — *Goodman Ace*

The paramount issue for our side is the one the other side doesn't like to have mentioned.
    — *Finley Peter Dunne*

Politics is a place where all are good who are not criminal, and all are wise who are not otherwise. — *Frank Moore Colby*

I have never found in a long experience in politics that criticism is ever inhibited by ignorance.   — *Harold Macmillan*

The world of politics is always twenty years behind the world of thought.   — *John Jay Chapman*

Politics is the diversion of trivial men who, when they succeed at it, become important in the eyes of more trivial men.
    — *George Jean Nathan*

Politics is the conduct of public affairs for private advantage.
    — *Bierce*

The whole art of politics consists in directing rationally the irrationalities of men.
    — *Reinhold Niebuhr*

Next to handshakings, nothing has been as overworked and successful as promising to reduce taxes.   — *Kin Hubbard*

To err is human, to blame it on the other party is politics.

Politics makes strange bedfellows—rich.

The more a man says he will do for politics, the more he expects politics to do for him.

Politics is made up of three parts: complaints, compliments and compromise.

Don't avoid politics because there are so many hypocrites—there's always room for one more.

Politics makes strange bad fellows.

Even grammarians have discovered that politics is singular.

In politics, some men have their price, while others give themselves away.

Most wives have no opinion about politics, but are very definite about it.

In politics it is more important to know everyone than to know everything.

Politics makes strange postmasters.

Some countries have a two-party system: while one party is in power, the other party is in jail.

The man who wants to clean up politics would make a good start by getting out of politics.

The man who goes into politics as a business has no business to go into politics.

In politics, truce is stranger than friction.

Mud and whitewash are the strange bedfellows of politics.

Politics is a profession where great skill is required, especially in making excuses.

There's a bright side to everything, and in politics it's the inside.

Politics is a strange game: you don't have to have a leg to stand on to run for office.

Keeping politics out of most things is a good idea, especially if we could keep politics out of politics.

In politics a man usually learns to rise below his principles.

Politics is played by people who want to clean up, but not to clean up politics.

Politics makes strange bedfellows, but they are always willing to lie on their own side.

In politicial matters much may be said on both sides—and always is.

POLL

By getting you to tell what you think, a pollster gets to tell you what others think.

A pollster resorts to the unverifiable to deduce the unwarrantable about the unpredictable.

The woman who can take *no* for an answer is probably conducting a survey.

Polls are usually unreliable because the real public opinion is only expressed in private.

A pollster first tells you how an election will turn out, and then tells you why it didn't.

POLYGAMY

Man is a natural polygamist: he always has one woman leading him by the nose, and another hanging on to his coattails.
— *Mencken*

Brigham Young originated mass production, but Henry Ford was the one who improved on it.
— *Will Rogers*

There is one advantage in a plurality of wives: they fight each other instead of their husbands.
— *Josh Billings*

Another type of married man who doesn't believe in divorce is the polygamist.

The reason polygamy would never work in this country is that the divorce courts couldn't stand the strain.

POPULAR

The louder a fellow laughs at nothing, the more popular he is.
— *Kin Hubbard*

Popularity is exhausting: the life of the party always winds up in a corner with an overcoat over him.
— *Wilson Mizner*

Popularity: the capacity for listening sympathetically when men boast of their wives, and women complain of their husbands.
— *Mencken*

The fellow that's mean around the home is always the life and sunshine of some lodge.
— *Kin Hubbard*

To his dog, every man is Napoleon; hence the constant popularity of dogs. — *Aldous Huxley*

If you want to be popular, don't think out loud.

Another way to be popular is to listen attentively to a lot of things you already know.

In a man, popularity comes from a wonderful sense of humor; in a woman, from a wonderful sense of rumor.

A fool and his money are soon popular.

Some girls always make a hit with the men, but never a home run.

If you want to be popular, never lie about yourself, and never tell the truth about others.

A better mousetrap is one way to get the world to beat a path to your door; another way is better claptrap.

Popularity consists mainly of allowing yourself to be bored by people most of the time while pretending to enjoy it.

In the order named, these are the most popular girls: the experimental, the sentimental and the ornamental.

POPULATION

We have been God-like in our planned breeding of our domestic plants and animals, but rabbit-like in our unplanned breeding of ourselves. — *Arnold Toynbee*

The world is populated in the main by people who should not exist. — *Bernard Shaw*

If people only made prudent marriages, what a stop to population there would be. — *Thackeray*

The solution of the population explosion lies in teaching people the value of good breeding rather than fast.

Getting married makes one out of two, but it doesn't seem to decrease the population.

There are many reasons for the population explosion, and sex is all of them.

Thanks to our high birth rate, people are being born faster than cars can kill them.

There would be no population explosion if people who are trying to keep the wolf from the door wouldn't let the stork fly in through the window.

The population explosion only goes to prove that to heir is human.

Half the world would like to see the other half get off the earth.

The population explosion is not an unmixed evil: think what it has done for toys, textbooks and television.

The population explosion is reaping a scarcity of food, but an abundance of food for thought.

The inhabitants of the United States come to their census every ten years.

Everyone talks about the population explosion, but no one does anything about it—except the homosexual.

The aim of birth control is to make the population less dense.

Man is never satisfied: millions who are against the population explosion are also against the depopulation of war.

The solution to the population explosion is a necessity, but not a stork necessity.

Many a nation would have more prosperity today if it had less posterity tomorrow.

There's no easy solution to the population explosion, but driving during the holiday weekends helps.

The biggest explosion that has ever been set off by matches is the population explosion.

PORNOGRAPHY

One man's biography is another man's pornography. — *Frank Harris*

Every age gets the pornography it deserves. — *V. S. Pritchett*

What is pornography to one man may be the laughter of genius to another.
— *D. H. Lawrence*

Many a novelist would be unreadable if he didn't resort to words that are unprintable.

A dirty book is seldom a dusty one.

Every generation breeds a novelist who becomes the fair-haired boy of the foul-mouthed set.

PORTRAIT

Are we to paint what's on the face, what's inside the face, or what's behind it?   — *Picasso*

Every time I paint a portrait, I lose a friend.   — *John S. Sargent*

A portrait is a picture in which there is something wrong with the mouth.   — *Eugene Speicher*

A beautiful woman can be painted as a totem only: not as a woman, but as a Madonna, a queen, a sphinx.   — *Saul Steinberg*

When you start with a portrait and try to find pure form by abstracting more and more, you must end up with an egg.
                                    — *Picasso*

Portraiture is the art of making a picture look exactly as you would look if you were handsomer than you are.

There are some men who very early in life begin to look like a family portrait.

A mirror shows people how they look, a portrait shows people how they think they look.

Men are seldom as black as they are painted, nor women as young.

POSITIVE AND NEGATIVE

Positive anything is better than negative nothing.
                        — *Elbert Hubbard*

Women are paradoxical creatures: a girl sometimes gives a positive answer in a decided negative.

A woman wears a sweater to accentuate the positive, and a girdle to eliminate the negative.

POSSESSION

The landscape belongs to the man who looks at it.   — *Emerson*

Fortune, talent, health: he had everything—but he was married.
                    — *Charles Gabriel Gleyre*

What belongs to everybody belongs to nobody.

Things not possessed are always best, but when possessed are like the rest.

No family has yet solved the problem of what to do with possessions that are not good enough to keep, and too good to throw away.

The man who has everything is probably not married to the woman who wants everything.

Some men keep the Sabbath, others keep everything they can lay their hands on.

A credit plan is a financial trick that enables you to possess things before you own them.

POSSIBLE

I am not an optimist, I am a possibilist.   —*Julian Huxley*

The airplane, the atomic bomb and the zipper have cured me of any tendency to state that a thing can't be done.   —*R. L. Duffus*

Youth is the time of life when you are not experienced enough to know that you cannot possibly do some of the things you are now doing.

Everything is possible: never use the word *never*.

POSTERITY

Why should we legislate for posterity—what has posterity ever done for us?   —*Sir Boyle Roche*

The Founding Fathers would not have talked so glowingly of posterity if they had known we were going to be it.

The chief disadvantage of being a descendant is that you pay more taxes.

If parents could read the future, posterity would be a thing of the past.

We used to do things for posterity, but nowadays we do things for ourselves and leave the bill to posterity.

The government may be working for posterity, but the trouble is that it insists on being paid by us.

POSTPONE

To the habitual procrastinator, it's never the right time to do the right thing.

Putting off for tomorrow what you can do today has one advantage: you may be dead tomorrow and then you won't have to do it.

Never put off till tomorrow what you can do today—there may be a law against it tomorrow.

Never put off till tomorrow what you can do today, unless someone else did it yesterday.

You have to put off some tasks a dozen times before they will completely slip your mind.

The job you're putting off till tomorrow probably got the same treatment yesterday.

There's no time like the present for putting off things.

Always put off till tomorrow what you shouldn't do at all.

Another bad habit most people put off giving up is the habit of procrastinating.

Do not put off till tomorrow what you can put off till the day after.

A procrastinator never has small problems because he always waits until they grow up.

Procrastination is the thief of time, and the loot can never be recovered.

POVERTY

I am never in during the afternoon, except when I am confined to the house by an acute attack of penury.   — *Oscar Wilde*

The poor have us always with them.   — *Saki*

I was once so poor I used to buy a pint of milk for breakfast and a loaf of bread for dinner, and eat them for supper.
— *Strickland Gillilan*

The greatest man in history was the poorest.   — *Emerson*

I wasn't born in a log cabin, but my family moved into one as soon as they could afford it.
— *Melville D. Landon*

Poverty is no shame, but being ashamed of it is.   — *Franklin*

I hate the poor, and look forward eagerly to their extermination.   — *Bernard Shaw*

The only advantage of being poor is that it doesn't take much to improve your situation.

Poverty is an allergy that makes a person unusually sensitive to paper money.

Poverty is no crime, but it is more certain in its punishment.

Another advantage of poverty is that your income tax is so small, you never have to borrow money to pay it.

Money talks, but poverty just pinches.

Poverty is an economic condition that prevents you from going anywhere—except into debt.

Poverty is a crime of which the rich are never guilty.

Money doesn't buy happiness, but that's not the reason so many people are poor.

You have no reason to be ashamed of your poverty if you acquired it honestly.

Being poor has its advantages: the car keys, for example, are never in your other pants.

Poverty is no crime: it is much worse.

When poverty comes in at the door, love should go out and hustle for a job.

Poverty is a condition you try to hide while you experience it, but brag about afterwards.

About the only thing today's children will be able to boast they got along without is poverty.

To be poor is no disgrace, provided no one knows it.

Americans who visit the Orient notice a lot of poverty there, and they usually bring home some of it.

A man never realizes the blessings of poverty until he gets over it.

Poverty is no crime, but that's all that can be said in its favor.

POWER

The power of man has grown in every sphere, except over himself.   — *Winston Churchill*

Power does not corrupt man; fools, however, if they get into a position of power, corrupt power.
                — *Bernard Shaw*

Power corrupts, and power politics corrupts absolutely.

They are building the new cars with more and more power, probably because too many pedestrians have been escaping.

Power is a tricky thing: first you use it, then you abuse it, and finally you lose it.

Might doesn't make right, but it never gives up trying.

Before marriage, her power over a man is in her lips; after marriage, it's in her tongue.

A woman is like a car: the body lines are of no value unless there is power under the hood.

A Congressman's staying power usually outlasts his stay in power.

If you want that strange power that some men have over women, have a rich relative leave you a fortune.

Beauty is potent, but money is omnipotent.

Horsepower was a lot safer when only the horses had it.

PRACTICAL

Practical men know where they are, but not always whither they are going; thinkers know whither we are going, but not always where we are.   — *Bernard Shaw*

When a girl can tell the difference between truth and flattery, she is too practical to be in love.

There's nothing less practical than a practical joke.

The man who keeps his feet on the ground never has far to fall.

The matter-of-fact person never dreams, except when he's asleep.

PRACTICAL JOKE

The point of a good joke you see, but the point of a practical joke you feel.

The best practical jokes are always played on someone else.

The trouble with the practical joker is that he allows his sense of humor to take the place of his other senses.

Beware of the practical joker: he shakes your hand one minute, and pulls your leg the next.

A practical joker is a person in good humor whose humor is seldom good.

A practical joker is one who never grows into his second childhood because he never grows out of his first.

To the practical joker every day of the year is April 1st.

A practical joker finds nothing funny in a joke unless it's at someone else's expense.

A practical joker spends half his time trying to get others into trouble, and the other half trying to get himself out of it.

A practical joker has a sense of humor that's made up of little sense and less humor.

When a practical joker puts his best foot forward, it is probably to trip someone.

Beware the practical joker: his idea of a good time is to give others a bad time.

A practical joker is a person in good humor who puts others in bad humor.

PRACTICE

Everbody ought to do at least two things each day that he hates to do, just for practice.
— *William James*

In music, practice makes perfect—nuisances.

If we practiced what we preached, most of us would work ourselves to death.

Every married woman is ready to practice economy if her husband would only give her enough money to practice with.

The world would be even worse than it is if more people preached what they practice.

Theory may raise a man's hopes, but practice raises his income.

All the world's a stage, and most of us need more rehearsals.

It's fortunate that most of us don't practice what we preach, or we'd be bigger fools than we are.

No matter how long a doctor has been treating patients, he is still practicing.

PRAISE

When someone criticizes me, I can defend myself, but against praise I am defenseless. — *Freud*

He who praises everybody, praises nobody. — *Samuel Johnson*

I accept a lot of praise I don't deserve and then make it right with myself by sacrificing a tithe of it to the Lord. — *Robert Frost*

If I were a rich man, I would employ a professional praiser.
— *Osbert Sitwell*

When a woman hears a man praising some other woman, she thinks to herself how easily some men are fooled. — *Ed Howe*

Woe unto me when all men praise me! — *Bernard Shaw*

Get someone else to blow your horn and the sound will carry twice as far. — *Will Rogers*

I don't really mind a little praise—as long as it's fulsome. — *Adlai Stevenson*

Instead of praising God so much, praise your friends a little more.

If a crazy man uttered a word in praise of a woman, she'd swear he had some sense left.

At twenty you blush when a man praises you; at thirty you think him clever; at forty you wonder what he wants.

The best way to knock the chip off your neighbor's shoulder is to pat him on the back.

Man lives by praise: most of us would rather be hurt by flattery than helped by criticism.

Some women are sane and normal, but others always have a good word for everyone.

Say something good about a man while he's up; even a tombstone will say something good about him when he's down.

Why praise the man who keeps both feet on the ground—he isn't getting anywhere.

Try praising your wife even if it does frighten her at first.

Faint heart never won fair lady, and neither did faint praise.

When a woman wants to know another woman's faults, she praises her highly among her female acquaintances.

The best thing to do behind a person's back is to pat it.

The wife who seldom praises her husband probably doesn't like to lie.

PRAYER

I don't know of a single foreign product that enters this country untaxed, except the answer to prayer. — *Mark Twain*

I have lived to thank God that all my prayers have not been answered. — *Jean Ingelow*

When the spirit rises, it lets the body fall on its knees. — *G. C. Lichtenberg*

There are few men who would dare make known to the public the prayers they make to God. — *Montaigne*

Prayer doesn't change God, but changes him who prays. — *Kierkegaard*

Pray: to ask the laws of the universe to be annulled on behalf of a single petitioner confessedly unworthy. — *Bierce*

The only time my prayers are never answered are on the golf course. — *Billy Graham*

If your prayers are not answered, the answer is no.

God may not be too busy to listen to your prayers, but that's no reason why you shouldn't keep them short.

Pray as though no work could help, and work as though no prayer could help.

Some people are greedy even when they pray: they expect a thousand-dollar answer to a one-minute prayer.

Some people are so busy asking God for favors, they have no time to thank Him.

When people pray, they are really asking God that two and two should not make four.

Good people pray, successful people advertise.

As long as there are final exams, there will always be prayers in our schools.

Some women are such bad cooks that their families pray before every meal.

Maybe the Lord lets people get into trouble because that's the only time they think of Him.

What this country needs are more people who pray more, and more people who prey less.

PREACHING

One of the proofs of the divinity of our gospel is the preaching it has survived. — *Woodrow Wilson*

The milk of human kindness should never be condensed, except when a preacher delivers it.

Clergymen are forever preaching about God who is forever silent.

The man who preaches by the yard usually practices by the inch.

A preacher is a clergyman whose sermons never apply to you but always to the other fellow.

Clergymen preach about many subjects, but the congregation generally prefers them to preach about half an hour.

The more a preacher appeases, the more he pleases.

There never was a man who practised half the things he preaches to his son.

The preacher who fills his church every Sunday is the one who tells you how to live rather than how to die.

A preacher is a man who must be able to talk louder than people can snore.

An evangelist is a traveling preacher who works to beat hell.

PREDICTION

Any astronomer can predict just where every star will be at half-past eleven tonight; he can make no such prediction about his young daughter.
— *James Truslow Adams*

Science can predict an eclipse of the sun years in advance, but cannot forecast the weather over the weekend.

PREFER

There is always something a woman will prefer to the truth.
— *Samuel Johnson*

Deep-seated preferences cannot be argued about: you cannot argue a man into liking a glass of beer.   — *Justice O. W. Holmes*

The world wisely prefers happiness to wisdom.   — *Will Durant*

PREGNANCY

There's no way to shorten pregnancy, not even by calendar reform.   — *Stanislaw J. Lec*

Oh, what a tangled web we weave when first we practice to conceive.   — *Don Herold*

Nowadays many a girl buys a maternity dress before she buys a bridal gown.

Sex is a drive where there are many accidents due to careless drivers.

Many a woman who is pregnant wishes her husband would bear with her.

Pregnancy is the only time when you can do nothing at all and still be productive.

Many a secretary quits when she gets too big for the job—figuratively speaking.

A maternity dress is designed to make you look pretty, considering the shape you're in.

An almost exclusively female disease is claustrophobia—the fear of confinement.

There would be less pregnancies among teenagers if they would resist the boyological urge.

The girl who is willing to do anything for a mink coat may soon find that she has trouble buttoning it.

PREJUDICE

Never try to reason the prejudice out of a man; it was not reasoned into him and cannot be reasoned out.   — *Sydney Smith*

Our prejudices are our mistresses; reason is at best our wife, very often needed but seldom minded.   — *Chesterfield*

A man's prejudice is mental, a woman's temperamental.

The difficulty in finding an ideal candidate is that no man can have prejudices enough to fit all sections.

The man who does not think as we do is apt to be prejudiced.

Many a man makes the mistake of developing his opinions in the dark room of prejudice.

Prejudice is merely a lazy man's substitute for thinking.

A prejudice is the easiest thing in the world to acquire, but the hardest thing to get rid of.

Some men change their minds, while others merely rearrange their prejudices.

What this country needs are more judges who weigh their words and keep their thumbs off the scales of justice.

You can always tell a prejudiced person: he is too stubborn to admit we are right.

Prejudice is an opinion that belongs to someone we dislike.

Prejudice is a matter of not only drawing your own conclusions, but of coloring them as well.

Another labor-saving device is prejudice: it enables you to form opinions without having to dig up the facts.

The only person who is unbiased is one who has the same bias we have.

The difference between a prejudice and a conviction is that you can explain a conviction without getting mad.

PRESCRIPTION

There's only one thing harder to read than the handwriting on the wall, and that's a doctor's prescription.

Doctors may write their prescriptions in illegible Latin, but their bills are always written in plain English.

Where ignorance is bliss, 'tis folly for a doctor to tell a patient what he has written on his prescription.

PRESENT

He to whom the present is the only thing that is present, knows nothing of the age in which he lives.   — Oscar Wilde

Times are not as bad as they seem—they couldn't be.

A few people are ahead of the times, many are behind the times, while the rest aren't even going in the same direction.

There's no time like the present—for those who enjoy worrying.

These are the good old days the next generation will hear so much about.

Now is the time for all good men to come to.

PRESIDENT

When things go wrong they like to blame the President, and that's one of the things that Presidents are paid for. — John F. Kennedy

I should like to be known as a former President who minded his own business. — Calvin Coolidge

The White House is the finest prison in the world.
— Harry S. Truman

The things I enjoyed most as President were the visits of children: they did not want public office. — Herbert Hoover

If I knew as much now as I thought I knew at nineteen, I'd

be the greatest President this country ever had.
— *Warren G. Harding*

When I became President, what surprised me most was that things were just as bad as I'd been saying they were.   — *John F. Kennedy*

A man can be right and President, but he can't be both at the same time. — *Finley Peter Dunne*

In youth I thought I might grow up to be President, but I soon dismissed it as the risk every American boy has to take.
— *Adlai Stevenson*

I would rather that the people should wonder why I wasn't President than why I am.
— *Salmon P. Chase*

Long ago I proposed that unsuccessful candidates for the Presidency be quietly hanged as a matter of public sanitation.
— *Mencken*

The President is always abused; if he isn't, he's doing nothing, and is of no value as the Chief Executive.   — *Harry S. Truman*

It's hard for the President to make a speech so that a bone-headed congressman and a high-brow mailman will both get what he means.   — *Will Rogers*

A man expects to be elected President of the United States for the fine qualities that the rest of us use to keep out of jail.
— *Finley Peter Dunne*

The President of today is the postage stamp of tomorrow.

Some men would rather be right than President, while others are not so particular.

What this country needs is two Presidents: one for the White House, and one for the road.

The man who would rather be right than President generally has his way.

In a democracy people are both elected and appointed: we, the people, elect the President; his critics appoint themselves.

The President of the United States serves a minimum four-year sentence, with no time off for good behavior.

It's better to be right than President, but it doesn't pay as well.

Many a President would have been more useful to society if he had been a cabinet maker instead of the maker of a cabinet.

PRESS

The hand that rules the press rules the country. — *Learned Hand*

The most important service rendered by the press is that of educating people to approach printed matter with distrust.
— *Samuel Butler*

Freedom of the press means freedom to suppress.
— *Bernard Shaw*

The greater part of whitewashing is done with ink.
— *George D. Prentice*

A free press is one that prints a dictator's speech but doesn't have to.

The vice of the people is the voice of the press.

PRESS AGENT

I never make a move without first ignoring my press agent.
— *Groucho Marx*

No man is a hero to his press agent.

A press agent never chooses the lesser of two evils, but the one most likely to be talked about.

The fool puffs himself up, the intelligent man hires a press agent.

A telescope will magnify a star a thousand times, but a good press agent will do even better.

Many a press agent keeps his client in the public eye like a cinder.

Freedom of the press is mostly freedom of the press agent.

A press agent is a man whose job is to discover genius where none exists.

It's hard to keep a good man down, especially if he has a press agent.

A press agent is a man who has discovered the secret of perpetual promotion.

The actor who publicizes himself has a fool for a press agent.

A press agent can exploit his talent only by exploiting the talent of others.

PRETENSE

Man is a make-believe animal: he is never so truly himself as when he is acting a part.
— *Hazlitt*

Half the people who make love could be arrested for counterfeiting.
— *Ed Howe*

To give up pretensions is as blessed a relief as to get them gratified. — *William James*

There are two motives in human life: the real motive and the pretended motive. — *Reinhold Niebuhr*

When some men take a position on high moral grounds, it is always a bluff.

Many a girl who plays smart to get a job has to play dumb to get a husband.

Thirty is the time in life when a woman's youth changes from present tense to pretense.

Another pleasant period in life is when your children grow up to the age when you don't have to pretend you know everything.

Nothing sets a man back like keeping up a front.

Beware of the girl who pretends to love you from the bottom of her heart—there may be another man at the top.

You can do a lot of bluffing by keeping your mouth shut.

PRICE

Nothing is as irritating as the fellow who chats pleasantly while he's overcharging you.

— *Kin Hubbard*

A cynic in a man who knows the price of everything and the value of nothing. — *Oscar Wilde*

Every man has his price, except the man who is really worth buying.

The gown that looks stunning on a woman usually has a price tag that leaves her husband stunned.

The highest price you can pay for anything is to get it for nothing.

Deflation is the period when prices decline on everything except what you want to buy.

Drink doesn't ruin a man today, it's the price that does.

There are two times when things go up in price: during inflation, and when you make a theft report to the insurance company.

Some restaurants get away with murder while leaving you to face the charges.

Some politicians ought to have a price tag attached.

There's always plenty of room at the top—for prices.

PRIDE

I'm proud to pay taxes in the United States; the only thing is, I could be just as proud for half the money. — *Arthur Godfrey*

It is as proper to be proud of ourselves as it is improper to proclaim it to the world.

— *La Rochefoucauld*

Pride goeth before destruction, except in the dictionary.

It isn't the things a man can do that he is proudest of, it's the things he thinks he can do.

Arrogance is a pose assumed by the body to hide the faults of the mind.

When you're on your high horse, the best thing to do is to dismount at once.

The difference between pride and vanity is that we have one and other people have the other.

So live that when a man says he's married to you, he'll be boasting.

Many a man is proud of his father and mother because they are the parents of such a wonderful person.

Pride goeth before a fall, but it goeth a lot quicker after one.

Would the boy you were be proud of the man you are?

PRIMITIVE

To most people a savage nation is one that doesn't wear uncomfortable clothes.

— *Finley Peter Dunne*

During primitive days women resembled men, and men resembled beasts. —*Anatole France*

Records show that no savage people ever invented an atom bomb.

The primitive African who beats drums to ward off evil spirits is ridiculed by the civilized American who blows horns to break up traffic jams.

An uncivilized country is one in which you can safely leave your house unlocked.

PRINT

There is a huge pile of printed matter, all to the effect that printed matter is in excess. —*Frank Moore Colby*

Why do publishers use large print in books for children, whose eyes are excellent, and small print in books for adults? —*William Lyon Phelps*

I wrote a short story because I wanted to see something of mine in print other than my fingers. —*Wilson Mizner*

Paper is patient, but the reader isn't. —*Joubert*

Printing broke out in the province of Kansu in A.D. 868: the early Chinese simply could not let well enough alone. —*Will Cuppy*

The older you get, the smaller the newspaper type gets.

PRISON

I recommend prison, where all my major works have been written, not only to aspiring writers but to aspiring politicians too. —*Nehru*

It is not the prisoners who need reformation, it is the prisons. —*Oscar Wilde*

Habeas corpus: a writ by which a man may be taken out of jail when confined for the wrong crime. —*Bierce*

There is no more independence in politics than there is in jail. —*Will Rogers*

There are more people than you realize who lead a simple life, but most of them are in jail.

Time is money and money is time—so get all the money you can without getting time.

A warden takes in a lot of guests that no one else would have.

Now that people live longer, life imprisonment is a longer sentence than it used to be.

The man who goes to prison for life will find little of it there.

In prison a person gets time off for good behavior while he serves time for bad behavior.

Stone walls do not a prison make, nor iron bars a cage, but they do help.

Another place where you can always tell a man by his clothes is prison.

In prison there are two sides to every question—the inside and the outside.

The only man who should not be judged by the company he keeps is a warden.

Time is money, but not when you're doing it in jail.

There are various stations in life, but the least desirable is the police station.

Prison reform will not work until we start sending a better class of people there.

The ideal place to read escapist literature is a prison.

The pen is mightier than the sword, or would be if we could get the criminals inside it.

Nobody is contented until he is in jail—then he has enough.

Prisons are full of criminals so foolish that even the police could catch them.

Life starts from a cell and, if you're found out, it also ends there.

PRIVACY

Things are coming to a pretty pass when religion is allowed to invade private life.
— Lord Melbourne

There's only one person who knows almost as much about you as your private secretary, and that is the switchboard operator.

As we stroll through life we come upon many flowery paths, but they are mostly labeled *Private*.

Two people in love suddenly discover that there are too many other people in the world.

Some women respect another's privacy: they never open their husbands' mail—unless it is marked *Personal*.

People who live in glass houses should pull down the blinds.

Girls shouldn't learn to love before twenty—it shouldn't be practiced in crowds.

PRIVILEGE

The war on privilege will never end; its next great campaign will be against the special privileges of the underprivileged. — *Mencken*

My political slogan is: Special privileges for all, equal opportunity for none.   — *Will Rogers*

What men value in this world is not rights but privileges.
— *Mencken*

What men prize most is a privilege, even if it be that of chief mourner at a funeral.
— *James Russell Lowell*

It's a woman's privilege to change things: her mind, her hairdo, and her age.

Do not resent growing old: many are denied the privilege.

It is a man's inalienable right to make a fool of himself, but he shouldn't abuse the privilege.

You often hear of a person who is underprivileged, but never of one who is overprivileged.

It's a husband's privilege to lay down the law, and a wife's to repeal it.

PRIZE

I don't care what people think of my poetry so long as they award it prizes.   *— Robert Frost*

Nobel prize money is a lifebelt thrown to a swimmer who has already reached the shore in safety.
— Bernard Shaw

A woman's values make no sense to her husband, especially when she thinks her bridge trophy is as important as his golf cup.

PRIZEFIGHT

A prizefighter has a limited choice: he either carries out his plans, or is carried out.

The only men nowadays who wake up and find themselves rich are professional boxers.

PROBLEM

Problems are the price of progress: don't bring me anything but trouble—good news weakens me.
— Charles F. Kettering

Men have more problems than women; for one thing, they have to put up with women.
— Françoise Sagan

Although some men are great mathematicians, woman still remains an unsolved puzzle.

Wouldn't it be wonderful if life's big problems occurred when we're seventeen—and know everything?

The world is full of problem children, and most of them are over twenty-one years of age.

We used to settle our problems over cigarettes and coffee—now they are our problems.

Many a father lives long enough to be as much a problem to his children as they were to him.

The two toughest problems in America today are: how to lose twenty pounds, and where to find a place to park.

Of all the problems facing wives, the biggest is usually the one sitting across her at the breakfast table.

Parents who ignore their children's problems breed problem children.

The woman who is interested in a book on marriage problems is probably married to one.

Life is a teacher that's always giving you new problems before you've solved the old ones.

A man's hardest problem is to find a girl attractive enough to please him and dumb enough to like him.

PROBLEM AND SOLUTION

Many a problem will solve itself if you'll forget it and go fishing. — *Olin Miller*

Science is always wrong: it never solves a problem without creating ten more. — *Bernard Shaw*

Man is forever striving to solve the problems of the world whose greatest problem he is.

The solutions of one generation are the problems of the next.

There is only one major problem today, and that is, how to deal with the people who are trying to solve it.

The trouble with the world is that there are always more problems than solutions.

To girls, men are not a problem but a solution; to wives, men are not a solution but a problem.

The biggest problem in the world could have been solved when it was small.

PRODIGAL SON

You can't expect the fatted calf to share the enthusiasm of the angels over the prodigal's return. — *Saki*

It hardly pays to be a prodigal son for the little veal there is in it. — *Ed Howe*

A money order would have saved the prodigal son the trouble of coming home. — *Arthur Baer*

The trouble with the prodigal son is that he won't stay at home after he returns.

The prodigal son returns home empty-handed, but the prodigal daughter usually carries an armful.

The prodigal son had to come to himself before he could come to his father.

The mistake was in killing the fatted calf instead of the prodigal son.

PRODIGY

A child prodigy is another person's child who is exceptionally talented, or your own grandchild who isn't.

The only thing more annoying than a precocious child is its mother.

A child prodigy is a youngster who is too young to be as old as he is.

The mother who thinks her child is a budding genius has neighbors who think he should be nipped in the bud.

A child prodigy is a youngster who knows how to go to his psychiatrist all by himself.

The child prodigy who begins as a genius at four often develops into a fool at forty.

PRODUCTION

Economics divides the world into two parts: one half suffers from too much production, and the other half from too little.

Communism has one advantage over us: they have long ago learned the secret of how not to produce too much consumer goods.

Trouble is usually produced by those who produce nothing else.

Man is constantly improving his methods of production in everything—except children.

In varying degree, every country suffers from an overproduction of non-producers.

PROFESSION

All professions are conspiracies against the laity.   —*Bernard Shaw*

Professional men, they have no cares; whatever happens, they get theirs.   —*Ogden Nash*

Medicine is my lawful wife and literature my mistress; when I get tired of one, I spend a night with the other.   —*Chekhov*

Lawyers, preachers and tomtit's eggs, there are more of them hatched than come to perfection.
—*Franklin*

A girl prefers a young man's profession of love to any other profession.

A man's profession is his practice, but he doesn't always practice what he professes.

The test of a profession is a love of the drudgery it entails.

PROFESSOR

I have known two professors of Greek who ceased speaking to one another because of divergent views on the pluperfect subjunctive.   —*Stephen Leacock*

In politics, the professor always plays the comic part. —*Nietzsche*

America believes in education: the average professor earns more money in a year than the professional athlete earns in a whole week.

The job of a professor of economics is to teach students how to solve the problems which he himself has avoided by becoming a professor.

The professor who comes in much too early is rare: in fact, he's in a class by himself.

PROFIT

It is a socialist idea that making profits is a vice; I consider that the real vice is making losses.
—*Winston Churchill*

The worst crime against working people is a company which fails to operate at a profit.
— *Samuel Gompers*

You can profit from your mistakes, but that does not mean the more mistakes, the more profit.

The chief ingredient that makes expensive merchandise so expensive is profit.

It's good to combine business with pleasure, but it's better to combine business with profit.

The one race bookmakers are sure to make a big profit on is the human race.

You are born into the world with nothing: everything you acquire after that is sheer profit.

Business prophets tell what is going to happen, business profits tell what has happened.

Clergymen should perform marriage ceremonies free of charge; they shouldn't profit by other people's mistakes.

PROGRESS

There has been lots of progress during my lifetime, but I'm afraid it's heading in the wrong direction.
— *Ogden Nash*

Progress: the search for the best possible product at the most possible mark-up with the shortest possible duration for the earliest possible replacement. — *John Ciardi*

Progress is the process whereby the human race is getting rid of

whiskers, the vermiform appendix and God.
— *Mencken*

Progress is the mother of problems.
— *Chesterton*

Democracy is ever eager for rapid progress but the only progress which can be rapid is progress downhill.
— *James Jeans*

Unquestionably there is progress: the average American now pays out twice as much in taxes as he formerly got in wages.
— *Mencken*

The reasonable man adapts himself to the world, but the unreasonable man tries to adapt the world to him—therefore, all progress depends upon the unreasonable man.
— *Bernard Shaw*

Progress might have been all right once, but it went on too long.
— *Ogden Nash*

What we call progress is the exchange of one nuisance for another nuisance. — *Havelock Ellis*

All my life affection has been showered upon me, and every forward step I have made has been taken in spite of it.
— *Bernard Shaw*

Progress is a continuing effort to make the things we eat, drink and wear as good as they used to be. — *Bill Vaughan*

All progress is based upon a universal innate desire on the part of every organism to live beyond its income. — *Samuel Butler*

All progress is initiated by challenging current conceptions, and executed by supplanting existing institutions. — *Bernard Shaw*

The art of progress is to preserve order amid change, and to preserve change amid order.
— *A. N. Whitehead*

The European talks of progress because he has established a society which has mistaken comfort for civilization. — *Disraeli*

The trouble with progress is that is goes forward, not backward. — *Oscar Wilde*

Progress always means change, but change doesn't always mean progress.

Progress is always uneven: as our driving manners become more crude, our gasoline becomes more refined.

What we call progress is merely a gradual falling in line with the ideas of minorities.

Progress is sometimes followed by a comma, never by a period.

We have finally reached a state of affairs where a man can fly into space safely, but cannot cross the street safely.

Progress comes from making people sit up when they want to sit down.

Progress is where one generation makes time payments on its cars, and the next generation makes time payments on its planes.

The world is progressing: it spends more money for gunpowder than for face powder.

The proof that we are making progress is that we are getting more one-way streets and two-way marriages.

The world moves rapidly: yesterday's radical is today's reactionary.

Progress has shrunk the earth so that all nations are now within shooting distance of one another.

The way of the progressor is hard.

Progress does not always go forward: city traffic, for example, moved much faster in the horse-and-buggy days.

PROHIBITION

A prohibitionist is the sort of man one wouldn't care to drink with—even if he drank.
— *Mencken*

Prohibition makes you want to cry into your beer, and denies you the beer to cry into.
— *Don Marquis*

At the beginning of Prohibition even those who disliked it, believed in it; at the end even those who liked it, disbelieved in it.
— *Chesterton*

Many a drinking man believes in prohibition but only for prohibitionists.

Where the drys have their law, the wets have their whisky, and the locality gets it taxes.

PROMISCUITY

Some men have no ambition, enterprise or ability, except about women. — *Ed Howe*

What I have seen of the love affairs of other people has not led me to regret that deficiency in my experience. — *Bernard Shaw*

Save a boyfriend for a rainy day, and another in case it doesn't rain. — *Mae West*

The easier a woman is to get, the easier she is to forget.

Variety is the spice of love.

A man can love more than one woman at the same time—if they don't find it out.

Many a girl lands on a psychiatrist's couch because she landed on too many couches before.

The easiest way to get out of one affair is to get into another.

Beware of the woman who is always willin', or you'll be takin' penicillin.

A man will forget most of his love affairs, while a woman will remember even some she has never had.

None but the brave deserve affairs.

A nymphomaniac is a woman who takes on the husbands of other women so as not to wear out her own.

A man is always ready to give up a passing fancy for something fancier.

Promiscuous girls make up in men what they lack in mentality.

Sex is a drive, and there are too many teenagers driving without a license.

A fool and her legs are soon parted.

The young man who makes a study of women at college often follows it up with a postgraduate course.

Some girls love too much, others love too many.

Many a man operates on the principle that there's a little bit of bed in every good little girl.

The girl who gives love to all doesn't give all to love.

Promiscuity is to be condemned more on medical than on moral grounds: it is turning us into a syphilized nation.

PROMISE

Whom the gods wish to destroy they first call promising. — *Cyril Connolly*

When a man gives his word to another man, it's his bond;

when he gives his word to a woman, it's his bondage.

A politician is known by the promises he doesn't keep.

There's a great deal of difference between a young man of promise and a young man of promises.

During courtship when a man promises never to look at another woman, remember it is just another campaign promise.

Many a man is as good as his word, but his word is no good.

During an election, all campaign speeches sound alike—like promissory notes.

If you are engaged to a promising young man, see that he keeps his promise.

When a politician breaks his promise to you, he usually replaces it with a better one.

If you don't like to make excuses or apologies, stop making promises.

No honest businessman ever goes back on his word, at least not without consulting a lawyer.

PRONUNCIATION

Every time we meet a schoolteacher we find that we have been pronouncing another word incorrectly.   — Ed Howe

A judge always pronounces words the same way, but pronounces sentences differently.

It is the rare foreigner who does not mispronounce words with a pronounced accent.

PROOF

If a man could say nothing against a character but what he could prove, history could not be written.   — Samuel Johnson

There is too much say it, and too little prove it, in the world.   — Ed Howe

A golfer has one advantage over a fisherman: he doesn't have to show anything to prove it.

The proof of the pudding is in the eating, but not if the eater is a bad judge of pudding.

A husband is the head of the household—until he tries to prove it.

When your date says he's not interested in marriage, he probably has a wife at home to prove it.

PROPERTY

No man acquires property without acquiring with it a little arithmetic also.   — Emerson

Private property began the instant somebody had a mind of his own.   — E. E. Cummings

All the world's a stage, and everyone wants to be the property man.

Life is a paradox: we must deliver the goods, yet not be caught with it.

The man who worships the ground his girl walks on probably knows her father owns the property.

When a girl is interested in a man less for his money than for his deeds, she's probably thinking about his real estate and mortgages.

PROPHECY

I always avoid prophesying beforehand because it is much better to prophesy after the event has already taken place.
— *Winston Churchill*

You can make a better living in the world as a soothsayer than as a truthsayer.
— *G. C. Lichtenberg*

A country is sometimes not without honor save for its own prophet.   — *Samuel Butler*

PROPOSAL

Proposals are usually so unromantic that most married women can't remember how or where they happened.
— *Helen Rowland*

I haven't found men unduly loath to say, "I love you"; the real trick is to get them to say, "Will you marry me?"
— *Ilka Chase*

Leibnitz contemplated marriage, but the lady asked for time to consider; this gave *him* time to consider, so he never married.
— *Fontenelle*

A proposal is an offer of marriage when even the man of few words talks too much.

After a man proposes on his knees, he spends years trying to get back on his feet.

When a man proposes to a girl and she gets mad, you can imagine what he proposed.

Man proposes and woman imposes.

When a man asks a woman to marry him, he pays her the greatest compliment possible, or else he needs her money.

If a man looks foolish when he proposes, it's because he's doing a foolish thing.

Sometimes the only thing that keeps a girl from marrying a man is her foolish pride—she is waiting for him to propose.

Men seldom win sweeties with tearful entreaties.

The woman who accepts a man the first time he proposes to her usually rejects every one of his proposals thereafter.

Man supposes he proposes.

The girl who doesn't accept a rich man the first time he proposes was probably not there.

Times have changed: in the old days, before you could pop the question, you had to question her pop.

The man who proposes is fishing for trouble, and generally gets hooked with his own line.

Many a girl would marry her boyfriend if he were rich or handsome—or if he'd ask her.

When a man proposes to a girl, he usually makes the best speech he'll ever regret.

A bachelor is always ready with a proposition, but never with a proposal.

Man proposes—but not always marriage.

PROSE AND POETRY

Poetry is able to say twice as much as prose in half the time while seeming to say half as much in twice the time.
— *Christopher Fry*

When you write in prose, you say what you mean; when you write in verse, you say what you must. — *Dr. O. W. Holmes*

In prose you might say a thing seven different ways; in poetry the words are not replaceable.
— *Stephen Spender*

Prose is words in their best order; poetry is the best words in the best order. — *Coleridge*

Prose is used to express things, poetry to caress them.

Free verse is a form of poetry where there's a great deal of prose license.

PROSPERITY

Prosperity has ruined many a man but, if a man has to be ruined, that is the most pleasant way.

Science is wonderful: you can hear speeches about our prosperity over a television set that isn't paid for.

The trouble with an expanding economy is that it usually leads to expanding waistlines.

Prosperity is the period when you can always get credit enough to live beyond your means.

Prosperity is a mixed blessing: it's when you've never had it so good, but also when you've never had it taken away from you so fast.

Affluence is the state in which you complain about the quality of the champagne.

Prosperity is a fleeting interval between the last installment and the next down payment.

It's hard to tell about prosperity: when the hog is fattest it goes to the butcher.

You may not know when you are well off, but the Internal Revenue Service does.

For one man who can stand prosperity there are a thousand who would like to try.

Prosperity is the period when you don't wonder where your next dollar is coming from, but where it has gone.

Most people cannot stand sudden wealth, but then most people do not have to.

PROSPERITY AND ADVERSITY

In prosperity our friends know us, in adversity we know our friends. — *John Churton Collins*

For one man who can stand prosperity, there are a hundred that will stand adversity. — *Carlyle*

During good times people accumulate debts that they can't pay back during bad times.

In the matter of making fools, prosperity has it all over adversity.

PROSTITUTION

Prostitutes are a necessity: without them, men would assault respectable women in the streets.
— *Napoleon*

No woman is worth money that will take money. — *John Vanbrugh*

Venus cunningly raised the price of her goods by making pimping illegal. — *Montaigne*

A prostitute may be good for nothing, but she's never bad for nothing.

A prostitute is the only healthy woman who wears out more sheets than shoes.

Play safe: remember that a call girl's reputation means less to her than yours does to you.

Nature abhors a vacuum, and human nature abhors a whore.

Whoring and hoarding never go together.

A prostitute is a woman who does the same thing for a living that other women do for pleasure.

Politics makes strange bedfellows, and so does prostitution.

Prostitution is a game where the man gets a little fun, and the woman gets a little fund.

The business of a prostitute is to make feminine capital out of masculine interest.

PROTECTION

I never lied save to shield a woman—or myself.
— *Ring Lardner*

The law protects everyone, especially those who can afford to hire a good lawyer.

PROVERBS

The Queen of Sheba never told what she thought of King Solomon's proverbs warning young men against women.
— *Don Marquis*

The recipe for making a good proverb is: take one gallon of truth, boil it down to a pint, sweeten with kindness, and lay away to cool. — *Josh Billings*

A proverb is a short sentence distilled from long experience.
— *Cervantes*

What are the proper proportions of a maxim? A minimum of sound to a maximum of sense.
— *Mark Twain*

A new broom sweeps clean, but never trust an old saw.
— *James Thurber*

All the good maxims have already been written; the only thing that remains now is to put them into practice.   — *Pascal*

A proverb is an expression that makes no impression.

A nation's proverbs are like itself—self-contradictory.

Solomon made a book of proverbs, but a book of proverbs never made a Solomon.

Proverbs are the literature of the illiterate.

Some proverbs are half-truths, but most are semi-falsehoods.

Another thing that everyone preaches and no one practices is a proverb.

A maxim is a saying of maximum repetition and minimum value.

PROVIDE

It's a woman's duty to provide for the inner man, and a man's duty to provide for the outer woman.

Some husbands are good providers, but only if you count children.

PRUDERY

Henry James was one of the nicest old ladies I ever met.
— *Faulkner*

Mrs. Grundy is the only deity officially recognized by the English state.   — *Aldous Huxley*

A prude gets most of her pleasure from being shocked by other people's pleasure.

Some mothers are so prudish that they teach their children the facts of life by starting with artificial flowers.

To the prude, all things are imprudent.

PSYCHIATRY

I do not want a psychiatrist for the simple reason that if he listened to me long enough he might become disturbed.
— *James Thurber*

A psychiatrist is the next man you start talking to after you start talking to yourself. — *Fred Allen*

If the Prince of Peace should come to earth, one of the first things he would do would be to put psychiatrists in their place.
— *Aldous Huxley*

A psychiatrist is fortunate: his patients never die and they never get well.

You go to a psychiatrist when you're slightly cracked, and keep going until you're completely broke.

A psychiatrist is a person who will listen to you as long as you don't make sense.

Psychiatry is a blessing: in the past a child who chopped up furniture was crazy; nowadays he's merely unstable.

Psychiatrists never seem to find out anything good about anybody.

Psychiatry is a branch of medicine that enables a person to suggest a wrong course of treatment with complete confidence.

A normal person is one who has not yet been examined by a psychiatrist.

A psychiatrist gets paid for asking you the same questions your wife asks for nothing.

A psychiatrist is a doctor who can't stand the sight of blood.

Psychiatry is the science that has turned the old-fashioned sins of yesterday into the emotional ills of today.

A psychiatrist is the only man who encourages the woman who talks too much to keep on talking.

Psychiatry covers a multitude of sins.

The psychiatrist who tells parents to spend more time with their children is probably trying to drum up business.

A psychiatrist is a man who tries to put you on your feet by putting you on a couch.

A psychiatrist is secure only as long as his patients aren't.

The psychiatrist who talks to himself should talk to another psychiatrist.

Anybody who goes to see a psychiatrist ought to have his head examined.

A psychiatrist is a man who goes to a burlesque show and watches the audience.

Psychiatry is a form of treatment where the doctor never pays visits but where the visits always pay the doctor.

PSYCHOANALYSIS

Psychoanalysis is confession without absolution. — *Chesterton*

A psychoanalyst is a man who, when a beautiful oversexed woman is lying on a couch, does nothing but talk to her.

Before psychoanalysis, everything a child did was the child's fault; now everything a child does is his parents' fault.

If your analyst understands you, there must be something wrong with him.

All analysts are psychological, but some are more psycho than logical.

Give the psychoanalyst his due: he is the only one who can make a domineering person take it lying down.

When two psychoanalysts get together, which one takes the couch?

A psychoanalyst is one who stops you from worrying about your problem, and starts you worrying about your bill.

Psychoanalysis begins with the analyst suspecting the sanity of the patient and ends with the patient suspecting the sanity of the analyst.

A psychoanalyst is a person who reads between the lines even when there is nothing there.

Another reason psychoanalysis is so popular is that only in an analyst's office are you allowed to put your feet on the couch.

A psychoanalyst can take any simple symptom and explain it in language no one understands.

Psychoanalysis is a sinecure that offers a cure for the insecure.

Psychoanalysis begins with a man losing his mental balance and ends with his losing his bank balance.

My analyst says I have a persecution complex, but he's just saying that because he hates me.

PUBLIC

The trouble with the public is that there is too much of it; what we need in public is less quantity and more quality.
— *Don Marquis*

The people are to be taken in very small doses. — *Emerson*

The average public is made up of people who think they are above the average.

Women's participation in public affairs keeps the affairs public.

Never underestimate the intelligence of the public, and never overestimate its knowledge.

PUBLIC AND PRIVATE

A Pharisee is a man who prays publicly and preys privately.
— *Don Marquis*

Many a family manages to live in public as the rich do by living in private as the poor do.

What this country needs is less public speaking and more private thinking.

The trouble with many candidates is that they have private opinions on public questions.

The taxpayer is a private citizen whose money belongs to the public.

The man who blows his own horn in public usually plays second fiddle at home.

There's nothing more public than the private life of a movie star.

What this country needs is more interest in public affairs and less interest in private affairs.

PUBLICITY

I don't care what is written about me so long as it isn't true.
— *Katharine Hepburn*

Some people commit a crime for no other reason than to see their name in print. — *Flaubert*

I don't care what they call me as long as they mention my name.
— *George M. Cohan*

A celebrity often creates publicity but is more often created by it.

The evil that men do lives after them, the good they publicize while they live.

If an actor bites a dog, it's not news—it's publicity.

Publicity is another thing you get when you are successful enough not to need it.

Publicity agents continually remind the public that their clients dislike publicity.

Many a man would give to charity anonymously, but only if it were well publicized.

The worst thing you can say about a movie star is—nothing.

A publicity hound is the breed that has the biggest mouth and the longest tale.

Truth is stranger than fiction, and publicity is strange than both of them.

Behind every successful entertainer there's a woman—working in a publicity agency.

Publicity is getting your private *I* in the public eye.

When a movie star stays married, it's probably a publicity stunt.

PUBLIC OPINION

Public opinion is the God of democracy and the journalist is his prophet.

Public opinion is what people think other people think.

At 20 we don't care what the world thinks of us; at 30 we wonder what it thinks of us; at 40 we discover it doesn't think of us at all.

In a democracy, a change in public opinion is a matter of degree; in a dictatorship, a matter of decree.

The weakness of public opinion is that most people express it only privately.

PUBLIC RELATIONS

Public relations is the art of doing what the public likes, or making it like what you do.

Many a man who makes money in public relations has to give it to private relations.

Public relations is the business of creating public opinion for private advantage.

Public relations is the art of not treating the public like relations.

PUBLIC SPEAKING

The hardest thing about making a speech is knowing what to do with your hands. — *Kin Hubbard*

Too many public speakers begin by saying they have nothing to say, and then take an hour to prove it. — *William Lyon Phelps*

No matter how much strong black coffee we drink, almost any afterdinner speech will counteract it. — *Kin Hubbard*

He loves afterdinner speaking so much, he starts a speech at the mere sight of bread crumbs. — *Fred Allen*

When a speaker adjusts his spectacles and begins to fumble around in his inside coat pocket, it's a good time to quietly leave the hall. — *Kin Hubbard*

The hardest thing to stop is a temporary chairman. — *Kin Hubbard*

The public speaker who drives home too many facts will also drive home too many listeners.

One of the chief evils of public speaking is to finish your speech before you stop talking.

Afterdinner speeches would be much shorter if they were given before dinner.

The job of the public speaker is to talk, the job of his audience is to listen, and the speaker must always finish his job first.

Public speaking is practiced by too many mouths putting too few ideas into too many ears.

The female of the speeches is more deadly than the male.

The trouble with some public speakers is that you can't hear what they're saying; the trouble with others is that you can.

Many a prepared speech delivered to prove something merely proves how badly it was prepared.

The first rule of public speaking is to speak up, the second is to sit down.

It's never so bleak that it can't be bleaker—there might have been a more boring speaker.

An impromptu speech is seldom worth the paper it is written on.

Oratory is the art of talking at length without letting on what you are talking about.

When a public speaker is lost in words, his audience is usually lost in thought.

The three B's of public speaking are: be brief, be interesting, be gone.

Many a public speaker knows just what not to say, but not when to quit saying it.

A public speaker never realizes how important timing is until he notices the audience looking at their watches.

It's much easier for a public speaker to talk a lot than it is for him to say something.

Advice to public speakers: Leave your audience before your audience leaves you.

Many a public speaker who needs no introduction needs a conclusion.

Some public speakers are applauded when they stand up, but most are when they sit down.

An orator is a man who seems to think that to be immortal a speech must be eternal.

The worst speechmakers are the ones with an addiction to diction.

A poor public speaker talks until he gets tired, a poorer one talks until his audience gets tired.

Public speaking is like drinking: knowing how to start is less important than knowing when to stop.

An afterdinner speaker eats what he doesn't like, tells stories he doesn't remember, to people who have already heard them.

Many a public speaker who speaks straight from the shoulder would be more interesting if his remarks started a little higher up.

If an afterdinner speaker wants to know what to talk about, tell him to talk about ten minutes.

Public speakers who talk like a book are seldom wise enough to shut up like one.

God gave eloquence to some, brains to others.

The best way to make a speech is to have a good beginning and a good ending—and to keep them close together.

Little boys who talk too much usually grow up to be public speakers.

Many a public speaker begins with not knowing what he is going to say, and ends with not knowing what he has said.

Many afterdinner speeches make people dull, and many dull people make afterdinner speeches.

In the recipe for public speaking, the most important ingredient is the shortening.

When a public speaker forgets his watch, he is likely to go by the calendar.

The surest way to stay awake during an afterdinner speech is to deliver it.

The trouble with many a public speaker is that every time he stands up before an audience, his mind sits down.

A public speaker should stand up to be seen, speak up to be heard, and shut up to be appreciated.

PUBLISHER

It is with publishers as with wives: one always wants somebody else's.　　　*— Norman Douglas*

A publisher of today would as soon see a burglar in his office as a poet. *— Henry de Vere Stacpoole*

In first novels the hero is usually the publisher.

PUNCH CARD

Universities are getting to be so big nowadays that the only way a student can show any individuality is to bend his punch card.

Automation has added a new fear to our lives—the fear of folding a punch card.

The eleventh commandment is: Don't fold, spindle or mutilate!

PUNCTUALITY

Women have a less accurate measure of time than men: there is a clock in Adam, none in Eve.
— *Emerson*

Punctuality is one of the cardinal business virtues: always insist on it in your subordinates.
— *Don Marquis*

The only good thing about punctuality is that it usually gets you an apology.

Punctuality is a virtue, if you don't mind being lonely.

Today's college student is more punctual than yesterday's—if he doesn't arrive at school early, he won't find a parking place.

The trouble with being punctual is that nobody's there to appreciate it.

Always being punctual has its drawback: people will think you never have anything to do.

Punctuality is the thief of time.

Another way to have a lot of leisure is always to be on time for appointments.

Punctuality is a virtue, especially if you want to avoid meeting people.

A woman on time is one in nine.

Installment buying is the only method known to get some people to do things on time.

Punctuality is the art of guessing how late the other fellow is going to be.

The man who is always on time wastes a lot of time waiting for other people.

Punctuality is a virtue, but only if it is combined with patience.

PUNCTUATION

All morning I worked on the proof of one of my poems, and I took out a comma; in the afternoon I put it back. — *Oscar Wilde*

Anyone who can improve a sentence of mine by the omission or placing of a comma is looked upon as my dearest friend.
— *George Moore*

I think of myself as a stylist, and stylists can become notoriously obsessed with the placing of a comma, the weight of a semicolon.
— *Truman Capote*

Many novelists use very little punctuation nowadays, probably because most of their characters stop at nothing.

It's all right to break your word if you use a hyphen.

At college you learn how to use punctuation marks, but not what to put between them.

Logic teaches that if an educated person knows how to use colons in writing, a semi-educated person must know how to use semi-colons.

The writer who gets paid by the word seldom uses hyphens.

The exclamation mark is being discarded because people aren't surprised at anything any more.

Stories about movie stars who get married should end with a comma.

PUNISHMENT

Many a man spanks his children for the things his own father should have spanked out of him.
— *Don Marquis*

Don't spare the rod, or you may some day find junior carrying one.

We punish children who aren't old enough to know right from wrong, but we don't punish parents who are.

The old-fashioned parent believes that stern discipline means exactly where it is applied.

An old-timer is one who remembers when the kid who got a licking at school, was in for another when he got home.

It is always permissible to spank a child if one has a definite end in view.

Spank your child every day; if you don't know the reason why, he does.

Life is an eternal childhood where experience starts to punish us even before our parents stop.

In the old days when a child misbehaved to get attention, he got it.

Never slap a child in the face: remember, there's a place for everything.

Nowadays it's dangerous to punish children—most of them are armed.

Some smart children should be praised, and others applauded—with one hand.

Another advantage spanking has over child psychology is that it makes the child smart.

A pat on the back develops character, but only if administered often enough, young enough, and low enough.

When a child throws a fit of bad temper, a sensible parent lets him catch it.

The Bible tells us the meek shall inherit the earth, but doesn't tell us what they've done to warrant such punishment.

To get the wild oats out of a boy, thrash him.

PUNNING

Hanging is too good for a man who makes puns; he should be drawn and quoted.   *— Fred Allen*

No one ever enjoys anybody else's puns, only his own.
— Louis Untermeyer

The inveterate punster follows conversation as a shark follows a ship.   *— Stephen Leacock*

A pun is a pistol discharged at the ear.   *— Charles Lamb*

The nation whose people go in for puns is on a high level of culture.   *— G. C. Lichtenberg*

Punning, like poetry, is something every person belittles and everyone attempts.
— Louis Untermeyer

The man who lacks the wit to pun, is sure to groan at every one.

A punster is a person whose sense of humor seldom makes sense.

One man's **pun** is another man's groan.

A pun is a short quip followed by a long groan.

To people below the norm of humor, the pun is the lowest form of humor.

The punster is a man who gets a kick out of hearing his friends groan.

The pun is mightier than the sword.

It takes two to put across a play on words: one to pun and one to groan.

A pun is something brief that always brings forth grief.

The irrepressible punster who always feels in good humor usually expresses it in poor wit.

Wits make puns, and half-wits groan at them.

PURE

To the pure all things are poor.
— Robert Frost

I am as pure as the driven slush.
— Tallulah Bankhead

Blessed are the pure for they shall inhibit the earth.

To the pure all things are impure.

PURIST

A purist sometimes drives slowly, but never fastly.

The person who corrects your grammar should be refuted with a hammer.

A purist is an educated person who has never learned whom to say whom to, and who who.

The purist who criticizes a mystery story probably objects because it's a who-dun-it instead of a who-did-it.

All purists are alike: they speak as if they were picking out their words with tweezers.

A purist never has any difficulty speaking English correctly, except when he mixes it with too much Scotch.

PURITAN

The puritan is one who uses the cross as a hammer to knock in the heads of sinners.   — *Mencken*

Every man has a touch of puritanism in him; in my case it takes the form of a dislike for smutty pictures.   — *Mencken*

Puritans like to wear the fig leaf over the mouth.   — *Aldous Huxley*

Puritanism: the haunting fear that someone, somewhere, may be happy.   — *Mencken*

The pagan of today is the puritan of tomorrow.

The Puritan's idea of religious liberty was to find some place where he could give his own intolerance a little more room.

To the puritan, all things are impure.

PUSH

I'm certainly not one of those who need to be prodded; in fact, if anything, I am the prod.
    — *Winston Churchill*

We all admire a pusher, provided he is pushing someone else.

You can't push yourself forward by patting yourself on the back.

The door to success is always marked *Push*.

The hardest thing about climbing the ladder of success is pushing your way through the crowd at the bottom.

All the world shoves a shover.

When you see a man pushing a baby carriage, it's a sign that there's trouble ahead of him.

A lazy person doesn't go through life—he's pushed through it.

PUSH AND PULL

Push will get you far, but pull will get you farther.

When you have the push, you don't have to have pull.

Push will get a person everywhere, except through a door marked *Pull*.

The man with pull is ahead at the start; the man with push, at the finish.

Push is more important than pull, especially if you are going through a revolving door.

QUARREL

I never take my own side in a quarrel.   — *Robert Frost*

There are two sides to the story when men quarrel, but at least a dozen when women quarrel.
— *Ed Howe*

Cut quarrels out of literature, and you will have very little history or drama or fiction or epic poetry left.   — *Robert Lynd*

People generally quarrel because they cannot argue.   — *Chesterton*

A domestic quarrel is a head-on collision where she loses her head and he blows his top.

Every married couple have a lot to contend with—they have each other.

It takes two to make a quarrel, and the same number to get married.

The worst thing about a domestic quarrel is that both husband and wife say what they think without thinking.

There are songs without words, but never quarrels without words.

During a family quarrel everyone talks and no one listens—except the neighbors.

In a quarrel when the wife hits the ceiling, she usually lands on her husband.

If it weren't for marriage, husbands and wives would have to quarrel with strangers.

A smart husband knows just the right thing to say when he quarrels with his wife, but a smarter husband doesn't say it.

If it weren't for marriage, there would be no quarrels between husbands and wives.

Language is sometimes used to conceal thought, but never in a domestic quarrel.

If marriage makes a husband and wife one, then it doesn't take two to make a quarrel.

In most domestic quarrels where there's nothing more to be said, both husband and wife keep on saying it.

When husband and wife quarrel, they make the mistake of thinking they couldn't have done any worse.

Many a husband takes all the joy out of a domestic quarrel by refusing to talk back.

The worst thing about a quarrel is that you always remember to bring up things you ought to forget.

When women aren't busy picking husbands, they are busy picking quarrels with them.

No man lives without quarreling with his wife, unless he is a bachelor.

In a domestic quarrel there's only one way to convince your wife, and that is to agree with her.

A word to the wife is sufficient —to start a quarrel.

A domestic quarrel often ends with the husband having his hands full—of flowers.

Two can live as cheaply as one, but not so peacefully.

People are always annoyed by quarreling neighbors, especially when they can't hear everything.

One of the few things left in married life that can still be made out of nothing is a quarrel.

In a domestic quarrel the wife may be the first to give in, but she is the last to give up.

The best way to avoid a domestic quarrel is to know the exact psychological moment when to say nothing.

QUESTION

How womanly it is to ask the unanswerable at the moment impossible. — *Christopher Morley*

I had six honest serving men who taught me all they knew; their names were Where and What and When, and Why and How and Who. — *Kipling*

No man really becomes a fool until he stops asking questions. — *Charles P. Steinmetz*

There are two sides to every question because when there are no longer two sides, it ceases to be a question. — *Herbert Samuel*

The wife who is forever asking her husband questions has to take a lot for grunted.

The question of the hour: what time is it?

The only ones who ask more embarrassing questions than children and wives are lawyers.

When you ask a chatterbox a question, it's like pulling your finger out of a dike.

A question may be queer, but the questioner is always the querist.

A man soon learns how little he knows when his child begins to ask questions.

QUESTION AND ANSWER

Judge a man by his questions rather than his answers. — *Voltaire*

By nature's kindly disposition most questions which it is beyond man's power to answer do not occur to him at all. — *Santayana*

No question is so difficult to answer as that to which the answer is obvious. — *Bernard Shaw*

It is better to ask some of the questions than to know all of the answers. — *James Thurber*

He must be very ignorant for he answers every question he is asked. — *Voltaire*

Why is it that a child usually asks questions that have no answers?

Just about the time you finally learn the answers, they change all the questions.

The classic alibi of the student who fails an exam is that the greatest fool can ask more questions than the wisest man can answer.

A politician's idea of an unfair question is one he cannot answer.

Adolescence is the period when children stop asking questions and begin to question the answers.

The more questions a woman asks, the fewer answers she remembers.

Some people are so smart, they even know the answers to rhetorical questions.

Four and sixteen are the most provocative ages: at four, you know all the questions; at sixteen, you know all the answers.

When a wife demands an explanation, a husband always has a choice of several wrong answers.

Many a man passes for wise because he asks questions which can't be answered even by himself.

Many a short question is evaded by a long answer.

It would take a father less time to answer his children's questions if he would simply admit he doesn't know.

Nothing is more flattering to a man than when a pretty girl asks the kind of questions he is able to answer.

Before marriage, he knows all the answers; after marriage, she knows all the questions.

Children who ask questions are sometimes as ignorant as adults who can't answer them.

QUEUE

People are judged by what they stand in line for.   — *Bill Vaughan*

An Englishman, even if he is alone, forms an orderly queue of one.   — *George Mikes*

Always try to put yourself in the other fellow's place, but not if you're queuing up for something.

There's nothing like a queue to keep a woman in line.

QUIET

The Antarctic is the most peaceful and quiet place on the face of the earth—no woman has set foot there.   — *Richard E. Byrd*

Very often the quiet fellow has said all he knows. — *Kin Hubbard*

A man will promise women and babies anything to keep them quiet.   — *Ed Howe*

An inability to stay quiet is one of the conspicuous failings of mankind.   — *Walter Bagehot*

Quiet people aren't the only ones who don't say much.

An old-timer is one who remembers when a quiet evening at home did not include television, dishwasher, stereo, washing machine, and garbage disposal.

Many a man who can't tell one note from another knows when to apply the soft pedal.

It's hard to keep a good man quiet about it.

Before marriage, she's glad when he tries to be the quiet, thoughtful type; after marriage, she thinks he's angry about something.

People quiet down as they grow older, probably because they have more to be quiet about.

QUIP

You've got to snap the quip to make Pegasus prance.
— *Robert Frost*

Clever men make quips, and clever columnists repeat them.

A quip is the quickest distance to the point.

The clever quips we might have made and didn't have saved us many a friend.

A word to the wise is sufficient, but not to the wisecracker.

When some men get off a clever quip, it's probably beginner's luck.

A proverb is practical wisdom; a quip, impractical wit.

A gagfile is the place where a good gag goes when it dies.

Everyone appreciates a clever remark, especially when it's his own.

QUIT

If at first you don't succeed, try, try again; then quit—there's no use being a damn fool about it.
— *W. C. Fields*

It's not hard to quit smoking; what is hard is to stay quit.

The trouble with many of us in trying times is that we quit trying.

Marriage is a poker game in which only the very wise quit at the right time.

The alcoholic is always going to quit after the next one instead of quitting after the last one.

Some people swear off gambling, while others stop entirely.

It takes a lot of will power, but many people finally succeed in giving up trying to give up smoking.

QUOTATION

You could compile the worst book in the world entirely out of selected passages from the best writers in the world. — *Chesterton*

Pretty things that are well said —it's nice to have them in your head. — *Robert Frost*

One learns little more about a man from the feats of his literary memory than from the feats of his alimentary canal.
— *Frank Moore Colby*

There are two kinds of marriages: where the husband quotes

the wife, and where the wife quotes the husband.
— *Clifford Odets*

I quote others in order the better to express my own self.
— *Montaigne*

I have made it a rule that whenever I say something stupid, I immediately attribute it to Dr. Johnson, Marcus Aurelius or Dorothy Parker. — *George Mikes*

Those who never quote, in return are never quoted.
— *Isaac D'Israeli*

If you look up a dictionary of quotations, you will find few reasons for a sensible man to desire to become wealthy. — *Robert Lynd*

If you want to be quoted, say something you shouldn't say.

Before marriage, they quote Shakespeare; after marriage, Junior.

Quotations also cover a multitude of sins.

You can always depend upon children to quote you correctly, especially when it's something you shouldn't have said.

RABBIT

Never serve a rabbit stew before you catch the rabbit.
— *James Thurber*

Many a man who is a wolf downtown is only a rabbit at home.

There's this to be said for the rabbit: he never tries to make somebody believe he is wearing a mink coat.

Two and two make four, but they make many more if you refer to two rabbits.

It takes at least twenty-five rabbits to make a sealskin coat for a woman.

There would be no population explosion if women wouldn't have children in rabbit succession.

RACE TRACK

If horses had a sense of humor, you would hear many a horse-laugh at the race track.

Another place where people never profit from their mistakes is the race track.

We arrive at the race track with faith and hope, and depart from it needing charity.

No matter what race course a gambler frequents, he is on the wrong track.

At the race track a man has his mind on money all the time, but his hands on it for a short time.

A race track always attracts people who have a special talent for backing the wrong horse.

The man who bets on a sure thing at the track should set aside enough money to get him back home.

The only person who is always sure to make money at the race track is the jockey.

The only two subjects of conversation at a race track are why you expect to win and how you happened to lose.

There are always less horses on the race track than asses in the stands.

The race track is another place where you never blame your ignorance when you lose, but always brag about your knowledge when you win.

The only sure way to pick a winner at the race track is not to bring any money with you.

The horse you put your money on usually runs away with it.

The race track is a place where the man who knows nothing about horses is always ready to back up his knowledge with money.

A race track is a place where the favorite horse wins only when you don't bet on him.

Men lose millions of dollars daily at the race track just to find out again that one horse can run faster than another.

The race track is another place where you can run your fortune into a shoestring.

You go to the race track in a state of happy expectation, and come from it in a state.

A race track is a place full of experts who can tell you which horse you should have backed after it has won.

Another place where a woman's intuition never seems to work is the race track.

RACKETEER

In every racket, the overhead is always less important than the underhand.

A racketeer sometimes goes away for a rest, but more often to avoid arrest.

RADICAL

I never dared be radical when young for fear it would make me conservative when old.
— *Robert Frost*

I am trying to do two things: dare to be a radical and not a fool, which is a matter of no small difficulty.
— *James A. Garfield*

Since it is now fashionable to laugh at the conservative French Academy, I have remained a rebel by joining it. — *Jean Cocteau*

Radicalism: the conservatism of tomorrow injected into the affairs of today. — *Bierce*

The trouble with radicals is that they are trying to make the world much better instead of trying to make it a little better.

A radical is one who thinks he votes right when he votes left.

RADIO

Too bad they invented radio when nobody had anything to say.
— Chesterton

Radio has succumbed to its first enemy: it has become static.
— Gilbert Seldes

After quitting radio I was able to live on the money I saved on aspirin.
— Fred Allen

A lot of modern music is improved by bad reception on radio.

Radio enables people who seldom have anything to say to talk to people who seldom listen.

Nowadays the voice crying in the wilderness is just a teenager with a pocket radio.

Radio static always seems to know just what program you prefer.

Every man has a right to his own opinion, but before radio came in he could bore only a few people at a time with it.

A transistor radio is a small, noisy plastic case with a teenager attached.

The radio is a wonderful gadget, and the most wonderful thing about it is the knob that turns it off.

Another advantage of radio over television is that it never shows old movies.

In the good old days radioactivity meant nothing worse than radio broadcasting.

Nowadays the still, small voice is more likely to be a pocket radio.

RAILROAD

A passenger train is like a male teat—neither useful nor ornamental.
— James J. Hill

Every railroad train has two ends, and the diner seems to be at the other one.

Another thing commuters miss when they move away from the city is the train.

RAILROAD CROSSING

The car always beats the train to the crossing—barring accidents.

Which are to be eliminated first —the grade crossings or all the people who don't stop, look and listen?

Another place where a motorist never makes the same mistake twice is a railroad crossing.

Don't race trains at crossings: if it's a tie, you lose.

You never know what you can do till you try, but don't experiment at a railroad crossing.

When approaching a railroad crossing, stop, look and listen— and you'll hear the car behind crashing into you.

Everybody makes a mistake now and then, but why pick out a railroad crossing for a background?

RAIN

Rain is good for vegetables, and for the animals who eat those vegetables, and for the animals who eat those animals.
— *Samuel Johnson*

It rained so hard that all the pigs got clean, and all the people dirty.   — *G. C. Lichtenberg*

It is best to read the weather forecasts before we pray for rain.
— *Mark Twain*

If I were running the world I would have it rain only between two and five A.M.—anyone who was out then ought to get wet.
— *William Lyon Phelps*

Rainy days come to those who save up for them.

Into each life some rain must fall, especially when you've left your umbrella at home.

Children prefer snow, but adults prefer rain because it is self-shoveling.

The surest way to bring spring showers is to hose the lawn and sprinkle the flowers.

About the only thing that seems to come down nowadays is the rain, and even that soaks you.

If it weren't for the sun, the rain would never be mist.

It rains on the just and unjust alike, but the unjust have the raincoats and rubbers.

Save up your money for a rainy day, and then stay home when it rains.

Into each life some rain must fall, but an optimist always expects a rainbow.

It never rains but it pours, especially on someone without an umbrella.

April showers bring May flowers —also headaches to mother from kids indoors for hours.

The rains that nourish the optimist's flowers make the pessimist's weeds grow.

The rainy days for which a man saves usually arrive during his vacation.

Primitive Indians used to do a snake dance when they wanted rain; civilized man just starts out on a picnic.

April showers bring May flowers, unless you're an amateur gardener.

Into each life some rain must fall, but seldom on the days when the weatherman forecasts it.

A rainy Sunday prevents many a nap in church.

RAISE

A gardener raises a few things, a farmer raises many things, and the middleman raises everything.

The easiest things to raise in a garden are weeds, and the hardest thing to raise is yourself.

Inflation is the period when less people raise food and more people raise food prices.

Nothing seems to make a woman's clothes go out of style faster than a raise in her husband's salary.

RARE

If you can speak what you will never hear, if you can write what you will never read, you have done rare things. — *Thoreau*

There is nothing so rare as a day in June, or a famous man who has not written a book.

There's a difference between the rare gift a woman receives before marriage, and the rare gift she receives afterwards.

Love at first sight is rare, and even rarer is love with insight.

The man who is not injured by flattery is as hard to find as the one who is improved by criticism.

Good authors are rare: they rarely make good husbands, rarely good fathers, and rarely good books.

June days may be rare, but they are seldom raw.

Things that are what they seem to be, are so rare that you cannot recognize them when you see them.

REACTION

I suspect my reflections, but respect my reflexes.
— *Yves Tanguy*

Every action has its reaction: a man's head turns when a woman's hips sway.

Life is an endless series of bounces, some as predictable as the rebound of a basketball, others as unpredictable as the rebound of a football.

A woman responds to a domestic crisis sometimes by having a good cry, sometimes by seeing a lawyer, but most often by rearranging the furniture.

Before marriage, he reacts to perfumes; after marriage, to cooking aromas.

There's no explaining human behavior: some people applaud at the movies, others nod at the telephone.

REACTIONARY

A reactionary is an elderly man who still retains the radical ideas of his youth.

The reactionary has an advantage over others: he always knows what his opinions will be tomorrow.

A reactionary always opposes anything new, and then claims there's nothing new under the sun.

Many a reactionary admires the great liberals of the past so much that he disapproves of the slightest change from their positions.

A die-hard is a reactionary who worships the ground his head is buried in.

A reactionary is like the man who sits in a train facing backward as he is carried forward.

Many a reactionary would rather be rightist than President.

A reactionary is a man who thinks that today's politics can operate tomorrow with yesterday's policies.

A reactionary is one whose opinions have been in his family for generations.

When offered a new idea, a reactionary will always turn it down before he turns it over.

A reactionary is one whose leanings to the right give him the wrong slant.

If the radicals of yesterday are the liberals of today and the conservatives of tomorrow, where do the reactionaries belong?

A reactionary is a man whose political opinions always manage to keep up with yesterday.

READING

Some people are as easy to read as the top line of an optometrist's chart. — *Budd Schulberg*

Lessing's confession that he had read too much for the health of his mind, shows how healthy his mind was. — *G. C. Lichtenberg*

There is a great deal of difference between an eager man who wants to read a book and the tired man who wants a book to read. — *Chesterton*

Reading is like permitting a man to talk a long time, and refusing you the right to answer.
— *Ed Howe*

If I had read as much as other men, I would have been as ignorant as they. — *Thomas Hobbes*

The ordinary man would rather read the life of the cruelest pirate that ever lived than of the wisest philosopher. — *Robert Lynd*

I would sooner read a timetable or a catalogue than nothing at all. — *Somerset Maugham*

If you read too fast or too slowly, you'll never understand anything. — *Pascal*

I have the reputation for having read all of Henry James, which would argue a misspent youth *and* middle age. — *James Thurber*

Those who don't read good books have no advantage over those who can't read them.

Every man is a volume if you know how to read him.

Reading maketh a full man, but the kind of reading determines whether he will be full of sense or nonsense.

Greater love hath no man than he who reads the books you insist upon lending him.

There are two common ways to avoid thinking: one is never to read, and the other is to do nothing but read.

At school we first learn to read, and we then read to learn.

The chief advantage of speed reading is that it enables you to figure out the cloverleaf signs in time.

The man who can read a woman like a book probably likes to read in bed.

He read so much about the dangers of smoking that he decided to give up reading.

READING AND WRITING

Foolish writers and readers are created for each other.
—*Horace Walpole*

When a man begins to write for money, he stops reading for pleasure. —*Lionel Strachey*

I never desire to converse with a man who has written more than he has read. —*Samuel Johnson*

The book that can be read without any trouble was probably written without any trouble also.
—*Oscar Wilde*

We read often with as much talent as we write. —*Emerson*

The hand of the writer should never be concerned with the eye of the reader. —*Jules Renard*

What is written without effort is read without pleasure.
—*Samuel Johnson*

Writing may make you eat your words, reading makes you eat another person's words.

How times change: the old-fashioned woman was ashamed to read the kind of books that modern women are now writing.

No books are as difficult to write as some books are to read.

If you cannot write things worth reading, you can at least read things worth writing.

Easy writing makes hard reading.

He can do two things at once: he can read writing.

Only one *i* is needed for reading, but two are needed for writing.

REAL ESTATE

The best part of a real estate bargain are the neighbors.

Another man who gets a little and gives a lot is the realtor.

A real estate agent is a man whose children learn division at school and subdivision at home.

Money isn't everything, but when buying real estate it can mean a lot.

REALISM

Realism is a corruption of reality. —*Wallace Stevens*

The man who learns to face reality soon realizes how well off he was before.

Everything is relative: the optimist thinks the realist is a pessimist, while the pessimist thinks the realist is an optimist.

A realist lets circumstances decide which end of the telescope to look through.

The realist tries to make a friend of his creditor, but never tries to make a creditor of his friend.

REASON

Man is a reasoning rather than a reasonable animal.
— *Alexander Hamilton*

We don't want a thing because we have found a reason for it; we find a reason for it because we want it. — *Will Durant*

Our prejudices are our mistresses; reason is at best our wife, very often heard but seldom minded. — *Chesterfield*

A man always has two reasons for doing something: a good reason, and the real reason.
— *J. P. Morgan*

Hear reason, or she'll make you feel her. — *Franklin*

He is no mean philosopher who can give a reason for one half of what he thinks. — *Hazlitt*

The heart has its reasons which reason does not understand.
— *Pascal*

If you follow reason far enough it always leads to conclusions that are contrary to reason.
— *Samuel Butler*

There is reason in all things, but not in all people.

Some men find dozens of reasons why they cannot do something when all they need is one reason why they can.

When a man brings his wife flowers for no reason—there's a reason.

A woman has three reasons for everything she does: the reason she says she has, the reason she thinks she has, and the reason she really has.

There's a difference between reasons that sound good and good sound reasons.

By the time children reach the age of reason, they have already driven their parents out of it.

Some men dislike women without any reason, while others like them that way.

When a man has no good reason for doing a thing, he has a good reason for letting it alone.

Some women will do almost anything for a reason, and the reason is money.

Even if your wife is willing to listen to reason, she doesn't like to hear the same one over and over again.

RECESSION

Economic recessions wouldn't be so bad if they didn't come when so many people were out of work.

A recession is when your neighbor loses his job, and a depression is when you lose yours.

During a period of bad business, it's bad business to talk about bad business.

A recession is when your in-laws have to move in with you, a depression is when you move in with them.

Economy doesn't always make sense: prosperity turns into recession when people stop buying things they cannot afford.

A recession is the period when you tighten your belt, while a depression is when you have no belt to tighten.

RECIPE

No woman ever lives long enough to try all the recipes she clips out of newspapers and magazines.

A girl has already baited the hook when she starts asking his mother for recipes.

Nature is wiser than human nature: there's a limit to the number of foods, but not to the number of recipes.

Some recipes are so fancy, they sound almost good enough to eat.

What makes the recipes look so appealing in the women's magazines is not the food but the photography.

When the bride gets a recipe from her mother, the groom should get a prescription from his doctor.

RECORD

The trouble with much modern music is that you can't tell when the record is worn out.

The politician who can't stand on his own record usually jumps on his opponent's.

A record that is never broken is the one the neighbors play after midnight.

Some people's records would not sound good on a phonograph.

Another cure for alcoholism is recording a drunk singing, and playing it back to him the next day.

A candidate is always willing to go on record, but not always on his record.

RED

When a man sees red, he's dangerous; when a woman sees red, she has to have one just like it.

Whether it's on the road or in an argument, when you see red, stop!

America has a long tradition of fighting Reds—redskins, redcoats, and Communists.

The man who goes out to paint the town red doesn't use water colors.

Color-blindness is rare among women: when a woman sees red, she sees red.

Red is a universal signal for *Stop,* except when you find it on a girl's lips.

REDUCING

The fastest way to reduce is to eat nothing and then walk it off.

Destiny shapes our ends, but a reducing diet also helps.

You can't win: every time a new reducing diet comes out, new and more tempting foods appear on the market.

Women spend their time in a reducing salon increasing expenses by reducing expanses.

A sure way to reduce is never to eat while your wife is talking.

The trouble with reducing is that your diet calls for less food while your appetite calls for more.

Walking will reduce your weight, jaywalking your years.

If you buy a book on weight reducing, you are sure to lose, if only the price of the book.

The easiest way to get rid of weight is leaving it lie untouched on the plate.

The diet that doesn't require dieting, and the exercise that doesn't require exercise are excellent for the reducer who doesn't like to reduce.

One of the best ways to reduce is to watch your step to the refrigerator.

The world is full of poor losers, especially those who are trying to reduce.

What this country needs more than another reducing diet for fat bodies is a reducing diet for fatheads.

A man always loses weight when his wife is dieting.

The best way to reduce is by the proper kind of exercise— the exercise of will power.

REFEREE

It is the referee in a prize fight who counts seconds when seconds count.

The mother who arranges a match for her daughter usually intends to referee it too.

REFORM

The church is always trying to get other people to reform; it might not be a bad idea to reform itself.   *— Mark Twain*

A man who reforms himself has contributed his full share towards the reformation of his neighbor.   *— Norman Douglas*

Most attempted reforms are only publicity for the evils they would reform.   *— Ed Howe*

I regret that before people can be reformed they have to be sinners.   *— Ogden Nash*

Every reform was once a private opinion.   *— Emerson*

It is essential to the triumph of reform that it shall never succeed.   *— Hazlitt*

Reformers decrease the world's contentment that they may better the world's condition.

— *Agnes Repplier*

If a man has a pain in his bowels, he forthwith sets about reforming the world. — *Thoreau*

After a woman has looked at a man three or four times, she notices something that should be changed. — *Ed Howe*

I own I never really warmed to the reformer or reformed.

— *Robert Frost*

The main dangers in this life are the people who want to change everything—or nothing.

— *Lady Astor*

The objection to reformers is that they spoil all the bad things of life.

Never marry a man to reform him: the rites never right him, and the altar won't alter him.

The motive behind all reformers is their joy in suppressing joy.

The world needs reformers because there is always the work of some former reformer to be undone.

Mothers make men, and wives mend them.

There's nothing more exclusive than a reform school: you can only get in through the recommendation of a judge.

What reformers don't butt into is nobody's business.

The two enemies of reform are the knaves who oppose it and the fools who favor it.

Reform in haste, and repent at leisure.

A wife will declare she got the best man living, and then will try to make a new man out of him.

Religion often gets credit for reforming sinners when old age is the real reason.

Many a man who is anxious to reform the world has a faucet that leaks.

If a woman had it to do over, she'd never marry a man she had to do over.

You never hear of a man marrying a woman to reform her.

We are all in favor of reform; what we dislike is being reformed by someone who is no better than we are.

Many a reformer would like to turn the world into a reformatory.

The world will never be as bad as reformers think it is, nor as good as they think it ought to be.

Marriage is an institution, but too many wives think it's a reform school.

Politicians never become reformers but reformers become politicians.

The woman who marries a man to reform him should remember that you cannot turn an old rake into a lawn mower.

Marriage is a partnership which a man forms, and his mother-in-law reforms.

Many a woman is determined to reform her husband even if she has to make herself a widow in the process.

REFUSAL

Take not the first refusal ill; though now she won't, anon she will.   — *Thomas D'Urfey*

He who refuses nothing will soon have nothing to refuse.
                  — *Martial*

He could refuse more gracefully than other people could grant.
                  — *Chesterfield*

Sometimes it's what a girl does that attracts a man, but more often it's what she won't do.

Where there's a won't, there's a way.

A favorite son sometimes declines, but more often declines to decline.

A smart girl knows how to refuse a kiss without being deprived of it.

When someone says, "I'll think it over and let you know," you already know.

REGRET

I have often regretted what I have eaten, but never what I have drunk.   — *Bismarck*

Remorse: regret that one waited so long to do it.   — *Mencken*

Regret is an appalling waste of energy; you can't build on it; it's only good for wallowing in.
                  — *Katherine Mansfield*

A man who regrets a love affair is a fool, a woman who regrets a love affair was a fool.

The bitterest remorse a married man feels is the extravagant fee he bestowed upon the minister in sentencing him.

It's better to have something to remember than nothing to regret.

You never know what you can do till you try, and then you're sorry you found out.

The follies which a man regrets most are those which he didn't commit when he had the opportunity.

Always put off till tomorrow what you might rue today.

Many a go-getter is afterward sorry he got her.

Even the man who thinks twice before he speaks is often sorry he said it.

If a man doesn't marry his first love, he is apt to regret it—also if he does.

RELATIVES

Every man sees in his relatives, and especially in his cousins, a series of grotesque caricatures of himself.   — *Mencken*

Before marriage, a girl complains of her kin to her lover, and after marriage he complains of them to her.   — Ed Howe

Don't criticize your wife's relatives; remember, you chose them.

Blood will tell: nobody criticizes your faults quicker than your relatives.

A close relative is one you see occasionally between family funerals.

If the knocking on the door goes on and on, it's not opportunity —it's relatives.

When it comes to trade relations, most of us would like to.

Some uncles have so much money you never see them at all.

Success is relative: the more success, the more relatives.

If at first you don't succeed, your relatives will tell one another just why you'll never succeed.

It's a wise child that resembles its rich relatives.

Always tell your rich relatives how fast you are making money, and your poor ones how fast you are losing it.

Some relatives are distant, some are close, but the wealthiest are usually both distant and close.

Never judge a man until you've spoken to his wife's relatives.

The best way to find relatives you've lost track of is to become very rich.

Neither a borrower nor a lender be: if you're a borrower, you'll have distant relatives; if you're a lender, you'll have close ones.

Blood will not always tell: it often refuses to speak to poor relations.

Even after a man loses his last friend he still has his relatives.

Progress isn't always improvement: the invention of the airplane did away with distant relatives.

In some marriages the problems are all relative.

Life is a balance sheet: you are probably disliked as much by your relatives as they are by you.

RELAXATION

The best time to relax is when you don't have time to relax.

Some men are not afraid of work: they'll lie down beside any job and relax peacefully.

Nowadays if you're too relaxed, you probably need an analyst.

How did people relax on holiday weekends before they had cars to kill one another with?

Many a man finds his office a good place to relax from his strenuous home life.

Another optimist is the doctor who tells the mother of six small children to relax.

RELIGION

Religion is becoming less and less a way to get to heaven, and more and more a way to get hell out of earth.
— *William Allen White*

All religions begin with a revolt against morality, and perish when morality conquers them.
— *Bernard Shaw*

Where it is a duty to worship the sun, it is pretty sure to be a crime to examine the laws of heat. — *John Morley*

Man is the only animal who's got the true religion—several of them. — *Mark Twain*

A churchman who never reads *The Freethinker* has no more real religion than the atheist who never reads the *Church Times*.
— *Bernard Shaw*

Religion has not civilized man, man has civilized religion.
— *Robert G. Ingersoll*

All religions must be tolerated, for every man must get to heaven in his own way.
— *Frederick the Great*

Some people think that all the equipment you need to discuss religion is a mouth.
— *Herman Wouk*

Erasmus laid the egg of the Reformation and Luther hatched it.
— *R. C. Trench*

A modernist married a fundamentalist wife, and she led him a catechism and dogma life.
— *Keith Preston*

There would never have been an infidel if there had never been a priest. — *Jefferson*

It is the test of a good religion whether you can joke about it.
— *Chesterton*

A religion that is small enough for our understanding would not be large enough for our needs.
— *Arthur Balfour*

God is for men, and religion for women. — *Joseph Conrad*

When a man says he can get on without religion, it merely means he has the kind of religion he can get on without.
— *Harry Emerson Fosdick*

Those who have loved God most have loved men least.
— *Robert G. Ingersoll*

Man's greatest blunder has been in trying to make peace with the skies instead of making peace with his neighbors. — *Elbert Hubbard*

My father was a God-fearing man, but he never missed a copy of the *New York Times* either.
— *E. B. White*

You can change your faith without changing gods, and vice versa. — *Stanislaw J. Lec*

Many have quarreled about religion that never practiced it.
— *Franklin*

Religion is tending to degenerate into a decent formula wherewith to embellish a comfortable life.
— *A. N. Whitehead*

Irreligion: the principal one of the great faiths of the world.
— *Bierce*

When the collection plate is being passed, some men are always ready to put in a good word for religion.

Some religions require to be wound up every seven days.

The only people who never quarrel about religion are the people who haven't any.

There would be more religion in business if there were less business in religion.

Too much perfume is in bad taste; even the odor of sanctity may be overdone.

Some people use their religion only on Sundays, others use it every time they can profit by it.

If you want to see man at his worst, observe what he does to his fellow men in the name of God.

A fundamentalist seems to know everything about religion, and nothing about anything else.

If some men were twice as religious as they seem to be, they wouldn't be half as religious as they ought to be.

The man who doesn't go to any church probably had a baptism that didn't take.

REMARRIAGE

Marriage is a very good thing, but it's a mistake to make a habit of it.   — *Somerset Maugham*

Marriage is hardly a thing one can do now and then, except in America.   — *Oscar Wilde*

Some men profit by their mistakes, others get married a second time.

A man can save himself a lot of trouble by marrying his second wife first.

Marriage is a lottery, and some people aren't satisfied with their luck until they've tried it several times.

The man who marries the second time doesn't deserve to lose his first wife.

Some girls never know just what they are going to do from one husband to another.

When a man marries again, he takes a new leash on life.

Today marriage is no longer a handicap—it's more likely to be a relay race.

The woman who is disappointed in her first marriage is usually disillusioned in her second.

A woman rarely misses her first husband until after she marries her second.

When a brilliant woman marries a dumb man it's probably because her first husband was a genius.

Nowadays when a man marries, the girl merely borrows his name for a while.

A movie colony is where, if a man's wife looks like a new woman, she probably is.

A woman gets over her first husband's death, but her second husband doesn't.

Marry in haste, and repeat at leisure.

The lifelong trips on the sea of matrimony are nowadays being replaced by short cruises.

REMEMBER

It isn't so astonishing, the number of things I can remember, as the number of things I can remember that aren't so.
— *Mark Twain*

I always have trouble remembering three things: faces, names, and—I can't remember what the third thing is.   — *Fred Allen*

A woman will always cherish the memory of the man who wanted to marry her; a man, the woman who didn't.

Remember the poor—it costs nothing.

It's more tactful for a man to say he knew her when she was a little girl than when he was a little boy.

The best way to be remembered by people is to owe them money.

Remember that your wife still enjoys candy and flowers; let her know that you remember by speaking of them occasionally.

The best thing that can be said for some people is that they remind us of others who are worse.

REMEMBER AND FORGET

A friend who at a pinch cannot remember a thing or two that never happened is just as bad as one who does not know how to forget.   — *Samuel Butler*

She was made to be an ambassador's wife: she has a wonderful faculty of remembering people's names and forgetting their faces.   — *Oscar Wilde*

The surest way to remember something is to try and forget it.

When a man forgets himself, he usually does something everyone else remembers.

A woman should never blame her husband for forgetting his mistakes: there's no need for both of them to remember the same things.

What you do for a woman she will forget, but what you fail to do she will always remember.

If you want to remember, tie a string around your finger; if you want to forget, tie a rope around your neck.

The older you grow, more things are harder to forget, and less things are easier to remember.

Woman is a paradox: she always wants some worthwhile remembrance to forget a man by.

A bachelor is plagued by two classes of women: those who can't forget him, and those who can't remember him.

Forgetfulness is a virtue only when you can remember the right things to forget.

A happy marriage is one where the man knows what to remember, and the woman knows what to forget.

REMINISCENCE

After a woman has had seven children, reminiscences of her past begin to sound like statistics.
    — Ed Howe

An old man's idea of a bright and intelligent woman is one who enjoys hearing reminiscences.
    — Ed Howe

It takes more than a good memory to have good memories.

Old age is the period when our memories grow shorter and our reminiscences grow longer.

The older you grow, the faster you could run as a boy.

RENT

A modern apartment house is one where the landlord and the tenant are both trying to raise the rent.

Nowadays many a family finds itself occupying a more expensive apartment without even having moved.

When a woman enjoys living in a fool's paradise, there's probably some man paying the rent.

REPAIR

For fixing things around the house, nothing beats a man who is handy with a checkbook.

Many a man who saves up for a rainy day is frustrated to find he has to put a new roof on his house.

A husband may be able to fix anything a handy man can, but the handy man does it now.

A do-it-yourselfer is always repairing things around the house to the best of his inability.

A household appliance may pay for itself, but you have to pay the repairman.

Many things that cost a few dollars a decade ago now cost twice as much just to have them fixed.

A do-it-yourselfer starts by making things, and ends by making repairs.

If you have a husband who is absolutely useless around the house, the chances are everything in it works.

A repairman usually fidgets with his gadgets while time fugits.

Give a do-it-yourselfer the proper tools, and in a few minutes a leaky faucet will turn into a running stream.

A man never knows what he can do until he tries to undo what he did.

Spring is the time of year when a good neighbor returns the lawnmower he borrowed so its owner can have it fixed.

When a repairman is unhappy, it's probably one of those days when nothing seems to go wrong.

REPARTEE

Repartee is a dual fought with the points of jokes.
— *Max Eastman*

Repartee is the brilliant remark the other fellow makes just before you think of it.

Repartee is a quick and witty retort that saves many a friendship, but only when it isn't made.

The clever retort you make becomes even more clever when you tell about it afterward.

Repartee is the art of saying what you think—and getting out of range before it is understood.

A good retort always puts the other person in a bad humor.

Repartee is a cutting remark made by a sharp tongue to slit someone's throat.

A clever person thinks of a witty retort in time to say it, but a cleverer person thinks of it in time not to say it.

Repartee is the art of insulting a person in public but making it sound like brilliant wit.

The secret of repartee is repertory.

Repartee is the art of making a point glitter while making a person bitter.

REPEAT

Repeating a mistake is sometimes excusable, but repeating the repetition never is.

You can always tell an eight-year-old, but you have to tell him twice.

Recipe for perpetual trouble: Believe all you hear and repeat it.

The difference between opportunity and importunity is that opportunity doesn't repeat.

Sometimes it's what a woman says that hurts, but more often it's the number of times she repeats it.

Out of the mouths of babes come words we adults should never have said.

History doesn't repeat itself as often as gossip does.

Women and telephones repeat what they hear, but the telephone repeats it exactly.

Death and taxes are equally inevitable, but death is not a repeater.

A fool is always taking the same courses over again in the school of experience.

A politician sometimes keeps a promise, but more often just keeps repeating it.

Another nice thing about babies is that they never go around repeating the smart things their parents say.

You can't believe everything you hear, but you can repeat it.

The man who doesn't make the same mistake twice probably repeats it more often.

Many a man wouldn't mind his wife having the last word if she didn't go on repeating it.

REPENTANCE

If a man's done something in his youth that he has to do penance for, let him marry.
— *Finley Peter Dunne*

To many people virtue is mainly a matter of repenting sins rather than avoiding them.
— *G. C. Lichtenberg*

It is much easier to repent of sins that we have committed than to repent of those we intend to commit. — *Josh Billings*

Repentance proves that only a good person can have a bad conscience.

You can't win: you'll repent if you marry, and you'll repent if you don't.

If you put off repentance till tomorrow, you have a day more to repent of and a day less to repent in.

Repentance is imagining heaven but feeling hell.

REPORTER

I believe in equality for everyone, except reporters and photographers. — *Gandhi*

The function of a good reporter is not to cover a story, but to uncover it.
— *Herbert Bayard Swope*

Journalists always apologize to one in private for what they have written against one in public.
— *Oscar Wilde*

Reporters' wives never believe what they read.

Another thing that covers a multitude of sins is a reporter.

REPUTATION

What people say behind your back is your standing in the community. — *Ed Howe*

A doctor's reputation is made by the number of eminent men who die under his care. — *Bernard Shaw*

When a person loses his reputation, the last place he looks for it is where he lost it.

Many a movie star doesn't get a reputation till she's lost one.

A man is known by the company he thinks nobody knows he keeps.

Any blow struck in defense of a woman's reputation is apt to leave a dent in it.

A man has as many reputations as he has friends.

You can patch overalls or a reputation, but it's hard to keep it from showing.

A man's reputation is the composite of what his friends, enemies and relatives think of him.

After a man once loses his reputation, it is very hard for him to lose it again.

A man is known by the company he shakes.

No man can understand why a woman should prefer a good reputation to a good time.

You cannot run up your own reputation by constantly running down other people's.

Many a has-been lives on the reputation of his reputation.

A man's reputation depends largely upon what the public hasn't found out about him.

RESEARCH

Research is to see what everybody else has seen, and to think what nobody else has thought.
– Albert Szent-Györgyi

Research is an organized method of keeping you reasonably dissatisfied with what you have.
– Charles F. Kettering

Basic research is what a scientist is doing when he doesn't know what he is doing.

RESIGNATION

It seems that nothing ever gets to going good till there's a few resignations.   *– Kin Hubbard*

Once in a while a government official resigns for the reason given in his letter of resignation.

The minister who preaches on the subject of resignation should practice what he preaches.

A cynic is the kind of man who would resign from the human race if he knew where to send his resignation.

RESISTANCE

Girls who offer no resistance lead a very nice existence.

The line of least resistance is usually the one we sign on.

The woman who has everything should be given a course in sales resistance.

The only thing harder to resist than a woman's wiles are her wails.

If you can't resist temptation, live in a small town: there everyone will help you resist it.

It's surprising how much hard work some men will put in resisting hard work.

Even if kisses don't spread viruses, they certainly lower a girl's resistance.

RESOLUTION

It is always during a passing state of mind that we make lasting resolutions.
— *Proust*

Good resolutions are simply checks that men draw on a bank where they have no account.
— *Oscar Wilde*

A good resolution for most people would be to swear off breaking them.

The only sure way to keep your New Year's resolutions is to keep them in a safe-deposit box.

If the good die young, what's the use of making New Year's resolutions?

Some resolutions are like some girls: easy to make but hard to keep.

The best way to keep a New Year's resolution is—to yourself.

A few days after New Year's is when most people find out that it's easier to break a resolution than a habit.

A man and his resolution are soon parted.

Don't worry too much if you've broken your New Year's resolution: you can always remake it next year.

Most New Year's resolutions go in one year and out the other.

A good resolution is always stronger at its birth than at any subsequent period.

Many a man who thinks it's silly to make New Year's resolutions resolves not to make any.

RESORT

There are two kinds of resorts vacationers should try to avoid: those that are deserted, and those that are crowded.

Men stay at a summer resort till their money runs out; women, till their clothes run out.

It's odd that most winter resorts are situated in places where it's always summer.

A resort is a place full of girls looking for husbands, and husbands looking for girls.

Never judge a resort by its postcards.

An ideal summer resort is one where fish bite and mosquitoes don't.

Another person who makes a mountain out of a molehill is the advertising copy writer for a summer resort.

In most winter resorts you will find the staff very friendly: they welcome you with open palms.

RESPECT

There was no respect for youth when I was young, and now I am old, there is no respect for age— I missed it coming and going.
— *J. B. Priestley*

One of the surprising things of this world is the respect a worthless man has for himself.
— *Ed Howe*

I have always thought respectable people scoundrels, and I look anxiously at my face every morning for signs of my becoming a scoundrel. — *Bertrand Russell*

A man of self-respect is one who still believes that nobody suspects him. — *Mencken*

No place in England where everyone can go is considered respectable. — *George Moore*

If fortune wishes to make a man respectable, she gives him virtues; if she wishes to make him respected, she gives him success.
— *Joubert*

All biological necessities have to be made respectable whether we like it or not. — *Bernard Shaw*

I don't know what a scoundrel is like, but I know what a respectable man is like, and it's enough to make one's flesh creep.
— *J. M. deMaistre*

If you stick to any opinion long enough, it becomes respectable. — *Bertrand Russell*

The man who doesn't treat women with courtesy and respect either doesn't know enough or knows too many.

Many a man thinks it's his chest measurements people respect when it's only his intellect.

No woman commands her husband's respect if she always makes him respect her commands.

Many a bearded artist's chief ability lies in showing his disrespect for respectability.

RESPONSIBILITY

You are not in charge of the universe: you are in charge of yourself. — *Arnold Bennett*

Some men always recognize their duty in sufficient time to side-step it.

The man who shirks responsibility to avoid making a mistake is making a bigger mistake.

It is the irresponsible adolescent who is responsible for much of the trouble nowadays.

It's the little things that count: many a safety pin carries more responsibility than a bank president.

Man thinks woman is irresponsible, yet holds her responsible for all his misfortunes since Adam and Eve.

Some men who hold highly responsible positions are responsible for more than you think.

The man who has his head in the clouds instead of his feet on the ground should carry more responsibility on his shoulders.

A woman of forty is responsible for her figure, a woman of fifty for her face.

Every husband soon learns not to hold his wife responsible today for what she said yesterday.

If you could kick the person responsible for most of your troubles, you wouldn't be able to sit down for months.

Some people grow under responsibility, while others merely swell.

REST

Rest is a good thing, but boredom is its brother. — *Voltaire*

Who remembers when we used to rest on Sunday instead of Monday? — *Kin Hubbard*

I shall need to sleep three weeks on end to get rested from the rest I've had. — *Thomas Mann*

Eternal rest sounds comforting in the pulpit; well, you try it once, and see how heavy time will hang on your hands.
— *Mark Twain*

Many a man rests up less on his own vacation than on that of his boss.

The man who sends his wife away for a rest certainly needs it.

Another sign of middle age is when, after painting the town red, you have to rest a week before applying the second coat.

Half a loaf is better than no loafing at all.

A vacation sometimes begins with your needing a rest, but more often ends that way.

In the old days when it was said that a man had gone to his everlasting rest, it didn't mean that he had secured a government job.

RESTAURANT

The man who opened the first restaurant must have been a person of extraordinary genius.
— *Brillat-Savarin*

Every wife ought to know her husband's favorite dish—and which restaurant serves it.

Some restaurants are so expensive that you have to find a pearl in an oyster in order to break even.

The way of a maid with a man usually leads to an expensive restaurant.

The nicest thing about eating in a dive is that you are never bored by the stuffed shirts who wouldn't be caught dead in them.

Hope springs eternal in the human breast—that's why a new restaurant is crowded.

The man who doesn't know which side his bread is buttered on probably eats at a drugstore lunch counter.

RESTRAINT

When half the men become fond of doing a thing, the other half prohibit it by law.
— *Ed Howe*

The girl who makes sure she's nobody's fool will probably be nobody's darling either.

Behind every successful man is a woman constantly telling him. what not to do and say.

RESULT

It has been my observation and experience, and that of my family, that nothing human works out well.   — *Don Marquis*

Results are what you expect, and consequences are what you get.

Perseverance is the result of a strong will, stubbornness is the result of a strong won't.

RETIREMENT

The worst of work nowadays is what happens to people when they cease work.   — *Chesterton*

Retirement is the time when you never do all the things you intended to do when you'd have the time.

When a professional golfer retires, what does he retire to?

The chief problem when you retire is how to spend a lot of time without spending a lot of money.

Retirement is the period in life when you stop quoting the proverb that time is money.

Two things are essential for a happy retirement: much to live on, and much to live for.

During retirement, many a man works harder at loafing than he used to loaf at working.

Retirement is the time in life when you have the time, but not the time of your life.

Look before you leap: before deciding to retire, stay home for a week and watch the daytime television shows.

The people hardest to convince that they should retire are children at bedtime.

Retirement is the time in life when you stop lying about your age and start lying about the house.

A good time to retire is before it's too late to have a good time.

Many a man in retirement hasn't a single thing to do but sit and look for trouble.

Retirement is the period when the rest of your days depend largely on the rest of your nights.

Retirement is a field of clover, but by the time you reach it, you're too old to climb the fence.

The man who looks forward to retirement when he can go fishing seven times a week, soon finds himself doing the dishes three times a day.

Another disadvantage of retirement is that you drink coffee on your own time.

Retirement is the period when a man who can now do anything he wishes wishes he could do something else.

If time is money, retired people should have a good deal more money than they know what to do with.

Retirement is the time in life when there is nothing so difficult as doing nothing.

Many a man has solved the problem of what to do during his retirement: he just sits around and criticizes the government.

Retirement is the time in life when a woman has twice as much husband on half as much income.

There's no such thing as equality between the sexes—whoever heard of a housewife retiring?

Life would be wonderful if a man could retire without telling his wife.

Retirement is the period when you exchange the bills in your wallet for snapshots of your grandchildren.

When does the man with a lifetime job retire?

Everyone would be able to retire in comfort if he could sell his experience for what it cost him.

Retirement is the period when you wake up in the morning with nothing to do, and go to bed at night with it still to be done.

RETRIBUTION

The man who asks a woman what she wants deserves all that's coming to him.   — Alec Waugh

In this world a man gets all he can, in the next world he gets all he deserves.

Sooner or later every brat gets what's coming to him: he grows up and becomes a parent too.

This would be a happier world if more of us got what we wanted and fewer of us got what we deserved.

RETURN

A woman doesn't spend all her time in buying things: she spends part of it in taking them back.
                    — Ed Howe

When going from bad to worse, provide yourself with a return ticket.

The best thing about being married is that you always have your wife to come home to after that blonde stands you up.

The man who lets himself go should remember to come back.

September is the month when the children go back to school, and their mothers go back to bed.

The public gets the returns on election night, the politicians get the returns the rest of the year.

Most of the time it is quite a relief to get back to where you were so glad to get away from.

Of all kindnesses, that of lending books is the one that meets with the least return.

REUNION

Class reunions are full of people who graduated from colleges they couldn't get into today.

There's no one so disconcerting at a class reunion as your old-time classmate with both money and hair.

The hardest promise to keep is the one you make at a family reunion to write oftener.

Many a man finally gets to a class reunion only to find his classmates so bald and fat that they don't recognize him.

Why is it that at a class reunion everyone your age turns out to be a lot older than you are?

REVEAL

Nothing reveals a man's character so much as the joke he takes offense at.   — G. C. Lichtenberg

In important matters, we expose our best sides; in trivial matters, we disclose ourselves as we really are.   — Chamfort

An X-ray reveals a lot about a man, but an ex-wife can reveal much more.

The seer tells fortunes, the lover tells lies, and a woman tells everything.

You can never tell about a woman, and if you can you shouldn't.

The man who tells his wife everything knows nothing.

REVENGE

The best way of revenging yourself on a man who has stolen your wife is to leave her to him.
                    — Sacha Guitry

It's far easier to forgive an enemy after you've got even with him.   — Olin Miller

Beware of the man who does not return your blow: he neither forgives you nor allows you to forgive yourself. — Bernard Shaw

Revenge does more for the legal profession than any other human emotion.

The longest odds in the world are those against getting even.

Every man has moments of vindictiveness when he wishes he were a truck driver.

Time spent in getting even is better used in getting ahead.

Revenge is like biting a dog because the dog has bit you.

People who want to get even with others are usually at odds with themselves.

Revenge is the only debt which it is wrong to pay.

Revenge is sweet—to the sour.

When you get even with people it always leaves them with the impression that they owe you something.

Some people do odd things to get even.

REVERSE

A poet's life is filled with verses and reverses.

Turnabout is fair play, except for the man who's been through a hurricane.

For success, keep your eyes open and your mouth shut; for eating grapefruit, reverse the process.

No husband has ever understood why his wife should want to buy a new hat when she can wear the old one backward.

REVISION

I can't write five words but that I change seven. – *Dorothy Parker*

The secret of good writing is to go through your stuff until you come on something particularly good—and then cut it out.
– *P. G. Wodehouse*

No writer puts the last touches to his work until he burns it.
– *G. C. Lichtenberg*

REVOLUTION

We have a lot of people revolutionizing the world because they've never had to present a working model.
– *Charles F. Kettering*

Revolutions are not made by men in spectacles.
– *Justice O. W. Holmes*

Revolutionary movements attract those who are not good enough for established institutions as well as those who are too good for them. – *Bernard Shaw*

I am for the restoration of order, but not for the restoration of the old order. – *Mirabeau*

Rebels are those unlucky persons who, when things have come to violence, have the misfortune to be of the weaker party.
– *Adam Smith*

You can never convince a revolutionist that a new upset may be even worse than the old setup.

REVOLVING DOOR

I don't know anything as willing and that seems to enjoy its work as a revolving door.
– *Kin Hubbard*

The way some people push others around, you'd think they came from a long line of revolving doors.

If it were not for revolving doors, there would be fewer married men going around with strange women.

A confidence man is one who goes into a revolving door behind you and comes out ahead.

REWARD

There's often a reward for finding something, but never for finding fault.

Human beings will never work as hard for money as for more money.

RHYME

Modern poets are bells of lead: they should tinkle melodiously, but usually they just klunk.
— *Lord Dunsany*

Inferior poets are absolutely fascinating: the worse their rhymes, the more picturesque they look. — *Oscar Wilde*

A little before my sixteenth year I first committed the sin of rhyme. — *Robert Burns*

RICH

I am indeed rich since my income is superior to my expense, and my expense is equal to my wishes. — *Edward Gibbon*

The greatest luxury of riches is that they enable you to escape so much good advice.
— *Arthur Helps*

The only thing I like about rich people is their money.
— *Lady Astor*

There is no get-rich-quick scheme equal to a poor girl marrying a rich man. — *Ed Howe*

It is not what we take up but what we give up that makes us rich. — *Henry Ward Beecher*

God must love the rich or he wouldn't divide so much among so few of them. — *Mencken*

There are two types among the rich: the haves and the have-mores.

Some people are so rich, they have no neighbors.

If a fool and his money are soon parted, why are there so many rich fools?

Keeping on your toes and being well heeled usually go together.

When riches come in at the door, love flies around and bars all the exits.

It is harder for a rich man to enter heaven—or jail.

Another advantage of being rich is that all your faults are called eccentricities.

There are only two ways to be rich: have much, or be content with little.

Some people may have their first dollar, but the man who is really rich is the one who still has his first friend.

Many an optimist has become rich simply by buying out a pessimist.

Rich are those who have many friends—they have to be.

RICH AND POOR

The leaders of the French Revolution excited the poor against the rich; this made the rich poor, but it never made the poor rich.
— *Fisher Ames*

The best condition in life is not to be so rich as to be envied, nor so poor as to be damned.
— *Josh Billings*

Extravagance is the luxury of the poor, penury the luxury of the rich. — *Oscar Wilde*

I've been rich and I've been poor; rich is better.
— *Sophie Tucker*

Two classes of people worry about money: those who have too little and those who have too much.

The poor have more children, but the rich have more relatives.

The man who goes through a fortune in a few years will find it difficult to go through his poverty that fast.

The poor we have always with us because the rich go away for the summer and winter.

It's hard to be poor, but much easier than to be rich.

The rich are always giving advice to the poor, but the poor seldom return the favor.

What troubles the poor is the money they can't get, and what troubles the rich is the money they can't keep.

There's no one so unhappy as the poor man who has nothing, except the rich man who has nothing to do.

If it were not for the fools in this world the poor would never get rich.

Money talks, and poverty also has a way of telling.

It's about as hard for a rich man to enter heaven as it is for a poor man to remain on earth.

God help the rich—the poor can sleep on the park benches.

The poor have to work so hard to make a living, they don't have time to get rich.

Not enough people like to help the poor, while too many people like to help the rich.

The trouble with the very rich is that they live without working, and the trouble with the very poor is that they work without living.

There are two classes of people: the have-nots and the have-yachts.

A rich husband is always a rich man, but a rich man is often a poor husband.

The rich man employs a secretary, a butler, a valet, a cook, a laundress and a housekeeper; the poor man just gets a wife.

People know you when you become rich, but you know them when you become poor.

If everybody were rich, the world would be poorer.

More of the poor would not feel want if more of the rich did not want feeling.

The rich man has the better food, but the poor man has the better appetite.

RID

A never-failing way to get rid of a fellow is to tell him something for his own good.
— *Kin Hubbard*

There are ninety-nine ways of getting rid of a bore, and every single one of them is right.

RIDDLE

The riddles of God are more satisfying than the solutions of man.   — *Chesterton*

It's a wise parent who never knows the answers to his child's riddles.

RIGHT

There is no mistake so great as that of being always right.
— *Samuel Butler*

Doing right doesn't come as hard as getting credit for it.
— *Ed Howe*

The greatest lesson in life is to know that even fools are right sometimes.   — *Winston Churchill*

It's an odd thing that though we all disagree with each other, we are all of us in the right.
— *Logan P. Smith*

I can think of no blissfuller state than being treated as if I was always right.   — *Robert Frost*

To do the right thing is not always the right thing to do.

Some people always say the right thing at the right time; others are bores too.

Success in marriage is much more than finding the right person; it is a matter of being the right person.

The world's shortest sermon is preached by the traffic sign: *Keep Right.*

No one has a right to all his rights.

It takes two to make a quarrel —two people who are both right.

It's an advantage to be right in politics, but an even greater advantage to be in right.

The pedestrian who has the right of way gets little satisfaction out of being dead right.

By the time a man learns to stand up for his rights his arches have caved in.

There would be fewer arguments if more of us tried to determine what's right instead of who's right.

The man who would rather be right than President is probably neither.

Another trouble with marriage is that it allows you to claim as a right what formerly you asked as a favor.

The man who is always right and knows it is always unpopular and doesn't know it.

When a politician does what he thinks is right, it's probably because he can't get out of it.

It's not enough to say the right thing at the right time; it must be said to the right people.

A good motto for married men is: be sure you're right, and then ask your wife.

RIGHT AND WRONG

The more uncivilized the man, the surer he is that he knows what is right and what is wrong.
— *Mencken*

I do not greatly care whether I have been right or wrong on any point, but I care a good deal about knowing which I have been.
— *Samuel Butler*

Whenever you're wrong, admit it; whenever you're right, shut up.
— *Ogden Nash*

There is nothing more certain than that age and youth are right, except perhaps that both are wrong. — *Robert Louis Stevenson*

A man may be intellectually right though being morally wrong.
— *Chesterton*

If some people got their rights, they would complain of being deprived of their wrongs.
— *Oliver Herford*

He who says nothing, says nothing wrong; he who does nothing, does nothing right.

Why does the person who doesn't know right from wrong always do wrong?

If you're willing to admit you're all wrong when you are, you're all right.

When you set out to right some people's wrongs, first make sure you don't wrong other people's rights.

If a man is right, he cannot be too radical; if wrong, he cannot be too conservative.

A man expects an apology when you're in the wrong; a woman expects one when you're in the right.

Many a man confuses his right to be wrong with his right to be a wrongdoer.

Nothing wrong ever happens at the right time.

Two wrongs don't make a right, and two rights don't make a pair.

There is something always wrong with the man who is always right.

When you're right, no one remembers; when you're wrong, no one forgets.

Half the world spends its time to set right what the other half has done wrong.

If you're in the right, argue like a man; if you're in the wrong, argue like a woman.

Even when a politician does the right thing, he probably does it for the wrong reason.

The easiest way to get into trouble is to be right at the wrong time.

Nothing is ever all wrong: even a watch that won't run is right twice a day.

You can't win: if you do something wrong, the government fines you; if you do something right, the government taxes you.

A lot more people would try to do right if they thought it was wrong.

Two wrongs don't make a right, but they often make a riot.

Many a man would rather be right than President, and many a woman would rather be wrong than reasonable.

Never confuse right and left in politics with right and wrong in life.

RIGHTEOUS

There are two classes of people: the righteous and the unrighteous; the classifying is done by the righteous.

Some men spend so much time hunting after righteousness, they haven't any time to practice it.

The man who pretends to be clothed in righteousness is always a misfit.

RING

The longer a wedding ring is worn, the harder it is to remove.

When a young man gives his girl a ring, he gives it with all his heart and most of his savings.

Every girl wants a ring on her finger, but not a thimble at the end of it.

An engagement ring is a symbol that a woman will eventually twist a man around her next-to-little finger.

The three-ring circus of matrimony: engagement ring, wedding ring, and teething ring.

The best way for a woman to preserve her wedding ring is to dip it in dishwater three times a day.

The advantage of giving your girl the engagement ring grandmother wore is that grandfather has probably completed the payments on it.

A girl uses soft soap to get a ring off her finger—and also to get one on.

To the bachelor, a wedding ring symbolizes a vicious circle.

An engagement ring is a piece of jewelry that usually turns a right-handed girl into a left-handed one.

A ring on the finger is worth two on the phone.

Some girls get rings with large diamonds, others get rings that look as if they were all paid for.

A wedding ring may not be as tight as a tourniquet, but it stops the wearer's circulation.

The bright sparkle of a diamond ring often renders a woman stone-blind to the defects of the man who gives it.

During courtship a girl is unpredictable until she gets an engagement ring—then she shows her hand.

Opportunity knocks for every man, but a woman gets a ring.

A wedding ring is a circle around a woman's finger, but a noose around a man's neck.

RISK

A man sits as many risks as he runs.   *— Thoreau*

Don't be afraid to take a big step if one is indicated; you can't cross a chasm in two small jumps.
— Lloyd George

I've run less risk driving my way across the country than eating my way across it.
— Duncan Hines

The man who never stubs his toe is probably standing still.

Don't hesitate to go out on a limb sometimes—after all, that's where the fruit is.

There are lots of ways to become a failure, but never taking a chance is the most successful.

Nothing is ever gained without risk: you can't steal second base and still keep one foot on first.

Take a chance! Even a turtle gets nowhere until he sticks his neck out.

ROAD

Our national flower is the concrete cloverleaf. *— Lewis Mumford*

Detour: something that lengthens your mileage, diminishes your gas, and strengthens your vocabulary.   *— Oliver Herford*

The pioneers who blazed the trails now have descendants who burn up the roads.

A highway is a road where a lot of cars are moving rapidly until your car joins them.

If we cannot leave footprints on the sands of time, the least we can do for posterity is to leave good roads.

Our highway system has been making steady progress: we can now drive virtually everywhere and see practically nothing.

A highway is a main road surfaced with concrete and cars.

You can always tell when you are on the right road—it's upgrade.

Life is a highway full of cloverleaf intersections with no road signs pointing out where they lead to.

The old narrow roads where the cars could barely pass are being replaced by wonderful new highways where eight cars can collide at one time.

The superhighways have made driving easier, but they do take their toll.

The three most famous highways are the primrose path, the straight and narrow, and the road to ruin.

A highway is full of careless motorists who are always driving too close ahead of you.

ROAD HOG

A road hog is entitled to half the road, and he always takes it right out of the middle.

A car brings out the beast in some men, usually the road hog.

Mix tin and copper and you have bronze, mix tin and brass and you have a road hog.

Another person with a one-track mind is the road hog.

A road hog should be put in the pen like other hogs.

A road hog is a motorist who thinks he owns the highway simply because his taxes helped pay for it.

ROMANCE

To a romantic girl, all roads lead to Romeo.

Many a man who makes hay while the sun shines would prefer to make love while the moon shines.

No man is a romantic hero to a widow.

The right person at the right place makes moonlight and music unnecessary.

Every romantic young man is bound to love beyond his means.

Many a girl spoils a perfectly good romance by falling in love with the man.

A romantic girl is always dreaming of being swept off her feet by a strong man she has eating out of her hand.

The paths of romance lead but to the cradle.

The biggest deterrent to a budding romance is the blooming expense.

A summer romance usually comes to an end by fall—or marriage.

Many a romance begins when you find the girl of your dreams, and ends when you wake up.

Every romantic girl likes to be taken with a grain of assault.

A romance is a short period when two people cannot see too much of each other, followed by a long period when they do.

Romance makes the heart flutter and the tongue flatter.

There are many girls who would fall in love with some man even if there weren't a single man on earth.

Romance begins with a prince kissing an angel, and ends with a bald-headed man yawning at a fat woman.

ROME

Rome has more churches and less preaching in them than any other city in the world.
— *Will Rogers*

When in Rome do as the Romans do, unless your wife is with you.

Rome wasn't built in a day, probably because it was a government job.

All roads lead to Rome, and all detours lead to profanity.

When in Rome, do as the Romans do: order spaghetti.

Rome wasn't built in a day— they had their labor troubles too.

ROOM

It takes a man to make a room silent.
— *Thoreau*

The dining room is the place where the family eats while the kitchen is being painted.

There's always room at the top because the top keeps getting higher all the time.

The proper study of mankind is a room where womankind can't get in.

There is always room at the bottom.

The biggest room in the house is always the room for self-improvement.

ROOSTER

I love a rooster for two things: the crow that's in him, and the spur that's on him to back up the crow.
— *Josh Billings*

Have you ever noticed that a rooster runs with his hands in his pockets?
— *Lucien Guitry*

Patience is a virtue, but it will never help a rooster lay an egg.

Don't be like the rooster that thinks the sun rises to hear him crow.

Hens lay eggs only in the daytime because they're all roosters at night.

The rooster isn't unpopular because he gets up early; it's because he has so much to say about it.

ROOT

Money is the root of all evil because so many people root for it.

Money doesn't grow on trees because the Bible tells us it's a root.

The hardest thing to do in the garden of life is to dig up the root of evil.

ROPE

Usually you don't buy string; it comes to you, and you take it off, and send it out again.
— *A. A. Milne*

Give a man enough rope and he skips; give a woman enough rope, and she makes a marriage knot.

Life is a process with all sorts of strings attached to it: apron, heart and purse.

Training is everything: a rope gets tight because that's the way it's taut.

Give a jealous woman enough rope, and she's fit to be tied.

ROSE

Won't you come into the garden? I would like my roses to see you. — *Richard Brinsley Sheridan*

A rose by any other name would cost as much.

Don't divorce your wife: bring her a dozen roses; the shock will kill her, and you can use the roses for the funeral.

Some people are always grateful for the roses, while others always grumble at the thorns.

A rose by any other name would smell.

RUIN

I never heard or knew of a woman who was ruined by a book. — *James J. Walker*

Many a home is ruined by the husband backing horses, and many a garage by the wife backing cars.

The first half of our lives is ruined by our parents, and the second half by our children.

Whom the gods would destroy, they first make other people mad at.

RULE

It's a good idea to obey all the rules when you're young just so you'll have the strength to break them when you're old.
— *Mark Twain*

My soul hates the fool whose only passion is to live by rule.
— *Santayana*

The tyrant dies and his rule ends, the martyr dies and his rule begins. — *Kierkegaard*

When I read some of the rules for speaking and writing English,

I think how any fool can make a rule, and every fool will mind it. — *Thoreau*

Life is a game in which, if you break the rules, the rules will eventually break you.

It's a poor rule, as a rule, that doesn't work both ways.

In school we have the rule of three, in courtship the rule of two, in marriage the rule of one.

There are many hard and fast rules for success, but the trouble is all are hard and none are fast.

It's a good rule that works even one way.

Every rule has its exception, including this one.

It's a poor rule that won't work both ways, but a poorer one that won't work our way.

RUMOR

There's only one thing as difficult as unscrambling an egg, and that's unspreading a rumor.

"They say" is the biggest liar in the land.

There's nothing that grows so fast as the rumor that comes in at both ears and hurries out of the mouth.

Some women are born gossips, while others have a well-developed sense of rumor.

Nothing travels faster than a rumor, especially one that hasn't a leg to stand on.

When a group of women get hold of an idle rumor, they soon put it to work.

A groundless rumor covers ground rapidly.

A rumor without a leg to stand on will get around some other way.

RUN

Liszt belongs to the school of runs—after women. — *Nietzsche*

Honesty may be the best policy in the long run, but most of us are only sprinters.

Politics is a game where a man is always running for office or running for cover.

The man who enjoys running after women doesn't have to find women who will run.

RUSH HOUR

The rush hour is when a motorist travels the shortest distance in the longest time.

During the rush hour a motorist has the choice of hitting the car ahead or being hit by the car behind.

The rush hour is the time of day when the traffic rushes at a snail's pace.

The rush hour is when you can't avoid anywhere a long line of cars going nowhere on their way to somewhere.

The rush hour is the only hour when all the cars downtown are laid end to end.

It's called the rush hour because that's when traffic is at a standstill.

RUSSIA

If I wanted to start an insane asylum, I would just admit applicants that thought they knew something about Russia.
— *Will Rogers*

The trouble with Russian roulette is that the right Russians never play it.

Russia claims she wants peace in Asia and Africa, but doesn't say how big a piece.

Russia is a country that lies behind the Iron Curtain—and lies in front of it too.

Russia talks as if she wants to make up with the rest of the world, but acts as if she wants to make off with it.

SACRIFICE

One half of knowing what you want is knowing what you must give up before you get it.
— *Sidney Howard*

A woman will always sacrifice herself if you give her the opportunity; it is her favorite form of self-indulgence.
— *Somerset Maugham*

America is a land of opportunity where a plumber can become an executive—if he is willing to make the financial sacrifice.

A miser sacrifices the present to the future, a spendthrift sacrifices the future to the present.

No man can acquire money without making sacrifices—not even when he marries for it.

SAFETY

Women have got to make the world safe for men because men have made it darned unsafe for us women.   — *Lady Astor*

The only way you can pass speeding motorists at a safe distance is to travel by plane.

Know the traffic laws, but don't learn them by accident.

There's only one kind of safe car, and that's the one that can go no faster than its driver can think.

The driver is safer when the roads are dry, and the roads are safer when the driver is dry.

The highways would be much safer if an ounce of prevention were added to every gallon of gasoline.

Another thing that cannot be preserved in alcohol is safety.

Every year there are a million more cars on the roads—so if you want to cross the street, you'd better do it now.

Drive carefully—and the life you save will probably belong to a speed maniac.

For safety's sake, keep at least five car lengths behind the car ahead, and don't allow more than two cars in between.

Drive carefully—the other fellow's car may not be paid for either.

Man's ability to travel safely under water and fly safely in the air is no proof that he'll ever learn to cross the street safely.

Another lifesaver is the motorist who does not drive the way his wife tells him to.

A safety island is a marked-off area in a street that permits cars to strike you only from the side.

SAILOR

The man who has a girl in every port is not a sailor but a wholesaler.

Not all wolves wear sheep's clothing: some wear navy uniforms.

There's nothing more fleeting than a sailor's love.

If a sailor had a wife in every port, he'd also have a wife in every court.

SAINT

Plaster saints are always more honored than living ones.

A saint is as big a liar as the rest of us when he is making love.

Another trouble with the world is that it's run by people who think St. Francis of Assisi had a low standard of living.

There's no one so uncomfortable as the bishop who has a saint in his diocese.

SAINT AND SINNER

The saints are the sinners who keep on trying.
                    —Robert Louis Stevenson

There are only two kinds of men: the saints who think they are sinners, and the sinners who think they are saints.   *—Pascal*

The problem is how to tell the sinners from the saints when you know them both intimately.

Saints are intolerant of sinners, but none so intolerant as sinners just turned saints.

Hell can have no terror for the poor sinner who has got himself married to a saint.

Not all hypocrites pretend to be saints; some pretend to be sinners.

SALAD

To make a good salad is to be a brilliant diplomat: one must know exactly how much oil one must put with one's vinegar.
                    —Oscar Wilde

A woman is like a salad—much depends on the dressing.

In making a salad, become a spendthrift for oil, a miser for vinegar, a diplomat for salt, and a maniac for mixing.

SALARY

Half the world doesn't know how the other half lives on the husband's salary.

The man who gets as large a salary as he thinks he deserves is probably overpaid.

Many an employee is not only paid what he's worth but is also given a salary.

A man commands a salary and his wife commandeers it.

Another thing that goes in like a lion and out like a lamb is a man asking for a raise.

The good old days were the days when your greatest ambition was to earn the salary you cannot live on now.

Salary is the amount of money you are underpaid.

SALE

A woman will buy anything she thinks a store is losing money on.
— *Kin Hubbard*

It's amazing how many things a woman manages to do without until she sees them on sale.

A bargain sale is an event at which a woman often ruins one dress while buying another.

SALESMAN

In salesmanship, a foot in the door is worth two on the desk.

The chief advantage of being a traveling salesman is that you don't have to do your children's homework.

Opportunity sometimes knocks on your door, but more often it's a salesman.

Conversation isn't a lost art; it's simply been made practical and turned into salesmanship.

Another person who is here today and gone tomorrow is the traveling salesman.

A good salesman treats his customer as if she were his girl friend, not his wife.

A traveling salesman wishes he could have as good a time when away from home as his wife imagines he has.

A soft answer turneth away wrath, but not the door-to-door salesman.

Salesman's secret of success: Live well within your means, but dress far beyond your means.

A traveling salesman directs part of his enterprise and imagination to his business accounts, but most to his expense account.

The job of a door-to-door sales-man is to canvass homes to find out that people don't want to buy his product.

SALT

The flavor of a pinch of salt can be improved by dropping it into a glass of beer.

If the politicians knew that the voter always takes their state-ments with a grain of salt, they would probably put a tax on salt.

The world is full of people who salt away money in the brine of other people's tears.

When friends tell you how to cure a sore throat, take it with a grain of salt: the advice won't do you any good, but the salt may.

SAMSON

There's nothing worse than a homemade haircut—look what it did for Samson!

Samson's weakness was his fondness for showing off his strength.

Very few of us are Samsons, so we ought to be careful how we use the jawbone.

SANITY

No man is sane who does not know how to be insane on proper occasions. *—Henry Ward Beecher*

What frightens us most in a madman is his sane conversation.
—Anatole France

SANTA CLAUS

Santa Claus has the right idea: visit people once a year.
—Victor Borge

Santa Claus may be the world's best navigator, but he is also the world's worst judge of size and color.

Some girls never grow up: they think every man they meet is Santa Claus.

No wonder Santa Claus is a jolly old fellow: Dad pays for all the toys, and Santa gets all the credit.

Many a man has to leave home when his wife finds Santa Claus kissing the maid.

Under a welfare state there is always the danger that adults as well as children will believe in Santa Claus.

By the time a girl can fill a stocking she knows the truth about Santa Claus.

Christmas is always a problem to the man who has to convince his kids that there is a Santa Claus, and his wife that there isn't.

Santa Claus is a Christmas crea·ture by whom children are some·times confused, often amused, but never refused.

By the time a man grows fat enough to look the part, his kids no longer believe in Santa Claus.

SARCASM

When one woman praises another, people think she is sarcastic.

Nothing is more discouraging than unappreciated sarcasm.

The worst way to cultivate friendships is by giving people little digs.

To the victors belong the spoils, and to the vanquished the privilege of indulging in sarcasm.

The keener a man is intellectually, the more cutting remarks he makes.

Experience is a good teacher, though she is often sarcastic.

Many a wife sends her husband to an early grave with a series of little digs.

SATELLITE

Nowadays it isn't always true that whatever goes up must come down—sometimes it orbits.

A satellite is an artificial body revolving about the earth that falls without landing anywhere.

With all the satellites flying around in space nowadays, it may be very dangerous to hitch your wagon to a star.

A satellite is another thing that's always on the go without getting anywhere.

SATIRE

Satire is the soured milk of human kindness.
— *A. N. Whitehead*

Of all debts, men are least willing to pay taxes—what a satire is this on government! — *Emerson*

In literature it is the satirist who rules with an irony hand.

Satire is a form of humor enjoyed by some and misunderstood by many.

A satirist is a man who is always knocking the stuffing out of stuffed shirts.

SATISFACTION

An entirely satisfactory man is one who gives his heart to God, his money to his wife, and asks nothing for himself. — *Ed Howe*

Man wants but little here below, but woman isn't so easily satisfied.

Half the world, dissatisfied with what it has, doesn't know how the other half can be satisfied with what it hasn't.

Honesty is the best policy, but many people are satisfied with less than the best.

Satisfaction is what a woman feels when she hears herself praised or another woman criticized.

SAVINGS

Saving is a very fine thing, especially when your parents have done it for you.
— *Winston Churchill*

Another good way to save money is to be too busy to spend it.

Many a man saves his money so that by the time he is too old to enjoy it, he has plenty.

Save your money—you never know when your friends will need it.

It's all right to save for a rainy day if you don't forget to enjoy the dry ones.

If everyone saved money, how would anyone get money to save?

At twenty, he thinks he can save the world; at thirty, he begins to wish he could save part of his own salary.

The most important thing to save for old age is yourself.

The problem of how to save money affects only those who have no money to save.

Don't marry until you have saved some money; and if you wish to keep it saved, don't marry.

Try to save some money—it may be worth something again someday.

It's remarkable how much money a man can save merely by getting sleepy before midnight.

It's hard to figure out how much money you save by not drinking or smoking, and even harder to figure out what became of it.

Take care of your pennies, and the high cost of living will take care of your dollars.

There are many advantages in saving money, the chief one being that you can pay your taxes without borrowing.

When saving up for your old age, don't forget to lay up a few pleasant thoughts.

Some people have a lot of money because they save it, and others because they don't spend it.

A savings club is a useful weapon with which to beat the cost of living.

Work hard and save your money, and when you are old you can have the things only young people can enjoy.

A penny saved is a penny earned—and taxed.

Save something while your salary is small; it will be impossible to save after you begin earning more.

SCALE

The person who steps on a scale after dieting usually finds that he has taken off nothing more than his coat.

What this country needs is a bathroom scale that lies.

The woman who weighs herself every day on a penny scale is bound to lose—pennies.

The only thing that gives you more for your money than it used to is a weighing machine.

The best place for your bathroom scale is in front of the refrigerator.

SCANDAL

Think how many blameless lives are brightened by the blazing indiscretions of other people. — *Saki*

The objection to a scandalmonger is not that she tells of racy doings, but that she pretends to be indignant about them.
— *Mencken*

The woman who is always mixed up in a scandal never gets the details straight.

There's no one so annoying to a scandalmonger as the woman who never talks about anyone.

You sometimes meet a woman who talks for hours about things that leave her speechless.

A scandalmonger always distorts the truth, except when the truth can do more damage.

Gossips relish scandal as delicious, especially when it's most malicious.

Sooner or later every scandalmonger is bound to get caught in her own mouthtrap.

A scandalmonger is a person that puts who and who together and gets—whew!

A scandalmonger is a woman who tries to be first with the worst.

There's no fun listening to scandal unless you believe it.

The scandalmonger chooses not the lesser of two evils, but the one likely to cause more trouble.

Truth, crushed to earth, will rise again—if it is sufficiently scandalous.

One woman's past is another woman's pastime.

Scandal is a fifty-fifty proposition—half the people enjoy inventing it, and the other half enjoy believing it.

To a scandalmonger the worst scandal is the best.

Nothing makes a scandal grow like a grain of truth.

A scandalmonger is always sure to give you the benefit of the dirt.

When some women can't find something malicious to say about someone, they change the subject.

Scandal is an ill wind that blows nobody good.

SCATTERBRAIN

A scatterbrain finds it hard to think of less than a dozen things at once.

A scatterbrain goes through life never remembering what trump is.

A scatterbrain is unable to concentrate on anything, except a toothache.

SCENERY

Along the highways, you can't see the scenery for the signery.

If all the world's a stage, it's putting on too many changes of scenery.

Summer driving can be monstrous: after all, when you've seen one beer can, you've seen them all.

About the only way to get some motorists to look at scenery is to have it painted on the billboards.

SCHOLAR

The world's great men have not commonly been great scholars, nor its great scholars great men.
— *Dr. O. W. Holmes*

Learning preserves the errors of the past as well as the wisdom.
— *A. N. Whitehead*

The most learned differ from the ignorant only by their ability to find pleasure in hairsplitting.
— *Anatole France*

A good scholar will find Aristophanes and Hafiz and Rabelais full of American history.
— *Emerson*

A bluestocking is a woman who has a mania for intellectual subjects without having a ray of intellect.
— *Bernard Shaw*

Learning: the kind of ignorance distinguishing the studious.
— *Bierce*

Many a scholar with a pound of learning lacks an ounce of common sense to appy it.

The public always has greater respect for scholars who use language it cannot understand.

A scholar is like a foghorn: he calls attention to a fog without doing anything to dispel it.

The trouble with many a scholar is that the more he knows, the less he understands.

Scholarship is the attempt to exhaust a subject by first exhausting the reader.

A scholar is someone who owns more hard-cover books than paperbacks.

Knowledge is knowledge, but scholarship is a form of ignorance.

Women don't become bluestockings until men are no longer interested in their legs.

A scholar lives to learn, but seldom learns to live.

A classical education helps you to look down on the wealth it prevents you from earning.

The trouble with much scholarship is that it covers the ground without cultivating anything in it.

A scholar is a man who uses more words than he needs to tell more than he knows.

SCHOOL

I have never let my schooling interfere with my education.
— *Mark Twain*

When I was at school I knew all the dates in French history, but unhappily not what happened on them.   — *Sacha Guitry*

My schooldays were the period when I was being instructed by somebody I did not know about something I did not want to know.
— *Chesterton*

When a teacher calls a boy by his entire name, it means trouble.
— *Mark Twain*

If schools are overcrowded, it's because the building rate cannot keep up with the breeding rate.

Laugh, and the class laughs with you, but you stay after school alone.

The disadvantage of having a son or daughter in high school is that one has to attend the high school plays.

In elementary school, many a true word is spoken in guess.

A high school is an educational institution full of schoolboys who are sure they know more than their parents.

Some school children excel in social adjustment, activity participation and initiative, while others learn to read and write.

The money that is saved on schools this year will be spent on jails ten years later.

When little boys grow up, they change their minds and think that teachers ought to be paid enough to live on.

Public schools are usually run by men but overrun with women.

The first time many of us realize that a little learning is a dangerous thing is when we bring home a poor report card.

The man who drives fastest past a school was probably the slowest one getting through it.

Progress is not always advancement: in the past we had the little red schoolhouse; now we have the little-read schoolboy.

What most youngsters object to about school is the principal of the thing.

We provide buses so that children don't have to walk to school, and provide gymnasiums for the exercise they miss from not walking.

Behind every successful man is some fellow who once went to school with him.

School days are among the happiest days of your life, provided of course your children are old enough to attend.

The boy who is always at the foot of the class ought to become a chiropodist.

The community that claims it cannot afford to spend more

money for schools always has thousands of unpaid-for cars to prove it.

SCIENCE

The man of science does not discover in order to know; he wants to know in order to discover.
— *A. N. Whitehead*

The science of today is the technology of tomorrow.
— *Edward Teller*

Scientists regard it as a major intellectual virtue to know what not to think about. — *C. P. Snow*

Science is what you know, philosophy is what you don't know.
— *Bertrand Russell*

The only man with anything to say is the man of science, and he can't say it. — *James M. Barrie*

Science is a first-rate piece of furniture for a man's upper chamber, if he has common sense on the ground floor.
— *Dr. O. W. Holmes*

Science is a collection of successful recipes. — *Paul Valéry*

Science has always been too dignified to invent a good back-scratcher. — *Don Marquis*

Frogs will eat red-flannel worms fed to them by biologists; this proves a great deal about both parties concerned. — *Will Cuppy*

Aristotle discovered all the half-truths which were necessary to the creation of science.
— *A. N. Whitehead*

In science the credit goes to the man who convinces the world, not to the man to whom the idea first occurs. — *William Osler*

When I find myself in the company of scientists, I feel like a shabby curate who has strayed into a drawing room full of dukes.
— *W. H. Auden*

The space scientist is a most remarkable man: he has his feet on the ground and his head in the clouds.

Science is wonderful: for years uranium cost only a few dollars a ton until scientists discovered you could kill people with it.

A mineralogist is the only living creature who belongs to the mineral kingdom.

The ways of science are unpredictable: it can get men up to the moon, but it cannot get pigeons down from public buildings.

A metallurgist is an expert who can look at a platinum blonde and tell whether she is virgin metal or common ore.

SCIENCE AND RELIGION

Science without religion is lame, religion without science is blind.
— *Einstein*

Science commits suicide when it adopts a creed. — *Thomas Hardy*

There is more religion in men's science than there is science in their religion. — *Thoreau*

The church saves sinners, but science seeks to stop their manufacture.   — *Elbert Hubbard*

I prefer the man who calls his nonsense a mystery to him who pretends it is a weighed, measured, analyzed fact.
   — *Bernard Shaw*

Religion will not regain its old power until it can face change in the same spirit as does science.
   — *A. N. Whitehead*

No path leads from a knowledge of that which is to that which should be.   — *Einstein*

Science is wiser than religion: it never tries to do the humanly impossible, like making you love your neighbor like yourself.

SCOLD

Every time a woman gives a man a piece of her mind she loses a piece of his heart.
   — *Helen Rowland*

There are far too many women who can dish it out better than they can cook it.

A married woman's ignorance of the law never prevents her from laying it down.

All scolds are alike: they tell their husbands off by going on and on.

Before giving others a piece of your mind, make sure you can spare it.

Every time a man quarrels with his wife, words flail him.

The woman who can read her husband like a book seldom skips the disagreeable parts.

The worst way of giving another person peace of mind is by giving him a piece of your mind.

SCOTLAND

The noblest prospect which a Scotchman ever sees is the high road that leads him to England.
   — *Samuel Johnson*

A Scot is the only man who sings about auld lang syne and knows what it means.

SCOUT

Many a male is a boy scout until he's sixteen, and a girl scout thereafter.

Why is it you never hear about a girl scout helping an old man across the street?

SCRATCH

A man doesn't love a woman because he thinks her clever or admires her, but because he likes the way she scratches her head.
   — *Yeats*

A busy man is usually a happy man, unless he is busy scratching.

Scratching is nature's way of giving you something to do while you itch.

When a dog has fleas he doesn't start drawing up an indictment against the world—he starts to scratch.

Don't itch all over—learn to itch where you can scratch.

With automation making such rapid strides, we'll soon be doing nothing by hand except scratching ourselves.

'Tis better than riches to scratch when it itches.

SCULPTURE

We sculptors are generally less nervy than painters because we get a chance to hammer out our neuroses. *— Henry Moore*

Seldom is a Gothic head more beautiful than when it is broken. *— Malraux*

The more my sculptured bust resembles me, the worse it looks. *— Emerson*

Modern sculpture is a form of sculpture often mistaken for art, especially by the man who has created it.

Abstract sculpture is a form of modern art which the sculptor doesn't understand, but expects the spectator to.

The sculpture of today is odd if it is not odd.

A modern sculptor can take a rough block of stone, work on it for months, and finally make it look like a rough block of stone.

The realistic sculptor cuts less of a figure in contemporary art than the non-objective sculptor.

SEASICK

I was so seasick, my stomach was ejecting meals I had hoped to eat the following week. *— Fred Allen*

Seasickness is a condition which is never helped by sherry, but always helped by port.

Travel often brings out what is good in a man, especially ocean travel.

The best place on a ship for a hang-over is the rail.

You can't eat your cake on shipboard and have it too.

Seasickness is the only thing that can make a tourist look like his passport photograph.

A hypochondriac is a woman who is seasick during the entire voyage of life.

It's better to give than to receive, but not when you're seasick.

SEASONS

Nature cannot jump from winter to summer without a spring, or from summer to winter without a fall.

When a girl is being courted in the spring, the man is heading for a fall.

You can't beat the weather: spring is too rainy and summer's too hot; fall is soon over and winter is not.

If you're cold in April it's because winter has stolen a March on spring.

Clock-setting formula for daylight-saving time: Man springs forward and falls back.

SEAT

We're about to enter the age of flight before we've even developed a chair that a man can sit in comfortably.
— *Philip Wylie*

The most common of all antagonisms arises from a man's taking a seat beside you on the train, a seat to which he is completely entitled.
— *Robert Benchley*

Girls who eat a lot of sweets soon develop bigger seats.

When a man doesn't give his seat to a lady in a bus, it's because he has no manners, or because he has no seat.

The seats of the mighty vary in width.

American men look up to women—from their seats in the bus.

Another mystery of life is why people will always ask if the empty seat beside you is occupied.

There are always plenty of seats in the subway; the trouble is, people are always sitting on them.

You can't keep trouble from coming, but you needn't give it a chair to sit on.

The man who always gives up his seat in a bus to others probably walks to work.

SEAT BELT

More women would use them if the seat belts in cars were covered with mink.

Buckling a seat belt takes much less time than a ride in the ambulance.

The reason seat belts are installed in cars is to keep people alive until they make their last payments.

Seat belts often save lives—it's hard to fall asleep while sitting on the buckle.

The man who won't diet when he outgrows his belt probably will when he outgrows his seat belt too.

A glutton is a man who is constantly adjusting his seat belt.

Seat belts were invented to keep you from suddenly leaving the scene of an accident.

SECRET

There are some occasions when a man must tell half his secret in order to conceal the rest.
— *Chesterfield*

Never tell a secret to a bride or groom; wait until they have been married longer. — *Ed Howe*

The secret of the sphinx is that she has no secret. — *Chesterton*

How can we expect another to keep our secret if we cannot keep if ourselves? – *La Rochefoucauld*

Men have been living a long time, and the most important thing they have learned is that some things should be kept from their wives.   – *Ed Howe*

A person may be very secretive and yet have no secrets.
             – *Elbert Hubbard*

A man keeps another person's secret better than his own, a woman keeps her own better than another's.   – *La Bruyère*

Secrets are things we give to others to keep for us.
             – *Elbert Hubbard*

It's hard for a woman to keep a secret without getting a few friends to help her.

The secret of a lot of happy marriages is a lot of secrets.

Any woman can keep a secret if she wants to, but where can you find a woman who wants to?

Where a secret is concerned, a woman makes every word tell.

A secret is best kept by keeping the secret of its being a secret.

There are four ways to transmit a secret to a woman: to write, telephone, wire, and tell another woman not to tell her.

Some women can keep a secret —they never tell who told them.

Most of us can keep a secret —it's the people we tell it to that can't.

When a woman is asked not to tell a secret, she never knows whom not to tell it to first.

A woman never betrays a confidence without first imposing the strictest secrecy.

It's such a nuisance to keep a secret—let someone else do it for you.

The man who thinks his wife doesn't understand him is lucky —she knows how to keep a secret.

The secret of a secret is to know when and how to tell it.

The way a woman keeps a secret is to tell everybody not to tell anybody about it.

Any woman can keep a secret —until she meets another woman.

A secret is something that is not only told in strict confidence, but also repeated in strict confidence.

Secrecy with women consists in telling a thing to only one person at a time.

Women can keep a secret as well as men—it just takes more of them.

The man who has no secrets from his wife either has no secrets or no wife.

The most fascinating of all things to a woman is a secret, but only if she doesn't know it.

Women never give a secret away—they exchange it for another.

Keeping a secret from some people is like trying to smuggle daylight past a rooster.

Every woman can keep a secret, especially in circulation.

The better half is usually the half that has not been told.

You do people a good turn when you trust them with a secret: they feel so important while telling it.

The only woman who never betrays a friend's secret is she who has never been entrusted with it.

SECRETARY

In America, I had two secretaries: one for autographs, the other for locks of hair; within six months one had died of writer's cramp, the other was completely bald. *— Oscar Wilde*

The only difference between a secretary and a private secretary is that one knows more and tells less.

When a secretary is fired, it's because she either knows too little or too much.

You can fool some of the people some of the time, but not your private secretary.

A man has arrived when his secretary feels flattered that he's kissed her.

Another thing overlooked in the curriculum of secretarial schools is a course in how to brew coffee.

A secretary is a clever girl who can add or a cute girl who can distract.

The man who labors under a heavy burden at the office should hire a lighter secretary.

The first thing a new secretary types is her boss.

Another unsung hero is the businessman who first hired a female secretary.

Advice to pretty secretaries: take your shorthand at arm's length.

Many a secretary enables an executive to combine more pleasure with business than pleasure with vacation.

The test of a good secretary is her ability to think up excuses that her employer's wife will believe.

SECURITY

More people might live to a ripe old age if they didn't work so hard to provide for it.

To some husbands financial security means having a place to hide money where their wives can't find it.

As the world becomes more and more civilized, it puts more and more things under lock and key.

SEDUCTION

A woman will sometimes forgive the man who tries to seduce

her, but never the man who misses an opportunity when offered. *— Talleyrand*

No one with a particle of taste seduces a young girl nowadays; they wait till she is married—it saves time and trouble.
— James G. Huneker

I can safely affirm that I never in my life seduced a woman.
— Lord Byron

I must seduce her so as to save myself from being ridiculed for falling in love with her.
— Choderlos de Laclos

After you persuade her, 'tis easy to invade her.

Sometimes an executive fires a pretty secretary for a mistake she refuses to make.

It takes two bodies to make one seduction.

The favorite trick of some men is to keep a girl out till the *oui* hours of the morning.

SEED

Unless you have a green thumb, about the only thing you can raise with a seed catalogue is your hopes.

Faith will never die as long as colored seed catalogues are printed.

The illustrations in a seed catalogue are intended to show you what the flowers will not look like when they come up.

An old-timer is one who remembers when all a farmer wanted from the government was a free packet of seeds.

The widespread occurrence of backaches will continue as long as the laws permit the mailing of seed catalogues.

Save your empty seed packets after you've planted your garden; they are just about the right size for storing the crop.

Nature is an original artist; that's why she never copies the pictures on seed packets.

SEEK

Money and women are the most sought after and least understood things of any we have.
— Will Rogers

The search for happiness is one of the chief sources of unhappiness. *— Eric Hoffer*

You don't have to take out a search warrant to look for trouble.

SEGREGATION

Segregation is the offspring of an illicit intercourse between injustice and immorality.
— Martin Luther King

You can't hold a man down without staying down with him.
— Booker T. Washington

To like an individual because he's black is just as insulting as to dislike him because he isn't white. *— E. E. Cummings*

If human beings were as wise as animals, the only creature they would segregate is the skunk.

A segregationist is not blind to principle, but blind on principle.

SELF

I have never seen a greater miracle or monster than myself.
— *Montaigne*

Make the most of yourself for that is all there is to you.
— *Emerson*

The least pain in our little finger gives us more concern than the destruction of millions of our fellow-beings.   — *Hazlitt*

I should not talk so much about myself if there were anybody else I knew so well.   — *Thoreau*

Don't discuss yourself, for you are bound to lose: if you belittle yourself, you are believed; if you praise yourself, you are disbelieved.   — *Montaigne*

When a man tries himself, the verdict is usually in his favor.
— *Ed Howe*

If we weren't all so interested in ourselves, life would be so uninteresting we couldn't endure it.   — *Schopenhauer*

Man is the only animal that suffers from the disease of self-hatred and self-contempt.
— *Montaigne*

It is as hard to see oneself as to look backwards without turning around.   — *Thoreau*

Many a woman who feels she is bearing a cross is merely putting up with herself.

No one you meet in life ever gives you as much trouble as yourself.

The woman who is all wrapped up in herself is always overdressed.

Some people try to make something for themselves, others try to make something of themselves.

A windbag is an empty man who is always full of himself.

About the worst advice you can give some people is *Be yourself!*

Don't feel sorry for yourself: feel sorry for those who have to live with you.

The only successful reform is that accomplished in the first person.

When a man complains about not being himself, it is probably a great improvement.

Don't be yourself—be what you ought to be.

A married man's best friend is his wife's husband.

SELF-CONTROL

The best time for you to hold your tongue is the time you feel you must say something or bust.
— *Josh Billings*

Self-control is the ability to keep cool while someone is making it hot for you.

Don't sell parents short: the fact that children live to be adults is a great tribute to their self-control.

The reason why self-discipline is hard to learn is that you need self-discipline to learn it.

Many a man's wonderful self-control is due to the fact that he has a wife.

If you can keep your head when all about you are losing theirs—maybe you just don't understand the situation.

It is hard to be silent when you have nothing to say.

There are times in most men's lives when they lose control of themselves—others remain bachelors.

Self-control is a virtue you never knew you had until you argue with the boss.

The best test of self-control is the power to listen to another person describe the same ailment you have—and not mention it.

Try to see yourself as others see you, but try not to get angry about it.

Another thing that is most needed when it is exhausted is self-control.

SELF-DECEPTION

Man shows no greater talent than in his ability to deceive himself.   —Anatole France

Young men are apt to think themselves wise enough, as drunken men are apt to think themselves sober enough.
—Chesterfield

The worst tumble of all is when you fall over your own bluff.

You can fool some of the people all of the time, and all of the people some of the time, but the rest of the time they will fool themselves.

It would serve no purpose to see ourselves as others see us —we simply wouldn't believe it.

SELF-DENIAL

The parents of today are making it hard for their children to tell their children what they had to do without.

The best advice to a dieter is: No thyself.

These are trying times: most of us have to do without the things our parents never heard of.

SELF-ESTEEM

The most difficult secret for a man to keep is his own opinion of himself.   —Marcel Pagnol

All the extraordinary men I have ever known were chiefly extraordinary in their own estimation.   —Woodrow Wilson

Self-respect: the secure feeling that no one, as yet, is suspicious.
—Mencken

We do not deal much in facts when we are contemplating ourselves.   —*Mark Twain*

Self-esteem is the confidence which a person has in himself even though there's no one he has fooled more often.

Of all the opinions which people entertain, the best one is that which they have of themselves.

There's plenty of room at the top, but not enough for the people who think they ought to be there.

The proof that many a man is a poor judge of human nature is the good opinion he holds of himself.

The man who is sure to make others boil is the one who is always letting off esteem.

A woman who deflates her husband's ego inflates another woman's chances of getting him.

When we have self-esteem, we call it self-respect; when others have it, we call it self-conceit.

Every now and then you meet a man who enjoys the reputation of being the most remarkable person he knows.

There would be no more room at the top if those who reach it were half as big as they think they are.

SELF-IMPORTANCE

There is nothing that you and I make so many blunders about,

and the world so few, as the actual amount of our own importance.   —*Josh Billings*

If you don't think too much of yourself, you are much more than you think.   —*Goethe*

Appearances are deceiving: there's a lot less to a stuffed shirt than meets the eye.

Many a man who thinks he's too big for the little job turns out to be too little for the big job.

SELF-INDULGENCE

Let me have my way exactly in everything, and you will find that a pleasanter creature does not exist.   —*Carlyle*

I never smoked and never drank until I was twelve years old.   —*DeWolf Hopper*

If you want to get somewhere, you must let yourself go.

SELFISH

Selfishness speaks all languages and plays all sorts of parts, including that of unselfishness.
—*La Rochefoucauld*

Next to the very young, the very old are the most selfish.
—*Thackeray*

Selfishness sometimes gets a person what he wants, but more often gets him what he deserves.

When it comes to doing things for others, are you one of those who stop at nothing?

People who are self-centered always live in unpleasant surroundings.

If you are merely looking out for yourself, look out!

Know thyself, and *no* thy selfishness.

SELF-KNOWLEDGE

When I am reading my lectures I often think to myself, "What a humbug you are!" and I wonder the people don't find it out.
— *Thackeray*

It's not only the most difficult thing to know oneself, but the most inconvenient. — *Josh Billings*

We are what other people say we are: we know ourselves chiefly by hearsay. — *Eric Hoffer*

Fortunate is the man who knows as much about himself as some woman thinks she knows about him.

Know thyself, but tell no one what thou knowest.

It's strange how much you have to know before you realize how little you know.

Some people really ought to know themselves: they never think about anything else.

SELF-LOVE

Love is blind, but self-love is full of *I*'s.

If a man can't marry himself, how can he ever marry his first love?

Only love can make two people think as much of each other as they think of themselves.

The man who is in love with himself won't find many rivals.

The reason we can't see ourselves as others see us is that love is blind.

The girl who falls in love with herself may find herself alone with her sweetheart forever after.

Love is full of faith, but no love is so faithful as self-love.

You can always get someone to love you, even if you have to do it yourself.

Many a man won't marry because he can't find a girl who will love him as much as he does.

The course of true love never runs smooth, except when it's self-love.

A man in love with himself never wavers in his devotion.

SELF-MADE MAN

Self-made men are most always apt to be a little too proud of the job. — *Josh Billings*

Everyone is a self-made man, but only the successful men are willing to admit it.

When a man says he's a self-made man, is he boasting or apologizing?

The self-made man can always point to Frankenstein as an example of the failure of the other type.

If all people descended from Adam, what about the self-made man?

The only way to account for some self-made men is that the building inspectors must have been bribed.

Some are self-made men, but most are the revised work of a wife and children.

The trouble with most self-made men is that they know how to make money better than they know how to make a man.

Why is it we never hear of a self-made woman?

The self-made man who boasts about it has not finished his job.

SELF-PRAISE

I always like to hear a man talk about himself because then I never hear anything but good.
— *Will Rogers*

The advantage of doing one's praising for oneself is that one can lay it on thick.
— *Samuel Butler*

He was as shy as a newspaper is when referring to its own merits.
— *Mark Twain*

A man is never more serious than when he praises himself.
— *G. C. Lichtenberg*

We are all so near the Day of Doom that everyone, even Gabriel, has to blow his own trumpet.
— *Robert Frost*

When a man starts singing his own praises, it's pretty sure to be a solo.

Nature is wise: she has arranged your anatomy so as to make it hard for you to pat yourself on the back.

The man who blows his own horn has everyone dodging when he approaches.

SELF-SATISFACTION

Why is it that the man who is satisfied with so little in himself demands so much in others?

The man most easily satisfied is the self-satisfied man.

Self-satisfaction is the smug feeling we get from comparing other people's faults with our own virtues.

The man who is always satisfied with himself never seems to satisfy anyone else.

SELL

A man never knows how many friends he hasn't got until he tries to sell them something.

The only time in life when nobody is trying to sell you anything is your prenatal period.

Selling is easy, but only if you work hard at it.

There are two kinds of businessmen: one kind is selling out and the other is out selling.

You can't take it with you, probably because everyone is trying to make you spend it.

The business with a slow turnover generally overturns fast.

He who sells what isn't his'n, must buy it back or go to prison.

SENATE

There ought to be one day—just one—when there is open season on senators. — *Will Rogers*

The Senate is a body of elderly men charged with high duties and misdemeanors. — *Bierce*

The average senator is honest as they come; it's after he gets to the Senate that you have to watch him.

In Congress, senators are a luxury: that is why the law of the land limits them to only two from each state.

Senators always examine an issue after they've reached a conclusion, and investigate a problem after they've made up their minds.

SENILITY

First childhood begins with Mother Goose, and second childhood with Father Time.

The pace of modern living is increasing so fast that our second childhood arrives nowadays before we are ready for it.

Old age is the period when a woman is in her dotage, and a man in his anecdotage.

The child is father to the man, but there's no second manhood for second childhood.

Many a man has a much better time in his second childhood than he had in his first.

SENSE

The trouble with fiction is that it makes too much sense, whereas reality never makes sense.
— *Aldous Huxley*

There is nothing a man of good sense dreads in a wife so much as her having more sense than himself. — *Henry Fielding*

When I see something that makes absolutely no sense whatever, I figure there must be a damn good reason for it.
— *Peter De Vries*

One of the wisest things my daddy ever taught me was that "so-and-so is a damned smart man, but the fool's got no sense."
— *Lyndon B. Johnson*

Good sense about trivialities is better than nonsense about things that matter.   —*Max Beerbohm*

A man may be disconsolate with everything, but he is never discontented with the amount of sense he has: it is always enough.   —*Ben Hecht*

The world makes no sense, and neither do most of the people in it.

Man is the only sex that thinks it has more sense than woman.

The less sense a girl has, the more sense she seems to make to some men.

How many cents a dollar is worth depends on how much sense the spender has.

A frivolous woman makes life mighty interesting to a man while he's searching for a sensible one.

In order to make sense out of anything, you must put some sense into it.

A man always has more sense after he's married, but it's too late then.

Many people have horse sense, but few have more sense.

There are many ways to damn a woman with faint praise, and one of them is to say she's sensible.

The man who has more money than sense isn't always rich.

A psychiatrist's job is to make sense out of a patient who doesn't make sense.

There's nothing so rare as a man talking sense and his wife agreeing with him.

Already we can travel faster than sound—now all we have to do is to catch up on sense.

A sensible girl is more sensible than she looks because a sensible girl has more sense than to look sensible.

SENSE OF HUMOR

Whenever I indulge my sense of humor, it gets me into trouble.   —*Calvin Coolidge*

The man who tries to define a sense of humor proves nothing except that he has not got a sense of humor.   —*Chesterton*

It's great to have a sense of humor so you can get a laugh out of your friends' misfortunes.

You can tell that women have no sense of humor by the way they look at their hats without laughing.

Man was given a sense of humor to compensate for nature's law of gravity.

The best of humor is the kind that enables you to see at once what it isn't safe to laugh at.

Women do have a sense of humor—look at the men they marry.

The sense of humor is a subject that never fails to interest scholars who haven't any.

The one great thing needed in golf is a caddie with no sense of humor.

The only thing worse than being married to a woman without a sense of humor is being married to a woman with one.

The sense of humor is the only one of man's senses that doesn't always make sense.

We have imagination to compensate us for what we aren't, and a sense of humor to console us for we what we are.

Many a woman goes on a diet and loses nothing but her sense of humor.

Few people admit that they lack sense, and even fewer that they lack a sense of humor.

If you were to list the half-dozen people with the best sense of humor, who would the other five be?

In spite of what men say, women have a keen sense of humor—the more you humor them, the better they like it.

You can't explain the sense of humor: a man will split his sides over the family album, and then look in the mirror without cracking a smile.

Your sense of humor is what enables you to laugh at something —unless it happens to you.

A man with a good sense of humor seldom laughs at his own jokes, especially when his wife tells them.

SENSES

I never know whether to pity or congratulate a man on coming to his senses.   — *Thackeray*

Half of us are blind, few of us feel, and we are all deaf.
        — *William Osler*

Love sharpens all the senses, except common sense.

We moderns have eyes for television, ears for the radio, a nose for news, and the personal touch—all we lack is taste.

The five senses are horse sense, innocence, common sense, concupiscence, and nonsense.

SENTENCE

Caress every sentence gently, and soon it will turn into a smiling expression.   — *Anatole France*

A sentence should read as if its author, had he held a plow instead of a pen, could have drawn a furrow deep and straight to the end.   — *Thoreau*

With 60 staring me in the face, I have developed inflammation of the sentence structure and a definite hardening of the paragraphs.
        — *James Thurber*

SENTIMENT

The world makes up for all its follies and injustices by being damnably sentimental.
        — *Thomas H. Huxley*

A sentimentalist is simply one who desires to have the luxury of an emotion without paying for it.
— *Oscar Wilde*

Sentimentality—that's what we call the sentiment we don't share.
— *Graham Greene*

No woman ever falls in love with a man unless she has a better opinion of him than he deserves.
— *Ed Howe*

Sentimentality is only sentiment that rubs you the wrong way. — *Somerset Maugham*

A sentimentalist is a woman whose heart is always going to her head.

Sentimentality is no indication of a warm heart; nothing weeps more freely than a block of ice.

Sentimentality is 99 per cent sentiment, and 1 per cent mentality.

SEPARATION

The girl who marries for money sometimes separates from her husband, but never from the money.

If divorce didn't separate some couples, the police would have to.

Truth is more of an estranger than fiction.

A fool and his money are soon parted, but you never call him a fool till the money is gone.

Nothing in the world can break the bond of true friendship, except moving to the suburbs.

A woman should leave her husband long enough to increase his appreciation, but not long enough for him to seek consolation.

A man's best friend is money, but the trouble is the best of friends must part.

Some married couples are inseparable—it requires a dozen people to pull them apart.

A fool and his father's money are soon parted.

The man who takes things philosophically doesn't always part with them that way.

A woman never really treats her husband like a doormat until she walks out on him.

A confirmed bachelor believes that what God has put asunder, no man should join together.

If a man keeps his friends, it's a sign they don't see much of him.

A flirt sometimes separates the men from the boys, but more often the husbands from their wives.

A fool and his money are soon parted because he has more dollars than sense.

SERIOUS

People are much too solemn about things—I'm all for sticking pins into episcopal behinds.
— *Aldous Huxley*

It is not so important to be serious as it is to be serious about important things.
— *Robert M. Hutchins*

We are growing serious and, let me tell you, that's the very next step to being dull.
— *Addison*

Satan fell by the force of gravity—taking himself too seriously.
— *Chesterton*

Blessed is he who takes himself seriously for he shall create much amusement.
— *Strickland Gillilan*

Thou sayest such an undisputed thing in such a solemn way.
— *Dr. O. W. Holmes*

Nobody on earth is as serious as a student of comedy.
— *Brendan Gill*

In love, no man begins to be serious until he begins to be foolish.
— *Helen Rowland*

Some people think that everything others do with a serious face is sensible. — *G. C. Lichtenberg*

There's nothing like a solemn oath—people always think you mean it. — *Norman Douglas*

Some people are serious about everything, even about fun.

Many a true word is spoken in jest, but the majority of lies are uttered in earnest.

A teen-ager can tell that her boy friend is serious about her by the way she calls him up every day.

A person who is too serious to take a joke should take a vacation.

The real trouble with the world is that we don't take too seriously the reformers who take things too seriously.

Always take your work more seriously than you take yourself.

SERMON

Few sinners are saved after the first twenty minutes of a sermon.
— *Mark Twain*

You can preach a better sermon with your life than with your lips.
— *Oliver Goldsmith*

Americans are so tense and keyed up that it is impossible even to put them to sleep with a sermon. — *Norman Vincent Peale*

A good sermon helps people in different ways: some rise from it strengthened, others wake from it refreshed.

The length of a sermon depends on whether you are awake or asleep.

The minister who has to preach a sermon is never so convincing as the minister who has a sermon to preach.

A sermon is a long talk about sin, with the minister always against it.

The man who walks in his sleep should get back before the sermon is finished.

A good sermon does two things: it comforts the afflicted, and it afflicts the comfortable.

If you want to hear one man talk and keep fifty women silent, go to church.

So live that when a sermon is pointed, it's not at you.

When people sleep in church, maybe it's the preacher who should wake up.

The half-baked sermon causes spiritual indigestion.

A sermon often wearies a churchgoer by its length, but seldom by its depth.

The difference between a good sermon and a poor one is a nap.

If a minister wants to practice what he preaches, he should rehearse his sermons.

If you stay awake and listen to the Sunday sermon at church, it will do you good—you'll probably sleep better that night.

Many a sermon is finished long before it stops.

The eternal gospel does not require an everlasting sermon.

The only way some men can keep awake during a sermon is by playing golf.

A churchgoer's idea of a good sermon is one that goes over his head and hits someone else.

The length of a sermon often determines how late a person sleeps on Sunday morning.

SERVANT

Robinson had a servant who was even better than Friday—his name was Crusoe.   *— Nietzsche*

It is easier to serve two masters than to master two servants.

Another person who is here today and gone tomorrow is a maid.

A man is known by the company he keeps, and a woman by the maids she can't keep.

One of the easiest roles for an actress to play is a maid, because few people nowadays know what a maid looks like.

There are two types of servants: those who resent criticism and those who ignore it.

People who keep servants would like to know how to keep them.

Men may come and men may go, but for coming and going domestic help has a record that will never be equaled.

Train up a servant in the way she should go, and the first chance she gets, she goes.

The only woman who can keep a maid longer than a husband is a movie star.

A woman sometimes has to let her pretty maid go because her husband won't.

They have a wonderful old family maid; she has been with them for the past twenty meals.

SERVE

The ability to allow others to serve him is not the least of the talents that produce a great ruler.
— *Richelieu*

No man can serve two masters, unless he has a wife and grown-up daughter.

Some people are always willing to serve you, but only in an advisory capacity.

There are many good ways to serve leftovers, but the best way is to serve them to someone else.

Youth must be served, and cleaned up afterward.

All things come to him who waits—on himself.

No man can serve two masters, but a yes man can serve hundreds.

It serves no useful purpose to use the cliché that it serves no useful purpose.

SERVICE

Of all the domestic animals invented for the service of man, the most useful is woman.
— *Max O'Rell*

The only person who is shunned for serving his fellow man is the process server.

SETTLE

No one really knows how many times a man should marry before he settles down.

The best way to settle an argument is to step outside before you're invited to.

Girls used to dream of a plumed knight in shining armor, but nowadays they will settle for anyone in a sweat shirt and a sports car.

A century ago our country was largely unsettled; today conditions are the same.

It is better to debate an important matter without settling it than to settle it without debating it.

Marry a poor girl if you want to settle down; marry a rich one if you want to settle up.

SEWING

A sewing circle is a group of women who meet regularly to needle their absent friends.

A stitch in time saves embarrassment.

Many a girl who weaves a romantic spell before marriage won't even darn a sock afterward.

Some women go through life forever knitting, while others are forever needling.

As ye sew, so shall ye rip.

Some husbands are so helpless that when they want their socks darned, their wives have to thread the needle for them.

SEX

Of the delights of this world man cares most for sexual intercourse, yet he has left it out of his heaven.   — *Mark Twain*

The basic impulse to propagate our race has propagated a lot of other things as well.
— *G. C. Lichtenberg*

Women become attached to men by the intimacies they grant them; men are cured of their love by the same intimacies.
— *La Bruyère*

The only unnatural sex act is that which you cannot perform.
— *Alfred Kinsey*

The female sex today is beginning to take a little interest in sex whereas mine is beginning to take little interest in anything else.
— *James Thurber*

To the Latin, sex is an hors d'oeuvre; to the Anglo-Saxon, it is a barbecue. — *George Jean Nathan*

In the duel of sex, woman fights from a dreadnaught and man from an open raft.
— *Mencken*

Unless we gratify our sex desire, the race is lost; unless we restrain it, we destroy ourselves.
— *Bernard Shaw*

Sensuality is the vice of young men and old nations.
— *William Lecky*

Some things are better than sex, and some things are worse, but there's nothing exactly like it.
— *W. C. Fields*

When he will, she won't; and when he won't, she will. — *Terence*

When will the world know that peace and propagation are the two most delightful things in it?
— *Horace Walpole*

Sexual intercourse is a slight attack of apoplexy.   — *Democritus*

After coitus every animal is sad, except the human female and the rooster.   — *Galen*

If a man and woman, entering a room together, close the door behind them, the man will come out sadder and the woman wiser.
— *Mencken*

Continental people have a sex life, the English have hot-water bottles.   — *George Mikes*

The old-fashioned girl yielded to a man's embraces as if she were slowly lowering herself into a tub of cold water.   — *James Thurber*

When a man beats only his wife, it's merely a sex drive.
— *G. C. Lichtenberg*

Sexual relationships are often like an hourglass; one single point of contact.   — *Bernard Berenson*

To err is human, but it feels divine.   — *Mae West*

We have too much sex on the brain, and too little of it elsewhere.   — *Norman Douglas*

To the poet, sex is love; to the psychiatrist, love is sex.

Another reason sex is so popular is that it's centrally located.

If sex is such a driving force, why is so much of it found parked?

Girls who like to show their knees, know all about the birds and bees.

The odds are usually two to one in favor of sex: you and she against her conscience.

Sex is a drive where there are just as many women drivers as men.

Statistics show that the three favorite things in life are a martini before and a nap after.

Of all creatures hunted for sport, woman is first.

Sex is the proof that it is easier to get two bodies together than two souls.

The difference between a bachelor girl and a spinster is sex.

If four bare legs in bed were the main thing, mighty few marriages would last.

Two's company, three's the result.

In the art of love it is more important to know when than how.

Never make love to a woman when you have something better to do, but what is better?

Middle age is the first time you discover you can't do it the second time; old age is the second time you discover you can't do it the first time.

Sex is the most fun you can have without laughing.

Sex is a drive where there are too many reckless drivers.

There are only two kinds of girls: those that do, and those that are never asked.

The trouble with matrimony today is that too many couples marry at too early an urge.

SEX APPEAL

Men and women do little else but make trouble for each other, yet if a high wall separated them they would break it down to get through.　　—Ed Howe

We throw the whole drudgery of creation on one sex, and then imply that no female of any delicacy would initiate any effort in that direction.　　—Bernard Shaw

A woman loses her sex appeal when she becomes the opposing instead of the opposite sex.

There's nothing worse than the girl who is considered charmless, except the man who is considered harmless.

A flirt is a girl whose sex appeal springs from her eye cue.

Lives there a fellow so abnormal that he can't be stirred by a low-necked formal?

When some men meet a pretty girl they never give her a second thought—they are far too busy with the first.

All is not sex that appeals.

Many a man leaves the straight and narrow path to follow a woman who isn't built that way.

You can't explain sex appeal: many a man falls in love with a woman without a fraction of attraction, a trace of grace, or a glimmer of glamour.

Beware of the girl with the baby stare—a man is safer in the electric chair.

Sex appeal is partly what a woman has, but mostly what a man thinks she has.

Breathes there a man with soul so dead, who never has turned round and said, "Hmm, not bad!"

It is the same when angling for men or fish—your lines should be well baited.

The woman with sex appeal usually wears a dress that holds on tight going around the curves.

When a woman puts a little sway in her walk, it is to sway the opposite sex.

Sex appeal is the mystery behind the mastery of woman over man.

Some women are so seductive as to make a bachelor dissatisfied with bachelorhood and a married man dissatisfied with marriage.

The woman with sex appeal can always make feminine capital out of masculine interest.

Girls with low necks are apt to have sex.

Every girl should use what Mother Nature gave her before Father Time takes it away.

SEXES

If you wonder which is the stronger sex, watch which one twists the other around her little finger.

I love the idea of there being two sexes, don't you?
— *James Thurber*

The battle of the sexes can be a most enjoyable scrimmage if you'll only stop trying to create woman in your own image.
— *Ogden Nash*

The three sexes are men, women and professors.
— *J. E. Spingarn*

The battle of the sexes is sometimes won by the man's resistance, but more often by the woman's persistence.

Men are the weaker sex, not women; otherwise why are they afraid to get married?

In the war of the sexes, there are no conscientious objectors.

Every Jack has his Jill: if one won't another will.

The battle of the sexes really begins when a man and woman marry and become one, and then try to decide which one.

The three sexes are masculine, feminine and nuder.

The war of the sexes is not between man and woman but between women and other women.

When it comes to women, no man can be both logical and biological.

In the battle of the sexes women rely on two weapons—cosmetics and tears.

The three sexes are masculine, feline and neuter.

In the battle of the sexes, men are more deceitful, but women are more deceptive.

Each of the sexes has one trait the opposite sex vents its hate on; women were made to make men wait, and men were made to wait on.

The battle of the sexes is often caused by a man's earnings and a woman's yearnings.

There are three sexes: those who whistle, those who turn around, and those who do neither.

In the battle of the sexes, the captivating male is often turned into a captive.

Another difference between the sexes is that a woman's slip always pulls down while a man's shirt always creeps up.

In the battle of the sexes, every woman has her curves and every man his angles.

The war between the sexes will never be ended successfully: there's too much fraternizing with the enemy.

SEXOLOGY

We are not taught to think decently on sex subjects, and consequently we have no language for them except indecent language.
— *Bernard Shaw*

The only thing that the sex psychologists can't read a sexual significance into is trap-shooting, and they are working on that now.
— *Robert Benchley*

To a sexologist there are only two kinds of people—men and women.

A sexologist is a man who is more interested in high frequency than high fidelity.

There's nothing wrong with a person's sex life that the right psychoanalyst can't exaggerate.

The affairs of sexology are the affairs of the sexes.

Sexology is the science which deals a little with sexual behavior, but a lot with sexual misbehavior.

SHAKESPEARE

If Bacon wrote Shakespeare, who wrote Bacon?
— *George Lyman Kittredge*

To know the force of human genius we should read Shakespeare; to see the insignificance of human learning we may study his commentators.
— *Hazlitt*

Poets like Shakespeare knew more about psychiatry than any $25-an-hour man. — *Robert Frost*

Macbeth is a tale told by a genius, full of soundness and fury, signifying many things.
— *James Thurber*

Shakespeare never has six lines together without a fault.
— *Samuel Johnson*

I don't know if Bacon wrote the works of Shakespeare, but if he did not, he missed the opportunity of his life. — *James M. Barrie*

To this day I cannot read *King Lear,* having had the advantage of studying it accurately in school.
— *A. N. Whitehead*

The final proof of Shakespeare's genius is that he forced Broadway managers to recognize him.

It is much easier to quote Shakespeare than to read him.

In a Shakespearean play, no one ever gets a chance to sit down, unless he's a king.

Another reason Shakespeare turned out as much work as he did was that he didn't have to answer the telephone.

Shakespeare was right about show business—display's the thing.

SHAME

As soon as a woman begins to be ashamed of what she shouldn't, she ceases to be ashamed of what she should. — *Livy*

A woman is usually not ashamed to do for love what she is ashamed to describe.

Always put off till tomorrow what you are ashamed to do today.

If a woman deceives a man once, she should be ashamed; if she deceives him twice, he should be ashamed.

Some men are ashamed of nothing, except being ashamed.

A man starts to cut his wisdom teeth the first time he eats crow.

Any man who guesses a woman's age correctly ought to be ashamed of himself.

When a person is humiliated, he suddenly shrinks to his normal proportions.

SHAPE

Destiny may shape our ends, but we shape our own middles.

A girl may be both ignorant and shapely, but she is never ignorant of the fact that she is shapely.

A man is getting old when he starts to watch his own shape instead of hers.

A girl likes to be shipshape in everything but her figure.

Some women buy clothes that give them the shapes they dieted to avoid.

When you see the odd shapes of some human beings, it's hard to believe that they all come from the same pattern.

A girl with a good figure can often shape her own destiny.

Human beings come in only two forms, but in millions of shapes.

A girl in good shape is often the reason why a man is in bad shape.

Statesmen have less influence than fashion designers in determining the shape of things to come.

A girl's plans for the future seldom take shape until she does.

Time is the destiny that shapes our ends while it ends our shapes.

SHARE

Grief can take care of itself, but to get the full value of a joy you must have somebody to divide it with. *— Mark Twain*

All children share things with others, even if it is only a contagious disease.

When a woman promises to share a man's lot, she never suspects that it may be just a lot of trouble.

Pull your own weight, but keep your thumb off the scales.

Happiness adds and multiplies as we divide it with others.

A gold digger may not share a man's interests, but she is interested in everything he has shares in.

If you feel down in the mouth, make liquor share it with you.

The person who always borrows trouble is usually generous about sharing it with others.

Beware of the woman who, when you ask her to share your lot, wants to know the size of it.

What every woman needs is a husband to share her joys and sorrows—and her friends' secrets.

SHAVING

The best reason I can think of for not running for President of the United States is that you have to shave twice a day.
— Adlai Stevenson

A commuter shaves and takes a train, and then rides back to shave again. *— E. B. White*

Another advantage of an electric razor is that you don't have to sober up to shave.

Never get up in the morning with a long face, or you'll have that much more to shave.

Man is better off than woman in many ways: for one thing, he never has to kiss someone who needs a shave.

A man usually shaves his face in the morning when it's his mind that's fuzzy.

SHAW, BERNARD

Bernard Shaw is an excellent man; he has not an enemy in the world, and none of his friends like him.   —*Oscar Wilde*

I am genuinely free from envy, but how can I be envious when I pity every other man for not being Bernard Shaw.   —*Bernard Shaw*

If I am sane, the rest of the world ought not to be at large.
—*Bernard Shaw*

I lay my eternal curse on whomsoever shall make schoolbooks of my works and make me hated by schoolboys as Shakespeare is hated.   —*Bernard Shaw*

Things have not happened to me; on the contrary, it is I who have happened to them.
—*Bernard Shaw*

It has taken me nearly twenty years of studied self-restraint to make myself dull enough to be accepted as a serious person by the British public.   —*Bernard Shaw*

I am the unquestioned lawful heir of my mother's property and my father's debts. —*Bernard Shaw*

With the single exception of Homer, there is no eminent writer whom I can despise so entirely as Shakespeare when I measure my mind against his.   —*Bernard Shaw*

I yield to no man in the ingenuity and persistence with which I seize every opportunity of puffing myself and my affairs.
—*Bernard Shaw*

I have solved practically all the pressing questions of our time, but they keep on being propounded as insoluble, just as if I never existed.
—*Bernard Shaw*

I cannot learn languages; men of ordinary capacity can learn Sanskrit in less time than it takes me to buy a German dictionary.
—*Bernard Shaw*

People are usually born twenty years after I create them in fiction.
—*Bernard Shaw*

I know a great deal more about economics and politics than Jesus did, and can do things he could not do.   —*Bernard Shaw*

I shall be remembered as a playwright as long as Aristophanes and rank with Shakespeare or be a forgotten clown before the end of the century.   —*Bernard Shaw*

SHEEP

The older a lamb grows, the more sheepish it becomes.
—*Henry Erskine*

The first in a flock is still a sheep.   —*Bernard Berenson*

If a cure for insomnia were found it would put thousands of sheep out of work.

Families that have a black sheep always try to keep it dark.

Counting sheep is no fun; most men would rather count calves.

It is better to be a dark horse than a black sheep.

SHERIFF

The wicked flee when no man pursueth, but they make better time when the sheriff is after them.

It's always nice to know that someone is thinking about you, unless it's the sheriff.

SHIP

Anyone who has to ask about the annual upkeep of a yacht can't afford one. —*J. P. Morgan*

Being in a ship is being in jail, with the chance of being drowned.
—*Samuel Johnson*

The only thing some men know about ships is that port is red.

An ocean liner is a night club and swimming pool that also crosses the high seas.

A ship in harbor is safe, but that is not what ships are built for.

A submarine is the only ship that can travel overseas underseas.

Many a man waits for his ship to come in even though he never sent one out.

SHIRKER

Some men are still looking for a job with the responsibility of an office boy, the hours of an absentee, and the income of an executive.

Some people are like blisters—they don't show up until the work is done.

A goldbricker earns his daily bread by the sweat of another man's brow.

Among the chief problems of a business executive is the number of unemployed he still has on the payroll.

A shirker is always looking for less to do and more time to do it in.

A shirker is a worker who acts as if he were on a pension instead of a salary.

A goldbricker puts more hours in his work than work in his hours.

A goldbricker never does anything, yet gets criticized just the same.

There are still too many people whose idea of a job is nothing but a series of coffee breaks with retirement benefits.

A goldbricker is a man who, to say the least, is always ready to do the least.

SHIRT

Women may be smarter than men, but did you ever see a man wearing a shirt buttoned in the back?

From shirt sleeves to shirt sleeves takes two generations and one degeneration.

The husband who is willing to give his wife the shirt off his back probably wants her to sew a button on it.

A stuffed shirt never buys his shirts that way, but stuffs them himself.

Some men lose their shirts by playing the horses, some by speculating in the stock market, and others by sending them to the laundry.

People are illogical: when a man has lost his shirt, they expect him to roll up his sleeves.

SHOCKING

It is not only good for people to be shocked occasionally, but necessary to the progress of society that they be shocked often.
— *Bernard Shaw*

It is discouraging to think how many people are shocked by honesty and how few by deceit.
— *Noel Coward*

Did it ever occur to you that there is a good deal of fun in being shocked?   — *Ed Howe*

If things go on as they have, imagine the horrifying things the children of the next generation will have to do to shock their parents.

Many a scandalmonger finds it hard to believe people do the shocking things she tells others they do.

Men used to be shocked listening to the kind of stories women nowadays are telling.

About the only thing nowadays that can still be shocked is grain.

There are two kinds of women: those who pretend to be shocked when they're not, and those who pretend not to be shocked when they are.

SHOES

There's one good thing about tight shoes: they make you forget your other troubles.
— *Josh Billings*

If the high cost of living goes any higher, we'll be buying our shoes one at a time instead of a pair.

There's nothing smaller than some women's feet, except the shoes they're in.

The first thing a woman would do if she were in a man's shoes is kick them off.

What this country needs is a pair of shoes that will increase in size along with the growth of children's feet.

A woman's little feet usually run up a big shoe bill.

Another way to find out where the shoe pinches is to foot your wife's shoe bills.

There was an old woman who lived in a shoe—naturally, several sizes too small.

A popular girl needs a closet full of shoes, probably because young men come in different heights.

Why does a woman buy shoes at a shop where the only comfortable ones are worn by the salesmen?

No man is indispensable: even a pair of shoe trees can fill your shoes.

Women's taste in shoes differ, but they all like to buy shoes that are larger inside than they are outside.

The only woman who doesn't wear shoes that are too tight is a mermaid.

If shoes have a small hole, that's poverty; if they are mostly holes, that's style.

Every little girl is eager to grow up and wear the kind of shoes that are killing mother.

No man ever learns to shop properly: if he likes the first pair of shoes he tries on, he will buy them simply because they fit.

Never judge a woman's feet by the shape of her shoes.

A shoe store is where a woman tries on many pairs of shoes, hoping to find something larger in the same size.

SHOPPING

A woman is a creature that's always shopping.   *— Ovid*

A woman spends the first part of life shopping for a husband, and the rest of her life shopping for everything else.

Time is money, so when you go shopping take lots of time.

The most a man can hope for when he goes shopping with his wife is that her feet will start to hurt before his wallet does.

Another optimist is the man who double-parks while his wife is shopping.

After trying on a few dresses and a dozen hats, a woman begins to wish she had brought some money along.

All things come to him who waits, especially shopworn things.

The successful shopkeeper depends not on the number of customers who come in, but on the number who come back.

At the end of a shopping spree a woman is tired as well as spent.

When a man ridicules a woman for shopping all day and buying nothing, you can be sure he's a bachelor.

A woman has many good reasons for shopping, one of which is that she cannot afford it.

SHORT

Brevity may be the soul of wit, but there's very little fun in being short.

It's an advantage for a fisherman to be short: the fish look bigger when they are photographed together.

Christmas is the season when the days are the shortest, and so are most people.

In courtship, women are the smarter sex: a woman can look up to a man shorter than she is.

SHOW BUSINESS

In show business, you can't live on things made for children—or critics.
— *Walt Disney*

Everybody has two businesses —his own, and show business.
— *Eddie Cantor*

The man who provides the interruptions of a good musical comedy is called the librettist.
— *George Ade*

There's only one man in the theater that can count on steady work—the night watchman.
— *Tallulah Bankhead*

In show business, sex rears its ugly head in the shape of a beautiful body.

Another thing a musical comedy must have for a long run is good legs.

Show business is the only business where you can get up in the world without having to get up in the morning.

In show business, it's the box office that counts, not the applause.

Fools rush in where angels fear to tread—especially in show business.

If a musical comedy takes off enough clothes in the summer, it usually runs through the winter.

A command performance is a show given for the benefit of the overprivileged.

Some types of entertainment have to be sin to be appreciated.

SHOWGIRL

Showgirls are so beautiful, it is sad to think that twenty years from now they will all be five years older.
— *Will Rogers*

In show business, more showgirls are kept than promises.
— *Fred Allen*

It takes all kinds of people to make a showgirl.

Showgirls usually go for only one kind of man—the strong, solvent type.

A college girl gets her education by degrees, a showgirl by stages.

SHREW

Many a woman's idea of keeping her house in order is to put her husband in his place.

A shrew is a strong-minded woman who is usually minded by a weak-minded man.

When a wife reigns, she often storms.

A shrew is a special kind of wife: she takes her husband to have and to scold.

It's impossible to live with a battle-ax: she always misunderstands what her husband isn't saying.

A shrew is the one nag you can always bet on.

Every man can tame a shrew, except the man who is married to her.

A shrew's strong will always dominates over her husband's weak won't.

SHUT

The man who has a closed mind ought to keep his mouth shut too.

The best way to save face is to keep the lower half of it shut.

Another way to lose weight is to keep both your mouth and your refrigerator shut.

A closed mind is only closed to things coming in, not to things going out.

Take a tip from nature: your ears weren't made to shut, but your mouth was.

SHY

He was like one of those men who are too shy to talk to strangers, but not too shy to hold up a bank. —*Joseph Mitchell*

Nothing keeps a girl's hair so neat as a bashful boy friend.

Faint heart never won fair lady, nor dark one either.

A woman is always shy about telling her age—several years shy.

There's no one so bashful as the young man who never gets his face slapped.

When a girl is reserved, a man wonders whom for.

Faint heart never won fair lady, or escaped one either.

SICK

In literature a man is ill, but in real life he is sick.

We wouldn't mind so much the woman who is always talking about her ailments, if she'd only take our advice.

A hypochondriac is a person who has no disease but many complaints.

Nothing ruins friendship quicker than one woman infringing on another woman's symptoms.

Convalescence is the period when you are still sick after you get well.

It takes longer for a person to get over an illness if compensation sets in.

The worst thing about a hypochondriac is not that her ailments are chronic, but that they are chronicles.

No one can feel worse than the man who gets sick on his day off.

SIGHT

We see things not as they are, but as we are. — *H. M. Tomlinson*

A wise man sees as much as he should, not as much as he can. — *Montaigne*

After marriage a woman can see right through her husband without looking at him, and he can look right through her without seeing her. — *Helen Rowland*

Many a woman who is a vision at night is a sight in the morning.

An oculist is the doctor you go to see when you can't see.

Hindsight is good, foresight is better, but insight is the best of all.

If we could see ourselves as others see us, we'd never speak to them again.

A man doesn't need 20–20 eyesight to appreciate a 36–24–36 vision.

The man who sees things as they ought to be is much happier than the man who sees them as they are.

If a girl gives up wearing glasses, she looks better but doesn't see as well.

An egotist may be all I's, yet he cannot see anything but himself.

The difference between nearsighted people and shortsighted ones is that the nearsighted can be corrected.

It would also help if we had the gift of seeing others as they see themselves.

Many a case of love at first sight involves a nearsighted man.

When your vision begins to blur, you should use stronger glasses and weaker drinks.

Oh wad some power the giftie gie us to see some people before they see us.

The man who sees eye to eye with his wife has probably had his vision corrected.

SIGN

When a woman says she won't, it is a good sign she will; and when she says she will, it is an even better sign. — *Mencken*

The most effective of all highway safety signs is on the car marked *Police*.

The worm always turns, but he doesn't always give you the signal in advance.

Actions speak louder than words, especially in sign language.

Nowadays everything is done by machinery, except gestures, which are still being made by hand.

The longest line in the dollar sign is crooked.

You cannot stop people from thinking—even if you display a THINK sign.

SIGNATURE

The only thing some men can do better than anyone else is to read their own signature.

The surest way to tell whether you like a modern painting or not is first to see who painted it.

A signature always reveals a man's character—and sometimes even his name.

Money talks, but a credit card uses sign language.

Many a man is simple and straightforward in everything but his signature.

SILENCE

For God's sake! Hold your tongue and let me love.
— *John Donne*

If nobody ever said anything unless he knew what he was talking about, what a ghastly hush would descend upon the earth!
— *A. P. Herbert*

Silence is not always tact, and it is tact that is golden, not silence.
— *Samuel Butler*

I believe in the discipline of silence and can talk for hours about it. — *Bernard Shaw*

Nothing so stirs a man's conscience or excites his curiosity as a woman's silence.
— *Thomas Hardy*

Silence is foolish if we are wise, but it is wise if we are foolish. — *C. C. Colton*

I have been breaking silence these twenty-three years and have hardly made a dent in it. — *Thoreau*

Silence has been given to woman to better express her thoughts. — *Desnoyers*

Silence is become his mother tongue. — *Oliver Goldsmith*

It isn't a bad plan to keep still occasionally even when you know what you're talking about.
— *Kin Hubbard*

Silence is the wit of fools.
— *La Bruyère*

I have never been hurt by anything I didn't say.
— *Calvin Coolidge*

There is only one way by which man can express the inexpressible, and that is by silence.

Before she marries, every girl should take a course in domestic silence.

The hardest thing to keep in this world is to keep still.

There's nothing wrong with having nothing to say; the trick is not to say it aloud.

When you want a group of women to be silent, ask the oldest lady to speak up.

The most convincing argument in the world is intelligent silence.

Silence is golden—that's why there is so little of it.

Silence is often broken but never when it falls.

The difference between a fort and a fortress is that a fortress is harder to silence.

There's no one so wise as the man who says nothing at the right time.

The best thing for anyone who has nothing to say is to say nothing and stick to it.

Many a man thinks that only the silent woman is worth listening to.

Silence is only golden when you cannot think of a good answer.

Another advantage that silence has is that it cannot be repeated.

When a man suddenly acquires a lot of money in one way or another, he is usually reticent about *another*.

When a woman suffers in silence she is in a critical condition.

Silence is the college yell of the school of experience.

Another thing that marriage brings out in a man is silence.

The only thing that can force some women to suffer in silence is laryngitis.

The trouble with silence is that too much of it is mixed with words.

In domestic quarrels it is important to know how to say nothing, but even more important to know when.

SIMPLE

The whole is simpler than the sum of its parts. — *Willard Gibbs*

Everything should be made as simple as possible, but not simpler.
— *Einstein*

God created woman to satisfy man's craving for the simple things in life.

Another thing so simple that a child can operate it is a grandparent.

SIMPLE AND COMPLEX

Everything is simpler than you think, and more complex than you imagine. — *Goethe*

Psychoanalysis was a wonderful discovery; it makes quite simple people feel they are complex.
— *S. N. Behrman*

The great man is too often all of a piece; it is the little man that is a bundle of contradictory elements.
— *Somerset Maugham*

Simple pleasures are the last refuge of the complex.
— *Oscar Wilde*

There's nothing more complicated today than trying to lead a simple life.

A politician simplifies everything before he is elected, and complicates everything afterward.

Oedipus was a simple man who became a complex.

Knowledge leads us from the simple to the complex; wisdom leads us from the complex to the simple.

SIN

Men are not punished for their sins, but by them.
— *Elbert Hubbard*

It is public scandal that gives offense: it is no sin to sin in secret.   — *Molière*

It is funny but true, a man will sin most when he is happiest.   — *Peggy Hopkins Joyce*

The world's as ugly as sin, and almost as delightful.
— *Frederick Locker-Lampson*

If there is an unpardonable sin, it is to believe that there is an unpardonable sin.

A moralist criticizes other people's sins, a saint criticizes his own.

All your sins may be forgiven and never trouble you again—unless you run for office.

One of the reasons why sin is so attractive is because it is so well advertised.

There are many synonyms for sin, and a good preacher knows most of them.

Some women are most happy when confessing the sins of other women.

One man's sin is another man's singularity.

The sins of the father are visited on the son, but the sins of the son are visited on the whole family.

The wages of sin are sables.

Remember, before you can expect forgiveness of sin, you must sin.

All of us sin sometimes, but the unpardonable sin is always committed by the other person.

Epigrams cover a multitude of sins.

The wages of sin have one redeeming feature: they are always paid.

SING

Ask singers to sing, and you can't get them to start; don't ask them to sing, and you can't get them to stop.   — *Horace*

Whether or not the tenor is castrated, he sings like a eunuch.
— *James G. Huneker*

When something is not worth saying, it's sung. — *Beaumarchais*

Whoever heard a married man coax his wife to sing? — *Ed Howe*

People who have heard me sing, say I don't.   — *Mark Twain*

If you must sing while bathing, do it under a shower, not in the tub; the sound of running water is a great help.

There are times when a quartet is a greater menace than a triangle.

There's no one worse than the singer who can't carry a tune, except the one who won't drop it.

Two pints make a quartet.

When a man sings his own praises he always gets the tune too high.

Singing is every man's bathright.

SINGLE

Celibacy has the advantage of involving submission to the wants and wishes of a single tyrant.
— *Lionel Strachey*

A girl always knows when the right man comes along—he's single.

A woman is resigned to remaining single when she starts buying her shoes for comfort and her sweaters for warmth.

A bachelor girl is a girl who is still looking for a bachelor.

Some people never marry because they do not believe in divorce.

A bachelor is one who has never been married, a spinster is one who has never been married or anything.

The great majority of men who go around looking for arguments are single.

A rolling stone gathers no Mrs.

The advantage of being single is that it's a wonderful experience —until your wife finds you out.

When a bachelor tells a girl he likes her just the way she is, he means *single*.

Advice to men who are single —stay!

Two can live as cheaply as one, but it's worth the difference to stay single.

Another advantage of being a bachelor is that a single man doesn't have to lead a double life.

SISTER

A young man is always more interested in someone else's sister than his own.

The only one of your uncle's sisters who is not your aunt is your mother.

SIZE

You can tell the size of a man by the size of the things that make him mad. — *Adlai Stevenson*

Here in Texas maybe we got into the habit of confusing bigness with greater. — *Edna Ferber*

In everything that matters the inside is much larger than the outside. — *Chesterton*

Gifts and people come in different sizes, and they seldom match.

Size isn't everything: it's the big fish that gets caught in the net.

It isn't that little men always marry big women, it's the big women who marry the little men.

It isn't the size of the dog in the fight that counts, it's the size of the fight in the dog.

When a man can't contain himself, is he too large or too small?

There are two good ways to determine how big a man is: by the size of his friends, and the size of his enemies.

Size isn't everything: the little woman often has a big man under her thumb.

The size of your troubles generally depends on whether they are coming or going.

SKEPTICISM

A skeptic doesn't believe everything he hears, or even everything he says.

It is the lot of the skeptic to doubt his beliefs but believe his doubts.

Give a skeptic an inch, and he'll measure it.

If some skeptics thought seeing is believing, they wouldn't look.

When the skeptic who doesn't believe in the hereafter gets to heaven or hell, does he believe in the heretofore?

A skeptic is a man who has faith in nothing, except in his own lack of faith.

SKIING

The mold out of which good skiers are cast is usually plaster of Paris. *— Art Buchwald*

The skier who gets a lucky break is the one who breaks a ski instead of a leg.

A ski jump is a leap made by a person on his way to the hospital.

Skis are a pair of wooden strips sometimes used as snow gliders but more often as splints.

A ski resort is usually known for its setting of snow and mountains—and bones.

Skiing is best when you have lots of white snow and Blue Cross.

Skiing must be a great sport: many a person has been known to ski for hours on end.

In learning to ski it's important to have a good instructor; otherwise, you're liable to break a ski instead of a leg.

SKIN

The finest clothing made is a person's own skin. *— Mark Twain*

A thick skin is a gift from God.
— Konrad Adenauer

A girl's best friend is a clear white skin, especially if it's ermine.

The difference between a tax collector and a taxidermist is that the taxidermist leaves the hide.

Charity also covers a multitude of skins.

Most people are born lucky: the average baby at birth has about a thousand square inches of skin—just enough to cover him all around.

SKIRT

A sarong is a simple garment carrying the implicit promise that it will not stay long in place.
— *E. B. White*

No skirt should be so short as to expose the *knee plus ultra.*

The proper length of a woman's skirt is a little above two feet.

Short skirts have reduced the number of daydreamers: there aren't as many men nowadays with their heads in the clouds.

Short skirts make women look shorter and make men look longer.

Another advantage of short skirts is that they make it easier for the man who can't remember faces.

No one knows what the short skirt will be up to next.

Fashions change behavior: it used to be improper for a girl to cross her legs in company—then came short skirts.

The proper length for a skirt is just above reproach.

SKUNK

The habits of skunks are phew! but unique.   — *Josh Billings*

If you want to keep the neighbors' noses out of your business, raise skunks.

The skunk is the only animal that's more often smelled than seen.

No one likes a skunk because it puts on such awful airs.

Nobody can act like a skunk without someone getting wind of it.

A skunk in the bush is worth two in the hand.

Many a girl who marries for mink later discovers that what she really got was a skunk.

SLANG

The language of the street is always strong: what can describe the folly and emptiness of scolding like the word *jawing?* — *Emerson*

Slang is the vengeance of the anonymous masses for the linguistic thralldom imposed on them by the educated classes. — *Mario Pei*

Slang has its place, and its place seems to be everywhere.

Most American teen-agers speak a foreign language—it's called slang.

To the purist, all slang is impure.

SLEEP

There is only one thing people like that is good for them: a good night's sleep.   — *Ed Howe*

Living is a disease from which sleep gives us relief eight hours a day.   — *Chamfort*

I never take a nap after dinner but when I have had a bad night, then the nap takes me.
— *Samuel Johnson*

I must marry—if only to get to bed at a reasonable hour.
— *Benjamin Constant*

Of all things that are better late than never, going to bed ranks first.

Frequent naps will keep you from getting old, especially if you take them while driving.

Sleep is something you do when you do nothing.

The amount of sleep required by the average person is about half an hour more.

To the idealist, sound sleep means a good conscience; to the realist, it means a good mattress.

Sleep is the only thing that keeps a glutton from eating twenty-four hours a day.

Monday is the day when many a girl goes to work with her sleep showing.

Man is the only animal that goes to sleep when he's not sleepy, and gets up when he is.

The proof of the pudding is not in the eating but in the sleeping.

Next to a beautiful girl, sleep is the most wonderful thing in the world.

Sleep is a form of death on the installment plan.

It is impolite for a man to fall asleep while his wife is talking, but a man has to sleep some time.

The best time to attend to your neighbor's affairs is in your sleep.

About the only time the modern youngster can be seen but not heard is when he's asleep.

Sleep cancels out all the difference between the wisest man and the biggest fool.

The only virtue in sleepwalking is that you get your exercise and your rest at the same time.

No wonder Rip Van Winkle was able to sleep for twenty years—his neighbors had neither a radio nor television.

SLEEP AND WAKE

I fell asleep reading a dull book and dreamed I kept on reading, so I awoke from sheer boredom.
— *Heine*

Sleep is such a wonderful thing that it's a shame you can't keep awake to enjoy it.

The man who falls asleep holding a steering wheel will probably wake up holding a harp.

It is better to sleep on what you are going to do than to stay awake over what you have done.

A bore talks long enough to put you to sleep, but loud enough to keep you awake.

People never find fault with others except when they're awake, and never find fault with themselves except when they're asleep.

While sleeping, it is best to lie on the right side—also while awake.

The United States spends more money than any other country on coffee to keep people awake, and on sleeping pills to put them to sleep.

The man who sleeps like a top must wake up and find the bedclothes wound around him.

The irony of life is that by the time you retire and can sleep late, you're too old to be able to.

SLEEPTALKING

A sleeptalker is a man who talks in his sleep or a man who sleeps in his talk.

If you talk in your sleep, be careful what you do when you're awake.

The man who has no secrets from his wife probably talks in his sleep.

When a sleeptalker gives no secrets away to his wife, it's the triumph of mind over mutter.

When a married man talks in his sleep, it's probably the only chance he gets.

Some husbands talk in their sleep; others just grin, and it's even more exasperating.

If you want to make sure that your wife will listen to what you have to say, do your talking in your sleep.

SLIM

During middle age half the women talk about how slim they used to be, and the other half about how slim they're going to be.

Exercise is a popular form of reducing, with the chances of getting slim being slim.

To the slim, all years are lean years.

Little girls should obey their mothers and eat their cereal or they are liable to grow up and become fashion models.

Middle age is the time when the only thing that's slim about a woman's figure is her chance of getting it back.

SLIP

Better slip with foot than with tongue.   *—Franklin*

The Irish bull differs from the bulls of all other islands in that it is always pregnant. *— R. Y. Tyrrell*

There's many a Freudian slip 'twixt the cup and the lip.

A slip at the right time is better than a quip on the wrong occasion.

There's many a slip 'twixt editor and contributor.

When some men open their mouths, you never know which foot they're going to put in.

Embarrassment is often caused by a slip that shows, especially a Freudian slip.

There's many a cup 'twixt the lip and the slip.

SLOW

Haste makes waste: give time time.

Driving as if you were late to a dental appointment is a good safe speed.

Slow and steady may win the race, but history records that the tortoise won only one race with the hare.

Sometimes the only thing to do about the slow driver in front of you is to wait for the worm to turn.

Some women are so slow, they take an hour to prepare a pot of instant coffee.

Motorists should do as they used to do in childhood—approach the schoolhouse slowly.

A slowpoke is a man who strains to advance in order to remain where he is.

Statistics show that the general run of pedestrians is a little too slow.

SLUM

God made the country, and man made the town, and the politician made the slum.

Opportunity knocks very timidly when it gets to the slums.

SMALL

Life is too short to be small.
— *Disraeli*

It's the little things that bother us: we can dodge an elephant but not a fly.

The reason conscience is a small voice is that it tells you only when you've done something small.

It's the little things that annoy us: we can sit on a mountain but not on a tack.

It's the little things that matter most: what good is a bathtub without a plug?

SMALL TOWN

In a small town every face rhymes with every other.
— *G. C. Lichtenberg*

In a village a rich man is respected, a great man suspected.
— *Bernard Shaw*

In a small town, when you see a girl dining with a man old enough to be her father, he is.

A small town is a place where nothing happens every minute.

Another reason it is harder to become rich in a small town is that everyone is watching.

A small town is a place where you don't need a credit card to get credit.

Another thing about a small town is that everyone who leaves is a success.

A small town is one where the postmaster knows more than the schoolmaster.

Although everyone in a small town knows what everyone else is doing, they still read the newspaper to find out who's been caught at it.

A small town is the only place that takes pride in its traffic congestion.

Every small town is famous for something even if it didn't happen there.

A small town is the place where a fellow with a black eye doesn't have to explain—everyone knows.

If you don't know what's going on in a small town, you can be sure that nothing is.

A small town is where you can get a week's rest in half the time.

If nobody knows the troubles you've seen, you're probably not living in a small town.

A home town is the place where they wonder how you ever got as far as you did.

Half the world doesn't know how the other half lives, but not in a small town.

A small town is a place where you chat for a while on the phone even when you get the wrong number.

In a small town everyone knows whose check is good, and whose husband isn't.

Many a two-car family lives in a one-horse town.

A small town is a village where there is no place to go where you shouldn't.

Nothing ever happens in a small town, but what you hear makes up for it.

A village is a small out-of-the-way place that uses something called money instead of credit cards.

SMART ALECK

A smart aleck knows everything, except how to keep others from thinking him a fool.

What this country needs are a few men in government as smart as we were at sixteen.

A smart aleck is a know-it-all who really knows nothing, and is the last one to find it out.

You are never too old to learn, unless you're a smart aleck.

A wiseacre knows more about everything than you know about anything.

Some guys are wise, and some are wise guys.

A smart aleck takes so much pleasure in telling what he knows, it's a pity he knows so little.

If a smart aleck were twice as smart as he tries to be, he wouldn't be half as smart as he thinks he is.

A smart aleck is the only person who knows things without having to learn them.

SMELL

If a disinfectant smells good, it isn't a good disinfectant.
— *Ed Howe*

Every stinking smell that fights it out with a ventilator imagines itself Don Quixote.
— *Stanislaw J. Lec*

The only thing stronger than a mother's love is sometimes a father's breath.

The man who sticks his nose into other people's business usually smells.

A woman first uses a deodorant to smell less, and then uses a perfume to smell more.

You can never tell whether some cheeses are imported or deported from Italy.

The man who has a girl on his mind and liquor on his breath probably also has a wife on his hands.

Smelling salts won't revive a man half as quickly as smelling brandy.

Those who smell least, smell best.

Many a woman who has a dozen perfumes that smell differently is married to a man with a dozen pipes that smell the same.

SMILE

If you haven't seen your wife smile at a traffic cop, you haven't seen her smile her prettiest.
— *Kin Hubbard*

It's better to make the world smile at what you say than laugh at what you do.

Sometimes when a woman smiles, she means it.

Good manners require that a winning smile should always be seen on the face of a good loser.

A sourpuss has nothing to lose by smiling, but is afraid to take a chance.

Keep smiling!—and everyone will wonder what you've been up to.

It's good to smile when everything goes wrong, but it's better to stop smiling and do something about it.

Be your own florist: wreathe your face in smiles.

We all learn from experience: no man wakes up his second baby just to see it smile.

A smile is a curve that helps to set things straight.

Show me a man who smiles when everything goes wrong—and I'll show you an idiot.

You are not fully dressed until you wear a smile.

A person who is two-faced usually wears the one with a smile.

The man who falls in love with a smile often makes the mistake of marrying the rest of the girl.

A smile is a language that even a baby understands.

If you want to spoil the day for a sourpuss, greet him with a broad smile.

Some girls can't even wear a smile without looking in the mirror to see if it fits.

There are a lot of people who would never be recognized if they were caught smiling.

SMOKING

Pipe-smokers spend so much time cleaning, filling and fooling with their pipes, they don't have time to get into mischief.
— *Bill Vaughan*

Smokers and non-smokers cannot be equally free in the same railway carriage. — *Bernard Shaw*

The wife who doesn't smoke always figures out how much her husband would save if he didn't smoke.

Will power is what a woman must have for her husband to give up smoking.

It's better for a person to be smoking here on earth than in the hereafter.

Some men smoke between meals, others eat between smokes.

Many a man's idea of giving up smoking cigarettes is merely giving up buying.

Learning to smoke is almost as painful as trying to give it up.

As ye smoke, so shall ye reek.

Smoke and the world smokes with you, swear off and you smoke alone.

A chain smoker is a person who is always smoking, or who is always giving up smoking.

If you don't think smoking makes a woman's voice harsh, try dropping cigarette ashes on her rug.

Many a high-strung person who gives up smoking keeps on fuming.

Another way to stop the smoking habit is always to light the filter end of the cigarette.

The most difficult thing for a woman is to cut out smoking, especially her husband's.

The greatest tobacco evil is the man who continually quits smoking.

Don't smoke in bed if you don't want to make an ash of yourself.

No one gives up smoking without substituting something for it, like boasting.

If you smoke your cigarettes shorter, you'll smoke them longer.

Another class of people who ought to cut down on smoking are those who are always borrowing cigarettes.

SNAKE

If you see a snake coming toward you in a jungle, you have a right to be anxious; if you see it coming down Park Avenue, you're in trouble.   — *Theodor Reik*

The fact that a snake wags its tail at you doesn't mean it wants to be petted.

The first thing a student of reptiles learns is never to pick up a live rattlesnake till it's dead.

Cleopatra should have taken an aspirin instead of an asp.

SNEEZE

He possesses more power than anyone else on earth, but he cannot stop a sneeze.   — *Mark Twain*

Nothing is really impossible, except keeping your eyes open when you sneeze.

A convalescent is usually so full of antibiotics that if he sneezes, he's bound to cure somebody.

SNOB

A snob has to spend so much time being a snob that he has little time left to meddle with you.
— *Faulkner*

If it were not for the intellectual snobs who pay in solid cash, the arts would perish with their starving practitioners.
— *Aldous Huxley*

A snob gets the wrong slant on people by looking down from her family tree.

It takes all kinds of people to make a world, and a snob is glad she's not one of them.

A snob regards himself as the equal of his superiors, and the superior of his equals.

To a snob, happiness consists of being asked everywhere and going nowhere.

A snob is one whose grandfather made money and who therefore refuses to associate with persons who have made it themselves.

A snob doesn't want to know anyone except those who don't want to know her.

The children of those who are snubbed today become the snobs of tomorrow.

A snob is a man standing on a ladder, licking the feet of the man above, and stepping on the hands of the man below.

Many a man would be a snob —if he had a suit of clothes to go with it.

A snob spends half her time telling how superior she is, and the other half telling how inferior others are.

Don't misunderstand: snobs are in favor of equality, but only with the right people.

A snob is one whose eyes look down on others while his nose turns up.

SNORE

Every executive should sit back and meditate sometime during the day—and try not to snore.
— *Bill Vaughan*

He snored so loud that we thought he was driving his hogs to market. — *Swift*

Laugh, and the world laughs with you; snore, and you sleep alone.

Another mystery that has never been solved is why people who snore are always the ones who fall asleep first.

Marriage to some people is nothing but a delusion and a snore.

Usually when a woman wakes her husband out of a sound sleep, it's on account of the sound.

The best cure for the man who snores so loud that he wakes himself up is to put cotton in his ears.

The first thing that a man learns after he's married is that he snores.

If you cannot cure your husband's snoring, try kindness, patience, and stuffing an old sock in his mouth.

SNOW

Each snowflake in an avalanche pleads not guilty.
— *Stanislaw J. Lec*

Snow is beautiful—when you are watching the other fellow shovel it.

The snow falls alike upon the just and the unjust, after which the just falls upon the snow the unjust hasn't cleared away.

Every boy knows that snow is good for nothing except to throw it away.

Snowflakes would be lovely if they weren't so shovely.

Nothing in nature is more beautiful than a single snowflake, and nothing in nature is more rare.

Shoveling the snow off your walk may be hard work, but it's easier than to get your teen-age son to do it.

One good thing about a snowfall is that it makes your lawn look as good as your neighbor's.

Some women make so much noise shoveling the snow, their husbands cannot even nap in peace.

SOAP

We may live without faith, we may live without hope, but civilized man cannot live without soap.

Few children fear water, unless soap is added.

Another example of unrequited love is that of the soap manufacturers for children.

Watching a boy use soap, you'd think it came out of his allowance.

SOBER

The worst thing about him is that when he's not drunk, he's sober.   — *Yeats*

The best test of sobriety is being able to remove your trousers while standing up.

It's not getting drunk that's so bad, it's waking up to all the horrors of sobriety.

SOCIABLE

If you wish to become known as a good fellow, lend your ears to the bores and your money to the incompetents.   — *Don Marquis*

A good mixer is anyone who prefers the society of others to himself.

If you want to be a social success, remember that it is more important to say than to do good things.

SOCIALISM

Many people consider the things government does for them to be social progress, but the things government does for others as socialism.   — *Earl Warren*

We should have had socialism already, but for the socialists.
— *Bernard Shaw*

Socialism is workable only in heaven where it isn't needed, and in hell where they've got it.
— *Cecil Palmer*

I am probably the only man in Christendom who has never been a socialist even for an instant.
— *Mencken*

There's something else I dislike just as much as creeping socialism, and that's galloping reaction.
— *Adlai Stevenson*

Socialism is a form of government under which too many adults, and not enough children, believe in Santa Claus.

Socialism is bureaucracy of the people, by the people, and for the people.

Socialism works, but nowhere as efficiently as in the beehive and the anthill.

SOCIETY

To get into the best society nowadays, one has either to feed people, amuse people, or shock people.   — *Oscar Wilde*

Of the best society it used to be said, its conversation affords instruction while its silence imparts culture.   — *Goethe*

There are no social differences —till women come in.
— *H. G. Wells*

Society is a madhouse whose wardens are the officials and the police. — *August Strindberg*

Society is divided into two classes: the shearers and the shorn; we should always be with the former against the latter.
— *Talleyrand*

A society woman is known by the company she gets rid of.

Man is attracted to society by a desire to improve himself, and he leaves it for the same reason.

Society is built on four types of people: performers, conformers, reformers and misinformers.

The upper crust is made out of the same dough as the lower, only more of it.

One should never open one's mouth in polite society unless one has nothing to say.

The cream of society seldom rises on the milk of human kindness.

Society is made up of two classes: the haves who are up and doing, and the have-nots who are down and doing without.

After a woman arrives in society she often wants to forget how she got there.

Society is made up of a small group of people who dress for dinner, or the rest of us who dress for breakfast.

Loneliness is the greatest of bores, otherwise there would be no accounting for society.

A man is known by the company he can't get into.

Society is divided into two classes: those in the swim, and those in the soup.

SOCIOLOGY

There's doing good—that's sociology; there's also doing well—that's art. — *Robert Frost*

History never repeats itself; if it did, it would be sociology.

A sociologist is a scientist who blames crime on everything and everyone, except the person who commits it.

It takes two to make a criminal: one individual and one society.

In sociology, the needy are deprived, underprivileged or disadvantaged, but never poor.

SOCRATES

Socrates was famed for wisdom because he realized at the age of seventy that he still knew nothing. — *Robert Lynd*

Socrates was a wise man, but he knew less about American history than the most ignorant schoolboy.

SOLDIER

I could have become a soldier if I had waited; I knew more about retreating than the man who invented retreating. — *Mark Twain*

I rose by sheer military ability to the rank of corporal.
— *Thornton Wilder*

A GI is a young American whose combat training in the army prepares him for marriage.

Advice to soldiers: When arguing with your sergeant, be sure you're right—then let the matter drop.

A paratrooper is the only member of the armed forces who starts at the top and works his way down.

The longer a soldier stays in the army, the ranker he gets.

A GI is a man who wakes up to music every morning.

SOLITUDE

I have a great deal of company in my house, especially in the morning when nobody calls.
— *Thoreau*

I enjoy solitude—even when I am alone. — *Jules Renard*

Solitude is a good place to visit but a poor place to stay.
— *Josh Billings*

I would rather sit on a pumpkin, and have it all to myself, than be crowded on a velvet cushion. — *Thoreau*

If you are afraid of being lonely, don't try to be right.
— *Jules Renard*

It is not good for man to be alone; he must have somebody to quarrel with to be happy.

You don't have to go off somewhere by yourself to find solitude; another way is always to tell the truth.

There's no one so lonesome as the woman who arrives at a party on time.

One thing worse than being alone is to be with someone who makes being alone a pleasure.

The psychiatrist believes you shouldn't keep too much to yourself, and so does the tax collector.

Solitude is sometimes a matter of isolation, but more often of insulation.

If you can't stand solitude, maybe you bore others too.

The only thing a woman needs to keep a secret is solitude.

Great deeds are generally done when a man is alone, especially when he's fishing.

Solitude is more enjoyable if you get someone to share it with.

SOLUTION

There's always an easy solution to every human problem—neat, plausible and wrong. — *Mencken*

Wouldn't it be wonderful if our officials in Washington could solve our money problems the way we keep solving theirs?

The job of the younger generation is to find solutions to the solutions found by the older generation.

The man who knows how to solve the world's problems fortunately lacks the authority to do so.

A know-it-all always seems to have the solution to every problem right in the hollow of his head.

Many a man solves in ten minutes a problem that goes on being unsolved for centuries.

The only men who can solve the world's problems can be found sitting around on park benches.

Parents have lots of trouble solving their children's problems, and children have even more trouble solving their parents' problems.

SONG

The best thing about most popular songs is that they are not popular long.

Many a song would be on the hit parade except for two things— words and music.

The most difficult problem in writing a drinking song is to get beyond the first bar.

Lots of girls can be had for a song, but the trouble is, it's the wedding march.

It is better to forget all of an old song than only half of it.

There are songs that never die, but it isn't the fault of radio.

The worst thing about expanding our educational program is that the more colleges we build, the more alma mater songs we'll have.

The old popular songs are best, especially those that are not sung any longer.

Nothing is as old as last year's song hit nor as new as the song hit of a generation ago.

Is a popular song bad music set to worse grammar or bad grammar set to worse music?

The life of a popular song is brief, but never brief enough.

A popular song lasts only a few months, after which it has to have its name changed.

The worst thing about a popular song is that it makes us all think we can sing.

Current popular songs are forgotten too quickly to be used against us by future generations.

SOPHISTICATION

Sophistication is knowing how smart you are, but wisdom is understanding how foolish.

Children are so sophisticated nowadays they don't even believe that the stork brings baby storks.

The man who is really sophisticated is too sophisticated to pretend he's sophisticated.

You have had enough to drink when you feel sophisticated and cannot pronounce it.

SOPRANO

There's one strange thing about a soprano: her solo is always so high.

You hardly ever hear sopranos practicing any more, except over the radio.

There are thousands of dialects in the world, excluding the one used by lyric sopranos.

Television permits a soprano a wide range—from high C to low V.

SORROW

It is foolish to tear one's hair in grief, as if grief could be lessened by baldness. — *Cicero*

Woman makes half the sorrows which she boasts the privilege to soothe. — *Lord Lytton*

When I hear that a friend has fallen into matrimony, I feel the same sorrow as if I had heard of his lapsing into theism.
— *Swinburne*

Sorrow grows less and less every time it is told, just like the age of a woman.

The sincerest mourning for husbands is done by women who have never been wives.

You can avoid a lot of sorrow if you'll work today and worry tomorrow.

There are many cures for grief, but careful nursing isn't one of them.

Man was made to mourn, and woman was made to make him.

SOUL

Most people sell their souls and live with a good conscience on the proceeds. — *Logan P. Smith*

When a woman unhappily yoked talks about the soul with a man not her husband, it isn't the soul they are talking about.
— *Don Marquis*

One of the proofs of the immortality of the soul is that myriads have believed it—they also believed the world was flat.
— *Mark Twain*

The soul too has her virginity and must blend a little before bearing fruit. — *Santayana*

The man who claims he is captain of his soul probably has a wife who is the colonel.

SOUND

Sound at the wrong time and place is noise, and at the right time and place is music.

With radio, television and records, American family life has never before been on such a sound basis.

People who make the soundest arguments usually make the least noise.

The pioneer of stereophonic sound was a candidate talking out of both sides of his mouth.

The most beautiful sound is never heard—the sound of falling prices.

SOUP

It was as thin as the homeopathic soup that was made by boiling the shadow of a pigeon that had starved to death.
— *Lincoln*

The poor man eats potato soup; the rich man, vichyssoise.

There's only one thing more difficult than finding a needle in a haystack, and that is finding a clam in clam chowder.

SPACE

I'll put a girdle round about the earth in forty minutes.
— *Shakespeare*

If man had heeded the advice always to keep both feet on the ground, we wouldn't be living in the space age.

In most homes, the father is concerned with parking space, the children with outer space, and the mother with closet space.

The exploration of outer space has a bright future; it will never run out of space to explore.

Space travel is the only way now known to man of leaving this world without dying.

There's nothing so expensive as the government space program because there's no limit to the overhead.

Space travel originally started with hitching your wagon to a star.

Space is being conquered by man while man is being conquered by time.

The most important space in the world is not beyond the earth, but between the ears.

Scientists are trying to find intelligent beings on other planets, probably because they have given up the search here on earth.

Nowadays no one seems to believe the sky's the limit.

The space age has almost solved the problem of travel to the moon, but cannot solve the problem of traffic on earth.

SPADE

The man who could call a spade a spade should be compelled to use one: it is the only thing he is fit for. — *Oscar Wilde*

Sometimes you have to call a spade a spade to get it back from your neighbor.

There's no one more exasperating than a bridge partner who calls a spade two spades.

Many a man who is candid enough to call a spade a spade is not courageous enough to call a liar a liar.

Before starting a garden, there are several things to consider: one of these is where to borrow a spade.

Many a man calls a spade a spade until he accidentally trips over one.

The man who boasts he calls a spade a spade is usually giving someone a dirty dig.

SPECIALIST

A specialist is the only man who can afford to be ignorant on all subjects but one.

If you want a thing to be well done, don't do it yourself—hire a specialist.

The difference between a physician and a specialist is that one treats what you have while the other thinks you have what he treats.

The man we call a specialist today was formerly called a man with a one-track mind.

If you are sick, go to a specialist and he will do you good—and plenty.

SPECULATION

A speculator is a man who observes the future, and acts before it occurs.   — Bernard Baruch

It takes three generations to make a gentleman, but only one lucky guess on the stock market.

A friend in need is a friend who has been playing the stock market.

SPEECH

The true use of speech is not so much to express our wants as to conceal them.
                    — Oliver Goldsmith

British broadcasters speak as if they had Elgin marbles in their mouths.   — Dylan Thomas

A good speech, like a woman's skirt, should be long enough to cover the subject and short enough to create interest.

Short speeches are not always the best, but the best speeches are always short.

It should take two weeks to prepare a half-hour speech, one week an hour speech, but no time at all a two-hour speech.

A filibuster is a long speech about nothing by an authority on the subject.

Parents who can't get their teen-age daughter off the phone wonder why they waited so impatiently for her to say her first baby word.

If you see it in the *Congressional Record* it's true, unless it happens to be a speech.

When a woman develops an impediment in her speech, it's probably because she stops to think.

If speech is the index of the mind, what some men need is an Index Expurgatorius.

Speeches are like the horns on a steer: a point here, a point there, with a lot of bull in between.

Many a glib talker has a lot of depth on the surface but way down deep is very shallow.

A speech is like a bad tooth: the longer it takes to draw it out, the more it hurts.

SPEED

Life can be pretty grim when you pass eighty, especially if there's a state trooper behind you.

Cars continue to be driven at just two speeds: lawful and awful.

The speed maniac is the only type of jet pilot who operates on the ground.

Sooner or later the speed maniac is bound to be overtaken by the state trooper or undertaken by the mortician.

The way many a motorist speeds through traffic, you'd think he was late for his accident.

Laying down the law to some motorists is merely an incentive for them to step on it.

If you want to get a good look at a speed maniac, the best place is the morgue.

Every American is entitled to the pursuit of happiness, but not at the rate of eighty miles an hour.

Speed records are always made by people who aren't going anywhere in particular.

A speed maniac is a man with a light head but a heavy foot.

The motorist who rushes to cover the earth faster than others ends with the earth covering him sooner than others.

Some men never want to make up for lost time until they get behind a steering wheel.

The race is not always to the swift, but the navy is always willing to put its money on the fleet.

If it wasn't for the highway tollbooths, some motorists would never slow down.

If you want to live to see ninety, don't keep looking for it on the speedometer.

The speed maniac always brings two places closer together, especially this world and the next.

With many a driver it is a case of the more hurry, the less need.

The faster you drive, the sooner the ambulance will overtake you.

The violation of traffic laws by speeders often leads to a death sentence.

Some men hold fast that which is good, while others hold good that which is fast.

There are two kinds of speeders: those who drive too fast, and those who fly too low.

SPELLING

Simplified spelling is all right but, like chastity, you can carry it too far. — *Mark Twain*

The trouble with the dictionary is that you have to know how a word is spelled before you can look it up to see how it is spelled. — *Will Cuppy*

Chaucer had talent, but he couldn't spell. — *Artemus Ward*

The man who is busy with public matters cannot be bothered with spelling. — *Napoleon*

No man has a right to be a litrary man onless he knows how to spel. — *Artemus Ward*

A chrysanthemum by any other name would be easier to spell.

Some of the hardest words in English are spelled with *e*'s.

Some people are good at spelling; others know how to spell the synonyms for the words they don't know how to spell.

L-o-v-e spells romance, m-a-r-r-i-a-g-e dispels it.

There's more than one way to skin a cat, and according to some secretaries, there's more than one way to spell a word.

The average man is never troubled with dyspepsia, at least not until he tries to spell it.

Some stenographers spell abominably, while others cannot spell it.

SPEND

A successful man is one who earns more than his wife can spend, and a successful woman is his wife who has no trouble spending it. — *Sacha Guitry*

Persons who have never made or saved a dollar are always telling me how to spend a million. — *Henry Ford*

People don't mind spending their money if they know it isn't going for taxes. — *Will Rogers*

I would rather be a beggar and spend my money like a king, than be a king and spend my money like a beggar. — *Robert G. Ingersoll*

If a man didn't spend all his money on his family, he'd probably lose it some other way.

Money has wings, but can fly in only one direction—away.

Many husbands spend most of the time after money because their wives spend money most of the time.

The best test of blood pressure is to watch a man being liberal with the money he owes you.

Many a man manages to be pound-foolish without being penny-wise.

Some women don't believe in saving up money for a rainy day, because that's the worst day for shopping.

Some people are in debt because they spend what they tell their friends they earn.

Many a man's ambition is to be able to afford to spend what he is already spending.

To maintain our high standard of living, we must continue to spend more, and no one is so eager to help out as the teen-ager.

No one spends money like a drunken sailor—except a sober congressman.

Money doesn't talk—it just goes without saying.

The woman who spends 90 per cent of her husband's income is usually very critical about how he spends the other 10 per cent.

No law can keep a fool and his money from exceeding the speed limit.

You spend by the month, not by the day: a month's salary goes just as fast in February's 28 days as in March's 31.

Time is money, and some people spend one just as foolishly as the other.

When a man meets a girl and soon finds he can't eat or sleep or drink, it's because he's broke.

Another reason you cannot take it with you is that it goes before you do.

God has to take some people out of this world in order to set their money in circulation.

Some wives are always breaking things, like fives, tens and twenties.

A woman can never understand what her husband does with his money, even when she gets it herself.

Once upon a time the fool and his money were soon parted; now it happens to everyone.
where in particular.

SPEND AND SAVE

Everyone is always in favor of general economy and particular expenditure.   *—Anthony Eden*

He practiced the utmost economy in order to keep up the most expensive habits.   *—Bernard Shaw*

Saving is a habit; extravagance, an art.

Every man ought to save up enough to buy himself a home in the country, and then do something else with the money.

A woman's idea of economy is to save money in one shop so she can spend it in another.

If we want to have national prosperity, we must spend; if we want to have individual prosperity, we must save.

What this country needs is a new kind of money that would be easier to save than to spend.

It isn't enough for a married couple to like the same thing if he likes to save it and she likes to spend it.

False economy is saving what is left after spending instead of spending what is left after saving.

The hardest part of being poor is trying to save while spending as much as the rich do.

SPENDTHRIFT

A spendthrift is a person who considers it a disgrace to die rich.

The spendthrift spends his money right and left, but seldom spends it right.

It takes three generations of thrift to make one spendthrift.

A spendthrift not only can't take it with him, he can't even hold on to it while alive.

A spendthrift is the only person who cannot economize even when he is broke.

Spendthrifts act as if living within your income is a fate worse than debt.

A spendthrift is a fellow who treats some of his friends lavishly with the money he owes other friends.

The spendthrift is a man who is all spend and no thrift.

The man who offers you a penny for your thoughts is probably a spendthrift.

A spendthrift is the one that two can live as cheaply as.

Many a man at first can't live within his income, and then can't live within his credit.

SPINSTER

It isn't dying a spinster that worries women, it's living that way.

A spinster remains unmarried out of choice—but not always her choice.

The difference between a bachelor girl and a spinster is nobody's business.

Spinsters live longer than married women because where there's hope there's life.

A spinster is probably a woman who was never in the right place at the right time with the right man in the right mood.

Spinsterhood is sometimes a misfortune but more often an achievement.

Many a woman is unmarried because she cannot stay awake long enough while some man is bragging about himself.

Spinsters are born, not made.

A spinster is a miss who does not always miss as much as others think she does.

The woman who knows all the answers never gets asked.

A spinster is usually a woman who regrets that she was so sensible.

A spinster is a woman who gave up before she gave in.

A young spinster is a menace, a middle-aged one a misfortune, but an old one a delight.

A spinster makes mistakes like other women, but not at the marriage license bureau.

SPINSTER AND MARRIED WOMAN

There would be more spinsters marrying if other women didn't marry so often.

A man shouldn't marry a girl for her money, but neither should he let her remain a spinster just because she has money.

The unmarried woman is always looking for a husband, and so is the married woman.

Women will not stay single, and they won't stay married either.

When spinsterhood is bliss, 'tis folly to be wived.

SPIRIT

The worst way to keep your spirits up is by pouring spirits down.

An excessive drinker always feels out of spirits when he is out of spirits.

Another man who is never low in spirits is the liquor salesman.

SPITE

We call it malice when others bear it, but righteous indignation when we do.

A favor is never so long-lived as a grudge.

Women who make up a bridge club are usually friendly in spite of their spite.

No matter how much you nurse a grudge, it won't get better.

SPLIT PERSONALITY

The man with a split personality is his own worst enemy, and the psychiatrist's best friend.

Another case where one half doesn't know how the other half lives is the man with a split personality.

The man who has a split personality feels like a king one day and like the deuce the next.

Many a woman wouldn't mind having a split personality—if the other one did the housework.

A good example of a split personality is an egotist with an inferiority complex.

The man with a split personality probably takes a pep pill one day and a tranquilizer the next.

Many a woman has a split personality—a catty disposition and a dogged determination.

When a psychoanalyst treats a person with a split personality, does he use a double couch?

The man with a split personality is the only one who can go out on a double date by himself.

Another case where two equals one is the split personality.

The man with a split personality ought to go chase himself.

When a psychiatrist treats a person with a split personality, does he charge him double?

A split personality is the only case where two can live as cheaply as one.

SPONGER

A freeloader always accepts an invitation to a party, even when he doesn't get one.

Not every absorbing personality is a welcome guest—he may just be a sponger.

A freeloader is the only type of man who saves money by eating out.

A sponger could earn a lot of money with the effort he spends trying to save a little.

The only thing a freeloader has ever been known to pay is a visit.

A sponger will continue to get and forget as long as others will continue to give and forgive.

SPORTS

The only way of preventing civilized men from kicking and beating their wives is to organize games in which they can kick and beat balls. —Bernard Shaw

It's hard for the modern generation to understand Thoreau, who lived beside a pond but didn't own water skis or a snorkel.
—Bill Vaughan

The most interesting sport to watch is the contest between an irresistible blonde and an immovable bachelor.

Many a girl thinks she is fond of sports until she marries one.

Some colleges have a strict rule on sports: no student athlete may be awarded a letter unless he can tell which letter it is.

If you enjoy the sport of seeing horses run without losing money on them, attend a polo game.

One of the most popular winter sports is taking a plane to Florida.

The woman who is always losing the ball while golfing should try taking up bowling instead.

An athlete is as young as he feels but seldom as important.

A favorite winter sport is looking at the pictures you took last summer.

The one disadvantage of an outdoor life is that it cannot be enjoyed indoors.

Every athletic team has a coach and Charley horses to pull it.

SPORTSMANSHIP

Always imitate the behavior of the winners when you lose.
— *George Meredith*

Don't criticize a poor loser— he still is a better opponent than any kind of winner.

The only drawback in being a good sport is that you have to lose to prove it.

Some players are good losers, while others don't pretend.

Sportsmanship requires that a loser grip the winner's hand even though he wishes it were his throat.

Win as if you were used to it, lose as if you enjoyed it for a change.

Everyone admires a good loser —except his wife.

There are less winners than losers, but more good winners than good losers.

SPRING

Treat spring just as you would a friend you have not learned to trust.   — *Ed Howe*

What's good about March? Well, for one thing, it keeps February and April apart.
— *Walt Kelly*

No one objects to March coming in like a lion—it's the hanging around like a polar bear that's depressing.   — *Bill Vaughan*

In the spring a young man's fancy, but a young woman's fancier.   — *Richard Armour*

The course of the seasons is a piece of clockwork, with a cuckoo to call when it is spring.
— *G. C. Lichtenberg*

Nothing makes a poet as mad as a late spring.   — *Kin Hubbard*

The best thing about spring is that it always comes when it is most needed.

April showers bring May flowers—with the help of spading, fertilizing, planting, watering and weeding.

Spring comes unusually late or unusually early every year—as usual.

When spring comes, many a man who is retired wishes he were still working so he could take the day off.

Spring is the season of the year that makes you wish you were alive.

The only difference between April and March is that you expect it in March.

Spring is the glorious season when the grass grows up along the roadside and hides the discarded beer cans.

In the spring a young girl's fancy turns to thoughts of love

—the same ones she has been thinking about all winter.

Spring is the time of year when the weather seldom gets together with the season.

There's something bad in everything good: when spring comes, can spring cleaning be far behind?

In the spring many a husband is transferred from the doghouse to the garden.

Spring is the season when you can rely very little upon the weather, and even less upon the weatherman.

Take a lesson from spring: say it with flowers.

Spring was once a forerunner of flowers and nectar, but now is a herald of the tax collector.

In the spring a young man's fancy lightly turns from thoughts of work.

There's no accounting for taste: spring is a divine season to the poet, and nothing but sleet and rain to the weatherman.

April is the month when the green returns to the lawn, the trees and the Internal Revenue Service.

Spring hasn't really reached the suburbs until you are awakened by the first lawn mower.

Spring is the silly season when men plant grass in order to slave in the summer keeping it cut.

Another of life's ironies is to have house cleaning, gardening and spring fever all come at the same time.

SPY

An intelligence service is, in fact, a stupidity service.
　　　　　　　— E. B. White

The all-seeing eye of a totalitarian regime is usually the watchful eye of the next-door neighbor.
　　　　　　　— Eric Hoffer

When he's on our side, he's an intelligence officer; when he's on the enemy's side, he's a spy.

A secret agent holds his job as long as he holds his tongue.

STAMP

You can be a Senator or a Congressman today, but tomorrow you are liable to be paying for you own stamps.
　　　　　　　— Will Rogers

He used to be known in the office as a lad who could lick his weight in postage stamps.
　　　　　　　— Franklin P. Adams

A postage stamp sticks to nothing so closely as another stamp.

STAR-SPANGLED BANNER

There are two occasions when the voice of the people is heard: when they vote, and when they sing the national anthem.

The only piece of music the public will stand for all the time is "The Star-Spangled Banner."

The best way some Americans can show respect for the Star-Spangled Banner is by not trying to sing it.

Probably the only man who ever knew all the words of "The Star-Spangled Banner" was Francis Scott Key.

The man of few words is he who joins in the chorus of "The Star-Spangled Banner."

Americans stand up when they hear the national anthem played, and they fall down when they try to sing it.

The only way to get some people to stand on their own feet is to play "The Star-Spangled Banner."

There's only one thing harder to remember than the words of "The Star-Spangled Banner," and that's the name of the last Vice-President.

STATESMAN

The heart of a statesman should be in his head.   — *Napoleon*

Since most statesmen cannot see farther than their own noses, the statesman with a short nose is at a disadvantage.   — *Paul Claudel*

A genuine statesman should be on his guard; if he must have beliefs, not to believe them too hard.   — *James Russell Lowell*

Nature abhors a vacuum, even in the heads of statesmen.
   — *Clare Boothe Luce*

You admire a statesman for the enemies he has made, but not when you're included among them.

History wouldn't repeat itself so often if statesmen would only listen.

Statesmanship is the conduct of foreign affairs that tries to cure the conflicts which its statesmen create.

A statesman is a politician who has mastered the art of holding his tongue.

The best that can be said for some of our statesmen is that they remind us of other statesmen who are worse.

A statesman should have gray hair to make him look distinguished, and an ulcer to make him look thoughtful.

STATISTICS

He uses statistics as a drunkard uses a lamppost, for support, not for illumination.   — *Chesterton*

Statistics prove that you can prove anything by statistics.

Statistics are like witnesses: you can always get them to testify for either side.

A statistician can use facts and figures to support anything, especially himself.

Sunday drivers make Monday statistics.

A statistician is a man who comes to the rescue of figures that cannot lie for themselves.

Another thing that cigarette smoking causes is statistics.

A statistician carefully assembles facts and figures for others who carefully misinterpret them.

Statistics have taken all the fun out of driving over a holiday weekend.

Don't put too much stock in figures: a man can drown in a stream that averages only two feet in depth.

Statistics is the science of producing unreliable facts from reliable figures.

Facts are stubborn things, but statistics are more pliable.

A statistician is a specialist who assembles figures and then leads them astray.

Safety sign: Slow Down Before You Become A Statistic.

Statisticians assemble facts and figures for everything, except for the time wasted in assembling facts and figures.

If all the statisticians were placed end to end, they would reach endless conclusions.

To a statistician, fractions speak louder than words.

Statistics can be made to prove anything—even the truth.

STATUE

Men who deserve monuments do not need them. — *Gene Fowler*

The statue of a hero usually stands outdoors, with a pedestal below him and a pigeon above.

Blessed are the peacemakers: nobody erects hideous statues of them.

The car will never completely replace the horse until there are bronze statues of generals behind a steering wheel.

Statues are never erected in honor of comedians—they get laughed at enough while they are alive.

Statues are erected to the memory of famous people, but they are really for the birds.

The reason that statues of politicians look so unnatural is that statues keep their mouths shut all the time.

No statue has ever been erected to the memory of a man who let well enough alone.

STATUS

You can tell the people who are in your class: they are the ones you hate to see get ahead of you.   — *Carey Williams*

The happiness of the great consists only in thinking how happy others must think them to be.
— *Francis Bacon*

The person who needs a status symbol has no status.

When a man finds he can keep up with the Joneses, it's time for him to move to a more expensive neighborhood.

Some people own so many status symbols, they're absolutely in awe of themselves.

Don't worry about finding your station in life; there's always someone who will tell you where to get off.

A status symbol is anything your neighbor has and which you can't afford.

In the suburbs the neighbors are trying to keep up with the Joneses while the Joneses are trying to keep up with the payments.

There's no one so insecure of his status as the man who goes in for status symbols.

STEAK

What is so rare as a day in June, or the steak you order well done?

Some men want their steaks rare, some very rare, and others just want the body heat restored.

More people in restaurants would order filet mignon if they knew how to pronounce it.

If you stop to think what you pay for steak, it is easier to understand why cows are sacred in India.

STEAL

Never steal more than you actually need, for the possession of money leads to extravagance, foppish attire, frivolous thought.
— Dalton Trumbo

Men are not hanged for stealing horses but that horses may not be stolen. — Halifax

Never steal a doormat: if you do, you'll be arrested, hanged, and maybe reformed; steal a bank.
— Finley Peter Dunne

Men are not arrested for stealing, they are arrested for being caught at it.

In positions of trust, women are more honest than men; they have no women to steal for.

The man who steals another man's wife is no better than a horse thief.

The real reason why Robin Hood robbed only the rich was that the poor had no money.

It is easier to rob a million men of a dollar each than to rob one man of a million.

A juvenile delinquent gives up stealing bases when he starts stealing cars.

You can be robbed of what you have, but not of what you are.

Some men rob Peter to pay Paul, while others rob Peter to pay Pauline.

STICK

Dogs are faithful: they will stick to a bone after everybody has deserted it.   —*Josh Billings*

Money is a friend only while you stick to it.

Because a woman is a clinging vine, it doesn't mean that she can hang onto a dollar.

Summer is the season when everything that's supposed to stick together comes apart, and everything that's supposed to come apart sticks together.

Poverty is a wonderful thing: it sticks to a man even when all his friends forsake him.

Women are not inconsistent: when they reach a certain age, they stick to it.

STINGY

The height of folly is to live poor so you can die rich.

Some people are so stingy you'd think they were saving their money for a rainy century.

Stinginess is merely practicing economy before you have to.

Stingy is a word whose pronunciation depends upon whether it's applied to a person or insect.

Stinginess generally limits its contributions to good advice.

Getting money from some husbands is like taking candy from a baby—they put up a terrific yell.

Many a man who gives till it hurts is extremely sensitive to pain.

Another of life's ironies is that your close friends are seldom wealthy, while your wealthy friends are usually close.

Many a man thinks nothing is too good for his wife, and nothing is what he gives her.

The closer a man is, the more distant his friends are.

STOCKBROKER

A stockbroker is a man who is smart enough to tell you what stocks to buy, and too smart to buy them himself.

A stockbroker is always ready to back his judgment with your last dollar.

A stockbroker advises you what to do with money you wouldn't have if you had followed his advice.

A stockbroker spends his time planning how others should spend their money.

A broker is a man who runs your fortune into a shoestring.

STOCK MARKET

The stock market has spoiled more appetites than bad cooking.
    —*Will Rogers*

Many a man would lose more in the stock market if his wife spent less in the supermarket.

The man who butts his head against the stock market soon learns why it is called Wall Street.

The stock market is a place where some men operate, but more men are operated on.

Wall Street is made up of three types of investors: bulls, bears and asses.

Many a man is badly burned in the stock market by picking up a hot tip.

In Wall Street it's hard to be successful without having ulcers, but easy to have ulcers without being successful.

Every time the stock market takes a tumble, another class graduates from the School of Experience.

In Wall Street the bulls sometimes make it and the bears sometimes make it, but the hogs never do.

The best way to make a thousand dollars in the stock market is to start with five thousand and quit when you've only lost four.

The only way to beat Wall Street: Beat it.

The secret of success in the stock market is known only to those financial advisors who sell their advice cheaply.

The most dangerous animal in Wall Street is not a bull or a bear, but a bum steer.

People who play the stock market are often led astray by false profits.

STOCKS AND BONDS

Don't gamble: buy some good stock, hold it till it goes up and then sell it—if it doesn't go up, don't buy it!   — *Will Rogers*

There's many a slip 'twixt the stock and the tip.

Many a man is a pessimist because of the stocks an optimist has sold him.

The best time to buy stocks and bonds is always in the past.

A gentleman farmer is one who has more stock in the bank than in the barn.

The sins of the fathers are often visited upon the children in the shape of stocks and bonds.

A financier is a man who would rather own than come from a good stock.

A government bond is a financial device to give you back some of the money you paid in taxes.

Buying stocks on margin is all very well as long as you minimize the margin of error.

STOMACH

God designed the stomach to eject what is bad for it, but not the human brain.
          — *Konrad Adenauer*

I can reason down or deny everything, except this perpetual belly: feed he must and will, and I cannot make him respectable.
— *Emerson*

Before I was in love I always had stomach trouble. — *Swift*

He who does not mind his belly will hardly mind anything else.
— *Samuel Johnson*

The way to a man's heart is through his stomach, but not by jumping down his throat.

Woman's waistline moves up and down: man's expands in a horizontal line only.

Middle age is the time in life when, after pulling in your stomach, you look as if you ought to pull in your stomach.

Too many men tighten their belts by pushing expanding stomachs against them.

The poorest way to keep food down on an empty stomach is to bolt it down.

Girls often wear bathing suits with bare midriffs because the way to a man's heart is through the stomach.

Exercise reduces fat, except when you exercise your stomach.

A man will ask a hundred questions about the oil he puts into his car, but not one about the things he puts into his stomach.

A paunch is a protruding stomach often used by a man instead of an ash tray.

During middle age it's not the man that grows too big for his breeches, but his stomach.

STONE

The two stones most commonly associated with marriage are the diamond and the grindstone.

People who live in glass houses shouldn't live within a stone's throw of one another.

One person's stumbling block is another person's steppingstone.

The Stone Age is about twenty: and the bigger the stone, the better she likes it.

A timid person never casts the first stone, probably because he is too petrified.

STOP

Never let a difficulty stop you: it may be only sand on your track to prevent skidding.

Talent is not the art of knowing, but the art of knowing when to stop.

When you stop to think, don't forget to start again.

Once upon a time there was a lawyer's daughter who told her boyfriend: "Stop, and/or I'll slap your face."

There's no known way to stop a chatterbox's flow of words: you can't even dam it with faint praise.

STORK

About the only thing that actually discriminates in favor of the poor is the stork.

Most people could manage the wolf at the door if only the stork wouldn't fly in at the window.

The man who has eight or more children may be said to be stork mad.

STORY

We may be willing to tell a story twice, but are never willing to hear it more than once.
— *Hazlitt*

When a friend says, "Well, to make a long story short," it's too late. — *Don Herold*

In telling a story, it should be just true enough to be interesting, but not true enough to be tiresome. — *Saki*

The stories some people tell are stranger than both truth and fiction.

Love is always the same old story, but some men tell it better than others.

There are three sides to every story—his, yours, and the truth.

The best way to make a long story short is to stop listening.

"That's the end of my tale," as the monkey said when he backed into the lawn mower.

STRAIGHT

A fairly decent man does not need laws to keep him straight— his competitors and patrons usually tend to that. — *Ed Howe*

The effort to keep straight used to be a moral struggle instead of a diet.

When a man is bent on marriage, there's always a girl around to straighten him out.

It is difficult to remain straight if you move in political circles.

There's no virtue in going straight if you're going straight to hell.

STRANGE

Though a good deal is too strange to be believed, nothing is too strange to have happened.
— *Thomas Hardy*

Truth is stranger than fiction— to some people. — *Mark Twain*

Of all odd crazes, the craze to be forever reading new books is one of the oddest.
— *Augustine Birrell*

All the world is queer save thee and me, and even thou art a little queer. — *Robert Owen*

Many an author is stranger than his fiction.

People are strange: they want the front of the bus, the back of the church, and the center of attention.

To parents of teen-agers, youth is stranger than fiction.

STRANGER

Be kind to your friends: if it weren't for them, you'd be a total stranger.

A flirt never talks to strangers— unless they are men.

The gold digger who never accepts gifts from perfect strangers has probably never met anyone who is perfect.

A stranger is a friend whose acquaintance you haven't made yet.

STRENGTH

The best time for parents to put a child to bed is while they still have the strength.

The man who is as sound as a dollar is not as strong as he used to be.

STRENGTH AND WEAKNESS

The weakest link in a chain is its strongest because it can break it.   — Stanislaw J. Lec

Strengthen me by sympathizing with my strength, not my weakness.   — Bronson Alcott

Many a man's weakness is his fondness for showing off his strength.

The modern girl is no stronger than her weakest moment.

It's the weaker sex that puts the caps on jars so tight that the stronger sex can't get them off.

An adolescent always weakens when a pretty teen-ager tells him how strong he is.

New Year's resolutions prove that our weaknesses are usually too strong for us.

The golfer who is strong enough to lug a hundred pounds of equipment around a mile-long course is often too weak to reach for a two-ounce ash tray.

Courtship is the period when a girl finds out that her strength lies in her weakness.

The weaker sex is often the stronger sex because of the weakness of the stronger sex for the weaker sex.

STRETCH

Man's mind, stretched to a new idea, never goes back to its original dimensions.
          — Justice O. W. Holmes

Since the invention of stretch garments, women take up one-third less space.

Many a man thinks he is broadening his mind when he is merely stretching his conscience.

There's only one thing more elastic than a rubber band, and that is the human conscience.

Truth is fiction—if you stretch it far enough.

STRIKE

The computer will never replace man entirely until it learns how to strike for shorter hours.

If you think both sides in a dispute cannot win, just interview management and labor after a strike is settled.

The good old days were those when the only strikes in the country were gold, silver and oil.

Whatever their merits, labor disputes are unpopular with the public because a strike cannot be a hit.

The best way to settle a strike is to strike a settlement.

STRUGGLE

When a girl has made up her mind to marry a struggling young man, he might as well stop struggling.

Nothing ages a woman faster than the eternal struggle of trying to remain young.

Some girls struggle for years to get a mink coat, while others get them by not struggling.

There's a great struggle between vanity and patience when we meet a person who admires us and also bores us.

STUBBORN

A man will do more for his stubbornness than for his religion or his country. — *Ed Howe*

The person who won't take advice is often less stubborn than the one who is giving it.

Some people will have their own way even when they don't know what it is.

The man who does not think as you do is apt to be stubborn.

The only use some people make of their will power is to support their won't power.

The husband who acts like a mule is bound to turn his wife into a nag.

No creature is as stubborn as a mule, except the man who says so.

STUDY

From his earliest years, he studied how to avoid study.
— *Anatole France*

Except it be a lover, no one is more interesting as an object of study than a student.
— *William Osler*

The proper study of mankind is woman. — *Coventry Patmore*

No student knows his subject: the most he knows is where and how to find out the things he does not know. — *Woodrow Wilson*

It doesn't make much difference what you study so long as you don't like it.
— *Finley Peter Dunne*

I would live to study, and not study to live. — *Francis Bacon*

Men always study women, and know nothing about them; women never study men, and know all about them.

The best way to haze freshmen is to make them study.

It's foolish to study, because the more we study, the more we discover our ignorance.

Some students never amount to anything at college—they don't do a thing but study.

The proper study of mankind is man, but the most popular is woman.

Never let your studies interfere with your college education.

If you study all your life, you can know at eighty almost half as much as you thought you knew at eighteen.

Many a parent has a son at college who does well in everything, except his studies.

The proper study of mankind is a room where womankind can't get in.

STUPIDITY

You must have taken great pains, sir; you could not naturally have been so very stupid.
— *Samuel Johnson*

Men are born ignorant, not stupid; they are made stupid by education. — *Bertrand Russell*

Against stupidity, the gods themselves fight in vain. — *Schiller*

Every day I hear stupid people say things that are not stupid.
— *Montaigne*

Education leaves the mass of mankind pretty nearly as it found them, with this single difference: it gives a fixed direction to their stupidity. — *Thomas Love Peacock*

The stupid you always have with you. — *Thoreau*

It takes a thoroughly good woman to do a thoroughly stupid thing. — *Oscar Wilde*

There is nothing so stupid as the educated man, if you get off the thing he was educated in.
— *Will Rogers*

What people lack in intelligence they usually make up for in stupidity.

The man with nothing between the ears usually falls for the woman with nothing between the earrings.

There is nothing in the world that can give man a sense of the infinite like human stupidity.

STYLE

Style is the mind skating circles round itself as it moves forward.
— *Robert Frost*

Literary people are forever judging the quality of the mind by the turn of expression.
— *Frank Moore Colby*

Every style that is not boring is a good one. — *Voltaire*

The greatest possible mint of style is to make the words absolutely disappear into the thought.
— *Hawthorne*

In literature the ambition of the novice is to acquire the literary language; the struggle of the adept is to get rid of it.
— *Bernard Shaw*

We are surprised and delighted when we come upon a natural style, for instead of an author we find a man. — *Pascal*

If you can tell stories, create characters, devise incidents, and have sincerity and passion, it doesn't matter a damn how you write. — *Somerset Maugham*

All the fun's in how you say a thing. — *Robert Frost*

A good writer should be so simple that he has no faults—only sins. — *Yeats*

There is such an animal as a nonstylist, only they're not writers —they're typists. — *Truman Capote*

Read carefully what the first critics don't like about your work, then cultivate it: it's the only thing that's individual and worth keeping. — *Jean Cocteau*

Style is to the book what a smile is to the look. — *Ivan Panin*

The four greatest novelists the world has ever known—Balzac, Dickens, Tolstoy and Dostoevski —wrote their respective languages very badly. — *Somerset Maugham*

In matters of grave importance, style, not sincerity, is the vital thing. — *Oscar Wilde*

The Epistles of St. Paul are so sublime, it is hard to understand them. — *Voltaire*

Crisp writing usually has a good deal of shortening in it.

SUBJECT

The man who knows only one subject is almost as tiresome as the man who knows no subject.
— *Dickens*

One advantage many public speakers enjoy is that they're unhampered by any knowledge of their subject.

Some women can talk for hours on any subject, others don't even need a subject.

If you want to know what's the subject matter of most popular songs, it doesn't.

Before marriage, he is the main subject of her conversation; after marriage, she wants to change the subject.

The man who can talk on a hundred different subjects generally does.

Where money is no object with a wife, it's usually the subject.

SUBMISSION

Render unto Caesar the things that are Caesar's, and unto God the things that are God's; and unto human beings—what?
— *Stanislaw J. Lec*

The man who gives in when he is wrong, is wise; the man who

gives in when he is right, is married.

Our country is full of meek men who will stand for anything, except a woman in the subway.

A married man's home is his castle, with him being the vassal.

The chief objection to turning the other cheek is that is leaves the chin wide open.

If at first you don't succeed, try, try again; then resign yourself to being like other people.

For most people the hardest thing to give is—in.

You can always judge a man by the woman's thumb he is under or the little finger he is wound around.

SUBSTITUTE

Youth thinks intelligence a substitute for experience, and age thinks experience a substitute for intelligence.   —*Lyman Bryson*

Of all the substitutes, a substitute speaker is the worst.
              —*Kin Hubbard*

There is a substitute for everything, especially for original thinking.

A rabbit's foot is a poor substitute for horse sense.

Experience is the best substitute for trial and error, but some people refuse to accept any substitute.

Marriage by proxy is all right if you could stay married that way.

There's a substitute for everything, but no one has yet figured out a substitute for hard work.

There's no substitute for brains, but the next best thing is silence.

The bigger a man's head gets, the easier it is to fill his shoes.

Technology is replacing things with substitutes at such a rapid rate that it will soon have to replace the substitutes with substitutes.

Money isn't everything, but it's the best substitute for credit.

SUBURBS

A suburban mother's role is to deliver children: obstetrically once, and by car forever after.
              —*Peter De Vries*

Suburbia is where the developer bulldozes out the trees, then names the streets after them.
              —*Bill Vaughan*

There's only one thing worse than living in the suburbs, and that is living in the suburbs of the suburbs.

By the time you've finished paying for your home in the suburbs, they are no longer the suburbs.

The suburbs are a place where a man owes more on his cars than he does on his house.

Many a man prefers to live in suburbia because of the city people he doesn't have to meet.

Don't laugh at the people who live in the suburbs: you may get a raise some day and live there yourself.

Many a farmer wakes up one morning and finds himself in the suburbs.

The suburbs are being built up so fast, its inhabitants are coming to the city for solitude.

The spread of suburbia is transforming large fields of country into small plots of crab grass.

In the suburbs the station wagons are sometimes bigger than the station.

Having a home in the suburbs is a problem of location: it's usually on the outskirts of your income.

There's no need for you to keep a dog in the suburbs if all your neighbors have one.

The suburbs are full of white-collar employees who work a week to earn enough to hire a repairman for a day.

An optimist is a man who moves to the suburbs to get away from the noise.

A frontiersman nowadays is one who moves into a house at the edge of a new subdivision.

SUBWAY

The subway may not serve a humanitarian purpose but it certainly brings people closer together.

The subway during the rush hours is a good example of freedom of the press.

Subway travel is the most uncomfortable distance between two points.

If subway passengers oiled themselves they would pack better —sardines do.

Travel is broadening, but for the subway traveler it is flattening.

Another place full of people who have no trouble making ends meet is a crowded subway.

The subway has put women on an equal standing with men.

The gentleman in the subway is always recognized by his get-up.

SUCCESS

Success has always been a big liar. —*Nietzsche*

The secret of success is this: there is no secret of success.
—*Elbert Hubbard*

When a man succeeds, he does it in spite of everybody, and not with the assistance of everybody.
—*Ed Howe*

Success is that old ABC—ability, breaks and courage.
—*Charles Luckman*

If A equals success, then the formula is A equals X plus Y plus Z, with X being work, Y play, and Z keeping your mouth shut. —*Einstein*

Success often depends upon knowing how long it will take to succeed.   — *Montesquieu*

There would be more incentive to success if successful men seemed to enjoy life more.

Five things are essential to success: one is wealth, and the other four are money.

For a man, success in life consists in getting the money; for a woman, in getting the man who gets the money.

Success gives some people big heads, and others big headaches.

The ladder of success is made up of many rounds, and many of these are rounds of drinks.

The road to success is always under construction.

God help the man who thinks he has succeeded, for there is nothing more he can do for himself.

There's plenty of room at the top, but there's no place to sit down.

It isn't the man who takes things as they come that succeeds, but the man who also grabs them as they go.

The secret of success: never let down and never let up.

It is the rare individual who can stand success—especially a close friend's.

Behind every successful man can be found three people: his wife, and Mr. and Mrs. Jones.

Success is the difference between doing good and making good.

The road to success is always rough because those who pass over it never drag their feet.

None of the secrets of success will work unless you do.

Success means making a lot of money to pay the taxes you wouldn't have to pay if you weren't so successful.

Success does not always go to a man's head; it often goes to his mouth.

Nothing shows the price of success more clearly than the income tax tables.

Why is it that the man your wife gave up to marry you always turns out to be more successful?

There's plenty of room at the top, but not much company.

Success often goes to a man's head, but the money that accompanies it goes to the government.

Success brings poise, especially avoirdupois.

There is no short cut to success: if you want to reach the Promised Land, you must go through the wilderness.

Women are seldom as successful as men—they had no wives to advise them.

Sometimes it's harder to be a success than to become one.

The two leading recipes for success are building a better mousetrap and finding a bigger tax loophole.

Success is largely a matter of keeping in the groove while keeping out of a rut.

Success comes to two kinds of men: those who are always on their toes, and those who are always stepping on the other fellow's.

Nothing recedes like success.

A successful man is one who earns more than his wife can spend; a successful woman is one who marries such a man.

SUCCESS AND FAILURE

It sometimes happens that when a man fails in doing anything else well, he marries well. — *Ed Howe*

Success goes to your head, failure to your heart.

There are three kinds of men: successful men, unsuccessful men, and those who tell the second group how the first group did it.

Are you a success, or do you still lie to your wife?

The formula for success is a secret, the formula for failure is to try to please everybody.

Many a short cut to success turns out to be a trap door to failure.

Many a man who is busy making a success of his business is busy making a failure of himself.

Nothing succeeds like success, and nothing fails like failure.

Yesterday's formula for success is tomorrow's recipe for failure.

Failure is the result of not knowing what to do; success is the result of knowing what not to do.

Success comes in cans, failure in can'ts.

The man who always criticizes others for his failures never credits others for his successes.

It is hard to admire a man who makes a success out of what you gave up as a failure.

If you fail, it's because you took a chance; if you succeed, it's because you grasped an opportunity.

Failure is the prize drawn by the man who wastes all his time talking about success.

The secret of success: don't fail.

Man is never given his due: if he fails, it's his own fault; if he succeeds, his wife made him.

To get anywhere, you must strike out for somewhere, or you'll get nowhere.

Nothing succeeds like success, and nothing fails like reading a book on how to attain it.

As soon as success turns a man's head, he's facing failure.

Success results from making more profits from less mistakes; failure, from making less profits from more mistakes.

Just when you think you have it in the bag, the bag breaks.

To be a success, you have to work hard about twenty years; to be a failure, you have to work hard about twice as long.

Success is only a matter of luck —ask any man who has failed.

Many men have made success out of failures, and success has made failures out of many men.

Remember that the only way to skip rungs on the ladder of success is on the way down.

SUFFERING

How little it takes to make life unbearable: a pebble in the shoe, a cockroach in the spaghetti, a woman's laugh.   — *Mencken*

The young suffer less from their own mistakes than from the wisdom of the old.   — *Vauvenargues*

It is a glorious thing to be indifferent to suffering, but only to one's own suffering.
— *Robert Lynd*

I have suffered too much in this world not to hope for another.
— *Rousseau*

Somewhere in the shadow cast by every famous man is a feminine victim.   — *Jules Renard*

Some tortures are physical and some are mental, but the one that is both is dental.   — *Ogden Nash*

The woman who suffers in silence really does.

SUGGESTION

Every man has some weakness; a common one is making suggestions to his wife about how to run the house.

When everything else fails, try doing what the boss suggested.

A word to the wise is sufficient, a word to the wife never is.

SUICIDE

There are many who dare not kill themselves for fear of what the neighbors will say.
— *Cyril Connolly*

The thought of suicide is a great consolation; with its help you can get through many a bad night.   — *Nietzsche*

No matter how much a woman loved a man, it would still give her a glow to see him commit suicide for her.   — *Mencken*

There is only one truly philosophical problem, and that is suicide.   — *Camus*

If I were not afraid my people might keep it out of the newspapers, I should commit suicide tomorrow.   — *Max Beerbohm*

Suicide is belated acquiescence in the opinion of one's wife's relatives.   — *Mencken*

SUICIDE

There's one thing in favor of suicide: it never becomes a habit.

More people commit suicide with a fork than with any other weapon.

To get out of the world for the sake of getting out of debt is suicidal.

Killing time is not murder—it's suicide.

Life is as you take it, and there are many ways of committing suicide.

An alcoholic spends his life committing suicide on the installment plan.

The man who hangs himself dies of his own free will and accord.

SUIT

Nothing lasts as long as a suit you don't like.

The best way for a man to make his suit last longer is to get married.

If you remove the bodice of some summer outfits, you have a playsuit; if you remove the skirt, you have a sunsuit; if you remove anything else, you have a lawsuit.

Clothes make the man, and suits make the lawyer.

SUMMER

The weather in the month of Aug. shouldn't happen to a dog.
— *Bill Vaughan*

Summer has set in with its usual severity. — *Coleridge*

Do what we can, summer will have its flies. — *Emerson*

Summer is the season when it is sometimes hard to tell whether a man is wearing shorts or merely forgot his pants.

Summer is here when the chair you're sitting on gets up when you do.

Summer is the time when you discover that the television show you missed last winter wasn't worth watching in the first place.

Summer is the season when you ride bumper to bumper to get to the beach where you sit the same way.

Summer is the long season of uncomfortable weather between a pleasant week in the spring and a pleasant week in the fall.

Summer is the season when there's not much on radio, television or the girls at the beach.

Summer is the season that you look forward to all year, gripe about when it arrives, and are sorry when it's gone.

Summer is the time of year when a mother appreciates nothing so much as a teacher's patience.

Summer is the season when the women who aren't at the beach get undressed anyway and go to the supermarket.

Summer is a season divided into three parts: anticipation, vacation, recuperation.

Summer is the season of the year when the dog days don't bother us as much as the mosquito nights.

Summer is the season when the air pollution is much warmer.

SUMMER AND WINTER

Summer is the time when it's too hot to do the job that it was too cold to do last winter.

Summer is the time of year when children slam the doors they left open all winter.

Winter is when you turn up the furnace to keep the house as hot as it was last summer when you turned on the air conditioner.

Summer brings leaves of absence, and winter brings absence of leaves.

During the summer months you feel too lazy to work, and during the winter months you feel too good to work.

Winter is the season of the year when you always decide that you like summer best.

Nature is perverse: when we need heat most, she gives us winter; and when we need cold most, she gives us summer.

A loafer is a man who likes to mow the lawn in the winter and shovel snow in the summer.

SUN

One must stand on his head to get the best effect in a fine sunset, to bring out all its beauty.
— *Mark Twain*

The sun rises before I do, but I break even by retiring after it does. — *Jules Renard*

The man who makes hay while the sun shines often gets sunstroke.

A sun bath is the only bath that requires neither soap nor water.

Make your own sunshine—it may not tan the skin, but it will warm the heart.

If a fee were charged to see the sun rise, almost everybody would be up to watch it.

The goldenrod makes hay fever while the sun shines.

One man's sunset is another man's sunrise.

SUN AND MOON

It is only during an eclipse that the man in the moon has a place in the sun.

The man who makes hay while the sun shines would prefer to make love while the moon shines.

A bathing beauty in the sun kindles as much romance as the man in the moon.

After millions of years of getting light from the sun, man

finally decided to get enlighten-
ment from the moon.

SUNDAY

Other Sundays could be made
as popular at church as Easter
Sunday if you made them into
fashion shows too. — *Will Rogers*

When the weather is bad on
Sunday, many people would
rather endanger their souls than
their health.

Sunday is the day when the gas
stations get the money that the
collection plates at church formerly did.

Sunday has become the day of
the week when you either get
scolded by a preacher or bawled
out by a traffic cop.

Sunday is what it takes to make
a house look lived in.

If all the cars in the world
were placed end to end, it would
be Sunday afternoon.

Any golfer can be religious on
a rainy Sunday.

SUPERIOR

Always obey your superiors—
if you have any. — *Mark Twain*

Nothing strengthens a friendship as much as the conviction
by each one that he is superior
to the other. — *Balzac*

The trouble with a superiority
complex is that the wrong people
always have it.

Many a man thinks he's the
greatest thing alive even though
there are lots of others as small
as he is.

The girl with a jutting exterior
isn't always her sister's superior.

Man's superiority to other animals lies in his ability to talk,
especially his ability to talk himself into trouble.

A superiority complex makes a
nobody think himself a somebody,
and everybody else a nobody.

The woman who thinks no man
is good enough for her may be
right, but she is more likely to
be left.

A henpecked husband doesn't
have to believe in God to recognize the existence of a superior
being.

The sexes are alike in one way:
they both try to conceal the superiority of women over men.

Having a superiority complex
makes it easier for a person to
talk about his inferiors than to
find any.

SUPERMARKET

A supermarket is the only place
that issues more stamps than a
post office.

The man who says woman's
place is in the home ought to be
made to do the marketing.

The only place where men don't
find fault with women drivers is
the supermarket.

In a supermarket it's important to decide which products to buy, but even more important which checkout line to queue up at.

The supermarket is the only place where everyone follows the straight and narrow path.

Don't pull all your eggs in one basket, unless you're at the supermarket.

Money goes very fast nowadays, and one of the places it goes fastest is the checkout counter of a supermarket.

The most expensive vehicles to operate per mile are the carts found in a supermarket.

SUPERSTITION

Let me make the superstitions of a nation and I care not who makes its laws or its songs either.
— *Mark Twain*

Many a man is not superstitious because he thinks it brings bad luck.

You don't have to be superstitious to think it's unlucky to have thirteen children.

If horseshoes are lucky, how is it that every horse that loses has four of them?

Superstition rushes in where knowledge fears to tread.

Depend upon the rabbit's foot if you will, but remember that it didn't work for the rabbit.

Our superstition is faith, the other person's faith is superstition.

Superstition turns a four-leaf clover into a better omen of success than ambition.

The man who frees you from your superstition makes you adopt his own.

A horseshoe is a symbol of good luck, but only when it's on the winning horse.

SUPPLY AND DEMAND

If the law of supply and demand is responsible for existing prices, the law should be amended.

When demand is scarce, supply is ample, like good advice and bad example.

Men believe in the law of supply and demand; women, in the law of demand and supply.

Talk is cheap because the supply always exceeds the demand.

The law of supply and demand doesn't always hold true: there are always more reformers than reform.

Another thing where the demand always exceeds the supply is sex.

According to the law of supply and demand, when buyers don't fall for prices, prices must fall for buyers.

If there is a relation between supply and demand, why are there more kinds of headache remedies than headaches?

The law of supply and demand never seems to apply to money.

SUPPORT

Any man who, having a child or children he can't support, proceeds to have another should be sterilized at once.   *—Mencken*

Every human couple should be able to support by its labor at least three unproductive, greedy, mischievous brats as well as themselves.   *—Bernard Shaw*

Many a man looks to his father for support until his children are old enough to take care of him.

The girl who can support a husband doesn't have much trouble finding a husband to support.

Some wives support their husbands, others hold them up every payday.

The most serious impediment to marriage nowadays is the difficulty of supporting both a family and the government on one salary.

Don't judge a man by the clothes he wears—he may have a wife and three daughters to support.

A father first supports his daughter to the altar, and then supports his son-in-law.

The wife of Atlas probably supported him while he supported the world.

A husband is supposed to support a wife even if she is insupportable.

Many a man who has his B.A. and M.A. is still living on his PA.

The man who believes in the economic emancipation of women probably thinks his wife has as much right to support the family as he has.

What can't be cured supports the doctor.

Atlas supported the world, but it takes a hundred million Americans to support just the U.S.A.

None but the brave deserve the fair, but only the rich can support them.

A father-in-law is the only man who often supports two wives without being a bigamist.

Many a man marries a girl because he can no longer support her in the style to which he has accustomed her.

All the world's a stage, and every father plays a supporting role.

When young people rush into matrimony, they hope their parents will be good supports about it.

The man who has trouble supporting his wife doesn't know what trouble is—he should try not supporting her.

A man will sometimes stand on his dignity when he has no other visible means of support.

When it costs you more to support the government than it does to support your family, you're really a success.

In marriage the upkeep of woman is often the downfall of man.

SUPREME COURT

Isn't it funny that anything the Supreme Court says is right?
— *Robert Frost*

Women always have the last word, except on the Supreme Court where the last word really counts.   — *Tom Clark*

Some families have more differences of opinion than the Supreme Court.

There are some American citizens who would like nothing better than to have the Supreme Court declared unconstitutional.

The last guess of the Supreme Court becomes the law of the land.

SURE

I wish I were as sure of any one thing as Macaulay is of everything.   — *Lord Melbourne*

It is the dull man who is always sure, and the sure man who is always dull.   — *Mencken*

Self-evidence: evident to one's self and to nobody else.   — *Bierce*

There is nothing sure in politics but censure.

It's better to be sure than sorry, but if you're too sure, you're sure to be sorry.

The surest thing about first love is that it is not likely to be the last.

Never be sure unless you know.

The only thing an agnostic is sure of is that he doesn't know.

SURGEON

She got her good looks from her father—he's a plastic surgeon.
— *Groucho Marx*

Surgery separates the patient from the disease by putting the patient back to bed and the disease in a bottle.
— *Logan Clendening*

A surgeon is a doctor accustomed to take out tonsils, appendixes and nurses.

Middle age is the period when your doctor tells you that if you don't cut out something, the surgeon will.

At the prices they charge, no wonder surgeons wear masks when they operate!

A good surgeon can always perform a serious operation in less time if he is not in a hurry.

Never argue with your surgeon: he has inside information.

When a man talks more than a woman about his operations, he is probably a surgeon.

SURPLUS

If I were a girl, I'd despair: the supply of good women far exceeds that of the men who deserve them.
— *Robert Graves*

In the order named, these are our country's largest surpluses: grain, advice, and wire hangers.

The only thing harder to get rid of than the government's surplus wheat is its citizens' surplus fat.

When the government does it, it's stockpiling; when you do, it's hoarding.

The United States always has at least three unmanageable surpluses: corn, cotton and calories.

SURPRISE

The only thing that should surprise us is that there are still some things that can surprise us.
— *La Rochefoucauld*

By God, Mr. Chairman, at this moment I stand astonished at my own moderation. — *Robert Clive*

Time changes everything, except something within us which is always surprised by change.
— *Thomas Hardy*

Show me a man who understands women, and I'll show you a man who is in for a big surprise.
— *Burton Hillis*

There is no greater evidence of superior intelligence than to be surprised at nothing. — *Josh Billings*

Women have been so highly educated that nothing should surprise them, except happy marriages. — *Oscar Wilde*

Some couples surprise their friends by getting married; others, by staying married.

If you want to give your fiancé a surprise for his birthday, tell him your real age.

At the turn of the century people were amazed when someone drove 20 miles an hour—they still are.

Behind every successful man is a woman who couldn't be more surprised.

Don't tell her you are unworthy of her: let it come as a surprise.

The goodness of bad people and the badness of good people is less surprising than the ignorance of educated people and the knowledge of the uneducated.

The unexpected doesn't always happen, but it always happens when you least expect it.

Nothing upsets a housewife more than when her friends drop in unexpectedly to find the house looking as it usually does.

SUSPENSE

The suspense is terrible; I hope it will last. — *Oscar Wilde*

Some girls like to be kept in suspense, others simply like to be kept.

SUSPICION

Half the declarations of love a man makes to a woman are to quiet her suspicions. *— Ed Howe*

We are always paid for our suspicion by finding what we suspect. *— Thoreau*

Nothing can happen but the suspicious man believes that somebody did it on purpose.
— Robert Lynd

The louder he talked of his honor, the faster we counted our spoons. *— Emerson*

Some men are so nice to their wives that it arouses the suspicion of the neighbors.

Half the world doesn't know how the other half lives, but it has its suspicions.

Some marriages are failures because the wife is suspicious, and others because she isn't.

If you suspect a woman, don't marry her; if you marry her, don't suspect her.

Watch out for those who fall at your feet: they may be reaching for the edge of the rug on which you're standing.

The politician who has never been suspected of graft is a proper subject for suspicion.

Many a teenager wonders what her parents were up to at her age that makes them so suspicious of her.

There are two things that are always under suspicion: how a man got his black eye, and how a girl got her mink coat.

If we could be aroused as easily as our suspicions, we wouldn't need alarm clocks.

When a man suddenly becomes kind and loving to his wife, she doesn't always know whom to suspect.

A woman is always suspicious of another woman who can keep a secret.

A suspicious wife will spend a long time trying to find out something, and then an even longer time trying to forget it.

No matter how high some girls go in life they never get above suspicion.

What you don't know doesn't hurt you: it's what you suspect that causes all the trouble.

Many a brilliant husband who seems to know everything, doesn't suspect anything.

Suspicion is what drives a woman to find out something she would rather not know.

SWEARING

In certain trying circumstances, urgent circumstances, desperate circumstances, profanity furnishes a relief denied even to prayer.
— Mark Twain

Swearing was invented as a compromise between running away and fighting. *— Finley Peter Dunne*

There ought to be a room in every house to swear in.
—*Mark Twain*

Swearing is a bad habit, and it should not be indulged in by other people.

A sailor's wife gets used to hearing strong language, a clergyman's wife gets used to doing without it.

Advice to men who indulge in profanity: Swear off.

The three things that inspire the most profanity are an alarm clock, a road hog, and a wife.

If you must swear while typing, confine your remarks to the top line of the typewriter.

Out of the mouths of babes come words father should never have said in their hearing.

Before marriage, men swear to love; after marriage, they love to swear.

The woman who swears she has never been intimate with any man, can hardly be blamed for swearing.

They also swear who only stand and wait.

By the time you've cured yourself of swearing, it's time to make out another income tax return.

The average man has a vocabulary of 10,000 words—until he barks his shin.

Some of us swear off on New Year's, but most of us swear off and on the rest of the year.

What you say is always more important than how you say it, except when you're swearing.

Before entering office public officials are sworn in; before leaving, they are cussed out.

There's many a damn 'twixt the door and the jamb.

Swearing is natural to man: you swear at the pedestrian when you are a driver, and at the driver when you are a pedestrian.

SWEAT

It is not necessary that a man should earn his living by the sweat of his brow, unless he sweats easier than I do. —*Thoreau*

Genius is one per cent inspiration and ninety-nine per cent perspiration. —*Thomas A. Edison*

Perspiration is the only liquid it is impossible to drown in.

Glands have a great deal to do with a person's success, especially the sweat glands.

A beautiful garden requires a lot of water, much of it in the form of perspiration.

Success often depends less on aspiration than perspiration.

SWEATER

A sweater is a knitted garment worn by a child when his mother feels cold.

The girl who wears a sweater is probably trying to pull a man's eyes over the wool.

If the sweater fits, a girl buys a size smaller.

Many a man's favorite yarn is the kind that's worn in sweaters.

All a sweater does for some girls is to make them look warm.

Women's sweaters come in four sizes: small, medium, large, and WOW!

SWIMMING

Some girls go in for swimming, while others know every dive in town.

It is better to keep your skeletons in the closet than to take them to the swimming pool.

All women ought to know how to swim: it's good training and besides, it keeps their mouths shut.

The duck is nature's proof that swimming does not always improve the figure.

SYMPATHY

When you are in trouble, people who call to sympathize are really looking for the particulars.
— *Ed Howe*

In any combat between a rogue and a fool, the sympathy of mankind is always with the rogue.
— *Mencken*

If there was less sympathy in the world, there would be less trouble in the world.
— *Oscar Wilde*

Sympathy is such a wonderful thing, it's a crime to waste it on others.

No woman can do anything with a man so long as some other woman feels sorry for him.

Some women are so sympathetic, they are never happy unless they are feeling sorry for someone.

The man whose wife doesn't understand him deserves far less sympathy than the man whose wife does.

To feel sorry for yourself is to waste sympathy on someone who doesn't deserve it.

A neighbor's sympathy in time of trouble usually consists of a little compassion and a lot of curiosity.

Marriage brings sympathy: every woman feels sorry for some other woman's husband.

Sympathy is your pain in my heart.

Some women are so sympathetic, if you're in trouble they'll tell everyone about it.

TACT

Tact consists in knowing how far to go too far. — *Jean Cocteau*

Women and foxes, being weak, are distinguished by superior tact.
— *Bierce*

Tact: to lie about others as you would have them lie about you.
— *Oliver Herford*

Tact is the art of remembering not to forget yourself.

Tact is giving a person a pat on the back when you feel like giving him a kick in the pants.

Never hesitate to say what you think, but take care to say some things only to yourself.

Tact is the art of dressing the bare facts and draping the naked truth.

Tact is the art of knowing when not to tell the truth, where not to tell the truth, and how not to tell the truth.

When people lie about a matter of fact, it's generally a matter of tact.

Tact is the art of putting your foot down without stepping on anyone's toes.

If you are tactful for an hour, nobody notices it; if you are tactless for a minute, everybody notices it.

Tact is the ability to shut your mouth before someone else does it for you.

Married life teaches many lessons: one of them is to think of things far enough in advance not to say them.

Tact is the art of showing that you don't dislike a person as much as you do.

Tact is the fine art of never thinking the way we speak, or the finer art of never speaking the way we think.

People with tact have less to retract.

Tact is the ability to change the subject when you can't change your mind.

Tact is the art of making a point without making an enemy.

A tactful person never opens his mouth wide enough to put his foot in it.

Tact is the art of saying the right thing while thinking the wrong thing.

Tact is the ability to avoid saying what comes naturally as if it were natural.

Another person who says what he thinks without thinking is the tactless one.

Tact is the ability to see others as they see themselves.

Tact is the art of thinking twice before saying nothing.

TALENT

The luck of having talent isn't enough; you must also have a talent for luck.
— *Berlioz*

This God-given talent which I have must be tossed aside like an old mistress—or is it mattress?
— *Robert Benchley*

Everyone has talent at 25—the trick is to have it at 50. — *Degas*

Talent is a matter of quantity: talent doesn't write one page, it writes three hundred.
— *Jules Renard*

Talent is like an arm or a leg— use it or lose it.

The most important talent an artist can have is to be contented with a little money.

The secret of success is a talent —the talent for hard work.

Use whatever talents you possess: the woods would be silent if only those birds sang that sing best.

TALK

Lots of people act well but few people talk well, which shows that talking is the more difficult of the two.   — *Oscar Wilde*

Most of the time in married life is taken up by talk.   — *Nietzsche*

Talking is a hydrant in the yard, and writing is a faucet upstairs in the house; opening the first takes the pressure off the second.
— *Robert Frost*

He suffered occasionally from a rush of words to the head.
— *Herbert Samuel*

War talk by men who have been in a war is interesting, but moon talk by a poet who has not been in the moon is dull.
— *Mark Twain*

Women prefer to talk in two's, while men prefer to talk in three's.
— *Chesterton*

I hate people who talk about themselves as you do, when one wants to talk about oneself as I do.   — *Oscar Wilde*

I'd rather be guilty of talking over a person's head than behind his back.   — *Adlai Stevenson*

Great talkers are so constituted that they do not know their own thoughts until they hear them issuing from their mouths.
— *Thornton Wilder*

When we love, we always have something to say.
— *Mary Wortley Montagu*

Before a man speaks, it is always safe to assume that he is a fool; after he speaks, it is seldom necessary to assume.   — *Mencken*

Talk to every woman as if you loved her, and to every man as if he bored you.   — *Oscar Wilde*

To babble is to make a feminine noise somewhat resembling the sound of a brook, but with less meaning.   — *Oliver Herford*

Talk about others and you're a gossip; talk about yourself and you're a bore.

After all is said and done, more is said than done.

It always takes a person much longer to tell you what he thinks than what he knows.

A woman never puts off till tomorrow what she can say today.

To say the right thing at the right time, keep still most of the time.

In childhood we learn the evil of backtalk; in adulthood, the evil of behind-back talk.

What this country needs is not more fast readers, but less fast talkers.

When a woman lets a man do most of the talking, watch out: she's up to something.

Talk is cheap, but not when money does it.

When women speak of love, how they love to speak!

If you want to know how she will talk to you after marriage, listen while she talks to her younger brothers.

Where there is much to be said on both sides, there is seldom anything omitted.

It's not true that women do all the talking, not at least when Congress is in session.

The only way a man can be sure of getting the last word is to talk to himself.

Money talks, but it doesn't always speak when spoken to.

An egotist talks to you about himself, a gossip talks to you about others, and a brilliant conversationalist talks to you about you.

The man who says that it goes without saying, goes right ahead and says it anyway.

Telling all you know is as bad as believing all you hear.

The man who marries money soon finds out that he has married something else that talks.

Some people think they have something to say, others think they have to say something.

What this country needs are less wide-open spaces entirely surrounded by teeth.

It's unfriendly to talk about people behind their backs, but it's safer that way.

Talk is cheap, but not if you're buying a good tape recorder.

Marriage transforms a girlfriend from a fascinating conversationalist into a wife who is better still.

TALK AND LISTEN

When a woman is talking to you, listen to what she says with her eyes.   — *Victor Hugo*

The surest way a man can make his wife listen is by talking to another woman.

Every woman is fond of listening in, but not half as much as she is of talking out.

Never write when you can talk, and never talk when you can listen.

A windbag expects others to listen to him attentively while he says nothing.

Women don't talk all the time; they must listen part of the time, otherwise how could they associate with other women.

The more a chatterbox talks, the less you listen.

It isn't true that some wives do all the talking and never listen; they listen to every word they say.

There's nothing wrong when you talk to yourself, but watch out when you start to listen.

What this country needs are more good listeners and less poor speakers.

Women don't talk more than men; they're listened to more, that's all.

If nature intended us to talk more than listen, she would have given us two mouths and one ear.

When your wife says she has nothing more to say, prepare to spend an hour listening to her say it.

TALKATIVE

I have never met a woman who talks as much as I do.
— *Herbert Bayard Swope*

The trouble with me is that I like to talk too much.
— *William Howard Taft*

Loquacity is a disorder which renders the sufferer unable to curb his tongue when you wish to talk.
— *Bierce*

People who like to shoot off their mouths never run out of ammunition.

If men who did things talked half as much as men who know how things ought to be done, life would not be worth living.

Some people would say more if they talked less.

The housewife who leaves nothing unsaid probably leaves everything undone.

Don't talk too much: a stiff lower jaw is as useful as a stiff upper lip.

TALL

The oftener you see Toulouse-Lautrec, the taller he grows.
— *Jules Renard*

Another advantage in marrying a tall girl is that the top of your refrigerator will always be dusted.

People are growing taller nowadays, but they are still up to their necks in trouble.

When you grow tall enough to reach the jam on the pantry shelf, the craving for jam has disappeared.

A tall girl may not attract all men but she is seldom overlooked.

Another person who lies in bed longer than others is the six-footer.

TALL AND SHORT

A short man looking up sees much farther than a tall man looking down.

Size isn't everything: tall men are just as short at the end of the month as anyone else.

'Tis better to have loved a short girl than never to have loved a tall.

TASK

Old age is ready to undertake tasks that youth shirked because they would take too long.
— *Somerset Maugham*

The man who does more each day than his allotted task will soon find himself rewarded with an increased allotted task.

No man ever lived long enough to do all the things his wife wants him to do.

When there are unpleasant chores to be done, some husbands go far beyond the call of duty.

Nothing reminds a woman of all the things her husband has to do around the house like the sight of him resting.

TASTE

I'm a man of very simple tastes: the best of everything is quite good enough for me. — *Michael Arlen*

Good taste is the worst vice ever invented. — *Edith Sitwell*

Good taste is the excuse I've always given for leading such a bad life. — *Oscar Wilde*

No one ever went broke under-estimating the taste of the American public. — *Mencken*

Men lose their tempers in defending their taste. — *Emerson*

There is no disputing tastes—with the tasteless.
— *James G. Huneker*

Good taste is better than bad taste, but bad taste is better than no taste at all.

There's no accounting for taste, especially bad taste.

Some men drink whiskey to take away the taste of tobacco, and then smoke tobacco to take away the taste of whiskey.

The Lord loves everyone, which shows His heart is better than His taste.

Tasteless is a word which means in bad taste, used by people with good taste.

Too much taste makes waist.

The self-admiration of some people proves that there's no ac-counting for taste.

Many a married couple have similar tastes: he doesn't care for her, and she doesn't care for him.

TAXES

To tax and to please, like to love and be wise, is not given to men. — *Edmund Burke*

The tax collector must love poor people—he's creating so many of them. — *Bill Vaughan*

What the government gives, the government can take away, and

once it starts taking away it can take more than it gives.
— *Samuel Gompers*

If crime could be taxed, there would be no need for other taxes.

Taxation without representation was tyranny, but it was a lot cheaper.

The less the government cuts down on its spending, the more it makes us cut down on ours.

A taxpayer can claim depreciation on all sorts of things—except himself.

The more a tax expert taxes his imagination, the less the government taxes his client.

The primary requisite for any new tax law is for it to exempt enough voters to win the next election.

The way taxes are today, you may as well marry for love.

The average taxpayer believes in only one kind of government handout—the kind that takes the government's hand out of his pocket.

When the meek inherit the earth, they will have very little left after paying inheritance, capital gains and other taxes.

Earning money would be a pleasure—if it wasn't so taxing.

Another man who doesn't have to pass a Civil Service examination to work for the government is the taxpayer.

Taxation is the most common means adopted by a government to prevent its people from hoarding.

There is only one person more interested in taxes than the tax collector, and that is the taxpayer.

Only in a democracy have the citizens complete freedom in deciding how to pay their taxes— by check, cash or money order.

The taxpayer is anxious to know where his tax money is going to, and even more anxious to know where it is coming from.

Of all our natural resources, the first one to be exhausted will probably be the taxpayer.

The reason there's so much grumbling about taxes is that it's about the only thing that isn't taxed.

The government should be glad the taxpayers have what it takes.

The taxpayer is always opposing old taxes but elects officials who are always proposing new ones.

There's no such thing as a small taxpayer.

Because he pays taxes, a taxpayer thinks he's entitled to a voice in deciding what they should be.

If farmers are paid not to raise crops, why can't we pay Congress not to raise taxes?

The tax collector believes not only what he's told but twice as much.

Some taxpayers close their eyes, some stop their ears, some shut their mouths, but all pay through the nose.

Every man should feel indebted to his country, but that doesn't mean he shouldn't pay his taxes.

A taxpayer is a desperate man who is constantly being pushed to the wall while the wall keeps receding.

When your ship comes in, it's always docked by the government.

The only person who gets paid for sticking his nose into other people's business is the tax collector.

TAXI

The way they are driven, nothing is more certain than death in taxis.

A taxi is a vehicle that disappears when it rains.

Existence is a taxi-ride through life, with the meter running whether we are going somewhere or just standing still.

All things come to him who waits for a taxi on rainy days, except a taxi.

The average taxi covers over a hundred miles a day, excluding pedestrians.

To a taxi driver a rainy day is always fare weather.

TEA

If I had known there was no Latin word for tea, I would have let the vulgar stuff alone.
— *Hilaire Belloc*

Tea should not be brewed so weak that it can't get up to the spout of the teapot.

To an Englishman the only thing lukewarm in America is tea.

Take a lesson from tea: its real strength comes out when it gets into hot water.

The reason the English are such great tea drinkers is on account of their coffee.

TEACHING

What we want is to see the child in pursuit of knowledge, and not knowledge in pursuit of the child.   — *Bernard Shaw*

A schoolmaster is a man among boys and a boy among men.
— *C. E. M. Joad*

Most subjects at universities are taught for no other purpose than that they may be retaught when the students become teachers.
— *G. C. Lichtenberg*

Everybody is now so busy teaching that nobody has any time to learn.   — *Agnes Repplier*

A teacher who is not dogmatic is simply a teacher who is not teaching.   — *Chesterton*

A teacher is a person who knows all the answers, but only when she asks the questions.

A teacher's lot is not a happy one: the worst behaved schoolchild usually has the best attendance record.

Good teachers cost a lot, but poor teachers cost a lot more.

A schoolteacher handles many more children than a parent, and is given two-months' vacation every year to recuperate.

It is more important for a teacher to be a stimulant than to be important.

Many a woman who teaches at school part of the time, continues to teach everywhere else the rest of the time.

One of the important duties of a teacher is to keep a roomful of live wires grounded.

Schoolteachers are the only women who have learned to ask questions and keep quiet long enough to hear the answers.

Experience is a great teacher, and sometimes a pretty teacher is a great experience.

A teacher is a person who faces a bunch of desperadoes with her back to the wall and no gun in her hand.

A self-taught man usually has a poor teacher and a worse student.

A smart mother suggests that her child bring an apple to his teacher; a smarter mother suggests that he bring a couple of aspirins.

Teaching is the fine art of imparting knowledge without possessing it.

TEARS

There's only one woman who sheds more tears than a grieving wife, and that's a cunning one.

In an argument with a man, one sniffle is worth a thousand words.

Tears are a form of feminine waterpower used to overcome masculine will power.

A wife's tears are sometimes wiped away with a handkerchief, sometimes with a tissue, but most often with a greenback.

A woman always resorts to tears when she wants to get something out of her system—or out of her husband.

Drying a widow's tears is one of the most dangerous occupations known to man.

TECHNOLOGY

Where there is the necessary technical skill to move mountains, there is no need for the faith that moves mountains. — *Eric Hoffer*

The Industrial Age had to wait centuries until people in Scotland watched their kettles boil and so invented the steam engine.
— *A. N. Whitehead*

Technology enables man to gain control over everything except technology.

Technology improves things so fast that by the time we can afford the best, there's something better.

Technology has created everything necessary in a kitchen, except a woman who will stay in it.

Technology is rapidly filling our homes with appliances smarter than we are.

Technology has made improvements in everything, except the weather and people.

TEENAGER

Like its politicians and its wars, society has the teenagers it deserves. — *J. B. Priestley*

There's nothing wrong with teenagers that trying to reason with them won't aggravate.

A teenager is a daughter whom you understand only a little, but who misunderstands you a lot.

The only way to tie down a teenager is with a telephone cord.

The teenager who is an eyeful for the boys at school is often a handful for her parents at home.

You are never too old to learn, unless you're a teenager.

Teenagers are hard to figure out: after spending all day at school together, they hurry home so they can call one another on the phone.

A teenager is an adolescent who is constantly irked by her disobedient parents.

All that keeps parents from having a home, a car and a phone of their own is a couple of teenagers in the house.

A teenager always puts things back where she didn't find them.

Nothing can make the world beat a path to your door like a teenage daughter.

A teenager is always too tired tc hold a dishcloth, but never too tired to hold the phone.

Nowadays teenagers would rather be uncouth, unkempt and disgruntled than couth, kempt and gruntled.

Teenage is the awkward time in life when a girl is too old for fairy tales and too young for cocktails.

Teenagers accept being ruled by their parents, but object to being overruled by them.

By the time a girl becomes a teenager, her parents have stopped trying to bring her up and have started trying to keep up with her.

A teenager is a girl who occasionally interrupts her telephone conversations with a little homework.

By the time a girl becomes a teenager, her parents are so old that she cannot do anything with them.

A teenage daughter is so unpredictable, you can never tell what she is going to do next to upset you.

A teenager usually spends half her time on the telephone talking, and the other half at the television listening.

Don't worry about unhappy, confused teenagers: in a few years they'll grow up into unhappy, confused adults.

About the only thing teenagers will take lying down these days is a telephone call.

Nowadays too many teenagers suffer from severe cases of hefever.

A teenager may not know how to raise children, but is sure she knows how to raise parents.

TEETH

Aristotle could have avoided the n.istake of thinking that women have fewer teeth than men by simply asking Mrs. Aristotle to open her mouth.
— *Bertrand Russell*

It is after you have lost your teeth that you can afford to buy steaks.   — *Pierre A. Renoir*

Many a true word is spoken through false teeth.

The girl who uses kisses as a weapon is armed to the teeth.

False teeth help many a man to keep a stiff upper lip.

TELEPHONE

Half the phone calls would never be answered if we knew in advance who was calling.

A woman's place is in the home because that's where the telephone is.

The telephone enables you to hold a long, relaxed conversation without being interrupted by the ringing of the telephone.

Why is it that the wrong number on a telephone is never busy?

It was a lucky thing for all of us that when Alexander Graham Bell made his first telephone call, the line was not busy.

The telephone is a handy instrument that's always at your beck and call, except in a home with a teenager.

The telephone is the greatest nuisance among conveniences, and the greatest convenience among nuisances.

Women are the weaker sex: they automatically reach for a chair when they answer the phone.

When a girl marries, her mother loses a daughter but gains a telephone number.

Most women prefer the telephone to television because you can't talk back on television.

Telephones formerly stood upright but now through overuse have to rest in a cradle.

College students away from home consider the family telephone a collector's item.

A teenager on the phone rarely stops to think, and even more rarely thinks to stop.

Progress works both ways: in the old days you could dial wrong numbers only locally; nowadays you can dial them all over the country.

Talk is cheap, but not on the long-distance telephone.

About the only thing the father of a large family gets out of the telephone is the monthly bill.

If there were no such thing as extrasensory perception, how would people know you're in the bathtub when they call?

A woman can stay longer on the telephone than on a diet.

A party line is a telephone over which subscribers indulge in both private and public speaking.

One man's telephone is another man's wrong number.

Youth calls to youth, which is why their parents never get a chance to use the phone.

The only time a woman suffers in silence is when her phone is out of order.

One way to shorten the phone conversations of teenagers is to bring back the old-fashioned wall phone where you had to stand to talk.

TELEPHONE BOOTH

If you think the art of conversation is dead, you have probably never stood waiting outside a public telephone booth.

Some women can talk themselves out of anything, except a telephone booth.

All the world loves a lover, except when you're waiting to use the phone.

It's no fun to kiss a girl over the phone, unless you both happen to be in the same booth.

An optimist is a man who thinks a woman in a phone booth will be right out when he hears her say good-bye.

If you think money doesn't talk, just try to telephone from a booth without a dime.

TELEPHONE DIRECTORY

The real test of fame is when your name appears in print everywhere, except in the telephone directory.

Another book that carries alliteration too far is the telephone directory.

TELEVISION

Time has convinced me of one thing: television is for appearing on—not for looking at.
            —*Noel Coward*

I hate television; I hate it as much as peanuts, and I can't stop eating peanuts.   —*Orson Welles*

Television is now so desperately hungry for material that they're scraping the top of the barrel.
            —*Gore Vidal*

Television is a daily menace to housework, and a nightly menace to homework.

Another thing that's wrong with television is that it goes in for movies that are not worth going out to see.

Television is a medium of first-grade entertainment, at least for persons who have not gone beyond the first grade.

Television is a medium of entertainment, and a tedium of advertising.

Schoolchildren spend too much time watching television; their interests are directed toward the wrong channels.

You can always enjoy television if you have a big enough screen: just put the screen in front of your television set.

Television is a form of entertainment which you continue to watch in the hope that it will turn into a form of entertainment.

The modern appliance that has done more than any other to reduce a woman's working hours is the television set.

Television is called a medium because so little of it is rare or well done.

The evil that men do lives after them—especially when they're television reruns.

Television stimulates conversation, but only when the set is broken.

A big television set makes a bad program that much worse.

Even the bad of television has its good: the worse the program is for children, the quieter it keeps them.

Television gives people who do nothing a chance to watch people who can't do anything.

The trouble with being a television star is that you wind up in everyone's home but your own.

Television is a wonderful form of entertainment that has only two things wrong with it—the commercials and the programs.

The Westerns on television would be vastly improved if they were shown live, including the ammunition.

Television has changed the American child from an irresistible force to an immovable object.

Television is a half-baked art produced by the half-hearted and written by the half-witted for the half-educated.

Two minds seldom run in the same channels—at least, not where there's only one television set at home.

Television is the only form of entertainment that usually puts you to sleep before you go to sleep.

Some people always keep their television sets turned on out of fear that they might miss something bad.

Television would be more enjoyable if the commercials showed less gravity and the programs more levity.

The chief virtue of television is that it does away with a lot of useless conversation.

A television set is an object in the home entirely surrounded by schoolchildren dodging their homework.

A soap opera is a television serial about a family that never spends its time watching a television serial.

Television is a form of entertainment where old movies never die, no matter how long ago they were shot.

Many a child who watches television will go down in history— and also in English and arithmetic.

Television mysteries have had so many variations that the only murder suspect left now is the sponsor.

Another thing that's wrong with television is that it sneaks into your home the movies you've been trying to avoid for years.

The more you see of television, the more you like it less.

Television will never give the people the programs they want because neither television nor the people know what the people want.

A sponsor is the only television viewer who enjoys the commercials more than the programs.

Television is more educational than you realize: think of all the repairmen's children it is putting through college.

On television the crime shows are often worse than the crimes they show.

There's no better test of how your children stand up under disaster than when the television set goes out of order.

Some television programs are so bad, you get annoyed when they interrupt the commercials.

Television is a predictable medium: the good guys always win on the Westerns, and the bad guys on the news programs.

TEMPER

Man is a rational animal who always loses his temper when called upon to act in accordance with the dictates of reason.
— *Oscar Wilde*

The worst-tempered people I've ever met were people who knew they were wrong. — *Wilson Mizner*

Another man who should have his head examined is the one who is always hitting the ceiling.

Temper never shows itself in a man until it has been lost.

When a child in a tantrum loses his head, it is usually followed by a mother losing hers.

The worst way to handle a woman is to fly off the handle.

When your temper rises, remember that the higher it goes the further it must drop on the return journey.

The time you need your temper most is after you lose it.

A woman never loses her temper: she keeps it and uses it over and over again.

When right, you can afford to keep your temper; when wrong, you cannot afford to lose it.

Control your temper: remember, the emptier the pot, the quicker it boils.

If there's a cool spot in hell, hot-tempered people should get it.

A man should never lose his temper, especially when he blows his top.

A man is never in worse company than when he flies into a rage and is beside himself.

The most dangerous high explosive known to man is a woman's temper.

Men are like steel: they are of little value when they lose their temper.

You can never get rid of a bad temper by losing it.

When a husband loses his temper, he usually finds his wife's.

Never marry a man who loses his head more often than his hat.

Keep your temper: no one else wants it.

TEMPERATURE

Friends are the thermometers by which one may judge the temperatures of our fortunes.
— *Countess of Blessington*

Man is a thermometer, woman the temperature; the thermometer is always subject to change of temperature.

The right temperature at home is maintained by warm hearts, not by hotheads.

A thermostat is an apparatus that keeps a house too warm for one parent and too cold for the other.

When you have low temperature, your feet are cold; when you have high temperature, your head is hot.

TEMPTATION

Temptation is woman's weapon and man's excuse.   — *Mencken*

I can resist everything except temptation.   — *Oscar Wilde*

There are several good protections against temptation, but the surest is cowardice. — *Mark Twain*

The only way to get rid of a temptation is to yield to it.
— *Oscar Wilde*

Anyone who has to be led into temptation doesn't deserve to enjoy it.

Some men flee from temptation, but others just crawl away from it hoping it will overtake them.

The average number of times a girl says *no* to temptation is once weakly.

Flirts and philanderers are never bothered by temptation—except when they can't find any.

Why should we resist temptation—there will always be more.

During the first half of life it is hard to avoid temptation, and during the second half it is even harder to find it.

Most of us keep at least one eye on the temptation we pray not to be led into.

Opportunity knocks only once, but temptation bangs on the door for years.

Many a man is virtuous because he is neither clever enough to avoid temptation nor wise enough to yield to it.

Lead us not into temptation—just tell us where it is and we'll find it.

It's much easier to resist temptation if you're broke.

Temptation would be a lot easier to avoid if we didn't meet it in such gay company.

When you meet temptation, turn to the right.

The only trouble with resisting temptation is that you may not get another chance.

When you flee temptation be sure you don't leave a forwarding address.

TEN COMMANDMENTS

An efficiency expert is the kind of man who thinks he can improve on the Ten Commandments by cutting them down to five or six.

Man has made millions of laws, but hasn't yet improved on the Ten Commandments.

Moses was a great lawgiver: his keeping the Ten Commandments short and to the point shows he was no ordinary lawyer.

A man isn't wholly bad if he has only broken nine commandments.

Ever since the Ten Commandments, legislators have been busy passing millions of laws trying to enforce them.

The straight and narrow path doesn't detour around the Ten Commandments.

TENNIS

When I was 40, my doctor advised me that a man in his forties shouldn't play tennis, and I could hardly wait until I was 50 to start again. — *Hugo Black*

They also serve who only stand and wait, unless they're playing tennis.

Tennis is one of the few pastimes where *love* means nothing.

TENSION

The trouble with most of us is that we are living in the present —tense.

Gelatin is the only food a high-strung person can eat that's more nervous than he is.

If every generation nowadays is a tense generation, where is the past tense generation?

TEST

What is the purpose of an examination—to find out what you know or what you don't know?

An aptitude test is one where a student is apt to do anything.

Whenever you wish you were young again, just think of having to take school exams.

One of the worst tests you can flunk is a Wassermann.

The only thing to give the man who claims he has everything is a lie detector test.

An aptitude test shows that a young man is most likely to succeed in a business where his father is the boss.

What you don't know doesn't hurt you, except during an examination.

Nowadays a student has to pass more tests to get into college than his dad had to pass to get out.

Life is a test that has more questions than there are answers.

TEXTBOOK

Most textbooks tell you more about the subject than you are interested in knowing.

Another book that's much harder to read than it was to write is a textbook.

THANKSGIVING

The Puritans gave thanks for being preserved from the Indians, and we give thanks for being preserved from the Puritans.
—Finley Peter Dunne

Thanksgiving Day is a day devoted by persons with inflammatory rheumatism to thanking a loving Father that it is not hydrophobia.   *—Mencken*

Thanksgiving is a day set apart every year to acknowledge God's favor, especially by parents whose sons have survived the football season.

After Thanksgiving dinner, the man who has trouble making ends meet ought to get himself a longer belt.

Thanksgiving is a day off that's usually followed by an off day.

THEATER

A good many inconveniences attend playgoing in any large city, but the greatest of them is usually the play itself.   *—Kenneth Tynan*

In order to fully realize how bad a popular play can be, it is necessary to see it twice.
—Bernard Shaw

I have never regarded any theater as much more than the conclusion to a dinner or the prelude to a supper.   —*Max Beerbohm*

If you want to help the American theater, don't be an actress, be an audience.
—*Tallulah Bankhead*

The New York playgoer is a child of nature, and he has an honest and wholesome regard for whatever is atrocious in art.
—*Frank Moore Colby*

One can play comedy, two are required for melodrama, but a tragedy demands three.
—*Elbert Hubbard*

It isn't a shortage of good scripts that ails the theater; it is a shortage of producers who know a good script when they see one.   —*George Jean Nathan*

The theater is a great equalizer: it's the only place where the poor can look down on the rich.
—*Will Rogers*

When they have a success, theatrical producers think they are brilliant, but when they have a failure, they think the public are fools.   —*Sacha Guitry*

Every fool who is connected with the theater thinks he knows better than an author how to make a play popular and successful.   —*Bernard Shaw*

If a farmer fills his barn with grain, he gets mice; if he leaves it empty, he gets actors.
—*Bill Vaughan*

A theater requires two good producers: one to produce the play, and the other to produce the cash.

To really enjoy a play at the theater, a woman must have her hat on and her shoes off.

In the theater, the worst crimes are a low voice on the stage and a high hat in the audience.

There's only one thing worse than to hear people come in while a play is in progress, and that's to hear them go out.

The teenager who thinks she should be on the stage is really going through one.

When some plays open, the audience shouldn't call for the author, but for the authorities.

The only place where a person answers the phone and never gets a wrong number is the stage.

The people you can see through easily are never the ones who sit in front of you at the theater.

THEOLOGY

Theologians always try to turn the Bible into a book without common sense. —*G. C. Lichtenberg*

Doctors differ, especially Doctors of Divinity.

Isn't it strange that those who profess the most knowledge of the next world should display so little knowledge of this one?

A theologian is a blind man in a dark room searching for a black cat that isn't there—and finding it.

THEORY

Some theories are good for nothing except to be argued about.
— *G. C. Lichtenberg*

Even for practical purposes theory generally turns out the most important thing in the end.
— *Justice O. W. Holmes*

Socrates thought and so do I that the wisest theory about the gods is no theory at all.
— *Montaigne*

The isms of youth are the wasms of age.

The quickest way to kill a good theory is to put it into practice.

THEORY AND FACT

Science is organized common sense where many a beautiful theory is killed by an ugly fact.
— *Thomas H. Huxley*

A theory is no more like a fact than a photograph is like a person.
— *Ed Howe*

In scientific work, those who refuse to go beyond fact rarely get as far as fact.
— *Thomas H. Huxley*

A young man is a theory, an old man is a fact.   — *Ed Howe*

THIEF

A burglar is merely a man who feels that he isn't as rich as he ought to be.   — *Struthers Burt*

He had 63 ways of getting money, the most common and most honorable ones being stealing, thieving and robbing.   — *Rabelais*

Many a man is saved from being a thief by finding everything locked up.   — *Ed Howe*

A thief is another man who believes that heaven helps those who help themselves.

A sneak thief can't seem to tell the difference between opportunity and temptation.

A burglar always tries to live within another man's means.

With some thieves the safest safes are unsafe.

THIN AND FAT

Imprisoned in every fat man is a thin one wildly signaling to be let out.   — *Cyril Connolly*

Most of us are either too thin to enjoy eating, or too fat to enjoy walking.   — *Ed Howe*

It's easy to make women happy: just tell the fat ones they're thinner, and the thin ones they're getting fatter.

Worry makes people thin, except when they worry about being fat.

Middle age is the period in a man's life when his hair is getting thin while the rest of him is getting fat.

Slim girls have to be seen to be appreciated, fat girls have to be lean to be appreciated.

THINK

Thinking isn't to agree or disagree—that's voting.

— *Robert Frost*

Where all men think alike, no
man thinks very much.

— *Walter Lippmann*

There is no expedient to which
a man will not go to avoid the
labor of thinking.

— *Thomas A. Edison*

I think, therefore Descartes exists.   — *Saul Steinberg*

Life has taught me to think,
but thinking has not taught me
to live.   — *Alexander Herzen*

A man thinks as well through
his legs and arms as his brain.

— *Thoreau*

Ours is an age which is proud
of machines that think, and suspicious of the men who try to.

— *Howard Mumford Jones*

There are two ways to slide
easily through life: to believe
everything or to doubt everything;
both ways save us from thinking.

— *Alfred Korzybski*

Thinking is more interesting
than knowing, but less interesting
than looking.   — *Goethe*

He that thinks himself the happiest man, really is so; but he
that thinks himself the wisest, is
generally the greatest fool.

— *C. C. Colton*

I think that I think; therefore,
I think I am.   — *Bierce*

Life always gives you plenty
to think about, but seldom enough
to think with.

The man who is afraid to think
for himself usually chooses the
wrong woman to think for him.

The more we think of some
people, the less we think of them.

For every man who is always
telling you what he thinks, there
is another who is always telling
you what others think.

Many a man who thinks he is
thinking, is merely digesting yesterday's newspaper.

Some men learn to think on
their feet by being public speakers,
but most men learn to do so by
being pedestrians.

The man who thinks too much
of himself doesn't think enough.

The best way to win a man
is to make him think you think
as much of him as he does.

A few people think, many think
they think, and the rest use clichés
so they won't have to think.

One of the few projects that do-
it-yourselfers have not yet tackled
is thinking.

Don't wonder what people are
thinking about you; they aren't
thinking about you but wondering
what you are thinking about them.

When a man sits and thinks,
his television set is probably
broken.

The man who thinks twice before acting, often has to think a third time to play off the tie.

The less a man thinks of his neighbors, the more he thinks of himself.

Half the trouble in the world arises because you can't stop people from thinking, and the other half because you can't start them.

THINK AND SPEAK

How can I tell what I think till I see what I say.
—*E. M. Forster*

In America we can say what we think, and even if we can't think, we can say it anyhow.
—*Charles F. Kettering*

If we are not ashamed to think it, we should not be ashamed to say it.   —*Cicero*

There isn't anything anybody can say about you that hasn't already been thought.

When men talk, they seldom stop to think; when women talk, they seldom think to stop.

Think twice before you speak, and you'll find that someone has changed the subject.

It is really impossible to say what we think; the best we can do is think what we say.

Women generally speak as they think—only oftener.

The law of compensation also applies to thinking: the smaller

the ideas, the bigger the words used to express them.

Speaking without thinking is shooting without aiming.

Some people always finish a sentence before starting the thought which it expresses.

A woman often speaks without thinking, but never thinks without speaking.

If people would speak only when they think, you would always be able to hear a pin drop.

Too many people mistake connected words for connected thought.

Think twice before you speak —especially to a friend in need.

Women don't talk without thinking: even a chatterbox keeps on talking while she thinks of something to say.

The man who boasts that he always talks the way he thinks, should either talk less or think more.

THIRST

Some men thirst for fame, some thirst for money, while others just thirst.

What is there about hearing his parents snore that makes a little child so thirsty?

Some men drink when they are thirsty to cure their thirst, and drink when they are not thirsty to prevent it.

Some men thirst after fame, some thirst after power, but all men thirst after salted peanuts.

THOUGHT

Everything has been thought of before, but the problem is to think of it again.   *— Goethe*

I've known countless people who were reservoirs of learning, yet never had a thought.
— Wilson Mizner

If I held all the thoughts of the world in my hand, I would be careful not to open it.
— Fontenelle

The deeper the thought, the higher you must climb to grasp it.

The only food for thought is more thought.

A girl is always sure she can read a man's thoughts, especially when he hasn't any.

Second thoughts are best, but split-second thoughts are often better.

It is a waste of time for some men to collect their thoughts.

Many a train of thought carries no freight.

A woman thinks of a dozen things at once, a man has a dozen thoughts on one thing.

Second thoughts are best, especially in cases of love at first sight.

There are two schools of thought: one school always claims there are two schools of thought, while the other doesn't.

When a man is lost in thought, it's probably because he's in unfamiliar territory.

Nowadays most food comes canned and packaged, including food for thought.

Some men never give girls a second thought because the first thought covers everything.

If second thoughts are best, forethoughts ought to be twice as good.

The proverbial penny for your thoughts has now become $25 an hour at the psychiatrist's.

THRIFT

Teach thrift to all with whom you come in contact; you never know when you may need their savings to finance one of your ventures.   *— Don Marquis*

To recommend thrift to the poor is like advising a man who is starving to eat less.
— Oscar Wilde

Economy is a kind of thrift that's easiest to practice when your wife does it.

Frugality is the practice of making money go the farthest by barely letting it go at all.

A penny saved is a girlfriend lost.

When a woman stints, you never know whether she does it to save or to spend.

The secret of thrift is to live as economically the day after pay-day as you do the day before.

Some people practice thrift to make ends meet; others, to make them overlap.

Take care of the pennies, and the dollars will take care of your heirs and their lawyers.

Thrift is a necessity elevated by the poor to the rank of a virtue.

A penny saved is a penny earned, but it's usually a dollar's worth of time wasted.

THUMB

The man with a green thumb is sometimes a good gardener, but more often a careless painter.

A do-it-yourselfer is a man who stands out in a crowd like a sore thumb with his sore thumb.

The man who is all thumbs never seems to have a green one.

The only way a do-it-yourselfer can stop hitting his thumb is to have his wife hold the nail.

The man who is all thumbs has one advantage: he doesn't have to lift a finger around the house.

There's nothing so rare as a woman who has sprained the thumb she holds her husband under.

THUNDER AND LIGHTNING

Thunder is impressive, but it is lightning that does the work.
— *Mark Twain*

The same battle in the clouds will be known to the deaf only as lightning, and to the blind only as thunder.   — *Santayana*

TIE

I have a hankering to go back to the Orient and discard my neck-tie—neckties strangle clear think-ing.   — *Lin Yutang*

Family ties are stronger at Christmas—and louder too.

Whenever there's a beautiful tie between father and son, the son is probably wearing it.

Everything in life eventually adjusts itself, except a bowtie.

The chief difference between a tie and a noose is that one is worn without a collar.

The only way some men can make themselves heard is by their ties.

The advantage of a polka-dot tie is that one more spot doesn't matter.

A bachelor is a man with no ties, except those that need clean-ing.

Women are wiser than men: they refuse to wear ties so that men cannot get even with them at Christmas.

If you have trouble making both ends of your tie come out even, wear a vest.

TIME

Time is a dressmaker specializing in alterations.
— *Faith Baldwin*

Time is that which man is always trying to kill, but which ends in killing him.
— *Herbert Spencer*

Time is money says the proverb, but turn it around and you get a precious truth: money is time.   — *George Gissing*

You cannot kill time without injury eternity.   — *Thoreau*

When men are not regretting that life is so short, they are doing something to kill time. — *Ed Howe*

Time goes, you say? Ah no! Alas, time stays, we go.
— *Austin Dobson*

Take care of the minutes, and the hours will take care of themselves.   — *Chesterfield*

Half our life is spent trying to find something to do with the time we have rushed through life trying to save.   — *Will Rogers*

Time makes friendship stronger, but love weaker.   — *La Bruyère*

People who cannot find time for recreation are obliged sooner or later to find time for illness.
— *John Wanamaker*

One can always trust to time: insert a wedge of time, and nearly everything straightens itself out.
— *Norman Douglas*

Time changes with time: in youth, time marches on; in middle age, time flies; and in old age, time runs out.

Those who kill time eventually mourn the corpse.

Time heals all things—except leaky faucets.

Time waits for no man, but it usually hesitates a while for a woman of twenty-nine.

How time flies with love!—and how love flies with time!

All things come to him who waits, except the precious time lost while waiting.

Time is money, especially time-and-a-half.

A bore's idea of killing time is to talk it to death.

Time waits for no man—it is too busy waiting for woman.

Some people count time, others make time count.

No wonder time flies—there are so many people trying to kill it.

All bores are alike: they always take your time taking their time.

Time is ungallant—it tells on a woman.

Time is the greatest of healers, but the poorest of beauticians.

The three principle kinds of time are standard, daylight saving, and over.

Time is money, except when it's on your own time.

Time heals all wounds and wounds all heels.

TIMESAVER

A timesaver is a household device that enables a mother-in-law to spend more of her time interfering with her children.

Throughout history man's inventions have been timesavers—then came television.

The greatest timesaving device is not resisting temptation.

The disadvantage of timesavers in the home is that they leave wives more time to think up more chores for their husbands.

The more timesaving devices a man accumulates, the less leisure he has.

TIMID

Let the meek inherit the earth —they have it coming to them.
— *James Thurber*

Blessed are the meek for they shall inherit the earth—after all the other people in the world are dead.

Some men are born meek, others get married.

The meek shall inherit the earth —that's the only way they'll ever get it.

A timid man never differs from his wife but always differs with her.

The meek shall inherit the earth, but they won't stay meek after they get it.

TIP

I wonder if it ain't just cowardice instead of generosity that makes us give tips. — *Will Rogers*

If you're too busy to take a vacation, you can get the same effect by tipping every other person you meet.

The tip you leave for lunch today would have bought a dinner a generation ago.

All tips come to him who waits.

Poor men give big tips pretending to be rich, and rich men give small tips pretending to be poor.

Another man who serves you and never gets tipped is the process server.

Only a doorman can open your car door with one hand, help you in with the other, and still have a hand left waiting for the tip.

All the world loves a lover because he tips so generously.

The human touch is not always what it's alleged to be—sometimes it's merely an itching palm.

Waiters are different: when you
don't tip them, they become upset.

The traditional rate of tipping is
10 per cent, but 15 per cent in-
sures better service, which is why
some people give 20 per cent.

TIRED

The man who says he has exhausted life generally means that
life has exhausted him.
— *Oscar Wilde*

The girl who marries because
she's tired of working is in for a
surprise.

When a man looks tired, don't
tell him he needs a vacation—he
has probably just had one.

The only thing some men seem
able to grow in a garden is tired.

Nothing tires a chatterbox more
than having to listen.

Some men always look tired,
probably from constantly looking
for a place to rest.

A man may not always know
whether he's tired or lazy, but his
wife does.

Another difference between the
rich and the poor is that the rich
are tired in the morning and the
poor are tired in the evening.

Many a man who is tired of life
is merely tired of married life.

It's a rare executive who is so
tired that he can hardly lift his
feet to the top of the desk.

TITLE

The Ancient Mariner would not
have taken so well if it had been
called *The Old Sailor*.
— *Samuel Butler*

Books with absurd and far-out
titles are seldom worth reading.
— *G. C. Lichtenberg*

TOAST

The girl men toast is usually
the one women roast.

If you drink to other people's
health too often, you'll ruin your
own.

The most popular toast people
drink to at a ski resort is *Bot-
toms Up*.

Toast is the strangest of all
foods: it is eaten in the morning
and drunk at night.

The difference between a toast
and a roast is presence and absence.

TOASTMASTER

The duty of a toastmaster is to
be so dull that the succeeding
speakers will appear brilliant by
contrast.
— *Clarence Budington Kelland*

A toastmaster is the man at a
banquet who flatters every afterdinner speaker with a buttered-up
toast.

Many a public speaker has the
tough task of waking up the audience after the man who introduces him has finally finished.

When a toastmaster is original, he is dull in a new way.

TODAY AND TOMORROW

So often we rob tomorrow's memories by today's economies.
— *John Mason Brown*

Don't do everything today— save some mistakes for tomorrow.

Never put off till tomorrow what you can get someone else to do for you today.

Being foolish today makes it easier to be wiser tomorrow.

What a wonderful world this would be if we all did as well today as we expect to do tomorrow.

The puppy love of today leads to the doghouse of tomorrow.

A worrier always seems less troubled by what happens today than by what might happen tomorrow.

Today's scandals, crimes and exposés become tomorrow's good old days.

TOLERANCE

Since others have to tolerate my weaknesses, it is only fair that I should tolerate theirs.
— *William Allen White*

Broad-minded is just another way of saying a fellow's too lazy to form an opinion. — *Will Rogers*

I have seen gross intolerance shown in support of tolerance.
— *Coleridge*

People are very open-minded about new things—as long as they're exactly like the old ones.
— *Charles F. Kettering*

It is easy to be tolerant of the principles of other people if you have none of your own.
— *Herbert Samuel*

Broad-mindedness is the result of flattening out high-mindedness.
— *George Saintsbury*

The man who wants someone to tolerate his faults should not get himself a wife but a dog.

Tolerance is the ability to smile when someone else's child behaves as badly as your own.

The more a girl tolerates a man's shortcomings, the more she tolerates his long stayings.

Nature is strange: you seldom meet a broad-minded man with a swelled head.

There's nothing that proves the infinite tolerance of human nature as a golden wedding anniversary.

The trouble with being tolerant is that people think you don't understand the problem.

Tolerance is a wonderul thing: it enables the rich to declare that there is no disgrace in being poor.

It's much easier to be tolerant of someone you don't like than of someone who doesn't like you.

Most of us are in favor of tolerance, but it is difficult to tolerate the intolerant, and impossible to tolerate the intolerable.

Tolerance is the belief that people who disagree with you have the right to be wrong.

Always tolerate other people's opinions, but don't be too broadminded to take your own side in a dispute.

The first part of your life your parents learn to stand you, and the last part you learn to stand them.

No man is so charitable that he ever becomes bankrupt making allowances for others.

TOMBSTONE

The tombstones of a great many people should read: *Died at thirty, buried at sixty*.
— *Nicholas Murray Butler*

Dead men tell no tales, but their tombstones are awful liars.

The tombstone is the only thing that can stand upright and lie on its face at the same time.

Some people are so anxious to get ahead in the world that they succeed only in getting a headstone.

A cemetery is a place where monuments are put up to perpetuate the memory of the forgotten.

TOMORROW

All things come to him who waits, except tomorrow.

Tomorrow ought to be the longest day in the week—judging from the number of things we are going to do then.

Tomorrow is two days late for yesterday's job.

Tomorrow is the day on which loafers work, fools act sensibly, and drunks swear off.

Some men are always going to make hay while the sun shines—tomorrow.

TONGUE

Actions don't always speak louder than words—your tongue can undo everything you do.

In a battle of tongues a woman can always hold her own, but she never does.

There's many a man whose tongue might govern a multitude if he could only govern his tongue.

Women sometimes go after men, hammer and tongues!

The tongue is located only inches away from the brain, but it often sounds as if it were miles away.

One of the first things you learn when studying a foreign language is that the word *tongue* is feminine.

A fool's tongue is always long enough to cut his throat.

One tongue is enough for two women.

The first screw to get loose in a person's head is usually the one that controls the tongue.

A linguist can master any tongue, except his wife's.

TOOL

Lo! Men have become the tools of their tools.   — *Thoreau*

The rake's progress is slowest when there's a boy at the end of the handle.

A do-it-yourselfer is always spending a lot of money on tools to save a little money.

The gardening tool still unmatched is a simple spade with wife attached.

When a do-it-yourselfer is not at home, he is probably at the hardware store.

When buying garden tools, remember to get only those that are very strong, yet not too heavy for your wife.

The most popular do-it-yourself kits will always be a checkbook and a ballpoint pen.

TOOTHBRUSH

Another of life's tough decisions is to determine just when to discard a toothbrush.

The only exercise some people get is when their electric toothbrushes break down.

The electric toothbrush is a device which requires that you also see the repairman twice a year.

Religion is like a toothbrush: everyone should have one and make use of it daily, and no one should try to force it on anyone else.

If you use an electric toothbrush and still get cavities, it may be a weak battery.

TOP AND BOTTOM

You cannot get to the top by sitting on your bottom.

There's always room at the top, but there's always more room at the bottom.

In food, fat settles at the top; in folk, fat settles on the bottom.

Some people blow their top, but all people blow their bottom.

TOUCH

To touch a man's heart, sympathize with him; to touch his wallet, flatter him.

The thing bachelors dread most about marriage is that feminine touch.

One touch of nature makes the whole world kin, except when it's poison ivy.

Love is blind, which is why it has such a keen sense of touch.

TOURIST

A tourist first travels to learn, and then learns to travel.

The most interesting thing to a tourist thousands of miles from home is another tourist.

A tourist is a person who travels abroad to be overcharged by foreigners instead of by his own countrymen.

Breath-taking scenery usually leaves tourists speechless, but only until they reach home and friends.

A tourist finds it quite a relief to get back to where he was so glad to get away from.

The only crop that is grown in America and harvested abroad is the American tourist.

Tourists are all alike: they want to go places where there are no tourists.

Half the world doesn't know how the other half lives, but it tries to find out during the tourist season.

A tourist is a person who travels to find things that are different, and then complains when they are.

TOWEL

In this cynical age nothing is sacred, except a guest towel.

A towel is the only thing that gets wet as it dries.

You are not really at home in a friend's house until you use his guest towel.

A guest towel is what often persuades people that their hands don't need washing at all.

TOY

Most modern toys are educational: they teach us how little we can get nowadays for our money.

Mechanical toys should always be bought in duplicate so that the children can play at the same time as their fathers.

An unbreakable toy is one a child uses to break all his other toys.

Another difference between men and boys is not the size but the price of their toys.

An educational toy is so called because it educates a parent in what not to buy for his child next time.

Some men put away childish things, others drive over them coming into the garage.

When the psychiatrist's child plays with toys, it's probably a set of mental blocks.

The first thing a child tries to find out about a new toy is how it breaks.

There are two types of educational toys: those that take a few hours to fall apart, and those that take a few days to put together.

TRADE

You never learn a trade thoroughly until you learn the tricks of the trade.

He's a jackass of all trades and a master of none.

TRADING STAMPS

The more it costs, the more trading stamps you get; the more trading stamps you get, the more it costs.

Many a woman won't give up cigarettes not because she is hooked on smoking, but because she is hooked on trading stamps.

It takes the average housewife about three checkbooks to fill up one trading-stamp book.

The way some women go out of their way to look for trouble, you'd think trading stamps came with it.

If wives would save money as eagerly as they save trading stamps, most of us would be very rich.

With groceries you get trading stamps for which you can get everything but groceries.

Pity the poor housewife: she must not only cook, clean and shop, but must also be able to lick her weight in trading stamps.

The chief drawback of being a shoplifter is that you never get trading stamps.

TRADITION

Traditionalists are pessimists about the future and optimists about the past.   *— Lewis Mumford*

Tradition does not mean that the living are dead, but that the dead are living.   *— Chesterton*

Tradition is the handicap by means of which yesterday keeps up with today.

Tradition is the tyranny of the dead over the living.

TRAFFIC

One way to solve the traffic problem would be to keep all the cars that are not paid for, off the streets.   *— Will Rogers*

Traffic jams are often caused by the construction of new highways to relieve traffic jams.

In traffic, it is better to be careful a hundred times than to be killed once.

Drivers are always in a hurry so that they can get in front of you so that they can slow down.

They're called traffic arteries probably because there's always blood flowing in them.

Year by year it takes less and less time to fly around the world, and more and more time to drive to work.

The only way to get ahead in a large city is to stay out of traffic.

Experts have thought up every possible solution to the traffic problem, except the one of keeping the cars home.

The motorist who stops, looks, and listens will hear another car bump into his rear.

There are three kinds of traffic problems—urban, suburban and bourbon.

Nowadays there are altogether too many people in too many cars, in too much of a hurry, going in too many directions.

As traffic increases, road manners become more crude and gasoline becomes more refined.

Some people get what's coming to them by waiting, and others while crossing the street.

Even if the country were on the road to ruin, it would never get there as long as we have our present traffic jams.

The grass is always greener in the next lawn, and the traffic always moves faster in the next lane.

The trouble with traffic is that the car of tomorrow is driven by the motorist of today on the highway of yesterday.

Any car you buy now can go eighty or ninety miles an hour, except on Sundays and holidays.

If all the cars in the country were placed end to end, some fool would still pull out and try to pass them.

TRAFFIC COP

The judgment of a traffic cop is not always right, but his customers are always wrong.

Don't take one for the road, unless you want a state trooper for a chaser.

An American doesn't dare say things to a traffic cop that he doesn't hesitate to say about the President.

Always drive as if a traffic cop were looking.

A traffic cop is a harassed policeman who considers pedestrians as mental defectives, and motorists as homicidal maniacs.

All men are born equal, but some grow up and become traffic cops.

A traffic cop first compels speeders to curb their cars, and then their emotions.

To make a long story short, tell it to a state trooper.

Talk is cheap, except when you're talking to a traffic cop.

One of the most trying of all jobs is being a traffic cop: you have to stay mad all the time.

The traffic cop who suffers from insomnia probably counts cars.

Another expense seldom anticipated by the motorist is having his car overhauled by a state trooper.

A man will allow only one person to talk to him like his wife—a traffic cop.

TRAFFIC LIGHT

If you think the younger generation isn't interested in getting ahead, just watch them at a traffic light.

The principle behind the timing of traffic lights is to trick the pedestrian into the middle of the street.

To the reckless motorist, safe driving means honking your horn while going through a red light.

Many traffic signals which tell the pedestrian to walk ought to tell him to run instead.

TRAGEDY

What the American public wants in the theater is a tragedy with a happy ending.
— *William Dean Howells*

The tragedy of life is not so much what men suffer, but rather what they miss.   — *Carlyle*

There are two tragedies in life: one is to lose your heart's desire, the other is to gain it.
— *Bernard Shaw*

TRAILER

The only kind of a home with no place to put anything except where it belongs, is a house-trailer.

The advantage of a house-trailer is that it provides you with a place to live while you look for a place to park.

In house-trailer living, many a husband expects his wife to fix the flats because it's a woman's job to take care of the house.

TRAINING

Training is everything: the peach was once a bitter almond; cauliflower is nothing but cabbage with a college education.
— *Mark Twain*

The first of all unions to go in for on-the-job training is marriage.

It takes some kind of training in every special field except being an expert in international affairs.

TRANQUILIZER

If everyone took tranquilizers, no one would need them.

Nowadays people have learned how to meet a crisis face to face —they take a tranquilizer.

The time a man needs a tranquilizer most is when his wife forgets to take hers.

The trouble with taking tranquilizers is that you soon find yourself being nice to people you dislike.

A tranquilizer is a pill for the body to treat an ill of the mind.

Parents would be better off if they gave up taking tranquilizers and gave them to their children instead.

Most tranquilizers are not habit-forming, not at least if you take them every day.

What this country needs is a new tranquilizer that will not make a grouch less miserable, but will make him enjoy feeling miserable.

TRANSGRESSOR

The way of the transgressor is hard—on his family.

The way of the transgressor is hard, and so is every other well-beaten path.

The way of the transgressor is soft enough; it's the place he arrives at that's hard.

TRANSLATION

Reading a translation is like looking at a tapestry on the wrong side. —*Cervantes*

Poetry is what is lost in translation. —*Robert Frost*

Pope's translation of Homer is a portrait endowed with every merit except that of likeness to the original. —*Edward Gibbon*

It is as impossible to translate poetry as it is to translate music. —*Voltaire*

The Latin translations of the Bible are not versions but perversions. —*St. Jerome*

Translations are like women: if they are faithful, they are not beautiful; if they are beautiful, they are not faithful.

Some writers are so obscure, they are untranslatable even into their own language.

The way of the transgressor is hard, and the way of the translator even harder.

Prose can be translated, but poetry can only be transmutilated.

TRAP

Like any other trap, marriage is much easier to get into than to get out of.

Woman is a delusion and a snare, and man is snared by the delusion.

Matrimony is a trap devised to make men think they are getting what they want when they are really getting what they deserve.

TRAVEL

I should like to spend the whole of my life traveling, if I could borrow another life to spend at home. —*Hazlitt*

A man travels the world over in search of what he needs, and returns home to find it. —*George Moore*

The traveler sees what he sees, the tourist sees what he has come to see. —*Chesterton*

Only the traveling is good which reveals to me the value of home and enables me to enjoy it better. —*Thoreau*

The world is a book, and those who do not travel, read only a page. —*St. Augustine*

There are many famous monuments in Europe that tourists should travel hundreds of miles to miss.

Travel develops a man's mind, especially his imagination.

Americans go abroad for three reasons: to study, to travel, and to get into trouble.

Travel is a pleasure, and space travel is out of this world.

The less good will in the world, the more goodwill tours.

A tourist goes abroad to discover foreigners, a traveler goes abroad to discover himself.

The woman who travels light probably has a husband who carries all the suitcases.

Travel sometimes broadens the mind, more often lengthens the tongue, but most often flattens the wallet.

Travel enlarges the minds of some people, but swells the heads of others.

Travel by air is no problem: now let us see if we can do something about travel by road.

You can't take it with you, but just try to travel without it.

The best travel slogan still is: let yourself go.

When people from all walks of life want to go anywhere, they ride or fly.

A few reels of your vacation pictures soon put your guests in a traveling mood.

Travel is broadening, especially if you stop at all the recommended eating places.

In traveling abroad with your family, it is easy to lose your children, and even easier to lose your mind.

TREE

A home without a tree isn't fit for a dog.

A tree surgeon breaks his leg every time he falls out of a patient.

Money doesn't grow on trees, but many suburbanites soon discover that trees grow on money.

Today's mighty oak is just yesterday's little nut that held its ground.

You can always tell a dogwood tree by its bark.

TRIAL

When both judge and jury are against a man, thirteen is an unlucky number.

In times of trial, nothing brings so much comfort to a man as an acquittal.

Every man thinks he possesses intelligence until he is tried by a jury of his peers.

Another place where truth is stranger than fiction is at a court trial.

Anyone can sit on a jury, but it takes a lawyer to sit on a witness.

TRIANGLE

Two's company and three's a divorce.

If a man is still in love after many years of married life, his wife probably doesn't know who she is.

In a triangle the other woman is always the cute angle.

In show business, the typical triangle consists of an actor, his wife, and himself.

The right angle from which to approach any problem is the try angle.

The problem with a love triangle is to keep it from turning into a wreck-tangle.

You cannot keep your family circle on the square with a triangle.

The infidelity of a wife is usually a triangle, while that of a husband is usually a hexagon.

The course of two loves never runs smooth.

A triangle consists of three people, two of whom fool around with love as if it wasn't loaded.

One man's chicken is another man's meat.

TRIPLETS

Triplets prove that you can have too much of a good thing —two too much.

The only blessed event that you never begrudge an enemy is triplets.

It's sometimes very hard to keep up with the Joneses, especially when Mrs. Jones has just had triplets.

There's only one thing in life more surprising than twins, and that's triplets.

TROUBLE

Hot water is my native element: I was in it as a baby, and I have never seemed to get out of it ever since. — Edith Sitwell

All the trouble that some people have in life is that which they married into. — Ed Howe

Nobody every grew despondent looking for trouble.
— Kin Hubbard

Some women like to sit down with trouble as if it were knitting.
— Ellen Glasgow

Trouble creates a capacity to handle it. — Justice O. W. Holmes

The way out of trouble is never as simple as the way in.
— Ed Howe

Queer thing how trouble acts different on folks: it's like hot weather—sours milk but sweetens apples. — Joseph C. Lincoln

Half the trouble in the world is caused by what some people have done, and the other half by what others have failed to do.

The trouble with most women is their trouble with most men.

Instead of trying to drown their troubles, some people take them out and give them swimming lessons.

Forget your old troubles—there are a lot of new ones coming.

To a little child all troubles are big.

The man who always laughs at his trouble will never have trouble finding things to laugh at.

A person who fishes in troubled waters always gets a good catch.

Don't bore your friends with your troubles; tell them to your enemies who will enjoy hearing about them.

A lot of trouble is one thing you can get without a lot of trouble.

Most of the world's troubles arise from workers who don't think and thinkers who don't work.

Some women never borrow trouble—they prefer to give it.

When you tell people your troubles, half of them are not interested, and the other half are glad to learn that you're getting what you deserve.

You don't need help to get into trouble, but you usually have it.

The best way to hatch out trouble is to brood over it.

If you want to get rid of trouble it shouldn't be difficult; there are lots of people who are always looking for it.

A troublemaker never has any trouble making trouble.

The easiest way to get into trouble is to be right at the wrong time.

People who haven't enough trouble of their own usually make a lot of trouble for others.

People who invite trouble find that it's the one guest who always accepts.

The man who marries in order to have someone to tell his troubles to, soon has plenty to talk about.

Never meet trouble halfway; it's quite capable of making the entire journey alone.

A fool and his money can make a lot of trouble before they are parted.

Some people are so congenial, they will sympathize with you in trouble, and if you haven't any trouble, they will hunt some up for you.

Those who look for trouble never have much trouble finding it.

TROUSSEAU

A girl always spends a lot of money on her wedding gown because she thinks it's the last dress she'll have to pay for herself.

A woman may put on a riding habit and never go riding, a swim suit and never go swimming, but when she puts on a wedding dress, she means business.

Movie stars are all alike: they never wear the same wedding gown twice.

If a girl would spend as much time and thought in choosing a husband as she does a trousseau, there'd be more happy marriages.

You can't live on love—unless you own a bridal shop.

TRUST

If women believed in their husbands they would be a good deal happier—and also a good deal more foolish. — *Mencken*

When a man has no reason to trust himself, he trusts in luck.
— *Ed Howe*

Put your trust in God—but keep your powder dry.
— *Oliver Cromwell*

Half the world becomes disillusioned by its trust in men, and the other half by its trust in women.

The most disappointing period of a man's life is when his wife begins to trust him.

There's only one thing finer than to have a friend you can trust, and that is a friend who will trust you.

Among your friends there is always one you can trust to be unworthy of your trust.

There's only one person more unreasonable than the man who trusts nobody, and that's the man who trusts everybody.

A faithful husband is any man who is married to a trusting wife.

A woman will trust her body and soul to a man whose own mother wouldn't trust him with a dollar.

The only friends we can trust are the ones who never ask us to trust them.

The woman who trusts her husband everywhere is probably the woman who goes everywhere with her husband.

TRUTH

If you are out to describe the truth, leave elegance to the tailor.
— *Einstein*

Never tell the truth to people who are not worthy of it.
— *Mark Twain*

How awful to reflect that what people say of us is true!
— *Logan P. Smith*

Ye shall know the truth, and the truth shall make you mad.
— *Aldous Huxley*

Truth is a torch that shines through the fog without dispelling it. — *Helvétius*

Everyone wishes to have truth on his side, but not everyone wishes to be on the side of truth.
— *Richard Whately*

The pure and simple truth is rarely pure and never simple.
— *Oscar Wilde*

The pursuit of truth shall set you free, even if you never catch up with it. — *Clarence Darrow*

There is no such source of error as the pursuit of absolute truth.
— *Samuel Butler*

I tell the truth, not as much as I'd like to but as much as I dare, and I dare more and more as I grow older. — *Montaigne*

The truth is more important than the facts.
— *Frank Lloyd Wright*

No real gentleman will tell the naked truth in the presence of ladies. — *Mark Twain*

Truth: something somehow discreditable to someone. — *Mencken*

It is the customary fate of new truths to begin as heresies and end as superstitions.
— *Thomas H. Huxley*

Truth is a fruit which should not be plucked until it is ripe.
— *Voltaire*

Truth makes many appeals, not the least of which is its power to shock. — *Jules Renard*

Though I can always make my extravaganzas appear credible, I cannot make the truth appear so.
— *Bernard Shaw*

When you want to fool the world, tell the truth. — *Bismarck*

Between truth and the search for truth, I choose the second.
— *Bernard Berenson*

The truth would be told more often if it were as safe to tell as to hide.

Always tell the truth—if you want to make trouble.

Teach your child always to tell the truth, but not always to be telling it.

Beware of a half-truth: you may have gotten hold of the wrong half.

One of the nicest things about telling the truth is that you don't have to remember what you said.

Some of the things that seem too good to be true, aren't.

Parents always want their children to tell the truth, the whole truth, and nothing but the truth —unless there are visitors present.

As long as the truth is naked, men will continue to take liberties with her.

Children and fools speak the truth: children because they don't know any worse, and fools because they don't know any better.

An honest person tells the truth, a tactless person tells the whole truth.

Another trouble with the world is that we're always urged to tell the truth, but we're never urged to hear it.

Truth often lies at the bottom of a "well, well!"

TRUTH AND FICTION

A writer is congenitally unable to tell the truth, and that is why we call what he writes fiction.
— *Faulkner*

Truth is stranger than fiction, but seldom as convincing.

Most of the fiction in this world comes from people who are repeating true stories.

The reason truth is stranger than fiction is that there is less of it.

Truth has only to pass through a few persons to become fiction.

Truth is stranger than fiction, except science fiction.

TRUTH AND LIES

One should be just as careful about lying as about telling the truth.   — *Lionel Strachey*

I never could tell a lie that anybody would doubt, nor a truth that anybody would believe.
— *Mark Twain*

If you want to be thought a liar, always tell the truth.
— *Logan P. Smith*

A truth that's told with bad intent, beats all the lies you can invent.   — *William Blake*

Never lie when the truth is more profitable.   — *Stanislaw J. Lec*

History is strewn thick with evidence that a truth is not hard to kill, but that a lie, well told, is immortal.   — *Mark Twain*

All men are born truthful and die liars.   — *Vauvenargues*

It is twice as hard to crush a half-truth as a whole lie.
— *Austin O'Malley*

In real life truth is revealed by parables, and falsehood supported by facts.   — *Bernard Shaw*

A new untruth is better than an old truth.
— *Justice O. W. Holmes*

The chief advantage of being truthful is that your lies are believed.

The man who is always inventing lies is a liar, and so is the man who is always inventing the truth.

Women never lie more cleverly than when they tell the truth to those who don't believe them.

Lie and the world lies with you; tell the truth and the world lies about you.

There are lots of lies being told everyday, and the worst of it is that many of them are true.

Some people love the truth, and some hate to get caught in a lie.

The reason truth crushed to earth will rise again is that truth cannot lie.

If you cannot tell the truth when it sounds like a lie, nor a lie when it sounds like the truth, what are you to say?

The safest of all lies is sometimes the truth.

If you never lie, your friends will stop speaking to you, and your enemies will think you are lying anyway.

The most important part of lying is to know when to tell the truth.

The man who claims he always tells the truth deserves the woman who claims she never tells a lie.

Nothing can be falser than a truism.

Truth lies at the bottom of a well, but if it lies, how can it be the truth?

Don't mind the lies people tell about you—be thankful they don't tell the truth.

A lie can travel halfway round the world while truth is putting its pants on.

You can't win: if you tell lies, people will distrust you; if you tell the truth, people will dislike you.

The truth cannot be told without words, but lies can be told in silence.

Some people are so addicted to falsehood, they can't even tell the truth without lying.

Truth is what's left over when you run out of lies.

The couch is where the patient in a psychiatrist's office lies to tell the truth.

TRY

A man spends part of his time before marriage trying to get ahead, but most of his time after marriage trying to get along.

Trying to be happy is like trying to fall asleep; you won't succeed unless you forget you are trying.

A teenager is an adolescent who is going through a trying period —trying to avoid study and trying to avoid work.

The man who never tried has no sympathy for the man who has tried and failed.

Marriage is a trying institution in which a woman tries to make a man do as she thinks, and a man tries to make a woman think as he does.

It is always trying times for the person who is always trying to get something for nothing.

TURKEY

Lots of Thanksgiving Days have been ruined by not carving the turkey in the kitchen.
— *Kin Hubbard*

Coexistence is what the farmer does to the turkey until Thanksgiving.

TURN

When a woman claims she has just turned thirty, it is probably a U-turn.

Life is a labyrinth in which there are a dozen wrong turns for every right one.

A well-turned leg means a well-turned neck—but seldom on the same person.

TWINS

If you have twins, the chances are you're not enjoying single blessedness.

When a man loses his job, the next baby will probably be twins.

There's a good side to everything: when your son is behaving badly, you are lucky he wasn't twins.

All men are created equal—especially twins.

There's only one thing more helpless than a baby, and that is twins.

Of two evils, it isn't always possible to choose the lesser—sometimes they are twins.

The only pair of twins who are unable to sleep in twin beds are Siamese twins.

Two heads are better than one, but not when your wife gives birth to twins.

TYPEWRITER

The biggest obstacle to professional writing is the necessity for changing a typewriter ribbon.
— *Robert Benchley*

I know so little about the typewriter, I once bought a new one because I couldn't change the ribbon on the one I had.
— *Dorothy Parker*

The pen is mightier than the sword, and the typewriter is mightier than both.

Everything works well on paper, except a broken typewriter.

The typewriter will never achieve maximum utility until it stops making mistakes in spelling.

Another dangerous combination is a fool and a typewriter.

What this country needs is a typewriter that will strike an indefinite letter when you aren't sure of the spelling.

UGLY

A woman may be as wicked as she likes, but if she isn't pretty it won't do her much good.
— *Somerset Maugham*

It is the plain women who know about love; the beautiful women are too busy being fascinating.
— *Katharine Hepburn*

Be it ever so homely, there's no face like one's own.

Some women have natural beauty along with a special talent for making the worst of it.

Some people are better than they look—and they ought to be.

Age comes before beauty—at least with some women.

Many an unattractive girl appeals to men, but none of them respond.

Handsome is as handsome does —is the motto of all unattractive people.

If you're not pretty, cultivate your voice: at least you'll look better on the telephone.

Ugliness is a point of view: an ulcer may be beautiful to a pathologist.

A mud pack improves the appearance of some women—until they take it off.

There's compensation in everything: unattractive girls are generally the best cooks.

There's a use for everything, even jealous wives; otherwise unattractive secretaries would never get jobs.

Beauty is only skin deep, but ugliness goes to the bone.

ULCER

Don't envy the man who has everything because, if he does, he has an ulcer too.

The trouble with success is that its formula is the same as the one for ulcers.

There are many ways to get ulcers, but the most common is from mountain-climbing over mole-hills.

The person with an ulcer doesn't diet to reduce, but is reduced to dieting.

One of the worst things that can happen to a businessman is to have ulcers and still not be a success.

When a man doesn't want to talk about his ulcer, it's probably a sore spot with him.

He who keeps his mind on his work, gets ahead; he who keeps his work on his mind, gets an ulcer.

The really smart businessman is the one who doesn't get ulcers, but whose competitors do.

We don't get ulcers from what we eat, but from what's eating us.

The yesman who is always saying "Yes sir" when he should be saying "No sir," usually ends up with an ulcer.

UMBRELLA

I judge how much a man cares for a woman by the space he allots her under a jointly shared umbrella.   —*Jimmy Cannon*

The only thing some people save up for a rainy day is an umbrella.

Another man who seldom has an umbrella when it rains is the weatherman.

A fair-weather friend lends you an umbrella when the weather is fair, and takes it back when it rains.

The first deadly warhead ever invented was an open umbrella carried by a woman.

Money saved for a rainy day buys a much cheaper umbrella than it used to.

There's always room for a good man, except under the same umbrella with his wife.

UMPIRE

Umpires are like women: their decisions are hasty and irreversible, and even when they're wrong, they're right.

A baseball fan sitting five hundred feet from the plate can see better than an umpire standing five feet away.

Umpires aren't always wrong: sometimes they give the home team the best of it.

An umpire's job is to see that baseball is played on the square as well as on the diamond.

Every baseball fan knows that it rains on the just and the umpires alike.

In baseball, the greatest applause an umpire ever gets is silence.

UNCLE SAM

Inheritance taxes are so high that the happiest mourner at a rich man's funeral is usually Uncle Sam.
— *Olin Miller*

She was going to complain to the President about something, and if that didn't do any good she was going to write to Uncle Sam. — *Peter De Vries*

Uncle Sam was formerly a tall and slender fellow who has recently developed a shamefully large waste.

The good old days were those when Uncle Sam lived within his income, and without ours.

The reason Uncle Sam has to wear such a tall hat is that he is always passing it around.

UNDERSTAND

There are three things I have always loved but never understood: art, music and women.
— *Fontenelle*

It was not until I was seventy-three that I almost understood the form and character of birds, fish and plants. — *Hokusai*

There is a great difference between knowing and understanding: you can know a lot about something and not really understand it. — *Charles F. Kettering*

To understand one woman is not necessarily to understand any other woman. *—John Stuart Mill*

No one is ever old enough to know better. *—Holbrook Jackson*

For a man to pretend to understand women is bad manners; for him really to understand them is bad morals. *—Henry James*

It takes more than the understanding of man to understand woman.

There are two periods in a man's life when he doesn't understand a woman: before marriage and after marriage.

The only thing men can't understand about women is how women understand so much about men.

No man really understands a woman, no matter how young he is.

It takes years of married life before a man learns to understand every word his wife is not saying.

It's strange how much easier it is for a man to understand a woman when he's not married to her.

What would it avail a man if he understood women—he'd still fall in love.

Some people understand nothing better than anything else.

Men don't understand women because they can't; women don't understand men because they don't have to.

The man who says he understands women probably lies about other things too.

If men understood women better, or if women understood men better, things would be just as they are.

When a man finally gets to understand women, his wife won't let him make use of his knowledge.

There are only three kinds of men who don't understand women: the young, the old, and the middle-aged.

Marriage originates when a man meets the only woman who understands him, and so does divorce.

No man will ever understand a woman, but he can have a lot of fun trying to find out.

UNDERTAKER

What a scandal it would cause if an undertaker gave way to cheerfulness and whistled at his work! *—Ed Howe*

There's nothing wrong with some men that an undertaker can't fix.

Another man who is not affected by the number of do-it-yourselfers is the undertaker.

Undertakers look solemn because the world is full of dead ones who are holding out on them.

The man who follows the medical profession is either a doctor or an undertaker.

Whose funeral parlor does he use when an undertaker buries another undertaker?

Be guided by an undertaker and he'll put you in a hole.

UNDRESS

Every time a woman leaves off something she looks better, but every time a man leaves off something he looks worse.
— *Will Rogers*

Everyone is always stripping: after all, a lady taking off her gloves is removing her garments.
— *Gypsy Rose Lee*

At a burlesque show the attendence falls off if nothing else does. — *Wilson Mizner*

The stripper who has little on her mind usually has even less on her body.

After all is said and undone, a woman retires for the night.

A stripper is an actress who doesn't let her right hand know what her left hand is undoing.

People who live in glass houses should undress in the dark.

A stripper is a woman who starts out with a strapless gown and ends up with a gownless strap.

UNEMPLOYMENT

There's no telling how good business would be if all the people studying unemployment would go to work.

If time is money, the unemployed should have more money than the employed.

Unemployment hits the man with no trade hardest—he doesn't even know what trade he's unemployed at.

Another way to solve the unployment problem is to invent a machine that does the work of one man and takes a dozen men to operate.

Some men are so conscientious, they just sit at home and worry because they don't go out and look for a job.

UNHAPPY

Men are the only animals who devote themselves assiduously to making one another unhappy.
— *Mencken*

Men who are unhappy, like men who sleep badly, are always proud of the fact.
— *Bertrand Russell*

You don't have to suffer to be a poet; adolescence is enough suffering for anyone.
— *John Ciardi*

Unhappiness is not knowing what we want, and killing ourselves to get it. — *Don Herold*

People should be sufficiently discontented to feel there is something to live for. — *Bernard Shaw*

Call no man unhappy until he is married. — *Socrates*

There's enough misery and unhappiness in the movies without having it in real life too.

There's no one so unhappy as a woman with a secret that nobody wants to know.

Half the world is unhappy because it can't have the things that are making the other half unhappy.

The pursuit of happiness is often a sure way to unhappiness.

There are as many women unhappily married as there are women unhappily unmarried.

All the world's a stage, and some women are always rehearsing their woes.

Most of the unhappiness of the world is caused by the belief that the rest of the people are happy.

UNITED NATIONS

The United Nations was set up not to get us to heaven, but only to save us from hell.
— *Winston Churchill*

The United Nations is made up of states that cannot tolerate injustice or oppression—except at home.

The only thing the member states of the UN have in common is their ability to see one another's faults.

The United Nations always seems up in the air, just like the skyscraper it's housed in.

The United Nations is a concert of nations with too many wind instruments.

What the United Nations needs most are united notions.

The United Nations is made up of one part protocol, one part alcohol, and one part vitriol.

The trouble with the United Nations is that while its problems are getting bigger, its delegates remain the same old size.

The United Nations was set up to make nations behave like friends instead of relatives.

The purpose of the United Nations is to get countries to draw together so that one won't draw first.

The United Nations is made up of national delegates who could promote more peace by giving less advice.

The United Nations spends so much time on procedure that it has no time left to proceed.

Nothing reveals how disunited nations are like a session at the United Nations.

The United Nations is a stage, with Communism trying to turn it into a puppet show.

The reason they pay regular salaries to UN delegates is that they are not very good at peacework.

The United Nations is an international organization whose problems are multiplied by division.

The United Nations was organized with the purpose of helping nations to make up rather than to make off with one another.

UNITED STATES

If you don't know what a great country this is, I know someone who does—Russia.
— *Robert Frost*

The United States is a land where men govern but women rule. — *John Mason Brown*

The trouble with this country is that there are too many people going about saying, "The trouble with this country is—"
— *Sinclair Lewis*

America is a great country, but you can't live in it for nothing.
— *Will Rogers*

There are no institutions in America—there are only fashions.
— *Mencken*

America is a nation that conceives many odd inventions for getting somewhere, but can think of nothing to do when it gets there. — *Will Rogers*

America is the best half-educated country in the world.
— *Nicholas Murray Butler*

Rabelaisian looseness is just as characteristic of America as Puritanical strictness. — *Aldous Huxley*

The President is the head of the United States, the Supreme Court is its backbone, and Congress is its lungs.

America is a land that glories in its great poets as long as it doesn't have to read them.

The United States is a nation that tops the rest of the world in automation, education—and taxation.

America is still the land of opportunity: everyone can become a taxpayer.

There are more cars than families in the United States, and more fools than cars.

America is a government of checks and balances: Congress writes the checks, and the people supply the balances.

The United States is a country that achieves more triumphs with its spacecraft than with its statecraft.

America is a land where most citizens vote for Democrats, but hope to live like Republicans.

The history of the United States: splitting logs, splitting hairs, splitting atoms.

America is a land of freedom where everyone is free to complain about the lack of freedom.

The United States produces more food than any other country, and more diets to prevent us from eating it.

In the United States, the farmer is the backbone, the reformer is the wishbone, and the politician is the jawbone.

The best way to get ahead of Russia is to get behind America.

The United States is the only land where the poor have a parking problem.

America is dedicated to life, liberty, and the pursuit of happiness—so long as it's pursued respectably, secretly, and without too much noise.

Historians are still trying to convince us that the United States was founded to avoid taxation.

America is a land of such easy credit that even the underprivileged are overfinanced.

The United States can do anything any other country can do, except borrow money from the United States.

What this country needs is less talk about what America makes, and more talk about what makes America.

The United States has more cars than any other country in the world—and also more hospitals.

America is a land inhabited by millions of people surrounded by tax collectors.

The thing that impresses foreigners most about the United States is the way parents obey their children.

UNLUCKY

Whether or not a black cat crossing your path brings bad luck depends on whether you are a man or a mouse.

It's unlucky to postpone a wedding, but not if you keep on postponing it.

Some men are so unlucky that when their ship finally does come in, there's sure to be a dock strike.

Bad luck never lasts; it continues for a while, and then gets worse.

Pity the unlucky person who looks forward all year to his vacation and then returns with mosquito bites over poison ivy on top of sunburn.

Lighting three cigarettes on one match isn't unlucky—it's unlikely.

The height of hard luck is being shipwrecked on a desert island with your own wife.

UNPLEASANT

Something unpleasant is coming when men are anxious to tell the truth. — *Disraeli*

A person should do one unpleasant duty every day just to keep himself in moral trim. — *William James*

Some women are so disagreeable, they always stick up for people you want to talk about.

When a wife has nothing more to say, she always finds a very unpleasant way of not saying it.

UNPOPULAR

My definition of a free society is a society where it is safe to be unpopular. — *Adlai Stevenson*

The only person more unpopular than a holier-than-thou is a cleverer-than-thou.

Many a has-been believes that he's still as popular as he never was.

USE

The question of common sense, "What is it good for?" would abolish the rose and be answered triumphantly by the cabbage.
— *James Russell Lowell*

A fellow's usefulness frequently ends when he gets an assistant.
— *Kin Hubbard*

Knowledge and timber shouldn't be much used till they are seasoned. — *Justice O. W. Holmes*

It is almost as great a misfortune to be of use to everybody as to be of use to nobody.
— *Baltasar Gracián*

Constant use will wear away anything, especially friends.

Another nice thing about money is that it has so many different uses.

Beware the opportunist: he has no use for people he cannot use.

USELESS

Music is essentially useless, as life is. — *Santayana*

We have too much knowledge of useless things, and too much ignorance of useful things.
— *Vauvenargues*

He is useless on top of the ground; he ought to be under it, nourishing the cabbages.
— *Mark Twain*

A friend who is very near and dear may in time become as useless as a relative. — *George Ade*

The punishment of criminals should serve a purpose: when a man is hanged he is useless.
— *Voltaire*

The only purpose some men serve in life is to prove the futility of existence.

Every daughter finds her mother's advice useless until she can pass it on to her own daughter.

No matter how worthless a man is, there's always a woman and a dog that love him.

It's hard to keep a good man down, and even harder to keep a good-for-nothing up.

UTOPIA

The Utopian is a poet who has gone astray. — *W. R. Inge*

Utopia is the good old days— plus all the modern conveniences.

Utopia is the place where all women get married, and all men remain bachelors.

If all the reckless drivers were laid end to end, that would be Utopia.

Utopia is a land where there are no Joneses for the neighbors to keep up with.

Utopia must be a faraway place full of people who would like to be back home again.

Utopia is a land where there's an equal distribution of wealth, and everyone gets more than he has.

The only place where adults act like adults is—Utopia.

Utopia is a land whose population is made up of engaged couples only.

Utopia is the only place where all a government does is govern.

Utopia is a land where the government always does something for you, and never does anything to you.

Utopia is a land that is run without crime or treason.

Most people have good intentions, but the only place where they carry them out is Utopia.

Utopia is an ideal state where you love your enemies instead of loving your enemies' enemies.

Utopia is a place where the Joneses are trying to keep up with you.

VACATION

A vacation is over when you begin to yearn for your work.
— *Dr. Morris Fishbein*

In planning a vacation the rule is: take along half as much baggage and twice as much money.

Maybe you can't take it with you, but have you ever seen a car packed for a vacation trip?

A vacation starts a few days before it begins and lasts a few days after it ends.

A travel book sometimes helps you decide where to spend your vacations, but more often it's a bankbook.

Many men go on vacations for the fishing, but many more girls go on vacations for the hunting.

A vacation is a way of getting into the pink by going into the red.

Some people's idea of roughing it on a vacation is to have a cabin without television.

You never have total recall about your vacation: you know where you went, but not where your money did.

The best place to spend your vacation is just inside your income.

Despite jets, missiles and electronic devices, man has still not invented anything that goes faster than a vacation.

Vacations are holidays when people are immersed in fun, bathed in sunshine, and washed by waves before they are soaked.

The only real vacation many a man gets is when his wife goes away on hers.

School vacation is a mixed blessing: when it begins for children, it ends for their mothers.

The trouble with most vacations is that the two weeks off are followed by two off weeks.

A vacation should be long enough for the boss to miss you, but not long enough for him to discover he can get along without you.

The trouble with a vacation is that it's such a long time paying for such a short time playing.

A man doesn't have vacation problems: his boss tells him when to take them, and his wife tells him where.

A vacation is a period during which you learn where to stay away from next year.

Marriage is a business in which a man takes his boss along on his vacation.

One always needs a vacation, even if it's only to recover from the exhaustion of packing for it.

Many a person returns from his vacation broke: while he was getting away from it all, it was getting away from him.

A vacation is like love: anticipated with pleasure, experienced with discomfort, and remembered with nostalgia.

Some people never learn: they still think they can have a wonderful vacation on what they can afford.

VACUUM

A vacuum of ideas affects people differently than a vacuum of air, otherwise readers of books would be constantly collapsing.
— *G. C. Lichtenberg*

Nature abhors a vacuum: when a head lacks brains, she fills it with conceit.

Some women use a vacuum cleaner to pick up dirt, while others use the telephone.

VAGRANT

How is it that a vagrant can always find liquor, but can never find a job?

A vagrant is a nobody on his way from nowhere to nothing.

VALUE

The chief value of money lies in the fact that one lives in a world in which it is overestimated.
— *Mencken*

People exaggerate the value of things they haven't got: everybody worships truth and unselfishness because they have no experience with them.
— *Bernard Shaw*

Cherish all your happy moments: they make a fine cushion for old age.   — *Booth Tarkington*

If husbands had trade-in values, there would be many more divorces.

The only time a man objects to being overrated is when he pays his income tax.

A mother-in-law always accepts her daughter's husband at his own valuation—if it is low enough.

A man may be worth more than others, and still be worthless.

The average man's opinions are generally of more value to himself than to anyone else.

Character is a man's worth, success is what a man's worth.

If you think the younger generation doesn't know the value of a dollar, just ask a teen-ager how many gallons of gas it will buy.

Never tell a woman you are unworthy of her love—she knows.

How much would you be worth if you lost all your money?

VANITY

Man that is born of woman is apt to be as vain as his mother.
— *Robert Frost*

A man who is not a fool can rid himself of every folly except vanity.   — *Rousseau*

Vanity is so secure in the heart of man that everyone wants to be admired: even I who write this, and you who read this. — *Pascal*

The best way to turn a woman's head is to tell her she has a beautiful profile.
— *Sacha Guitry*

The only cure for vanity is laughter, and the only fault that's laughable is vanity.
— *Henri Bergson*

My vanity is excessive: wherever I sit is the head of the table.
— *Mencken*

An ass chosen to carry the statue of Isis, before which the people kneeled in reverence, thought the homage was paid to him.
— *G. C. Lichtenberg*

Vanity is the magic mirror that gives many an unattractive woman delusions of glamour.

When a nobody thinks himself a somebody, he thinks everybody else is a nobody.

Many a man could easily support a wife if he didn't also have to feed her vanity.

Vanity is what makes the man in a rut think he's in the groove.

When success turns a man's head, it should wring his neck at the same time.

A man's high opinion of himself is usually increased by everyone except the rest of the world.

If it isn't vanity, what is it that drives a man to make his son grow up just like his father?

The hardest secret for many a woman to keep is her overweening opinion of herself.

VARIETY

There is no greater variety than in amatory pleasures, yet they are always the same.
— *Ninon de Lenclos*

Only two of God's creatures, the dog and the guitar, have taken all sizes and shapes so as not to be separated from man.
— *Andrés Segovia*

With me a change of trouble is as good as a vacation.
— *Lloyd George*

Variability is one of the virtues of a woman: if you have one good wife, you are sure to have a spiritual harem. — *Chesterton*

It is foolish to make the same mistake when there are so many varieties to choose from.

VEGETABLE

If there were only turnips and potatoes in the world, someone would complain that plants grow the wrong way.
— *G. C. Lichtenberg*

The most enjoyable way to follow a vegetable diet is to let the cow eat it and take yours in roast beef.

Cabbage is a friendly vegetable: when you cook it in your apartment it goes up and down the hall and visits your neighbors.

VEGETARIAN

Ferocity is still characteristic of bulls and other vegetarians.
— *Bernard Shaw*

Most vegetarians look so much like the food they eat that they can be classified as cannibals.
— *Finley Peter Dunne*

There are people who so arrange their lives that they feed themselves only on side dishes.
— *José Ortega y Gasset*

The vegetarian is the only living creature who belongs to the vegetable kingdom.

Vegetarians have never been able to explain why the first sin was the result of eating fruit.

A vegetarian never eats meat on a Friday, or in any week that has a Friday in it.

The first thing that missionaries should teach cannibals is to become vegetarians.

Eschewing meat can be tougher than chewing it, unless you're a vegetarian.

A vegetarian eats oysters only during the months that have an X in their spelling.

VENDING MACHINES

What this country needs is a credit card that will fit into a vending machine.

The vending machine will never replace the cheerful waitress until it learns to give service with a smile.

VENUS DE MILO

Venus de Milo shows what will happen to you if you keep on biting your nails. — *Noel Coward*

Venus de Milo typifies the beauty of women: when they're

beautiful, they're probably not all there.

Never use harsh detergents: look at what happened to Venus de Milo.

The world has always believed in rearming, except in the case of Venus de Milo.

VETERINARIAN

The only doctor who never sends any of his patients a bill is the veterinarian.

A veterinarian is the only doctor who can diagnose without asking questions.

Another doctor who never bothers about cultivating a bedside manner is the veterinarian.

VICE

One big vice in a man is apt to keep out a great many smaller ones.   — Bret Harte

It is impossible to root out of an Englishman's mind the notion that vice is delightful, and that abstention from it is privation.
— Bernard Shaw

The next best thing to leading others astray is to be led astray oneself.   — Norman Douglas

Every man should have enough vices to keep him from being a menace to society.

Many a man loves vice for the enemies it has made.

Cultivate vices when you are young, and when you are old they will not forsake you.

We are not punished for our vices, but by them.

Many of us are misled by our vices, but most of us follow them without any leading at all.

The most common vice of some people is to be forever giving advice.

VICE AND VIRTUE

He has all the virtues I dislike, and none of the vices I admire.   — Winston Churchill

The virtue of some people consists wholly in condemning the vices of others.   — Herbert Samuel

Some people with great virtues are disagreeable, while others with great vices are delightful.
— La Rochefoucauld

We know God will forgive us our sins; the question is, what will He think of our virtues?
— Peter De Vries

Men do not vary much in virtue; their vices only are different.   — Elbert Hubbard

The vices of some people suit them, while the virtues of others don't.   — La Rochefoucauld

One good vice will get you more publicity than a dozen virtues.

Virtues are learned at mother's knee, vices at some other joint.

The difference between other people's children and your own is the difference between vice and virtue.

The only vice some men have is their claim to being virtuous.

Virtue is more to be feared than vice because its excesses are not subject to the regulation of conscience.

He who hesitates is probably torn between vice and virtue.

When virtue hides her face it is called modesty; when vice does so, it is called shame.

Only a true friend overlooks your virtues and appreciates your faults.

The man who has no vices probably has some of the worst virtues.

VICE-PRESIDENT

Once there were two brothers: one ran away to sea, the other was elected Vice-President—and nothing was ever heard from either of them again.
— *Thomas R. Marshall*

The Vice-Presidency of the United States isn't worth a pitcher of warm spit.
— *John Nance Garner*

After a lifetime of devoted service, the statesman's declining days were clouded by great sorrow: he became Vice-President of the United States.
— *Finley Peter Dunne*

Some men would rather be right than President, others would rather be wrong than Vice-President.

The only labor trouble some banks have is keeping the vice-presidents busy.

Some men are born obscure, some achieve obscurity, and others become Vice-Presidents.

Blessed are the meek for they shall be vice-presidents.

If a boy is lucky, he may grow up to be President of the United States; if he is unlucky, he may grow up to be Vice-President.

America is the only financial institution which is run with only one Vice-President.

Some men become a success in a bank, some a failure, while most become vice-presidents.

VICTIM

A confidence man gets rich quick by finding a victim who gets poor quick.

When a man makes a mistake in his first marriage, the victim is his second wife.

Revenge is sweet, but not when you're the victim.

Hard work never killed anybody, but why take a chance on being its first victim?

The reason a confidence man makes money without working is that he finds suckers who want to do the same.

No matter how often it is plucked, the human goose grows a new crop of feathers.

VICTORY

A conqueror is always a lover of peace: he would like to make his entry into our state unopposed.   — Karl von Clausewitz

The victor belongs to the spoils.   — Scott Fitzgerald

In the battle of the sexes, woman gains her greatest victories by surrendering.

You can generally win if you are careful not to triumph.

To the victors belong the privilege of fighting over the spoils.

VIGOR

It's not the men in my life that counts—it's the life in my men.
— Mae West

It's healthier to have women on your lap than on your mind; that's why you're more vigorous at twenty than at seventy.

Many a woman marries a man for life, and soon finds out that he doesn't have any.

VIOLIN

I occasionally play works by contemporary composers to remind myself how much I appreciate Beethoven. — Jascha Heifetz

Playing the violin must be like making love—all or nothing.
— Isaac Stern

Had I learned to fiddle, I should have done nothing else.
— Samuel Johnson

The ideal gift for a musician living upstairs is a violin—with no strings attached.

One of the most difficult instruments to play well is second fiddle.

The violin is the proper musical instrument for a wedding: after the romantic music is over, the strings are still attached.

VIRGINITY

One of the superstitions of the mind of man is believing that virginity can be a virtue. — Voltaire

Breathes there a woman with soul so dead, who never lost her maidenhead?

Eternal vigilance is the price of virginity.

A man seldom robs a woman of her virginity without an accomplice.

Virginity is a balloon in the carnival of life that vanishes with the first prick.

VIRTUE

When you can't have anything else, you can have virtue.
— Don Marquis

What we should really beg of our neighbors is: "Forgive us our virtues." — *Nietzsche*

A virtue, to be serviceable, must like gold be alloyed with some commoner but more durable metal. — *Samuel Butler*

I have never seen a man as fond of virtue as of women. — *Confucius*

Mona Lisa is the only beauty who went through history and retained her reputation. — *Will Rogers*

Virtue must be valuable, if men and women of all degrees pretend to have it. — *Ed Howe*

Virtue is its own reward, and usually the only reward.

Some men would be models of virtue if it weren't for their thoughts, words and deeds.

The straight and narrow path wouldn't be so narrow if more people walked on it.

Be virtuous and you will be happy—as well as quaint and queer.

One trouble with being virtuous is that you can't tell your friends about it afterwards.

There's a vast difference between a girl's virtue and her virtues.

The straight and narrow path is never congested by heavy traffic.

Marriage teaches a man thrift, punctuality and many other virtues he wouldn't need if he stayed single.

It always pays for a girl to be good, but not much.

The trouble with the straight and narrow path is that there's no place to park.

For a girl to remain friendly with some men is virtuously impossible.

Virtue is its own punishment.

Many a person cannot follow the straight and narrow path without becoming straight-laced and narrow-minded.

VISION

We call loudly for a man of vision, and when we get one we call him a visionary. — *Thackeray*

The farther backward you can look, the farther forward you are likely to see. — *Winston Churchill*

You see things, and you say "Why?"; but I dream things that never were, and I say "Why not?" — *Bernard Shaw*

The obscure we see eventually, the completely apparent takes longer. — *Edward R. Murrow*

Vision is definitely affected by glasses, especially after they have been filled and emptied a few times.

The man with vision always gets ahead of the man with visions.

When it comes to spotting a blonde hair on a man's coat, every wife has 20-20 vision.

VISIT

Visit, that ye be not visited.
— *Don Herold*

There's no place like home, especially when your wife wants you to go with her to visit her relatives.

Only when a gadabout is out visiting is she really at home.

The reason a man doesn't like his wife to go home to her mother is because it will then be her mother's turn to visit him.

Friends are lost by calling too often or too seldom.

Unwelcome guests never guess they're unwelcome.

A man is getting old when he no longer cares where his wife goes provided he doesn't have to go along.

Eternal visitation is the price of relatives.

When a woman visits, she drops in for a call; when a man visits, he calls in for a drop.

Man is a paradoxical creature who longs to visit the moon, but hesitates to visit his next-door neighbor.

VITAMIN

No matter how thorough her knowledge, a dietician can never know her vitamins from A to Z.

Nature is perverse: it puts most of the vitamins in the foods we don't like.

Vitamin ads are so attractive, they make a man who has his health feel that he's missing something.

VOCABULARY

The last thing a political party gives up is its vocabulary.
— *Tocqueville*

The most common method of acquiring a large vocabulary is by marrying it.

If you add a word a day to your vocabulary, at the end of a year your friends will wonder who the hell you think you are.

The average woman has a smaller stock of words than the average man, but the turnover is greater.

VOICE

Every woman is endowed with three voices: one for the telephone, one for company, and the voice she reserves for her husband.

When a woman lowers her voice, it's a sign she wants something; when she raises it, it's a sign she didn't get it.

It's sad when an opera singer realizes she's lost her voice, but not half so sad as when she doesn't realize it.

The male voice changes once in a lifetime, but the female voice changes every time a woman stops scolding her husband to answer the phone.

The more liquid a man pours down his throat, the less chance there is of drowning his voice.

Science can magnify the human voice enormously, but it can't do a thing with the voice of conscience.

About the only voice a man gets in running his home is the invoice.

The man who talks the loudest generally lets his voice keep working while his mind rests.

VOTING

Vote for the man who promises least—he'll be the least disappointing.　　— *Bernard Baruch*

Giving every man a vote has no more made men wise and free than Christianity has made them good.　　　　　— *Mencken*

When a fellow tells me he's bipartisan, I know he's going to vote against me.
　　　　　— *Harry S. Truman*

Clever and attractive women do not want to vote; they are willing to let men govern as long as they govern men.
　　　　　— *Bernard Shaw*

There ain't any finer folks living than a Republican that votes the Democratic ticket.　— *Will Rogers*

If a large city can choose for its mayor a man who merely will not steal from it, we consider it a triumph of suffrage.
　　　　— *Frank Moore Colby*

I always voted at my party's call, and I never thought of thinking for myself at all.
　　　　　— *W. S. Gilbert*

Think well before voting, but not too well—there are already too many abstainers.

The drawback in voting for the man of your choice is that he is seldom a candidate.

The citizen who never votes probably doesn't want to feel responsible for what goes on in Washington.

The people who criticize unintelligent Congressmen are the intelligent voters who elected them.

Our democracy was created by men who fought for the right to vote so that their descendants could exercise their right not to vote.

It's always right to vote for the best man, but the chances are that the best man is not running.

The man who never bothers to vote is always ready to tell you what's wrong with the government.

There will always be some people who prefer to vote for what they want rather than work for it.

The chief difficulty of cutting down the expenses of government is that so many of the expenses can vote.

Generally about half the citizens vote, and generally the wrong half.

What this country needs is a Congress capable of voting more intelligently than the voters who elect it.

A good citizen is one who continues to vote for new schools even after his children have grown up.

Many a man will drink wet and vote dry so long as he can stagger to the polls.

The citizen who doesn't vote because he wants nothing to do with crooked politics, does have something to do with it.

Our politics would be vastly improved if the millions of young people who want to vote but can't, would exchange with older folks who can vote but don't.

In elections, the undecided vote is usually the deciding factor.

It is always the man who doesn't vote who spends his time criticizing the officials other men have elected.

VULGARITY

Vulgarity is the garlic in the salad of taste. — *Cyril Connolly*

A vulgarian is usually a person who doesn't know the meaning of the word.

It is only the rare vulgarian who isn't fit to live with pigs— the majority of them are.

WAGES

The definition of a living wage depends upon whether you are getting it or giving it.

Nowadays a man is given a raise to enable him to live the way he is already living.

In the old days the biggest deduction from a man's pay envelope took place after he got home.

A man's wages are usually equal to about half of what he thinks he deserves.

It is called take-home pay because it is seldom big enough for you to go anywhere else with it.

WAIT

There are two kinds of people in one's life: people whom one keeps waiting, and people for whom one waits. — *S. N. Behrman*

In this world truth can wait; she's used to it. — *Douglas Jerrold*

All things come to him who waits, especially things not worth waiting for.

The woman who says she won't be a minute is usually right.

A man is known by the company he keeps, but a woman is known by the company she keeps waiting.

Everything comes to him who waits—if he waits till it comes.

Time and tide wait for no man, but woman expects all three to wait for her.

Husbands have always had a leisure problem—it's called waiting.

Some men never achieve anything because they spend most of their lives waiting for their wives to dress.

All things come to him who waits, but they come faster if he meets them halfway.

A woman's promise to be on time carries a lot of wait.

Only two kinds of men will wait for a woman—husbands and single men.

Another thing that comes to him who waits is a second notice.

All things come to him who waits, especially sickness, disillusion and old age.

The man of the hour is the husband whose wife told him to wait a minute.

All things come to him who waits, but they are mostly leftovers from those who didn't wait.

WAITER

I must be getting old because nowadays I find I'm more interested in the food I eat than in the girl who serves it.
— *John Steinbeck*

Some are born great, some achieve greatness, and some have a bowing acquaintance with headwaiters.

In some restaurants the only good waiters are the customers.

No man likes to be put in his place, except by a headwaiter.

The youngster who never pays attention when he is called, will probably grow up to be a waiter.

WALKING

A pedestrian is a man in danger of his life; a walker is a man in possession of his soul.
— *David McCord*

I am a slow walker, but I never walk backwards. — *Lincoln*

Man must look just as ridiculous to the crab when it sees him walk forward. — *G. C. Lichtenberg*

Man is a walking creature: one generation walks to school, the next walks to the school bus.

When you see a married couple out for a walk, the one who is two steps ahead is probably angry.

Walking is the best form of exercise, but only if you can dodge those who aren't.

Some motorists insist that if God had intended us to walk, we would not have been born with cars.

If it weren't for dogs, some people would never go for a walk.

Walking is a pleasure only when you can afford to ride if you want to.

Walking on an empty stomach is a wonderful aid to digestion, but be careful whose stomach you walk on.

If walking is such good exercise for health, why do you seldom see a mailman who looks stronger than a truckdriver?

Walking is a lost art: nowadays people in every walk of life don't.

Walking is a wonderful exercise that is sure to prolong your life, unless you try to cross the street.

WALLET

His money corrects his judgment: he keeps his mind in his wallet. — *Molière*

Formerly the bulging billfold meant lots of money; today it merely means lots of credit cards.

The way to a woman's heart is through his wallet.

You pay an income tax on what you put into your wallet, and a sales tax on what you take out of it.

You can always tell a family man: he has more snapshots in his wallet than bills.

After you've spent all your money on Christmas gifts, the one gift you are sure to receive is a wallet.

In the order named, the most valuable contents of a wallet are: family photos, credit cards, paper money.

WAR

The War World after the next one will be fought with rocks.
— *Einstein*

Diplomats are just as essential in starting a war as soldiers are in finishing it. — *Will Rogers*

The only war where the men knew what they were fighting for was the Trojan War: it was fought over a woman.
— *William Lyon Phelps*

Wars teach us not to love our enemies, but to hate our allies.
— *W. L. George*

The supply of uranium is very limited, and it is feared that it may be used up before the human race exterminates itself.
— *Bertrand Russell*

Soldiers usually win the battles, and generals get the credit for them. — *Napoleon*

The trouble with war is that all the preliminaries are arranged by matchmakers, and all they have left for fighters to do is the murdering. — *Finley Peter Dunne*

How good bad music and bad reasons sound when we march against an enemy! — *Nietzsche*

We are glad to have God on our side to maul our enemies when we cannot do the work ourselves.
— *Dryden*

War is little more than a catalogue of mistakes and misfortunes.   — *Winston Churchill*

The tragedy of war is that it
uses man's best to do man's
worst.   — *Harry Emerson Fosdick*

The hero of the next war will
be the one who prevents it.

War does not determine who is
right, but only who is left.

Wars will always continue to
abolish nations until nations finally
abolish wars.

A warmonger is a person who
is invincible in peace and invisible in war.

We haven't paid for our last
war because we haven't had our
last war yet.

The worst thing about war is
that it seldom kills off the right
people.

War makes human life cheap,
and everything else dear.

If the people of the world will
not learn to get along without
nuclear warfare, nuclear warfare
will teach the world to get along
without people.

Those that live by the sword
shall perish by the taxes.

Naturally war doesn't pay; it's
never even paid for.

A warmonger is a man who is
always ready to lay down your
life for his country.

There is only one sure way to
abolish war forever, and that is
to have World War III.

WAR AND PEACE

I don't know whether war is an
interlude during peace, or peace
an interlude during war.
                      — *Clemenceau*

In peace, sons bury their fathers; in war, fathers bury their
sons.   — *Herodotus*

War makes rattling good history, but peace is poor reading.
                   — *Thomas Hardy*

Vice foments war, while virtue does the fighting; thus, if not
for virtue, we should always have
peace.   — *Vauvenargues*

More war, more gore; more
pax, more tax.

Hammering swords into plow-
shares is more difficult nowadays
because no one seems to know
what a plowshare looks like.

Whoever heard of a civilized
country preparing for peace instead of for war?

Peace would last longer if no
new wars could be started until
all the generals of the previous
wars were dead.

In wartime it's the law of the
jungle, in peacetime it's the law
of the bungle.

A pacifist believes peace should be everyone's business because war may be everyone's funeral.

The peace of today costs more than the war of yesterday.

Nations work for peace by toiling to pay for the last war and by financing the next.

The nation that's always prepared for war isn't always prepared for peace.

In time of peace prepay for war.

World War III is unique because it will never be mentioned in history books.

The only way to stop all wars is to get all the nations to outlaw peace.

The best argument for everlasting peace is that it would enable us to pay for past wars.

Peace on earth is not an impossible ideal: all we have to do is keep wars from breaking out.

WASH

Republicans have been peddling eyewash about themselves and hogwash about Democrats— what they need is a good mouthwash. — *Lyndon B. Johnson*

The classes that wash most are those that work least. — *Chesterton*

Every time a boy shows his hands, someone suggests that he wash them. — *Ed Howe*

Man is rapidly learning to wash everything by machine, except himself.

WASHINGTON, D.C.

Washington is a city of Southern efficiency and Northern charm. — *John F. Kennedy*

How prophetic L'Enfant was when he laid out Washington as a city that goes around in circles! — *John Mason Brown*

Washington is the seat of the government, and the taxpayer is the pants pocket.

Another reason many Americans visit Washington is that they like to see the people they're working for.

Many more servants than Presidents have lived in the White House.

Once upon a time only Washington's face was on our money; now Washington's hands are on it too.

The Washington Monument is one of the few things in Washington that's always upright.

The most common form of capital punishment is having to live in Washington, D.C.

Washington is full of go-getters who go there solely to get.

Washington is the place where money is printed, shipped all over the country, and soon finds its way back.

Half the politicians in Washington are trying to get investigations started, and the other half are trying to get them stopped.

Millions of Americans visit Washington yearly: some like to see the sights, while others like to be near their money.

Half the people in Washington are hoping to be discovered, and the other half are afraid they will be.

WASHINGTON, GEORGE

George Washington as a boy was ignorant of the commonest accomplishments of youth—he could not even lie. — *Mark Twain*

Old George Washington's forte was not to have any public man of the present day resemble him.
— *Artemus Ward*

America's lack of imagination is due to its having adopted for its national hero a man who was incapable of telling a lie.
— *Oscar Wilde*

No wonder George Washington is the father of his country: look at all the beds he slept in!

The stern expression of George Washington on the dollar bill shows his disapproval of the huge increase in our national debt since he left office.

It was much easier for George Washington never to tell a lie: there were no income tax forms in his day.

At school we learn that Washington never told a lie—the man, not the city.

George Washington must have had total recall—look at all the monuments to his memory!

George Washington was first in war, first in peace, and first in the hearts of his countrymen—but he married a widow.

George Washington may have slept in more beds than any other American, but he was always awake at the right time.

George Washington was the first and last man elected President of the United States without telling a lie.

One thing you can still get for a dollar is an engraved portrait of George Washington.

Another remarkable thing about George Washington was that he was born on a national holiday.

If George Washington never told a lie, how did he manage to go so far in politics?

Don't complain that you can't sleep in a strange bed: think of George Washington—he slept in a different bed almost every night.

George Washington never told a lie, but then he was never stopped by a state trooper for speeding.

WASTE

I wish I could stand on a busy street corner, hat in hand, and beg people to throw me all their wasted hours. — *Bernard Berenson*

Everyone should keep a mental wastepaper basket, and the older he grows, the more things will he promptly consign to it.
     — *Samuel Butler*

Most of us don't want the government to squander our money because we want to do it ourselves.

A Congressman's idea of government waste is the money spent in another Congressman's district.

Men waste time, and time wastes men.

An efficiency expert is a man who wastes a lot of time figuring out the little time others are wasting.

The dog is man's best friend, and the wastepaper basket his next best.

Another optimist is the citizen who votes for a candidate who promises to eliminate government waste.

WATCH

When a man retires, and time is no longer a matter of urgent importance, his colleagues present him with a watch.
     — *Robert C. Sherriff*

Women whose time is worth the least generally have the most expensive watches.

There's a right time for everything, but not for the man who has a cheap watch.

A man with one watch knows what time it is, but a watchmaker with dozens of watches can never be sure.

The person who gives a watch as a gift probably thinks there's no present like the time.

Never ask a bore the time, or he will start to tell you how watches are made.

The only thing wrong with a watch that's waterproof, shockproof and crushproof, is that you can still lose it.

If it weren't for the watch-repairman, we wouldn't have such a good time.

The times are out of joint; O cursed spite: one place your watch is wrong; another, right.

WATER

I never drink water—I'm afraid it will become habit-forming.
     — *W. C. Fields*

You can't trust water: even a straight stick turns crooked in it.
     — *W. C. Fields*

I never drink water—that's the stuff that rusts pipes.
     — *W. C. Fields*

In winter you can't get the kids into a bathtub, and in summer you can't get them out of a pool.

Flowers are grateful for watering; whiskey is not.

The best way to prevent the water from coming into your house is not to pay the water tax.

The only way an alcoholic can keep above water is by not drinking anything else.

Many a woman drives a man to drink—water.

It's a lucky thing that water is a liquid; if it were a solid like coal or marble, how could we get it to run through faucets?

When a man tries to drown his troubles, he never uses water.

Economics makes no sense: no matter how much it rains, you always get a water bill.

If you want to liquidate your debts, don't spend your money like water.

Some men are in favor of fluoridation, some are against it, while others just don't drink water.

Still waters run deep—but how can they run if they are still?

If you want to make something tender, keep it in hot water, unless it's your husband.

Many an argument holds water no better than a newborn puppy.

WAY

A wise woman will always let her husband have her way.
— *Richard Brinsley Sheridan*

Some men are on their way to marriage, some are on their way to success, but most are merely on their way.

Middle age is the interlude between the time you are on the way up and on the way out.

Where there's a woman, there's a way—and she usually gets it.

The people most difficult to get along with are those who object to our having our own way.

Life is a continuous process of learning new ways to make the same old mistakes.

Women are unpredictable: you can never tell how they are going to manage to get their own way.

Where there's a will, there's a way; but where there are many wills, there's no way.

A typical politician, when he comes to the parting of the ways, goes both ways.

Every woman is all right in her own way—but not if she always wants it.

WEAKNESS

The greatest weakness of all is the great fear of appearing weak. — *Bossuet*

A girl's weakest moments come when she's plied with strong drinks.

WEALTH

The only thing wealth does for some people is to make them worry about losing it. — *Rivarol*

Superfluous wealth can buy superfluities only.   — *Thoreau*

Wealth is what gives you the right to preach about the virtues of poverty.

God shows his contempt for wealth by selecting the *nouveau riche* to give it to.

The Scriptures first taught the futility of riches, but it took an income tax to drive the lesson home.

Ignorance is bliss only when you have more money than you know what to do with.

About the only thing the average taxpayer can accumulate by a lifetime of labor is a wealth of experience.

The trouble with the affluent society is that it keeps on wanting more affluence.

It's hard for a rich man to enter the kingdom of heaven, but it's easy for him to get on the church board of trustees.

Wealth has a way of attracting many rich friends, and even more poor relatives.

WEAPON

The best armor is to keep out of gunshot.   — *Francis Bacon*

A man may build himself a throne of bayonets, but he cannot sit on it.   — *W. R. Inge*

The best weapon against an enemy is another enemy.
— *Nietzsche*

Life is a battle of wits which most people fight unarmed.

America will never be invaded —its juvenile delinquents are too well armed.

A car is the only weapon against which there is no defense.

There are only two types of weapons in modern warfare: the obsolescent and the experimental.

WEAR

Behind every successful man is a woman—who has nothing to wear.

Life is a process in which your nerves wear out as your years wear on and your illusions wear off.

If a girl is pretty enough, she can wear almost anything or almost nothing.

Many a husband would like his wife to wear her dresses a little longer—about a year longer.

What the well-dressed woman will wear: Less.

While many a father is wearing out a pair of shoes, the rest of the family is wearing out a set of tires.

In the good old days you saw less of a woman on the beach than you now see on the street.

The woman who says she hasn't a thing to wear usually spends hours deciding what to put on.

The women of today wear more clothes than their grandmothers, but not at the same time.

WEATHER

Bad weather always looks much worse through a window.
                              —John Kieran

In New England in the spring I have counted 136 different kinds of weather inside of twenty-four hours.   *—Mark Twain*

Whether it's cold or whether it's hot, we must have weather, whether or not.

When some people don't like the weather, they act as if their friends were to blame for it.

Don't knock the weather—without it, how would we start conversations?

You can generally tell what the weather is going to be by what you plan to do that can be hurt by it.

There are five kinds of weather: spring, summer, fall, winter, and unusual.

The pessimist expects every change in the weather to be a change for the worse.

This is a free country: if you don't like the weather where you live, you can go elsewhere and not like the weather there also.

No matter how bad the weather is, it's always better than none.

It is difficult to get the weather of any season to live up to the poetry that is written about it.

When the weather lacks dryness, you first feel it in your sinus.

The weatherman can never be sure about the weather, and we can never be sure about the weatherman.

WEATHER BUREAU

The Weather Bureau is a place where everybody talks about the weather, but nobody does anything about it.

Many a man would rather be right than work for the Weather Bureau.

The man who can't tell what kind of a day it is on account of the fog belongs in the Weather Bureau.

Another place where no one is ever ruined by success is the Weather Bureau.

The Weather Bureau is a department of the government that issues unreliable forecasts which everyone relies on.

WEATHERMAN

The weatherman is a prophet who is always right, except for his timing.

Pity the poor weatherman: he is hired by the government to predict the unpredictable.

In theory the weatherman is weatherwise, but in practice he is otherwise.

When his charts say fair, but his corns hurt, what kind of weather does the weatherman forecast?

The weatherman is a man you can never depend upon to be always wrong.

The weatherman's reports would often be more accurate if he would only stick his head out of the window.

The wife of the weatherman never knows what weather to expect.

The weatherman is smart enough to get paid for predicting the weather, but too smart to bet on it.

The only man who changes his mind as often as a woman is the weatherman.

The weatherman is another tipster who is paid for his predictions and not for their accuracy.

Everybody talks about the weatherman, but nobody does anything about him.

A weatherman is able to forecast - changes in weather due to his experience, knowledge and rheumatism.

Another person who never seems to learn from his past mistakes is the weatherman.

Another prophet who can read the past better than he can the future is the weatherman.

Nothing worries the weatherman: he gets his salary, rain or shine.

The trouble with the weatherman is that he's appointed, not elected.

It isn't the frequency or the inaccuracy of the weatherman's forecasts that's so annoying as the frequency of the inaccuracy.

A weatherman makes the mistake of forecasting the weather before it happens.

The weatherman is the leading writer of fiction employed by the government.

Every now and then the weatherman makes a mistake—and guesses right.

It is his knowledge of barometric pressures and wind velocities that enables the weatherman tc forecast the weather incorrectly.

The weatherman is always right about one thing: there's some kind of weather every day.

A weatherman is so called because you never know whether he is right or wrong.

WEDDING

Generally the only one who can cure a lovesick young couple is a Doctor of Divinity.

There are no words in the English language that lead to as many quarrels as "I do."

A wedding is a ceremony at which a woman acquires another mind of her own.

The trouble with being best man at a wedding is that you get no chance to prove it.

Many a husband lives to regret the extravagant fee he bestowed upon the minister who sentenced him.

The happiest days in a movie star's life are her wedding days.

A wedding is a ceremony at which a man chooses the woman he wants to spend his life listening to.

At a wedding a father gives his daughter up with reluctance, and a mother gives her up with relief.

The altar is the place where many a man and woman are mispronounced man and wife.

Doesn't the bride look stunning, and doesn't the groom look stunned?

A wedding is a ritual marking the time when a woman stops dating and starts intimidating.

Love should be behind every wedding, but not too far behind.

Divorce has become so easy nowadays that women have stopped crying at weddings.

Before the wedding, you expect too much of marriage; after the wedding, you get too much of it.

A wedding takes only a few hours, but the arguments go on forever.

A good many things are easier said than done—including the marriage vows.

Ministers who are opposed to games of chance somehow don't object to performing marriage ceremonies.

The only wedding that is sure to go off without a hitch is where the groom doesn't show up.

A wedding is the formality a man has to go through before going to work for a new boss.

When a bride walks into the church she thinks: *Aisle, Altar, Hymn.*

It may be hard for a girl to love her enemies, but she usually sends them an announcement of her wedding.

At a wedding the bride is usually well groomed and the groom well bridled.

A wedding is the ceremony that altars a man's life, liberty and pursuit of happiness.

After paying for the wedding, about the only thing a father has left to give away is the bride.

A shotgun wedding is one in which the bride's father says, "He does."

When a man likes a girl he likes her just as she is, but the girl always wants to altar his status.

A wedding is a put-and-take exchange where the groom takes your daughter off your hands while you put him on his feet.

Every wedding leads to happiness, if not for the married couple, then for their enemies.

The only time you can depend upon a woman not to change her mind is at her wedding.

A noon wedding is a good idea: if the marriage doesn't work out, at least you haven't ruined a whole day.

In spite of all the propaganda for world peace, there will probably be the usual number of weddings in June.

A wedding marks the time when a woman stops putting her best foot forward and starts putting her foot down.

There's only one sure way the groom can get publicity on his wedding, and that is to stay away from it.

At a wedding the happiest couple in the world are sometimes the bride and groom, but more often the bride's parents.

Every bride and groom would do well to remember that in *wedding,* the *we* comes before the *I.*

A wedding is the bridal day when a woman leads a man to the halter.

The best man is one chosen to keep the bridegroom from escaping before the ceremony.

The bride who takes a man for better or for worse often finds him much worse than she took him for.

Many a wedding takes place when a man can't afford to go steady with a girl any longer.

A wedding is a ceremony at which a woman surrenders before she proceeds to dictate her own terms.

WEED

A weed is a plant whose virtues have not yet been discovered.
– Emerson

An amateur gardener is one who knows how to make two weeds grow where only one grew before.

Some people are like weeds— always showing up where they are not wanted.

Work well done never needs redoing, unless of course it's weeding.

The grass next door may be greener, but it's just as hard to weed.

Another difference between annual and perennial plants is that the perennials are usually weeds.

A weeding job that's once completed must soon thereafter be repeated.

An amateur gardener never seems to learn that everything that grows like a weed is one.

You cannot get something for nothing—unless it's a weed.

If you pick one weed less every day, by mid-summer you'll probably have the habit licked entirely.

One of the first lessons a gardener learns is that many things grow that were never planted.

A weed is the only plant a gardener can grow without the aid of a packet of seeds.

The best way to tell the difference between young plants and weeds is to pull up everything in sight—those that grow again are weeds.

WEEK

A week is the shortest distance between two Mondays, and the longest distance between two paydays.

What this country needs is a shorter week for working, and a longer week for thinking.

WEEKEND

A family's worst problem is the rainy weekend: after the children have played in, the parents are played out.

Nobody knows where the television repairman goes on weekends, but he probably goes off somewhere with the doctor and the plumber.

Most traffic accidents occur on Saturday and Sunday: it's a great life, if you don't weekend.

Few marriages are really compatible: most people who like to rest on weekends are married to people who don't.

WEEP

She would have made a splendid wife, for crying only made her eyes more bright and tender.

– O. Henry

A sob is a sound made by women, babies, tenors, clergymen, actors and drunken men.

– Mencken

If you must cry over spilt milk—condense it.

A woman never knows what she can do till she cries.

At first a husband will give his wife anything if she cries a little; after a while she has to go into hysterics.

Laugh and the world laughs with you, cry and they say you are drunk.

If at first you don't succeed, cry, cry again.

Character doesn't change: the little cry-baby eventually becomes a groan man.

The reason mothers cry at weddings is that girls tend to marry men like their fathers.

To cope with a husband successfully, a wife must keep on crying.

WEIGHT

In her lover's arms, a woman weighs but a feather; in her husband's, a ton.

Women are never satisfied: they are always trying to take off weight, put it on, or rearrange it.

It's not the minutes you take at the table that add to your weight —it's the seconds.

Take a lesson from the elephant: it lives to a ripe old age without ever worrying about its weight.

It isn't how much a woman weighs that's important—it's where she carries the weight.

Avoid unpleasant restaurants if you don't want to gain weight in the wrong places.

Losing weight is no problem; the trick is to lose it so that it doesn't find its way back.

Many a woman's fondest wish is to be weighed and found wanting.

A banana is a fruit whose flesh brings your weight up but whose skin brings your weight down.

WELCOME

I appreciate your welcome: as the cow said to the Maine farmer, "Thank you for a warm hand on a cold morning."
—John F. Kennedy

There's no way to recondition a welcome when it's worn out.
—Kin Hubbard

Life would be wonderful if everyone were as glad to see us as a candidate seems to be before election.

The glad hand doesn't always have a genuine ring to it.

The early bird catches the worm—and he is welcome to it.

WELFARE

If people are fit to live, let them live under decent human conditions; if they are not fit to live, kill them in a decent way.
—Bernard Shaw

A government that robs Peter to pay Paul can always depend upon the support of Paul.
—Bernard Shaw

The chief problem of the welfare state is to prevent the unemployed from becoming the unemployable.

People on welfare have all they can do to keep body and soul and television together.

The man who wants the government to take care of him should first consider the American Indian.

People on welfare should be happier than the well-to-do because they are less likely to experience a change for the worse.

Half the citizens of a welfare state believe they should support the government, and the other half believe the government should support them.

In a welfare state it is the rich, not the poor, who live on the wrong side of the tax.

WESTERN

In some Westerns, the only ways the bandits can elude the posse is by crossing over to another station.

The hero of a Western usually wears a .45 Colt, and the heroine a 38 sweater.

In the typical Western, the heroine is prettier than the hero, and the horse is smarter.

In television millions of dollars are spent on horse operas that could be better spent on abolishing them.

WHALE

Consider the whale: it never gets into trouble until it comes up and starts spouting.

The whale never takes a chance: although it is constantly in water, it always carries around its own shower.

WHEEL

The wheel enabled man to get ahead—until he got behind it.

Every adolescent hates to put his shoulder to the wheel, but loves to get his hands on it.

WHISKEY

I like whiskey, I always did, and that's why I never drink it.
— Robert E. Lee

No married man is genuinely happy if he has to drink worse whiskey than he used to drink when he was single. — Mencken

Too much of anything is bad, but too much of good whiskey is barely enough. — Mark Twain

Man ages whiskey, and whiskey ages man.

Mix whiskey and water—and you spoil two good things.

When a dog bites a man, that's that, but when a man bites a dog, that's too much whiskey.

Of all the remedies that won't cure a cold, whiskey is the most popular.

Whiskey has killed more men than bullets, but most men would rather be full of whiskey than bullets.

At a party it's not your host's English that matters, but his Scotch.

The trouble with whiskey is that you take a drink and it makes a new man out of you, and then the new man has to have a drink.

Though a fifth will go into three with none left over, there may be one to carry.

The proof of whiskey is in the drinking: some men drink all their lives and live to be 90-proof.

Whiskey is merely legal though some people seem to think it's compulsory.

Whiskey is a good treatment for a cold, but don't treat it so eagerly that you can't tell where the cold ends and the hangover begins.

Whiskey drowns some troubles, but floats a lot more.

WHISPER

What I like in a good author is not what he says but what he whispers.   *— Logan P. Smith*

Some women will believe anything you tell them—if you whisper it.

Money talks with such power that even its whisper can be heard.

WHISTLE

Sometimes a pretty girl is so shy, you have to whistle at her twice.

Opportunity knocks but once, but for a pretty girl it whistles all the time.

Whistling to keep up your courage is easy enough; the difficulty is to get up enough courage to whistle.

The ideal gift for the girl who has everything is a police whistle.

You're middle-aged if the girls you whistle at think you're calling your dog.

If some censors had their way, a man couldn't even whistle an off-color song.

WIDOW

When a woman becomes a widow, she always tells you how young she was when she married.   *— Ed Howe*

A widow is a battleship whose first captain has been shipwrecked.   *— Alphonse Karr*

A self-made man deserves credit, but not as much as a self-made widow.

So many widows look so happy, we often wonder.

Many a widow finds it easy to marry again because dead men tell no tales.

When a widow remarries and starts talking about her first husband, her second husband should start talking about his next wife.

Widows rush in where spinsters fear to tread.

If a widow is rich and pretty, she soon gets over being one.

The disadvantage of marrying a widow is that she has more to talk about.

Many a man is soon forgotten after he is dead, unless you should happen to marry his widow.

It takes a tender young widow to capture a tough old bachelor.

The widow's mite is never so fully realized as when she is looking for a second husband.

Many a dull wife will make a merry widow.

The most dangerous thing about a widow is her predilection for marrying the innocent bystander.

A widow often turns her second husband into the most sincere mourner of her first.

A gold digger is a woman whose ambition it is to become the widow of a rich man.

Rich men build fine homes, and wise men marry their widows.

A widow is fortunate: she knows all about men, and the only man who knows all about her is dead.

A young widow has a peculiar way of seeing a man without looking at him.

Widows are not the only women who have late husbands.

Many a widow is more devoted to her grief than she had ever been to her husband.

WIDOWER

When a man loses his wife, it doesn't take long before he finds himself under new management.

Many a widower remarries soon after his wife's death because he doesn't believe in holding a grudge long.

Henry VIII was probably the greatest widower the world has ever known.

The widower who marries his wife's sister, bestows the highest possible praise on his mother-in-law.

WIFE

Wives are people who feel that they don't dance enough.
— Groucho Marx

Whenever I hear a woman offering fond banter to her mate, I know she has another bed for more serious exchanges.
— Ben Hecht

To want a wife is better than to need one, especially if it happens to be only your neighbor's.
— Norman Douglas

A good wife is good, but the best wife is not so good as no wife at all.   — Thomas Hardy

How can a woman be expected to be happy with a man who treats her as if she were a perfectly natural being? — Oscar Wilde

It's always better to have your wife with you than after you.

A wife may not be the only woman a man ever loved, but she's the only woman who made him prove it.

A wife is called the better half because she usually gets the better of the other half.

A wife sometimes has eyes that see not, sometimes ears that hear not, but never a tongue that talks not.

Some wives are like fishermen: they think the best ones got away.

Wives of great men oft remind us that we ought to be satisfied with the ones we've got.

A wife is a great comfort during all the troubles which a bachelor never has.

Every married man sooner or later discovers that the wife who has given in, has not given up.

Many a half-truth is told about marriage, with the wife always the better half.

A wife is usually satisfied with only two things: a mink over her shoulders, and a husband under her thumb.

A wife is a woman who singles out a man, doubles his joys, and triples his expenses.

A man shouldn't look for too much in a wife—just someone to spend with the rest of his life.

Wife a mouse, quiet house; wife a cat, awful that.

Many a marriage runs into trouble when the better half starts believing she's the better three quarters.

There's only one kind of wife who likes to talk a lot—the married one.

A wife is a creature remarkable for her ability to live on very little compared with her craving to live on very much.

Don't speak of your private ailment in public—she might hear you.

Wives can be divided into two types: those who do the improbable, and those who expect the impossible.

There's no such thing as a wife who cannot think of a better man she could have married.

There's no one worse than the wife who leaves her husband and takes everything, except the wife who takes everything and doesn't leave.

The typical wife spends half her time ignoring her husband's virtues, and the other half deploring his faults.

It is easier to procure a wife than to cure one.

A loyal wife is one who sits up with you when you are sick, and puts up with you when you are well.

Half the married men do not half appreciate their better half.

Some wives realize they talk to themselves, while others think their husbands are listening.

An intelligent wife sees through her husband, an understanding wife sees him through.

Formerly a man got a wife who could cook like his mother; nowadays he is more likely to get one who can drink like his father.

The wife who enjoys being put on a pedestal usually objects to being put on a scale.

There are two kinds of wives: those who have wealthy husbands, and those who act as if they have.

Half the world doesn't know how his better half lives.

If you do housework for money, you're a servant; if you do it for nothing, you're a wife.

Every man should have a wife —preferably his own.

Matrimony is a partnership in which many a woman who starts out as the better half ends up as the whole works.

WIFE AND SECRETARY

The man who claims his wife doesn't understand him, usually picks a pretty secretary to tell it to.

Behind every successful man is a wife who tells him what to do, and a secretary who does it.

An executive's wife wishes she knew as much about his affairs as his private secretary does.

If wives only knew what secretaries think of their husbands, they would cease to worry.

When a man treats his secretary better than his wife, it's because he can dictate to her.

An executive always finds it hard to convince his wife that he hired his pretty secretary on account of her experience.

A confidential secretary is one the wife never finds out about.

The difference between a wife and a secretary is the difference between passive acquiescence and active co-operation.

A man's secretary seldom has reason to be jealous of his wife.

When a secretary marries the boss, she gives up being a secretary and he gives up being the boss.

Never complain to your wife that your secretary doesn't understand you.

The executive who has a secretary do his thinking for him at the office usually has a wife do his thinking for him at home.

WIG

We do not mind having our hair ruffled, but we will not tolerate any familiarity with the toupee which covers our baldness.
— Eric Hoffer

A man is as young as he feels— until he buys a toupee.

A toupee always fools people, but only those people who wear it.

About the only advantage of a wig is that it doesn't have dandruff.

There are lots of men sixty and seventy years old who haven't a single gray hair in their toupees.

If you buy an expensive wig on credit, you're in debt over your ears.

It is easier for a man to put a toupee over his bald spot than to put it over the public.

The more natural a toupee, the less you can tell it from a wig.

WILD

There are no wild animals until man makes them so. — Mark Twain

There is one thing about a crop of wild oats: it harvests itself.
— *Ed Howe*

A fly is as untamable as a hyena.   — *Emerson*

Wild life is not disappearing; it is merely affecting a merger with domestic life.

The wild younger generation of yesterday simply cannot understand the wild younger generation of today.

The wilder a man is about a woman, the easier it is for her to tame him.

It's hard to be both a good mother and a good gardener: either the flowers or the children are apt to run wild.

Formerly wild life was found only in the country; nowadays it is found commonly in the city.

Some men have wild times, others have wild imaginations.

Man's destruction of wild life has been going on for centuries in preparation for the destruction of the wildest animal of all—himself.

The best way to curb a wild young man is to bridal him.

A naturalist is the only one who knows that there is a difference between wild life and child life.

The younger generation is wilder than the previous one because the previous generation had better parents.

The naturalist who thinks our wild life is disappearing probably hasn't attended any collegiate parties recently.

WILL

The man who waits to make an entirely reasonable will, dies intestate.   — *Bernard Shaw*

The will of the people, like other wills, is often contested bitterly.

Where there's a will, there's a way—to get even.

A will is a legal statement indicating how a person wants his property divided among his errors.

Many a wife succeeds in breaking a man's will both before and after he dies.

There are only two sides to an argument, except among the surviving relatives of a rich man who has left no will.

When lawyers work with a will, there is trouble in store for the heirs.

Where there's a will, there's an inheritance tax.

The man who dies intestate leaves the world the same way he came into it—without his will.

The man who makes his own will is the best friend of the legal profession.

A will is a person's last whim and testament.

Where there's a will, there's a why.

Success depends more often on your own will than on a rich relative's.

Before a man can dispose of his property foolishly, he has to begin his will, "I, being of sound mind . . ."

Where there's a will, there are dissatisfied relatives.

A woman admires a man with a will of his own, but only if it's made out in her favor.

To make a will is the wont of every prudent man.

Only a person of sound mind can make a valid will, and only a lawyer of sound mind can break it.

Where there's a will, there's a lawsuit.

Some husbands leave incontestable wills, others have them.

A will is a legal device to get people to execute the wishes of the dead more faithfully than the wishes of the living.

Where there's a will, there's a way; where there are many wills, there's no way.

Everyone should have enough will before his death to leave a will after his death.

Where there's a will, there's a way—out for the lawyers.

WILL POWER

Will power is to the mind like a strong blind man who carries on his shoulders a lame man who can see.   — *Schopenhauer*

In government, as in marriage, in the end the more insistent will prevails.   — *Learned Hand*

Free will and determinism are like a game of cards: the hand that is dealt you is determinism; the way you play your hand is free will.   — *Norman Cousins*

Many a man has a will of iron, but it's in his wife's name.

If a man will use sufficient will power, he can become anything in life—except a child prodigy.

The man with enough will power to give up smoking and drinking seldom has enough will power to stop talking about it.

Will power is what every man has—until he tries to give up smoking.

Good fortune often comes from will power—sometimes your own, and sometimes a deceased relative's.

A weakling is a man who doesn't let his will power get the best of him.

A good test of will power is the self-control to buy in the supermarket only those items which are on your shopping list.

Will power is the ability to keep on dressing for church after the Sunday paper arrives.

The wiles of most women are stronger than the wills of most men.

Another good test of will power is to meet a friend with a black eye and not ask any questions.

All that most people lose when they go on a diet is will power.

Will power is what makes you do what you have to do when you hate to do it most.

When a man of strong will makes up his mind to tell his wife to do something, he usually does it.

The best inheritance that a parent can give a child is a will—to work.

When a woman will, she will; but when she says she will, she probably won't.

Will power is that admirable quality in ourselves which is detestable obstinacy in others.

The man who marries a wisp of a girl may soon be surprised at the will o' the wisp.

WIN

Anybody can win, unless there happens to be a second entry.
— *George Ade*

You never can tell: every now and then the best man wins.

You can always tell the golfer who's winning: he's the one who keeps telling his opponent that it's only a game.

WIN AND LOSE

If you argue with a woman and win, you lose.

It is better to lose in a cause that you know will someday win than to win in a cause that you know will someday lose.

The wrangler is always winning arguments—and losing friends.

It's unpleasant to play poker with a poor loser, but it's much better than playing with any kind of a winner.

The less you bet, the more you lose when you win.

Women who are the easiest to win are the most difficult to lose.

WIND

It's more refined to say "break wind."
— *Don Marquis*

Man produces three kinds of wind: sneezing from the head, belching from the mouth, and farting from the bowels. — *Montaigne*

Some men have the idea that they are breezy when they are merely windy.

The woman who is married to a windbag always knows how the wind blows.

Listening to some public speakers is like aiming at a target: allowance has to be made for the wind.

Another blow-hard that's hard to take is a hurricane.

Winds blow on cold days to make them colder, but keep away on hot days to make them hotter.

It's a small world, but not to the man who chases his hat on a windy day.

A windbag is a talkative man who blows more wind than he breaks.

The wind is ill-tempered to the shorn lamb.

WINDOW

Better keep yourself clean and bright—you are the window through which you see the world.
— *Bernard Shaw*

Marriage is an alliance entered into by a man who can't sleep with the window shut, and a woman who can't sleep with the window open.   — *Ogden Nash*

When you open a window yourself, you get fresh air; if someone else opens it, you get a draft.

Housewives would have a brighter outlook on life if they kept their windows clean.

Winter is the season when you can't close the window you couldn't open in the summer.

WINE

One of the disadvantages of wine is that it makes a man mistake words for thoughts.
— *Samuel Johnson*

Wedlock's like wine: it's not to be properly judged till the second glass.   — *Douglas Jerrold*

Whether a man gives up wine or women depends on the vintage.

Bacchus has drowned more than Neptune.

There is no comparison between wine and women: wine improves with age.

The more claret, the less clarity.

Any port in a storm—preferably expensive port.

Age improves all wines except the whine of man.

WINK

Men get rich by winking at laws, women by winking at men.

Girls who wink at men past forty are either dumb, or plain, or naughty.

There have been many spectacular advances in communications recently, but the quickest is still the wink.

It takes the eye only a split second to wink—the world's quickest way for a man to get into trouble.

When a girl winks it means she either has something in her eye or someone in it.

Why talk about not sleeping a wink, when people in their sleep never wink?

The light that lies in women's eyes is often a wink.

A flirt will begin an affair with a wink, often in the hope it will end with a mink.

WINTER

The most serious charge which can be brought against New England is not Puritanism but February. — *Joseph Wood Krutch*

Winter is not a season, it's an occupation. — *Sinclair Lewis*

It's just plain bad planning on nature's part, having the days shortest when there is most to do. — *Bill Vaughan*

The old-fashioned winters were not worse, but the old-fashioned heating systems were.

Winter is the time of year when most people have more off days than days off.

Another sign of success is reaching for your suitcase instead of your overcoat when the cold weather sets in.

If fashion designers continue to advance the season it won't be long before winter hats are again worn in winter.

Winter is a strange season: it freezes your hands and feet, but thaws your nose.

Why go South for the winter when you have so much more of it where you are?

Winter always seems to last too long, probably because it comes in one year and out the other.

The man who claims the old-fashioned winters were tougher probably has a son who shovels the sidewalk for him.

Winter is the season when gentlemen befur blondes.

WISDOM

Be wiser than other people if you can, but do not tell them so. — *Chesterton*

He swallowed a lot of wisdom, but all of it seems to have gone down the wrong way. — *G. C. Lichtenberg*

The only one who is wiser than anyone is everyone. — *Napoleon*

No matter how long he lives, no man ever becomes as wise as the average woman of forty-eight. — *Mencken*

To my extreme mortification, I grow wiser every day. — *Lord Byron*

A wise woman puts a grain of sugar into everything she says to a man, and takes a grain of salt with everything he says to her. — *Helen Rowland*

We can be knowledgeable with other men's knowledge, but we cannot be wise with other men's wisdom. — *Montaigne*

The art of being wise is the art of knowing what to overlook. — *William James*

It's surprising how much wisdom every man possesses—if not for his own affairs, then for the affairs of others.

Wisdom lies in knowing how ignorant we are, and keeping the knowledge to ourselves.

A word to the wise is—unnecessary.

You can only become wise by noticing what happens to you when you aren't.

The man who sacrifices his health in the search for wisdom would be wiser if he didn't.

Many a wise word is spoken in ignorance.

The smart man can always catch on, the wise man knows when to let go.

The way to be wise is not to be otherwise.

What this country needs is less wise guys and more wise men.

Without wisdom, knowledge is more stupid than ignorance.

If you want to live wisely, ignore wise sayings—including this one.

Wise men change their minds when they grow wiser.

An intelligent man believes only half of what he hears, a wise man knows which half.

He's a wise man who knows what not to say—provided he doesn't say it.

The disadvantage of becoming wise is that you realize how foolish you've been.

A word to the wise is sufficient, but they seldom escape that easily.

The man who stays unmarried is a great deal wiser than he will ever know—unless he gets married.

WISE AND FOOLISH

A fool often fails because he thinks what is difficult is easy; a wise man, because he thinks what is easy is difficult.
— *John Churton Collins*

Wise people are foolish if they cannot adapt themselves to foolish people. — *Montaigne*

It takes a wise man to handle a lie, a fool had better remain honest. — *Norman Douglas*

A wise man who stands firm is a statesman, a foolish man who stands firm is a catastrophe.
— *Adlai Stevenson*

The cleverest woman on earth is the biggest fool on earth with a man. — *Dorothy Parker*

The man who lives without being foolish on occasion is not as wise as he thinks.
— *La Rochefoucauld*

If forty million people say a foolish thing it does not become a wise one, but the wise man is foolish to give them the lie.
— *Somerset Maugham*

Matrimony and bachelorhood are both equally wise and equally foolish. — *Samuel Butler*

The mistakes of the fool are known to the world but not to himself; the mistakes of the wise man are known to himself but not to the world. — *C. C. Colton*

It is better to speak wisdom foolishly like the saints than to speak folly wisely like the dons. — *Chesterton*

He dares to be a fool, and that is the first step in the direction of wisdom. — *James G. Huneker*

A wise man learns more from his enemies than a fool from his friends. — *Baltasar Gracián*

Age doesn't bring wisdom, it merely makes you less foolish.

Travel makes a wise man wiser, and a fool more foolish—and so does everything else.

A man will often do something wise simply because he hasn't the money to make a fool of himself.

The wise man says it can't be done, but the fool goes and does it.

You can learn more from a wise man when he is wrong than from a fool when he is right.

Fools rush in where wise men want them to tread.

For every wise man who gives advice to a fool, there are a hundred fools who give advice to wise men.

When a wise man tries to teach a fool, he comes nearest to being one.

The fool is never so stingy with his folly as the wise man is with his wisdom.

Any fool can make a woman talk, but only a wise man can make her listen.

WISH

Our necessities are few but our wants are endless. — *Bernard Shaw*

A woman never knows what she really wants until she finds out what her husband can't afford.

If you don't get everything you want, think of the things you don't get that you don't want.

Man wants but little here below —but you'd never guess it.

When a woman has something she wants to talk to her husband about, it's about something she wants.

If a man could have half his wishes, he would double his troubles.

There's nothing that cures people from wanting things like being able to afford them.

You can get almost anything you want if you'll just wait until you don't want it.

Before marriage, she wants a man; after marriage, she wants a maid.

If you want money, go to strangers; if you want advice, go to friends; if you want nothing, go to relatives.

Many a woman doesn't know what she wants, and won't give her husband any peace until she gets it.

Man wants but little here below —usually a little of everything.

Many of us spend half our time wishing for things we could have if we didn't spend half our time wishing.

The modern teen-ager has been tried and found wanting—everything under the sun.

A clever woman knows how to get what she wants by pretending she doesn't want it.

Any man who doesn't want what he hasn't got, has all he wants.

Man is a strange animal: when he gets what he wanted he wonders why he wanted it.

Man wants but little here below, and he usually gets it.

Most of us keep wishing for things we don't have, but what else is there to wish for?

A woman never knows what she wants until she knows she can't get it.

Success is getting what you want; happiness is wanting what you get.

A man with ten children is better off than a man with ten million dollars because the man with ten children doesn't want any more.

Man wants all he can get; woman wants all she can't get.

WIT

It's not enough to be witty; you must also have enough wit to avoid having too much.
— *André Maurois*

A wise man will live as much within his wit as within his income. — *Chesterfield*

There's no possibility of being witty without a little ill-nature; the malice of a good thing is the barb that makes it stick.
— *Richard Brinsley Sheridan*

Next to being witty yourself, the best thing is being able to quote another's wit. — *Bovee*

There are no fools so exasperating as those who have wit.
— *La Rochefoucauld*

Those who cannot miss an opportunity of saying a good thing are not to be trusted with the management of any great question.
— *Hazlitt*

Wit ought to be a glorious treat, like caviar; never spread it about like marmalade. — *Noel Coward*

Wit lies in the likeness of things that are different, and in the difference of things that are alike. — *Madame de Staël*

A wit should be no more sincere than a woman constant.
— *William Congreve*

Brevity is the soul of wit, and laughter is the goal of it.

One man's wit is another man's poison.

The fool who thinks himself a wit is probably half right.

Children often say bright things, but only their parents think they are bright enough to be repeated.

Brevity is the soul of wit, and wit is the brevity of levity.

Many people live by their wits but few by their wit.

If you try to analyze what makes people laugh, you'll soon discover that there's more to wit than you realize.

WIT AND HUMOR

The humorous story is American, the comic story is English, the witty story is French.
                    —Mark Twain

The man who sees the consistency in things is a wit; the man who sees the inconsistency in things is a humorist. *—Chesterton*

Brevity is the soul of wit, and levity is the soul of humor.

Only his wife knows that a good wit is not always in good humor.

WITNESS

A witness in court always has to swear to tell the truth before he starts to lie.

You never know how much a man can't remember until he is called as a court witness.

Some witnesses in court tell half-truths while others tell whole lies.

There are two types of witnesses in court: one remembers everything, and the other remembers nothing.

Eye-witnesses at a trial never seem to see eye to eye with other eye-witnesses.

You can be sure that witnesses in court are lying when they tell different stories; also when they tell exactly the same story.

Witnesses will testify to anything, even the truth.

Half the people on the witness stand suddenly have a lapse of memory, while the other half suddenly remember things that never happened.

Many a witness makes a jury wonder what lies ahead.

It takes two to make a bargain, but it helps if there's a third to witness it.

WOMAN

After thirty years of research into the feminine soul, the great question which I haven't been able to answer is: What does a woman want?   *—Freud*

A bad woman raises hell with a good many men, while a good woman raises hell with only one.
                    —Ed Howe

Next to the wound, what women are best at making is the bandage.   — *Barbey d'Aurevilly*

The proper function of women is to make reasons for husbands to stay at home, and still stronger reasons for bachelors to go out.
    — *George Eliot*

As soon as women belong to us, we no longer belong to them.
    — *Montaigne*

Being a woman is a terribly difficult task since it consists principally in dealing with men.
    — *Joseph Conrad*

It's the nature of women not to love when we love them, and to love when we love them not.
    — *Cervantes*

There are three things a woman can make out of almost anything —a salad, a hat and a quarrel.
    — *John Barrymore*

Fifty percent of the world are women, yet they always seem a novelty.   — *Christopher Morley*

To be a woman is something so strange, so confusing and so complicated that only a woman could put up with it.
    — *Kierkegaard*

He gets on best with women who knows how to get on without them.   — *Bierce*

The strongest propensity in woman's nature is to want to know what's going on, the next strongest is to boss the job.
    — *Josh Billings*

Next to the dinosaur, woman is nature's most outstanding failure.
    — *I. A. R. Wylie*

I know what women expect, and give it to them without disagreeable argument—they'll get it anyway.   — *Ed Howe*

When I say I know women, I mean I know that I don't know them.   — *Thackeray*

A good woman inspires a man, a brilliant woman interests him, a beautiful woman fascinates him, but a sympathetic woman gets him.   — *Helen Rowland*

A woman never loafs; she shops, entertains, and visits.
    — *Ed Howe*

Women have simple tastes: they can get pleasure out of the conversation, of children in arms and men in love.   — *Mencken*

A woman has a dozen different ways to make a man happy, and a hundred ways to make him unhappy.   — *James G. Huneker*

Women are the sex which believes that if you charge it, it's not spending; and if you add a cherry to it, it's not intoxicating.
    — *Bill Vaughan*

In France, women are a passion, in England a pleasure, in America a pursuit.

Woman is the tender and the spender gender that longs to be the slender gender.

Half the world doesn't know how the other lives, but that isn't the half that's made up of women.

Woman is a paradox who pleases when she puzzles, and puzzles when she pleases.

It's a good thing that men don't understand women: women understand women, and they don't like them.

Women are attractive at 20, attentive at 30, and adhesive at 40.

There are two kinds of women: those who wish to marry, and those who haven't the slightest desire not to.

There's really nothing on earth like a woman—except another woman.

Women are unreasonable creatures who wear hats that are unattractive, dresses that are unbecoming, and shoes that are uncomfortable.

It takes a magician to saw a woman in half, but it takes a husband to make her go to pieces.

Women are divided into two classes: those who don't believe everything their husbands tell them, and those who haven't any husbands.

Some people have no trouble separating the men from the boys —these people are called women.

Woman is a being—therefore let her be.

Woman is the only creature that can be found with wool over its body, fur on its shoulders, leather on its feet, and feathers on its head.

There's only one thing that keeps men from understanding women, and that's women.

A woman will probably never be the President of the United States, but she never has any trouble being speaker of the house.

Another thing stranger than fiction is woman.

Woman was first created from man's side, but has never been on his side since.

There are two things a woman wants to be: the gleam in a man's eye, and the green in a woman's.

Woman is a creature that urinates once an hour, defecates once a day, menstruates once a month, procreates once a year, and copulates whenever she can.

There has never been a man yet who could tell what a woman was thinking by listening to what she was saying.

Woman is a strange creature: her legs are longer than her stockings, and her feet are bigger than her shoes.

The feminine mind has many phases, and the man who tries to understand them is sure to be fazed.

Another reason why women aren't what they used to be—they used to be girls.

The best combination for a woman is an old head, a young heart, and a baby face.

Women love men not because they are men, but because they are not women.

The man who admits he doesn't understand women must have had considerable experience with them.

Women are like thoroughbred horses: you have to speak kindly to them before you bridle them.

The last thing God made is the first thing man looks at—a pretty woman.

Women are divided into two classes: those who want husbands, and those who desire single men.

Up to 20, a woman needs good parents; from 20 to 40, good looks; from 40 to 60, good humor; and from 60 up, good stocks and lots of them.

God made woman beautiful and foolish: beautiful, that man might love her; and foolish, that she might love him.

No man living knows more about women than he does—and he knows nothing.

WOMAN DRIVER

Time, tide and women drivers wait for no man.

If a woman driver ahead of you signals a left turn, be careful—she may turn left.

Lightning and a woman driver never strike twice in the same place.

Many a woman who can get an eight-inch foot into a six-inch shoe cannot get a six-foot car into an eight-foot garage.

The woman who changes her mind while making a U turn, makes an O turn.

Giving a woman driver the right of way may be chivalry, but it is more often prudence.

Nothing confuses a man more than to drive behind a woman who does everything right.

You can't trust women: how often have you criticized a woman driver, only to find her a minute later turn into a man!

The woman who doesn't drive a car doesn't know what she's missing.

Not only do women drive as well as men, but they can also drive in both directions on a one-way street.

Which is the lesser of two evils: the woman driver, or the woman reading the road map?

There are two kinds of women drivers: those who run into trouble, and those who back into it.

A good woman driver is one who can miss anything that will get out of her way.

Give some women drivers an inch, and they'll take a fender.

The only time some women drivers give you more than half the road is when they're walking.

Hell hath no fury like a woman driver.

In teaching your wife to drive, the first thing she should learn is that a car must be steered—not aimed.

Among women drivers, one bad turn deserves another.

A woman driver is a person who drives the same way a man does, only she gets blamed for it.

WOMAN-HATER

No man is as anti-feminist as a really feminine woman.
— *Frank O'Connor*

Misogynist: a man who hates women as much as women hate one another. — *Mencken*

A woman-hater is a man who believes that marriage is a woman's way of getting revenge.

A woman-hater is seldom a bachelor.

The misogynist who thinks very little of women thinks more about them than anyone else.

A woman-hater is the only man above and beyond the call of beauty.

A misogynist hates only two kinds of women: those who are married, and those who aren't.

A misogynist is a woman-hater who gloats that the world is run by men, but gripes that it is over-run with women.

Another class of women-haters seems to be the men who design women's clothes.

A man sometimes becomes a woman-hater because he couldn't get a woman to marry him, but more often because he did.

Every woman-hater is under the delusion that there is something wrong with women but nothing wrong with him.

WONDER

The world will never starve for want of wonders, but for want of wonder. — *Chesterton*

Niagara Falls are wonderful, but the wonder would be greater if the water did not fall.
— *Oscar Wilde*

The eighth wonder of the world is wondering what will happen next.

WOOD

Wood is a remarkable material which burns so easily in a forest and with such difficulty in the fire-place. — *Bill Vaughan*

The unfailing mark of the blockhead is the chip on the shoulder.

Chop your own wood and it will warm you twice.

WOOL

The man who has the wool pulled over his eyes is generally fleeced.

If you are trying to pull the wool over your wife's eyes, you had better use a good yarn.

It makes all the difference whether the shepherd loves the fleece or the flock.

WORDS

I am paid by the word, so I always write the shortest words possible. — *Bertrand Russell*

He has a genius for compressing a minimum of ideas into a maximum of words. — *Winston Churchill*

Nine times out of ten it is the coarse word that condemns an evil, and the refined word that excuses it. — *Chesterton*

Words should be only the clothes, carefully custom-made to fit the thought. — *Jules Renard*

Words are like money: there is nothing so useless, except when put to use. — *Samuel Johnson*

The two most beautiful words in the English language are: "Check enclosed." — *Dorothy Parker*

All paraphrases and expletives are so much in disuse that soon the only way of making love will be to say, "Lie down." — *Horace Walpole*

Among all the famous last words none is better known than "I never felt better in my life." — *Joseph Wood Krutch*

Words are the coins making up the currency of sentences, and there are always too many small coins. — *Jules Renard*

I am not yet so lost in lexicography as to forget that words are the daughters of earth, while deeds are the sons of heaven. — *Samuel Johnson*

What a vast amount of paper would be saved if there were a law forcing writers to use only the right words! — *Jules Renard*

Why do social workers use five-syllable words when dealing with juvenile delinquents?

A woman's last word is usually semifinal.

When a man claims he always keeps his word, it's probably because nobody will take it.

Many a beautiful girl ruins her charm by the use of four-letter words—like *don't* and *stop*.

The man of few words is probably married to the woman of a few million.

People who usually have the last word are seldom the ones who have the first thought.

A picture is worth a thousand words, especially if they are your wife's words.

Procrastination is the thief of time, and so is every other big word.

How can you take a woman's word when you never know which is her last word?

When one word leads to another, it generally ends up in a quarrel, a speech, or a dictionary.

The man of few words generally keeps them mighty busy.

The noblest words in English are the four-letter words, like love, hope and pity.

A woman's last word never is.

The man of few words doesn't have to take so many of them back.

With some people emphasis is not putting more stress on one word than another, but more distress.

All wives have the last word: some have it in arguments, others have it in clothes.

To understand others and be understood by all, know the big words but use the small.

No man objects to a woman having the last word if she doesn't also have all the words which precede it.

A word to the wise: *speak;* two words to the unwise: *shut up.*

When a man says his word is as good as his bond, get the bond.

The last word is often a word that lasts.

Sometimes a husband has to resort to sharp words as the only kind he can get in edgewise.

A woman's last word always differs from the one that follows.

The man of few words probably got that way after saying "I do."

WORK

Life is just a dirty four-letter word: w-o-r-k.   — *J. P. McEvoy*

Nothing is really work unless you would rather be doing something else.   — *James M. Barrie*

I do not like work even when someone else does it.
                    — *Mark Twain*

When a man tells you that he got rich through hard work, ask him *whose?*   — *Don Marquis*

If you don't want to work, you have to work to earn enough money so that you won't have to work.   — *Ogden Nash*

Labor disgraces no man, but occasionally men disgrace labor.
                — *Ulysses S. Grant*

Anyone can do any amount of work, provided it isn't the work he is supposed to be doing at that moment.   — *Robert Benchley*

Like every man of sense and good feeling, I abominate work.
                — *Aldous Huxley*

No man is obliged to do as much as he can do; a man is to have part of his life to himself.
                — *Samuel Johnson*

A woman's work is never done, especially the part she asks her husband to do.

The people who claim that brain work is harder than physical labor are generally brain workers.

Many a man works himself to death by burying himself in his work.

Many thousands of people are already working a four-day week, but the trouble is that it takes them five days to do it.

Men who lead double lives never do the work of two.

Keep your eye on the ball, your ear to the ground, and your shoulder to the wheel—now in that position try working.

Hard work never hurt anyone who hired someone else to do it.

Some men are so eager for success that they are even willing to work for it.

Doctors think people ought to do some work after retirement, while employers think some people ought to do work before.

A workhorse is a man who spends too much time minding his own business.

The man who puts his hand to the grindstone doesn't have to keep his nose there.

Work is good for you—it's labor that kills.

In the good old days when a man finished his day's work, he needed rest; nowadays he needs exercise.

It isn't the hours you put in your work that count, it's the work you put in the hours.

Some men know only one way of killing time, and that is by working it to death.

Formerly when a man worked ten hours a day, it was called economic slavery; nowadays it is called moonlighting.

There's nothing like hard work —thank God there isn't!

There's only one thing worse than to live without working, and that is to work without living.

The only time some people work like a horse is when the boss rides them.

What will happen to work when the trend toward longer education meets the trend toward earlier retirement?

The working day should be further reduced, if only to enable men to finish the work they bring home from the office.

Some girls are working girls, and some are working men.

Hard work never hurt anybody who spent his time telling how hard work never hurt anybody.

Always keep your mind on your work by day, but not your work on your mind by night.

More people become crooked from trying to avoid hard work than become bent from too much of it.

Many men are hard workers: they're always looking around to find something for others to do.

A workhorse is a man who works himself to death in order to live better.

WORK AND PLAY

All work and no play makes Jack a dull boy—and Jill a wealthy widow.

They are two common mistakes in life: to play at work and to work at play.

All work and no play makes Jack a dull boy—to everyone but his employer.

WORLD

The world is like a mirror: frown at it and it frowns at you; smile, and it smiles too.
— *Herbert Samuel*

Intelligent people make many mistakes because they cannot believe that the world is really as foolish as it is.   — *Chamfort*

God should not be judged on the basis of this world—it is just one of his rough sketches.
— *Van Gogh*

The world is not growing worse and it is not growing better—it is just turning around as usual.
— *Finley Peter Dunne*

The world is a play that would not be worth the seeing if we knew the plot.
— *Frank Moore Colby*

It's a man's world, and you men can have it.
— *Katherine Anne Porter*

We are told that when Jehovah created the world he saw that it was good—what would he say now?   — *Bernard Shaw*

The universe is like a safe to which there is a combination, but the combination is locked up in the safe.   — *Peter De Vries*

The world is a spiritual kindergarten where bewildered infants are trying to spell God with the wrong blocks.
— *Edwin Arlington Robinson*

The world is getting to be such a dangerous place, a man is lucky to get out of it alive.
— *W. C. Fields*

The telescope makes the world smaller; it is only the microscope that makes it larger. — *Chesterton*

The most incomprehensible thing about the world is that it is comprehensible.   — *Einstein*

If there was nothing wrong in the world there wouldn't be anything for us to do.
— *Bernard Shaw*

Your sense of humor makes the world a comedy; your sense of honor, a tragedy.

The world is a jigsaw puzzle with a peace missing.

What if the world is destroyed by atom bombs; after all, we got on very well without it before we were born.

This is the best of all possible worlds—and everything in it is a necessary evil.

It takes all kinds to make the world, and the world certainly looks it.

Maybe the trouble with the world is that it took God six days to create it while we are trying to run it on a five-day week.

The more you see of this world, the less you worry about the next.

With the passing of time the world grows better and better—one by one our enemies die.

Love makes the world go round, and divorce makes it wobble.

The world seems little to the man whose wife is a nag, but it seems still less to him when his wife is a widow.

It may be a man's world, but most of it is in his wife's name.

No scientist knows where the center of the universe is, but every man in love does.

Every day the world turns over on someone who has just been sitting on top of it.

Young lady, he may be all the world to you, but you'd better see more of the world first.

If all the world's a stage, it's putting on a mighty poor show.

This world is mostly concerned with right and left; the next world, with above and below.

Take the world as it is, not as it ought to be.

The world is a paradox: too many people have too much of everything, and too many people have too little of anything.

Formerly people used to wonder where the world was going; now they just wonder when.

The world which took only six days to make, will probably take six thousand years to make out.

It takes all kinds of people to unmake the world.

The way the world is going, the future of humanity is not on the knees of the gods, but across them.

WORM

What good does it do the worm to turn—he's the same on all sides.

All the animals came on the Ark in pairs, except the worms—they came in apples.

A wise worm turns in before the early bird turns out.

Some husbands are book worms, others are just ordinary worms.

If a man lets a woman make a worm out of him, he deserves to squirm.

Many a poor worm doesn't know which way to turn.

The early bird catches the worm, so the wise worm gets up late.

Finding a worm in your apple is not so bad as finding only half a worm.

It takes some worms a mighty long time to turn.

WORRY

One of the commonest mistakes is thinking your worries are over when your children get married.
— *Kin Hubbard*

There are two days in the week on which I never worry: one is yesterday and the other is tomorrow. — *Robert Jones Burdette*

Set aside half an hour every day to do all your worrying—then take a nap during this period.

Worry all you want to; it's the one thing that hasn't gone up in price.

If you can't help worrying, remember that worrying can't help you either.

Many people worry a lot today about tomorrow because they didn't worry a little yesterday about today.

The man who worries constantly will soon look old enough to be his father.

Stop worrying about getting older because when you stop getting older, you're dead.

If you must worry, always do your worrying in advance; otherwise you'll miss most of the chances.

No matter how many worries a pessimist has, he always has room for one more.

Worry is a sign of sanity: the mentally unbalanced never worry.

A psychiatrist has nothing to worry about as long as others have something to worry about.

Worry is the interest paid by those who borrow trouble.

Blessed is the man who is too busy to worry by day, and too sleepy to worry at night.

It is just as useless to worry as it is to tell others not to.

Worry is like a rocking chair: it gives you something to do, but it doesn't get you anywhere.

Worrying does a person good: the things he worries about usually don't happen.

Some people worry about three kinds of trouble: all they ever had, all they have now, and all they expect to have.

A lot of people worry about nothing—especially when it's in the bank.

America is a land where many worry about their income tax, and even more worry about their income.

There's no need of worrying if you can help it; and if you cannot, there's no use in worrying.

WRECK

Every life is a wreck among whose ruins we have to discover what the person should have been.
— *José Ortega y Gasset*

After witnessing an auto wreck you always drive carefully—for several minutes.

A ship may be wrecked at sea, but it's the shore that wrecks a sailor.

When bigger and faster cars are made, bigger and faster fools will wreck them.

Sooner or later every reckless young blood becomes a bloodless old wreck.

An automobile wreck is a bad thing, but it does give some drivers a chance to look at the scenery.

The car is chiefly responsible for changing recreation into wreck-creation.

WRESTLE

Women are a problem, but they are the kind of problem men like to wrestle with.

Nowadays you never meet anyone who becomes exhausted from wrestling with his conscience.

WRINKLE

Nothing good lasts: every dimple winds up as a wrinkle.

As soon as time starts putting wrinkles on the brows of men, it also starts putting more brow on them.

Nowadays everything seems to be wrinkle-resistant, except people.

Father Time is a great artist but women don't care for the lines he draws.

Your dimples you get from your parents; your wrinkles, from your children.

A hypochondriac is always looking in the mirror and reading between the lines.

WRITING

He is a writer for the ages—the ages of four to eight.
— *Dorothy Parker*

The tools I need for my trade are paper, tobacco, food, and a little whiskey. — *Faulkner*

Nature, not content with denying him the ability to think, has endowed him with the ability to write. — *A. E. Housman*

How vain it is to sit down to write when you have not stood up to live! — *Thoreau*

A good writer is not *per se* a good book critic, no more so than a good drunk is automatically a good bartender. — *Jim Bishop*

To write simply is as difficult as to be good. — *Somerset Maugham*

The physical business of writing is unpleasant to me, but the psychic satisfaction of discharging bad ideas in worse English makes me forget it. — *Mencken*

I write fast because I have not the brains to write slow.
— *Georges Simenon*

Writing is the hardest way of earning a living, with the possible exception of wrestling alligators.
— *Olin Miller*

Writing is an act of faith, not a trick of grammar. — *E. B. White*

I have tried simply to write the best I can; sometimes I have good luck and write better than I can.
— *Hemingway*

I write in order to attain that feeling of tension relieved and function achieved which a cow enjoys on giving milk. — *Mencken*

People do not deserve good writing, they are so pleased with bad.
— *Emerson*

The secret of good writing is to say an old thing in a new way or to say a new thing in an old way.
— *Richard Harding Davis*

I always start writing with a clean piece of paper and a dirty mind. — *Patrick Dennis*

If you are in difficulties with a book, try the element of surprise: attack it at an hour when it isn't expecting it. — *H. G. Wells*

The profession of book-writing makes horseracing seem like a solid, stable business.
— *John Steinbeck*

Writing is a wholetime job: no professional writer can afford only to write when he feels like it.
— *Somerset Maugham*

An essayist is a lucky person who has found a way to discourse without being interrupted.
— *Charles Poore*

I shall live bad if I do not write, and I shall write bad if I do not live. — *Françoise Sagan*

The purpose of writing is to hold a mirror to nature, but too much today is written from small mirrors in vanity cases.
— *John Mason Brown*

Write without pay until somebody offers pay; if nobody offers within three years, sawing wood is what you were intended for.
— *Mark Twain*

The writings by which one can live are not the writings which themselves live. — *John Stuart Mill*

Word-carpentry is like any other kind of carpentry: you must join your sentences smoothly.
— *Anatole France*

Whenever I apply myself to writing, literature comes between us. — *Jules Renard*

If I had to give young writers advice, I'd say don't listen to writers talking about writing or themselves. — *Lillian Hellman*

I never think when I write; nobody can do two things at the same time and do them well.
— *Don Marquis*

Read over your compositions and, when you meet with a passage which you think is particularly fine, strike it out.
— *Samuel Johnson*

The most essential gift for a good writer is a built-in, shock-proof shit detector. — *Hemingway*

It's not wise to violate rules until you know how to observe them.   — *T. S. Eliot*

Writing isn't hard—no harder than ditch-digging.
— *Patrick Dennis*

If a young writer can refrain from writing, he shouldn't hesitate to do so.   — *Gide*

How can anyone do better than that—after all, I wrote it myself.
— *Molière*

The man who lives by his writings eats his own words—indirectly.

Some men write for publication, others just write for circulation among editors.

Two wrongs don't make a writer.

WRONG

We ought never to do wrong when people are looking.
— *Mark Twain*

A man should never be ashamed to own he has been in the wrong, which is but saying that he is wiser today than he was yesterday.   — *Swift*

If you have always done it that way, it is probably wrong.
— *Charles F. Kettering*

There are people who say I have never really done anything wrong in my life; of course, they only say it behind my back.
— *Oscar Wilde*

The man who says "I may be wrong but—" does not believe there can be any such possibility.
— *Kin Hubbard*

When some husbands are wrong, they make up for it by being the last to admit it.

Some people would rather be wrong than quiet for a minute.

Brevity is a virtue: the man of few words can tell you in one sentence what's wrong with the world.

The best measure of your ability is the length of time it takes you to find out when you're wrong.

A woman's place is in the wrong.

A brat doesn't know right from wrong, yet always manages to do the wrong thing.

A psychoanalyst can always find something wrong with you if there is nothing wrong with you.

Some husbands can do no wrong —they wouldn't dare.

There are only two things wrong with the world—men and women.

In a domestic quarrel two people say the wrong things after one of them does the wrong thing.

When things go wrong, don't go with them.

The way reformers distinguish between right and wrong is, if you enjoy doing a thing, it's wrong.

Many a man who doesn't want to get married changes his mind when the wrong woman comes along.

A telephone number is never wrong: it's the wrong person who gets it.

The man who is busy telling what's wrong with the world never seems to have any time to try to improve it.

YAWN

Love is a fever that ends with a yawn.   — *Edgar Saltus*

Imitation is the sincerest form of flattery, except when you yawn.

A yawn is nature's method of giving the person listening to a bore an opportunity to open his mouth.

A polite person never yawns, and never notices when another does.

No man likes to see a girl yawn, but it's much less dangerous than her sigh.

Yawning is opening your mouth when you should be shutting your eyes.

One yawn usually makes two yawners, but one bore makes many more.

You would yawn too if you saw as many tourists as the Grand Canyon sees.

A yawn may be bad manners but it's an honest opinion.

Yawning is a trick devised by nature to open a person's mouth as a hint to others to shut theirs.

YEAR

This is the next year you expected so much from last year.
                    — *Ed Howe*

The years teach much which the days never know.   — *Emerson*

A woman's years are always fewer than her age because the first few years of her life she is too young to count.

The best ten years of a woman's life are between the ages of 29 and 30.

A year consists of 365 days no matter how many days you take off.

The years that a woman subtracts from her age are not lost: they are added to the ages of her friends.

The ten best years of a man's life are the ten just before he stumbles and Mrs.

No matter how well a woman carries her years, she's bound to drop a few sooner or later.

When you are 50 years old, you will have slept through 17 of them and spent 6 in eating.

The best years of a man's life usually come after the best years of his life have been wasted.

YES

A word to the wife is sufficient, but only if the word is *yes*.

It's a bad habit for a girl to keep repeating herself, especially if she always says *yes*.

Talk is cheap, but one word sometimes, like a woman's *yes*, can cost you thousands.

Another popular creature is the girl who is famous for her beautiful ayes.

YES AND NO

Yes and *no* are the oldest and simplest words, but they require the most thought. *— Pythagoras*

I like the sayers of *no* better than the sayers of *yes*. *— Emerson*

When dealing with politicians, remember that a politician's *yes* means no more than a woman's *no*.

At home a teenager rarely says *yes*; away from home she rarely says *no*.

Always say *no*, and you'll never be married; always say *yes*, and you'll never be divorced.

In show business some girls get nowhere while others get yes-where.

Never answer a question with a *yes* or *no*, except a proposal of marriage.

With a man two negatives make an affirmative, but with a woman, one does.

Nowadays the difference between a popular girl and an unpopular one is *yes* and *no*.

When a lady says *no*, she means *maybe;* when she says *maybe*, she means *yes;* when she says *yes*, she is no lady.

When a diplomat says *yes*, he means *maybe;* when he says *maybe*, he means *no;* when he says *no*, he is no diplomat.

YESMAN

I was once in no man's land during the war, but now that I'm in Hollywood I'm worse off—I'm in yesman's land. *— Irvin S. Cobb*

Don't be a yesman; when the boss says *no*, you say *no* too.

A yesman is a somebody who remains a nobody because he tries to please everybody.

A yesman and a no-woman seldom mean it.

By trimming himself to suit everybody, the yesman soon whittles himself away.

A yesman thinks he is giving service when he is merely giving servility.

The yesman is unpopular, but not the yes-girl.

YESTERDAY

Avoid hurry: always do it yesterday.

The trouble with fishing is that you seldom get there yesterday when the fish were biting.

YESTERDAY AND TODAY

The politician's promises of yesterday are the taxes of today.
— *Mackenzie King*

Now that it's behind you, what did you do yesterday that you're proud of today?

What we didn't do yesterday causes most of the trouble today.

YESTERDAY, TODAY AND TOMORROW

I am not afraid of tomorrow for I have seen yesterday and I love today. — *William Allen White*

Yesterday is a cancelled check; tomorrow is a promissory note; today is the only cash you have— so spend it wisely.

Time is a patient observer waiting for tomorrow to turn today into yesterday.

With some people there's no relation between what they thought yesterday, what they say today, and what they do tomorrow.

Eat, drink and be merry for today is the tomorrow you worried about yesterday.

Yesterday is experience, tomorrow is hope, and today is getting from one to the other as best we can.

YOUNG

Ask the young: they know everything.
— *Joubert*

Youth is about the only thing worth having, and that is about the only thing youth has.
— *Ed Howe*

No man knows he is young while he is young.   — *Chesterton*

Youth is that period when a young boy knows everything but how to make a living.
— *Carey Williams*

During childhood, they never hang up their clothes; during adolescence, they never hang up the telephone.

You are only young once, but you can stay immature indefinitely.

Why do they call it the coming generation when it spends most of its time going?

Women are not as young as they look—they can't all be under thirty.

You'll always stay young if you eat properly, sleep sufficiently, exercise daily—and lie about your age.

Youth is born to be disillusioned and, when the process is over, youth is also over.

Life to the younger generation today is just meet and drink.

The best way for a girl to keep her youth is not to introduce him to other girls.

You are only young once—after that you merely think you are.

Youth would be more interesting if it came later in life.

Stop worrying about the younger generation: they too will grow up, get married, and start worrying about the younger generation.

Youth is glorious but it isn't a career.

A woman is young when she doesn't look a day older than she says she is.

Youth is the wonderful time of life which only the young are strong enough to endure.

Another trouble with the youth of today is that they prefer a poor excuse for getting married to a good reason for staying single.

Alarmists always regard the rising generation as a falling one.

It's all right to think you're as young as you used to be as long as you don't try to prove it.

YOUNG AND OLD

The young have aspirations that never come to pass; the old have reminiscences of what never happened.
— *Saki*

We are happier in many ways when we are old than when we are young: the young sow wild oats, the old grow sage.
— *Winston Churchill*

The young man who has not wept is a savage, and the old man who will not laugh is a fool.
— *Santayana*

In youth we run into difficulties, in old age difficulties run into us.
— *Josh Billings*

The denunciation of the young is a necessary part of the hygiene of older people, and greatly assists the circulation of their blood.
— *Logan P. Smith*

At sixteen, you think you will live forever; at sixty, you wonder how you've lasted so long.

Youth is the happiest time of all, but only age knows it.

An old man who marries a young girl is buying a book for someone else to read.

There's only one thing worse than the old who think nothing matters but the past, and that's the young who think nothing matters but the present.

The older your generation gets, the wilder the younger generation becomes.

In youth, every temptation is an opportunity; in age, every opportunity is a temptation.

A man is as young as he feels, a woman is as old as she looks.

The younger generation knows best until it becomes the older generation, and then it knows better.

A man is never too old to learn, but he is sometimes too young.

No matter how old you are, you're younger than you'll ever be.

When a man's young, he doesn't think much about women; and when he's older, he doesn't know what to think.

Nowadays the rising generation retires when the retiring generation rises.

When your friends begin to flatter you on how young you look, it's a sure sign that you're growing old.

In youth we pursue physical culture; in age, fiscal fitness.

The older the woman, the more experience she has had in staying young.

The trouble is that the young don't know what to do, and the old can't do what they know.

A man is as old as his arteries, a woman is as young as her art.

In youth, everything matters too much; in old age, nothing matters much.

The present generation blames everything on the older generation, and expects it to be corrected by the younger generation.

Some people grow old gracefully, while others keep disgracefully young.

ZEAL

If at first you don't succeed with a girl, try a little ardor.

When you put a little ready money aside, you find it's not only ready, it's downright eager.

Some people get carried away by the sound of their own voice, but not far enough.

Beware the reformer who can't conceal his vehement zeal for the commonweal.

ZERO

Don't swell yourself with vanity; remember that the zero is the fattest of all numerals.

No man is a hero to his valet, but many a man is a zero to his secretary.

The nearest thing to nothing that anything can be and still be something is zero.

Cynicism is the practice of reducing every hero to zero.

ZIPPER

Girls who wear zippers shouldn't live alone.   —*John Van Druten*

Home cooking would be speeded up fifty years by the use of zippers on canned goods. —*Russel Crouse*

Zippers get stuck on women more often than men do.

Zippers are more popular in automated offices than elsewhere—if you wear a button, someone's liable to push it.

Of all the things that tax a man's patience, there's nothing to compare with a stuck zipper.

There's no such thing as an ideal husband, but the nearest thing to one is the husband who can fix a zipper.

A woman needs both luck and pluck when she's alone and her zipper gets stuck.

Nothing has done so much to bring husbands and wives together as the dress that zips up the back.

ZOO

A zoo is a place devised for animals to study the habits of human beings. — *Oliver Herford*

Evolution has developed man to such a high degree that he builds zoos to keep his ancestors in cages.

The quizzical expression of the monkey at the zoo comes from his wondering whether he is his brother's keeper or his keeper's brother.

If prizes were given at the zoo, the giraffe would probably win by a neck, or the anteater by a nose.

The little girl who goes to the zoo to look at the animals will grow into the woman who goes to the shops to look at their skins.

Look at a chimpanzee or monkey in the zoo long enough and it will remind you of someone you know.

If animals kept zoos, would they keep the men and women in separate cages?

Author and Name Index

Ace, Goodman, 615
Adams, Franklin P., 181, 197, 427, 565, 763
Adams, Henry, 329, 433
Adams, James Truslow, 625
Addison, Joseph, 719
Ade, George, 732, 838, 871
Adenauer, Konrad, 54, 739, 768
Adler, Alfred, 117
Adler, Mortimer J., 478
Agate, James, 184, 527, 563
Alcott, Bronson, 409, 771
Alexander the Great, 484
Algren, Nelson, 195
Allen, Fred, 7–8, 16, 40, 47, 68, 136, 142, 155, 196, 209, 225, 233, 328, 359, 370, 378, 395, 399, 412, 446, 462, 477, 554, 643, 647, 651, 659, 672, 705, 732
Allen, Frederick Lewis, 85
Allen, Grant, 269
Allston, Washington, 162
Alvarez, Walter C., 382
Ames, Fisher, 685
Anderson, Sherwood, 44, 484
Angell, Norman, 158
Anouilh, Jean, 431
Aragon, Louis, 339
Archer, William, 194
Aretino, Pietro, 325
Aristotle, vii, 178, 212, 469
Arlen, Michael, 794
Armour, Richard, 253, 316, 515, 569, 762
Arnold, Matthew, 607, 609
Artzybasheff, Boris, 44
Astor, John Jacob, 517
Astor, Lady Nancy, 18, 572, 667, 684, 694
Attlee, Clement, 578
Auden, W. H., 87, 562, 703
Augustine, Saint, 822
Austen, Jane, 18, 552
Austin, Alfred, 479
Austin, Mary, 610

Bach, Johann Sebastian, 540
Bacon, Francis, vii, x, 6, 271, 362,

548, 564, 725, 726, 765, 772, 857
Baer, Arthur, 74, 179, 337, 338, 634
Bagehot, Walter, 655
Baldwin, Faith, 812
Balfour, Arthur, 670
Balzac, Honoré de, 102, 273, 489, 774, 782
Bangs, John Kendrick, 57
Bankhead, Tallulah, 218, 651, 732, 806
Barbey d'Aurevilly, Jules, 576, 878
Barkley, Alben, 38
Barrie, James M., 218, 310, 408, 455, 703, 726, 883
Barrymore, Ethel, 138, 460
Barrymore, John, 96, 878
Barton, Bruce, 16
Baruch, Bernard, 84, 195, 375, 520, 585, 755, 848
Baudelaire, Charles, 91, 475, 541
Baum, Vicki, 430
Beaumarchais, Caron de, 119, 221, 737
Beecham, Thomas, 539, 561, 568
Beecher, Henry Ward, 243, 684, 697
Beerbohm, Max, 45, 194, 242, 299, 397, 603, 716, 779, 806
Beethoven, Ludwig van, 165, 845
Behan, Brendan, 556
Behrman, S. N., 736, 849
Belloc, Hilaire, 527, 553, 796
Benchley, Robert, 42, 235, 238, 268, 303, 496, 558, 706, 725, 790, 830, 883
Ben-Gurion, David, 520
Benn, Anthony Wedgwood, 578
Benn, Ernest, 473
Bennett, Arnold, 79, 143, 611, 678
Bennett, James Gordon, 447
Berenson, Bernard, 173, 406, 722, 728, 827, 855
Bergson, Henri, 6, 841
Berlin, Irving, 561
Berlioz, Hector, 790
Bernard, Claude, 44
Bernstein, Henri, 388
Bibesco, Elizabeth, 344
Bierce, Ambrose, 17, 76, 81, 88, 93,